D1238127

432

DATE DUE

The Virginia Experiment

THREE SHIPS AT JAMESTOWN

The *Susan* (*Sarah*) *Constant*, in foreground, maneuvers off the site of Jamestown with the *Godspeed* (*Goodspeed*), left, and the *Discovery*.

THE
Virginia
Experiment

THE OLD DOMINION'S ROLE
IN THE
MAKING OF AMERICA
1607-1781

Alf J. Mapp, Jr.

Hamilton Press

LANHAM • NEW YORK • LONDON

Hamilton Press

4720 Boston Way
Lanham, MD 20706

3 Henrietta Street
London WC2E 8LU England

British Cataloging in Publication Information Available

This edition published in 1987 by
Hamilton Press.

Library of Congress Cataloging-in-Publication Data

Mapp, Alf J. (Alf Johnson), 1925-
  The Virginia experiment.

  Bibliography: p.
  Includes index.
  1. Virginia—History—Colonial period, ca. 1600-1775.
2. Virginia—History—Revolution, 1775-1783. I. Title.
F229.M28   1987   975.5   87-105
ISBN 0-8191-5779-1 (pbk. : alk. paper)

All Hamilton Press books are produced on acid-free
paper which exceeds the minimum standards set by the National
Historical Publication and Records Commission.

Foreword to Second Edition

M^Y gratitude goes out to the public, whose reception of the first edition of *The Virginia Experiment* made this second edition possible. It goes out also to those well established professional historians whose tolerance and generosity in 1957 toward a newcomer to their ranks made possible the book's present status as a standard in its field.

The passage of seventeen years has not necessitated any reversals of judgement or radical changes in the first edition, but it has provided a cornucopia of works on Virginia and American history from which I have drawn to enrich the retelling of my story. I am grateful for the contributions of all of my colleagues, but especially for Richard Lee Morton's masterful *Colonial Virginia* and Virginius Dabney's lively *Virginia the New Dominion*.

ALF J. MAPP, JR.

Portsmouth, Virginia
May, 22, 1974

Foreword to Third Edition

ONCE again I express my gratitude to readers of *The Virginia Experiment,* this time for keeping it alive for thirty years. Together with scholars in the field of American history, they have helped to make it the standard work in its field. Interpretations that provoked lively controversy when the first edition appeared have since gained general acceptance. *The Virginia Experiment* has appeared in successive printings in both hardback and paperback. In 1974 the book was modified in its second edition to include later findings that enriched the story. In this, the third edition, a few minor changes are made to include the results of more recent research.

I hope that, in its new costume, this first-born of my books will continue to win friends.

ALF J. MAPP, JR.

Willow Oaks
Portsmouth, Virginia
February 1, 1987

TO MY PARENTS
AND FIRST TEACHERS
ALF JOHNSON MAPP
AND
LORRAINE CARNEY MAPP

Contents

Acknowledgments

FOR encouragement in the writing of this book, I am indebted to the late Dr. Douglas Southhall Freeman, Pulitzer Prize-winning biographer of *R. E. Lee* and *George Washington* and a historian of international reputation, who persuaded me to widen the scope of the work originally planned; the late Clayton Torrence, executive secretary of the Virginia Historical Society and editor of the *Virginia Magazine of History*, who studied my outline and assured me that the projected volume would meet a real need; and Virginius Dabney, author, historian, and formerly Pulitzer Prize-winning editor of the *Richmond* (Va.) *Times-Dispatch*.

For careful reading of parts of the manuscript of the first edition, I am indebted to the late Dr. Earl Gregg Swem, compiler of the monumental *Virginia Historical Index*, former editor of the *William and Mary College Quarterly Historical Magazine*, and publications editor for the Jamestown 350th Anniversary Commission. The manuscript of that edition was read in its entirety by Dr. W. Edwin Hemphill, then director of the Virginia Division of History, and now editor of the John C. Calhoun Papers. Both of these gentlemen made helpful suggestions.

I am deeply appreciative of the helpfulness, while I was working on both editions, of staff members of the Virginia State Library and the library of the Virginia Historical Society in Richmond, the Alderman Library of the University of Virginia in Charlottesville, the libraries of the College of William and Mary and Colonial Williamsburg, Inc. in Williamsburg, Virginia, the Sargeant Room of the Norfolk Public Library, and the Hughes Library of Old Dominion University in Norfolk, and the Library of Congress.

Edward M. Riley, Jr., director of research for Colonial Williamsburg, Inc. and my colleague on the Publications Committee for the 350th Anniversary of the Beginning of Representative Government in the Western World and the editorial boards for both the Jamestown Foundation and the Virginia Independence Bicentennial Commission, has been particularly helpful in obtaining research materials in preparation for the revised edition.

Aid in assembling illustrations has come from the Division of History, the Virginia State Chamber of Commerce, and Colonial Williamsburg, Inc.

My wife, Ramona Hartley Mapp, and my son, Alf J. Mapp, III, have helped with the proofreading for the revised edition.

A. J. M., JR.

List of Illustrations

. . . And Cauldron Bubble

Fire burn and cauldron bubble.
—SHAKESPEARE, *Macbeth*, Act IV, Scene 1

Their sweat, their tears, their blood . . .
—SIR WINSTON CHURCHILL, *The Unknown War* (1931)

... And Cauldron Bubble

ON May 6, 1607 an experiment began. Into that experiment have been poured the blood of valiant, dreaming men, the tears of patient, believing women, and the sweat of both. At times the crucible of experiment has seethed under the catalysis of war and threatened to overflow in the violence of its ebullition. But always the great experiment has gone forward. The vibrations of its force have been felt in every continent of the earth. Great empires have trembled and toppled to their doom, and new nations have been thrust up amid the smoke and chaos of the mighty upheaval. But no one living can tell the final result of the great experiment, for it is even now in progress. Even if the work were complete, no one could weigh and measure the result with scientific precision, for intangibles have gone into the crucible and the success of the experiment must be assayed in terms of human values. But we can profitably examine the ingredients—human and material—which have mingled and mixed in the making of this potent brew.

The great experiment began on a day in May of 1607 when an Englishman—standing amid the ageless, windswept dunes of Cape Henry, flanked by a hostile, unknown continent and a treacherous, little-known ocean—opened at once a small sealed box and a new era in world history.[1] Scarcely more than a hundred men were present at the dramatic scene, but many eyes in Europe were riveted on the little group. For this motley company of distinguished gentlemen, artisans, and laborers comprised the beginnings of the first permanent English settlement in America, and that tiny box contained instructions that were to provide the governmental foundation of the new colony. None of that little band, waiting in tense expectation, had seen the document, for King James I had expressly ordered that the seal on the box not be broken until the colonists had landed on the Virginia shore. That small foundation was to grow and expand until it produced the first legislature in North America, until it became a free and independent government, until eventually it merged its sovereignty in a great federal union whose democratic influence was to spread to every quarter of the globe.

The Virginia experiment has become the American experiment. It has merged with the traditions of New England, the influence of the Middle Colonies and the spirit of the ever-moving Western

3

'frontier to form the American expression of democracy. It is our purpose to trace in the pages that follow the evolution and expansion of the Virginia experiment in the story of American government. We must ever bear in mind that this governmental expression *is* a great, continuous experiment—an experiment even now in progress— and that from this fact it derives its vital, virile and expanding force.

ALF J. MAPP, JR.

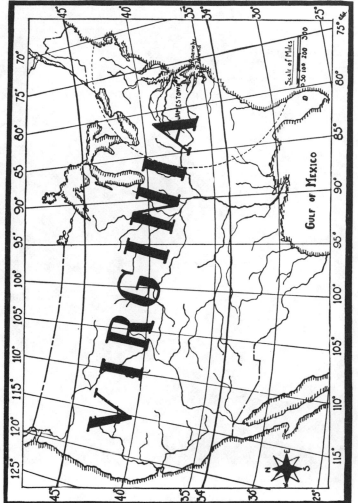

From M. P. Andrews, Virginia, the Old Dominion.

EXTENT OF VIRGINIA TERRITORY UNDER CHARTERS OF 1606 AND 1609

PLATE I

Photo courtesy Sir Ronald Lechmere, Bart., and Virginia Historical Society.

SIR EDWIN SANDYS
"The father of colonial self-government."

PLATE II

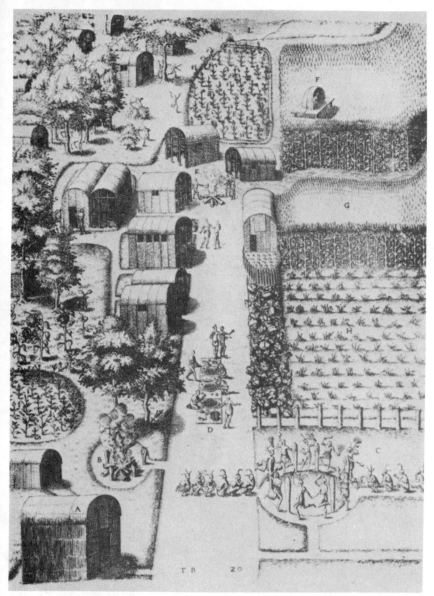

INDIAN VILLAGE

Indian villages in Tidewater Virginia were like Secota, located in what is now North Carolina, and shown in the famous engraving by Theodore de Bry. Key to the picture is as follows:

(a) Tomb of the chiefs; (b) Prayer circle;
(c) Dancing arena; (d) Feasting place; (e) Gardens;
(f) Platform with watchmen for fields;
(g) (h) and (i) Crops; (k) Cooking fire; (l) River.

PLATE III

Photo from Virginia Cavalcade, *courtesy Virginia State Library.*

DEFENSE OF JAMESTOWN

These scenes of early colonial conflict with the Indians, painted by Sidney King, are based on artifacts unearthed by archaeologists at Fort Raleigh and have been authenticated through research by the National Park Service and the Smithsonian Institution.

Plate IV

THOMAS WEST, THIRD LORD DE LA WARR (DELAWARE)

PLATE V

SIR THOMAS DALE, HIGH MARSHAL OF VIRGINIA

PLATE VI

Photo by Dementi Studio from portrait in State Capitol.

ALEXANDER SPOTSWOOD,
VIRGINIA'S GREATEST COLONIAL GOVERNOR

PLATE VII

FIRST CAPITOL AT WILLIAMSBURG

This structure, carefully restored by Colonial Williamsburg, Inc., is like the on
which served as capitol of the colony from 1704 until its destruction by fire in 174

PLATE VIII

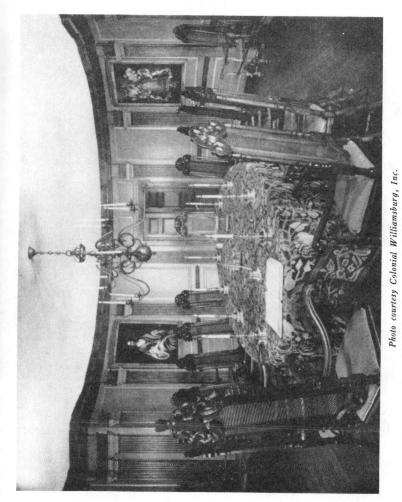

Photo courtesy Colonial Williamsburg, Inc.

COUNCIL CHAMBER OF THE COLONIAL CAPITOL AT WILLIAMSBURG

PLATE IX

HALLWAY AT CARTER'S GROVE

This mansion on the James is representative of great planters' homes in eighteenth century Virginia.

PLATE X

ST. JOHN'S CHURCH, RICHMOND
Here Patrick Henry spoke of liberty and death.

Plate XI

VIRGINIA'S REVOLUTIONARY CAPITOL

In this building, Virginia's capitol from 1752 until 1780, the Virginia Declaration of Righ
and the first written State constitution in the world were adopted. The painting sign
"E.R.D.," was painted either before or shortly after the building's destruction by fire.

PLATE XII

Photo from Virginia Cavalcade, *courtesy Virginia State Library.*

RICHARD HENRY LEE, "THE CICERO OF AMERICA"

Plate XIII

Photo by Dementi Studio from portrait in State Capitol.

PATRICK HENRY, "THE FIREBRAND OF THE REVOLUTION"

PLATE XIV

GENERAL DANIEL MORGAN

The "Old Wagoner" here wears the fringed hunting shirt which was the uniform of many of Virginia's best fighting men.

PLATE XV

Photo from Virginia Cavalcade, courtesy Virginia State Library.

YORKTOWN AFTER THE BATTLE

In left foreground is the badly damaged Nelson house, Cornwallis' headquarters. The photograph is from an eighteenth century water color by Benjamin Latrobe.

PLATE XVI

Chapter I

BRAVE NEW WORLD

(1603-1611)

Chapter I

~~~~~~

(1603-1611)

WHAT manner of men were these who stood unabashed upon the storm-swept threshold of a new era?

Posterity does not answer with one voice. Some imaginative romanticists have insisted that the first settlers invaded the wilderness clad in claret velvet[1] and armed with pedigrees of prodigious length. Some would-be realists, in over-zealous attempts at refutation, have suggested that the records of Newgate Prison might yield much information concerning the personal and genealogical history of the first Virginians. Authentic evidence reveals both generalizations to be erroneous. There was no uniform type of early settler.

In the vanguard of exploration came younger sons of noble lineage, denied material inheritance by the law of primogeniture of the Old World, but ready to pit their physical inheritance against the wilds of the new. With them came small tradesmen and merchants of meager means, men afire with the promise of a new land where they might carve out their separate destinies free from the fetters of England's unwritten caste system.

Of the more than one hundred[2] members of that group, forty-eight, among them a surgeon, are listed as gentlemen by one source.[3] There was another surgeon not listed as a gentleman. Four of the colonists were carpenters. Twelve were laborers. The presence of a clergyman, a blacksmith, a tailor, a barber, a bricklayer, a mason, a sailor and a drummer made the group fairly representative of English urban society. The names of three of the company have been preserved without occupational classification, and four were mere boys. The rest remain anonymous.[4] There were no women. Obviously, it was thought that woman had no place in the grim and often grisly business of subduing a continent.

That original band, for the most part, were destined for immortality as a group but for obscurity as individuals. And this was, in a sense, symbolic of their character. Most of them were ordinary persons endowed with ordinary talents, subject to the common faults and foibles, and possessed of the virtues and surprising latent nobility and latent cruelty of the ordinary man in any continent and in any century. But collectively they were great: when they erred, they erred greatly; but when they triumphed, they triumphed grandly. Their minds did not comprehend the staggering significance of the task which engaged their efforts, but their hearts felt the fierce tug of forces beyond their comprehension. A new century was opening, a century of exploration that would discover new lands, new peoples, and new ideas—a century that would open a new world.

Only the most phlegmatic soul could have been sluggishly unaware of the spirit of inquiry and exploration that swept like a fresh wind over a restive, feverish world grown weary of the old and impatient for the new.

There were in that little band a few men who, though denied the benefit of historical perspective that is ours today, grasped imperfectly but almost instinctively the significance of the tremendous enterprise upon which they were embarked. Looking back across the cluttered sweep of the centuries, we see them standing forth in bold and bright relief from the gray mass of anonymity.

First to claim our attention are the stocky figure, bluff, ruddy countenance, and lush beard of Captain John Smith,[5] who makes his entrance to the clanking of prison chains. Now in his twenty-eighth year, he is old in the ways of the world, having traversed strange nations and strange seas, seen civil war and religious war, and killed more than his share of Turks and Christians in the interim. His present annoying state of captivity is no new experience. But we must not allow the colorful young captain to divert our attention for long from other figures equally significant and perhaps even equally deserving of our commendation. For he is, in theatrical parlance, a "mugger," and centuries will roll by before the public sees him as one of the greatest scene-stealers of all time.

There is Christopher Newport, commander of the expedition, one of six masters of the Royal Navy—not yet an admiral, though already regarded as one. The hero's role is old to him. A decade and a half ago he led against the Spaniards in the New World an expedition that destroyed or captured twenty enemy vessels and, in the same grand sweep, sacked four towns in the West Indies and Florida.[6] His efforts and his fame as a colonizer are destined to exceed the confines of a single hemisphere. At present, however, perhaps his greatest prestige derives from the fact that he is the guardian of the mysterious sealed box.[7]

There too is middle-aged Captain Edward Maria Wingfield, a loyal servant to king and country with important connections[8] in England, but lonely among ardent Protestants who believed he was a Catholic.

We see Captain John Martin, brother-in-law to the influential Sir Julius Caesar, and a man of enterprise with a keen eye for business, a royalist to the core.[9]

Present, too, are stolid Captain Bartholomew Gosnold, veteran mariner who saw service under Sir Walter Raleigh; Captain John Ratcliffe, also a mariner of standing; ill-fated Captain George Kendall; adventurous George Percy, youngest of the Earl of Northumberland's eight sons and a veteran of the wars in the Low Countries; and ambitious Captain Gabriel Archer, who studied law at Gray's Inn.

A man apart and yet a sharer of every common burden is the Reverend Robert Hunt, Anglican clergyman—ever hopeful, ever striving, ever animating his flagging comrades.

Young Captain Smith is quick to note the "mildnesse of the ayre, the fertilities of the soyle, and situation of the rivers, . . . safe harbours, much merchantable fish, and places fit for Salt coats, building of ships, making of Iron . . ."[10] in the new land that augur well for its future development as another England beyond the seas. Christopher Newport, we may be sure, is aware that he is advancing the majestic course of empire. Captain Wingfield is acutely conscious of his role in furthering his Majesty's dominions and prestige. Captain Martin's eyes gleam with realization of the new land's tremendous commercial possibilities, and perhaps with a dream of economic empire.

But what of that idealist, the Reverend Mr. Hunt? Who can divine his thoughts and emotions at this dramatic moment?

For this moment is at once a culmination and a beginning.

It is the culmination of a saga that began in the year 1000 A.D. when the stout oak keel of a storm-battered Viking ship scraped on a sandy strand of the North American coast. It is the climax of an epic that saw a ridiculed Genoese navigator plant the standard of Spain in the exotic Bahamas, that saw an Italian merchant and his son near the dawn of a day in June of 1497 claim for England all that lay beyond the fog-wrapped rocks of Newfoundland, that saw courtly Sir Walter Raleigh found a colony that vanished as suddenly and completely as the earthly estates and honors of that ill-fated courtier.

But we may be confident that thoughts such as these do not fill the minds of this small band of Englishmen. They do, however, have a sense of destiny. For the shore on which they stand is the theme of England's greatest masters of prose, poetry, and the dramatic arts.[11] More stimulating still to the seventeenth century imagination is the awful portent of a blazing firetailed comet which swung ominously low and glowering in the heavens as the three tiny ships *Susan Constant, Godspeed,* and *Discovery* plowed their lonely way through the vast and silent world of night and ocean.[12]

But if this moment is a culmination, it is also a beginning—the inception of a project that may disintegrate and fade into the mists of obscurity as did the Roanoke Colony, or that may grow in extent and influence even beyond the generous limits of contemporary imagination.

The tiny band on this savage coast are now without a legally sanctioned leader. Captain Newport was placed in "sole charge and command" of the Virginia expedition only "until such time as they shall fortune to land upon the coast of Virginia."[13]

Who will the new leader be? The seal is broken and the lid is lifted. The tense silence is broken by a voice reading the names of those appointed to the Council in Virginia—Captain Bartholomew Gosnold, Captain Edward Maria Wingfield, Captain Christopher Newport, Captain John Smith, Captain John Ratcliffe, Captain John Martin, Captain George Kendall. The roll is ended and no single chief official has been named. Is this then an anti-climax? Far from it! The royal failure to designate a leader for the colony has provided the perfect climax. It must choose its own executive. A few days later Wingfield is chosen by the Council in a free election[14] on American soil, and American democracy begins.

* * *

For the modern observer, gazing in retrospection across the stretch of centuries, the granting to the London Company of the charter of 1609 brings sharply into focus the contending personalities and ideologies of a distant day in the far-removed little rustic settlement by the turbid James. The London-Plymouth patent of 1606 signified the termination of the romantic and colorful period of individual adventuring in colonization, and the beginning of the fruitful, but still far from prosaic, period of corporate enterprise. The charter of 1609 marked a radical departure from the autocratic tradition of its predecessor. In it were embodied prerogatives that made possible the evolution of self-government under the guiding hands of the company rather than the despotic sway of the royal scepter. Thus was made possible the evolution that became revolution. Within scarcely more than a decade and a half the colony developed, in penumbral but perceptible outline, a form of government and legal administration that today prevails, with the exception of the Province of Quebec and the State of Louisiana, throughout the vastness of the Continent of North America.

The charters of 1606 and 1609 designated as Virginia territory all land "along the Sea Coasts, between four and thirty degrees of *Northerly* Latitudes from the Equinoctial Line, and five and forty degrees of the same Latitude, and in the main land between the same four and thirty and five and forty Degrees, and the Islands thereunto adjacent, or within one hundred miles of the coasts thereof."[15]

This tremendous tract included, in addition to the area of the present state of Virginia, in part the states of Maine, Michigan, Wisconsin, Minnesota, South Dakota, Montana, Idaho, Oregon, North Carolina, South Carolina, Georgia, Alabama, Mississippi, Arkansas, Texas, New Mexico, and Arizona; and in their entirety or very nearly their entirety, the states of Maryland, Delaware, New Jersey, Pennsylvania, New York, Connecticut, Rhode Island, Massachusetts, New Hampshire, Vermont, Ohio, West Virginia, Kentucky, Tennessee, Indiana, Illinois, Missouri, Iowa, Oklahoma, Kansas, Nebraska, Wyoming, Colorado, Utah, Nevada, and California. In short, this vast virginal tract included all or part of each of forty-two of the present fifty states. The territory embraced as well Lake Ontario and Lake Erie and much of Lakes Huron and Michigan. In addition, its boundaries encompassed part of what is today the Canadian province of Ontario. This transcontinental grant stretched approximately two thousand five hundred miles in an eight hundred mile wide belt from the Atlantic to the Pacific. It also extended one hundred miles into each of those oceans, and by March 12, 1612 included all islands within nine hundred miles of the shore between the thirtieth and forty-first degrees.[16] Among these islands were the Bermudas, then commonly known as the Summer Isles. ". . . This Virginia is a country in America between the degrees of 34 and 45, of the North latitude," wrote Captain John Smith. "The bounds thereof on the East side are the great Ocean: on the South lyeth Florida: on the North nova Francia: as for the West thereof, the limits are unknowne."[17] Even then men in America looked questioningly, hopefully, to the West in quest of the last great frontier.

The London Company were not at liberty to settle anywhere in Virginia that fancy might dictate, for the limits of their jurisdiction were not coterminous with the boundaries of this wilderness empire. The charter of April 10, 1606 gave royal sanction to the incorporation of the London and Plymouth Companies. The London Company were designated as the "first colony"[18] and were enjoined to plant their first "Habitation" "at any Place upon the said coast of *Virginia* and *America*, where they shall think fit and convenient, between the said four and thirty and one and forty Degrees of the said Latitude . . ."[19] Within their jurisdiction was all territory running fifty English statute miles north along the coast from the point of first settlement and fifty south from the point "together with all the Islands within one hundred miles, directly over against the said Sea Coast . . ."[20] This coastwise stretch extended one hundred miles inland. The Plymouth Company, designated as the second colony, were permitted to settle at any point along the coast between the thirty-eighth and forty-fifth parallels and enjoyed a comparable jurisdictional grant.[21] Article VI of the charter provided that "the Plantation and Habitation of such of the said colonies, as shall last plant themselves, as aforesaid, shall not be made within one hundred like *English* miles of the other of them, that first began to make their Plantation as aforesaid."

Article VII of the charter provided for a council of thirteen in each of the colonies to "govern and order all matters and causes, which shall arise, grow, or happen, to or within the same several colonies, according to such Laws, Ordinances, and Instructions, as shall be, in that behalf, given and signed with Our Hand or Sign Manual, and pass under the Privy Seal of our Realm of *England*." Each of the councils was authorized to use a special seal, and was given the power to coin money "for the more Ease of Traffick and Bargaining between and amongst them and the nations . . ." Article VIII provided for a royally-appointed council of thirteen sitting in England to be known as the Council of Virginia. In the hands of this council was placed the "superior managing and Direction" of all matters concerning the government of both colonies and of the entire Virginia territory. This supreme council was likewise granted the use of an official seal.

The charter contained one guarantee that was later to be the theme of debate and Revolution. Article XV made the promise that all subjects dwelling within the colonies and all children born to them within the "Limits and Precincts" of the colonies should "Have and enjoy all Liberties, Franchises, and Immunities, within any of our other Dominions, to all Intents and Purposes, as if they had been abiding and born, within this our Realm of *England*, or any other of our said Dominions." "The rights of Englishmen" was to become a familiar rallying cry in American history.

On March 19, 1607 King James issued an ordinance enlarging the number of the council in England by twenty-six.[22] Among those named was Sir Edwin Sandys,[23] who deserves special consideration. Though hailed by at least one distinguished historian as "the father of colonial self-government,"[24] Sandys only recently has begun to receive the measure of acclaim and appreciation which is his due.

When we first see him in this year of 1607 he is a dignified councillor of forty-five—a bold-featured, mustached and bearded man in the prime of life, the severity of whose countenance is relieved by large, full eyes and ennobled by an expansive brow. This is an arresting face—a face to delight a Rembrandt or a Rubens. And back of this face is an arresting personality. Many people will hail him as their champion, and his sovereign will avow a preference for Satan, if need be, instead.

Let us probe into the past of this commanding figure at the council table, and learn how he came to occupy his present seat of influence. Destined to gain fame from political conflict, he was born and reared amid dissension. For he is the second son of Archbishop Edwin Sandys, whose puritan conscience kept him for so long embroiled in private squabbles and public disputes. Love of learning carried young Edwin Sandys to Oxford, already mellow with age and tradition.[25] It is pleasant to imagine this man, so soon to become a leading protagonist in the violent social and political eruptions of his time, strolling in light-hearted conversation through the arbored walks of the University or idling with companions by the gently-flowing Cherriwell. George Cranmer and Richard Hooker, then a tutor, must have frequently accompanied him, for between them and Edwin Sandys there grew a warm friendship of long duration.

On the thirteenth of October, 1586, Sandys—not yet twenty-five—took his seat in Commons as member of Parliament for Andover. His penetrating logic, rich fund of learning, and native eloquence soon distinguished him and, despite his youth, he quickly assumed an active part in legislative proceedings.

Soon after the dissolution of Parliament in 1593, he embarked with Cranmer on a European tour of three years' duration, visiting France, Italy, and Germany. He must have found France pleasant, for in 1599 he was back in Paris writing a book entitled *Europae Speculum*. The work was religious in character and remarkably tolerant for the period. Apparently his father's staunch puritanism had not engendered in Sandys a hatred for Catholicism.

The story of Sandys' literary career is not the traditional one of the unknown author striving to secure publication of his first book. It is that of a man struggling to prevent its publication. Perhaps careful reflection convinced him that the extremely liberal tone of his completed manuscript might endanger the success of a highly promising political career. Nevertheless, Sandys did not destroy the work. Possibly he wished to preserve the manuscript for publication after retirement from the political arena, or perhaps he was motivated only by a natural affection for his brain-child. Eventually, despite the author's vigilance, a copy of the manuscript was stolen and published without his consent in 1605 under the title *A Relation of the State of Religion*. Sandys himself is said to have secured an order of the high commission condemning the book to be burnt. The order was executed November 7, 1605. The volume, nevertheless, enjoyed considerable success and was later translated into Italian, French, and Dutch.

The years from 1599 to 1605 were not entirely consumed by Sandys in efforts to prevent or suppress publication of his book. They were crowded with political activity. He returned to England in 1599. There is a record of his having resigned as prebend at Wetwang in 1602. The following year he journeyed to Scotland to meet James VI, now James I of England—first of the Stuarts, and to accompany the pudgy, awkward monarch to London. An auspicious beginning, indeed, for the aspiring politician's relations with the new ruler! Sandys must have listened patiently to the slovenly enunciated pedantry of the royal Scot, but even then the dogmatic king's divine right sentiments must have loomed ominously large in his conversation with the vigorous liberal.[26] Sandys entered James I's first Parliament (1603-4) as member for Stockbridge Hampshire and quickly became a leader in the House of Commons. The future opened bright and promising before Edwin Sandys in the spring of 1603. Once again in a position of political leadership, he stood high in the respect of Parliament and the regard of his sovereign. Moreover, on the eleventh of May, Edwin Sandys became *Sir* Edwin Sandys, for on that day he was knighted at the Charterhouse.

In this same month, Sandys assumed a position that was to indicate the course of his political career and to invite the opposition of those forces who would make that career such a turbulent one. He became chairman of the Commons committee appointed to confer with the Lords with a view to abolishing the court of wards, feudal tenures, and purveyance. He himself appears to have been the sole author of the committee's reports. Sir Edwin Sandys, son of an archbishop, friend of a king, had entered the lists against special privilege. The hostile opposition of the Lords defeated the proposed liberal measures, but their champion did not retire from the field. Soon afterwards Sandys was made chairman of a special investigating committee to study business conditions. He emerged as a vigorous advocate of open trade and a stubborn foe of the great trusts. Still later he voiced opposition to one of King James' favorite measures. In June of 1607 he demanded that all prisoners be allowed benefit of counsel. Conservatives trembled with rage and fear at the suggestion, and Hobart labeled it "an attempt to shake the corner stone of the law." In the same session, Sandys successfully carried a motion providing for the regular keeping of the "Journal" of the House of Commons—a hitherto unprecedented procedure.

In April, 1610, he was placed on a committee to study the "great contract" for commuting the king's feudal rights for an annual grant, and on April 10 delivered a speech on the subject in the Commons.

Sandys' political independence proved a thorn in the royal side, and the uncompromising liberal began to fade from political prominence. In 1613, however, Francis Bacon reported to his sovereign that Sandys had deserted the opposition faction. Apparently James I accepted his henchman's statement without question, and sought to woo Sandys into the royalist fold. Sir Edwin was granted a moiety of the manor of Northbourne, Kent. He was returned to the next session of Parliament, apparently as member for Rochester and for Hindon, Wiltshire.

If James I thought that he had purchased Sandys' support, he must have been severely jolted into realization of his error. In the first days of the session, Sandys plunged furiously into debate and proved himself still a fighting liberal. Not only did he forcefully attack pending royally-sponsored legislation, but he also urged with tenacious persistence that the grievances presented to the preceding parliament be referred to the Committee on Petitions. He was the dominant, determined, moving spirit of a committee appointed "to consider imposition." It was Sandys who presented the committee's report and on May 21 delivered before an undoubtedly startled House of Commons one of the most remarkable speeches of parliamentary history. The origin of every monarchy, he declared, lay in election. The people, he asserted, gave their consent to the king's authority only with the clear understanding that there were "certain reciprocal conditions" which "neither king nor people could violate with impunity." Climaxing this flood of unrestrained liberal sentiment came the assertion that a monarch who pretended to rule by any other title might be forced to relinquish his throne whenever there was sufficient force to compel his abdication.

The report of Sandys' speech fell with explosive impact on a shocked House of Lords. The stern, be-wigged Lords of Justice trembled on their benches, and Britain's complacent monarch must have rocked in astonishment upon his throne. Through all the hierarchy of conservative officialdom passed a great convulsive shudder. Here was treason! Here was heresy! The whole fabric of English government was endangered. The warp and woof of English political tradition, woven by countless numbers of the dead and living through five and one-half centuries, was in danger of being torn to shreds by the insane shouting of a liberty-intoxicated intellectual. Why, there was no knowing to what violence this ranting demagogue might incite that powerful but lethargic beast—the feared, the mighty mob. Fear was followed by hatred, for men instinctively hate that which they fear. Sir Edwin Sandys became at once the central object of England's conservative ire and the foremost champion of her liberal aspirations.

The Royal Scot, angered at the thwarting of his well-laid plans, determined to crush the political ambitions of a man who so rashly challenged the divine right of kings—a theory that was the cardinal principle of the proud monarch's political philosophy. Upon the dissolution of parliament on the seventh of June, Sandys was summoned before the royal council to answer for his parliamentary utterances. The charges against Sir Edwin were dismissed, but he was ordered not to venture beyond the limits of London without official permission, and to be prepared to give bonds for his appearance whenever demanded.

It is strange, indeed, that Sandys' great speech which, in its time, excited such varied and violent opinions should have faded from the memory of successive generations. For in this speech was enunciated the social contract theory of government nearly four decades before Locke attained his majority and one hundred sixty-two years before a young Virginian inserted the line about governments "deriving their just powers from the consent of the governed" in a document destined to become immortal as the Declaration of Independence. Ironically, also embodied in this speech made long before the parliament of 1680, was what would become the cardinal Whig dogma—a doctrine which subsequently would draw its chief adherents from the great landed nobility of England and particularly the venerable and properly conservative members of the House of Lords. Apparently James I's fears of the growth of anti-divine right sentiment were fully justified. However, the fabric of English political tradition not only survived without suffering serious mutation, but was greatly enriched by subsequent additions in what became, with the passage of centuries, an ever more clearly defined, though irregular, pattern.

One of the immediate results of parliamentary independence was that the frightened and angered king did not convoke another session of parliament before the expiration of a period of more than six years. Though intended as a deterrent to the growth of democracy, royal failure to summon parliament accelerated the transplantation of democratic sentiment to the western hemisphere and made possible, in large measure, the growth of the world's greatest democracy. When James I sought an easy solution to his problems, he created headaches for his successor George III. For Sir Edwin Sandys, no longer occupied in legislative activity, now directed his attention to colonial affairs. He became a member of the East India Company before August 1614 and on June 29, 1615 he became a member of the Somers Islands Company. It is from Sir Edwin that the Sandys tribe of the Bermudas derives its name. To the work of the Virginia Company, Sandys devoted most of his time and energy as a colonizer. Sandys' formal connection with the corporation began March 9, 1607 with his appointment to the Council in England. His first great service to the struggling Virginia Colony was rendered in 1609 when he wrote for it a new and more liberal charter which won the approval of Company and King.[27]

Only the confusion and conflict resulting from colonial operation under the autocratic charter of 1607 persuaded haughty King James to submit to the delegation of authority implicit in acceptance of the Charter of 1609.[28]

Almost before the last log was added to the stockade of the little frontier capital of Jamestown, the innate weakness of its government became glaringly obvious. President Wingfield, devoid of the

weapons of coercive authority, was powerless to enforce executive policy or even to bring harmony to his quarreling Council. The energies of that body, so essential to the vigorous pursuit of an established policy, were expended in violent debates. Less than a month after landing on Virginia soil, the confusion and inefficiency of the government were so great as to provoke from the harried colonists a petition to the Council for redress. Only the good judgment and diplomacy of Captain Newport were sufficient to persuade the angry settlers to submit to the authority of their government. But the colony was deprived of its mainstay when Newport, early in July, set sail with his small fleet for England.[29] The hand of Newport had been the hand of authority, and its restraining influence was no sooner removed than dissension erupted again with renewed fury. Captain Kendall, charged with exciting discord, was expelled from the Council and imprisoned. Membership was thus reduced to five. Wingfield, Gosnold, Ratcliffe, and Martin had sat in Council since its inception. Captain Smith, who made his entrance upon the Virginia scene to the clanking of prison chains, had not at first been permitted to sit in Council and had been kept under restraint until his acquittal of a mutiny charge on the twentieth of June. The membership of the governing body was further reduced by the death of Captain Gosnold, who succumbed to the dread "sicknesse" which mystified seventeenth century physicians.[30] Diminution in membership was accompanied by increase in dissension.

In September Ratcliffe, Smith, and Martin formed a cabal for the purpose of ousting Wingfield not only from the presidency of the Council but also from its deliberations.[31] Anxious for their own positions, the three conspirators mutually pledged that with the ousting of Wingfield expulsion should cease. What feelings of insecurity must have plagued each party to this plot! The members of the Virginia Council united only to accomplish the elimination of one of their number. Perhaps Captain Wingfield was not greatly surprised, on peering through the entrance of his tent, to find Ratcliffe, Smith, and Martin confronting him with a warrant of deposition declaring him "very unworthy to be eyther President or of the Councell."[32] Wingfield was charged with misappropriation of funds, improper division of the public funds, atheism, intended desertion of the colony, and connivance with Spaniards to effect destruction of the Virginia settlement. The deposed President was summoned to answer these charges. Wingfield resorted to the only practical expedient. He demanded a hearing before the king, a privilege which his enemies dared not deny him. The unhappy ex-president was temporarily imprisoned aboard the pinnace in which it was charged he had planned to desert the struggling colony.

Ratcliffe was chosen to succeed Wingfield. But Dissension, the real master of the colony, continued to reign without interruption. If the testimony of a deposed president may be believed, there followed an epidemic of "whipping, lawing, beating, and hanging."[33] We do know that James Read, a smith, was brought to trial, convicted, and sentenced to be hanged for striking the newly-elevated Ratcliffe. He saved his life only by the eleventh hour revelation of a plot against the government, allegedly led by Captain Kendall. Kendall, long a potential threat to the reigning three, was immediately tried by jury for mutiny, found guilty, and executed.[34] The hungry maw of "justice" had found a victim, and Read was permitted to escape with his life.

Not so easily satisfied was the very real hunger of the colony in the bitter December of 1607. The plight of Jamestown became so desperate that Captain Smith, seeking grain at any risk, led an expedition into the territory of the fierce Chickahominies. His departure left a vacancy on the Council which was soon filled by Captain Gabriel Archer, who was admitted at the insistence of President Ratcliffe over the earnest protests of Captain Martin. Immediately upon gaining his seat, the litigious Archer sought to secure the execution of his predecessor. He indicted Smith "upon a Chapter in Leviticus for the death" of two men under his command.[35] The two men in question had been slain by the Indians. Smith's trial was set for the day of his return, and his conviction and immediate execution were confidently anticipated. At the very time that his fate was being decided, Smith, cheered by breathtaking escapes from the Indians and doubtless confident of a hero's welcome, was rapidly pressing forward to the proposed scene of his execution.

The narrative has not a few of the elements of melodrama. Smith was about to stride unawares into the camp of his executioners. No effective voice of protest was raised in his defense. Suddenly a cry rang out. Someone had sighted a sail on the James. The First Supply from England was arriving. With it was Captain Newport, who quickly grasped the situation, and acted with characteristic wisdom and dispatch. Newport persuaded the Council not only to withdraw the charges against Smith, but even to reinstate him as a party to its deliberations.

Newport's dramatic eleventh hour arrival saved the life of

Captain Smith, but caused the death of a liberal movement for free government. The ambitious and wily Archer, alive to the opportunity presented by a hungering and oppressed citizenry, had prepared to summon a Parliament.[36] It is highly probable that his parliamentary government, if actually put into operation, would rapidly have degenerated into dictatorship or anarchy. Royal discovery of its existence would almost certainly have brought harsh repressive measures. Nevertheless, it is a highly significant fact that the temper of the colonists was such that in the very year of their arrival they would dare to throw aside their constitution in bold defiance of Company and King.

With Newport came a newly commissioned Councillor, Matthew Scrivener. A semblance of order prevailed temporarily. When Newport returned to England, he carried with him Archer and the imprisoned Wingfield. Councillor Martin left the colony a few months later. Thus Jamestown was governed by a Council of three—two of whom, Ratcliffe and Smith, were enemies, and one of whom, Scrivener, was inexperienced.

By the summer of 1608, dissension and machinations were once again rampant. Ratcliffe was deposed—because of "pride and unreasonable needlesse cruelty" and waste of public stores, according to Captain Smith.[37] But the testimony of a man's enemies should be taken with a grain of salt. Ratcliffe, like his predecessor, suffered imprisonment, and it is probable that Scrivener served as President in the interim between Ratcliffe's arrest and Smith's return in September from a voyage of exploration in the Chesapeake Bay. Upon Smith's arrival in Jamestown, he became President and, by virtue of his casting vote, was supreme in the Council of two and hence in the colony.

Smith's dictatorship was interrupted in October by the arrival of two new Councillors—Richard Waldo and Peter Wynne. The subsequent reinstatement of Ratcliffe enlarged the Council to such proportions that Smith, though he remained its President, could no longer dominate its deliberations.

Two months later, Smith sent Ratcliffe back to England, branding his old enemy a "poore counterfeited Imposture" and declaring that he was returning him "least the company should cut his throat."[38] By the summer of 1609, Waldo and Scrivener had drowned in an accident on the James River and Wynne had fallen victim to the dread "sicknesse" carried by the mosquitoes bred in its marshes. Smith had eliminated one Councillor; the James had eliminated the other three. The ambitious captain, as President and sole member of the Council, was once again dictator.

It was at this point that the London Company realized that the Councillor system it had initiated must be abandoned in favor of a more practicable scheme. The complaints of Smith, of Newport, of Ratcliffe, of Wingfield, of Archer were overwhelming evidence that harmony could not be achieved under a directing Council. Following a special meeting of the managers of the London Company, the Charter of 1609 was drawn up by Sir Edwin Sandys and approved by the Company. As we have seen, King James, appalled by the utter failure of colonial operation under the autocratic Charter of 1607, begrudgingly assented to the more liberal Charter of 1609.

By his assent, the King relinquished active control of the Virginia colony, and placed powers of direct supervision in the hands of the Company. So sweeping were the changes made possible by the new charter that the Company was actually legally empowered to establish in Virginia any system of government which it deemed efficacious. The immediate establishment of representative government was legally possible. Sandys was anxious to see the growth of liberal institutions in the New World. But he was a practical man as well as an idealist. He saw that the colony was perhaps not yet ready for representative government. Even had it been ready, the sudden appearance of popular institutions would doubtless have frightened King James into immediate nullification of the new charter. Nevertheless, the goal of representative government remained a living ideal in the minds of Sandys and his more liberal associates on the board of the London Company.

Proceeding with the work of reform made possible by the new charter, Company managers, under Sandys' leadership, abolished the Council and created the position of Governor and Captain General—an office embracing all executive functions in the colony and designed to serve as the center of gravity in colonial government.[39] The office of Lieutenant-General, or Lieutenant-Governor, was also created, with the idea that its occupant should serve as chief executive in event of the absence or incapacity of the Governor.[40] Power was granted the Governor to appoint a new Council to serve as an advisory body or cabinet. The Chief Executive was to possess removal as well as appointive power. He was empowered to "rule, punish, pardone, and governe."[41] The archetype of the office of State governor and President of the United States is clearly evident in the office of colonial Governor. The colonial chief executive was not absolute. The exercise of his powers was "according to such directions" as he received from the London Company.[42] Only in the event of rebellion might the Governor institute martial law.[43]

The granting of the Charter of 1609 aroused among Englishmen new interest in the Virginia enterprise, and gave fresh hope to many who had despaired of its success.[44] New subscribers and prospective settlers were secured. Robert Johnson, London alderman and Deputy Treasurer of the Company, published, probably in collaboration with Sandys, *Nova Britannia*, an advertisement for the Virginia Colony that has much in common with modern chamber of commerce bulletins. *Nova Britannia*, though intended to boost the progress of the New World settlement, is remarkable for its veracity. Nevertheless, its authors employed many ingenious techniques in their euphemistic descriptions. The hesitant would-be adventurer was induced to brave the dread Atlantic by the assurance that the ocean was free of "rocks, shallows," and "narrow straits."

Perhaps the whole-hearted support which the colony received at this time was due in part to the fact that no less a personage than the distinguished and able Thomas West, Lord De la Warr (Delaware) was appointed its first Governor. Sir Thomas Gates was appointed Lieutenant-General. Sir George Somers was commissioned Admiral, with Christopher Newport serving as Vice-Admiral. De la Warr was unable to sail to Virginia with Gates, Somers, and Newport when they left Plymouth with a fleet of nine ships June 12, 1609. The three did not reach their destination till ten months had passed. A pinnace and all its passengers and crew were lost at sea. Yellow fever further depleted the expedition during passage through the tropics. Crossing the Gulf Stream, the fleet was caught in a terrific West India hurricane which for forty-four hours battered the eight remaining vessels, and eventually wrecked the flagship *Sea Venture* on a Bermudan coral reef. Aboard the stranded vessel were Gates, Somers, and Newport. The accident which detained the new leaders, and hence delayed the institution of the new government, suggested to Shakespeare many elements of plot and vivid passages of description which would enthrall generations of readers of *The Tempest*.[45]

The seven remaining vessels reached Jamestown in August. Though apprised of the new charter by the freshly-arrived settlers, Smith refused to resign from the Presidency until presented the official papers relative to the transfer of authority. The documents alluded to were, of course, aboard the ill-fated *Sea Venture*. Smith's obstinacy provoked a bitter dispute, but the domineering captain stood firm, and his opposition eventually conceded that the colony should continue to be governed according to the old charter until the arrival of the ship-wrecked vessel. Smith, it was agreed, would continue as President until September 20, at which time Captain Francis West would succeed to leadership.[46]

West, jealous of Smith's continued assertion of power in defiance of the wishes of the London Company, ignored the President's pretensions to authority. The slighted President and dictator was filled with fury. It is even charged, though without adequate confirmation, that Smith went so far as to plot with the Indians the destruction of an expedition led by West.[47] If Smith fathered such a design, its execution was prevented by a serious accident. The President was the victim of an explosion which "tore the flesh . . . in a most pittifull manner."[48]

Among the new arrivals were three returning veterans of colonial affairs—Ratcliffe, Martin and Archer—each of whom had commanded a vessel of the storm-battered fleet. They now saw a chance for revenge upon their old enemy. The three former Councillors maintained that if Smith was still President by virtue of the provisions of the old charter, they were, by the same token, still members of the Council. This bit of legal sophistry seems to bear the peculiar stamp of wily Gabriel Archer. The three conspirators held a Council meeting, deposed Smith from the Presidency, and sent him back to England. Thus, by a species of poetic justice, Ratcliffe was permitted to have a part in according his old rival the same treatment which he had received at his hands. Francis West, despite his exertions, was not chosen to head the interim government. The honor went to George Percy.

Eventually, some of the company stranded in the Bermudas managed to reach the mainland in two pinnaces which they had constructed during their exile. Upon his arrival at Jamestown in May of 1610, Lieutenant-Governor Gates formally received the old patent and seal from President West and, in the absence of Governor De la Warr, assumed command of the colony.

The new executive had almost every reason to be appalled at the state of his bailiwick. The fear-ridden, disease-stricken colonists moved in clammy silence within the suffocating envelopment of the "dread sicknesse." One by one they succumbed in the damp nights, and in the mornings their bodies were "trailed out of their cabines like Dogges, to be buried." "There were never Englishmen left in a forreign country," Captain George Percy had written, "in such miserie as wee were in this new discovered Virginia."[49] That was in the first awful summer. Others equally fearful had followed. Sporadic Indian raids claimed as victims many who had survived the terrors of the unknown plague. The energetic foraging of Captain Smith had not always preserved the colonists from famine that left only roots, herbs, acorns, nuts, and berries to nourish their suffering bodies and sustain their feeble lives. Even cannibalism, that most savage assertion of the will to self-preservation, rose again from the dark recesses of primitive nature. The buried corpses of slain Indians were exhumed from the marshy soil of Jamestown and greedily devoured. The gaunt, chill-racked, fever-tortured survivors had not the energy to repair the ports, replace the gates, or raise again the fallen palisadoes of their stricken community. Sir Thomas Gates was met not by an enthusiastic and cheering citizenry, but by a pitiable handful of wretched beings who begged deliverance from the miseries of Jamestown. Gates felt that he had no alternative.

His only provisions were the meager and depleted stores that had been salvaged from the dwindling supplies of Devil's Island in the Bermudas. He told the pleading colonists that they might return. Wearily they climbed aboard the pinnaces the dismal day of June 17, 1610. Some lingered with the intention of setting fire to the gaping ruins of Jamestown. Only with the aid of Captain George Yeardley did Gates dissuade them from the attempt. Finally, all of the colosists were accounted for aboard the vessels. Gates was the last to board ship. He directed the firing of a farewell salute. The empty wilderness echoed the report. That night the vessels cast their moorings, and drifted with the black tide of the James out to the open sea.[50]

Apparently, Jamestown was to be another "lost colony." Spain had long cast a covetous eye on Virginia territory. As early as 1570, Spanish settlers dispatched by Don Pedro Menendez de Aviles had founded a short-lived settlement near the falls of the James.[51] Since the settlement of Jamestown, a Spanish vessel had been sent north from Florida to determine the strength of the Virginia Colony. Exaggerated reports from the Indians had deterred the Spaniards from aggressive action.[52] The Virginia settlers, occupied with the actual trials of colonization, were nevertheless constantly aware of the potential menace of Spain. Had not a French colony established north of St. Augustine been completely obliterated by the Spaniards? Zúñiga, Spanish Ambassador in London, was dispatching almost daily pleas to his sovereign to wipe out Jamestown. James I was anxious to avoid war with Philip III. Some thought that the British monarch's action in transferring to the London company authority for colonial administration was due in part to his desire to free himself from direct responsibility for the colony's welfare, and hence from the possible necessity of waging war to avenge Spanish depredations upon the infant settlement. It is quite likely that, had the Spaniards discovered Jamestown deserted, they would have proceeded to colonize the Chesapeake Bay area in the name of Philip III. James I probably would have disclaimed responsibility for any enterprise of the London Company, and Virginia would have gone by default to Spain. How different might have been the history of America, and of the world!

Fortunately, as Gates' ships sailed down the James on the morning of June 17, 1610, they were met by a pinnace dispatched by Lord De la Warr under Command of Captain Edward Brewster. The Governor, upon reaching Cape Comfort June 16, had learned of the proposal to abandon the colony, and had sent Brewster ahead with orders to forestall any attempt at desertion. Gates' ships turned about and sailed back for Jamestown, there to await the arrival of Lord De la Warr, immigrants, and direly needed provisions.

The Governor, upon arrival, severely rebuked his people for vanity and idleness, and pledged to invoke stern measures if necessary. He inspired the colonists to new hope and new endeavor. Factional controversy vanished. The authority of the administration was unquestioned. Comfortable houses were built. The fort was repaired. The chapel was restored and refurnished, partly at the Governor's personal expense. Practical Lord De la Warr, busy with matters of defense and housing, was not one to neglect the light touch. At his order, the chapel was kept decorated with flowers.[53] The frontier community soon grew accustomed to pomp and pageantry. Every Sunday the Governor marched down the little dirt street with an official party composed of the Councillors, officers, and "all the gentlemen." To the left, right, and rear of them marched the Governor's guards—fifty halberds gleaming, fifty bright red cloaks tossing in the warm Virginia sunshine.[54]

Chapter II

A PRINCESS AND A PURITAN

(1611-1616)

Chapter II

(1611-1616)

THE beneficent administration of Lord De la Warr could not cure all the ills of the struggling colony, nor was that administration destined to continue for long. Soon the ravages of the unknown "sicknesse" removed no less than one hundred fifty settlers, and incapacitated the vast majority of the new arrivals, so that the burden of labor fell upon the seasoned veterans of Virginia colonization.[1] The destructive forays of the Indians continued with unabated ferocity. In the face of all these difficulties, Lord De la Warr managed to maintain order in the settlement.

The Governor, however, soon left his official post at Jamestown because of failing health. We can hardly blame the poor old man. During his stay in the colony, he had suffered from violent attacks of the ague, the flux, cramp, gout, and scurvy.[2] When Thomas West, Lord De la Warr, hopeful of regaining his health, set sail for the West Indies April 11, 1611, Virginia lost one of the ablest governors it would ever know.

Despite the tremendous reverses experienced, the London Company scorned the idea of abandoning the experiment in colonization. Their persistence is evidence of the virility of the age. As early as the preceding January, the Virginia Company had secured the recall of Sir Thomas Dale from the Netherlands so that he might be appointed deputy governor of Virginia. On March 27, 1611, while Lord De la Warr was still resident governor in the colony, Sir Thomas Dale, standing on the poop deck of an English sailing vessel, saw the grim, rocky cliffs of Land's End fade into distance and merge with the horizon. With him were three hundred colonists bound for the New World. No devil-may-care crew of gentlemen adventurers were they! They were drawn from the better class of working men, and had been meticulously selected by the London Company with a view to their ability to survive in the New World. Arriving at Jamestown May 19, 1611, Sir Thomas Dale was met by Captain Percy, who delivered to him the letters patent, thus formally signalizing the transfer of command.

So began the stern, puritanical rule of Sir Thomas Dale. Marshal Dale he was called in Virginia, and there was significance in the title, for he subjected to military discipline all under his command. That the new deputy governor was truly a man of action was almost at once made evident. He quickly perceived that Jamestown was no fit site for settlement. This perception evidenced no unique insight. Several leaders objected to the location in 1607 before the palisades of the town were ever raised. Others had complained of the site since. The unique contribution of Marshal Dale was constructive action. Other governors had bitterly bemoaned conditions at Jamestown, but had hesitated to seek another site, despairing of finding a second location so well suited for defense against the Indians. It is also possible that an unconscious psychological impulse caused them to plant the seat of government near the ocean—the broad avenue of escape that led to home—rather than in the engulfing depths of the hostile wilderness. Marshal Dale was restrained by no such inhibition. Sailing up the James to a point about fifty miles above the capital, he found "a convenient strong, healthie and sweet seate to plan the new towne in, from whence might be no more remove of the principall seate."[3] The idea of establishing a settlement in the vicinity of this site previously had been entertained by at least two of the colonists. In the summer of 1609 Captain Francis West had commanded a company dispatched by Captain Smith, then President, to make preparation for a settlement at the falls. However, Captain Smith, upon personally viewing the site pronounced it "inconsiderately seated in a place, not only subject to the rivers inundation, but round invironed with many intolerable inconveniences."[4] He therefore gave orders to abandon the location and establish a settlement at Powhatan instead. Captain West, angered at the President's peremptory action, abandoned Powhatan, and the attempt at settlement came to nought. The following year Captain West's brother, Lord De la Warr, erected, at the falls of the James, Laware's Fort, which was intended to serve as a base for mineral-hunting expeditions. It is quite possible that, had Lord De la Warr remained longer in Virginia, he would have expanded the fort into a settlement of the proportions envisioned by Marshal Dale.

Marshal Dale, however, sprang to the task with greater energy and persistence than his predecessors. No doubt he was goaded to unusual exertions by the apparently urgent necessity of establishing a settlement farther inland, and hence less vulnerable to Spanish attack. The French colony on the St. John's River had been wiped out by the Spanish in 1565. Suspicions that the Spaniards plotted such a raid on the Virginia settlement were far from groundless. The marvelous espionage system of the King of Spain kept him constantly informed of the Virginia colony's progress. In February of 1607, before the English colonists had ever set foot on Virginia soil, he considered steps to hinder the enterprise, should it prove more than an ephemeral venture.[5] In May of that year the Spanish Board of War of the Indies reportedly concurred in the belief that "with all necessary forces this plan of the English should be prevented."[6] The following November the Spanish Council of State won their sovereign's assent to the proposal that a fleet be sent to seize the colony.[7] But months of inaction followed, and revival of the plan a year later resulted in no decisive action. Shortly before, the Spanish had received a report on Jamestown defenses from an Irishman who had stayed in the colony.[8] This man was undoubtedly the first "fifth columnist" in American history.

The Spanish menace was brought home to Marshal Dale with striking force when, shortly after his arrival, a Spanish caravel sailed into Chesapeake Bay, dropping anchor just beyond range of the guns at Point Comfort. Three men put out from the vessel in a Biscay shallop and made their way to shore, where they were immediately taken into custody by a Captain John Davis. A request that an English pilot be sent to the caravel was granted. The Spanish then threatened to bombard the English fort unless the three men were returned. Captain Davis flung back the answer, "Go to the Devil!" With the English pilot aboard, the Spanish ship weighed anchor and headed for the sea. The three Spaniards who had come ashore were retained as prisoners. Questioning failed to divulge the nature of their activity, but it was reasonable to assume that they were spies, as subsequent events would prove.

It was therefore quite natural that Deputy-Governor Dale, freshly arrived from England with instructions from the Company to build a second town and receiving convincing proof of the urgent necessity for such action, should immediately assume the task with energy and dispatch. But before Marshal Dale could leave Jamestown, the colony was plunged into fear by the sight of six unidentified ships, three of them caravels. The fact that the vessels were assumed to be Spanish is convincing evidence of Virginia's consciousness of the Spanish threat. Fortunately, the ships were revealed to be English. Aboard one of them was Sir Thomas Gates, returned to the colony to serve a second time as its chief executive. With him came more settlers, and in the three caravels which had caused such alarm were livestock.[9]

Dale immediately communicated to Gates his intention to build a town near the falls of the James, and received the new executive's enthusiastic approval. Three hundred men were placed under Dale's command, and in September the stern marshal began the task of clearing ground for Henrico—for so the company had decreed the town should be named.[10] Within ten days he had completely cleared and impaled seven acres. Oppressing "his whole compayne with such extraordinayre labors by daye and watchinge by night, as may seem incredible to the eares of any who had not the experimentall triall thereof,"[11] he quickly raised five high watch towers and built a church and a storehouse. Not until these structures were complete was the building of lodgings begun.

Two years later, Dale seized the Indian town of Appomattox and the territory claimed by its inhabitants. Thus Dale won the entire peninsula between the Appomattox and James rivers, naming it Bermuda.

The colony began to flourish for the first time. Great numbers of the colonists moved from Jamestown to more healthful Henrico, gaining a large measure of relief from the "dread sicknesse" which had so often reduced their ranks. Marshal Dale's military experience and his observation of fortifications in the Netherlands had taught him much about defense, and the strength of Henrico was proof that he had learned the lessons well. For the first time, great numbers of the colonists enjoyed effective protection from the Indians. Blessed with the vigor of health and undiverted by necessity for constant watchfulness, they turned their attention and energy to the production of bumper crops.

By 1614 Henrico boasted three streets and neat homes with brick foundations. Armor from the Tower of London gleamed on its battlements.[12]

But, though the colonists prospered, it is doubtful that they were happier than before. Material progress had been gained at the expense of lost liberty.

The construction and maintenance of Henrico constituted the first major public works project in American history. From the standpoint of creating full employment, supplying the necessaries of life in great abundance, and providing buildings for community use, it was a huge success. From the standpoint of its effect on the general welfare, it was in many respects an abysmal failure. Was fear of one's leaders more conducive to peace of mind than fear of the hostile wilderness? Was torture at the hands of English officers more endurable than that inflicted by the Indians? Was hunger suffered as punishment easier borne than famine induced by scarcity? Apparently most of Dale's contemporaries thought not, and consequently found his rule abominable.[13] The slightest negligence in the performance of appointed tasks was punishable. George Percy declared that the penalties meted out by Marshal Dale were extreme and cruel.[14] Percy was no squeamish judge. He had once attached weights to a man's feet and suspended him by his thumbs for a quarter of an hour in order to obtain a confession.

Dale's contemporaries charged that, in inflicting punishment, he engaged in "the slaughter of his Majestys free subjects by starveing, hangeinge, burninge, breakinge upon the wheele and shootinge to deathe . . ., besides continuall whippings, extraordinary punishments, workeing as slaves in irons for terme of yeares (and that for petty offenses) weare dayly executed."[15]

Not all of Dale's contemporaries, however, were critical of the stern measures he employed. Reverend Alexander Whitaker, who had come to the colony with the marshal, declared, "Sir Thomas Dale our religious and valiant governor, hath now brought that to passe, which never before could be effected."[16] In a sense, Dale was religious. Like Lord De la Warr, he sought to restrain blasphemy, breach of the Sabbath, and sacrilege of all forms. Unlike the good Lord De la Warr, his rigid morality was apparently untempered by Christian benevolence and tolerance. Under Dale's direction and Sir Thomas Gates' general supervision, "blue lawes" were strictly enforced. It was decreed that "every man and woman daly twice a day upon the first towling of the Bell shall upon the working daies repair into the Church, to hear divine Service upon pain of losing his or her dayes allowance for the first omission, for the second to be whipt, and for the third to be condemned to the Gallies for six Months."[17] Evidently in support of the belief that cleanliness is next to Godliness, it was ordered that "no man or woman . . . dare to wash any unclean linen . . . within the Pallizadoes, . . . nor rench, and make clean, any kettle, pot or pan . . . within twenty foote of the old well . . . upon pain of whipping."[18]

Apparently, so long as Gates remained acting governor of the colony the punishments provided in these exacting orders were used chiefly as threats, to secure obedience, except in the case of the colonists under Dale's direct leadership at Henrico. When Dale became acting governor after Gates' return to England in 1614, the harsh punishments set forth were frequently inflicted. How the Massachusetts settlers—destined to plant a colony on New England soil but a few years hence—would have loved stern, puritanical Marshal Dale! Of course, the orders enforced under Dale's administration completely violated the charter rights of the Virginia colonists.

During the Gates and Dale administrations, a planned economy was placed in operation for the first time in American history. Supervision of crop production was the very least of the economic controls imposed. It was decreed that "No man shall dare to kill, or destroy any Bull, Cow, Calfe, Mare, Horse, Colt, Goate, Swine, Cocke, Henne, Chicken, Dogge, Turkie, or any tame Cattel, or Poultry, of what condition soever, . . . without leave from the Generall, upon paine of death."[19]

Virginia's economy was essentially communistic. To the colony accrued the products of its lands. To the government fell the task of distribution. This rigid authorization system must have appealed to Dale's domineering, precision-craving temperament. But to the marshal's pragmatic mind, inefficiency was anathema. Consequently, when he perceived that communism was inefficient, he immediately abandoned the system. Thus, the age of capitalism came to Virginia.

"Sir Thomas Dale hath taken a new course, throughout the whole Colonie," wrote Secretary Ralph Hamor, "by which meanes the generall store (apparell onely excepted) shall not be charged with any thing . . ."[20] To each man were allotted three acres of "cleere Corne ground" which he was to hold as his own. It was provided that he not be "called unto any service or labour belonging to the Colonie, more than one moneth in the yeere," and that not at "seed time, or in Harvest." The settler, however, was not exempt from taxation. Each landholder was required "yeerely to pay into the store two barrels and a halfe of Corne."

From the purely practical standpoint of increased material prosperity, the new program initiated by Deputy Governor Dale was a great reform. Within a short period after its institution, the colony was flourishing as never before and sending valuable exports to the mother country.

The energetic marshal, though busy with domestic affairs, found time to assume additional responsibility in the matter of foreign relations. Activity in this latter field was complicated and enlivened by the presence at Jamestown of a number of prisoners. Among them was suave and clever Don Diego de Molina—one of the

Spaniards seized by Captain John Davis in 1611. The wily grandee, incredible though it seems, was able during his confinement to send espionage reports to his native country.[21]

Both Gates and Dale took quite seriously Virginia's claim, as set forth in the charters of 1606 and 1609, to all land "along the Sea Coasts, between four and thirty degrees of *Northerly* latitude from the Equinoctial Line, and five and forty degrees of the same latitude." Hence, they conceived it their duty to guard the colony's thousand miles of sea coast. Consequently, when word was received that the French had planted a coastal settlement in territory today embraced by the state of Maine, Gates' lieutenant, Admiral Samuel Argall, sailed with sixty musketeers to remove the trespassers from Virginia soil.[22] Moving northward up the Atlantic seaboard in a ship of fourteen guns, they came upon the French settlement in June 1613 and immediately attacked it. Admiral Argall gave the French commandant and fourteen of his men leave to sail for France. The other colonists were carried back to Jamestown as prisoners.

The event is memorable for more than its dramatic character. It is tremendously significant even aside from the fact that it was a bold assertion that Virginia would permit no trespassing upon her soil. How different might have been the course of the French and Indian Wars if France had been allowed to gain a firm stronghold on the New England coast! Another result of Dale's action was to become apparent in the succeeding decade. For the attack on the French settlement, together with a mopping-up expedition that followed, removed a foreign menace from a potential area of English settlement. Thus, Dale's and Gates' boldly executed foreign policy made that part of the New World safe for New England democracy.

Spanish and French prisoners were not the only ones to lend a cosmopolitan air to Jamestown. There were also captured Indians—among them Pocahontas, daughter of the powerful werowance Powhatan. That Pocahontas was the favorite daughter of the mighty Indian enemy was well known to the colonists. Therefore, when Argall heard in 1613 that the young princess was visiting at the seat of Patawomack, he conceived the idea of seizing her as a hostage to secure an end to hostilities with her father. The capture was effected, and a precarious peace prevailed. Several months later, colonist John Rolfe, won by the charms of the graceful and comely captive, was united with her in marriage. In a letter to Marshal Dale requesting permission to wed the daughter of an alien race Captain Rolfe urged that he was motivated by a desire "for the good of this plantation, for the honour of our countrie, for the glory of God, for my own salvation, and for the converting to the true knowledge of God and Jesus Christ, an unbeleaving creature, Pokahontas."[23] Undoubtedly, he revealed an even stronger motive when he confessed that Pocahontas was she "to whom my heartie and best thoughts are, and have a long time been so intangled, and inthralled in so intricate a laborinth, that I was awearied to unwinde myself thereout."

The marriage ceremony, performed in the Jamestown church in the presence of Englishmen and Indians, signalized the beginning of a stable period of peace. Powhatan was an imposing figure of innate majesty who frequently, by appearance and manner alone, struck with awe the Englishmen to whom he granted audience. No less than thirty or forty tribal chiefs from the mountains to the sea, and from north of the Potomac to Roanoke Island, owed him allegiance.[24] Hence, peace with Powhatan meant much. Only one hostile tribe—the fierce, independent Chickahominies—remained a threat to security, and when they learned of the league with Powhatan they sent two messengers with peace offerings to Dale.[25]

In 1616, Sir Thomas Dale returned to England. His administration had founded a new town on a healthier location than the capital, had inaugurated a capitalistic system that brought prosperity to the colony, had made the New England coast safe for English settlement, and had concluded peace with the Indians. Notable contributions, indeed! Of course, the record of achievement is marred by the evidence of cruelty. Yet some of his ablest contemporaries credited Dale's hard measures with saving the colony. Secretary Ralph Hamor wrote, "It was no mean trouble to him, to reduce his people, so timely to good order, being of so il a condition as may well witnesse his severe and strict imprinted booke of Articles, then needefull with all severity and extremity to be executed, . . . so as if the law should not have restrained by execution, I see not how the utter subversion and ruine of the Colony should have bin prevented."[26] In the year of Dale's departure, Captain Rolfe declared that the marshal's "worth and name, in concluding this peace, and managing the affairs of this colony, will out last the standing of this plantation."[27] Sir Edwin Sandys, liberal humanitarian, said, "Dale building upon those foundaçons with great & constant severity, reclaymed almost miraculously those idle and disordered people and reduced them to labour and an honest fashion of life."[28] Certainly, we may agree with John Ferrar's conclusion that he was a "greate advancer of the Virginia Action."[29]

Chapter III

LEGISLATORS, AFRICANS AND "TIGER" GIRLS

(1616-1621)

Chapter III

~~~~~~

(1616-1621)

WHEN Sir Thomas Dale sailed from Jamestown in 1616, the administration of the colony fell to the Deputy Governor, Captain George Yeardley (Yardly).[1] If we may accept the appraisal by the usually objective Robert Beverley,[2] Yeardley's first term of office contributed little to Virginia's welfare.

"Captain Yardley," says Beverley, "made but a very ill Governour, he let the Buildings and Forts go to Ruine; not regarding the Security of the People against the Indians, neglecting the Corn, and applying all Hands to plant Tobacco, which promised the most immediate Gain. In this condition they were when Capt. Samuel Argall was sent thither Governour, Anno 1617. who found the Number of People reduc'd to something more than Four Hundred, of which not above Half were fit for Labour. In the mean while the Indians mixing among 'em, got Experience daily in Fire-Arms, and some of 'em were instructed therein by the English themselves, and employ'd to hunt and kill wild Fowl for them. So great was their Security upon this marriage (of John Rolfe and Pocahontas)."[3]

Yet Yeardley's administration must have seemed quite successful to most of the colonists. The interlude of peace gained by exertions under Marshal Dale was far happier for the complacent settlers than the strenuous period in which it had been won. No longer was every nerve strained in vigilance against the approach of a stealthy enemy. Hunger was but a memory that added piquancy to the pleasure of the housewife as her eye rested on her fat fowls, or the contentment of her spouse as he surveyed his sleek herds. If Jamestown or Henrico palled, there was a possibility of a visit to the other. Just the knowledge that there were two towns, that one was not living in the only settlement in a vast wilderness, was a comfort to many. Cultivation of tobacco for European markets had been begun by John Rolfe as early as 1613. In 1617, *The George's* cargo of 20,000 pounds of tobacco was grabbed by English merchants at five shillings and three cents a pound. A seven-year exemption from customs duties upon goods brought from Virginia, granted to the

Company by the Crown, had two more years to go. Hastening to take advantage of the remaining time, the Company bought the entire Virginia crop. Profits from resale of the tobacco were used by the Company to advertise and enlarge the colony. The promise of a new and profitable industry quickened English hopes for the success of the colonial experiment. New vessels were fitted out to bear the anticipated commerce, and hundreds of good yeomen responded enthusiastically to the call for more men to build an England beyond the seas.[5]

In April 1618 the beloved Lord De la Warr set sail for Virginia to relieve Captain Argall who was serving as interim chief of the colony's government. The return of the good governor must have seemed a crowning blessing to many optimists.

But Lord De la Warr never reached Virginia. He, with about thirty of his company, died en route.

In the same month that Lord De la Warr embarked on his last voyage, the Emperor Powhatan died. Succeeding him was his brother Itopatin. Upon his accession, the peace pact between the English and the Indians was reaffirmed.[6] Again the optimists failed to detect any threat to their security. Itopatin was not of his late brother's mold and he was no match for the crafty and ambitious Opecancanough, werowance of Chickahominy and already fretting within the narrow confines of his satrapy.

Another old enemy—far more powerful—still threatened to reach out across the sea and add the Virginia Colony to Philip III's growing collection. King James could not be relied on to defend the settlements on the James from Spanish attack. The proud navy of Drake, Hawkins and Grenville, which had routed Philip II's "Invincible Armada" only thirty years before, had been allowed by James I to degenerate into a feeble instrument requiring rather than affording protection.[7] Count Gondomar, Philip's ambassador to London, was intimidating King James with threats of war, and thus exercising more influence at court than most Englishmen surrounding the Stuart monarch. In this very year, he proved his power by securing the execution of Sir Walter Raleigh, sponsor of the first English attempt to colonize Virginia.[8]

The Virginia Colony, counting security in terms of material prosperity, must have seemed to shrewd foreign observers like some poor animal being fattened for the slaughter. The question seemingly was whether it would fall victim to the Indians and be completely obliterated, or to the Spaniards and become a new base for exploitation in the New World. Had the latter occurred, two of the world's greatest political entities probably would not have come into being. The United States, as we know it today, a nation of English institutions and English speech, doubtless would not exist. Within what now are the borders of the United States might today be a number of Latin republics, such as we find in South and Central America. But, since even these governments to the South are modeled after that of the United States, such speculation is vain. Very likely there would be no British Commonwealth of Nations, for the Commonwealth system was the logical culmination of colonial reformation set in force by the American Revolution.

But these very threats to security were to prove, as once before, a blessing to the colony in its stumbling progress toward liberal government. King James coveted the New World riches pouring into Philip's coffers and hence was eager to encourage development of Virginia. Yet his fear of Spain made him increasingly loath to assume responsibility for the Colony. While a plantation on the Atlantic Coast was desirable, it was not worth going to war. After all, the Bermudan Colony which had resulted from the wreck of the Virginia-bound *Sea Venture* in 1609, and another Caribbean outpost now were bringing more wealth to England than the James River venture.[9] The rich promise of the tobacco industry did not gladden James, for he despised the plant as "a foul weed" and was even to go so far as to issue his famed "Counterblaste" against it. He probably looked to Virginia chiefly as a source of naval stores to relieve his dependency upon Sweden and Muscovy and as a doubtful source of gold. Hence it was that the Stuart monarch was in the mood to grant a more liberal charter to the London Company in 1618. "If it take not success," his advisors told him of the Company's experiment, "it is done by their owne heddes. It is but the attempt of private gentlemen, the State suffers noe losse, noe disreputation. If it takes success, they are your subjects, they doe it for your service, they will lay all at your Majesty's feet and interess your Majesty therein."[10]

So Sir Edwin Sandys was able to secure a greater transfer of authority to the Company in 1618. But the new charter never reached Jamestown, for it was sent over in the keeping of Lord De la Warr on the ill-fated voyage that cost him his life. But another plan of government, perhaps more liberal than the first, was to be instituted.

On the night of November 18, 1618, superstitious London sky-gazers became excited over the appearance of a comet. This phenomenon, ever associated with fateful events, inevitably recalled its fire-tailed counterpart which had hung low in the heavens only eleven years before as three small vessels, carrying a bit of England, clove an ocean path to a new world. The colony built by that little band commanded the attention of some of England's ablest men, gathered in London on that very November 18. The London-Virginia Council decided on that historic day to transfer its governmental prerogatives to the Virginia Colony itself.[11] Thus the appearance of celestial portents, a classic dramatic device for impressing an audience with the cataclysmic importance of the events portrayed, lent an authentically histrionic note to the beginning of the drama of colonization and to its first real climax.

Basically, the changes—which were to have world-wide import— were as follows:

The Colony was to be governed by "two Supreme Councils":

(1) The Council of State, consisting of "the Governor and his Counsellors," these to be chosen by the Company in England.

(2) The General Assembly, consisting of "the aforesaid Council of State and two Burgesses chosen out of each Town Hundred or other particular Plantation."[12]

This bicameral assembly was to convene annually and to "have power to make and ordaine whatsoever lawes and orders should by them be thought good and proffittable for our subsistence."[13]

The Assembly's powers to legislate for the welfare of the Colony were subject to the proviso that they not contravene the laws of England, the charter, or the instructions of the London Company.[14] Actually, there were other checks as well on the exercise of legislative authority. The Governor was empowered to veto any measure which he did not approve, and no legislative vote would suffice to override that veto. He, however, was no absolute monarch. The Company in London could always veto laws to which he had given assent. Furthermore, the Governor was empowered only to reject, not to initiate legislation. The dependence of the executive upon the legislature for enactment of those measures which he desired, together with the fact that the Assembly included the principal members of the only society that he was to know during his exile from England, must have made a thoughtful Governor reluctant to antagonize either Councillors or Burgesses.

Apparently, there was no dichotomy of duties corresponding to the bicameral division of the Assembly itself. Matters of defense and of finance appear to have originated in either house. The main difference between the two houses was that of personnel. The royally appointed Councillors and the popularly elected Burgesses were the representatives of different political philosophies. While greater prestige attached to the position of Councillor, it must not be assumed that Councillor and Burgess necessarily stood at opposite ends of the social scale. On the contrary, one family might have a member in each of the two chambers. True it is that more younger sons or representatives of less privileged branches of prominent families might be found in the lower house. But, for all practical purposes, Burgesses and Councillors met socially as equals.

As might be expected, the more exclusive house was the smaller. Thus, while the Council consisted of six men, under the Charter of 1619 there was a twenty-two-member House of Burgesses.

These Burgesses were to be elected from nine "plantations" and three "cities." Actually, there were at first eleven electoral districts variously called cities, hundreds, or plantations.[15]

Cities, so-called, were really areas assigned for the development of cities. Though inhabited, they could boast nothing more urban than a village.

A hundred was a territorial division adopted from the mother country. In England a hundred was a county division sufficiently large to have its own court or hundred moot. The word comes to us from the Anglo-Saxons. Some philologists think that the term was originally used to designate an area comprising one hundred hides. In old Saxon nomenclature, a hide was enough land to support a family. Other etymologists think that "hundred" was used to designate a territory which could be counted on to furnish a hundred warriors.[16] The term, as has been suggested, was particularly appropriate because of the plan of 1616 under which "Particular Plantations" were granted to stockholders who bore the cost of sending one hundred settlers to Virginia. It was natural that Englishmen, faced with the necessity of describing sparsely-settled tracts not designated as cities, should appropriate the time-honored and familiar English name for a division of a county.

The plantations referred to in the charter were not large estates such as came to bear that name in the American South and in tropical regions. The word was used in the older meaning of "a place colonized." Thus, at times, the entire colony was referred to as "his Majesty's plantation in Virginia."

Each of the electoral districts was denominated a "borough" and lay within one of the four "general boroughs" or "corporations" into which the settled portion of the colony was divided. Like other designations listed, the term "borough" was borrowed from England. In the mother country, the borough was a unit with citizenship rights of its own and with the privilege of sending representatives to Parliament.

On April 29, 1619, George Yeardley returned to Virginia with the title of Governor-General, a "Sir" before his name and the London Company's "general instructions for the better establishing of a Commonwealth."[17]

He issued a proclamation setting forth that "it was granted that a General Assembly should be held yearly once, whereat were to be present the Governor and Counsell, with two Burgesses from each Plantation freely to be elected by the inhabitants thereof; this assembly to have power to make and ordaine whatsoever lawes and orders should by them be thought good and profittable for our subsistence."[18]

Then, pending the holding of elections, he organized the Council of State as prescribed. The government of the colony remained in the hands of this Council of State, consisting of the governor and his counselors, until the convention of the General Assembly Friday, July 30, 1619 (O.S.) or August 9, 1619 by the modern calendar.[19]

That date is one of the most momentous in world history, for it marks the beginning of legislative government in the New World. On that day, says James Truslow Adams, "political self-government was formally inaugurated on the American continent."[20] John Fiske calls the Virginia General Assembly of 1619 one of the ancestors of "the bicameral legislatures of nearly all the world in modern times."[21]

What excitement must have prevailed that day in little Jamestown, or James City, as the settlers called it when in a pretentious mood! Planters from Bermuda Hundred, thirty-five miles up the James, and Kecoughtan, about thirty miles down river, and from other points between, converged on the colonial capital.[22] Their ladies, clad in the silks of England and wearing ruffed collars like millstones around their necks, were helped ashore from the barges that arrived at intervals. Pioneer life provided few dress occasions, and they were determined to make the most of the opportunity presented. Down the dirt street of Jamestown they went, turning their white-coifed heads in search of acquaintances, lifting their puffed-out prunella skirts from the dust and revealing brocaded petticoats of blue, green and canary. No less respendent were the men. Tight doublets of silk or velvet encased their chests like red, purple or blue armor. Gleaming swords rattled against the bright velvet of their stuffed knee-pants, which terminated in large garter bows where the silk stockings began. (This padding served more than vanity; it could cushion an arrow or sword thrust.) Long bright oversleeves, vestigial reminders of the cloak, tossed as their wearers walked. Little more than the goatees and mustaches of the planters appeared beneath the rakishly-dipped, wide brims of high-crowned felt hats. Elaborate dress was not merely a frivolity. For these English settlers in a wilderness, it was almost a necessity. With them, as always with Englishmen in colonial territory, correct dress was an important tie with the amenities of civilization.

Any gathering of the colonists in those days when a neighbor sometimes was somebody who could be reached within a day was an exciting occasion. But this day brought with it a stronger, albeit sobered, excitement. All thoughtful men of the newly-elected General Assembly must have been aware that they were making history.

"The most convenient place we could find to sit in," one of them wrote, "was the Quire of the Church."[23] The church here referred to is not the building to which Lord De la Warr used to march in such style with his red-cloaked guard, but one completed only about two years before the convening of the Assembly. "Built wholly at the charge of the inhabitants of that cittie [Jamestown]," it was a frame structure measuring fifty by twenty feet.[24]

"Sir George Yeardley, the Governour, being sett downe in his accustomed place," read the minutes of that historic meeting, "those of the Counsel of Estate [Council of State] sat next him on both handes, except onely the Secretary, then appointed Speaker, who sat right before him; John Twine, clerk of the General Assembly, being placed next the Speaker; and Thomas Pierse, the Sergeant, standing at the barre, to be ready for any service the Assembly should commaund him . . .

"But forasmuche as men's affairs doe little prosper where God's service is neglected, all the Burgesses tooke their places in the Quire till a prayer was said by Mr. Bucke, the Minister, that it would please God to guide and to sanctify all our proceedings to his owne glory and to the good of this Plantation."[25]

The Rev. Richard Buck, a good and faithful man weighed down with many personal disappointments,[26] stood before that brightly arrayed little assembly, a contrasting figure in his white surplice and close cap of black.[27] "Prayer being ended," say the minutes, "to the intente that as we had begun at God Almighty, so we might proceed with awful and due respect toward the Lieutenant, our most gracious and dread Soveraigne James I, all the burgesses were entrated to retyre themselves into the body of the Churche."[28] To those seventeenth century Englishmen who shared King James' belief in the divine right of Kings, there was reverence, not blasphemy, in those words.

▷ Before the Burgesses joined the Council of State in the body of the church, however, they responded to a roll call, each taking the Oath of Supremacy, "none staggering at it."[29] Members of the Council of State, having occupied their offices since soon after Governor Yeardley's return, had previously been sworn in.[30]

The legislators then took their seats facing the choir. Governor Yeardley, sitting in his green velvet chair with his back to the choir, looked down on rows of high-crowned hats like so many inverted flower-pots among waving plumes, for the Burgesses—true to English parliamentary tradition—sat with their heads covered.[31] Lady Yeardley, the former Temperance Flowerdew, must have regarded her husband with satisfaction. According to rumor, family pride had made her hesitate in marrying him.[32] Now he was a man of consequence. Within eight months,[33] he had been knighted and been appointed Governor General of Virginia, and today was presiding over the first legislative assembly in the New World.

Only one other man present rivaled Sir George's pre-eminence in the Assembly. That man was his wife's cousin, the capable John Pory, whose experience as a member of the Parliament in London, made him intimately familiar with procedures of which most others had only read or heard.[34] He was thus the logical choice for speaker of the Assembly. Nevertheless, he was an adherent of the Warwick faction that opposed Sandys' liberal ideas for Virginia development.[35]

This convention must have been much like the dramas of the period, acted by elegantly costumed players in the stark simplicity of a plain and well-nigh bare interior.

No mere perfunctory opening session was this. Tempers flared on that hot[36] August day. Speaker Pory himself objected to the admission of the elected representatives from Warde's Plantation on grounds that the settlement had been made without a commission from the London Company. The objection was waived, however, when Captain Warde promised to obtain a patent as soon as possible.[37]

▷ Not so easily resolved, however, was the issue of seating Burgesses from Martin Brandon. Captain Martin, upon the Governor's own motion, was summoned before the Assembly and requested to relinquish those special privileges, rendering him almost independent of the Jamestown government, which had been granted him by reason of his long services to the Colony. Enjoying the hard-won prerogatives of a feudal baron, Captain Martin was naturally unwilling to surrender them. "I hold my patent," he said, "for my service done, which no new or late comer can merit or challenge."[38]

The Assembly, on the other hand, was quite unwilling to grant a part in making the laws of the Colony to a constituency not fully subject to those laws. The legislature, therefore, acting as the judge of its members' qualifications, refused to seat the representatives of Martin Brandon.

Handling all business with a dispatch found only in the concluding hours of modern legislative sessions, the General Assembly sat but five days.

Before adjourning Wednesday, the legislature recorded the following address:

"In conclusion, the whole Assembly comanded the Speaker (as nowe he doth) to present their humble excuse to the Treasurer Counsell & Company in England, for being constrained by the intemperature of the Weather & the falling sick of diverse of the Burgesses to breake up so abruptly—before they had so much as put their lawes to the ingrossing."[39]

The Assembly was prompt to exercise its powers of taxation. In order to obtain funds for the payment of its officers, the legislature ordered "That every man and manservant of above 16 years of age shall pay into the handes and Custody of the Burgesses of every Incorporation and plantation one pound of the best tobacco."[40] This, of course, was the first poll tax levied by an American government.

The Assembly also asserted the exclusive right to levy general taxes. Such authority was not expressly granted to that body, but it was quick to take advantage of the latitude afforded by the grant of "power to make and ordaine whatsoever lawes and orders should by them be thought good and proffittable for our subsistence." Most important of the general taxes was the "quit-rent," a land tax paid to the King by all freeholders. This was not a levy peculiar to the colonies, but one exacted from all landholders subject to the Crown.[41]

The Virginia legislature, like the British House of Lords, also assumed judicial functions. A committee including both Burgesses and Councillors was named to study cases submitted to the General

Assembly as the highest tribunal of the Colony and recommend decisions to be voted on by that body in plenary session.[42]

While the Councillors and Burgesses of 1619 knew that they were making history, they had neither the leisure nor the perspective to see how their deliberations fitted into the grand design of parliamentary history on a global scale. Let us note for a moment the precedents which they had followed or established.

The most notable fact of all was that a legislature had been established. No other colony in the world had one. Thus the Virginia General Assembly of 1619 was England's first experiment in allowing self-government in a colonial possession. Upon the results of this experiment depended much of subsequent British colonial history. No colony of any world power except England was to have a legislature until the nineteenth century.[43]

The most obvious feature of the legislature brought into existence at Jamestown was its bicameral character. This feature was derived directly from British precedent. In Virginia, as in England, one of the two houses was an especially exclusive body, the members of which obtained their seats from the Crown, while the other was composed of members obtaining their seats by popular election.

At first, the members of the two bodies sat together, "after the manner of the Scots' Parliament," Robert Beverley observed.[44] Someone might have reminded Beverley that the two houses of the English Parliament had sat together when the bicameral system was first instituted. Simon de Montfort, who led the revolt against Henry III, summoned in 1265 an English national assembly which differed from its predecessors in that representatives of the boroughs were summoned. The lords spiritual and temporal, constituting one house, and the borough representatives, constituting another, continued to sit in the same chamber until the reign of Edward III in the fourteenth century. By that time diversity of interests and the Commons' desire for a place in the sun, rather than in the shadow of the Lords, forced a separation.[45]

After a few joint sessions, the two houses of Virginia's General Assembly were also to separate, apparently for much the same reason. Thus Virginia's early parliamentary history duplicated in large part that of the mother country. In each place, the upper chamber ante-dated the lower. In each, the two bodies first met together and then separated.

There are other striking parallels. In each case, the upper chamber evolved from a royal advisory council. Antecedent to the English

House of Lords were the Anglo-Saxon Witenagemot and the later Curia Regis.[46] The Virginia Council, as we have seen, originally advised and aided the Governor in his capacity as King's deputy.

The judicial functions of the Virginia General Assembly were a logical inheritance from England. The old Curia Regis had exercised judicial authority and the House of Lords, as its amplified successor, continued to sit as a high tribunal. A departure from British tradition, however, was the sharing of judicial authority between the two houses.

Now let us examine the precedents followed and established in the organization and procedure of the General Assembly.

First of all, the legislature began the day's activities with a prayer from the chaplain.

By what means the officers of the Assembly were first chosen, we do not know. But the Assembly began with a speaker, a clerk and a sergeant-at-arms as well as a chaplain.

The Assembly at once established its right to judge the qualifications of its own members when it admitted the representatives of Warde's Plantation only after deliberation and the representatives of Martin Brandon not at all. By its refusal to admit the representatives of Martin's hundred, the legislators also established the precedent of denying representation to those enjoying special privilege.

The concurrence of a simple majority sufficed for the passage of any legislation. The Governor's relationship to the Assembly was a dual one. As a member of the Assembly, he participated in making the laws. As a deputy of the King, he was the actual head of state and enforcer of royal directives in the colony. As the executive agent of the government, he was responsible for the enforcement of the laws enacted by the Assembly. As we have seen, he possessed an absolute veto that could be exercised as a brake on the legislature.

Almost as notable as the character of the General Assembly itself was the manner in which membership in the House of Burgesses was apportioned. Since Jamestown and Henrico were the only Virginia settlements which could be called towns, the first constituencies corresponded to counties. Thus the county became the basic unit of the new government.

* * *

The father of Virginia's new government, and so of self-government in America, was Sir Edwin Sandys. Its godfather was Henry Wriothesley, third earl of Southampton. It was Southampton who

helped Sir Edwin to obtain the Charter of 1618 which permitted the
summoning of a legislature. In 1619, Sir Edwin succeeded Sir
Thomas Smith as head of the London Company. An able and
devoted friend of Virginia, Smith ill deserved the opprobrium
heaped upon him by some colonists, but he had been more interested
in putting Jamestown on a sound economic basis than in making it
a political laboratory.[47]

On July 24, 1621 (O.S.), almost two years after the convening
of the General Assembly in Jamestown, the small stockholders, as a
result of Sandys' and Southampton's work, obtained the seal of
James I on an Ordinance for Virginia confirming the provisions for
representative government.[48] This document of 1621 may contain
some provisions not made in that of 1618. Comparison is impossible,
since no copy of the original is known to be in existence.[49] The 1621
ordinance did include a provision, perhaps not present in its predecessor, that the House of Burgesses "be called by the Governor, once
yearly, and no oftener, but for very extraordinary and important
occasions."[50] Here was laid the basis for special sessions.

The joint labors of Sir Edwin Sandys and Henry Wriothesley,
Earl of Southampton, might lead one to suppose that they were
kindred spirits. Such, however, was not the case.

In 1619, Southampton was forty-six years old. Auburn-
haired, with lively blue eyes, this handsome man loved life
and believed that it was compounded of adventures. In his own
career, he proved that to be true.

A great lover of the theater, he was the patron of many dramatic
poets, among them William Shakespeare. *Venus and Adonis*, which
appeared in 1593, and *Lucrece*, which appeared the following year,
were both dedicated to Southampton, the first in conventional terms
of appreciation, the second in glowing words of tribute. "The love
I dedicate to your lordship," Shakespeare inscribed in *Lucrece*, "is
without end . . . What I have done is yours, what I have to do is
yours, being part in all I have, devoted yours."

Southampton accompanied that scheming courtier Essex on his
two expeditions to Cadiz and the Azores (1596 and 1597), distinguishing himself on the second by his daring tactics.

In 1598, he was undiplomatic enough to get in a brawl at court,
and later the same year accompanied Sir Robert Cecil on a diplomatic mission to Paris.

The next year he went to Ireland as general of Essex's cavalry,
but returned to London when Queen Elizabeth had his commission
cancelled.

Southampton's association with Essex got him deeply involved in the conspiracy against the queen. Elizabeth, who did not let feminine emotion prevent her from ordering Essex's execution, naturally had few inhibitions about meting out such a sentence to a subordinate implicated in the plot. Hence, Southampton was condemned to death in February 1601. Cecil, by as adroit diplomacy in behalf of his friend as he ever exercised in the interest of his country, obtained commutation of the sentence to life imprisonment.

Lifetime confinement, to a man of Southampton's temperament, must have seemed more intolerable than death. But he was not long to remain a prisoner. The accession of James I in 1603 not only brought his release, but also restored him to his place at court.

In that same year, he further cemented his relations with the Royal family by entertaining Queen Anne at a special performance of *Love's Labors Lost* played by the famous Richard Burbage and his company.

Later during the year, Southampton—who must have quarreled as easily as he made friends—again gave offense to Royalty and was returned to prison for a short time.

In 1614, he fought on the Protestant side in the religious war in Germany. Three years later he was eager to outfit an expedition against the Barbary pirates, but the following year he seems to have found release for his pugnacious spirit in meetings of the London Company. He there joined hands with Sir Edwin Sandys for a good rousing fight against entrenched reaction.

In 1621, the year that their joint efforts brought forth the Ordinance of 1618, Southampton fell into official disgrace as a result of his opposition to George Villiers, first Duke of Buckingham.[51]

Opposition to Buckingham was a challenge to the King, since the twenty-nine-year-old peer then was the bosom companion of the madcap young Prince Charles and James' own favorite courtier.

The charming younger son and namesake of Sir George Villiers was introduced to the King at about the time of his twenty-second birthday by a friend who hoped that the young man would become a court favorite. He could not have selected a more propitious time. James was tiring of his chief advisor, Robert Carr, Earl of Somerset. The King apparently concluded that a man who could dance, fence and talk as well as George Villiers might be fit for high office. Accordingly, the young man was made a gentleman of the bedchamber on April 23, 1615. That September Somerset's downfall was precipitated by the charge that he had murdered Overbury and Villiers became his successor. Beginning with January of 1617, the start of every year brought him an honor. First he was made an earl, then Marquess of Buckingham, and then—in the very year that the First General Assembly convened in Jamestown—Lord High Admiral of England.

Buckingham rewarded so many of his friends with naval commissions that the already weak English fleet declined still further. His sympathy for the continental Protestants, increased when James' son-in-law accepted the crown of Bohemia, was dissipated before the end of the summer of 1620, perhaps partly by his wife's influence and partly by injuries inflicted on English sailors by the Dutch in the East Indies. The end of the year found him so much under the influence of Gondomar, the Spanish ambassador who had designs on Virginia, that the Spaniard was perhaps the real first minister of England's King.

Southampton's feud with Buckingham must have increased the vehemence of his fight for an increasing measure of self-government in Virginia. Southampton's cooperation made possible the realization of Sir Edwin Sandys' dream of a government in the New World in which the Geneva ideals of popular sovereignty could be united with the English traditions of legislation. Thus, as a result of London court intrigues related to struggle for supremacy among the great powers of the earth, the most important world event of 1619 took place in Jamestown, Virginia, a stockaded village on the edge of a trackless wilderness.

* * *

The ship that brought the new plan of government to Jamestown was not the only vessel freighted with destiny to discharge its cargo in Virginia in 1619.

"About the latter end of August," John Rolfe wrote to Sir Edwin Sandys soon after the start of the year 1620, "a Dutch man of Warr of the burden of 160 tunes arrived at Point Comfort, the commanders name Capt. Jope, his pilott for the West Indyes, one Mr. Marmaduke an Englishman. They met with the Treasurer in the West Indyes, and determined to hold consort shipp hetherward, but in their passages lost one the other. He brought not anything but 20 and odd Negroes, which the Governor and Cape Marchant bought for victualle (whereof he was in great need as he ptended) at the best and easiest rates they could. . . ."[52]

This account has, until recent years, led even historians to suppose that Negro slavery in what is now the United States began in

1619 and that the Dutch initiated the trade. A change in terminology wrought by the years and a strategy employed by an unscrupulous nobleman are responsible for the confusion.

The word "slavery" did not carry so harsh a connotation in 1619 as it does in our time. It was frequently used to describe "indenture," a process by which one person worked in the service of another, or of the colony, for a specified period in return for certain specified benefits. It was commonly said elliptically that a man had been "bought" when his services had been purchased. Virginia's first indentured servants were white.[53] There is no indication that the Negroes who arrived in 1619 entered bondage under circumstances anywise different from those under which many whites entered apprenticeship.

The *Treasurer*, an English vessel, had sailed from Virginia in the summer of 1618 "under pretense of getting salt and goats for the colony." It was equipped, however, with "powder, shott, wast clothes, ordynaunce streamers, flagges and other furniture fitt for the man of warre."[54]

The English vessel met a so-called "Dutch man-of-war" off the coast, and, proceeding together, they came upon and captured a Spanish frigate carrying a cargo of Negroes to the Spanish West Indies. Finding no bullion aboard the frigate, the captors seized the human cargo.

The cargo was landed in Virginia by the so-called Dutch man-of-war. The *Treasurer* was owned by Robert Rich, Earl of Warwick, who was engaged in piracy.[55] Naturally, he could not risk having his own vessel unload at Jamestown a cargo gained in a piratical raid. The boat was too well known. It was in the *Treasurer* that Argall had raided the French settlement on Mount Desert Island in 1613. It was the *Treasurer* that had carried to England the famous shipload of tobacco which created great demand for the product in the mother country. The vessel was too closely identified with the history of the colony to escape identification. Therefore, it was the *Treasurer's* consort, and not the *Treasurer* itself, which unloaded the stolen cargo.

The consort was probably not a Dutch vessel. As Matthew Page Andrews relates, the term "Dutch man-of-war" was "a convenient pseudonym for any English-named vessel engaged in anti-Spanish aggression."[56]

The "man-of-war" departed in haste after landing its cargo, evidently having been warned that the conscientious Sir George

Yeardley had succeeded Argall in the governorship since the *Treasurer* set sail from Virginia in 1618.[57] Though Governor Yeardley was not able to take action against the vessel, officials of the London Company learned of the exploit.

A generation before, piratical raids on Spanish commerce had been laughed off as jolly adventures by the best of Englishmen. The hearty laughter of England's red-haired queen had often mingled with that of Drake, Hawkins and other dashing "seadogs" when tales were told of plunder on the Spanish Main. But Sir Edwin Sandys was not disposed to regard with levity the *Treasurer's* piratical activities. Viewing them as a threat to relations between Spain and English colonial territory, he apologized to Ambassador Gondomar and disclaimed responsibility for the incident involving the "Dutch" consort.[58]

Warwick, fearing that Sandys' statements had jeopardized his position in a court dominated by the Spanish ambassador, was smitten with rage. He determined to vent his spleen upon Sandys' favorite project—self-government in Virginia. Thus the Earl of Warwick, an entrepreneur in piracy upon Spain, was brought by revenge to ally himself with the faction of Sir Thomas Smith and Alderman Johnson, the group that acquiesced with the King in his obeisance to Philip.[59]

So Sandys' apology to Gondomar made a new enemy for self-government in Virginia. But it may also have saved the colony. For, had Warwick succeeded in his scheme to make the Bermudas and Jamestown bases of supply for expeditions against Caribbean ports and depredations on Spanish commerce, Philip III might have retaliated by wiping out Virginia.

Many other immigrants had come and were yet to come in 1619. About fifty London orphans and outcast waifs arrived in Virginia in the spring, having been sent to the colony with the humanitarian aim of taking them off the streets.[60] Frequent references to them as "the Dutye boys" have caused many persons to suppose that they were sent as slave labor. The name however derives from the ship *Duty* which bore them to a superior environment, and one where they might earn decent livings.

The Crown also resorted to the expedient of sending to Virginia persons convicted of crimes and misdemeanors.[61] This policy, however, did not people the colony with cut-throats. Many of the "crimes" were offenses that would be regarded as trivial today. Some of Virginia's best yeoman stock arrived as criminals.

No less than 1,261 persons poured into the colony in 1619. One hundred of these were tenants for the College reservation, a portion of land having been set aside at Henrico for the establishment of a college, primarily for the benefit of the Indians that they might be schooled in Christianity. Fifty were tenants for glebe lands. Tenants to till the lands of the Colony and of the Governor, who was now provided with an official residence, numbered 210. Among the immigrants were one hundred boys as apprentices and fifty servants. Probably most of the servants were indentured, having obtained their passage to a new land of opportunity in exchange for two or three years' "slavery" (service) to the colony.[62]

But by far the most interesting immigrants arriving in 1619 were ninety "young maids to make wives for former tenants" now freed from indenture. The Company, in its "Declaration" of June 1620, referred to the sending out of "one hundred young maids to make wives . . . as the former ninety."[63] Other shipments followed.

The Jamestown colony had at first consisted entirely of men. But it was the desire of the London Company to establish a permanent colony, not a mere trading post. So white women began to enter Virginia, and, as we have seen, accompanied their planter husbands to sessions of the General Assembly. But women still were few in the colony. Many artisans and laborers lacked wives. So the arrival of shiploads of women was a matter of great importance. It gave stability to the infant settlements.

The Earl of Southampton, realizing that women were needed to halt the return of colonists to England, was an earnest promoter of projects to secure wives for the settlers. Much confusion over the status of these "maids," comparable to that over the status of the first Negro arrivals, has arisen from the recorded fact that their prospective husbands were to give 120 pounds of "the best leaf tobacco for each of them, and in case any of them die that proportion must be advanced to make it upon those that survive."[64] Many persons have the impression that these "maids" were shipped to Virginia as slaves, and there purchased like any other commodity.

On the contrary, their passages were paid by the Company or by groups of sponsors. Upon arrival in Virginia, they might reject any or all suitors. But if any man desired to marry one of them, it became incumbent upon him to reimburse the company or sponsors for the cost of her passage. The sponsors for maids setting forth in the *Warwick* and the *Tiger* wrote:

"We hope [they] shall be received with the same Christian piety and charity as they are sent from hence; the providing for them at their first landing, and disposing of them in marriage (which is our chief intent) we leave to your care and wisdom to take that order as may most conduce to their good, and satisfaction of the adventurers for the charges disbursed in setting them forth, which, coming to twelve pounds and upwards, they require one hundred and fifty of the best tobacco for each of them." (Tobacco, the true measure of a man's wealth in Virginia, had supplanted other currency.)

"If any of them shall unwarily or fondly bestow herself (for the liberty of marriage we dare not infringe) upon such as shall not be able to give present satisfaction; we desire that at least as ability shall be they be compelled to pay the true quantity of tobacco proportioned, and that this debt may have precedence over all others to be recovered; for the rest, which we hope will not be many, we desire your best furtherance for providing them fitting services, till they may happen upon good matches."[65]

Despite precautions for the safety of these "maids," those aboard the *Tiger* nearly became slaves. Passengers on the forty-ton pinnace, which had become separated from its consort, the 160-ton *Warwick*, were apprehensive when a strange sail was sighted. Apprehension flared into alarm when the unidentified vessel fast gaining upon them was seen to be a Turkish craft. The Turks were not alone in piracy, but they were more feared than most sea-roving predators, because they did not confine their looting to inanimate cargoes, or even to black slaves as did the more extreme western privateers. Young women were the most precious prizes of all. They would bring huge prices in the slave marts of the East. Blondes, of whom there would be a sizeable proportion in any English group, brought the highest prices of all. Their rarity in the East made them much sought after. Hence, the *Tiger's* cargo was a prize indeed.

The corsairs overtook the English pinnace and, scrambling onto its deck, quickly made themselves masters of the ship and went about their business in methodical fashion. They transferred most of the *Tiger's* food, serviceable sails, tackling and anchors to their own craft, and were preparing to make prisoners of the English girls when the sudden appearance of another ship caused them to flee the scene.[66] Thus these girls were spared the oppressive luxury of slavedom in a seraglio, and learned instead the hardships of homemaking in a wilderness.

* * *

What a year was 1619!

This year saw the beginning of representative government in the new world when the first legislative assembly ever to convene in North America met at Jamestown on a hot August day. That same month saw the Negro enter Virginia, and when he stepped on the little wharf at Jamestown he stepped also on the stage of American history. In the same year, women first came to the colony in large numbers and began to exert an important stabilizing influence. Indentured servants were beginning to pour into Virginia. The components of colonial society were assembled, and the building was beginning in earnest.

One group of settlers who headed for the Chesapeake Bay region were driven off their course by unfavorable winds and arrived instead at a point far north of their intended destination.[67] These men were the Separatists, or religious dissenters, who had found refuge in the Netherlands during their exile. Sir Edwin Sandys eventually obtained permission for them to settle in Virginia.[68] And to Virginia they came, even though carried far from the settled southern part. On November 11, 1620, a group of their leaders, apparently alarmed by the "anarchistic" sentiments of one Stephen Hopkins who had been punished in Jamestown for sedition, gathered around a table in the cabin of the wave-tossed *Mayflower* and by flickering candlelight drew up a compact of government.[69] The land off which they anchored was part of a large tract of Virginia officially named New England.

Thus in 1620 a settlement was planted between the Jamestown area and the French outposts, planted in fact in a region cleared of French colonists by an expedition of war sent out from Jamestown.

The southern colony was growing in numbers and in prosperity. In 1620 and 1621, the settlers could catch their breath after the rapid succession of events in 1619. A kind and upright Governor was in office. The "sicknesse" still took a heavy toll, but it was believed that restriction of immigration to the autumn months would diminish its effect. Between the thriving communities of Jamestown and Henrico lay productive plantations with neat frame houses. To some optimists, it must have seemed that the affairs of the colony were running on as steadily and as surely to their ultimate destination as were the waters of the James which flowed majestically past their homes.

Still there were some who feared that this sense of security was not well grounded. During the first session of the General Assembly of 1619, Secretary-Speaker John Pory had recorded Governor Yeard-ley's "particular opinion to my selfe in private . . . that in these doubtful times between us and the Indians, it would behoove us not to make as lardge distances between Plantation as ten miles, but for our strength and security to drawe nearer together."[70]

Chapter IV

TOMAHAWK AND SCEPTER

(1622-1624)

Chapter IV

(1622-1624)

SPRING came to an unhappy Virginia in 1622. Nearly twelve hundred settlers had perished in the interval since the dogwood last had bloomed along the banks of the James.[1]

So great were the ravages of the dread "sicknesse" that, as Thomas J. Wertenbaker has commented, "it was like condemning a man to death to send him to the colony."[2] Seventy-five or eighty percent of the laborers that left England for Virginia homes, the same historian tells us, died before the expiration of their first year.

Many perished en route. Lady Wyatt—who sailed to Virginia to join her husband, Sir Francis Wyatt, named to succeed Sir George Yeardley as Governor in November 1621—wrote her "Sister Sandys" that the ship in which she traveled had been "so pestered with people and goods . . . so full of infection that after a while they saw but little but throwing folks overboard."[3] Few of her fellow passengers, she reported, were alive when the vessel anchored off Jamestown.

Lady Wyatt was the former Margaret Sandys, niece of Sir Edwin. The ship in which her husband arrived had an escort of eight vessels.[4] More impressive than any pomp, however, was the fact that the new governor brought with him the confirmation, for which Sir Edwin and Southampton had contended, of those political privileges promulgated in 1619 by Sir George Yeardley.[5]

Sir George, who previously had only with difficulty been dissuaded from resigning, relinquished the governorship with good grace. Consistent with his generous spirit, he lavished praise on the associates who had aided him in his administration.[6]

The new Governor, Sir Francis Wyatt, seemed to have the equable temper of his predecessor. Moreover, as a couple to the manner born, he and his wife graced Jamestown society in a way that was pleasing to many of the colonists who were starved for the elegancies of life in the mother country.

So 1622 found Virginians distressed by the growing toll exacted by the "sicknesse," but consoled in some measure by the character of their Governor.

The race who shared Virginia with the English were also disturbed. The Indians, even more than the settlers along the James, feared extinction.

With anxious eyes they watched the constant encroachment of the white man upon the lands of their fathers. The Indian found himself fenced out of more and more of the territory which he regarded as his communal birthright. And still the great winged canoes of the English bore settlers in increasing numbers. Soon the Powhatans would find themselves squeezed in between the land-hungry white men on one side and the enemy tribes of the mountains on the other.

The wily Opecancanough plotted the destruction of these invaders of his realm. Past successes against other enemies fed his confidence.

Opecancanough was not a Powhatan by birth. He sprang from a foreign tribe, from the far Southwest.[7] There the white man, it is believed, had intruded upon his dominion. Suffering defeat at the hands of the well-armed and heavily-armored Spaniards, and seeing that further resistance was useless, he led his people toward the home of the rising sun. In the eastward course of the great migration, Opecancanough encountered many tribes who sought to bar his path, but apparently he defeated all of them from what is now Mexico to Virginia.[8]

Arrived in Powhatan's empire, which stretched from the mountains to the great waters, Opecancanough was face to face with a man of equal stature. He found it prudent to accept the post of werowance, or lord of a satrapy, under Powhatan's imperial sway, and opportunities for advancement.

There were occasions for a man of Opecancanough's courage and craft. Powhatan's brother, perhaps too long under the emperor's complete domination, was weak. Opecancanough had been building up his personal prestige during Powhatan's declining years. So the ineffectual Itopatin was soon displaced as Emperor by Opecancanough. The other heirs to the throne never had a chance.[9]

Plotting and biding his time, the crafty werowance had at last attained the goal which he had set years before. But this goal was actually only a stepping stone to realization of a greater one. It was Opecancanough's dream to lead the Powhatans into a campaign that would completely wipe out the white invaders. For this too he had plotted and waited. Now the time to strike was near at hand.

But the general complacency of the colonists, nurtured in eight years of peace, must not be disturbed. Surprise, the essential element in Indian tactics, must be used this time on a strategic scale. Opecancanough had expressed satisfaction upon the accession of Governor Wyatt, assured the English that he welcomed them and suggested an exchange of citizens to promote good will.

This plan, formulated by the Indian Emperor to get his agents inside the English settlements, was welcomed by the unsuspecting London Company.

"We exceedingly approve yor course," said a Company directive, "in takinge in of Indian families as being a great meanes to reduce that Nation to Civility and to the imbraceing of our Christian religeon; the blessed end wee have proposed to o^r selves in this Plantation. We doubt not of yor vigilancie that youe be not hereby entrapp'd, nor that the Savadge have by this accesse meanes to surprize you."[10]

One of the Indians thus gaining access to Jamestown was Opecancanough himself. Indeed, the subtle savage succeeded so well in convincing the idealistic George Thorpe of his sincere interest in Christianity that the good man built the chief a frame house. Thorpe smiled at the apparent simplicity of this barbarian when he witnessed his childish glee in repeatedly locking and unlocking the door. He reported the humorous occurrence to others and all were reassured by the evident guilelessness of Powhatan's successor.[11]

George Thorpe, despite his gullibility, was no fool. A scholar, he was also a member of the London-Virginia Council and had been a member of Parliament before being sworn into the Virginia General Assembly. Even before selling his estate and coming to Virginia to give his wealth and labor for the new colony, he had personally educated an Indian youth in England.[12] Thorpe was but the most zealous of a number of Virginians who regarded the Christianization of the Indians as the only excuse for, if not the prime purpose of, colonization.

So, in March of 1622, the time was ripe for attack. The Indians had easy access, not only to the towns, but even to the homes of the English. They had been furnished with firearms so that they might provide more game for the markets of Jamestown and Henrico. They might freely borrow the settlers' boats.

Opecancanough realized, however, that if surprise was to play its essential part in the destruction of the English, a concerted attack upon the entire line of settlement along the James must be launched at an appointed instant. For this blow was to be no mere raid on an isolated tribe, but a large-scale offensive against settlements with established, albeit imperfect, lines of communication. If the attacks failed to fall as a single stroke along the attenuated backbone of settlement, the wounds inflicted would rouse the colony to shake off its foes and seek revenge.

Undismayed by the necessity of coordinating operations along a front of more than a hundred miles, the shrewd old chieftain set his zero hour for eight o'clock in the morning of April 1 (March 22, O.S.). Indians living within the English settlements, as well as those still with their tribes, were assigned roles. Some of the Powhatans borrowed from the English the boats which would enable them to transport their warriors to points of attack. Others arranged to be the over-night guests of hospitable settlers on the eve of the massacre.[13]

Among the Indians made a party to the plot was Chanco, a youth serving out his indenture in payment for a Christian education. The boy went to bed troubled that night. At "Pace's Paines" he had been treated as a son by the planter. Could he lie under Richard Pace's own roof, knowing that the Englishman was to be killed in the morning, and not warn him? On the other hand, the massacre was the only instrument that could save his people from extinction before the constantly encroaching English. If he saved Pace by apprising him of the plot, the planter would then carry the warning to other settlers. To act, was to betray his people; to fail to act, was to betray his benefactor.

'A little before dawn, the suspense became unendurable for Chanco. He waked Pace and informed him of the plot. Taking time only to secure his own house, the planter ran to his boat and rowed with the strength of desperation to Jamestown. Governor Wyatt, roused from his bed and galvanized by the report of impending doom, quickly dispatched couriers to the surrounding plantations. Thus Jamestown, and the farms within a radius of five miles, were ready for the Indians when they struck.[14]

The other settlers were completely surprised. In some homes, Indians were breakfasting with the English when the hour arrived. Immediately, the guests seized the domestic cutlery and butchered their host, his wife and family. Not even the cries of children stayed them in a bloody business that admitted no distinctions of age and sex. Some of the small planters were laboring in their fields, the Indians helping them, as the zero hour approached. The idyllic scene would have provided an excellent illustration for promotional tracts circulated in London to show how the two races could dwell in amity. No suspicions were excited as the Indians paused occasionally to squint at the climbing sun. But suddenly, when its position marked the eighth hour of day, the Indians raised their hoes and tools in unison and struck down the English. Then they fell upon the bodies, continuing to beat and mangle them long after they had been reduced to corpses.[15]

The Indians resorted to ingenious stratagems in some places. On the plantation of a Mr. Harrison, they set fire to a tobacco barn and then came running to the house to give the alarm. Six unsuspecting Englishmen rushed out but were felled in a hail of arrows. Thomas Hamor, still within the house, had been so intent upon the writing of a letter that he knew nothing of the fire. Jumping up at the sound of excited shouts, he dashed outside. An arrow struck him in the back, but he ran into the house and barricaded the doors. The Indians then set fire to the dwelling, but a boy inside—discharging a gun at random—frightened them off. Thus the eighteen or nineteen women and children in the house were saved.[16]

Hamor's brother and a party of English were surprised in a nearby house, but beat off their assailants with spades, axes and brickbats.[17]

The kindly and innocent George Thorpe was warned of the attack by his servant, who perceived what the Indians were about as the zero hour struck. But, refusing to harbor suspicions against the natives, he never believed the warning until confronted by his murderer.[18]

About 350 men, women and children who had greeted the sun that morning were dead before it reached its zenith.[19] The only really effective protection for those not forewarned had been a dark skin. None of the approximately twenty-two Negroes then in Virginia was killed.[20] Disease, in the preceding months, had taken a much heavier toll than the massacre, but the suddenness of the blow from an unexpected quarter and the additional tragedy that it portended struck terror in the colonists' hearts as had nothing else in years. They were abruptly aware of the appalling state of their defences. The stockades around the towns had been allowed to deteriorate and had not been extended to include expansion. The planters' homes, as Sir George Yeardley had observed three years before, were too far apart for safety.

Revenge now called the English to a war to the death with the Indians. Logic confirmed that defensive strategy would not suffice. Governor Wyatt himself sounded the tocsin with the assertion, "All trade with them must be forborne, and without doubt either we must cleere them or they us out of the country."[21]

Sir Francis immediately dispatched expeditions against four strong tribes that were members of the Powhatan Confederacy. The march against the Wyanokes was led by Sir George Yeardley, who was an experienced soldier and had gained the confidence of the colonists during his tenure as Governor. Captain William Powell led a force against the Chickahominies and the Appomattocks, and Captain John West headed another group sent against the Tanx-Powhatans. A more unusual choice for military command was George Sandys, secretary of the colony and brother of Sir Edwin, who laid aside his self-imposed task of translating Ovid's *Metamorphoses* to lead an expedition against the Tappahatomaks.[22]

Excited demands for immediate destruction of the Indians could not, however, be met. True, the Indian's light arrows glanced like straws off the Englishman's plate and mail, but this same armor burdened the settler when he sought to follow the retreating Powhatan into his woodland haunts. The English might drive the Indians from villages and burn their homes, but the insubstantial shelters were quickly replaced from the materials at hand.[23]

The English adopted the more practical plan of systematically burning the Indians' corn crops.[24] Though mighty hunters, the Powhatans were mainly an agricultural people. Destruction of maize, their staff of life, threatened them with starvation and reduced the endurance of their warriors. Even so, the war seemed destined to be one of attrition. The Indians and the English had both suffered bitter disappointment, the one in the hope of a sudden stroke of victory, the other in the hope of an avenging counterstroke.

The Powhatans continued to harass the colonists, burning, pillaging and killing, and making communication between the plantations hazardous. "The harmes that they do us," the Assembly summarized, "is by ambushes and sudden incursions, where they see their advantages."[25]

Sir Francis advised owners of outlying plantations to vacate their holdings, but some refused to comply with his admonition. Among these self-sufficient householders was a Mrs. Proctor who, with the aid of her servants, had effectively beaten off the attack of April 1 and felt quite capable of dealing with any that might follow.[26] Not so fortunate were some women on the fringe of settlement who were borne away as captives in surprise raids.[27]

When autumn's flambeaus lit the forests of Powhatan, other fires were transforming the landscape. Sir George Yeardley led three hundred men down river against the Nansemonds and Opecancanough himself. The Indians fled, putting the torch to some of their own houses. The Englishmen completed the incendiary work.[28] The colony could ill afford this expenditure of men and energy, necessary as it was to self-preservation, for the "sicknesse" was still claiming many victims. "With our small and sicklie forces," George Sandys wrote, "we have discomforted the Indians round about us, burnt their houses, gathered their corn and slain not a few, though they are as swift as Roebucks; like the violent lightning they are gone as soon as perceived, and not to be destroyed but by surprise and famine."[29]

The following year, the colonists exploited surprise to the fullest. In the spring of 1623, the Indians sent envoys to Jamestown to sue for peace. Istan, a werowance, promised to deliver up all captives and "his brother Opecancanough" if the Indians were permitted to plant their corn in safety.[30]

Fearing another plot and determined to foil subterfuge with subterfuge, Captain William Tucker, with twelve armed men, went out "in a shalope under colour to make peace with them." When they arrived at Opecancanough's capital, Pamunkey, on June 7, the tribesmen ran down to the shore to meet the Englishmen and witness the bargaining session.

The white men, however, refused to parley until all prisoners had been restored. Complying with this requirement, the Indians brought forth seven white prisoners who were taken aboard the boat. At a quick signal, the Englishmen fired, bringing down "some 40 Indians including three of the chiefest."[31]

Other raids on the Indians were made the same year. Captain Samuel Mathews led an expedition against one tribe. Captain Nathaniel West commanded men sent against the Appomattocks and Wyanokes. Captain William Pierce headed a group dispatched against the Chickahominies. Captain William Tucker, who had deceived the Indians at Pamunkey, also did battle with the Nansemonds and Warraskoyacks. Captain Isaac Madison set out against the Great Wyanokes.[32] Raids on the Indians became so much a part of life's routine that the House of Burgesses came to call them "marches."[33]

In 1624, the commander-in-chief decided to lead personally an expedition against the Pamunkeys.[34] Sir Francis must have believed that the tribe could offer little resistance after Captain Tucker's surprise assault on them the year before, because he took with him only sixty fighting men. Stealthy Indian reconnaissance was at work, and the approach of the English was detected.[35] Under ordinary circumstances, the tribe might have retreated into the forest. Now, however, the lives of all of them depended upon a large crop of corn which had been planted to supply not only their own needs, but also those of their confederates.[36]

Suddenly, as they approached the village, Sir Francis and his small band were confronted by more than eight hundred braves in battle array.[37] The English, though out-numbered more than thirteen to one, joined combat. Firing from cover whenever possible, the Indians and the whites fought on hour after hour. As the sun sank, the English kept wearily firing away. Fatigue brought an atmosphere of unreality to the combat, the colonists losing consciousness of all except the weirdly-painted, fiendish faces that continued to glare at them and at which they must keep firing. Darkness came on, and overwrought imaginations kept the same nightmare visages before them.

When dawn lit the landscape with its weird half-light, those same faces leered forth, unmistakably real. The superior firing power of the English was beginning to have telling effect. Some of the young warriors wavered before the fierce volleys, only to be chased back into the fight by their elders.[38] The English were able to spare twenty-four men from combat to destroy the corn. Despairing of victory, the Pamunkeys withdrew a discreet distance to view with rueful eyes the destruction of all for which they had fought. The English estimated that they cut down enough corn on that day "to have sustained fower thousand men for a twelvemonth."[39] They counted the cost of the victory and considered themselves fortunate indeed. Sixteen of their number had been wounded in the two days of combat, but none had been slain. Of the wounded, a contemporary chronicler recorded, "none miscarried of those hurtes."[40] As for the Indians, he was able to report that, after the battle, they had "not greatly troubled us, nor interrupted our labours." The strength of the Indian menace was broken, at least for the time being.

But other problems remained to plague the colonists. Another series of threats to the colony had been set in operation before the massacre of April 1, 1622. While the settlers in Virginia looked forward with hope to the dawn of the year 1622, Sir Edwin Sandys and his colleagues planned with equal optimism. They were preparing a new charter for Virginia, apparently a document providing for a government more liberal than that of the mother country.[41]

James had feared that Sir Edwin might be making of Virginia a "seminary of sedition."[42] There were many jealous courtiers eager to feed his fear. King James had consented to have the charter confirmed by act of Parliament, provided that it was acceptable to the Privy Council.[43] Some members of the Council were honestly afraid that Sir Edwin's experiments would threaten the world. And, indeed, they did offer a threat to the only world that these men had ever known—the world of the court and of those elements of English society which acknowledged the court as the sun of their solar system. Some of these honest royalists were willing, as intelligent and candid men, to admit that their world was not perfect. But they feared that, if it were destroyed, only chaos and violence would fill the vacuum.[44] Other members, of a more malicious turn, were obsessed with the desire to rid themselves forever of a troublesome fellow. The upshot was that Sir Edwin Sandys landed in prison.[45] Not only had representative government in Virginia been deprived of its father's helping hand, but the royal coterie could rejoice that they had "struck some terrour into most undertakers for Virginia."

The reports of sedition that had caused James to deal so harshly with Sir Edwin continued to fester in his brain. He had learned that the Sandys faction of the London Company had not confined its efforts to planting what the king considered germs of liberalism in the New World. They were spreading the same infection in England itself.[46] Every company meeting was a potential committee session to organize rebellion. The intelligence of the participants made their activities more dangerous. Obviously, destruction of the Company would be the most telling blow to organized sedition in his kingdom. He therefore determined to annul the Company's charter and make Virginia a royal Colony.

Though a fanatical believer in the divine right of kings, James was shrewd enough to realize that summary revocation of the charter without excuse would inflame those embers of discontent which some were so assiduously fanning. He therefore seized upon an opportunity afforded in June 1622 of hinting broadly to the Company that he expected to play a hand in their operations. When they were preparing to elect a treasurer, or president, he assured them that he had no desire to "infringe their liberty of free election," but submitted to them a list of nominees to fill the vacant post, asking that one of the names be put in nomination.[47]

The Company went even further than that. They placed two of

the names in nomination. But both of the King's candidates were soundly defeated.[48]

When James received the news, he "flung himself away in a furious passion."[49] After all, he had sacrificed a measure of regal dignity in even submitting his choices to a vote. If the Company had been gentlemen, they would have graciously accepted the form of free election which he had permitted them, while in fact honoring his decision. A master of understatement was that scribe who recorded that James was "not well satisfied that out of so large a number by him recommended they had not made any choice."[50]

James now prepared to kill the London Company. He began methodical preparations for the execution. First he ordered Captain Nathaniel Butler, a Warwick supporter who had spent several weeks or more in Virginia, to write a descriptive pamphlet on the colony.[51] Captain Butler understood his assignment. He faithfully recounted in his *Unmasking of Virginia*[52] the many misfortunes which had befallen the plantation and attributed all of them to mismanagement by the Sandys faction.[53]

Angered by Butler's charges, the Company framed "A True answer to a writing of information presented to his Majesty by Captain Nathaniel Butler."[54]

Virginia planters themselves were articulate in the Company's defense. A point by point answer to each of Butler's charges was prepared and attested to in signed statements by sixteen colonists and mariners.[55]

"I founde the Plantacions," Butler had written, "generally seated uppon meere Salt marishes full of infectious Boggs and muddy Creekes and Lakes, and thereby subjected to all those inconveniences and diseases which are soe commonly found in the moste Unsounde and most Unhealthy parts of England whereof everie Country and Clymate have some."[56]

The Virginians could not, in honesty, contradict this assertion. They did, however, attempt to explain. "Wee say that there is no place inhabited but is conveniently habitable . . . yett that there are Marishes in some places wee acknowledge, Butt soe as they are more Commodious for divers good respects and uses then if they were wantinge."[57]

The planters and mariners categorically denied the second charge, that the water around Virginia landings was too shallow for boats.[58]

Butler's third charge had been that new colonists arrived unseasonably in winter and were "seen dyinge under hedges in the woods."[59]

Replying, the sixteen spokesmen for the colony wrote: "To the first they Answere that the winter is the most healthfull time and season for arrivall of newCommers . . . As for dyinge under hedges there is no hedge in all Virginia."[60]

The planters admitted the truth of Butler's fourth complaint, that "The Colony was this winter in much distress of victuall" and that food prices were unreasonably high, but they absolved the company of responsibility for these hard conditions.[61]

Butler's fifth charge was: "Ther Howses are generally the worst that ever I sawe the meanest cottages in Englande beinge every way equall (if not superior with most of the beste, And besides so improvidently and scatteringly are they seated one from an other as partly by theire distance but especially by the interposicion of Creeks and Swamps as they call them they offer all advantages to their savadge enemys and are utterly deprived of all suddaine recollection of themselves uppon any tearmes whatsoever."[62]

The planters and mariners answered: "First that the houses there were most built for use, and not for ornament, and are soe farr from beinge soe meane as they are reported that throughout his Ma^ts Dominions here all labouringe men houses (wch wee cheifly professe our selvs to be) are in no wise generally for goodnes to be compared unto them. And for the howses of men of better Ranke and quallety they are soe much better and convenyent that noe man of quallety wth out blushinge can make excepcion against them; Again for the Creeks and Swamps every man ther that cannot goe by Land hath either a Boate or a Conoa for the Conveyinge and speedy passage to his neighbors howse. As for Cottages ther are none in Virginia, that they knowe."[63] The colonists had indignantly denied Butler's allegations about the quality of their housing, but had hedged on his very valid charge of the vulnerability of the locations on which they built.

"I found not the least peec of Fortification," Butler stated in his sixth charge. He cited "Three Peeces of Ordinance onely mounted at James Citty and one at Flowerdue Hundred, but never a one of them serviceable Soe that itt is most certaine that a smale Borke of one hundred Tunns may take its time to pass up the river in spite of them and comminge to an Anchor before the Towne may beat all their howses downe about their eares and so forceing them to retreat into the Woods, may land under the favour of their Ordinance and rifle the Towne at pleasure."[64]

"It is true, replied the sixteen defenders of the Colony, "ther is as yett no other artificiall Fortificacions than Pallisadoes whereof allmoste everie Plantacion hath one, and divers of them hath Trenches, And this year Capt. Eache was sent for that purpose. [Probably, the massacre prompted the assignment of this task.] As for great ordinance there are fower peeces mounted at James Citty and all serviceable, ther are six Mounted at Flowerdue Hundred all of them likewise serviceable, And three mounted at Kiccoutan and all of them serviceable, there are likewise at Newporte Newes three, all of them serviceable, ther are likewise att Henrico seaven peeces and at Charles hundred two, and in other places, besides Fowlers and Murders at divers places."[65]

"Expectinge accordinge to their printed Bookes a great forwardnes of divers and sundry Comodities," read Butler's seventh indictment, "At myne arrivall I found not any one of them so much as in any towardnes of being."[66]

The planters admitted the absence of industry, but attributed this deficiency to "the Infancie of the Plantacion, and this unexpected massacre."[67]

The Virginians did not attempt to answer the last three charges.

"I found the Atient Plantations of Henrico and Charles Citty," Butler had asserted in his eighth indictment, "wholly quitted and lefte to the spoile of the Indians, who not onely burned the howses saide to be once the best of all others, but fell uppon the Poultry, Hoggs, Cowes, Goats and Horses whereof they killed great numbers to the greate griefe as well as ruine of the Olde Inhabitants, who stick not to affirme that these were not onely the best and healthiest parts of all others, but might allsoe by their naturall strength of scituacion have been the most easefully preserved of all the rest."[68]

His ninth charge was:

"Whereas according to his Majesty's gracious Letters Patent his people in Virginia are as near as possibly may be to be governed after the excellent laws and customs of Englande, I found in the government there not only ignorant and enforced strayings in divers particulars, but wilfull and intended ones; Insomuch as some who urged due conformity have in contempt been termed men of law, and were excluded from those rights which by orderly proceedings they were elected and sworn unto here."[69]

"There having been as it is thought not fewer than ten thousand souls transported thither," he concluded in his tenth thrust, "there are not, through the aforenamed abuses and neglects, above two thousand of them at the present to be found alive, many of them also in a sickly and desperate state. So that it may undoubtedly [be] expected that unless the confusions and private ends of some of the Company here, and the bad executions in seconding them by their agents there be redressed with speed by some divine and supreme hand, that instead of a plantation it will shortly get the name of a slaughterhouse, and so justly become both odious to ourselves and contemptible to all the world."[70]

Of these last three charges, the planters and mariners said:

"All these we leave to be answered by the Governor and Company, some of them being unfit to be determined of by us, And for the last we being ignorant how many have been transported or are now living there.

"We whose names are hereunder and hereafter written have, upon mature deliberation and after full examination and consideration of the premises, drawn up these answers, being such as we find in our consciences to be true, and shall at all times justify them upon our oaths."[71]

The Virginia Company replied to those three charges which the planters considered themselves unable to answer. They admitted the truth of Butler's description of Henrico and Charles City, but blamed their condition on the massacre which was declared to have been unavoidable. They dismissed the accusation of arbitrary rule with the assertion that Captain Butler was a disappointed office seeker, having unsuccessfully sought a seat in the colony's Council. The number of immigrants, according to the Company, did not exceed 6,000, of whom 2,500 had been sent over during the twelve years of Sir Thomas Smith's leadership. Twenty-five hundred, they claimed, rather than only two thousand, survived.[72]

James had shrewdly maneuvered his opponents into the desired position. Contrary statements had been issued concerning conditions in the Colony. The King now had an excuse to appoint a royal investigating commission. This he did in April 1623, adjuring the members to determine the "true estate of the Plantations of Virginia and the Somers Islands," and in so doing to inquire into "all abuses and grievances . . . all wrongs and injuryes done to any adventurers or planters and the grounds and causes thereof, and to propound after what sort the same may be better managed."[73]

The Commission plunged into its work with enthusiasm, demanding from the Company all "Charters, Books, Letters, Petitions, Lists of names, of Provisions, Invoyces of Goods, and all other writing whatsoever." They summoned as witnesses the clerk of the Company, its messenger and the keeper of the house in which its deliberations were conducted. They went so far as to intercept private letters from Virginia and record any data in them which placed colonial operations in an unfavorable light. To preserve the appearance of impartiality, they heard testimony from both sides.[74] Such were the activities of America's first investigating committee appointed for political purposes.

The outcome of the hearings was predictable in advance. Sir Thomas Smith, Sandys' old foe, was criticized by the commissioners for alleged mismanagement of colonial funds, but his policies were upheld. Sir Thomas was glad to join Alderman Johnson in blaming the colony's misfortunes on the Sandys group. Captain John Martin, who enjoyed special privileges under the Crown and had been denied representation in the House of Burgesses, sided with the royalists. Secretary Pory, who had served as Speaker in Virginia's first General Assembly, was willing to testify against the faction which made that experiment in self-government possible. Captain John Smith obligingly recounted instances in which his judgment had proved superior to that of the Company, and blamed the massacre on colonial officials. Warwick, still smarting under charges of piracy as a result of the *Treasurer's* activities, was eager to testify against the administration of Virginia. Many of the accusations leveled against Sandys and his followers were fantastic, but they must have wriggled a little self-consciously under the censure that they were men "of discourse and contemplation and not of reason and judgment."[75]

The investigating commission made its report in July, stating in a condensed version of Butler's report that "the people sent to inhabit there . . . were most of them by God's visitation, sicknes of body, famine, and by massacres . . . deceased, and those that were living of them lived in miserable and lamentable necessity and want. . . . That this neglect they conceived, must fall on the Governors and Company here [in London], who had power to direct the Plantations there." They added "That if his Majesty's first Grant of April 10 1606, and his Majesty's most prudent and princely Instructions given in the beginning . . . had been pursued, much better effects had been produced, than had been by the alteration thereof, into so popular a course."[76]

Finding the report a fit instrument for his design to "resume the government, and to reduce that popular form so as to make it agree with the monarchial form," James offered the Company a compromise. In exchange for the old charter, he would give them a new one which, while restoring active control of the colony to the Crown, would not invalidate any private interests. The proffered "new" charter was actually a new version of the old charter of 1606. This revised plan called for "a Governor and twelve assistants, resident . . . in England, unto whom shall be committed the government." Resident in Virginia would be a Governor and twelve assistants to be nominated by the aforementioned corresponding body in England. This system was designed so that "all matters of importance may be directed by his Majesty." An immediate reply was ordered by the King, "his Majesty being determined, in default of such submission, to proceed for the recalling of the said former charters."

At a special meeting on October 30, 1623, London Company stockholders voted on the question of surrendering their charter to the Crown. Many of the stockholders were idealists, but nearly all of them were businessmen. They had been promised the protection of their financial interests if they would relinquish their charter in exchange for one restoring active control of the colony to the Crown. Refusal to return the charter would mean loss of the money that they had invested in the colony. Principle triumphed over cupidity, and a large majority of the stockholders voted to reject the royal offer.[77]

Meanwhile, a royal investigating committee was operating within the Virginia Colony. John Harvey, John Pory, Abraham Piersey and Samuel Mathews were named to this on-the-scene commission. This body requested that the Council and House of Burgesses subscribe to a declaration approving revocation of the charter and submission to active royal control.[78]

To this request the General Assembly drafted a reply in January 1624. Titled *The answere of the Generall Assembly in Virginia to a Declaratione of the state of the Colonie in the 12 yeers of Sir Thomas Smiths Government, exhibited by Alderman Johnson and others*, the declaration was singularly intemperate for a public document.

"Holding it a sin against God and our own suffering to suffer the world to be abused with untrue reports and to give unto vice the reward of virtue," read the introduction, "we in the name of the whole Colony of Virginia, in our General Assembly, many of us having been eyewitnesses and patients [sufferers] of those times, have framed out of our duty to this country and love unto truth this dismasking of those praises which are contained in the foresaid declarations."[79]

Then begins the counter indictment:

"In those 12 years of Sir Thomas Smith's government, we aver that the Colony for the most part remained in great want and misery under most severe and cruel laws sent over in print, and contrary to the express letter of the King in his most gracious Charter, and as mercilessly executed, oftentimes without trial or judgment. The allowance in those times for a man was only eight ounces of meal and half a pint of peas for a day, the one and the other moldy, rotten, full of cobwebs and maggots loathsome to man and not fit for beasts . . ."

Starvation, this declaration declared, "forced many to flee for relief to the savage enemy, who being taken again were put to sundry deaths, as by hanging, shooting and breaking upon the wheel; and others were forced by famine to filch for their bellies, of whom one for stealing 2 or 3 pints of oatmeal had a bodkin thrust through his tongue and was tied with a chain to a tree until he starved. If a man through his sickness had not been able to work, he had no allowance at all, and so consequently perished. Many, through these extremities being weary of life, digged holes in the earth and there hid themselves till they famished."

"We cannot for this our scarcity," the declaration continued, "blame our commanders here, in respect that our sustenance was to come from England, for had they at that time given us better allowance we had perished in general, so lamentable was our scarcity that we were constrained to eat dogs, cats, rats, snakes, toadstools, horse hides and what not. One man, out of the misery that he endured, killing his wife, powdered [salted] her up to eat her, for which he was burned. Many besides fed on the corpses (?) of dead men, and one who had gotten insatiable out of custom to that food could not be restrained until such time as he was executed for it."

The General Assembly then drove home the most savage thrust. "Indeed, so miserable was our state that the happiest day that some of them hoped to see was when the Indians had killed a mare, they [the settlers] wishing whilst she was a-boiling that Sir Thomas Smith were upon her back in the kettle."

There followed the complaint that, under Sir Thomas Smith's government "those who had adventured their estates and persons were constrained to serve the Colony, as if they had been slaves, seven or eight years for their freedoms" and that they "underwent as hard 'and servile labor as the basest fellow that was brought out of Newgate."

They claimed that exploration had not been pressed under Sir Thomas Smith. They went so far as to assert, "Nought was discovered in those twelve years."

Housing under Sir Thomas' government was unfavorably contrasted with that under Sir Edwin Sandys' administration, it being asserted that in earlier times the people had never gone "to work but out of the bitterness of their spirits threatening execrable curses upon Sir Thomas Smith."

The Assembly's declaration concluded:

"To what growth of perfection the Colony hath attained at the end of those 12 years we conceive may easily be judged by what we have formerly said. And rather than to be reduced to live under the like government, we desire his Majesty that commissioners may be sent over with authority to hang us.

"Alderman Johnson, one of the authors of this declaration, hath reason to commend him [Sir Thomas Smith] to whose offences and infamies he is so inseparably chained."

Before affixing their signatures, the Assemblymen wrote:

"By the general report of the country which we never heard contradicted, we affirm this to be true whereof all or the most part were eyewitnesses or resident in the country when every particular within written were effected." First among the signers was Sir Francis Wyatt, the Governor himself.

Circumventing the Royal Commission in the Colony, the Assembly dispatched its reply to the King himself by one of the signers, John Powntis. But sly John Pory obtained a copy from acting Secretary Edwin Sharpless. For this betrayal of faith, Sharpless suffered the loss of part of an ear and was pilloried.[80]

How accurate were the charges made by the investigators and the retorts made by the defense? The near-unanimity with which the colonists sprang to the defense of the Company would indicate that the investigators' charges, brought to gratify the King's political designs, were greatly exaggerated. On the other hand, most of them contained the germs of truth.

Credence is lent to the charge that Sandys and his associates were men "of discourse and contemplation and not of reason and judgement" by a private letter which Sir Edwin's own brother, George Sandys, addressed to two other brothers, Sir Samuel and Sir

Myles Sandys, in April 1623. "I pray God," he wrote, "their contemplations do not so overswaye our experience that all in the end come to nothing: who thinke every thing done as soon as conceived (how unfeasable soever) and so highten their proceedings that it is impossible for our Actions to go along with their reports. But men that are ambitious to bee counted wise will rather justifie then acknowledge their errors, and impute the fault to the execution when it is indeed in the project."[81]

Nathaniel Butler's charge that the plantations were generally seated near unhealthful marshes was valid. The colonists' reply that the advantages of such locations outweighed the disadvantages was inadequate. Marsh birds for the table and greater nearness to the river's mouth did not compensate for the fearful toll of the "sicknesse."

Butler's description of the housing, we may conclude from the uniform testimony of many men of excellent reputation, was an exaggeration. Apparently, living quarters were as good as could be expected in pioneer settlements.

Charges that the colonists had relaxed their defenses and had taught the Indians the use of firearms were true. Here both company and colonists had erred.

Complaints that Sandys and his followers were attempting to establish in Virginia a government freer than that of the mother country were justified. But whether the encouragement of democracy meant the maintenance of a "seminary of sedition" was a matter of opinion.

The temperate quality of the colonists' reply to Nathaniel Butler's charges argues well for its essential validity, as does the forbearance of its authors in declining to comment on those matters of which they had no personal knowledge.

The intemperateness of the General Assembly's reply to Alderman Johnson's criticisms suggests hyperbole. Furthermore, the indictment of Sir Thomas Smith's government, rather than being an argument for retention of Company control, tended to discredit Company operations under both the Sandys and Smith administrations. It served the purposes of the Sandys faction only to the extent that it impugned the motives of their accusers. The Governor's signature on the Assembly's declaration, it must be admitted, lent weight, but even this effect was diminished by the knowledge that the Governor's wife was Sir Edwin's niece.

In general, an impartial commissioner might conclude that costly errors had hurt the colony under Company management. At the same time, it would have to be admitted that these errors resulted not so much from the system employed as from the inexperience of Englishmen in dealing with the problems of North American colonization. The Sandys faction had sometimes acted too much upon theory, and hence had issued impractical directives. At the same time, in the absence of experience, theory furnished the only guide. It proved a false one in dealing with the Indian problem. The great fault of the Sandys faction was that, even after the colonists had begun to acquire experience in wilderness life, it continued to send them theoretical directives from London concerning nearly every phase of their activity.

Yet their very idealism which sometimes slipped the bridle transformed the Virginia enterprise from a mere expedition of exploitation into a noble experiment of social significance. Sandys' knowledge of government enabled him to direct the colonists to political institutions toward which they had, before his administration, made but stumbling and desultory progress. Furthermore, Sandys—by his convincing eloquence and courageous example—infused into the Virginia undertaking an inspiration, a sense of participation in a great movement, that attracted the interest and support of able and conscientious men. The enthusiasm with which representative colonists sprang to the Company's defense is impressive evidence that the men and women living under its government were not disposed to blame it for all their misfortunes. The Virginia experiment, though sometimes unnecessarily costly in goods and lives, had so far been a success.

But reason and justice were not to decide the Colony's fate. King James had instituted the investigations with one purpose in mind. He was not to be swerved from that purpose.

Nevertheless, the Company turned in desperate hope to Parliament. They drew encouragement from the fact that some of their number were members of the House of Commons and thus might enjoy the sympathy of their colleagues. A petition to that body was quickly drawn up. Humble in tone, the document pictured Virginia as a "child of the Kingdom, exposed as in the wilderness to extreme danger and as it were fainting and labouring for life." The House was begged to hear "the grievances of the Colony and Company and grant them redress."

The petition was brought before Commons in May 1624. But they never gave it official consideration. They were prevented by a message from the King adjuring them "not to trouble themselves

with this petition as their doing so could produce nothing but a
further increase [of] schisms and factions in the Company."

"Ourself," he added, "will make it our own work to settle the
quiet and welfare of the plantations." A contemporary reported that
this message was received by the Commons with "soft mutterings."[82]

The King already had entrusted the case against the Company
to Attorney General Coventry, who now issued a *quo warranto*, the
term then commonly applied to any writ of the Crown demanding
by what right an individual or group exercised any office, franchise
or liberty. Determined to fight to the finish, the Sandys faction
prepared to employ attorneys to plead their case before the King's
Bench. But when the *quo warranto* came up on June 26, 1624, the
Company's charter was revoked on a technicality, it being maintained that the Company had made an error in pleading.[83]

* * *

Thus Virginia reverted to the status of royal province. The
Colony had operated under three charters:

(1) The Charter of 1606, under which its government had consisted of a royally-appointed Supreme Council seated in
England and a subordinate Council functioning in Virginia;

(2) The Charter of 1609, under which Virginia was provided
with a Governor appointed by the Supreme Council in
England and entitled to act independently of the subordinate
Council in the colony;

(3) The Charter of 1612 which, while continuing the Governor
and Council in Virginia, vested supreme authority for the
colony in the London Company. The Company's rule may
be divided into two periods:

(a) 1612-1618—Sir Thomas Smith's administration as
Treasurer with the Warwick faction, favoring martial law, in the saddle.

(b) 1618-1624—Embracing Sir Edwin Sandys' and
Southampton's administrations as Treasurer with
the Sandys-Southampton faction, favoring development of liberal political institutions, dominant.

Now, with the return of the Colony to the King, the institutions
established under Sandys' aegis were threatened. Would they survive? The answer to that question lay in a number of factors, not
the least of which was the mettle of Virginians themselves.

Chapter V

DR. POTT TREATS THE GOVERNOR

(1624-1635)

Chapter V

~~~~~~

(1624-1635)

TO administer the royal province of Virginia, James I appointed a large commission "to confer, consult, resolve and expedite all affaires . . . of Virginia, and to take care and give order for the directing and government thereof."[1] Seated in London and headed by Viscount Mandeville, the commission corresponded roughly to the directing board of the Company when, under the proprietary system, it had met with the Treasurer as chairman. There may have been significance in the fact that the weekly meetings of the new body were held in Sir Thomas Smith's house.[2]

Immediately the Commission resolved to return to the plan of government in operation in 1606.[3] Since the announcement of resumption made no reference to the General Assembly, an institution not in existence under the Charter of 1606, it seemed to preclude continuance of the legislature.

Opposition of the colonists to restoration of royal control doubtless was responsible for the Commission's decision to refrain from making revolutionary changes in Virginia's government.[4] On August 26, 1624, exactly one month after annulment of the Company's charter, the Commission (acting for the King) reappointed Sir Francis Wyatt.[5] The Council of twelve was retained in the Colony, and most of the old members were reappointed.[6] Retention of these signers of the hotly-worded petition of January 1624 was a notable concession.

About twenty-five hundred persons, of whom twenty-two were Negroes, were subject to the royal government established for the Jamestown colony in 1624.[7] All territory as far as fifty miles to the north of the point of first settlement and an equal distance to the south of that point and one hundred miles both east and west of the mainland coastline had been designated in 1606 as the London Company's field of operations and was immediately under the administration of the southern colony.

Actually, however, only a small proportion of the area drained by tidal waters was settled. Jamestown was indisputably the nerve center of the colony and the James River was still its spine. Besides

83

being the capital and first settlement, Jamestown (with its environs), was probably the home of more than half of the colony's population.

About fifty miles upriver from Jamestown, Henrico, the community that once had rivaled the capital in growth, lay in ashes.[8] Charles City, between Henrico and Jamestown, had suffered the same fate in the massacre of 1622.[9] The exploratory westward finger of settlement had been withdrawn a little. But other fingers probed out north and south from the banks of the James. Eastward, toward the open sea and away from the forest fastnesses of the most dangerous Indian tribes, colonization progressed.

The Indians across the great Chesapeake Bay had always been friendly to the white settlers. Englishmen in this favored section were spared the horrors of the Massacre of 1622.[10] It was not strange that many settlers were attracted to this fertile peninsula where they would be protected under the benign reign of Debedeavon, the Laughing King of Accomack.[11] The first settlement on the narrow strip of land between Chesapeake Bay and the Atlantic Ocean was made in 1614 about eight miles north of the point of Cape Charles and was called Dale's Gift, in honor of the deputy governor. It consisted of twenty men sent out from Jamestown to establish salt works.[12]

Accomack, an Indian name applied to the entire peninsula, was selected as the name for a second settlement which merged with the first by 1630.[13] Since a minister was assigned to parish service on the Eastern Shore in 1621,[14] it is evident that Accomack had experienced a substantial growth of population by that time.

Expansion still followed the waterways. The fact that ships could come close enough to Jamestown to be moored to its trees was partly responsible for the tenacity with which the colonists clung to that unhealthful site.[15] Plantations were made on the rivers and creeks.

Yet the forests did not, in themselves, furnish the impediments to transportation that the fondness for river sites would indicate. The great stands of pine, walnut, oak, cedar and ash were interspersed with little undergrowth, so that it was said a coach might be driven through them in many places.[16] The Indians lurking among the trees lent the forests their formidability.

The number of Indians in Eastern Virginia had been estimated at ten thousand by Captain John Smith.[17] A later estimate by Secretary Strachey, based on more extensive explorations, would indicate that this number occupied the heart of the Powhatan settlements alone.[18]

The English population of the colony was estimated at twenty-five hundred or more in 1630.[19] This estimate, indicating a static population, must have been most conservative. The census of 1635 disclosed that 4,914 persons were then resident in the colony.[20] By that year, the Virginians were more widely dispersed than they had been a decade before, but James City and its environs continued to be the center of population. James City County was the home of 886 persons. Below Jamestown, the counties of Warwick River and Elizabeth City boasted a combined population of 1,670. About 522 persons resided in Warrasquoke County, across the river from James City. Henrico and Charles City counties were repopulated, reporting 419 and 511 inhabitants respectively. The most spectacular growth of population, however, was to be found along the York River and on the Eastern Shore. There were enough plantations lying along the York to form the county of Charles River with a population of 510. The population of the county of Accomack had grown to 396.[21]

To most pioneering Virginians in the period from 1624 through 1635, class divisions were not permanent barriers to be accepted with resignation, but obstacles which a man might prove his mettle by surmounting. Aristocrats, as in any society, were few. But this exclusiveness made aristocracy most desirable. The ambitious artisans and small farmers of the colony did not wish to abolish the upper class, but rather to gain admission to its ranks. Many of them confused the trappings of Britain's aristocracy with the quality itself. Virtually all believed that acquisition of its material symbols was the surest means of attaining the sought-for status.[22]

Was not land the most important symbol of English aristocracy? Most assuredly so. The untitled representatives of gentle families were referred to as the "landed gentry." Then the ambitious small-farmer or artisan in Virginia must acquire land, land and more land!

The possession of extensive tracts of land was coming more and more to be a symbol of influence and social priority in the colony as a result of a policy, inaugurated under the Company's management, of reserving extensive acreage for officeholders and others in positions of authority. Thus three thousand acres were reserved for support of the Governor and one thousand for maintenance of ministers of the gospel.[23] Under this program of providing support for colonial officials without drawing heavily upon English resources, the creation of each new office necessitated the reservation of more land. The Company, in 1619, had assigned twelve hundred acres in lieu of a regular salary to Thomas Nuce, the superintendent of its lands. The Treasurer, the Marshal and the Cape Merchant were each granted fifteen hundred acres. The Vice-Admiral received three hundred, the Secretary and the Physician five hundred each.[24] Because of this policy, the possession of land came increasingly to be regarded as the principal means of sustaining the dignity of high position.

The "ancient planters," a designation proudly assumed by those who had ventured to Virginia before Marshal Dale's departure in 1616, had been rewarded by special grants.[25] The effect of this policy was both to enhance the prestige of these earliest settlers, and at the same time to intensify in the colonial mind the association between position and land.

Seemingly land was illimitable and the means of obtaining it were infinite. Therefore every man of spirit saw distinction within his grasp. The contest for individual primacy consumed almost as much energy as the struggle with the wilderness and the Indians. A mariner might part with his Virginia friend and return on the next voyage to find the settler moving in an entirely different walk of life. Perhaps you could not have found among the average man's acquaintances any two who would have agreed precisely upon his rank in colonial society, and he would have been almost certain to disagree with both. The distinctions between the "landed" and the "just-landed" gentry in Virginia were fluid indeed.

Titular leader of Virginia society, as his Majesty's representative in the colony, was the Governor. Actually, however, proud planters with prominent connections in England were likely to regard him as "first among equals." And, though such titled aristocrats as Sir Francis Wyatt and Lord de la Warr had served as chief executive in Virginia, other occupants of the gubernatorial office had been excluded from some English circles in which planters subject to their proclamations had moved with ease. Even Sir George Yeardley, a newcomer to titled ranks, had possessed "save a good deal of worth in his person, nothing but his sword"[26] when he entered Virginia. If some of the Councillors working with him were inclined to forget that fact, their wives were sure to remind them.

The twelve Councillors, though representing a variety of backgrounds, were, only less than the Governor, titular leaders of society. In general, there were named to the Council during this period those planters believed to have the greatest stake in the colony's welfare— the greatest landowners.[27]

Great planters not named to the Council might serve in the House of Burgesses, or if they did not deign to sit in an assembly composed largely of the middle group of farmers, might secure the election of a spokesman to that body. A planter who was the master of a hundred or great plantation could, like his English counterpart who possessed a manor, control its politics.[28]

The middle group of farmers were sprung from even more varied backgrounds than the class of great planters. Some were relatives of the colony's foremost leaders or were unprivileged representatives of some of the noblest houses of the mother country. Others were pursuing a way of life that had been followed by their ancestors for generations. Some had been artisans in the old country, and now were engaged in an occupation new to them but made congenial by pride of ownership. Most had only recently graduated from the small farmer class.[29]

The small farmers, for the most part, were men enjoying such independence as they had never known before. Some were pallid-faced laborers from city warrens who gloried in an out-of-door life as their own masters. Many had graduated from the status of indentured servant.[30]

Independent artisans, as the list of first adventurers reveals, had been present in the colony from its earliest days. The carpenter, the bricklayer, the mason, the blacksmith—and, to a lesser extent, the tailor and the barber—plied their separate trades.[31] Most of these laborers aspired to become planters. Some had but lately been indentured servants.

The system of indentured servitude, far from degrading human personality, offered new opportunities for fulfillment of its promise. It brought hope to many poor persons, for it gave them something of which many had not even dared to dream—the chance to begin life in a new world. For the sacrifice of a few years of freedom, they could gain such independence as they would otherwise never know.

Feudal in many aspects, indenture—like feudalism—implied an obligation of master to servant as well as the reverse. Indenture was effected by a legal contract, the servant binding himself to serve the master for a given term either in certain specified employment or (depending upon the terms of the bargain) in the performance of such duties as the master might assign, and the master in return agreeing to transport the servant to the colony, supply him with the necessities of life and (in many instances) give him a specified reward upon completion of his service.[32]

Many individual covenants contained special provisions for the benefit of the servant. In at least one case, it was agreed that the worker would not be compelled to plant and tend more than two hundred weight of tobacco during any one year.[33] Some artisans, jealous of the status of skilled laborer, entered into indenture only when the contracts provided that they should not perform common field work.[34] Some even contracted to receive annual wages while in servitude.[35] A child's indenture sometimes required that he be instructed in a trade or taught to read and write.[36]

"Freedom dues," the promised reward of which the servant dreamed when his day's labor was ended and with which he consoled himself when he waked to his round of tasks on the morrow, varied according to the contracting parties. Sometimes it was a sum of money, sometimes a set of tools, or clothes or a plot of land.[37]

The term of service varied. The most common length for adults was four years, for children a longer period. Indentured servants imported into the colony without written covenants were to be bound for a period of four years if twenty-one or more years of age, five years if under twenty, and seven if under twelve.[38]

Indentured servitude, developed in response to the needs of the great experiment in colonization of the New World, was itself an experiment. The Virginia Colony and its promoters had created a new social institution.[39] In the growth of every custom and the enactment of every law defining its character they were establishing a precedent.

The system was not the sudden product of a single brain. Rather it was built so gradually through individual solutions of the labor problem that the Virginia planters themselves were not aware that a new order was emerging until it was already well established. Each colonist hoped to become a successful planter and realized that he must recruit laborers if this ambition was to be realized. He could not employ his fellow colonists because all were as ambitious as he to become the masters of estates. Obviously, labor would have to be recruited from the ranks of those who desired to enter Virginia but were too poor to have hopes of making the voyage and becoming planters.

In 1617, it will be recalled, the London Company had given certain favored men the right to transport settlers to the colony and establish them in hundreds, large plantations enjoying (as was illustrated in the case of Martin's Hundred) immunity from many of the regulations framed in Jamestown. An agreement dating from

1619 reveals that a Gloucestershire man covenanted on September 7 of that year to serve the masters of a Virginia hundred in "lawfull and reasonable workes and labors" for three years in return for passage to the colony, "convenient diet and apparell meet for such a servant" and a grant of thirty acres upon completion of his term.[40]

As early as 1618, the "headright system," whereby individuals were granted fifty acres of land for each person transported to Virginia, was already in operation.[41]

Laws governing the relationship between master and servant were passed by the first legislature at Jamestown. A statute of 1619 provided "that all contracts made in England betweene the owners of lande & their Tenants and Servantes wch they shall send hither, may bee caused to be duly performed, and that the offenders be punished as the Governr & Councell of Estate shall think just & convenient."[42] The General Assembly also provided for the registration of servants' contracts, forbade servants to trade with the Indians and made the marriage of women servants contingent upon their masters' consent.[43]

Justice, almost unavoidably, was unequal for master and servant. Freemen were fined for many crimes, but the servant was presumed to have no money and hence was meted corporal punishment for all offenses. Thus, the master might receive a fine and the servant a lashing for the same violation of the law.[44]

Even at its best, of course, servitude is not an enviable state. One indentured servant, Richard Frethorne, wrote to his parents in 1623, "I thought no head had been able to hold so much water as hath and doth daily flow from mine eyes."[45] Apparently the happiness of the servant varied according to his particular situation and disposition. There is reason to believe that most indentured persons considered themselves fortunate to have gained passage to a new world and a new life. That their hopes were justified in many cases is evidenced by the fact that seven servants from the muster of 1624 took their seats as lawmakers in the General Assembly of 1629.[46]

Lowest in the social scale were the Negroes. Though virtually all of them were indentured servants, they constituted a class apart from white servitors.

The twenty Negroes imported into Virginia in 1619 apparently were considered as in indenture to the colony and were farmed out to seven men—five of them officials, one serving in a semi-official capacity and the seventh a Burgess.[47] One of these Negroes, named Anthony, married a fellow passenger—Isabella—shortly after arrival in Virginia. The first issue of their marriage, baptized in 1624, was named for their master, William Tucker of Kecoughtan.[48]

By 1623, there were twenty-three Negroes in Virginia. All were described as servants. Their greatest concentration was at Flowerdew Hundred, where there were eleven. There were four at Warrasquoyack, three at James City, two at Elizabeth City, and one at each of three outlying plantations. In 1624, Virginia's Negro population was reduced by one.[49]

One Negro, named Anthony Johnson, achieved considerably greater success than his fellows. By about 1625, his indenture had ended and soon he was accumulating property.[50]

We may be sure, however, that his improved economic status did not elevate him socially above white indentured servants, or even raise him to their level. A white man involved in miscegenation in the 1620's was considered guilty of a crime "to the dishonour of God and shame of Christianity."[51]

Negroes and unskilled white indentured servants proved adequate for the colony's principal enterprise—the cultivation of tobacco. This type of farming, however, did require a large laboring force. This labor requirement was the main impediment to every small farmer's becoming a great planter. Land was so cheap that a man of moderate means might acquire considerable acreage. But, without the laborers to clear away the timber, break the soil and cultivate and cure the tobacco, he could not convert his property into a plantation.[52] Thus, in the census of landowners in 1626, twenty-five of the holdings listed were for fifty acres or less, seventy-three for one hundred and most of the others for less than three hundred acres. Since there were 224 proprietors and the acreage totaled 34,472, the average farm was 154 acres in extent.[53]

So integral a part of Virginia's economy did tobacco become that it even served as the medium of exchange. In reference to this fact, Philip Alexander Bruce, the economic historian, states:

"The history of Virginia in the seventeenth century furnishes perhaps the most interesting instance in modern times of a country established upon the footing of an organized and civilized community, with an ever-growing number of inhabitants and an ever-enlarging volume of trade, yet compelled to have recourse to a method of exchange which seems especially characteristic of peoples still lingering in the barbarous or semi-barbarous state."[54]

"In no similar instance," he adds, "has an agricultural product entered so deeply and so extensively into the spirit and framework of any modern community."[55]

Yet, this practice, unique in modern times, arose quite naturally. In the primitive economy of the first years of settlement, barter prevailed. The Virginians raised tobacco to trade for manufactured goods from the mother country. There was no necessity for coin in these exchanges. The method was simple for the planter. It was decidedly advantageous to the merchant. By the operation of the tobacco barter system, he secured profits both on the goods which he imported into the colony and on the tobacco which he exported from it. The English government approved the procedure because, unlike commerce with continental Europe, it created no balance of trade against the English people with consequent annual withdrawals from the kingdom of large quantities of coin to cover the balance. Since this system brought no coin into Virginia, and the colony had no mint, tobacco became the medium of exchange in domestic economy as well as foreign trade.[56]

One of the petitions drawn up by the General Assembly of 1619 reported that there was in Virginia "no money at all."[57] For a number of years before 1632, all articles apparently were valued in terms of tobacco.[58]

Despite the supremacy of tobacco some diversification of crops was achieved in the third decade of the century. This process was greatly stimulated by the adoption in March 1629-30 of a regulation requiring that at least two acres of grain be planted for every person engaged in agricultural labor.[59] At this time, the colonists were still dependent upon the Indians for part of their maize. Within a brief period, however, the crop was sufficient to furnish an abundance for all. In 1631, the Governor authorized one Nathaniel Basse to visit New England, Nova Scotia and the West Indies and offer Virginia grain for sale to the inhabitants. Virginia was fast becoming the granary of English colonists in North America.[60]

The multiplication of Virginia livestock beyond the number required to serve the colony's own needs is evidenced by commissions granted in 1631 which instructed the holders to offer for sale in New England cows, oxen, hogs and goats.[61]

The growing of grain and raising of cattle soon came into conflict. The old practice of letting the cattle forage for themselves in the woods, marshes and fields had to be restricted. In 1626, a legal requirement was imposed that planters enclose the fields in which their crops were growing to protect them from depredations by

livestock. Any fence shutting cattle out of a range not under cultivation was, however, to be destroyed. The fence law for succeeding
years continued to reflect the cheapness of land as compared with the
valuation placed upon cattle.[62]

As a result of the fencing laws, the rail or snake fence became
a familiar feature of the landscape. The prevalence of these ricrac
barriers was a reflection of the abundance of wood and scarcity of
nails.[63] Board fences, however, were also built.[64]

Unenclosed was the farmhouse yard. There, sheltered in a clus-
ter of tall trees left when the land was cleared, was the one-story
frame house of the planter. The better plantation houses were about
forty by eighteen feet in ground dimensions. Sometimes there would
be a chimney at either end. A small wing or two might be added.
Overhead was the loft. A little distance from the home stood the
barn, the henhouse and perhaps a dairy or separate kitchen.[65]

Less prosperous planters lived in houses measuring about twenty
by thirty feet. Some lived in one-room dwellings.[66] Whether prosperous or poor, the planter usually had a home garden where grew
both vegetables and flowers. Here the sight and scent of familiar
English blooms made his wife feel more at home in the raw new
land.[67]

One recalls Captain Butler's assertion in his *Virginia Unmasked*
that the houses in the colony were the "worst in the world," and the
reply of Governor and Council that the dwellings of laborers in the
colony excelled those of the same class in England. From these
statements, it seems reasonable to conclude that there were not great
differences in quality of construction between the homes of various
classes in Virginia. Most of the carpentry was rough.[68] Skilled labor
was scarce and expensive. Brick was employed, with rare exceptions,
only in foundations and chimneys.[69]

The furnishings of the homes, however, were much superior to
the structures themselves. Though sliding panels or special shutters
might take the place of glass windows in many cases, the small
furnishings that lent grace to English homes were ordered from the
mother country.[70] Beds were the most important articles of furniture,
and red or green-curtained ones graced otherwise plain interiors.
Second only in importance was the chest, sometimes a highly orna-
mented affair, the receptacle of the best linen, finest garments and
other personal treasures.[71]

Carpets were not a mere luxury. They compensated for some of
the deficiencies of clumsy carpentry, helped to protect the house-

holders from drafts.[72] Tables and chairs were substantial and sometimes ornamental.[73] There is every reason to believe that tableware
was the equal of that to which most of the colonists had been accustomed in England.[74] It must be remembered that this was a period
in which the fork had not gained currency in London, and indeed
was regarded by most persons who had seen one as an effeminate
Italian innovation.

Though the planter's house in the 1620's and 30's was plain, it
was a vast improvement over the dwellings erected in the first
decade of settlement. On long winter nights, when brass utensils
and pewter tankards[75] caught gleams from the roaring fire and
myrtle-wax or tallow candles[76] chased away gloom in the corners,
the planter's family must have felt quite snug.

England was the source of most of the tools and utensils used by
the Virginians. A profitable trade had grown out of the business of
supplying the needs of the colonists and exporting their agricultural
products to England. A traveler arriving in the James in the autumn
of 1635 reported that he sighted thirty-six sailing vessels at a single
point.[77]

The absence of glass windows in many colonists' houses and the
importation of innumerable items ranging from hardware to cloth
illustrated the frustration of official England's desire to foster major
industries in Virginia.

The doctrine of mercantilism, though not yet refined and labeled,
influenced the economic planning of England's leaders. This same
doctrine had plunged England, Spain, Portugal, France and Holland
into the great colonial race which engaged their energies. The cardinal tenet of mercantilism was that a favorable balance of trade
existed when exports exceeded imports. Colonial expansion was
necessary if these states were to attain self-sufficiency. Particularly
was this true of a small insular kingdom like England. It was
hoped that Virginia and other English colonies would produce for
the Crown goods which otherwise would have to be purchased from
rival nations. For example, England hoped that Virginia would relieve her from dependency upon Sweden, Russia, Poland and Prussia
for tar, hemp and other naval stores.[78]

Believing that the colony could produce better and cheaper
timber for shipbuilding than Prussia and Poland, the English officials
eagerly sought to promote the lumbering industry in Virginia. The
new land's forests also stimulated high hopes for the production of
pitch, tar, turpentine and potash. Dutchmen and Poles experienced

in the manufacture of ship-stores were imported to Virginia to carry on their trades and to instruct the colonists in the same work.[79]

Virginia's abundant timber, it was further argued, would furnish fuel for the smelting of copper and iron ore. Frustrated in the search for gold, the colony and its promoters had turned to baser metals in the pursuit of wealth.[80]

An attempt to operate a furnace at a spot a few miles above Henrico where ore had been discovered, although aided by a hundred skilled workmen brought over from England and supported by the outlay of thousands of pounds, yielded only a shovel, a pair of tongs and one bar of iron before the laborers were massacred and the machinery cast into the James. In succeeding years, repeated efforts were made to reestablish the industry.[81]

Virginia timber was also expected to furnish fuel for another industry, one which was already declining in England because of a growing scarcity of wood.[82] Moreover, the desirability of such an undertaking was impressed upon the Virginian every time he looked out of his window. Tidewater sand, it was almost universally believed, would be excellent raw material for the manufacture of glass.[83] Accordingly, Italian glaziers had been brought into the colony as early as 1621.[84] Virginia sand, it soon became evident, did not possess the hoped-for properties, and the Italians were so eager to return to the more genial climate of their homeland that they sought to impede the enterprise at every opportunity. Eventually they cracked the furnace with a crowbar. "A more damned crew," George Sandys expostulated, "Hell never vomited!"[85] Nevertheless, English hopes for establishing successful glass works in the colony survived this abortive effort.

Great hopes were held for the establishment of salt works and soap factories. The Commission to Sir Francis Wyatt, July 24, 1621, confirming provisions for the General Assembly admonished him to promote both of these industries which, it was declared, had been "so often recommended."[86] Salt works, as we have seen, had been established on the Eastern Shore as early as 1614. Great interest in such projects continued throughout the years of settlement with which this chapter primarily deals.

Governor Wyatt was also advised to see that the colonists "make oyl of walnuts, and employ apothecaries in distilling lees of beer, and searching after minerals, dyes, gums and drugs, &c. and send small quantities home."[87] Evidently hopes for these industries were less extravagant than for others, since no large exports to the mother country were expected immediately.[88]

Great hopes were entertained that Virginia vineyards would make England independent of Southern Europe for wine.[89]

The colonists were counseled by English authorities in 1621, "Next to corn, plant mulbury trees, and make silk, and take care of the French men and others sent about that work."[90] They were also advised "to try silk grass."[91]

William Waller Hening did not exaggerate when he said that the "Acts of the General Assembly of 1621 relate entirely to the introduction of such staple commodities as the Company in England recommended, particularly the article of silk, which seems to have engrossed nearly the whole attention of the legislature."[92] The Company instructed the Governor in the same year "not to permit any but the Council and heads of hundreds to wear gold in their cloaths, or to wear silk till they make it themselves."[93] Silk worms had been shipped to Virginia as early as the winter of 1613-1614.[94] Past the middle of the Seventeenth Century, the English government was enjoining all colonists to plant mulberry trees for the nourishment of the worms and offering a reward of fifty pounds of tobacco for each pound of silk.[95]

* * *

The agricultural, industrial and social changes which we have reviewed were interrelated with momentous political developments in both the Old World and the New.

On April 6, 1625 occurred an event which plunged England into official mourning and had a profound effect upon the government of Virginia. James I died and was succeeded by his son Charles I. Charles was as firm an upholder of the "divine right of kings" and as much under Buckingham's sway as his father had been. But Buckingham had embroiled himself and England in too many difficulties to spend time devising schemes to frustrate self-government in Virginia. Fancying himself the champion of Protestantism in Europe, he had dispatched expeditions to Spain, France and Germany to fight wars for which the English people had no enthusiasm. When James I died, official England was shocked at the news that three-fourths of an army sent by Buckingham to free the Palatinate from Spanish control were already dead of disease, exposure and starvation without ever reaching their destination. The remnants of this force of twelve thousand gradually dispersed. Thus England's armed intervention in the Thirty Years' War ended in a fiasco that has been called "the most shameful defeat in English military history."[96] It is not strange that Buckingham found little time in 1625 to concentrate on affairs an ocean away in the tiny colony of Virginia.

Charles I did not share his father's hostility toward the Sandys faction nor his unyielding opposition to the Assembly. Accordingly, shortly after his accession, Charles abolished the Mandeville Commission which James had appointed to "give order for the directing and government" of Virginia. To function in its place, he named a committee of the Privy Council.[97] He even went so far as to consult with Sandys concerning the best form of government for the colony and requested from him a prepared opinion.[98]

Nevertheless, he rejected the idea of entrusting the government of Virginia to any company or corporation, preferring to retain it in his own hands. Nor did he at first make any provision for restoration of the House of Burgesses.[99] He authorized the Council already in existence.[100] Sir Francis Wyatt was reappointed Governor.[101]

So sincere was Sir Francis' devotion to the cause of self-government in Virginia that even when royal decree left the government of the colony to him and the Council, he continued to appeal for restitution of the House of Burgesses and all the restriction of his authority implicit in that action. In the absence of legal provision for a representative assembly, he kept alive by informal means the original form of Virginia's popular government. From 1619 to 1624, the General Assembly had consisted of the Governor, the Council and the House of Burgesses. Since the revocation of the Company's charter, the same Governor and Council had continued to function as usual. Only a substitute for the House of Burgesses was required to maintain a semblance of the former government. Governor Wyatt supplied the deficiency by inviting certain leading citizens to meet with the Governor and Council to consider important matters. These citizens, though there is no direct evidence of the fact, may have been virtually the same ones who had composed the House of Burgesses. The convention thus assembled issued documents under the title "The Governor, Council, and Colony of Virginia assembled together."[102] The colony had legislation by proclamation.

Governor Wyatt and the Council repeatedly petitioned the King to permit the calling of an Assembly. The first such appeal recorded that the signers "humblie desire that the Governors that are sent over may not have absolute authority. We desire that the Governor may be restrayned as formerly to the consent of his Counsell, which tytle we desire may be retayned to the honor of this Plantation and not converted to the name of his Assistants."[103]

The Councillors' regard for their own prestige, though, was secondary. Having urged that nothing be done to lower their status, they added:

"But above all we humbly intreat your Lordships that we may retaine the Libertie of our Generall Assemblie, than which nothing can more conduce to our satisfaction or the publique utilitie."[104]

Meanwhile only the character and resourcefulness of the governor made possible the continuation of democratic forms of government. It must, therefore, have been with considerable apprehension that the Council, in the winter of 1625-26, notified the Virginia Commissioners:

"The Governor hath long expected a Successor, and the necessity of his private estate compelling him not to put off any longer his return for England, wee hope it is already provided for."[105] How that apprehension must have increased as they awaited the name of his successor!

Gratitude replaced tension when they learned that the beloved Sir George Yeardley would resume the governor's office. A resident of Virginia, he would be first a colonist and secondly a royal official. In 1625, he had made the long trip to England to plead with King Charles "to avoid the oppression of Governors there [in Virginia], that their liberty of General Assemblyes may be continued and confirmed, and that they may have a voice in the election of officers, as in other Corporations."[106]

Once again installed in the Governor's office, Sir George continued Sir Francis' custom of calling informal meetings of "The Governor, Council, and Colony of Virginia assembled together."

But Sir George, beloved exemplar of the common sense, honesty, industry and devotion to duty which the Anglo-Saxon likes to regard as peculiarly his own, was not to be with them long. He died in November of 1627. The Council testified that the colony had lost "a main pillar of this our building & thereby a support to the whole body."[107]

In the same autumn, King Charles, anxious to gain the planters' acceptance of a royal offer to buy all their tobacco, offered them that which they had professed to desire above all other favors within the gift of the Crown. On March 4, 1628, officials in Virginia received written instructions to hold an election of Burgesses and summon a General Assembly.[108]

When these orders arrived, Captain Francis West, brother of the late Lord De la Warr, was Governor. In compliance, he ordered the first election of Burgesses under the Crown, and summoned the General Assembly to convene at Jamestown March 20.[109] Despite the fact that the Assembly owed its revival to Charles' desire to press a tobacco bargain, that body demonstrated its independence by flatly rejecting the royal terms. Nevertheless, the King made no retaliatory move to abolish the Assembly.[110]

The colony had also departed from royal wishes in the character of its local government. This departure, however, was not by design but at the dictation of circumstances. The dispersion of settlement in Virginia doomed to failure his Majesty's dreams of municipal government on the English model.

Though local government in the colony began to assume form in 1624, its beginnings are traceable to 1618. The proprietor of each plantation or hundred enjoying a measure of autonomy was authorized by the General Assembly in the latter year to designate a "commander" who should be the manager of his tenants. The Assembly of 1619 seems to have assumed the functioning of a "magistrate" in each community. It seems reasonable to conclude that the "commander" in each locality exercised the duties of magistrate and captain of militia. Councillors appear to have served as magistrates in non-proprietary communities.

In what informal fashion these magistrates administered justice before 1624, we do not know. In that year, the Assembly provided for the holding of monthly courts in Charles City and Elizabeth City for the punishment of minor offenses and the disposal of civil suits involving sums not exceeding one hundred pounds of tobacco. The court was to consist of the commander and others commissioned by Governor and Council.

Special authorization of the Commander at Accomack in 1625 to administer oaths for the adjudication of petty causes, together with other references to judicial proceedings elsewhere, indicate the growth of a system similar to that by which justice was administered in the English counties.

The monthly courts, because of the dispersion of population, were circuit courts which met at several different points for the convenience of the people. By 1632, there were five of these tribunals. Their prestige was enhanced by the fact that a Councillor headed each and was one of the quorum.

In 1634 the Assembly took the logical step of inaugurating

county government in Virginia. The colony was divided into eight counties taking their names from territorial designations already current: Henrico, Charles City, James City, Warwick River, Charles River (York), Warrosquoake, Elizabeth City and Accomack.

In each of these new divisions functioned a monthly court commissioned by Governor and Council. Jurisdiction was limited to criminal causes not involving life and limb and civil causes not involving sums exceeding ten pounds. The men composing the monthly court continued to serve as local magistrates, counterparts of English justices of the peace, in their particular neighborhoods. The monthly court fell heir to many administrative responsibilities, and its members came to serve as county commissioners.

In the same year that it created counties, the Assembly also created the office of sheriff. This official, of course, was, like his English model, responsible for enforcing the decisions of the courts.

Also created by the General Assembly and based on an English prototype was the office of county lieutenant, whose holder was commander of the county's militia.

Establishment of these new offices did not increase the number of officeholders so much as one might suppose. The population of each county was small, and the number of able men in each was naturally even smaller. Therefore, "one man in his time [played] many parts." Comparison of a list of commissioners in the early 1630's with a list of the Assemblymen in a roughly corresponding period reveals that, of thirty-one commissioners, seven were Councillors and twenty-two were or had been Burgesses. The county lieutenant might be either a Councillor or a Burgess. A citizen without influence was wise to avoid giving needless offense to the chief man in his county. He might encounter the frowning features of the offended one as the face of authority in many places.

In the decade from 1625 to 1635 were formulated laws which determined the integration between church and government throughout Virginia's colonial history.[111]

In preceding years, little legislation had dealt with the church.[112] By executive proclamation, Marshal Dale's "Laws Divine Politique and Martiall" of 1610 decreed that every man attend church every Sunday unless illness prevented. Each minister was required to preach on Sunday morning and catechize in the afternoon, read morning and evening prayer daily and preach every Wednesday. He was also enjoined to record all christenings, marriages and burials.[113] Nowhere was the church referred to as an organization of clergy and laity.[114] The nearest approach to such designation was in that part of Article VII of Dale's Laws which declared:

"Every minister where he is resident, within the same Fort or Fortress, Townes, or Towne, shall choose unto him four of the most religious and better disposed as well to inform of the abuses and neglects of the people in their duties, and service to God, as also to the due reparation, and keeping the Church handsome, and fitted with all reverent observances thereunto belonging."[115]

The parish was, of course, the ecclesiastical unit. Originally, the parish was geographically identical to the township. Yet parishes were created in territories where some small settlement gave hope of the rise of a city. In most cases, this hope was disappointed and the parish was populated largely by scattered farm families. The parishioners, therefore, frequently were not sufficient in number to pay the salary of their minister except by the payment of excessively high taxes. For this reason, parishes were combined and enlarged.[116]

Although Dale's Laws were abolished when martial law was ended in the colony, requirements imposed upon clergy and laity remained essentially what they had been under the severe governor. The General Assembly in 1619 gave legal status to surviving custom in church affairs. Requirements for the holding of divine service and catechizing of "such as are not yet ripe to come to the Communion" were enacted. A specific month, March, was designated for submitting to the Secretary of State an annual account of all christenings, burials and marriages. All ministers and churchwardens were charged with the duty of trying to prevent "all ungodly disorders."[117]

If those guilty of "skandulous offenses such as suspicions of whoredoms, dishonest company keeping with women, and such like . . . or other enormous sinnes" persisted in their activities after two warnings, the churchwardens were enjoined to present them to the minister, who was legally obligated thereupon to "suspend the offender for a time from the Church."[118]

Continued "living in sin" was considered justification for excommunication by the minister. The governor was to be notified in all cases of excommunication and was required, upon receipt of notification, to issue a writ for arrest of the person and seizure of his goods. Excommunication, however, was not to be determined solely by the ministers. All members of the clergy were required to meet with the Governor four times a year at set intervals "to determine whom it is fitt to excommunicate, and . . . first present their opinion to the Governor ere they proceed to the acte of excommunication."[119]

These enactments of the General Assembly hold particular interest because of the references to the churchwarden and to cooperative action of church and state. The fact that the churchwarden first appears in Virginia legislation as one charged with presenting offenders against moral law would indicate that this lay official had been functioning in the colony for a number of years in accordance with English ecclesiastical practice. Originally, the primary responsibility of English churchwardens, two of whom might be appointed by every incumbent of a parish, was maintenance of the church building and its properties. The English churchwardens soon acquired the additional responsibility of "presenting to the proper courts certain classes of offenders against ecclesiastical laws."[120]

Far more specific provisions affecting the Church were enacted into law by the General Assembly of 1623/24. Another custom was translated into law when it was enacted "That there shall be in every plantation, where the people use to meete for the worship of God, a house or roome sequestered for that purpose and not to be for any temporal use whatsoever, and a place empaled in [sic] sequestered only to the buryal of the dead."[121]

Each colonist who failed to attend church on Sunday was to be fined one pound of tobacco if he could not produce an acceptable excuse. Fifty pounds were exacted for a month's absence. No planter was allowed to sell his tobacco before paying church dues, and in each plantation some layman was designated to collect the minister's share "out of the first and best of the tobacco and corne."[122]

A minister could not with impunity neglect divine functions. An absence of two months from his parish would cost him half a year's salary. A four months' absence would mean the loss of a year's pay and of his parish.[123]

Significant of social change were two acts of the General Assembly of 1623/24. The first provided "That there be an uniformity in our church as neere as may be to the canons in England: both in substance and circumstance, and that all persons yeild readie obedience unto them under paine of censure."[124]

Particularly noteworthy are the phrases "our church," showing the colonists were beginning to think of the church in Virginia as an institution rather than a mere arm of the Church of England, and "as neere as may be," constituting official recognition of the fact that not all of the forms used in England could be transplanted unchanged to the colony.

The second act emphasizing the growing independence of the

church in Virginia provided "That the 22d of March be yeerly solemnized as holliday [holy day] and all other hollidays (except when they fall two together) betwixt the feasts of the annuntiation of the blessed virgin and St. Michael the archangell, then only the first to be observed by reason of our necessities."[125] The colony had established for the Church in Virginia a holy day entirely its own.

This tendency toward independence was strengthened by the course of events. With the abolition of the London Company's charter, the colonists became dependent upon the civil government for regulation of ecclesiastical affairs. As Dr. G. Maclaren Brydon stresses, "The supreme difficulty of the situation arose from the fact that their whole experience of the church as an institution centered in a bishop and a diocesan organization."[126] Even such civil duties as the probating of wills, the appointment of notaries and the granting of special marriage licenses, besides such ecclesiastical functions as the induction of ministers as rectors of their parishes and performance of the sacramental rite of confirmation, had been discharged by bishops. Discipline of the clergy and formulation of rules for the orderly conduct of worship had been responsibilities of ecclesiastical canons of the dioceses.

So long as the London Company had retained control of the colony, its council had sought the advice of the Bishop of London in ecclesiastical matters pertaining to Virginia. But revocation of the Company's charter ended this arrangement.

As a royal colony, Virginia would be subject to no bishop unless the King chose to create a diocese in Virginia or authorize some English bishop to exercise certain functions in the new dominion.[127]

If the church was to function in Virginia under these conditions, some substitute for diocesan organization would have to be found. In the absence of ecclesiastical authority, the colonists turned to civil authority. So developed was their faith in popular institutions that they turned not to the Governor alone, but to the General Assembly: Thus, after restoration of the legislature in 1628, parishes were erected and ministers appointed by that body.[128] A vestry selected from the landowners of each parish became the governing body in temporal affairs of the church in each division. The vestries tended to become self-perpetuating and their civil duties to increase with the passage of time.[129]

Since there was no bishop to select ministers for the colony, a number of unworthy persons desiring to better their social status set out for Virginia to be clergymen. John Hammond, looking back to those days, recalled:

"Then they began to provide and send home for Gospel ministers, and largely contributed for their maintenance: but Virginia savouring not handsomely in England, very few of good conversation would adventure thither, (as thinking it a place where surely the fear of God was not), yet many came, such as wore Black Coats, could babble in a Pulpit, roare in a Tavern, exact from their Parishioners, and rather by their dissoluteness destroy than feed their flocks."[130]

Hammond records a more happy sequel. "These wolves in sheeps cloathing" were, he says, "by their Assemblies questioned, silenced, and some forced to depart the Country. Then began the Gospel to flourish."[131]

Nowhere was the growing spirit of independence, beginning to pervade every phase of Virginia life, better exemplified than in the changing character of the church in Virginia. A transplanted institution had become a native one.

A General Assembly that had assumed the duty of regulating ecclesiastical affairs and disciplining and deposing the clergy could not be expected to remain long tolerant of political tyranny. A train of events set in motion in 1629 and culminating in dramatic fashion in 1635 would prove this so.

Captain Francis West resigned from the office of Governor March 5, 1629 in order to return to England. Pending arrival of the King's choice of a successor, the Council (as it had in the case of Captain West himself) chose one of its own number for the chief executive post.[132] The colonial system did not then provide that the Lieutenant-Governor should immediately succeed to office if the Governor died or was incapacitated. "If a governor dies," the instructions to Sir Francis Wyatt had stated in 1621, "the major part of council [are] to choose one of themselves within fourteen days; but if voices be divided, the lieutenant governor shall have the place."[133]

Yeardley's commission in 1626 had named his successor, but the vacancy occasioned by his death in 1627 did not find the man named prepared to assume his duties. Thus it was that Captain West, and then Dr. John Pott, served *ad interim* by choice of the Council.[134] The colonists were by no means eager for the royal appointee to arrive, for he was none other than Sir John Harvey—a "Sir" before his name now, but still the same John Harvey who had made himself obnoxious as one of the commissioners conducting the special investigation of Virginia affairs in 1623. The Commission's report had furnished one basis for revoking the Company's charter.

Dr. Pott, chosen to serve as governor in the interim between Captain West's resignation and Sir John Harvey's arrival, was the subject of many a gossip session in Virginia. Of "ancient and honorable" Yorkshire lineage, he was, even according to the testimony of his worst enemy, by far the best physician in the colony.[135] He was further described as "a Master of Arts, . . . well practised in chirurgery and physic, and expert also in distilling of waters, [besides] many other ingenious devices."[136]

Ah, those "other ingenious devices!" It was those chiefly that made Dr. Pott the subject of so much shocked speculation. Some claimed that he had used his knowledge of chemistry to poison Indians.[137] Why such a rumor should have alarmed the Virginians in a period when they were sworn to exterminate the aborigines is not evident. Perhaps some feared that the doctor might try his chemical arts on white enemies. He was said to have dealings with the Indians, but no one knew what he was up to.[138] Some speculated that he was setting tribe against tribe. Sure it is that the doctor, with his knowledge of chemistry, should have been able to make the tribal medicine men look like bungling amateurs. There were many persons ready to agree that Dr. Pott was too fiendishly clever for either his own or the colony's good.

Besides, he behaved in a way that many well-bred people branded scandalous. The man was obviously a gentleman, and well-educated too, but he evidenced a startling affinity for vulgar company. In a fluid society where many of the gentry had only the most tenuous claim to gentility, such behavior was not merely eccentric but reprehensible. Dr. Pott was an embarrassing link between the lower orders and the upper classes. "At first," George Sandys wrote a friend in London, "he kept company too much with his inferiors, who hung upon him while his good liquor lasted. After, he consorted with Captain Whitacres, a man of no good example, with whom he has gone to Kecoughtan."[139] The feminine population of Jamestown, we may be sure, concluded that the two were off on a drunken carouse.

Despite these shortcomings, Dr. Pott, as we have seen, commanded sufficient respect to be named by his fellow councillors to the highest office in their gift. Besides being intelligent, he was devoted to Virginia's free institutions. His apparent enjoyment of company in which his superiority was unquestioned might suggest that he would gratify his ego by being autocratic in office. His own intense individualism, however, must have prevented him from pursuing any course which might lead to permanent restrictions on personal liberty. Indeed, he helped to protect freedom by playing the dominant role in the establishment of local courts.[140]

Dr. Pott continued in office until the spring of 1630 when Sir John Harvey arrived to assume his duties.

Perhaps Sir John still smarted with resentment toward the planters because of their criticisms of the investigating commission on which he had served. Perhaps he had heard with what distaste his arrival had been awaited in Virginia. Perhaps he was afraid that the colonists, having known him when he was simply one John Harvey, would not appreciate the dignity of his new position. But, whatever his motivation, he seems to have entered upon the duties of his office with a determination to impress all with the extent of his power.

He seemed to select Captain Samuel Matthews as a means of proving his ability to aid those who pleased him. Within a few weeks after his arrival in Virginia, Governor Harvey wrote to King Charles requesting that Captain Matthews be granted the privilege of shipping his tobacco to England completely free of customs for a year or two.[141]

Harvey chose his predecessor in office for an object lesson to those who might displease him. He leveled a number of grave charges against Dr. Pott and had him removed from the Council. Pending his trial, Dr. Pott was ordered to remain at Harrop, his James River home which perpetuated in Virginia the name of his ancestral estate in Yorkshire. He ignored the warning. Consequently Governor Harvey had him arrested and placed under guard. Some of Dr. Pott's friends promptly offered to stand sponsor for him, but the doctor preferred to become a martyr.[142]

He had become a popular hero and was determined to play the role to the hilt. The lower classes were delighted with a gentleman who seemed to prefer their company. Besides, Dr. Pott—though the owner of lots in Jamestown in addition to his river plantation—had championed the small farmer in his efforts to thwart the large planters who were attempting to gain waterfront tracts, leaving the less desirable hinterland for those of smaller means.[143] Perhaps the story that he had poisoned the Indians won him more favor than disrepute among the lower orders. Revolving around Dr. Pott as the date of his trial approached were all the elements of a class conflict that, in a society less fluid, might have flamed into actual rebellion. An acute observer, aware of the increasing gulf between great planter and small, might well have speculated concerning the day when opportunity would be more restricted and social institutions would become crystallized.

On July 9, Dr. Pott was brought to trial on charges of "pardoninge wilfull Murther, markinge other mens Cattell for his owne, and killing up their hoggs."[144] The two latter charges must have been common ones in inadequately fenced Virginia. The doctor was found guilty upon two indictments by a jury of thirteen men, three of them Councillors, and his entire estate was ordered confiscated.[145]

It should be remembered that at this time the administration of justice was dependent upon the Governor, and the character of the Chief Executive determined its quality. Only personal moral considerations prevented a Governor from decisively influencing a jury.[146]

Perhaps the Governor still feared Dr. Pott's popularity with the masses, and his quondam fellow councillors may have regretted the shabby treatment accorded the man they had helped to make Governor. Execution of the sentence was suspended "until his Majesties pleasure might be signified concerning him," and the entire Council gave security for his safekeeping.[147]

Dr. Pott appealed his case to the King and his loyal wife made the dreaded Atlantic crossing to plead her husband's cause at court. She was referred to the Commissioners for Virginia who heard her plea in the presence of Governor Harvey's agent.[148]

Sir John himself, in a surprising move, appealed to the King for clemency in behalf of the doctor. "For as much as he is the only Physician in the colony," the Governor wrote, "and skilled in the Epidemicall diseases of the planters, . . . I am bound to entreat your Majesty to pardon him."[149]

Inexplicable as this action may seem, one statement in Sir John's letter reveals his major motive in bringing charges against Dr. Pott. "It will be," he declared, "a means to bring the people to . . . hold a better respect to the Governor than hitherto they have done."[150] Governor Harvey's every act, whether beneficent or malign, seemed to be designed to emphasize his authority. He was determined to be far more than the mere presiding officer indicated by the Privy Council in 1625. "His Majesties . . . pleasure," a communication from that body had stated, "is that all judgments, decrees, and all important actions be given, determined and undertaken by the advise and voices of the greater part."[151]

The Commissioners for Virginia, after hearing Mistress Pott's plea, agreed with her in very nearly the same words she herself had used.[152] They not only announced that they found no justification for the proceedings against the doctor, but also commented that there seemed to have been "some hard usage against him."[153] Dr. Pott did not regain his seat on the Council, but he did retain his property.

Sir John's treatment of Dr. Pott must have served as a warning to many of the colonists that their liberties were endangered. The Councillors began to harass him with an obstructionist campaign.

Sir John grew more unpopular also as a result of the favors he accorded an unwelcome guest of the colony. George Calvert, first Lord Baltimore, had arrived in Virginia before Governor Harvey and was making minute observations on climate, topography and other features of the land. In 1627, he had sojourned in his Province of Avalon, a grant including all of the great southeastern promontory of Newfoundland. Here he had planned to found a colony of refuge for English Catholics. Having experienced its climate, however, he had written King Charles:

". . . I have found by too dear-bought experience, which other men for their private interests always concealed from me, that from the middle of October to the middle of May there is a sad (face) of winter upon all this land; both sea and land so frozen for the greater part of the time as they are not penetrable, no plant or vegetable thing appearing out of the earth until the beginning of May, nor fish in the sea; beside the air so intolerable cold as it is hardly to be endured . . . . My house hath been an hospital all this winter; of a hundred persons fifty sick at a time, myself being one, and nine or ten of them died. Hereupon I have had strong temptations to leave all proceedings in plantations, and being much decayed in my strength, to retire myself to my former quiet; but my inclination carrying me naturally to these kind of works, and not knowing how better to employ the poor remainder of my days than . . . to further, the best I may, the enlarging your Majesty's empire in this part of the world, I am determined to commit this place to fishermen that are able to encounter storms and hard weather, and to remove myself with some forty persons to your Majesty's dominion Virginia; where, if your Majesty will please to grant me a precinct of land, with such privileges as the king your father . . . was pleased to grant me here, I shall endeavour to the utmost of my power, to deserve it."[154]

Before Lord Baltimore could receive the King's reply urging him to abandon the arduous work of colonization for the comfort of his English home, he was enroute to Virginia with Lady Baltimore, their children and a retinue of servants and followers.

The Virginians were not likely to welcome anyone who had designs on part of their territory, least of all a Papist. Furthermore, Lord Baltimore had tried to arrange a marriage between Prince Charles and the Infanta of dreaded Spain. Some even feared that this Catholic peer might persuade Charles to place the colony in his hands. Had he not been one of the commissioners appointed by the King's father to investigate affairs in Virginia?

Before Sir John Harvey's arrival, Dr. Pott and the Council had asked Lord Baltimore to subscribe to the Oath of Supremacy. To this oath, which acknowledged the supreme authority of the King in all ecclesiastical matters throughout the English dominions, no conscientious Catholic could subscribe. Lord Baltimore proposed an alternative declaration which was unacceptable to the Virginians. Since he balked at the Oath of Supremacy, the peer was told that he must sail for England at once.[155] Actually, the colonists had quite carefully maneuvered Lord Baltimore into a position where they could request his departure.

At this time Governor Harvey appeared upon the scene and attempted to make Lord Baltimore welcome. Despite the fact that at least one Virginian threatened to knock him down, the English lord appears to have been treated quite decently by the majority of the colonists. When he sailed for England he left his wife and children to await his return.

Back in England, Lord Baltimore made application for a new grant. At first he applied for land south of the Jamestown colony, but he was persuaded in 1632 to accept property that would stand as a buffer between the settlement of 1607 and the Hudson River territory being colonized by the Dutch. His grant, north of the Potomac River, was officially referred to as the "Province of Maryland in Virginia," but it was for all practical purposes a palatinate independent of the Jamestown government. The proprietor agreed to pay to the king a token annual quitrent of two Indian arrows.[156]

Lord Baltimore gained his charter only over loud protests from prominent Virginians and then did not live to see the royal seal affixed to it. Among those protesting on behalf of the colonists was

Captain Francis West, who had been sent to England to represent Virginia in the tobacco monopoly question. He doubtless was the first American ambassador.[157]

The Virginians also had sent William Claiborne to London to protect their interests in the matter of the Baltimore charter. Claiborne in 1631 had abandoned as hopeless his efforts to block issuance of the document and had returned to Virginia and established a settlement upon Kent Island in the Chesapeake Bay. There he had built dwellings, mills and storehouses and laid out orchards and gardens.[158]

A few weeks after Lord Baltimore's death in April 1632, his son Cecilius Calvert, who succeeded to the title, was issued the patent for which his father had made applications.

Again the Virginians protested. They claimed that the Maryland grant fell "within the Limits of the Colony," that it would interfere with their Indian trade in the Chesapeake, and that a settlement of Catholics would cause "a general disheartening of the Planters."

Perhaps the protests irritated the King. He commanded the Governor and Council to assist Lord Baltimore in the establishment of the settlement. They were told that they must "suffer his servants and Planters to buy and transport such cattle and comodities to their Colonie, as you may conveniently spare . . . and give them . . . such lawful assistance as may conduce to both your safetyes."[159]

When Lord Baltimore's colonists arrived at Point Comfort, Virginia in February 1634 under the leadership of his brother Leonard Calvert, they received a welcome as "intolerably cold" as the first Lord Baltimore had found his province of Avalon. The people of Jamestown viewed the more than three hundred men aboard the two vessels as a threat to the size of their territories and to their economic security. Far from furnishing cattle for the new colony, the Virginians caused Sir John Harvey to write, "Many are so averse that they crye and make it their familiar talke that they would rather knock their Cattell on the heades than sell them to Maryland."[160]

The Governor, however, was eager to compensate for the inhospitality of the Virginia planters. "For their present accommodations," he wrote the Privy Council, "I sent unto them some cows of myne owne, and will do my best to procure more, or any thinge else they stand in need of."[161] Such behavior won for Harvey the approbation of authorities in England, but increased the contempt in which he was held in Virginia.

When Calvert left Point Comfort after a stay of several weeks to found the town of Saint Mary's, he was really planting the second settlement in Maryland. For Claiborne's Kent Island settlement was within the bounds of the province assigned to Lord Baltimore. Desiring to defend his brother's rights but cause as little ill feeling as possible in doing so, Governor Calvert sent word to Claiborne that he would not harm the Kent Island Colony but that the Virginian must hold it as a tenant of Lord Baltimore. Wishing to assure himself of official backing, Claiborne appealed to the Virginia Council for a decision in the matter. They expressed the conviction that, inasmuch as the Virginian's settlement had been established prior to the issuance of Lord Baltimore's patent, it was not only the right, but the duty, of Claiborne to recognize the authority of the government of Virginia over his outpost.[162]

Claiborne thus proceeded with his plans for expanding a profitable fur trade with the Indians and developing the great empire of the Northwest under the credentials of the Jamestown government.

Meanwhile, a false report that Claiborne was attempting to arouse the Indians to attack Saint Mary's excited Governor Calvert's fears. A joint commission of Virginians and Marylanders—the first such joint commission in the history of England's American colonies—examined the charges and pronounced them inaccurate.[163] Nevertheless, feeling ran high until at last Virginians and Marylanders were ready to believe almost anything derogatory about each other. In April 1635, the crisis approached a climax when Governor Calvert, accusing Claiborne of engaging in illicit trade, seized one of the Virginian's merchantmen. Inflamed at what they regarded as an act of piracy, Claiborne and his followers sent a vessel to make reprisals. The Kent Island ship was attacked by two pinnaces from Saint Mary's and was obliged to surrender after a hard fight. Burning for revenge, the islanders inflicted a defeat on the Marylanders at the mouth of the Potomac a few weeks later.[164]

As the struggle between the Kent Islanders and the inhabitants of St. Mary's had waxed hotter, anger had mounted proportionately in Virginia. There was even talk of sending an expedition to Saint Mary's to drive the Marylanders out. As Sir John Harvey persisted in displaying sympathy with Calvert, he drew to himself still more hatred from the people ·he sought to govern. By now even Samuel Matthews, for whom Sir John had sought special favors, was disgusted with the Governor. "The inhabitants," he declared in a letter to Sir John Wolstenholme, ". . . understood with indignation that the Marylanders had taken Capt. Claibornes Pinnaces and men . . . which action of theirs Sir John Harvey upheld contrary to his Majesties express commands."[165]

There were many other complaints against the Chief Executive. It was charged that he was disposed "to feed his avarice and rapacity, by assessing, levying, and holding the public revenue, without check or responsibility."[166] In a fit of temper, he had knocked out some of Councillor Stevens' teeth with a cudgel.[167] His bad behavior in Virginia was becoming common gossip at Court.[168]

The issue between the Governor on the one hand and the Council and people on the other was made irreconcilable by an event of 1634. The Governor permitted a Captain Young, who came to Virginia in that year upon a commission for the King, to seize a skilled servant of one of the planters to complete his labor force for building two shallops. Exactly a decade before, the Assembly had enacted into law a provision that "the Governor shall not withdraw the inhabitants from their private labors to any service of his own or upon any colour whatsoever."[169]

If the Governor's violation of this statute went unchallenged, the laws of the colony would no longer protect private property. Accordingly Captain Matthews and other members of the Council called on Sir John for an explanation. The group stood in the open, but the Governor must have felt cornered. Captain Matthews, truncheon in hand,[170] tensely awaited Sir John's reply. Though it may have been customary for some of the Jamestown officials to carry cudgels in the fashion of a marshal's baton, Harvey must have been reminded of the weapon with which he had struck one Councillor in the teeth. The cold civility of these men cloaked a fierce anger. He had better appeal to their loyalty to the Crown. The indentured servant had been taken, he explained, to enable Captain Young "to prosecute with speed the King's service."[171]

"His Majesty," the Governor added, "had given him authority to make use of any persons he found."

"If things are done in this fashion," Captain Matthews shot back, "it will breed ill blood in Virginia." Turning aside, he lashed off the heads of some high weeds with a few savage swings of his truncheon.

"Come, Gentlemen." Governor Harvey's tone was conciliatory now. "Let us go to supper and for the night leave this discourse."

The invitation was refused almost with one voice, and the Councillors strode away without further ceremony.

The Governor had reviled the Council in public and had insulted its members in private. Henceforth the struggle between Governor and Council would be as much a war to the finish as that between colonists and Indians.

Another circumstance added to the wrath of both Councillors and Burgesses. The King in this very year had renewed his proposal for a royal monopoly of the tobacco trade and this time had demanded assent through the General Assembly. The Burgesses composed a refusal in the form of a petition. Sir John detained this document, saying that he feared it would offend his Majesty. By this arbitrary act, the colonists—in the words of Captain Matthews— "were made sensible of the miserable condition of the . . . [government]."[172]

Intrigue is not a seasonal plant. It flourished in Virginia during the winter of 1634-35. Many leading citizens, some of them Councillors, met behind closed doors to discuss means of dealing with the Governor. A horseman galloped along frozen Virginia roads, pausing at each plantation to exhort the people to oppose Sir John. Dr. Pott, the man Harvey had once confined to his plantation, was now covering Virginia, collecting names on a petition for redress of grievances.[173]

In the spring of 1635, Dr. Pott was conducting secret meetings in various parts of the colony. One of these meetings, held April 27 at the home of William Warren in York, was in progress when someone rapped on the door. The servant who answered found three friends of the Governor. He told them that they could not enter and closed the door. They then took turns bending their ears to the keyhole. Above the muffled conversation rose occasional hotly worded protests against the Governor. Then they heard Dr. Pott reading his petition and assuring the assemblage that it had been signed by some of the Councillors. General expressions of enthusiasm followed as the planters rushed forward to affix their signatures.[174]

The next morning several leading participants were arrested and brought before the Governor. Dr. Pott himself was arrested upon his return from another indignation meeting. He was put in irons, and with the others, was brought before the Council. He did not seek to conceal his part in circulating the petition, and declared, "If I have offended, I do appeal to the King, for I am sure of no justice from Sir John Harvey."[175] One of the prisoners asked why he had been arrested. "You shall know at the gallows!" snapped Sir John.[176]

Soon the Council was summoned to sit as a court in the case

involving these men. Governor Harvey declared his intention of dispensing with trial by jury and asserted that martial law should be executed. The indignant Councillors stood firm. They would never consent to an illegal trial. Swollen with rage, Sir John paced back and forth like a caged beast, roaring imprecations and howling protests while the Councillors watched in silent fascination. Suddenly he flung himself into his chair and, scowling ferociously, commanded the others to be seated.

A suspenseful silence followed. Finally Sir John announced that he would pose a question to be answered separately and promptly, in writing, by each Councillor. "What do you think they deserve that have gone about to persuade the people from their obedience to his Majesty's substitute?"

"And I begin with you," he added, pouncing on young Minifie.

"I am a young lawyer and dare not upon the sudden deliver my opinion," was the discreet reply.

Mr. Farrar intervened to protest against the irregularity of the proceedings, but was silenced by the wrathful Governor. Captain Matthews then protested, and he and the other Councillors refused to answer the question. The Governor indulged in a fit of vituperation and the session adjourned.[177]

When the Council met again, Sir John had another question. Why was a petition circulated against him?[178]

This time Minifie did not hesitate. "Because of the detaining of the Assembly's protest," he replied.[179]

"Do you say so?" snarled Sir John, springing from his chair and striking the young man on the shoulder. "I arrest you upon suspicion of treason to his Majesty."

"And we the like to you, Sir!" exclaimed Captain John Utie, as he seized the Governor. Captain Matthews helped Utie force the furious executive into a chair. Dr. Pott signaled at the window and fifty musketeers rose from their hiding places and came running toward the house. As the Councillors crowded around Harvey, Dr. Pott told the guards, "Stay here until there be use of you."

Captain Matthews then addressed himself to the Governor. "Sir," he said, "there is no harm intended you save only to acquaint you with the grievances of the inhabitants, and to that end I desire you to sit down in your chair." Following this declaration, he recited the people's grievances.

After a pause, Captain Matthews resumed. "Sir, the people's

fury is up against you and to appease it is beyond our power, unless you please to go for England, there to answer their complaints."

Sir John spurned the suggestion. He had been made Governor by the King, and save by his command he would not leave his post.

But, after several days spent surrounded by guards and in the knowledge that sentries had been posted at strategic points to thwart his attempts to raise an army, he perceived the futility of his position. While he was thus guarded, Dr. Pott and the other prisoners were at liberty.[180] When a special Assembly convened at Jamestown to consider grievances against the Governor, Sir John made a last effort to assert his authority. He sent them a letter declaring the session illegal and ordering the participants to disperse. His orders were ignored. He sent a letter to the Council, demanding his royal commission and instructions, but was informed that these papers had been entrusted to Mr. Minifie.[181]

The Governor received reports of violent hostility toward him in the "lower parts" of the colony, and did not know what turn the people's fierce determination might take. Accordingly, he agreed to sail to England on the first ship available. Even in this extremity, however, he sought to bargain. Unsuccessfully, he tried to name his successor, sought to persuade Matthews, Pierce and Minifie to accompany him to England and attempted to extract from the Council a promise not to molest Maryland.[182]

The Council named as Harvey's successor Captain John West, brother to Captain Francis West, who had served as Governor before. It then took the unprecedentedly democratic step of submitting the choice to the House of Burgesses for ratification. Their approval was quickly given, and they drew up resolutions detailing the complaints against Sir John. These documents, addressed to the King, were placed in the keeping of one Thomas Harwood, who sailed for England on the same ship that bore Sir John from the colony. Also aboard was Dr. John Pott, who had appealed his case to the King. Hardly a congenial group of passengers!

What a wealth of drama lay behind the terse colonial entry:

"On the 28th of April, 1635, Sir John Harvey thrust out of his government; and Capt. John West acts as Governor till the King's pleasure known."

A bloodless revolution had taken place, an event the more notable because it had accomplished a complete overturn of executive authority without a life being lost. Moreover, those responsible had evidenced a scrupulous regard for legal principles involved. Equally striking was the fact that the Councillors, seeking confirmation of their actions, had turned to the representatives of the people.

* * *

As Arnold Toynbee has observed in his monumental *A Study of History*, institutions transported across an ocean undergo a "sea change." This fact was well exemplified in the development of English institutions in Virginia in the period 1624-1635, with which this chapter has dealt. The alteration undergone in transit became apparent in 1624, when local government in Virginia, in obedience to conditions imposed by the plantation system, began to assume forms quite different from the English models of municipal government which Charles had hoped would be copied in the colony. Another sign of the same trend became evident in that year when an act of the General Assembly provided for "uniformity in our church *as near as may be* to the canons in England." When revocation of the Company's charter caused Virginians to seek some substitute for diocesan authority, they turned to their own civil government—legislative as well as executive—and made still greater institutional departures from the English model. The gulf became evident even to the most obtuse in 1635 when Governor Sir John Harvey, who had misunderstood the temper of the new land, was summarily expelled by its citizens.

Chapter VI

BERKELEY, BACON AND REBELLION

(1635-1677)

Chapter VI

(1635-1677)

THREE nervous men stood on deck as the vessel from Virginia entered Plymouth Harbor. Dr. Pott and Thomas Harwood were tense because so much depended upon Harwood's plan of dashing to London and making a good case against Sir John before the ousted Governor arrived. Sir John himself was restless because he had devised a scheme to thwart the two Virginians and the time of its testing was near.

As the ship docked, Sir John sprang ashore and hurried, not to London, but to the mayor of Plymouth. There he hastily recited a tale of mutiny. Before Pott and Harwood could get out of the city, the doctor had been arrested and the courier's papers had been seized. With the legal evidence against him in his own hands, Sir John proceeded to London to tell his tale of "mutiny and rebellion."[1]

Upon learning that one of his own appointees had been thrown out of office, King Charles flew into a rage and vowed that Harvey should be Governor in Virginia again if for but a single day. To this determination he would adhere even if charges against Sir John were proved. But, if the Governor should be acquitted, Charles would send him back to serve as chief executive for an even longer term than his Majesty originally had envisioned.[2]

The Privy Council heard the case in December 1635. Harwood refrained from narrating the long list of arbitrary actions which had inflamed the people against the royal appointee. Perhaps he feared that the King, already angry in the belief that his authority had been flouted, would only be goaded to reprisal by mention of liberty. The Virginian, nevertheless, did not mince words. He declared that Sir John "had so carryed himself in Virginia, that if ever he retourned back thither hee would be pistolled or Shott."[3]

Harvey might well gloat. He was acquitted and restored to his office. Moreover, West, Utie, Matthews, Minifie and Pierce—whom he had denominated "chief actors in the mutiny"—were ordered to return to England to answer charges of treason before the Star Chamber.[4]

Sir John's sense of triumph, however, was not unalloyed with apprehension. Harwood's bold prediction of the fate that would await the Governor if he returned to Virginia must have troubled the official's thoughts. He requested permission to sail up the James in a royal vessel. King Charles complied with Harvey's request, but furnished him the *Black George*, a ship so unseaworthy that it had to return to port only a few hours after setting sail.[5]

Not trusting again to Charles' hospitality, Sir John embarked on a merchantman and reached Point Comfort in January 1637. Establishing a temporary capital at Elizabeth City, he ordered a reconstituted Council to convene in the church there. He published a proclamation of amnesty for all participants in the "mutiny" except its leaders, then removed many officials and appointed their successors.[6]

If these actions were designed to impress upon the colonists the fact that Sir John would be Governor in every sense of the word, they accurately forecast the character of his new administration. As master of the reconstituted Council, he now held in his hands legislative and judicial as well as executive power. Confiscation, the imposition of fines, and such traditional punishments as whipping and ear-cutting were employed to discourage opposition.[7]

Matthews, West, Utie and Pierce, in conformity with the Privy Council's orders, were returned to England. Their goods, cattle and servants were seized.[8]

Captain Matthews, Harvey's favorite in the early weeks of his administration, was now the chief object of the Governor's ire. Sir John had sworn that there was such bad blood between him and Captain Matthews that if one stood the other should fall. Eyeing Matthews' fine herd of cattle, Sir John vowed that he would leave the Virginian not "worth a cow tail." Shortly thereafter one John Woodall entered suit against Captain Matthews for the recovery of two cows. It was ruled that Matthews in 1622 had held two of Woodall's cows, and that the increase of the cows to the time of the inquiry might number fifty. Accordingly, fifty head of Matthews' cattle were transferred to Woodall.[9]

Matthews, who was in England when the decision was rendered, secured from the Privy Council an order enjoining the Governor to restore his seized property. Sir John told the Virginians that he had received expressions of approval from the Privy Council because of his action in confiscating Matthews' property. Not until January 1639 did Sir John report that he had restored much of the Virginian's property, and then only after a second injunction from the Privy Council. Meanwhile Sir John's new favorite, Secretary Kemp, and others had broken into Matthews' house, ransacked trunks and chests and carried off articles that pleased them.[10]

This same Kemp, so dearly beloved by Harvey, had been called a "jackanapes" by a clergyman named Anthony Panton. The poor parson was charged with "mutinous speeches and disobedience" to the Governor and disrespect to the Archbishop of Canterbury. He was fined five hundred pounds, forced to make public submission in every Virginia parish and banished "with paynes of death if he returned, and authority to any man whatsoever to execute him."[11]

Meanwhile, sentiment in England was turning against the petty tyrant of Virginia. Matthews, Utie, West and Pierce had been granted liberty under bail immediately upon their return to the mother country in 1637. Dr. Pott apparently enjoyed similar freedom. We may safely assume that they lost no opportunity to disparage Sir John in official circles. The charges against the Virginians seem to have been forgotten after being referred to the Lord Keeper and Attorney General. The Privy Council sub-committee directly concerned with Virginia affairs came to side with the Virginians against their Governor. English merchants, antagonized by special duties Harvey had imposed, added their voices to the clamor against him.[12]

Thus Governor Harvey was deposed and the popular Sir Francis Wyatt became his successor in the fall of 1639. By orders from England, those men then on the Council and Secretary Kemp were to retain their posts. Sir Francis summoned Sir John to answer for his offenses, and he immediately set about righting the wrongs committed by his predecessor, particularly in the cases of Matthews and Panton.[13]

Though Harvey begged permission to return to England, pleading that his "many infirmities and weaknesses of body" required "advice and help beyond the skill and judgment which this place can give," he was required to remain for some time.[14] Sir Francis feared that, once Sir John was permitted to gain official ears in England, he might bring fresh charges to unsettle the government in Virginia. Eventually, when Harvey and Kemp were permitted to return, events justified Governor Wyatt's apprehensions. Sir Francis was recalled in 1642, and Sir William Berkeley was named to succeed him.

Despite his qualifications, the arrival of Sir William Berkeley was awaited with some trepidation in the colony. In the first place, Sir Francis Wyatt was as popular as any Governor the Virginians had known, and was a man of proved character. Most of the colonists must have believed it unreasonable to hope that change could bring them a better chief executive. Besides, they feared that the new Governor was being sent into Virginia to punish Sir John Harvey's enemies. They were aware of the advantages of having a sympathetic leader who could command the King's ear. But what guarantee was there that Sir William would be sympathetic? His position at court might make him an opponent of popular government.

Anthony Panton, who had suffered under Harvey and been compensated under his successor, entered a protest against the change of administrations and maintained that no complaint against Governor Wyatt could be sustained.[15]

A measure of the royal caution engendered by the colony's summary ousting of Harvey is afforded by the seriousness with which Panton's protest was received in England.

At first, the new appointee was ordered to remain in the kingdom until an investigation could be conducted. He was permitted to sail, however, after signing an agreement to protect Wyatt's interests and those of his friends.[16] The Privy Council doubtless was tiring of the cycle of revenge and counter-revenge which had kept Virginia in turmoil.

Sir William's every action after setting foot in Virginia seemed intended to dispel any fears that he might be hostile toward the Wyatt faction or desire to play the autocrat. His easy courtesy was so in contrast to Harvey's rough arrogance that the colonists were disposed to like him from the first. Whatever his talents as an executive, this affable, urbane and witty man would be a most welcome addition to colonial society.[17]

He soon gave more solid indications of his goodwill. William Pierce, Samuel Matthews and George Minifie—all of whom had once been charged with treason because of their part in the ousting of Governor Harvey—were appointed to the Council.[18] Sir William gave his assent to an act strengthening the legal authority of the General Assembly by making it officially the supreme court in Virginia.[19] Apparently placing the colonists' welfare above self-interest, he successfully urged the abolition of an unjust poll tax that contributed to the payment of his own salary. He proposed that there be substituted for the levy on tithables "assessments proportioning in some measure payments according to men's abilities and estates."[20] As a result, Sir William gained great favor as the friend of popular government and the poor man.

The colonists were delighted with their Governor. Fiercely loyal to his King and to the established church, he was also intensely faithful to the responsibilities of his position. He seemed to be as much a friend of liberty as any chief executive Virginia had known, but at the same time maintained a friendly dignity and reserve. The Assembly expressed the general gratitude when it presented Sir William an "orchard with two houses belonging to the collony . . . as a free and voluntary gift in consideration of many worthy favours manifested towards the collony."[21]

In this same year, great events in England began to play a decisive role in the life of Virginia. Charles I had been faced with rebellion in Scotland in 1638 and revolt in Ireland in 1641. Now the rising tide of Puritanism brought him civil war in England in 1642. The King planted his standard in the castle yard at Nottingham on a rain-sodden August 22 and summoned all loyal subjects to his side in the struggle against a mutinous Parliament. The Earl of Essex, one of the House of Lords minority that sided with the Commons majority, was appointed general of the Parliamentary forces. Nearly all Southern and Eastern England, embracing the commercial areas of middle class dominance, was rising in opposition to the King.[22]

It was, therefore, with deep appreciation that Charles received a testimony of loyalty framed by the General Assembly of Virginia in April 1642. That body declared that George Sandys, who had been sent to England in 1639 as the colony's agent or ambassador, had acted on the basis of misunderstanding when he presented to the House of Commons on behalf of the Virginia planters an appeal for restoration of the Company charter. Placing their representative in a most embarrassing position, the Assembly declared that return to the management of a corporation was never "desired, sought after or endeavoured to be sought for either directly or indirectly by the consent of any Grand Assembly or the common consent of the people."[23]

Contrasting the advantages of royal rule with certain "sufferings" under corporate management, the Assembly concluded, "The present happiness is exemplified to us by the freedom of yearly assemblies warranted unto us by his majesties gratious instructions, and the legal trial per juries in all criminal and civil causes where it

shall be demanded. And above all by his majesties royal incourage-
ment unto us upon all occasions to address ourselves unto him by
our humble petitions which doth so much distinguish our happiness
from that of the former times that private letters to friends were
rarely admitted passage."[24] These strictly royalist sentiments, expressed by a colony which a few years before had bitterly contested
revocation of the Company's charter, are no doubt attributable to
Sir William's influence.

Charles acknowledged the communication as "very acceptable"
and added, "As we had not before the least intention to consent to
the introduction of any company over that our Colony, we are by it
much confirmed in our resolution, as thinking it unfit to change a
form of government wherein our subjects there . . . receive much
contentment and satisfaction."[25] The King must have reflected that
young Berkeley was doing a good job indeed to bring so much satisfaction to a colony perennially plagued with discontent.

The following year brought more reforms that pleased the people.
The Governor approved legislation making Burgesses exempt from
arrest during legislative sessions and for ten days following dissolution. Possible abuse of power was thwarted by provisions limiting
the fees of the Secretary of State. Another safeguard to liberty was
a law, also passed in 1643, which prohibited the Governor and
Council from levying taxes without the consent of the more popular
branch of the Assembly.[26]

Meanwhile, though the Cavaliers—as the king's forces were now
called—appeared to be winning in England, they had been successfully opposed in their effort to take London and had been forced to
withdraw to Oxford. With the mother country torn by conflict, Sir
William ceased to receive royal pensions and allowances. The Assembly promptly levied a special temporary tax of two shillings
per poll on all tithable persons so that the Governor might be
compensated.[27]

In only one instance had Sir William displayed any sign of
intolerance, and in this exception he was warmly supported by most
of the influential colonists. In 1642, Richard Bennett and other
members of a Puritan settlement on the Nansemond River sent
letters to Boston requesting that ministers be sent to Virginia to serve
non-conformist congregations. Virginia adherents to the Church of
England regarded the three clergymen who arrived from New England as emissaries of revolt. Were the Puritans not responsible for
the Civil War now raging? Despite the fact that they brought letters

of introduction from Governor Winthrop to Governor Berkeley, their presénce provoked speedy passage of legislation requiring conformity on the part of all ministers in Virginia and empowering Governor and Council to expel all dissenters. Nevertheless, one New England clergyman, William Thompson, was bold enough to remain and apparently suffered no molestation.[28]

Religious quarrels, however, were soon submerged in a war within the colony that made even the struggle between Cavaliers and Roundheads seem distant. Opecancanough was on the warpath again, and as before the English were caught unawares. The "war to the death" between the aborigines and the invaders had so far subsided that Captain Thomas Rolfe, son of John Rolfe and Pocahontas, had obtained permission from the Governor to visit "his aunt Cleopatre and his kinsman, Opecancanough."[29] The blow fell April 18, 1644. The toll was not so great in proportion to the white population as in the massacre twenty-two years before, for the Indians did not this time have access to the homes of the English. The second massacre, the son of one of the settlers later recorded, "fell severest on the South-side of James River, and on the Heads of the other Rivers; but chiefly of York River, where the Emperor Opecancanough kept the Seat of his government."[30]

The wily Indian whose agile brain conceived this plot was "now grown so decrepit, that he was not able to walk alone; but was carried about by his Men, wherever he had a mind to move. His flesh was all macerated, his Sinews slacken'd, and his Eyelids become so heavy, that he could not see, but as they were lifted up by his Servants."[31]

Sir William Berkeley, determined to put an end to the war by capturing the Indian leader, sallied forth at the head of a party of horse and surprised the aged chief in his quarters. There was great rejoicing in Jamestown when Sir William returned with the author of so much of their misery as his prisoner.

Sir William, it is reported, treated his captive "with all the Respect and Tenderness imaginable."[32] Nevertheless, it is recorded that Opecancanough "heard one Day a great Noise of the Treading of People about him; upon which he caused his Eye-lids to be lifted up; and finding that a Crowd of People were let in to see him, he call'd in high indignation for the Governor." When Sir William answered the summons, Opecancanough "scornfully told him, That had it been his Fortune to take Sir William Berkeley Prisoner, he should not meanly have exposed him as a Show to the People."[33] Small wonder that the curiosity of Jamestown should have been excited by the presence of a royal captive "who at his pleasure could call into the field ten times more Indians than Sir William Berkeley had English in his whole government."[34]

The aged monarch "continued brave to the last moment of his life, and showed not the least dejection at his captivity." That proud life ended when a common soldier shot him in the back.[35]

The Indians, deprived of their leader, were brought to terms. Once again the struggle in England engaged the colonists' attention.

In 1648 concern deepened to alarm. The royal forces had experienced many reverses in England. Even in the colony, Puritan influence seemed to be growing. When Thomas Harrison, formerly Sir William's own chaplain, was converted by the nonconformists, many conservative Virginians were shocked at the strength of the "enemy" in their midst. Harrison was expelled from his parish and later moved to New England. "We are sensible," read an official declaration of the General Assembly, "of the many disaffections to the government from a schismaticall party, of whose intentions our native country of England hath had and yet hath too sad experience." A special guard of ten men was granted Sir William as protection against assassins.[36]

When news reached Virginia that Charles I had been beheaded January 30, 1649 by the victorious Parliamentary forces and that a Protectorate demanding allegiance from all English dominions had been established, the General Assembly, spurred on by Governor Berkeley, refused to acknowledge the Commonwealth and pledged anew its loyalty to the House of Stuart. Upon being informed of this response, Parliament passed an act forbidding the colony to have "Commerce or Traffique" with any people whatsoever.[37] The Governor delivered before the Assembly in March of 1651 a vehement denunciation of the Parliamentary regime and a stirring appeal for support of the Crown.[38] Referring to the Protectorate's demands for obedience and threats of punishment, he asserted:

"If the whole current of their reasoning were not as ridiculous as their actions have been tyrannical and bloody, we might wonder with what brows they could sustain such impertinent assertions. For, if you look into it, the strength of their argument runs only thus: we have laid violent hands on your landlord, possessed his manor house where you used to pay your rents; therefore, now tender your respects to the same house you once reverenced. I call my conscience to witness, I lie not. I cannot in all their declaration perceive a stronger argument for what they would impose on us, than this which I have now told you . . .

"Surely, Gentlemen, we are more slaves by nature than their power can make us if we suffer ourselves to be shaken with these paper bullets, and those on my life are the heaviest they either can or will send us. 'Tis true . . . they have long threatened the Barbadoes, yet not a ship goes thither but to beg trade, nor will they do to us, if we dare honorably resist their imperious ordinance. Assuredly, Gentlemen, you have heard under what heavy burdens the afflicted English nation now groans and calls to Heaven for relief, how formerly unheard of impositions make the wives pray for barrenness and their husbands deafness to exclude the cries of their succourless, starving children. And I am confident you do believe, none would long endure this slavery, if the sword at their throats did not compel them to languish under the misery they hourly suffer.

"Look at their sufferings with the eyes of understanding, and that will prevent all your tears but those of compassion. Consider with what prisons and axes they have paid those that have served them to the hazard of their souls. Consider yourselves how happy you are and have been, how the gates of wealth and honor are shut on no man, and that there is not here an arbitrary hand that dares to touch the substance of either poor or rich. But that which I would have you chiefly consider with thankfulness is that God hath separated you from the guilt of the crying blood of our pious sovereign of ever blessed memory.

"But, mistake not, Gentlemen! Part of it will yet stain your garments if you willingly submit to those murderers' hands that shed it. I tremble to think how the oaths they will impose will make those guilty of it that have long abhorred the traitorousness of the act.

"But I confess having had so frequent testimonies of your truth and courage I cannot have a reasonable suspicion of any cowardly falling off from the former resolutions, and have only mentioned this last as a part of my duty and care of you, not of my real doubts and fears.

"Or, if with untried men we were to argue on this subject, what is it can be hoped for in a change which we have not already? Is it liberty? The sun looks not on a people more free than we are from all oppression. Is it wealth? Hundreds of examples show us that industry and thrift in a short time may bring us to as high a degree of it as the country and our conditions are yet capable of. Is it security to enjoy this wealth when gotten? Without blushing, I will speak it: I am confident there lives not that person [who] can accuse me of attempting the least act against any man's property. Is it peace? The Indians, God be blessed, round about us are subdued. We can only fear the Londoners, who would fain bring us to the same poverty wherein the Dutch found and relieved us, would take away the liberty of our consciences and tongues and our right of giving and selling our goods to whom we please.

"But, Gentlemen, by the Grace of God, we will not so tamely part with our King and all these blessings we enjoy under him. And if they oppose us, do but follow me. I will either lead you to victory or lose a life which I cannot more gloriously sacrifice than for my loyalty and your security."

Deeply moved by the Governor's appeal, the Council and Burgesses gave unanimous support to resolutions embodying the arguments he had used.[39]

At first, Sir William seemed to have been justified in assuring the colonists that "paper bullets" were the worst that would be sent against them. The Protectorate was itself too insecure to spare resources for a punitive expedition to Virginia. The blockade threat would have been an extremely severe one if Parliament had had the means to execute it. But, though English naval commanders were ordered to seize foreign vessels trading with the colony, facilities were not sufficient to enforce the trade restrictions adopted.

Meanwhile, Puritan elements in Virginia were urging the Commonwealth to dispatch a military expedition to the colony to enforce obedience. At length the Council in England ordered a dual mission, both military and diplomatic. Thus, prepared for war or peace, a well-armed British fleet, with Captain Robert Dennis in command and peace commissioners aboard, sailed up the James in March 1652.[40]

Sir William found himself in a desperate plight. Soon hostile guns would be turned on his capital and troops would pour ashore. Puritans in the colony stood ready to aid the invading Parliamentary forces. Even if these troops were defeated, others would be sent.

But the Governor was not a man to surrender easily. Assuming active command of the militia, he disposed his land forces in accordance with good military practice, then pressed into service a few Dutch vessels in the James.

These formidable preparations no doubt strengthened the Parliamentary commissioners in their desire to negotiate rather than fight. "At last," Robert Beverley wrote a half century later, "Dennis contrived a stratagem which betrayed the country. He had got a considerable parcel of goods aboard which belonged to two of the Council, and found a method of informing them of it. By this means, they were reduced to the dilemma either of submitting, or losing their goods. This occasioned factions among them, so that at last, after the surrender of all the other English plantations, Sir William was forced to submit to the usurper on the terms of a general pardon."[41]

An historian reading the "Articles at the Surrender of the Countrie" without any other knowledge of the event might wonder who surrendered to whom. The Parliamentary regime made as many concessions as the Virginians did.

The terms stated:

"It is agreed and cons'ted that the plantation of Virginia, and all the inhabitants thereof, shall be and remaine in due obedience and subjection to the common wealth of England, according to the lawes there established, And that this submission and subscription be acknowledged as voluntary act not forced nor constrained by a conquest upon the countrey, And that they shall have and enjoy such freedoms and priviledges as belong to the free borne people of England, and that the former government by the instructions be void and null."[42]

It was also provided that "the Grand Assembly as formerly shall convene and transact the affairs of Virginia, wherein nothing is to be acted or done contrarie to the government of the common wealth of England and the lawes there established."[43]

It was agreed that "there shall be a full and total remission and indemnity of all acts, words or writings done or spoken against the parliament of England in relations to the same."[44]

But Virginia gained much. All trade restrictions on the colony were lifted and it was guaranteed that Virginia, despite its defiance, "shall enjoy all priviledges equall with any English plantations in America." Most sweeping of all was the promise "that Virginia shall be free from all taxes, customes and impositions whatsoever, and none to be imposed on them without consent of the Grand Assembly, And soe that neither fforts nor castles be erected or garrisons maintained without their consent."[45]

Separate articles drawn up between the Commissioners and the Governor and Council, like the general articles of surrender, provided that anyone might remain in Virginia for a year without subscribing to the oath of allegiance to the Commonwealth and might sell his property and leave the country in the meantime. Neither Governor nor Councillor would be "censured for praying for or speaking well of the King for one whole yeare in their private houses or neighbouring conference." Sir William must have obtained the concession that "there be one sent home at the present Governour's choice to give an accompt [account] to his Ma'tie [Majesty] of the surrender of his countrey."⁴⁶

The established church in the colony fared better than one might have expected. Though adherence to the forms of the Anglican Church had been a major point of controversy, the use of the Book of Common Prayer for the ensuing year was permitted "provided that those things which relate to kingship or that government be not used publicly." The ministers were allowed to retain their posts for the same period.⁴⁷

The Parliamentary commissioners stayed in Virginia for an extended period. Empowered by the Council of State to hold an election of Burgesses in which all who had subscribed to the oath of allegiance might participate, they remained to consult with the Burgesses on the best means of establishing a new government that would be both satisfactory to the colonists and acceptable to Parliament. Following a special election, a new House assumed its duties on April 26.

As might have been expected, a system of government framed with the advice and assistance of the Burgesses accorded them a much larger role in colonial affairs. Indeed, that body became the center of gravity in Virginia government. Only the distant London government was to have the power to veto its decisions. The Council, which had existed before the popular branch of the legislature and had continued to function when the latter ceased to exist, now was to be dependent on the Burgesses for its very life. In their republican exuberance, the Burgesses even debated whether the Councillors should be admitted to the General Assembly. Individual Councillors would owe their office to election by the members of that more numerous, but formerly weaker body, which they had protected from the encroachments of autocracy in past years.⁴⁸

Even the Governor was to be elected by the Burgesses, and his continuance in office would be at their pleasure.⁴⁹

By unanimous vote of the House and approval of the Commissioners, that zealous Puritan, Mr. Richard Bennett, was made Governor. That he should have won the Commissioners' approval is not surprising. He was one of them, having left the colony when his earlier efforts to displace the Berkeley regime failed and returned only with the expedition sent out to subdue it in the name of Parliament.[50]

Believing that they were organizing a temporary government and that details of administration would be determined later by the Council of State in England, the Burgesses failed to define the powers of the Governor, stating only that he should exercise "all the just powers and authorities that may belong to that place lawfully."[51]

A Council of thirteen was elected by the Burgesses. On it we find such familiar names as John West, Samuel Matthews and Thomas Harwood. Also named to the Council was Nathaniel Littleton, son of Chief Justice Sir Edward Littleton and a representative of the rapidly growing Eastern Shore.[52]

Even before establishment of the new government, opposition to it flared on that peninsula. The Navigation Acts passed by Parliament severely threatened a people whose way of life was dependent upon the water. When war broke out between England and Holland in 1652, the inhabitants of the Shore became highly suspicious of a number of Dutch who had settled among them. Orders for the protection of the Dutch, issued by the Parliamentary regime, made the Protectorate still more unpopular with the Northampton planters.

When the Parliamentary commissioners notified the people of Northampton that they would be subject to a tax of forty-six pounds of tobacco per poll, men of the county met in protest and chose a committee of six prominent citizens to draft a complaint for presentation to the General Assembly.[53] The committee produced the following historic document:

"We the inhabitants of Northampton County do complain that from time to time we have been submitted and been obedient unto the payment of public taxations. For after the year 1647, since that time we conceive and have found that the taxes were very weighty, but in a more especial manner . . . the taxation of forty-six pounds of tobacco per poll this present year. And desire that the same be taken off the charge of the County.

"Furthermore, we allege that after 1647, we did understand and suppose our County of Northampton to be disjointed and sequestered from the rest of Virginia, therefore that law that requireth and enjoineth taxations from us to be arbitrary and illegal, forasmuch as we had neither summons for election of Burgesses nor voice in their Assembly during the time aforesaid but only the single Burgess in September 1651. We conceive that we may lawfully protest against the proceedings in the Act of Assembly for Public Taxations which have relation to Northampton County since the year 1647."[54]

The framers of this Northampton Declaration deserve a prominent place in American history. At an incredibly early period in colonial life, they formally enunciated the doctrine that taxation without representation is unjust. Furthermore, they asserted that when this principle was violated, they had a right to declare their independence. It is strange that the issuance of this bold statement should have become one of the neglected episodes of American history.

Infuriated by the Northampton Declaration, the Burgesses in 1653 pronounced it "scandalous and seditious" and claimed that it had "caused much disturbance in the peace and government of that county."[55]

Whether the Northampton Declaration was cause or result, there had been considerable disturbance. The independence movement had reached a climax in June 1653 at a mass meeting led by Colonel Thomas Johnson, of Occohannock Neck. Inflamed by Johnson's oratory, one man had cried out that the justices were a "company of asses and villains" and had brought an assenting roar from the crowd.[56]

The Burgesses decreed that "all the subscribers of the said paper be disabled from bearing any office in this country . . . and the honorable Governor and Secretary be entreated to go over to Accomack with such assistants as the House shall think fit, for the settlement of the peace of that county and punishing delinquents."[57]

Governor Bennett soon had troubles nearer home. When the Burgesses were preparing to elect a Speaker in July 1653, he sent them a respectfully phrased note suggesting that it would not be proper for them to consider for the post Lieutenant-Colonel Chiles inasmuch as that gentleman had an interest in a lately-arrived ship, concerning which there was "something to be agitated in . . . Assembly." Governor Bennett carefully explained that he did not wish "to intrench upon the right of Assemblies in the free choice of a Speaker, nor to undervalue Lefft. Coll. Chiles," but merely was giving advice in which the Council concurred. The complimentary closing read "Your real servant."[58]

The Burgesses not only elected Lieutenant Colonel Chiles but also ordered that, he having represented "to the House his extraordinary occasions in regard of the dispatch of some shipping now in the country in which he is much interested and concerned, the House upon his desire have given him leave to follow his private affairs notwithstanding the election aforesaid."[59]

Oliver Cromwell, now Lord Protector or dictator of England, had not yet found time to define the powers of a Governor of Virginia, and the Burgesses meanwhile were jealously guarding their prerogatives.

In 1655, Edward Digges was chosen to succeed Governor Bennett. Apparently Digges' term, extending into 1658, was unmarked by controversy with the House. On occasion, he won high praise from that body.[60]

Not so peaceful was the administration of his successor, Samuel Matthews. As his actions in the expulsion of Governor Harvey revealed, Matthews was not afraid to assert what he believed to be his rights.

In the first year of his administration, he and his Council ordered the dissolution of the House before that body was ready to conclude its business. The royal governors, as representatives of the King, had exercised the power of prorogation.

Under the Commonwealth, however, the chief executive had become the agent of the House. The Burgesses therefore replied with polite firmness:

"The House humbly presenteth, that the said dissolution as the case now standeth is not presidential, neither legal according to the laws now in force. Therefore we humbly desire a revocation of the said declaration, especially feeling we doubt not but speedily to finish the present affairs to the satisfaction of your honor and the whole country."[61]

It was then unanimously voted that any Burgess departing before adjournment of the Assembly should be "censured as a person betraying the trust reposed in him by his country." The Speaker was ordered to "sign nothing without the consent of the major part of the House." An oath of strict secrecy concerning the "transactions, debates or discourses" of the chamber was administered to each Burgess.[62]

The Governor and Council replied the next day, April 2, 1658. "Upon your assurance of a speedy issue to conclude the acts so near brought to a confirmation in this Assembly," they wrote, "we are willing to come to a speedy conclusion, and to refer the dispute of the power of dissolving and the legality thereof to his Highness, the Lord Protector."[63]

The Burgesses unanimously pronounced the reply "unsatisfactory," and a second answer from the Governor and Council was so unacceptable that a committee was empowered to frame a declaration "for vindication and manifestation of the Assembly's power."[64] This committee reported:

"We find by the records, the present power of government to reside in such persons as shall be empowered by the Burgesses (the representatives of the people) who are not dissolvable by any power now extant in Virginia, but the House of Burgesses."[65]

Retention of Samuel Matthews as Governor, but with a new Council "nominated, appointed and confirmed by the present Burgesses convened, with the assistance of the Governor for his advice," was proposed.[66]

The Burgesses then drew up a declaration stating, in part:

"We the . . . Burgesses do declare that we have in ourselves the full power of the election and appointment of all officers in this country until such time as we shall have order to the contrary from the supreme power in England, all which is evident upon the Assembly records.

"And for the better manifestation thereof and the present dispatch of the affairs of this country we declare as followeth:

"That we are not dissolvable by any power yet extant in Virginia but our own; that all former election of Governor and Council be void and null; that the power of Governor for the future shall be conferred on Col. Samuel Matthews, Esq., who by us shall be invested with all the just rights and privileges belonging to the Governor and Captain General of Virginia and that a Council shall be nominated, appointed and confirmed by the present Burgesses convened (with the advice of the Governor, for his assistance,) and that for the future none be admitted a Councillor but such who shall be nominated, appointed and confirmed by the House of Burgesses as aforesaid, until further order from the supreme power in England."[67]

Forestalling possible defiance from the Council, the Burgesses commanded Captain Robert Ellison, High Sheriff of James City County and Sergeant-at-Arms for the General Assembly "not to act or execute any warrant, precept or command directed . . . from any other power or person than the Speaker of this honorable House. . . ."[68]

The House of Burgesses had effectively demonstrated its supremacy in the government of Virginia.

The next challenge to that supremacy came the following year from England. The colonists learned that Oliver Cromwell had died the preceding September, but that shortly before his death he had proposed to place Virginia's government on a solid constitutional foundation. Though death had stayed his hand, it was believed by the Council of State that the Protector had intended that authority in the colony be centered in the Council, with the Governor as its presiding officer, rather than in the House.[69]

The Burgesses proposed to appeal to Oliver Cromwell's successor, his elder son Richard, for confirmation of the powers exercised by them. In this they were joined by the Governor who, coming before the House, reiterated his recognition of that body's supremacy and promised to "joyne his best assistance with the country in making an address to his Highness [the Lord Protector] for confirmation of their present privileges."[70]

Richard Cromwell, whose ineptness in comparison with his destiny-conscious father earned him the soubriquet "Tumbledown Dick," resigned in May 1659. An interval of confusion succeeded in England and Virginia. To whom would Englishmen turn for leadership? The homeland's plight not only aggravated colonial problems, but found its duplication in Virginia. In the midst of renewed controversy over the relative authority of Council and House, Governor Matthews died in January 1660.

The Assembly convened March 13 and adjudged that, "by reason of the late frequent distractions, there being in England no resident absolute and generally confessed power," a reiteration of the legislature's supremacy was necessary.[71]

Turning next to the election of a Governor, they thought of Sir William Berkeley. After circumstances had delayed his departure, he had elected to remain in Virginia. Perhaps, aside from his attachment to the colony, he had preferred to keep an ocean between him and the Parliamentary regime.

In asking Sir William to be their Governor, the people's representatives no doubt were influenced in part by rumors that the monarchy would be restored as well as by the memory of general happiness and prosperity during his administration. Mindful, however, that another Parliamentary regime might succeed to power in England, the Assembly offered Sir William the gubernatorial office on the condition that he give allegiance to whatever power established itself as the home government.

The proud former Governor, ever loyal to the Crown, was unwilling to accept leadership with such commitments. In an address to the Assembly, he reaffirmed his loyalty to the House of Stuart, paid tribute to his late sovereign and condemned his execution, and briefly listed the succession of temporary regimes.

"Under all these mutable governments of divers natures and constitutions," he declared, "I have lived most resigningly submissive. But, Mr. Speaker, it is one duty to live obedient to a government, and another of a very different nature to command under it."[72]

Later, in the course of his address, Sir William said:

"You have, Mr. Speaker, with great wisdom and providence taken care of my obedient prostrating to the supreme power [in England] the authority you would entrust me with, for which I give you my humble thanks; for this wisdom of yours hath animated my caution of assuming this burden, which is so volatile, slippery and heavy that I may justly fear it will break my limbs."[73] He would be willing to hold office temporarily from the people of Virginia, but he would never accept confirmation from any English authority except the Crown. He therefore declined the governorship.

Berkeley had made his position clear. The legislators were willing to accept him on his own terms. Sir William therefore accepted office from the Assembly on the condition that he would serve by their authority only so long as the contest for control in England remained undecided. He pledged to resign as soon as any government was established in the homeland.[74]

Sir William found being Governor in 1660 quite different from his previous experience in that capacity. The Assembly jealously guarded its ascendancy. Berkeley himself confessed to Governor Stuyvesant of New Amsterdam, "I am but a servant of the Assembly's."[75]

What Sir William had termed "the miserable distractions of England" ended May 29, 1660 when the monarchy was restored. As the Governor had predicted, the people of Virginia "immediately return[ed] to their own professed obedience." The newly crowned Charles II quickly sent Sir William a commission to govern in his name.

Berkeley's expression of appreciation is interesting as an illustration of his attitude toward the throne. "I . . . most humbly throw myself at your Majesty's feet," wrote this proud man, "in a dutiful thankfulness to your Majesty that you yet think me worthy of your royal commands. It is true I did something which, if misrepresented to your Majesty, may cause your Majesty to think me guilty of a weakness I should ever abhor myself for. But it was no more . . .

than to leap over the fold to save your Majesty's flock, when your Majesty's enemies of that fold had barred up the lawful entrance into it and enclosed the wolves of schism and rebellion ready to devour all within it. Nor did I adventure on this without the advice and impulsion of your Majesty's best subjects in these parts. . . . I always in all conditions had more fear of your Majesty's frowns than the swords or tortures of your enemies."[76]

Restoration of the monarchy did not, as some had hoped, bring immediate repeal of the navigation laws passed under the Commonwealth. Indeed, these restrictions were intensified. Under the Act of 1651, no Virginia (or, for that matter, American, Asiatic or African) goods could legally enter England except aboard English ships of which the owner, master and three-fourths of the crew were English. Now, in the very year of the restoration, an act was passed requiring that all goods sent to the American colonies, from whatever country they might issue, be exported from England. An additional provision required the colonists to ship only to England or English dominions all tobacco, sugar, wool and other commodities produced by them. These laws increased the freight rates paid by the colonists, since the English charged more than the Dutch carriers, and also deprived them of the privilege of finding the most profitable markets for their products.[77]

It is thought that Governor Berkeley protested against the Navigation Acts when he returned to England in 1661 to oppose a renewed effort to return the colony to the management of the Virginia Company.[78] If so, his efforts were of no avail.

Virginia became increasingly the chief victim of England's struggle with Holland over the world's carrying trade.[79] Excluded from Dutch markets for their products, the planters found it impossible to dispose of much of their tobacco. In exclusive trade with England, tobacco prices declined sharply. Since these economic reverses involved a product that was not only the chief crop of the colony, but also its medium of exchange, they were fraught with peril.

Some merchants joined with the planters in appealing to Charles II in 1662 to decree that no tobacco should be planted in Maryland and Virginia for the space of a year.[80] It was hoped that restricting the supply until demand could catch up with it would solve the tobacco problem. The appeal was not sympathetically received. Nevertheless, the colonists did not abandon their hopes of government crop control.

In 1663, a province was carved from Virginia territory south of the Jamestown Colony, just as one had been carved from that to the north thirty-one years before. Sir William Berkeley was one of six knights and nobles to whom the lands between the thirty-first and thirty-sixth parallels were granted. Charles II's father had granted this territory of Carolina to Sir Robert Heath, but the patent had lapsed and it was assumed that all of Virginia had reverted to the Crown upon abrogation of the London Company's charter in 1624.

Meanwhile, falling tobacco prices and rising costs of imported commodities held the average Virginia planter in what threatened to prove a death squeeze. By 1664, the Crown had relented sufficiently from its flat rejection of the planters' appeal for crop control to authorize the Assembly to appoint commissioners to confer with representatives from Maryland upon a plan for curtailment of tobacco production. Commissioners from the two colonies, meeting at Wiccocomico May 12, agreed upon a proposal for the prohibition of tobacco planting after June 20 of each year. Ratification by the Virginia Assembly was swift, but the Maryland legislature balked.[81]

All the while, tobacco accumulated in London and Bristol warehouses, inevitably forcing lower and lower the prices paid to Virginia planters. Prices for goods of English manufacture continued to rise.[82] For the great planter, this situation was inconvenient. For the small farmer, it was disastrous.

Yet desperate appeals to Maryland for one year's cessation of tobacco planting seemed to have no effect. Sir William Berkeley, deeply concerned over Virginia's plight, made a winter trip to Maryland (no small labor in that wilderness world) that he might argue the matter personally. His persuasive powers proved as effective with Marylanders as with Virginians. The Maryland Assembly enacted a prohibition against the planting of tobacco from February 1666 to February 1667, the act to become operative upon the passage of identical measures by Virginia and North Carolina authorities. Once again the Virginia Assembly was quick to act. This time North Carolina caused delay. Indian troubles in the southern colony took precedence over all other matters. When North Carolina finally took appropriate action, Lord Baltimore doomed the entire project by refusing to sanction his colony's participation.[83]

Confessing his disappointment to his sovereign, Governor Berkeley wrote:

"This overtook us like a storm and enforced us like distressed mariners to throw our dear bought commodities into the sea when we were in sight of our harbor, and with them so drowned not only our present reliefs but all future hopes of being able to do ourselves good, whilst we are thus divided and enforced to steer by another's compass, whose needle is too often touched with particular interest.

"This unlimited and independent power . . . of the Lord Baltimore doth, like an impetuous wind, blow from us all those seasonable showers of your Majesty's Royal cares and favors, and leaves us and his own province withering and decaying in distress and poverty . . . This unreasonable and unfortunate prohibition . . . hath not only increased the discontent of many of the inhabitants of his province, but hath *raised the grief and anger of almost all your . . . subjects of this colony to such a height as required great care to prevent those disturbances which were like to arise from their [d]eluded hopes and vain expenses.*"[84]

Secretary Thomas Ludwell wrote in similar vein in 1667. Reporting that the average tobacco farmer's income was reduced to only fifty shillings a year, he pronounced that sum "so much too little that I can attribute it to nothing but the mercy of God that he has not fallen into mutiny and confusion."[85]

Though failing to secure either Maryland's cooperation in crop control or amendment of the Navigation Laws, Sir William was still determined to relieve Virginia's economic plight. English mercantilists insisted that the depression in the colony was due not to the Navigation Acts but to the failure of the Virginians to diversify their industry. They blamed the planters for subjecting themselves to an economy dependent upon a single crop. By producing iron, glass, silk and other products, they argued, the Virginians could improve their own condition and at the same time serve the empire.[86] Sir William decided to act upon their advice.

In July 1668, the Governor and Council requested that the King send into Virginia men skilled in the manufacture of silk and apparently accompanied their appeal with a sample of silk already produced. Governor Berkeley also addressed a personal letter to his sovereign concerning hopes for promotion of the silk industry in Virginia.[87]

Unfortunately, Berkeley's efforts to stimulate industry, like those of his predecessor, met with little success. The failure of many costly enterprises further aggravated economic suffering.[88]

These economic reverses had wrought social changes. Virginia was no longer a land of opportunity for the man of slender financial resources. Society was ceasing to be fluid. The great planters, with their reserves of wealth, could maintain their way of life. But the small farmer, however hard he might work, saw no possibility of advancing in status. Indeed, like the Red Queen in *Alice in Wonderland*, he had to run as fast as he could to stay in the same place.

The prosperity of the great planter, so long as it was a reminder to the small farmer of what he might achieve, had fostered no strong resentment. Now that it had become a symbol of what he was denied, the yeoman felt hostility rankling within him. The fact that the great planters or their agents collected his taxes and generally governed his affairs in this time of distress aggravated his umbrage.

Some of this dissatisfaction began to center upon Governor Berkeley. He led what was, on the colonial scene, a life of unexampled luxury. When the tax-burdened farmer beheld Sir William riding in his coach from Jamestown to his estate, Green Spring, with its great hall, many servants and slaves, seventy horses and fifteen hundred fruit trees,[89] he must have reflected bitterly that his own meager earnings helped to maintain the Governor in such state. There were many who thought that Sir William should refuse the gift of two hundred pounds annually voted him by the Assembly in addition to his salary of 1,200 pounds.[90] But there is no record that Sir William ever refused the generous offer. The legislature, of course, would continue to vote excessive rewards to Sir William. By patient and skillful diplomacy, he had quite unobtrusively placed the Assembly under his domination. He had performed many personal favors for the lawmakers.[91] The individual indebtedness of the Assembly's members amounted to a collective obligation. These same men and their friends dominated every sphere—political, judicial, economic and religious—of the small farmer's life.

To the other economic problems that plagued the farmer was added an increasing uncertainty that the goods he shipped to England would arrive or that he would receive what he had ordered. The Navigation Acts, framed especially with Virginia and other American possessions in mind, had helped to provoke a second war with Holland in 1665.[92] A year before the declaration of war, an English squadron had forced the surrender of New Amsterdam and thus added New York to England's other American possessions— Virginia, New England, Maryland, Carolina and the West Indies.

English raids, of course, invited reprisals. In 1667, the very year that the Dutch took advantage of the inactive status of some English vessels to enter the mouth of the Thames and carry away a prize ship, they performed an almost identical feat in the James. His pride hurt by the Virginia incident, Sir William Berkeley himself sought to lead a naval attack on the Dutch, but was thwarted by the dilatory tactics of those he impressed into service.[93] Merchant ships found it necessary to travel in convoys. The war ended formally before the close of 1667, but English vessels still could not count themselves safe. The Virginia farmer cared nothing for the quarrels of empires. He only knew that forces represented by colonial authority were playing havoc with his life.

Another great blow fell in 1669. The instrument that struck had been forged more than two decades before. The hand that wielded it was the same that now held the scepter. The autumn of 1649 had been a bleak one for Prince Charles and his followers. Refugees at St. Germain-en-Laye, near Paris, just eight months after the beheading of Charles I, they were reduced to poverty. One by one, they pawned their jewels to purchase necessities.[94] But they were sustained by hope. Prince Charles had been proclaimed Charles II in both Scotland and Ireland, and in each country there was an army to fight for him. Charles thus determined to reward these faithful followers who shared his adversity by sharing with them the prosperity that would be his upon restoration of the monarchy. Especially deserving, in Charles' eyes, were Ralph Lord Hopton, Baron of Stratton, the courageous Commander-in-Chief of Royal Forces in the west of England; Sir John Berkeley, Hopton's Commissary General and a diplomat as well; Sir William Morton, a lawyer who had turned soldier and suffered imprisonment for his King; Sir Dudley Wyatt, who had served during the Civil War as confidential messenger between King Charles and Queen Henrietta; Henry Jermyn, Baron of St. Edmundsbury, a great favorite with the Dowager Queen; John Lord Culpeper, who had served Charles most successfully as a parliamentarian and ineptly as a soldier; and Thomas Culpeper, Esq., a cousin of the peer. To these seven on September 18, 1649, the exiled Charles granted all territory in Virginia "bounded by and within the heads" of the Potomac and Rappahannock Rivers.[95] Within this tract of about a million acres, the patentees would exercise the rights and privileges of barons of the realm. An annual rent of £6,135 4d was to be paid at Jamestown "in lieu of all services and demands whatsoever."

The triumph of the Roundhead forces and the enforced subordination of Virginia on March 22, 1652 placed the fate of the grant in doubt.

When Charles II returned to England in 1660, some of the patentees pressed him for the promised reward. John Lord Culpeper made no bones of his poverty. "The usurer and I," he confessed, "are not yet even; for I have only scratched the usurer, the usurer has stabbed me."[96]

Late in 1661, the patent was enrolled. Three wealthy citizens of Bristol applied for a lease on the proprietary. They successfully enlisted the support of the King, who in a letter of December 5, 1662 instructed Governor Berkeley to give aid to the Bristol gentlemen.

These Royal instructions were no more popular than the commands to aid another proprietor, Lord Baltimore, had been exactly three decades before. Loyal Royalist though he was, Sir William was as disturbed as his Council at this news. The Governor had issued in the King's name before 1661 no less than 576 grants of "headright" lands in the Northern Neck.[97] What would happen to these grants? Settlers were attracted to the beautiful peninsula between the Rappahannock and Potomac, lured by this land that combined the advantages of hill country with the delights of salt water. If their grants were invalidated, the prestige of the Jamestown government would be shaken and rising discontent among the colonists would mount still higher. Anger against Lord Baltimore's arbitrary action in the matter of crop control had caused the Virginians to be suspicious of all proprietors and hostile toward all proprietaries.

The colonists set forth their complaint in an address to the Crown, conveyed by Colonel Francis Moryson. This gentleman's skillful maneuvering, after several reversals, succeeded in so discouraging the Bristol lessees that their project was abandoned about 1664.[98]

The patient Moryson won a major concession from the proprietors five years later. Under a renewed and revised royal grant of May 8, 1669, the patentees promised recognition of all land titles issued in their proprietary before Michaelmas 1661 provided that the holders of such titles were in "actual possession" of the land as of May 8, 1669. It was also agreed that the usual quit rents would continue to be paid and that all reversions and escheats would become the proprietors'. The grant was not to be in perpetuity. The patentees could retain proprietorship only of those parts of the grant which they "possessed, inhabited or planted" prior to May 8, 1690. Most important of all to leading Virginians, the new grant prevented the exercise of those feudal privileges which would have made the Northern Neck independent of the Jamestown Government. It was specified that the Proprietors ". . . shall not act or intermeddle with the military affairs or forces in this tract of land hereby granted, or any part therein, or any forts or fortresses, or castles thereof, without the order and authority and consent of the Governor and Council of Virginia, and that the Governor and Council of Virginia shall have full power and authority to lay and levy any tax or imposition in and upon the said territory . . . and all and every the possessors and inhabitants thereof for the public and common defense of the said Colony of Virginia and the territory and lands thereby granted as upon other parts of Virginia, proportionable, and the [Proprietors] shall be in all subject and obedient to such laws as are and shall be made by the said Governor and Council and Assembly for or concerning the said Colony or government thereof."[99]

In 1670, the Northern Neck patentees entered upon the tasks of collecting quit rents and promoting settlement in their domain. The first endeavor was most difficult, even with the reluctant assistance of the Jamestown government.

The measure of that reluctance is indicated by the Secretary of the Colony's report to the Council for Foreign Plantations, June 26, 1671, in which it was declared that the transfer to proprietors of land long occupied by settlers had fomented "infinite discontents," beyond anything he had seen in the colony before.[100] The suspicion that the Proprietors were trying to free themselves from Jamestown authority was openly avowed. The Council for Foreign Plantations were begged to maintain the status quo until the Assembly had readied a protest.[101]

The legislative protest was framed at the session of September 1671. The King was petitioned to protect Northern Neck settlers from "alteration" of their tenures and "alienation from their immediate dependence upon his Majesty." Major General Robert Smith became the colony's agent in London.[102] Like any good ambassador, he was supposed to keep the colony informed of any threatened change in regard to the Proprietary and also to intercede diplomatically to protect the colony's rights.

A decision by the Proprietors to conduct a resurvey of all "head-rights" in the Northern Neck, the cost to be borne by the tenants, may have been partly responsible for the Virginians' decision to take more decisive action in regard to the Proprietary. In any event, the colonists determined to acquire for the Jamestown government the proprietary rights to the Northern Neck. By the autumn of 1673, they concluded that rights of three of the six patentees could be purchased for £1,200. At this point, Governor Berkeley's patriotism triumphed over his acquisitiveness, and he generously offered to lend the colony the requisite sum. Also generous, the Assembly offered to pay him eight percent interest.[103]

In the midst of negotiations for purchase of a half interest in the Northern Neck, the Virginians received crushing news from Major General Smith. He reported the discovery in the Signet Office of a patent, dated February 25, 1673, transfering to Thomas Lord Culpeper (one of the Northern Neck proprietors) and Henry Earl of Arlington for a term of thirty-one years all land in the colony not previously patented.[104] Not only would they be given the privileges of collecting quit rents and confirming and issuing land grants, but would also be permitted to establish counties, name local officials and organize courts. The Virginians, already sacrificing to regain a portion of their territory granted to Proprietors, were appalled to learn that virtually the entire Colony was delivered into private hands, and that without any forewarning to its citizens.[105]

A copy of the patent, forwarded by General Smith, appears to have reached Virginia in the summer of 1674.[106] Convening in September, the alarmed Burgesses ordered preparation of an appeal to the King to revoke the Arlington-Culpeper Patent and confirm the "liberties, privileges, immunities, rights and properties" of the Colony. The Council was wholehearted in support of the House. Governor Berkeley, ardent Royalist though he was, went so far as to declare in a letter to the King that his Majesty had acted "upon misinformation" in granting dominion over Virginia to "two private persons."[107]

Three commissioners were thought necessary to represent the Colony in England at this critical juncture. The Assembly levied a tax of 120 pounds of tobacco per tithable to defray their expenses. The colony's representatives were making progress with Lord Arlington, but the tax to support their efforts bore heavily on the struggling Virginia farmer. This unfortunate colonist resented also the tax-supported attempts, in accordance with instructions from England, to convert Jamestown into a real city by artificial means. Even more bitter were his protests against the costly construction of forts to protect Virginia from foreign foes. He felt that the tax system was unjust anyway. A high poll tax, levied in equal measure on rich and poor, was grossly unfair. Land should be taxed. To the troubles resulting from the Navigation Acts, the wars with the Dutch, conflict with Proprietors, and mounting taxes to support costly and often unwise and inefficiently executed policies, were added natural misfortunes. A killing winter, a devastating storm, and an epidemic that killed half the cattle in Virginia had increased the colony's woes.[108]

Governor Berkeley was well aware that his administration was imperiled. Sir William had written in 1673 that many of the farmers were in such desperate straits that, upon the promise of any advantage from the Dutch, they might "revolt to them in hopes of bettering their condition by sharing the plunder of the country with them."[109]

In 1674, the announcement that heavier levies would be imposed sparked rebellion in New Kent County. Ragged men with frayed tempers gathered in an angry meeting and, clutching their guns, swore that they would not pay the new taxes. The Governor issued a proclamation warning them that resistance to Royal authority was treason. Some colonial leaders who held their confidence persuaded them to forego violence.[110]

There must have been a similar incident elsewhere in the colony, for Sir William reported that he had "appeased" two mutinies "raised by some secret villains who whispered among the people that there was nothing intended by the fifty pounds (levy) but the enriching of some few people."[111]

Natural phenomena heightened the tight-chested apprehension which Virginians felt in 1675. Once again appeared the same ominous sign in the sky which had affrighted the original Jamestown settlers as they spied it from the rolling decks of the *Susan Constant*, *Godspeed* and *Discovery*. Small wonder that the colonists exchanged anxious glances when they beheld a comet "streaming like a horsetail westwards" toward the horizon.[112] The superstitious could easily believe that all nature was conspiring to warn of imminent disaster. From nowhere appeared a flight of pigeons so numerous that their "weight broke down the limbs of large trees whereon they roosted at night." A similar omen had heralded the massacre of 1644. Warnings came from the earth itself. Clouds of insects, each "about an inch long and big as the top of a man's little finger," rose out of the ground, devoured leafy treetops and within a month disappeared.[113]

Other signs of danger were obvious even to the most skeptical. The Susquehannock Indians, hard pressed by the fierce Senecas, were retreating from their lands at the head of Chesapeake Bay down into Maryland and Virginia. The Susquehannocks were counted valuable allies of the Maryland colonists. Accordingly, the Marylanders furnished this tribe the firearms and munitions with which they defended themselves against the Senecas. In 1674, however, Maryland had negotiated a separate peace treaty with the Senecas. Thus, left to battle alone, the Susquehannocks desperately appealed to the legislature at St. Mary's to allot them some portion of Maryland for refuge. Camped on the north bank of the Potomac just south of Piscataway Creek, the tribesmen awaited word from their former allies.

The legislators were in a dilemma. The size of the tribe—it claimed six or seven hundred warriors—made the Marylanders fear to let them remain where they might infect peaceful Indians with their warlike spirit. But the legislators also quailed before the prospect of evicting so numerous a tribe. Eventually, the assemblymen offered the Indians permission to inhabit lands on the Potomac above the great falls. To this proposal, the Susquehannocks reluctantly agreed.[114]

But, as weeks ran into months, it became obvious that they were in no haste to leave. Their proscrastination was understandable. So long as they remained where they were, they were protected from the Senecas by the formidable reputation of the neighboring Piscataways.

Even this situation presented one great difficulty. Their food supply was low and, far from their fields and hunting grounds, they had no means of quickly replenishing it. The only alternative to starvation was robbery of the English plantations.

The confused picture of racial conflict abruptly leaped into sharp focus. Church-bound citizens of Stafford County halted in horror one summer morning before a gory spectacle that profaned the Sabbath scene. Sprawled across the threshold of his house, his head spilling blood, was Robert Hen. Nearby lay a dead Indian. Hen was beyond human aid. His neighbors could only stand and listen as he gasped out "Doegs, Doegs." A terrified boy crawled from under a bed to inform the settlers that Indians had done the bloody deed.[115]

The Virginians required no further evidence. The Doegs, a warlike tribe, lived just across the Potomac in Maryland. Colonel George Mason and Captain George Brent, commanders respectively of Stafford's infantry and horse, quickly rounded up thirty or more men for a punitive expedition. The party proceeded along the river bank until exactly opposite the Doeg tribal grounds and, following the Indians' own tactics, crossed over to attack at dawn. Confronted with two forest paths on the Maryland shore, Mason and Brent split their forces. Each soon came upon a cabin and had his men surround it.

A Doeg chieftain emerged from the quarters encircled by Brent's men and made signs that he wished to negotiate. When he attempted to make a break for freedom, the captain grabbed him by the hair and accused him of murdering Robert Hen. Protesting his innocence, the chief again broke away from his captors. A bullet from Brent's pistol dropped him in the dirt. The Doegs within the cabin fired on the English and then fled, leaving ten of their number writhing on the ground after a fusillade from Brent's men.[116]

Not one, but many Indians, ran forth from the cabin surrounded by Mason when he ordered his men to fire a volley. Fourteen of the tribesmen were slaughtered. One Indian risked his life by running up to Mason and shouting "Susquehannocks, friends." Appalled at his mistake, the captain cried out: "For the Lord's sake, shoot no more! These are our friends the Susquehannocks."[117]

In the moment they were spoken, those words ceased to be so. The Susquehannocks, quite understandably, would no longer regard the English as friends.

Well aware of this fact, Englishmen on both sides of the Potomac began to prepare for war in earnest. Governor Charles Calvert justly complained to Governor Berkeley that the trouble was caused by "the intrusion of the Virginians" on his province.[118] Realistically, however, the Marylanders knew that they were threatened no less than the Virginians. Accordingly, the two colonies attempted to coordinate military preparations. A joint expedition was organized to drive the Susquehannocks far from the areas of white settlement.[119]

The Indians knew that they were endangered. While awaiting attack, they began to build a fort in open ground near the junction of Piscataway Creek and the Potomac River. The English were delighted that this site had been chosen by their foes. Commanded by the Piscataway tribe's fort and accessible by sloop from two sides, it promised to be an easy target.[120]

Major Thomas Trueman and his Maryland troops took their stand September 26, 1675 on the north bank of Piscataway Creek and awaited arrival of the Virginians under Colonel John Washington[121] and Major Isaac Allerton. In the meantime, the Maryland commander invited Chief Harignera of the Susquehannocks to a parley. Since that chieftain was dead, the Indians sent five "great men" in his place. Acting as hastily as the Virginia avengers of

Hen's assassination, the Maryland major charged the Indian representatives with murder and put them under guard.[122]

The Virginia forces arrived the next day. Both commanders, like the men who served under them, were citizens of the Northern Neck. Colonel Washington was a rising Westmoreland planter of the middle group whose growing land interests included a tract only fifteen miles from the Susquehannock fort.[123] Major Allerton was also a Northern Neck planter.[124]

The Virginia officers accused the five captive Indians in much the same manner that the Marylanders had. Protestations of innocence prompted pointed questions as to how the Susquehannocks obtained their provisions and why some of them had been seen clothed in the garments of recently murdered Virginians.[125] The interview was conducted under difficulties. Not only was an interpreter required, but Major Trueman kept interrupting: "Gentlemen, are you finished? When you are done I will say something." At last, the impatient major provoked Colonel Washington to exclaim, "When we have done, we will give you notice!"[126]

The Virginians eventually despaired of obtaining a confession from the Indians and Major Trueman resumed his futile efforts. Quitting in exasperation, he demanded of Washington, "Are not these impudent rogues to deny the murders they have done when their Indians lie dead at Mr. Hinson's plantation, being killed in a fight there?"

"It would be very convenient," replied Washington, "to carry them up thither and to show them their Indians that are there buried."

"And so I will," replied Major Trueman.[127]

The Indians never returned from that journey. Their skulls were smashed, and bitter debate raged over responsibility for the deed. Some Marylanders charged that Colonel Washington had ordered the execution, but other witnesses testified to the Virginian's innocence. Major Trueman was impeached by the lower chamber of the Maryland legislature, found guilty by the upper, fined and sentenced to a prison term. Great was the revulsion in both colonies against the savage act. The Maryland Council recorded that "not a man would own to have had a hand" in "so great and unheard of a wickedness." Sir William Berkeley vowed, "If they had killed my grandfather and my grandmother, my father and mother and all my friends, yet if they had come to treat of peace, they ought to have gone in peace."[128]

What were the fruits of this infamous campaign? The Susquehannock fort's survival of a seven-week siege taught the English the
folly of their derision. Indeed, the Indian fortifications were so much
stronger than those hastily raised by the English that the Susquehannocks were able to rush out on quick sorties and return with
their enemies' horses for food.[129]

Humbled by this experience, the English requested a parley, but
the Indians pointedly asked, "Where are our great men"?[130] The
Susquehannocks, though, were prudent enough to realize that the
English would soon bring up reinforcements. They therefore swept
out of their fort, making a dramatic break through surprised lines
of white men, and faded into the forest.

While the English marched home in humiliation, the Susquehannocks hurried to a ford on the upper Potomac, crossed over
into Virginia and raided exposed plantations. Besides the stigma of
defeat and misconduct, the militia now bore the blame for these
depredations. The responsibility, whether wholly theirs or not, was
a heavy one. Sixty men, women and children had been slaughtered
in the first few days of Susquehannock raids. Death by burning and
flaying came to others who were borne away as captives. One frontier parish, Sitterborne, was reduced from seventy-one plantations
to eleven within the space of three weeks.[131]

The lurid tales of those who escaped inflamed and frightened all
of Virginia. Palisades and redoubts rose in frantic haste, and the
alert sentry with his rifle symbolized the colony's people.[132]

Governor Berkeley had no trouble in obtaining the Council's consent for a punitive expedition. Sir Henry Chicheley, a Royalist
veteran of the Civil War, was Sir William's choice as commander
of a company of infantry and cavalry quickly assembled. These men,
however, were never dispatched against the foe. Hardly had the
troop been organized when the Governor ordered them to disband.[133]

Sir William's action was not as inexplicable as it appeared to the
Virginia frontiersman. The Governor had just received a peace
proposal from the new chief of the Susquehannocks. The Indian
ruler justly reproached the Virginians for invading another province
to attack his people and then murdering their peace delegation.
These crimes had been heavily avenged by recent Susquehannock
raids, and the chief informed the Governor that compensation from
the English would permit resumption of peaceful relations. Sir
William replied with an expression of his own desire for peace.[134]

Amid great public agitation, the Assembly—summoned by the

Governor—convened in Jamestown March 7, 1676. Unthinking hot-heads demanded that all Indians be wiped out.[135] But they did not stampede the legislature into advocacy of such a senseless policy. By this time, the Assembly was far more representative of the Governor than of the populace. Sir William was as apprehensive of his own people as of their enemies. This whole tragedy which the legislature had met to consider had risen from the irresponsible action of colonial militia. Now that feeling ran fanatically high, the Virginians might turn any military expedition into an orgy of slaughter that would send every tribe east of the mountains on the warpath.

In obedience to the Governor's wish, therefore, the Assembly approved a defensive policy. War was declared on those known "to have committed murders, rapines and depredations." New prohi-bitions were placed on the sale of firearms to the Indians, five hun-dred soldiers were enlisted and provision was made for the erection of forts on the frontiers in Stafford, on the Mattaponi, Pamunkey and Nansemond rivers and at the falls of the Rappahannock, James and Appomattox. Much reliance was placed upon the aid of friendly Indians. Any Indian ally who brought in a captured enemy could claim three coats of matchcloth. One coat was the reward for the head of a dead one. Decapitation was a clumsier process than scalp-ing, but it gained more reliable trophies. Having adopted these measures, the General Assembly set aside two days for "public fasting and humiliation."[136]

Even these inadequate defense preparations had been undertaken too late. The enemy did not wait for completion of the English forts before resuming attack. The paralyzing war whoop sounded again and again, not only where fortifications were being constructed, but well within the circle of completed forts. Always it was the signal for burning and killing and mutilation.

Grief-crazed men ran to the forts to gasp out reports that their children had been slaughtered or their wives dragged into the wilder-ness. These men could not accept philosophically the information that no action could be taken until Governor Berkeley's permission to deal with the specific case had been obtained. While a messenger hastened to the Governor, the Indians lost no time in making good their escape.[137]

It is not remarkable that Virginians should decide that they must counterattack the enemy. The only wonder is that, terrified and maddened with anguish, they should have resorted to the orderly and traditional process of petition.

Petitions, however, accomplished nothing. Particularly unhappy was the experience of a group of petitioners from Charles City. One of them, all humility before his Majesty's representative, declared himself to be "one of your honor's subjects."

"Fools and loggerheads!" Berkeley exploded, "You are the king's subjects and so am I . . . . Pox take you."[138]

After this incident, even the right of petition in matters relating to defense was denied.[139]

Meanwhile, the anger of the people rose. The enemy struck next near the falls of the James. Among the plantations laid waste was that of Nathaniel Bacon—a twenty-nine-year-old Councillor who, despite the fact that he was the aristocratic heir to Friston Hall estate in England, sympathized with the small planters in their complaints against the colony's great landowners.[140] Bacon's overseer —more than a servant, a friend—was killed.[141] Nearby plantations were quickly deserted as the owners and their families made their way back to the more populated areas. Bacon did not join the herds of refugees crowding the villages and imposing themselves upon the charity of others. "I sent to the governor for a commission," he explained, "but being from time to time denied . . . and finding the lives and fortunes of the poor inhabitants wretchedly sacrificed, resolved to stand up in this ruinous gap and rather expose my life and fortune to all hazards than basely desert my post."[142]

Now came the frightening report that the enemy, massed fifty or sixty miles above the falls of the James, were preparing for an assault in force. The men of Henrico and Charles City counties saw that retreat was no longer practical. An end must come to evacuations or they would find themselves pushed off the continent. If their government would not make a stand for them, they would make a stand themselves. A motley host reminiscent of those who planted the colony—gentlemen, artisans, small farmers—assembled on the south side of the James at Jordan's Point. They now felt as Bacon did about the necessity for vigorous action. Small wonder that the young Councillor's name was most often mentioned when they discussed the need for a leader.[143]

Meanwhile the subject of this speculation was across the river in the company of three planters—Captain James Crews, who had spread the word that Bacon would accept captaincy of an expedition against the Indians;[144] Henry Isham, master of Doggans Plantation; and William Byrd, a former apprentice goldsmith who had emigrated to the colony only six years before at the age of eighteen and now, by virtue of good sense, a sizeable legacy from his uncle and marriage to highborn Mary Horsemanden was fairly on the way to becoming an aristocrat.[145]

At the propitious moment, these four rowed across the James and joined the crowd at Jordan's Point. When the young Councillor appeared, someone yelled "Bacon! Bacon!" The cry became a chorus. Thus the leader was chosen by acclamation.[146] Bacon transformed a punitive expedition into a crusade. He promised to fight not only for security from Indian attack, but also for the rights of free men. He pledged himself to war on oppressive taxes, unequal laws and favoritism in the courts. For these grievances he blamed Sir William Berkeley, calling him "negligent and wicked, treacherous and incapable."[147] In a wild burst of enthusiasm, the citizen soldiers drank "damnation to their souls" if they should prove false to their leader. Then they subscribed to a formal oath, signing their names "circular wise that the ringleader might not be found out."[148]

What sort of man was Bacon, and what kind of army did he command?

Obviously, he was no ordinary man. Though many called him brilliant, he was a man of action rather than contemplation. A Master of Arts in spite of himself, he had rollicked his way through Cambridge, winning a degree incidentally. He had also, on his father's insistence, studied law at Gray's Inn. Despite his own dislike of academic labor, his quick intelligence and natural eloquence attracted the friendship of famous scholars. As a kinsman of Francis Bacon, Viscount Albans and adviser to James I, he had been accustomed to titled society. He was at home, however, in any group where manly qualities were prized.[149]

What of the young commander's army? Few of its members had had formal military experience, but some were accustomed to command. Some were frontiersmen whose hunting skill and knowledge of the forests would stand them in good stead. Unusual leadership would be required to weld these individual talents into a disciplined force.[150]

Bacon and his men were ready to march on the Indians. Word reached them that a considerable body of Susquehannocks had moved south to a spot on the Roanoke in the vicinity of Occaneechee Island, near the North Carolina border. The island derived its name from the tribe of Indians who held it as a fastness athwart the southwest trail used by both English and Indian traders and there exacted a profit as middlemen.[151]

The Susquehannocks might prove a formidable foe. More recruits were desirable for the war against them. Accordingly volunteers were sought and found in New Kent County and, at a later stage of the march, among the Meherrin tribe. An effort to secure the aid of the Nottoways proved unsuccessful. Since the Meherrins added only twenty-four warriors to his force,[152] Bacon's long detour to secure Indian allies was a move of questionable wisdom.

The lengthened expedition took a heavy toll of provisions and the young leader had to let many of his men return home before it was completed. When he reached the banks of the Roanoke, he had only seventy tired men and a three days' food supply.[153]

By negotiations with Chief Persicles (also called Rossechy), Bacon secured the Occaneechees as allies. They had no love for the tribe whose raids had brought prohibition of the profitable fur trade.[154]

Under the domination of the Susquehannocks, who had built a fort near the island and manned it with thirty warriors, were the Mannikins. These tribesmen had long enjoyed the protection of the English and now informed Bacon by secret messenger that they stood ready to aid him.[155]

The English were able to get the Indians to fight their battle for them. The Occaneechees assaulted the Susquehannock fort and the Mannikins worked havoc inside the defenses. The Susquehannocks were completely vanquished, many of those who survived the attack being tortured to death according to the code of the forest.[156]

Bacon was not free to enjoy the success of his plans. At least eighty miles from the nearest white settlement, with his men deserting him and his food supply perilously low, he was faced with the threat that a rise in the river would leave him stranded among allies of doubtful loyalty.[157]

His discomfiture was increased by the Occaneechees' refusal to supply him with provisions for the homeward trek. Indeed, both they and the Mannikins began to guard their food supplies with care. When they began to man their forts, their behavior seemed ominous.[158]

What followed in the next few days is not clear, but Bacon's relations with the Indians deteriorated rapidly. Some of the leader's enemies claimed that he aggravated trouble with the Occaneechees by demanding that they surrender the Mannikins to him. Bacon's men, as has been suggested, may have thought they recognized some old marauders among their new-found allies.[159] Even so, the Occaneechee chief must have considered any such demand presumptuous when his own tribe, with the aid of the Mannikins, had won the victory.

The English and the Indians became extremely suspicious of each other, probably with justification on both sides. When Chief Persicles placed some of his warriors on the north bank of the river, as though to cut off a possible flight by the white men, Bacon's band assumed a warlike posture. In that apprehensive moment, the Indian families fled from their cabins and rushed toward the shelter of their fort. But the white men blocked the gates and attempted to hold the excited warriors, squaws and children as hostages.

A shot was fired from somewhere and an Englishman fell dead. Immediately Bacon signaled his men to charge the palisades. Rushing right up to the log defenses, they thrust the muzzles of their muskets into the portholes and fired away at the inmates as though they had been so many animals confined in a huge barrel. Other Indians were burned to death as some quarters were set afire. Some of Bacon's band, not thus occupied, enthusiastically entered into the grimmer sport of slaughtering the hostages amid the agonized protests of the men and dying screams of the women and children.[160]

Many Indians had escaped, however, so the fight was resumed at dawn of the next day. At first the Indians sought to fire only from concealment, but this cautious strategy eventually yielded to a desperate encircling maneuver in which the chief and many of the great warriors were killed. At nightfall, those still alive retreated to their canoes and slipped away.[161]

Bacon was exultant in victory. He congratulated himself upon the destruction not only of a great division of the Susquehannocks, but also of many Occaneechee warriors, their chief and their trading post. Still more, he prided himself on the fact that the Indians had been duped and goaded into "civil war."[162]

*   *   *

As might be expected, an enraged governor awaited Bacon's return. Sir William had made repeated efforts to prevent the young Councillor from executing his bold plan. He had issued a proclamation of amnesty for Bacon and his followers, to take effect if they would lay down their arms immediately and "return to their duty and allegiance."[163] If read by the insurgents, the document was ignored. The Governor then quickly raised a company of three hundred mounted volunteers who set forth from Middle Plantation May 3 with the design of intercepting Bacon's band at the falls of the James. Sir William, acting with the vigor of his earlier years, rode at their head.[164]

When, upon reaching Henrico, he found that Bacon had already left the area and could not be overtaken before striking his blow against the Indians, Berkeley determined that this young upstart who defied royal authority should be severely punished. By proclamation of May 10, he suspended Bacon from the Council, the office of justice of the peace and "all other offices civil and military."[165] Even in this official document, he could not repress his own wounded feelings. He expressed amazement that any of his people could be led astray by a glib pretender. Were his own years of service in peace and war so lightly regarded? The governor obviously believed that he was exercising great restraint in granting pardon to all of Bacon's followers except John Sturdivant and Thomas Williford, "the chief promoters of this rebellion," if they would leave Bacon and return to the ways of obedience. As for Bacon himself, rumor declared that Berkeley intended to hang him.[166]

Seeing that war with the Indians was already an established fact, Berkeley now busied himself as commander-in-chief of the colony's forces. He personally inspected the fort on the Pamunkey and dispatched scouts to discover the disposition of Indian forces. The Queen of the Pamunkeys and her tribesmen, it was learned, had abandoned their village for a position in Dragon Swamp at the head of the Piankatank River, and there had raised fortifications. Colonel Claiborne, acting for the governor, ordered her to return with her tribe to their former home. Though promising not to lift a hand against the English, she said that she could not move since, if Sir William was unable to protect himself against Bacon, he certainly would not be able to protect her.[167]

Such words were infuriating to a royal official who had a high estimate of his own dignity. Berkeley was ready to march on the Pamunkeys when frightening news reached him. The "mutinies" which he had feared were exploding all over the colony.[168] Fired with long smoldering discontents, the people were prepared to rally to Bacon's standard.

Concessions to popular demands must be made at once. Sir William issued a proclamation. "Finding by the too frequent complaints that the so long continuance of the present Assembly is looked upon as a grievance," he declared that he must with reluctance dissolve that body and call a new election. "All persons are to have liberty freely to present to the said Burgesses all such just complaints as they or any other have against me as Governor . . . And supposing I who am head of the Assembly may be the greatest grievance, I will most gladly join with them in a petition to his Majesty to appoint a new Governor of Virginia, and thereby to ease and discharge me from the great care and trouble thereof in my old age."[169]

Sir William now counted heavily upon prominent members of the political organization he had built during his terms as Governor. These men sought to quell uprisings in the constituencies in which they resided and campaigned for the election of Burgesses favorable to the regime in power.[170]

Berkeley himself remained with an armed force at the falls of the James, awaiting Bacon's arrival. At length the opening of the Assembly compelled the Governor's return to Jamestown, and it was then that Bacon returned to Henrico and a hero's welcome.[171]

"The country does so really love him," Bacon's wife wrote his sister, "that they would not leave him alone anywhere; there was not anybody against him but the Governor and a few of his great men which have got their estates by the Governor. Surely if your brother's crime had been so great all the country would not have been for him . . . I do verily believe that rather than he should come to hurt . . . they would willingly lose their lives."[172]

Some of Bacon's chief men framed a defense of their march against the Indians, declaring: "(We have) so much English blood in us as to account it far more honorable to adventure our lives in opposing them . . . to the last drop of our blood, than to be sneakingly murdered by them in our beds."[173] They stated that they had not shouldered arms to overthrow the government.

In the meantime, while interest in the approaching election mounted and charges and countercharges flew, Governor Berkeley summoned Bacon to Jamestown to answer for his rebellion.[174] Guarded by some of his followers, the young leader ignored the order. Sir William, as always when direct physical action was impossible, issued a proclamation. This one reiterated the charges against Bacon. It brought action.

On election day, the sheriff was reading the Governor's proclamation before the justices and citizens assembled in the courthouse at Varina, county seat of Henrico. He never finished. Into the room strode Nathaniel Bacon. Crowding after him came about forty armed men. Bacon demanded surrender of the paper and no one was disposed to argue with him. The election proceeded. To no one's surprise, the victors were Bacon and his lieutenant, Captain James Crews.[175]

The sloop that bore them to Jamestown to take their seats in the Assembly carried with them an armed guard of forty or fifty followers. Anchoring a little above Jamestown, Bacon inquired of the Governor whether he might unmolested assume his place in the legislature. Sir William let the guns of the fort deliver his reply. Bacon then sailed out of range, but under cover of darkness he landed with a party of twenty and stole through the dark streets of Jamestown to the home of Richard Lawrence, a friend and supporter. After conferring for several hours with both Lawrence and William Drummond, a former royal official in North Carolina who was sympathetic with the rebels, Bacon crept back to the water's edge. Just as he was shoving off, the alarm was given and all Jamestown sprang awake. Several boatloads of armed men pushed off in pursuit, and the ship *Adam and Eve* prepared to cast off for the chase. Captain Gardner's instructions were to capture or sink the rebel sloop.[176]

Through the hours of darkness, the gray light of dawn, and well into the afternoon, Bacon played a desperate game of hare and hounds on the broad waters of the James. The unequal contest came to an end at three o'clock when the small pursuing boats drove their quarry under the guns of the *Adam and Eve*.[177]

When Governor Berkeley received Bacon as his prisoner, the old man's bent for drama asserted itself. Throwing up his arms and rolling his eyes heavenward, the portly Royalist exclaimed, "Now I behold the greatest rebel that ever was in Virginia."[178]

After a dramatic pause, he asked, "Mr. Bacon, do you continue to be a gentleman? And may I take your word? If so, you are at liberty upon your parole."

Probably no one was more astonished than Bacon himself. The young man's effusive expressions of gratitude and repentance moved Sir William to grant him a "free pardon." The Governor even offered him reinstatement on the Council and a commission to march against the Indians if he would publicly make humble submission.[179]

Thus it was that Sir William's dramatic instinct was once again gratified. At a joint meeting of the Council and Burgesses, his Majesty's representative rose portentously, and said, "If there be joy in the presence of the angels over one sinner that repenteth, there is joy now, for we have a penitent sinner come before us. Call Mr. Bacon."

Entering on cue, the young rebel dropped to one knee and announced his submission.

"God forgive you," intoned the Governor. "I forgive you."

"And all that were with him?" came a voice from the Council.

"Yea, all that were with him."[180]

Bacon that day took his seat with the Councillors. Freed on the Governor's order, his captured supporters left for home.[181]

Several days later Bacon himself left Jamestown, having first taken "civil leave" of the Governor, saying that he must visit his sick wife.[182] Someone must have reported to Sir William immediately afterward that the young man was acting suspiciously, because the Governor ordered Bacon's lodging house searched, only to find that the reinstated Councilor had already left town. Parties of men were sent out after him by river and road, but all were outdistanced.[183]

Bacon's arrival in Henrico was the signal for a great reassembling of his followers. He informed them that he had not yet received the promised commission and evidently harangued them to some effect, for it is recorded that they "sett their throats in one common key of oathes and curses, and cried out aloud, that they would either have a Commission . . . or else they would pull downe the Towne."[184]

Not many days afterwards, word reached Jamestown that Bacon was marching on the capital with five hundred men. While some fed their fears on successive rumors, others were disposed to regard the reports as gross exaggerations. On June 22, however, the approach of a rebel force was confirmed, and Berkeley dispatched messengers in repeated attempts to learn their intentions. Bacon's intentions became obvious early on the morning of the twenty-third when the Governor, personally directing the mounting of guns to cover the narrow isthmus that joined Jamestown to the mainland, was interrupted by the cry: "To arms! To arms! Bacon is within two miles of the town." Someone rushed up with the excited report that the rebel chief had threatened to "kill and destroy all" if a shot were fired. The Jamestown garrison boasted only thirty soldiers. Sir William ordered the guns thrown from their carriages, directed the men to lay down their arms and strode to the State House to await Bacon and his rebel army.[185]

Tense hours passed, and still there was no sign of Bacon. Sir William had leisure to reflect bitterly upon the fact that the conqueror he awaited had been on his knees to him only a few days before.

At two o'clock in the afternoon, four hundred foot soldiers and a company of horse rode down Back Street and massed on the State House green. After placing guards in the fort and at the ferry, Bacon sent word to the Governor that he desired to speak with some Councillors.[186]

When two emerged from the building, Bacon informed them that he had come for his commission as general. But he emphatically stated that he would not tolerate any attempt by the Assembly to levy taxes to support his army.

The rabble behind him took up the cry "No levies! No levies!"

The sound was too much for Sir William to endure in silence. Dashing out on the green, the old man confronted Bacon with charges that he was a traitor and swore that he would have his own hands cut off before he would sign a commission.[187] Tearing open his coat in almost apoplectic rage, he roared, "Here, shoot me—'fore God, fair mark!"[188]

"Let us settle this difference singly between ourselves," was his next appeal, and he drew his sword as he made it. But the rebel captain ignored the challenge and said:

"Sir, I come not, nor intend, to hurt a hair of your honor's head. And for your sword, your honor may please to put it up. It will rust in the scabbard before ever I shall desire you to draw it. I come for a commission against the heathen who daily inhumanly murder us and spill our brethren's blood."[189]

Bacon sent his written demands up to the Assembly, now in session on the second floor of the State House. Berkeley stood in frustrated silence, while Bacon paced nervously, exhausting the conventional vocabulary of cursing and then resorting to his own inventions. From the windows above him peered gaping legislators. "You Burgesses," yelled the rebel, "I expect your speedy result."

"We will have it, we will have it!" chorused his followers. At his order, they cocked their guns and aimed at the upper windows.

"For God's sake," screamed a Burgess, "forbear a little and you shall have what you please."

At length, the Governor yielded to the demands of his own supporters and angrily scrawled his signature on a commission.

The next morning Bacon, accompanied by an armed guard, marched into the House of Burgesses and laid a series of demands before the legislators. He named some of the Governor's staunch supporters who must be ousted from office. He stated emphatically that the "traitor" and "rebel" charges made by Sir William in a letter to the King must be publicly retracted. Upon hearing of these demands, the Governor flew into another rage and vowed that he would rather die than comply with them. Nevertheless, a letter vindicating Bacon and expressing confidence in his loyalty was signed by the Council and Burgesses and Sir William himself.[190]

The Governor had other pen work to do. His signature was affixed to blank commissions for Bacon's lieutenants. Influential men, Berkeley's personal friends, were committed to prison. Sir William confessed that he thought Bacon's departure with his mob so critically important that he signed all documents thrust before him "as long as they concerned not life and limb."[191]

The Assembly had discussed Bacon's commission with guns pointed at their heads. Figuratively, their further deliberations proceeded under the same expediting influence.

They voted repeal of the law of 1670 which restricted the voting franchise to men owning a house or freehold. Passed in its place was a measure extending the suffrage to all free men.[192] Here was the bold assertion that a man's property had nothing to do with his right to vote.

A blow was struck at special privilege when legislation was passed depriving the Councillors of their exemption from taxation.[193]

Favoritism, nepotism and class rule all suffered with passage of measures providing that popularly elected representatives from each county sit with the justices of the peace in assessing the county taxes, that no Councillor could sit with the justices of the peace, that vestries be chosen triennially by the voters of the parish rather than continue to be self-perpetuating, and that the sheriff's term be limited to one year. It was also provided that one man should not hold more than one of the following offices at a time: sheriff, clerk of the court, surveyor and escheator.[194] How Sir William must have fumed when he signed such legislation into law!

Thinking that these revolutionary reforms would placate the rebels, the Assembly, on closing, ordered the new laws read before them. The legislators had not yet learned the temper of the mob. The rebels swore that they would have no laws at all.[195]

A new threat to the rebels' homes saved Jamestown from the danger of anarchy. Eight persons were reported killed by Indians in the upper counties. The common danger united irresponsible radicals, respectable small farmers and some successful planters under Bacon's standard.[196] Thus the mob, greatly augmented, left Jamestown to press an offensive against the Indians.

Sir William awaited the opportunity to reassert the authority which he felt was rightly his, all concessions to Bacon having been forced from him at gun point. He had ample reason to believe that many of the people, though afraid of the Indians, would support him in a stand against Bacon. Foraging parties from the young man's army were riding up to plantations and summarily seizing stores of meat and corn, horses or anything else that caught their fancy. Protests provoked vehement cursing. Bacon himself displayed a similar lack of restraint, ordering the arrest of Major Lawrence Smith and Major Thomas Hawkins, both of whom had warred valiantly against the Indians and now were engaged in raising troops.[197] He would tolerate no leadership but his own. Perhaps, having himself gained power by force of arms, he feared that another might obtain ascendancy in the same way.

One of Bacon's officers had been so rash as to threaten that his general might overrun and ruin all Gloucester County with a hundred horse. When some citizens of the county appealed to the Governor for protection, he hastened to reply that their petition was "most willingly granted."

"Nathaniel Bacon, junior," he declared, ". . . never had any commission from me but that which with arms he extracted from the Assembly, which in effect is no more than if a thief should take my purse and make me own I gave it (to) him freely. So in effect his commission, whatever it is, is void in law and nature."[198]

Sir William was acting true to form. Having issued a proclamation, he mounted his horse and galloped off to Gloucester to raise an army. He was exultant in the role of man of action as he addressed the assembled citizens of the county from his saddle.[199] But, when he finished his call to arms against the rebels, there was an ominous silence. Then there rose from the crowd a murmur and rumble as of a storm approaching through the forest. The cacophony resolved into one word repeated over and over: "Bacon." The crowd shifted and then dispersed, leaving a lone figure on horseback. Suddenly the old Governor crumpled up and fell over unconscious.[200]

* * *

Sir William was never the same man after that day. Perhaps he had suffered a stroke when, after he had endured days of furious

anger and the exertion of a hard ride, his most precious illusion—
that he was popular in Virginia—had suddenly been crushed.

When Bacon and his army, having heard the Governor's proclamation, descended on Gloucester to do battle with Sir William, they
found that the old man had fled across the Chesapeake to the Eastern
Shore.[201]

There was much to nourish the hopes of both Berkeley and Bacon
at this juncture.

The Governor found a sympathetic audience on the peninsula
that had not suffered at the hands of the Indians. They saw Bacon's
resistance to his Majesty's representative as treason.[202]

Bacon now enjoyed a moment of high triumph. He held all of
Virginia except one narrow peninsula. Moving to make his province
secure, he established headquarters at Middle Plantation and from
there sent out parties of horse to stamp out any military activity in
behalf of the Governor. Some of Berkeley's chief supporters—among
them such influential planters as Colonel Richard Lee and Philip
Lightfoot—were taken prisoner. One of Sir William's supporters
was found in Bacon's own camp, tried by court martial and sentenced to death. Bacon offered to spare the man if anyone "would
speak a word to save him." No one spoke, and he danced out his
life at the end of a rope.[203]

Having issued a manifesto in justification of his conduct throughout the rebellion, Bacon planned with Richard Lawrence and William
Drummond to establish a government with the support, nominal at
least, of some of the more substantial planters.[204] Accordingly, he
summoned many influential men—sheriffs, burgesses and even Councillors among them—to a discussion of the Indian war and the
problem of preventing anarchy. Obedient to his command, seventy
met with him August 3 at the home of a Captain Otho Thorpe.[205]
Probably these men hoped that Bacon's summons was really an
invitation to conciliation.

This illusion was dispelled when the rebel, after a long speech
designed to justify his conduct, asked all present to subscribe to three
oaths. The first was a pledge to help in the Indian war, the second a
promise to oppose all efforts by the Governor or his supporters to
raise troops against the rebel army, and the third a sworn subscription to the statement that resistance to royal troops until Bacon
could communicate with his Majesty was consistent with loyalty
to the crown.[206]

Some of the gentlemen angrily protested that the young man

was proposing treason. Accounts of what happened afterward differ. Some say that Bacon had the doors locked and would allow no one to leave until all had signed the oaths. Others say that sudden arrival of a report that Governor Berkeley had stripped the Tindall's Point fort changed the group's attitude.[207] In any event, Bacon had the signatures of all the gentlemen at his meeting before the assemblage adjourned.[208]

Governor Berkeley had been no less zealous in rallying supporters. Making Colonel John Custis major general and commander of the loyalist forces, Sir William established his headquarters at Arlington, Custis' strategically located Northampton County plantation. To this spot were attracted not only the various militia groups of the Eastern Shore, but also many planters who fled the mainland in their private sloops.[209]

The Chesapeake Bay was potentially both a barrier and an avenue to attack. Command of this body of water would determine control of the colony.

Determined to acquire a navy by capturing and outfitting merchant vessels, Bacon seized two ships in the James. One of these, the *Rebecca*, he armed with sixteen cannon from the Jamestown fort and sent across the bay to the Eastern Shore. Aboard her were two hundred fifty of his troops in addition to the ship's captain and regular crew. With them sailed a sloop and a small bark of four guns. Anchoring near Cape Charles, they awaited the arrival of other vessels that might be added to the growing navy. They did not wait long before gaining a valuable addition—a vessel of ninety tons.[210]

While his navy was thus engaged, Bacon prepared to make good his pledge to protect the colonists from Indian attack. He was already headed toward Henrico, selected a second time as the point of departure for an expedition against the Susquehannocks and Occaneechees, when word came that the Pamunkeys had fallen upon the residents of Gloucester. Those slaughtered on the spot were fortunate. Some captives were roasted alive while pieces of their flesh were offered to fellow captives. Others were disemboweled, and their entrails were draped around the trunks of nearby trees.[211]

Bacon therefore turned about and marched against the Pamunkeys. He painted a somber picture of the hardships ahead and called on all unwilling to follow him to the end to leave now. Only three did. His force by this time was augmented by the arrival of troops from the northern counties, these under command of Colonel Giles

Brent, half Indian but no ordinary half-breed.[212] He was the son of a Maryland gentleman and the empress of the Piscataways.[213]

After being led astray by an old Indian squaw compelled to serve as his guide, discovering his error and having her knocked on the head, Bacon found his way to the principal Pamunkey settlement and destroyed it in a surprise attack. Fewer than one hundred fifty men shared in his triumph, for the northern troops had despaired of success and marched back to their homes before the battle.[214] The smaller the company of victors, the greater the share of triumph for each.

Leading with him forty-five prisoners in the fashion of a Roman conqueror, Bacon headed back to Jamestown.[215] When he and his band staggered out of the forest into a King and Queen County clearing, they were half-starved and nearly exhausted and Bacon himself was ill. But they were animated by the belief that they now were in complete control of the entire Virginia mainland from the mountains to the bay, having subdued both Royalist and Indian enemies.

Their illusion of triumph was abruptly shattered. Their world had turned upside down while they were in the wilderness. The English crews of Bacon's impressed fleet had connived with Berkeley supporters on the Eastern Shore to place the vessels in the Governor's hands. Enjoying control of the bay, Sir William had reoccupied Jamestown and recruited a force said to number a thousand.[216]

Though Bacon must have been staggered by the information that so formidable a contingent stood ready to oppose his fatigued force of one hundred thirty-six, he delivered the news to his followers in manly fashion. They responded with vows to stand by him to the last and begged him to lead them forth to battle.[217]

Inspired to eloquence by this moving demonstration, he exhorted his men in ringing tones:

"Gentlemen and fellow soldiers:

"How am I transported with gladness to find you thus unanimous, bold and daring, brave and gallant! You have the victory before you fight, the conquest before the battle! I know you can and dare fight, while they will lie in their place of refuge and dare not so much as appear in the field before you. Your hardiness will invite all the country along as we march to come in and second you.

"The Indians we bear along with us shall be as so many motives to cause relief from every hand to be brought to you. The infamous actions of our enemies cannot but so reflect upon their spirits, as they will have no courage left to fight you. I know you have the prayers and well-wishes of all the people in Virginia, while the others are loaded with their curses."[218]

The sight of the Indian captives had the effect that Bacon envisioned. Food was thrust upon his men as they marched past the farmhouses of New Kent County. Many women fell subject to the glamour of the young rebel's exploits and begged to be enlisted under his banner. Some of the husbands added themselves and their arms to his force. This march and recruiting activities during a one or two-day encampment in New Kent increased Bacon's forces to three hundred men.[219] These he led down the left bank of the Chickahominy to a camp site just a few miles from Jamestown. From the capital there came the word that Sir William's army was "well armed and resolute," but the report only provoked from Bacon a smile and the reply: "I shall see that, for I am now going to try them."[220]

On the eve of his march upon Jamestown, he delivered to his troops another one of the eloquent speeches which never failed to inspire them. This was perhaps the most effective of all.

"If ever you have fought well and bravely," he said, "you must do so now. They are fresh and unwearied, they have the advantage of position, they have a fortified town into which to retreat. But I speak not to discourage you, but to let you know what the advantages are which we shall wrest from them. They call us rebels and traitors, but we will see whether their courage is as great as their pretended loyalty. Come on, my hearts of gold! He who dies on the field of battle lies in the bed of honor."[221]

The Jamestown which confronted Bacon in this eventful September was far different from the ill-fortified capital which he had surprised the preceding May. The Governor controlled the waters about the peninsula and three heavy guns commanded the narrow isthmus that afforded the only land approach. Yet Bacon boldly directed the digging of trenches and piling up of earthworks not more than four hundred feet from the town's palisades. He kept his men working feverishly till dawn, and then six of the rebels initiated hostilities, charging the palisades and firing upon those within. They returned to their trenches and there were no replying shots. Sir William had ordered his men to withhold their fire.[222]

Eventually, however, Berkeley ended the period of watchful waiting and began a heavy bombardment of the rebel positions, the town's fortifications being supported by naval ordnance. Realizing that Sir William intended to follow up his advantage with a charge on the rebel entrenchments, Bacon resorted to ungallant but effective means to stall off a sally. He sent out several parties to kidnap the· wives of leading planters and placed the ladies upon his ramparts in full view of Jamestown's defending force. Bacon used the time gained to strengthen his breastworks and add three mounted guns to his fort.[223]

The long-awaited sally came on September 15 and was repulsed. Bacon then opened his own bombardment. There was panic in Jamestown and few of its ordinary citizens had any stomach for a battle over Berkeley's prerogatives. Sir William and his lieutenants tried manfully to raise the morale of the townsmen, but their efforts were in vain. Facing hard reality, the Governor gave permission for evacuation of the capital under cover of darkness. Only eleven days before he had kissed the earth of Jamestown and thanked God for the privilege of reoccupying his old capital.

September 19, the morning after Berkeley's fleet weighed anchor, Bacon took possession of the town. The rebel leader was intelligent enough to see that he had won only a Pyrrhic victory. There were rumblings of royalist resurgence in the Northern Neck, and Colonel Giles Brent was now moved to abandon Bacon and to muster a thousand men to oppose him.[224] With such an army on the move and Berkeley in control of the water, the rebel position was untenable.

Bacon resolved that, if he could not hold Jamestown, Sir William should not either. Orders were given to burn the town by night. Bacon himself set fire to the church where the colonists had prayed so often in time of peril.[225] The State House, pride of the little capital, was fired. House after house was set afire, Lawrence and Drummond applying brands to their own homes.[226] Flames climbed up the old church tower and transformed it into a torch. Blazes flared from the windows of more than a score of houses. Roaring flames sent the long-claw shadows of tree branches reaching out fantastically across Back Street. Soon a fiery pyramid illumined the surrounding woods, affrighted the creatures of the night, and lit the waters with its red glow. Jamestown looked like an island of flame surrounded by molten fire.

The glow that lit up the sky was visible from the deck of Berkeley's ship.[227] To him and to others aboard, it must have seemed the sunset of Jamestown. The vessel weighed anchor and glided down river.

*   *   *

On the morning of September 20, Bacon led his men away from the ashes and black skeletons of what had been a town conceived in high hope and preserved through great vicissitudes. Though some of his band may have exulted when the flames leaped high as they went about their incendiary work, they must have felt quite different in the cold light of morning as they marched away from a heap of ruins to an unknown fate.

From this day onward events moved fast. After establishing new headquarters at Warner Hall in Gloucester County, Bacon advanced to intercept Brent's army. But Brent's men deserted before meeting the rebel forces.[228] The rebel leader believed this the time to impose a strict oath of fidelity binding the men of Virginia to support him even in opposition, if need be, to his Majesty's troops. Bacon presented the oath in a mass meeting at Gloucester Court House and delivered an eloquent appeal. Silence followed and then a Mr. Cole stepped forth as spokesman to declare that the men of Gloucester preferred neutrality.

Bacon was stunned for a moment. Then he lashed out with savage fury. He shouted to his audience that they were like the worst of sinners, wishing to be saved with the righteous and yet unwilling to do anything to win salvation. He was turning his back upon them when an officer interrupted to say that the leader had addressed only the horse, not the infantry. Bacon snapped back that he had spoken to the men, not to the horses.[229]

When the rebel chief learned that the Reverend James Wadding was responsible for much of the prejudice against subscribing to the oath, he arrested him.[230] But this act did not change the minds of the Gloucestermen.

Mr. Wadding's arrest was only the first of a series. Man after man was tried by hastily arranged court martial and immediately imprisoned. Plantations were plundered.[231] As Bacon found the people slipping away from him and his own vigor declining, he grew desperate. He ordered one of his own supporters executed for desertion.[232]

These actions frightened Gloucester County into submission, and the militia subscribed to Bacon's oath at a second meeting.[233] He had their signatures, but he no longer held their hearts.

In October, Bacon—little more than a walking skeleton—found it necessary to delegate many of the tasks of leadership.[234] But his burning zeal was still the animating force of the rebel army, and his fevered brain still teemed with plans for recouping his losses.

The Eastern Shore might yet be won. He might win the support of discontented men in Maryland and Carolina.[235]

But the young man—the adjective "young" now seemed incongruous—was never able to execute any of these schemes. As October wore on and the fever burned and he tossed on a louse-ridden bed in the home of Major Thomas Pate, a loyal Gloucester County supporter, Bacon summoned the Reverend James Wadding, the first man made to suffer for the county's reluctance in subscribing to the oath. Time after time, when the rebel chief seemed to be sinking, apprehension would suddenly penetrate his consciousness and he would demand to know whether the guard around the house was strong. It was, but Death slipped through on October 26, 1676.[236]

* * *

The rebel movement did not collapse with Bacon's death, but it lost its impetus and its direction. Joseph Ingram was chosen his successor, but he was not a man of Bacon's stature. Local interests began to predominate over the general concern, and the rebel army established too many garrisons, sacrificing its mass of maneuver.[237]

Sir William now began to prosecute the war with renewed vigor. Those of Bacon's lieutenants who fell into the Governor's hands were ordered hanged, and tearful pleas from grief-crazed wives— even if sobbed out on bended knee—were ignored.[238] Berkeley's success in capturing these men deprived the rebel forces of badly needed leadership, leadership even more necessary because of their dispersion. A proclamation from the Governor forbidding merchant vessels to trade with the western shore of Virginia further weakened the insurrectionists. Meanwhile Bacon's followers began to quarrel among themselves, and their plundering of farms made them seem less patriots than knaves to some planters.[239]

Accordingly, when Berkeley invaded Gloucester County with one hundred fifty men, its citizens—so lately forced into Bacon's ranks— wearily fell in line behind the Governor's standard.[240]

After a series of engagements which brought some victories to each side, it became evident to the more level-headed rebels that they would be the losers in the war of attrition into which the conflict had resolved itself. Their men and supplies were decreasing whereas the Governor's forces were constantly supplied and soon would be augmented by the arrival of troops from England.

At this point Captain Thomas Grantham, merchant master of a five-hundred ton vessel, assumed the role of mediator. He first got from Governor Berkeley an expression of willingness to accept surrender of the rebels rather than carry on the war until they were exterminated.

His next appeal was to Ingram and his lieutenants. He delivered a forceful argument, climaxing it with the admonition:

"Consult, like men of sense, your own felicity and quietly lay down your arms, lest by persisting in this open hostility you force them at last to be sheathed in your own bowels."[241]

Grantham explained that the Governor's terms included a promise that all who surrendered not only would be pardoned but also would receive compensation for their service in Bacon's army. After protests, Ingram's lieutenants joined with him in accepting the terms of surrender. Ingram no longer possessed the authority to surrender in the name of the entire army, but he could accept the terms as commander of the principal body of troops, those centered about West Point, the strategic site where the Mattaponi and Pamunkey rivers joined to form the York. Sir William, therefore, might well feel triumphant when Ingram's men, herded aboard the Governor's ship, filed past to kiss his hand in token of submission.[242]

Grantham next secured the surrender of a rebel cavalry force maintained in Gloucester County and of troops in a stronghold at Green Spring. Both groups were accorded extremely generous terms, the cavalry commander (Gregory Wakelett) being offered a share in Bacon's plunder from the Indians. The three surrenders arranged by Grantham had regained for Berkeley control of most of Virginia between the James and the Rappahannock.[243]

Lawrence, Drummond and Whaley, however, were determined that he should not easily retake the rest of the colony. Combining their forces, they found they had only three hundred men—no, not even that many, for a great number of their recruits were mere boys. But these they led into New Kent, hopeful of increasing their number. Instead, daily desertions took a heavy toll until at last they found themselves virtually alone. Lawrence and Whaley escaped, but Drummond was captured and went coolly to his death.[244]

Scattered groups of rebels were cleaned up so that, when a British fleet arrived late in January of 1677 bearing troops and three commissioners to settle the "grievances and affairs of Virginia," the rebellion was already history. There would be no need for the additional thousand soldiers already aboard vessels headed for Virginia.[245]

Only a few months before, the presence of the commissioners would have been most welcome to the Governor. Now they were most unwelcome, for they brought with them Royal notification that Sir William's request of June 1676 that he be retired from office had been granted. He could retain the titular headship of the colony's government, but must return to England to report to his Majesty while one of the commissioners—Colonel Jeffreys—ruled in his stead. Even more disturbing was a proclamation from the king granting amnesty to all participants in the insurrection except Bacon.[246]

Sir William took advantage of a technicality, telling the commissioners (Sir John Berry, Colonel Herbert Jeffreys, and Colonel Francis Moryson) that he interpreted the word "conveniency" in his orders as permission to postpone his abdication indefinitely. The commissioners' protests were of no avail. The Governor continued to punish captive rebels, his only concession being the substitution of civil trials for courts-martial. Even in this orgy of vengeance, Sir William was stayed by veneration for the crown. One old rebel soldier who displayed wounds he received in the service of Charles I won the Governor's reprieve so that he might receive a royal pardon.[247]

Though powerless to prevent the Governor's continued exercise of power, the Commissioners informed the King of his conduct.

From his Majesty came orders for Sir William to abandon "passion or resentment" and return to England immediately. The King's impatient exclamation on Berkeley went the rounds of the court. "That old fool," he declared, "has hanged more men in that naked country than I did for the murder of my father!"[248]

Berkeley now had no excuse for not returning. He therefore determined that his influence should survive his rule in Virginia. He saw that the Assembly summoned to convene February 20 was packed with his own supporters.[249]

Sir William never had the opportunity to tell his story in person to his sovereign. He became critically ill after embarking for England May 5. Charles sent word that he would be glad to receive the old courtier when Sir William's health permitted. But Berkeley's condition never improved. He died July 13, 1677.[250]

*   *   *

Bacon's Rebellion was the focal point for the integration of events in Virginia, Maryland, North Carolina and England.

In Cromwell's rebellion, England provided an example for the colonists. Virginians were fully aware of the parallel—some calling the Old Dominion's rebel chief "Oliver" Bacon. England also contributed heavily to the discontent that exploded in rebellion in Virginia. The Navigation Acts that cut Virginia tobacco out of Dutch markets threatened economic ruin to a colony where tobacco was not only the chief product but also the medium of exchange. Charles II's grant of the Northern Neck to his friends alarmed Virginians, some of whom had already settled in that peninsula, and caused the Jamestown government to undertake costly efforts to purchase an interest in the grant. This expensive program resulted in tax increases that magnified Virginia's economic discontent. Forts constructed because of England's war with the Dutch added to the tax burden.

Virginia's colonial neighbors also contributed to the causes of Bacon's Rebellion. Governor Berkeley's efforts to ease the hardships of tobacco planters by getting Maryland and Carolina to enter into agreement with Virginia to cease planting of the crop for a year failed when the simultaneous cooperation of Maryland and Carolina could not be obtained. The Indian problem was aggravated not only by the mistakes of Virginians, but also by Maryland's policy of pushing the Susquehannocks back and Carolina's commercial activities which built up the Occaneechees as powerful middlemen in inter-colonial trade.

The effects of Bacon's Rebellion were felt beyond Virginia's borders. Marylanders, like Virginians, suffered under the Navigation Acts and complained of an autocratic government. Bacon's example inspired rebellion in Calvert County in September 1676. Though the movement got off to a rousing start with a written protest against violations of "the liberties of the freemen of Maryland" and a defiant beating of drums and waving of colors when the Governor ordered the laying down of arms, it died for lack of coordinated leadership.[251] If observers that day had been able to peer into the future, they would have seen this disturbance as the beginning of a succession of insurrections that, merging with a strong spirit of militant Protestantism, would help to end the proprietary and would accustom Marylanders to the idea of fighting for liberty even in defiance of royal authority.[252]

Bacon's Rebellion also helped to crystallize rebellious thought in Carolina's Albemarle County and there led to actual insurrection a year after Bacon's death.[253] There were no dramatic results, but here, as in Maryland, principles of independence were boldly asserted and were not forgotten.

Bacon's Rebellion has aptly been called the "false dawn" of American independence. The metaphor holds true in several particulars. The false dawn is the glow that appears over the horizon and then vanishes before the coming of dawn itself. It does not cause the dawn. Instead, it is caused by the same factors that later produce the break of day and hence is a herald of the true dawn. In the same way, Bacon's Rebellion, caused by substantially the same factors that produced the American Revolution, was a herald—exactly a century in advance—of the dawn of American independence.

Chapter VII

"LAND OF GAUNTLET AND GLOVE"

(1677-1722)

Land of the gauntlet and the glove . . .
—Vachel Lindsay, "The Virginians Are Coming Again."

Chapter VII

~~~~~~

(1677-1722)

JUST five days before Sir William Berkeley's death, Thomas Lord
Culpeper was appointed royal Governor of Virginia, his commission to become effective upon the incumbent's demise. When
Berkeley died, King Charles ordered Culpeper to proceed to the
colony "with all speed."[1] So confident was he that this royal favorite
would comply without question that he assured the Virginians they
might expect their new Governor by Christmas "without fail."[2]

But Lord Culpeper, while gratified with his new title, was loath
to forsake the comforts of the court for the rigors of a devastated
colonial capital. He therefore did not arrive at Jamestown until the
spring of 1680. Colonel Jeffreys and the beloved, but now senile,
Sir Henry Chicheley were successively interim chiefs of state.[3]

A difficult duty fell to Lord Culpeper in July 1680 when the
King instructed him to rebuke the General Assembly for their
conduct during Jeffreys' administration. The commissioners had
demanded in April 1677 that Major Robert Beverley, clerk of the
legislature, turn over to them the original journals and orders of
that body. Upon the Major's insistence, they produced the part of
their commission which empowered them to make use of the legislature's papers. He then said he would allow them to examine the
documents but had no authority to turn them over without the
Assembly's permission. The legislature was not then in session, but
the commissioners were not deterred. They seized the records by
violence.[4]

Upon convening in October, the House of Burgesses protested
this "great violation of our privileges" and asked assurance that it
would not happen again.[5]

Charles II, in his turn, viewed the legislative declaration as a
"great presumption." He appealed to the Lords of Trade and Plantations to recommend steps "for bringing the . . . Assembly to a
due sense and acknowledgment of their duty and submission."[6]

The Lords branded the Burgesses' message "seditious, even tending to rebellion," and suggested that Governor Culpeper be ordered

to rebuke the legislators and punish the "authors and abettors of this presumption."[7]

It was thus that Lord Culpeper, on July 3, 1680, found himself no longer able to postpone the difficult task of bringing the legislature to account. First he discussed the matter with his Council, and probably was stunned by their spirited defense of the Burgesses. The Councillors unanimously recommended that the Governor not comply with the King's order.[8]

Caught between two strong forces—his sovereign and his Council, the unhappy peer yielded to the nearer one. The issue was unloaded on the Privy Council. England now saw that the independent spirit of Bacon's Rebellion was not restricted to a single class in Virginia. The colony's foremost leaders, some of them Berkeley's friends, had dared to defy a royal order. The mother country did not wish to deal with an even more universal rebellion in Virginia. Charles rescinded the order, but with hurt pride commanded that all references to the affair be "razed out of the books of Virginia."[9]

The King was beginning to learn what his Royal Governor had already learned, that the people of Virginia could not be summarily commanded in matters concerning their elected representatives.

Charles had instructed Lord Culpeper:

"It is our will and pleasure that for the future no Grand Assembly be called without our special directions, but that, upon occasion, you do acquaint us by letter with the necessity of calling such an Assembly and pray our consent and direction for their meeting."[10]

He had also said:

"You shall transmit unto us, with the advice and consent of the Council, a draft of such acts as you shall think fit and necessary to be passed that we may take the same into our consideration, and return them in the form we shall think fit they be enacted in. And, upon receipt of our commands, you shall then summon an Assembly, and propose the said laws for their consent."[11]

Charles, seated on his throne in far-away England and insulated from the world by a circle of courtiers, was completely unaware of the climate of public opinion in which his appointee was forced to work. Lord Culpeper disregarded the royal instructions and eventually the Committee of Trade and Plantations bowed to necessity and "altered their measures therein."[12]

Only by threats of royal power was an act levying a duty of two shillings upon each hogshead of tobacco exported from Virginia forced through the House of Burgesses. The legislators objected to the fact that the revenue thus obtained was not to be administered by the Assembly, but was to go directly into the royal coffers.[13] The King won in the showdown, but he could not be sure of winning many more times.

In August 1680 Culpeper returned to England, leaving affairs of state to Lieutenant Governor Chicheley. This conscientious but aged man, once a vigorous leader, was unable to cope with the turbulence that threatened destruction of the government. By 1682 tobacco prices were so low and economic distress was so great that a repetition of Bacon's Rebellion seemed almost certain. The Council declared that the mass of people in Virginia were unable "to provide against the pressing necessities of their families."[14]

Demands for legislation enforcing a cessation of tobacco planting caused Sir Henry Chicheley to call a session of the Assembly to convene at Jamestown April 18, 1682. Between issuance of the writ and the day of convention, Sir Henry received a letter from the King forbidding such a session before November 10, by which date he hoped that Lord Culpeper would be in Jamestown. It also stated that the two companies of troops kept in the colony since Bacon's rebellion would no longer be maintained at royal expense.[15] Sir Henry sought to appease both sovereign and Assembly by allowing the legislature to convene but restricting its deliberations to consideration of whether the colony should appropriate money for continued maintenance of the troops. The Assembly were loud in their protests and, after seven days of contention, Sir Henry was provoked to prorogue them till November 10.[16]

When the summons for an Assembly had been issued, the people's hopes had risen to a high pitch. They did not now take disappointment placidly. Men destroyed their own tobacco plants and then banded together to work havoc in their neighbors' fields.[17] Insurrection was put down in Gloucester only to rear in New Kent, and suppressed in New Kent only to burst into the open in Middlesex.[18]

Major Beverley, the former clerk of the Assembly, was suspected of instigating the riots. In any event, Royalists saw him as a dangerous man because of the people's tendency to identify their interests with the activities of this Berkeley supporter.[19] From Royalist to rebel was the ironic story of Beverley's life, at least as it appeared to some reactionaries.

Alarmed over reports from the Colony, Crown authorities ordered Lord Culpeper to repair to Virginia at once. He arrived in January

1683, armed with instructions to punish "some person who shall be found most faulty" as an example to insurrectionists and to do something to alleviate the plight of the tobacco planters. To aid him in this latter project, he was given permission to grant a cessation if such seemed advisable and a letter to Lord Baltimore requiring his cooperation if it were needed. Though Lord Culpeper was diligent in punishing leaders of the tobacco insurrection, he did nothing to remedy the conditions which caused it. Indeed, he admitted to the Privy Council that he actually encouraged the planting of tobacco with the design of increasing royal revenues by "a greater crop by far than ever grew since (the colony's) first seating."[20]

That spring he "judged . . . a proper time to make a step home"[21] and so again left his post of duty. This time he had taken one liberty too many. His letters patent as Governor were declared void and on September 28, 1683 Francis Howard, Lord Effingham was commsisioned Lieutenant and Governor-General of Virginia.[21]

Like his predecessor, he was in no hurry to make his home in the colony. Though he took his oath of office October 24, 1683 he did not set sail till several months had passed.[22]

The colonists soon learned that the new Governor was no easy-going Culpeper. Lord Effingham announced to the Assembly his determination to carry out the King's orders forbidding appeals to that body from the inferior courts.[23] Culpeper had received similar instructions, but had postponed their execution indefinitely.

The Burgesses asked the Governor and Council to join them in an appeal to the throne for restoration of this privilege of appellate jurisdiction, which enjoyed the sanction of "Laws and antient Practice."[24] Lord Effingham remained adamant. Thus separation of the legislative and judicial functions of government—something foreign to the English system—was achieved. An acute student of politics could have perceived that this change might prove tremendously significant.

Undaunted, the Burgesses proceeded to fight for another right. They boldly protested against the King's practice of annulling acts of Assembly, and declared that their statutes should have the force of law until repealed by the legislature itself. The Governor, as might be expected, emphatically refused to voice an appeal for "soe great an entrenchment upon ye Royall authority."[25]

Undoubtedly, the Burgesses had anticipated Effingham's reaction. They appealed directly over his head to the King, transmitting the message by two of their members.[26]

A new monarch received the Assembly's petition. Charles II had died in the spring of 1685 and the Duke of York was crowned King James II. In October 1685, James deigned to notice the petition "received from some unknown persons" and commended Effingham for declaring it unfit to be presented. He directed the Governor "to discountenance such undue practices for the future, as also the contrivers and promoters thereof." The two men deemed most responsible for the Assembly's plea were "turned out of all imployments."[27]

In this same year the Burgesses contested with the royal representative for retention of their most cherished power—that of taxation. The mother country's parliamentary history, particularly under the Stuart dynasty, demonstrated the fact that this privilege was the main safeguard of their prestige and effectiveness. Exercise of control over taxation could act as a check on executive policy and also could force the calling of the Assembly whenever the official purse was lean.

The Privy Council had learned enough of the Virginian temper to advise his Majesty against any attempt to seize the power of taxation for the throne by royal proclamation.[28] They therefore had urged Effingham as early as 1683 to have the Assembly voluntarily relinquish its power of taxation. In 1684 Effingham laid the matter before the Burgesses as a royal recommendation and was ignored.[29] In 1685 he again urged passage of a law permitting the Governor to levy taxes on advice of the Council. The Burgesses politely informed the Governor that they could not comply with his request "without apparent and signal violation of the great trust with them reposed."[30] Lord Howard prorogued the Assembly without bending them to his will.

The colonists had come to associate the Crown and the Privy Council with many of their tribulations. More and more, they began to think of themselves as Virginians—Englishmen with common interests who were misunderstood by authorities in London.

It is not strange, therefore, that when Virginians heard that Monmouth, the handsome bastard son of Charles II,[31] was in rebellion against James II, there were rumblings of revolt in the colony. Monmouth's failure ended the turbulence in Virginia, but before that "tongues ran at large and demonstrated the wickedness of their hearts" to such an extent that the Governor found it necessary to issue a special proclamation and take action against some individuals.[32]

Effingham had a rough time of it as his Majesty's representative in Virginia. One of his most vexing problems stemmed from the King's decision in 1684 to assume for himself Arlington and Culpeper's rights to quitrents, and apply the revenue thus gained to support of the colony. This tax was paid in tobacco at the rate of two pence a pound, established by Act of Assembly in March 1662. Since then the price of tobacco had so drastically declined that the tax returns were no longer considerable.[33]

Therefore, after assuming rights to the quitrents, the King ordered Effingham to have the Assembly repeal the law of 1662. He wished the tax henceforward to be paid in currency. With the colony facing economic ruin, the prospect of a quadrupled tax was alarming. Since tobacco was the common medium of exchange, the Burgesses probably reported truthfully when they declared that a lack of coins made it impossible to obey the royal order.[34] The Assembly refused to repeal the law of 1662.

Royal appreciation of the independent spirit dominant in Virginia was evidenced by the fact that James II, jealous as he was of his "divine rights" and impatient of those who brooked them, waited until August 1686 before nullifying the law by proclamation.

The Burgesses did not let the matter rest. So determined were they to resist the royal order that the Governor resorted to compromise. The tax would be collected in tobacco, but at a new rate that doubled the amount.[35]

In that same August of 1686, a bitter quarrel between the Governor and the Assembly resulted in dissolution of the legislature at the King's personal order.

Of course, Effingham realized that other Assemblies would have to be convened in the future when funds were needed, but he declared, "The public debts being paid, . . . I shall not for the future have so frequent Assemblies."[36]

Major Robert Beverley, clerk of the Assembly, was charged by royal authority with defacing the records, and deprived of his office. In April 1688, the Governor, with the approval of his Council and in spite of the violent resentment of the Burgesses, appointed a clerk. The House was forced to submit to loss of the right to elect its own clerk, but it still declared that he was the servant of that body and insisted that the Governor's appointee subscribe to the House's oath of secrecy.[37]

The Burgesses assembled in that year firmly determined that they must make a stand for their rights and the liberties of the people. Uppermost in the minds of many was the importance of confronting the Governor with the fact that he had seized legislative prerogatives in imposing fees upon the impoverished population. Foremost among these levies was what might, with little stretch of the imagination, be described as a seventeenth century "stamp act." It required "a fee of 200 pounds of tobacco for the Seal affixed to Patents and other public instruments."[38]

The Burgesses were incensed and alarmed over the Governor's action in reviving by proclamation a certain law which had been repealed many years before. They feared that same Governor might "by proclamation revive all the laws that for their inconveniencies to the country have been repealed through forty years since."[39]

The Burgesses asked the Council to join them in a protest against the Governor's encroachment upon their prerogatives. This the upper chamber refused to do. The Burgesses then resolved to appeal directly to the King, naming Colonel Philip Ludwell their emissary. They must not have been too hopeful for the success of their mission. James II had certainly shown himself no friend of liberty, and had aroused the suspicions of many Virginians by seeming to favor the advancement of Catholics. Aside from their religious convictions, many of the colonists—like many persons in England—associated Catholicism with the Spanish threat. In this very year, his Majesty's governor had increased their alarm by saying that Burgesses should not be compelled to subscribe to the oaths of allegiance and supremacy, and by permitting a Catholic to sit in the Assembly.[40]

James II received the petition in September,[41] and the colony anxiously awaited his decision. The following month they learned that the King had far more pressing matters on his mind. His Majesty reported to the Governor that William of Orange, ruler of Holland, was preparing to invade Britain.[42] James' second wife, Mary of Modena, had given birth in the summer of 1688 to a son. This child, being a boy, would take precedence in regal succession over the feminine offspring of the King's first marriage. Since this second wife, Mary of Modena, was an Italian Catholic, the child would be of the same faith. Thus a subject of the Pope seemed sure to sit on the throne after James' death, unless the line of succession were changed. This feat some influential Englishmen of both major parties—Whig and Tory—united to accomplish. Holland's Protestant monarch, William of Orange, was the grandson of Charles I, and his consort, Mary, was the daughter of James II himself by his English wife, Anne Hyde.[43] Not surprisingly, the Englishmen determined to thwart Catholic succession to the throne turned to William and Mary.

After carefully weighing the factors involved, William accepted their invitation. There was much risk involved, and the tragedy of Monmouth's abortive effort must have given him pause. But possession of the crown of England was important to him for a reason outweighing the prestige to be gained. He had dedicated himself to the cause of freeing Europe from the threat of French domination. By accepting a throne he would add a nation to his alliance.[44]

News of William's threatened invasion of England did not "put Virginia in a posture of defense," unless one meant defense against further encroachment by royal authority. "Unruly and disorderly spirits," Effingham reported, "laying hold of the motion of affairs, and that under the pretext of religion, . . . betook themselves to arms."[45] False reports that the Catholics of Maryland were plotting with the Senecas to slaughter the Protestants of Virginia gained credence with repetition. Men of the type whom Bacon led, doubtless many of them veterans of the rebel campaigns, collected in angry groups. Tension mounted ominously until one day in March of 1689 word arrived that William and Mary had been proclaimed King and Queen. The energy of repressed apprehension and anger was spent in celebration.[46]

Both England and Virginia now entered upon a new era. The flight of James and the bloodless victory of William and Mary deserve perpetuation in history as the "Glorious Revolution." Happy circumstances played a part in this accomplishment without bloodshed of a major constitutional change, but unusual discretion on the part of both William and English parliamentary leaders was no negligible factor.

Of primary importance was the fact that the center of gravity in governmental authority had shifted from the throne to Parliament. Parliament had crowned the new monarchs, and had altered the order of succession to do it. Before becoming the rulers of England, they had subscribed to a Declaration of Rights in which they foreswore such prerogatives as the "dispensing power," under which previous Kings had declared certain laws inoperative for a time. They acknowledged the illegality of any royal attempt to make or suspend laws, levy taxes or maintain a standing army without the consent of Parliament. For recognition of these principles, Virginians had been battling—sometimes in the field and more often in the legislative chamber—since Governor Harvey's expulsion.

Royal action on the petition presented by Ludwell soon gave the Virginians to know that they were dealing with a very different regime from that of the Stuarts. William ordered an investigation by the Committee of Trade and Plantations, and that body took quite literally his Majesty's instructions that justice be done. Both the colonists' charges and Effingham's personally delivered defense were heard and deliberated upon. The Committee recommended that the Governor's tax for affixing the seal to patents be discontinued and that other executive measures at issue be abandoned or compromised.[47]

Pressing the advantage gained, Ludwell several months later laid before the Committee charges of misgovernment and oppression by Effingham. Their Lordships' decision made the colonists' victory complete. Effingham was permitted to retain the title of Governor General but directed to remain in England, leaving actual governmental administration to a Lieutenant-Governor.[48] (How Lord Culpeper would have loved such an arrangement!)

* * *

A "Bloodless Revolution" had been wrought in Virginia as well as in the mother country. Freed at the end of a long period of contention from the twin threats of Indian attack and royal usurpation, Virginia was now prepared to move forward politically and culturally in the liberal tradition. But the past, for good or ill, is inescapable. So the course of Virginia's development in the new era of freedom would be influenced by the tyranny of the years that had gone before. The colonists' long struggle against royal encroachment upon their liberties had begun as early as Harvey's administration to make Virginians think of themselves as having interests apart from those of the mother country. This feeling grew in Berkeley's second administration into a strong conviction on the part of many men that they were justified in opposing royal power by force of arms in defense of these colonial interests. Culpeper's frequent absences from Virginia during his administration allowed Virginians to get in the habit of resisting royal directives with impunity, and made oppression under Effingham the more unbearable for colonists of both high and low degree. As the colonists found themselves constantly in contest with his Majesty's representative, the consciousness of interests separate from those of England intensified.

A more subtle change had also come about since Bacon's Rebellion. Many great planters of the colony had come to regard the rights for which the yeomanry contended as identical in most cases with Virginia's interests. Thus the drive for greater colonial independence no longer divided, but rather united, all classes in Virginia. The movement drew its impetus from the yeomanry, but increasingly attracted leadership from the aristocracy.

* * *

In June 1690 Colonel Francis Nicholson became Lieutenant Governor of Virginia and, acting for Effingham, the executive head of the colony. The boundaries of Virginia were still in dispute, some insisting that Maryland lay within its borders, but for all practical purposes the colony was bounded on the north by the Potomac and on the South by North Carolina. It still stretched westward, however, from the Atlantic (called the Virginia Seas by loyal residents) to the Pacific or California Sea.[49]

It was still sparsely settled, the development of townships like those in New England having been attempted repeatedly in vain. This failure was a matter of concern both to authorities in England and to some of the Assembly leaders. Lord Culpeper, obedient to royal instructions, had proposed a law ordering the erection of towns on each principal river and this Bill of Ports was passed in 1680. One such town in each county was appointed the official place of export and import for all products entering or leaving that district in foreign trade.[50]

The Virginia rural system, however, had evolved obedient to economic laws that could not be gainsaid by legislative fiat. The plentitude of fertile soil and ideal climatic conditions for tobacco raising, together with eager English and European markets for that indigenous product, had combined to produce a tobacco economy. Nature had blessed this great agricultural country with deep rivers, inlets and creeks that enabled sea-going ships to come right up to individual plantation landings.[51]

This situation was far different from that of New England, where a boulder-laden and rock-strewn land discouraged large-scale agriculture. New England towns would not spring up in Virginia at the wave of a legislative wand. English merchant captains learned this fact in 1681 when they found no special trading centers awaiting them and therefore proceeded as usual to the familiar plantation wharves. The shipmasters were prosecuted for violation of the law, and the planters' anger flared so high that the King found it prudent to suspend the act.[52]

But the idea that Virginia could be urbanized by legislative action did not die easily. It was revived in 1685 and brought the passage of legislation amended to the point of confusion by both Council and Burgesses.[53] It was this particular act that Major Robert Beverley, the clerk of the House, was accused of defacing. And so, while legislative wrangles raged and royal commissions fumed, Virginians pursued the rural ways to which they were accustomed.

Virginia, while more populated than a decade before, was actually more rural than it had been then. Henrico had been reduced to a village and Jamestown had not recovered from the devastation of Bacon's Rebellion.

But buildings and towns were rising in Virginia imaginations and many of the dreamers were impatient to convert visions into realities. Though the plan for a college in the colony had been struck low by the massacre of 1622, the idea had never died and was resuscitated in February of 1690 when Colonel Page, a leading planter, called a meeting at James City of gentlemen interested in promoting such a project.[54]

Colonel Nicholson's arrival in Virginia gave impetus to the movement. The new chief executive was fiery tempered and tactless, but he was an able administrator whose burning energy expressed itself in a passion for building.[55] The drive for a college gained momentum after Colonel Nicholson threw the weight of his office behind it.

In 1691 a Board of Trustees was formed, and a remarkable man—Commissary James Blair—was sent to England to plead for a charter. A thirty-six-year-old Scot with a Master of Arts degree from Edinburgh, he had come to Virginia as a missionary in 1685 and four years later had been made the Bishop of London's commissary, or official representative, in the colony.[56] Blair stood high in the estimation of his bishop, that prelate having selected the Scot as his chief instrument for reforming the colonial church.

The commissary, therefore, had no difficulty in winning the support of this important church official and, doubtless with his aid, won the endorsement of the Bishop of Worcester and the Archbishop of Canterbury. As a result, he not only secured from William and Mary the charter for a college to be named in their Majesties' honor, but also returned to Virginia with assurances of considerable financial support. The charter specified that Blair, already the choice of the Assembly, should be president of the school "during his natural life." He would begin his tenure under conditions that might well be envied by many another educator. It was provided in the charter that he should be rector of the Board of Visitors for the first year.[57]

Blair returned to Virginia with new-won political prestige to help him push plans for the college. The King himself intervened to make him a member of the Governor's Council.[58] The Commissary already stood first in the colony in ecclesiastical prestige. His marriage four years earlier to Sarah Harrison had allied him with some of Virginia's most influential families.[59] He soon found need for all these advantages.

Francis Nicholson was replaced as Lieutenant-Governor and chief executive the following year by Sir Edmund Andros. The new official had served as governor of both New York and Massachusetts, and resented the strong influence exerted in his new bailiwick by the Commissary. He also thought that Blair was too successful in getting the legislature to appropriate funds for his favorite enterprises.

Chief among these projects was the proposed college. The weight of the governor's office, thrown behind this enterprise in Colonel Nicholson's administration, was used to oppose it under his successor.[60]

Sir Edmund may have discounted the significance of Blair's firm chin and jutting jaw.[61] Though facial features are not a reliable index to character, the Commissary's physiognomy certainly correlated with his. If Blair could not convince the Governor, he must have him removed. This formidable undertaking did not dismay the young Scot in the least.

Andros' interest in economy was genuine, not just an excuse for his efforts to thwart the Commissary. He simplified governmental administration in a way that saved the taxpayers' money.[62]

He was just as interested in saving lives. By establishing at the falls of the rivers garrisons including forest-wise scouting forces, he gave even the frontier the type of protection which only coastal Virginia had enjoyed before.[63] This accomplishment gave the colonists a chance to consolidate the gains they had won from the wilderness.

He did not neglect such practical matters as industry and agriculture. His efforts to promote manufactures were promptly discouraged by the English authorities who, once so persistent in prodding colonial officials to stimulate industry, were now reluctant to build up competition for the mother country's looms and forges. He was somewhat more successful in promoting the diversification of agriculture, for he persuaded some of the planters to cultivate cotton instead of tobacco.[64]

Sir Edmund, however, saw no sense in spending good money for cultural and religious projects. So the conflict between the Lieutenant-Governor and the Commissary waxed hotter on a policy, as well as a personal, basis. Eventually Andros suspended Blair from the Council. Blair had himself reinstated by special order of the King. But Sir Edmund removed him again.[65]

The battle was joined in earnest and Sir Edmund must go. Blair protested to the Bishop of London that the Lieutenant-Governor obstructed both the college project and the effort to reform the clergy. The Commissary well knew that the latter charge would stir the Bishop as few things could. Blair also reported that this administration had made the Virginians "as divided a people as is upon earth."[66] Pressure was applied in London, and before the close of 1698 Sir Edmund Andros was removed.[67] The scholar had triumphed over the practical businessman in the very practical business of politics.

Not only did Blair oust his enemy, but he also chose the man's successor. The Commissary remembered Colonel Nicholson's enthusiasm for the college, and it was the Scot's recommendation that won the post for Nicholson.[68] Again the chief executive would be known as Lieutenant-Governor, the title and emoluments of a Governor General having been accorded to George Hamilton Douglas, the Earl of Orkney. The earl had relieved his sovereign of a vexing personal problem by marrying the pregnant Elizabeth Villiers.[69]

When Colonel Nicholson returned to Virginia as Lieutenant-Governor, he found the State House in ashes, the structure having burned in October 1698 shortly before Sir Edmund's departure.[70]

Colonel Nicholson viewed this state of affairs as more of an opportunity than a misfortune. Jamestown had never really recovered from the devastation of Bacon's Rebellion. The Jamestown site had been selected for the first settlement because of strategic considerations that were valid when all else was wilderness, but which no longer applied in a growing colony with a western frontier some eighty to one hundred miles from the coast. Here was the opportunity to select a site more suitable to Virginia's present estate and there erect a capital that might compare favorably with an English county seat. He selected Middle Plantation, the site of the College of William and Mary, about seven miles inland from Jamestown, and proposed that the city erected there be named Williamsburg in honor of the King.

Williamsburg was to be superior to many English communities in that its growth would not be haphazard but planned.

In April 1699 the Assembly passed "An Act directing the building the Capitoll and the City of Williamsburgh." Privately owned buildings that occupied the three hundred acre site would be condemned to make way for a city "suitable for the accommodation and entertainment" of a considerable number of persons. The main street, a broad thoroughfare to be named in honor of the Duke of Gloucester, was to stretch eastward from William and Mary College about a mile. At the Eastern terminus of this street was to be erected a building "for ever hereafter to be called and knowne by the Name of the Capitoll of this his Mat^ies Colony and Dominion of Virg^a." The act specified definite standards for any structures, business or residential, to be erected on this street.[71] Here was a bold step forward in city building and an instance of Virginians taking advantage of their situation in a new world to proceed along unexplored lines of progress.

Meanwhile Colonel Nicholson did not neglect less material matters. His interest in education extended beyond the building of a college. He realized that primary education must be attended to if Virginians were to be prepared for higher education. He encouraged the establishment of public schools in various communities, offering to pay part of the salary of clergymen who were willing to double as schoolmasters.[72]

In other enterprises, the erection of public buildings for example, he displayed equal willingness to support his projects with his purse.[73] Certainly he was not avaricious of money.

Some thought, though, that he was avaricious of power. He was impatient when Councillors disagreed with him and his temper flared whenever opposition blocked his path.[74]

He vented some of his aggressiveness on the pirates that infested Virginia waters, personally leading dramatically successful assaults on some of the fiercest freebooters.[75]

Still Nicholson's outbursts of temper began to alienate many men, particularly the Councillors,[76] most of whom were proud and sensitive. The more fair-minded ones, however, had to admit that the Lieutenant-Governor was a humanitarian. He evidenced a deep concern for the Negro slaves, and encouraged their education and Christianization.[77] Though personally impatient of contradiction, he was tolerant in broader matters, according Presbyterians the same freedom enjoyed by Anglicans.[78]

Colonel Nicholson loved as tempestuously as he ruled. In the spring of 1700, he conceived a grand passion for one of the nine daughters of Major Lewis Burwell. Learning that the teen-aged girl was already betrothed to Edmund Berkeley, the forty-five-year-old Governor appealed to her parents to break the engagement. They were not sufficiently impressed with the prospect of a Royal Governor for a son-in-law to intervene in the matter. Infatuation, frustration and stung pride spurred Nicholson's famed temper to madness. He swore that if Lucy Burwell married young Berkeley, he would cut the throats of the groom, the justice who issued the license and the clergyman who performed the ceremony.[79]

Love, however, eventually triumphed over rage. In a letter which may never have reached Lucy, he expressed the desire that God would make her "one of the happiest & fortunatest women in all respects." He added that he hoped to meet her "in Abraham's Bosom, being I'm debarred by your father (from) the honor and happiness of meeting you in this world."[80]

Nicholson's passion was not of the sort that burns itself out. He had told Major Burwell that his suit for Lucy's hand was "the most important affair of my whole Life, being for aught I yet see, twill dispatch me into another world, or make the small remainder of my life most unfortunate and uncomfortable in this."[81] His subsequent conduct indicated that his words were not mere frenzied hyperbole.

He quarreled incessantly with the Council and with the world. Most of all, his temper seemed to be directed against Commissary Blair.[82] It seems quite possible that Colonel Nicholson may have suspected Blair of blackening his character before Lucy Burwell's parents. Some of the Governor's letters made it clear that he believed the girl's attitude was a reflection of her parents', and that they were influenced by some who painted an unflattering picture of his character. In a memorandum, the colonel referred to "a false, scandalous and malicious report" and, writing of himself in the third person, declared:

"Notwithstanding the hopes, intrigues, designs and suggestions of some persons, . . . he may chance to be Governor of Virginia when these persons may be neither parsons nor lawyers in it."[83]

Was Commissary Blair the "parson" referred to? Certainly Blair and Nicholson were enemies afterward, and the commissary seemed to be a favorite target for the anger born of Nicholson's frustration.

In 1697 William Byrd II—one of Blair's bitterest enemies—wrote that the Commissary made "unjust war upon Sir Edmond Andros with . . . (a) view . . . that if he could worm him out of his government, he might possibly get his righteous patron Mr. Nicholson to succeed him. And, could that be brought about, . . . he expects to be first minister and to succeed in all his selfish views, believing that he should be able to lead that worthy gentleman by the nose as much as he pleases. But, if he should prove restive, I expect he will blacken him as much as he has done Sir Edmund Andros."[84]

Nicholson had definitely grown "restive." He was certainly not the type of man to be led "by the nose" anyway. The wonder is that two such domineering personalities as Blair and Nicholson had been able to work in league so long.

Blair and the Council drew up charges against Nicholson and forwarded them to Queen Anne, who had succeeded to the throne upon William's death in 1702. The Governor filed countercharges, but the Commissary and his friends prevailed.[85] Nicholson was removed in 1705 and was succeeded by Colonel Edward Nott. Before leaving the colony, Nicholson had witnessed an Assembly session in his new capitol. So impatient were the legislators to sit in the new edifice that they convened there in 1704 before it was finished. Its completion in 1705 had been marked by special ceremonies.[86]

One of Governor Nott's first acts in 1706 was to secure, in obedience to instructions from the crown, passage of an act providing for a Governor's House. The Assembly, which desired to retrench financially after expenditure on the capitol, was unenthusiastic.[87]

Colonel Nott was replaced before the year's end by Colonel Edmund Jennings.

Robert Hunter was named Governor in 1707, but, since he was forced to spend his term as a prisoner of the French, Colonel Jennings was chief executive until the appointment of Colonel Alexander Spotswood in 1710.[88]

* * *

The Virginia to which Spotswood came in 1710 was quite different from the colony which Sir John Harvey had hastily left in 1635. Great social, political and economic changes had transformed it within three-quarters of a century from an English frontier outpost to a dominion with an individuality compounded of rusticity and elegance.

By 1702, there were in Virginia twenty-five counties. The

Northern Neck, which had witnessed only the beginnings of settlement by the middle of the seventeenth century, was now sufficiently populous to account for five of these counties and nine of Virginia's forty-nine parishes.[89] The acreage and population of these counties were undetermined, but the other twenty counties embraced 2,164,-232 acres and a total population of 60,606.[90] The Eastern Shore—divided into two counties, Accomack and Northampton—boasted a population of 4,885. James City County was now no longer the center of population, registering but 2,990 souls as compared with Gloucester's 5,834.[91]

Jamestown itself was described in 1705 as "almost deserted."[92] The double blows of Bacon's burning and Nicholson's removal of the capitol had been too much.

As for the new capital, it had little claim to the designation "city." Some persons still thought that removal of the seat of government to Middle Plantation had been a "wild project."[93] Nevertheless, many Virginians must have taken pride in the new public buildings in Williamsburg. Witness, for example, the eagerness of the Assemblymen to convene in their new quarters.[94]

By 1706, the capitol presented an appearance of elegance that would have excited admiration even in England. An H-shaped brick structure at the eastern end of Duke of Gloucester Street, its most impressive face actually was to the south where two of the wings terminated in squat round towers. Each was conical roofed and each had three round windows on the lower floor directly in line with three long rectangular ones above, so that each appeared to be punctured with exclamation marks. In 1705, a cupola with clock was added at the order of the legislature, and the following year this architectural feature was emblazoned with the royal arms. With England's flag fluttering from its mast atop the cupola, the building would have seemed a worthy symbol of her Majesty's government in any part of the world.[95]

Seven-eighths of a mile away, at the other end of Duke of Gloucester Street, was the college. Dominant on the scene was a large building of harmonious proportions adapted to the colony's modest requirements from designs furnished by England's great Sir Christopher Wren.[96] It was appropriate that this man who wished to turn London's great fire to advantage by redesigning the city should have a part in the building of this planned city of the New World. A college quadrangle was envisioned.

On either side of broad Duke of Gloucester Street and parallel to it were two narrower thoroughfares, Francis and Nicholson streets. About midway of Nicholson Street, but considerably to the west of the street proper, workmen were engaged in construction of a Governor's House.[97]

Other structures in the town were a modest church that antedated the college, a brick jail completed in 1704 and a number of dwellings, including a few brick ones—new or under construction.[98]

Except for Williamsburg and Jamestown, Virginia was completely rural, even the county seats being tiny villages scarcely populated. except on court and muster days. A foreign visitor to the colony might have concluded on cursory inspection that Virginians had made few incursions on the forest and that these were being repulsed. Virginia planters allowed their land to remain uncleared until it was actually needed for cultivation. The principal crop, tobacco, exhausted the soil rapidly. Used-up fields were abandoned to the recapturing forest.[99] In 1693, it was reported that "perhaps not the hundredth part of the country is yet cleared from the woods."[100]

The principal elements of the population were the same as in 1624—great planters, middle planters, small planters, artisans, indentured servants and Negroes. But the proportions were different. The great increase in Negro slaves sharply reduced the number of indentured servants and enabled the great planters to expand their operations to a point where some of them became masters of feudal domains. The middle planter was hard pressed in competition with these colonial barons and the small planter found little opportunity to become a large scale operator. The most fertile land in the settled part of Virginia was already preempted and he had insufficient capital to purchase enough slaves to compete with the great planter.[101]

It is not strange, therefore, that some of these farmers migrated to other colonies. Most seem to have gone to the Carolinas.[102] The line of English settlement now extended all the way along the Eastern seaboard from the Carolinas to Newfoundland. Besides Massachusetts, New Hampshire, Connecticut, Rhode Island, New York, New Jersey, Maryland, Delaware and North and South Carolina, there was the young colony of Pennsylvania, founded in high idealism in 1681.

Though England had successfully displaced the Netherlands in New York and New Jersey, and Sweden in Delaware, she was still in a contest with Spain, and especially France, for most of the continent. England was by no means certain of winning this contest. La Salle, as early as 1682, had claimed for France all lands drained by the Mississippi, and French traders, priests and adventurers had established outposts in this great wilderness basin. The French were already well-established in Canada, and clearly intended to make a New France. In 1696, Louis XIV issued an edict ordering the explorers and adventurers in this great territory to take wives and settle down.[103]

The Spaniards had established posts in Florida and Mexico as well as to the north of the latter country.

King William had dared to take the English crown mainly because of his desire to establish a Grand Alliance against French power, and his action had drawn the American colonies into Europe's wars.[104] The War of the League of Augsburg (1689-1697), known to the colonists as King William's War, and the War of the Spanish Succession (1702-1713), remembered by the colonists as Queen Anne's War, added to the troubles of Englishmen at either end of the seaboard line of settlement. Indian allies of the French plagued the New Englanders. Skirmishes with the French disturbed the peace of South Carolina, and the Franco-Spanish alliance after 1700 added to that colony's discomfiture.[105]

It was only natural that, with Virginia's western territory likely to become a battleground of empires, farmers leaving the settled areas of Virginia to found family estates should choose a neighbor colony rather than the Old Dominion's own western reaches.

The great planters who dominated the settled areas of Virginia were few in number. In 1704 a report to the Lords of Trade stated that there resided on each of the colony's four great rivers "ten to thirty men who by trade and industry had gotten very competent estates."[106] A modern historian estimates that fewer than a hundred families comprised the great planter class. [107] A still smaller number from this select few were represented on the Council and actually were Virginia's equivalent of England's titled aristocracy. They were entitled to write after their names "Esquire," an honorific which, in the general absence of formal aristocratic titles in Virginia, served the colonists as a mark of station for a group whose members ranged in significance from that of baronet to baron. "There are no lords," a Huguenot visitor wrote shortly before the eighteenth century, "but each is a sovereign on his own plantation."[108]

These plantations were easily comparable to English manorial establishments. A traveler in Virginia reported that on approaching one such country seat he thought he was "entering a rather large village."[109] In truth, it was a village. Near the master's house were the dwellings of tenants, servants and slaves—in all about twenty buildings housing about forty-six persons of whom twenty-six were Negro slaves. The plantation of a Virginia river baron was a community in itself, complete with lord and lady, a variety of artisans and a school for the children.[110]

Having attained in the New World a station comparable to that of peers in the old, the inner circle of Virginia aristocracy industriously set about the job of faithfully emulating their prototypes. They eagerly surrounded themselves with the symbols of caste. Land in considerable acreage was still the principal mark of a gentleman, but much money was now lavished on the great house which was the nerve center of the plantation community. Brick was frequently used in its construction. The seventeenth century plan of a central hall with a large room on each side was still followed, but the hall was longer and the rooms were more numerous. The windows were larger and had crystal panes. Elegant furniture was imported from England. Oriental rugs graced the floors of some of the great houses. The gleam of silver complemented the rich luster of polished mahogany. Family portraits and coats of arms—those ancient symbols of aristocracy—were much in evidence. Usually the paintings were quite new, often portraying the owners and sometimes their fathers. In some cases the armorial bearings were no older than the portraits, a rather uncritical acceptance of flimsily-based claims prevailing in this land an ocean away from the College of Heralds.[111]

Most of these esquires were not content with accumulating the material symbols of aristocracy. They wished to exemplify that quality in their own persons. They gave careful attention to etiquette and conformed to a rigid code of what they believed constituted a true gentleman. He should endeavor to be courteous at all times and to be truthful under the most trying circumstances. Drinking, as in eighteenth century England, was often carried to excess without injury to the heavy imbiber's social status. Gambling, both on cards and on the outcome of horse races, was a favorite recreation. Whoring was condemned from the pulpits, but the illegitimate offspring of some great gentlemen outnumbered their legitimate issue. Even the pleasures of gambling and sex, however, were subject to the code. A man who cheated at cards was a lout, and one who made no provision for his illegitimate children was no gentleman. In addition to other attributes, the gentleman should be a competent rider and dancer and a good conversationalist. While he did not have to be a scholar, and seldom was, he should have a knowledge of English history, an acquaintance with the principal classics of literature, the ability to write and speak his native tongue with clarity and accuracy if not always with grace, and a genuine or feigned interest in music.[112]

How astonished must have been the typical traveler from overseas who, assuming from superficial observation that Virginia was almost uninhabited, emerged from the forest and discovered a baronial establishment and polite society!

The devotion to aristocratic ideals, the suzerainty over a community, the necessity for dependence on one's own abilities and knowledge in any number of varied circumstances, together with participation in government of the colony, combined to produce a breed remarkable for self-reliance, resourcefulness, pride, sensitivity and the habit of command.[113]

Generalizations, proverbially inaccurate anyway, are especially unreliable in the case of a group as fiercely independent and individualistic as the Virginia river barons. Probably no one member of this class embraced within himself all the qualities associated with the class ideal. The individuals varied widely in temperament and in ancestral background. They were knit together, however, by a common interest in preservation of the social order which had elevated them and by complicated lines of kinship.

Virginia's top aristocracy was well on the way toward equalling the intermarriage record of European nobility. Good illustrations of this fact appear in membership lists of the Council. In 1695, the twelve-man council included two Wormeleys—Ralph, the secretary, and Colonel Christopher Wormeley. Councillor and Auditor was Colonel William Byrd, the son-in-law of another Councillor, Colonel Daniel Parke.[114] Ralph Wormeley's wife, Elizabeth, was the daughter of a former councillor, Colonel John Armistead, and after becoming a widow married William Churchill, who was appointed to the Council in 1703.[115] The social cohesiveness of the Council increased with the passing years. When three vacancies occurred in 1713, Governor Spotswood explained that he chose the three men he appointed because the other qualified men were "related to one particular family, to which the greatest part of the present Council are already near allied."[116]

The Huguenot Durand reported:

"The gentlemen called Cavaliers are greatly esteemed and respected, and are very courteous and honorable. They hold most of the offices in the country, consisting of twelve seats in . . . (the

Council), six collectors, the rank of Colonel in each county, and Captains of each company. It is not necessary to have studied law to be a member of Parliament. They sit in judgment with girded sword."[117]

The description was literal. From all parts of Tidewater these men would come riding into Williamsburg. "Booted and with belted sword," they sat around the green-covered council table, and under the watchful eyes of Queen Anne's portrait, dispatched the colony's business.[118] Some would reinforce their arguments with quotations from Roman statesmen or philosophers.[119] All could bring to the deliberations practical business experience on a considerable scale. They adjourned each day in time for a supper sparked with an infinite variety of wines and liqueurs, following which they repaired to the gaming table. An early riser might find them still playing in the morning. A few hours' sleep and they were ready for another day's work.[120]

There were no typical members of the inner circle of aristocracy —the twenty-five or so families who dominated the political, economic and social life of the colony. They delighted too much in diversity for that and their way of life encouraged the tendency. But there were representative members.

One of these was Secretary Ralph Wormeley.[121] Eight years before his death in 1701, he was described by a prominent opponent as "the greatest man in the government, next the Governor."[122] He was the master of Rosegill, the Middlesex County plantation that Durand had assumed to be "a rather large village." Representing the second generation of his family in Virginia, he was the son of Ralph Wormeley I, a planter and justice of York County, and finally Councillor, whose home had been an asylum for refugee royalists. Ralph II's step-father was the beloved Sir Henry Chicheley, deputy and acting Governor of Virginia. Wormeley himself was descended from ancient landed gentry of Yorkshire.

The future Secretary of the colony spent part of his youth in England, studying at Oxford. His father's enterprise had provided him with an excellent start as a great planter. His home plantation, embracing 5,200 acres, was the largest in Middlesex, and he owned land in other counties. His mansion was a nine-room frame structure with attic, but the rooms were spacious and Rosegill could sleep thirty guests. The household staff included eight white servants besides the Negro slaves. The countryside marveled over the mansion's great collection of silverware, all engraved with the family crest.

The lord of Rosegill was a magnificent embodiment of aristocracy when, mounted in a saddle of crimson velvet on a spirited horse, he rode forth to inspect his domain.

Wormeley's interest in learning went beyond his service as a trustee of the College of William and Mary. His library included three hundred seventy-five volumes, and was then the largest in Virginia. Though small by modern standards, it was comprehensive and an impressive index to the variety of its owner's interests. About eighty of the books were religious works, for Wormeley was a pious man, conscientious in the performance of his duties as a vestryman of Christ Church, Middlesex. There were sixty volumes of history and biography, including the writings of Plutarch and Lucan as well as of Raleigh and other Englishmen. Smith's *General History of Virginia* was present.

Wormeley's library reveals him to have been not only an active participant in public affairs, but also a serious student of government. As justice of the county court, commander of the militia for two counties, naval officer on the Rappahannock, receiver of duties, and Councillor and Secretary, he could call upon the wisdom of great men who through the ages had set down their thoughts on statesmanship. He had on his shelves Cicero's *Prince*, Sir Walter Raleigh's *Maxims of Government*, a collection of political aphorisms called *The Cabinet Council*, Henri duc de Rohan's *Treatise of the Interest of the Princes and States of Christendom*, William Penn's *No Cross, No Crown*, and John Locke's *Two Treatises of Government*, besides other works on political theory. There were also such practical aids to the business of governing as about thirty law books, including six volumes of Virginia laws, Sir Francis Bacon's *Elements of the Common Laws of England*, Michael Dalton's *Country Justice* and *The Office and Authority of Sheriffs*.

Wormeley's concern with effective expression was shown by his possession of two English dictionaries—no doubt a rare thing even in England. In all, he possessed more than thirty dictionaries, grammars and other works concerning the English, French, Spanish, Greek and Latin languages.

Doctors were few and far apart in Virginia, so each planter's library contained at least one medical book. Wormeley had twenty-six medical works. There were about a dozen other scientific volumes, including Bacon's *Sylva Sylvarum*, Burnet's *Theory of the Earth* and Boyle's *Some Considerations Touching the Usefulness of Experimental Natural Philosophy*.

There were atlases and geographies, books on business and finance, works on agriculture and the management of estates, and about twenty-five volumes in the belles-lettres category. Though few, these were select, including the writings of John Donne, George Herbert, Edmund Waller, Samuel Butler, Ben Jonson, Beaumont and Fletcher, Cervantes, Montaigne, Virgil, Ovid, Horace and Terence. Philosophy was represented by Bacon, Seneca and Pythagoras.

Though Wormeley's library showed him to be a man of broad intellectual interests, it also revealed that he was not a bookworm. The *English Horseman* was an appropriate volume for a man who delighted as Wormeley did in horse racing. Nor was it strange to find on the Secretary's shelves two volumes dealing with the preparation of alcoholic beverages. An aristocratic Frenchman—no stranger to strong drink—reported that Wormeley not only downed a draught so potent that he was afraid to join with him before diluting his own, but that the Virginian showed no effects whatsoever.[123]

The Secretary's position as a member of the river baronage was consolidated by his second marriage. In 1687, he wed Elizabeth, daughter of Colonel John Armistead, a Gloucester County planter and Councillor.

A Middlesex neighbor of Wormeley's and the husband of his widow was William Churchill, who was elevated to the Council in 1705 and there served until his death in 1710.[124] Unlike the Secretary, Churchill was a first generation Virginian who made the grade; but, like him, he was aided by his family background. A descendant of Oxfordshire country gentry, Churchill sprang from a family which for several generations before him had been prominent in the affairs of North Aston Parish.[125]

As the eleventh son of a country squire,[126] William Churchill would have been hard put to retain the station to which he was born had he remained in England. In Virginia, however, he sought an opportunity to advance farther than his grandfathers. Coming to the colony about 1669 when about nineteen or twenty years of age, he so rapidly improved his fortunes that five years later he was Deputy Sheriff of Middlesex County.[127] Eight years after this appointment, he was a substantial landowner and was made a Justice.[128] When he became vestryman of Christ Church Parish, Middlesex, he was assuming a role familiar to his forebears in North Aston.[129]

By the time he was a member of the Council, he owned a Middlesex County estate of 1,950 acres, besides a Richmond County estate of 2,280 acres and divers other grants of land in England and Virginia.[130] The Middlesex estate was first named "Churchill" in the strength of family pride, but later was renamed "Bushy Park."[131] The adoption of this name, made famous by the home of the Duke of Clarence, was symbolic of Churchill's ambition to recreate on the Rappahannock the way of life enjoyed by a great noble on the Thames.

He did bring elegance to his mansion. He terraced the grounds and apparently spent considerable care in their landscaping. He acquired silver plate and had it engraved with his coat of arms, a handsome design with lion rampant and ducal coronet.[132] He received great help in his improvement program when his close friend, Secretary Christopher Robinson, master of the famous plantation Hewick, willed him his household furnishings.[133] Churchill's wife, the former mistress of Rosegill, must have had an effective hand in reconditioning the interior.

When Christopher Robinson willed William Churchill his furniture, he also left him his finest horse. This gift was the start of stables that might well have been envied by many an English country gentleman.[134]

Despite his interest in horses, however, Councillor Churchill would not have been called—as was Secretary Wormeley—"one of the gayest men in the country." He was deeply concerned over the prevalence of heavy drinking and had a strong dislike of swearing.[135]

Like other great gentlemen of Virginia, he took a conscientious interest in his church. For many years, he paid the salaries of the minister and clerk and dictated the choice of sermons. He was determined that his domination should outlast his life. Accordingly, he willed the church a sum of money, the interest from which was to pay the rector "for preaching four quarterly sermons yearly against the four reigning vices, . . . atheism and irreligion, swearing and cursing, fornication and adultery, and drunkenness." These instructions, he said, were to be followed "forever."[136]

Proud as Councillor Churchill was, he adhered to the ideal of *noblesse oblige*. His philanthropy was exercised lavishly in Middlesex County; in Christ Church Parish, London; and in his native parish of North Aston, Oxfordshire.[137]

He also labored in behalf of his county. It was chiefly through his efforts that Middlesex obtained a new courthouse worthy of its general progress.[138]

Councillor Churchill's attitude toward heavy drinking provided sport for another river baron, Colonel William Byrd II, when the two of them attended Council sessions in Williamsburg. Byrd entered in his secret diary under date of October 27, 1709:

"We drank some of Will Robinson's cider till we were very merry and then went to the coffeehouse and pulled poor Colonel Churchill out of bed. I went home about one o'clock in the morning."[139]

The very next day, however, he recorded:

"About 3 [p. m.] we rose and had a meeting of the College in which it was agreed to turn Mr. Blackamore out from being master of the school for being so great a sot."[140]

Apparently, a gentleman could get drunk, but he was not supposed to let drinking interfere with the day's work. Byrd himself had risen that morning at six o'clock, after only five hours' sleep following the night's merrymaking, and had spent a busy day interrupted only by an early afternoon siesta.[141]

On November 1, Byrd confided to his diary:

"We were very merry and in that condition went to the coffeehouse and again disturbed Colonel Churchill."[142]

The next morning the James River baron was up again at six o'clock.[143]

Someone who saw Colonel Byrd only at play might easily conclude that he was a shallow fellow. How wrong the observation would be! Byrd was a man of many-faceted personality, a gentleman who would have been at home in Renaissance Venice. A scholar as well as a good liver, he took equal delight in a well-turned phrase and a well-turned ankle.[144]

The senior William Byrd, one-time apprentice to a goldsmith, had migrated to Virginia in 1670 at the age of eighteen and, with the aid of a considerable estate inherited from his childless Uncle Stagg and his own industry in the Indian trade, he graduated to the great planter class.[145] He had been a friend of Nathaniel Bacon's, but had broken with him and had returned his own family to England upon the outbreak of actual rebellion.[146]

Though the family came back to Virginia after Bacon's death, young William made the voyage to England at the age of seven to receive a gentleman's education. After instruction under the supervision of his maternal grandfather, he was apprenticed to a business firm which sent him to Holland. There a steady diet of business failed to satisfy his intellectual appetite and he was miserable until, shortly after his eighteenth birthday, he returned to England and began the study of law at London's Middle Temple. He became a good student, learning not only from his books but also from the society of such eminent men as Sir Robert Southwell, Charles Boyle, Earl of Orrery, and Hans Sloane, who were attracted by his merit and personality.[147] At the age of twenty-one he was admitted to the bar, and the following year his scholarship received unusual recognition when he was made a member of the Royal Society.[148]

Returning to Virginia at the age of twenty-two, he took a seat in the House of Burgesses.[149] This auspicious start was due more to his father's influence than to his own merit, the elder Byrd having become a member of the Council. By this time the Councillors, like lords of the manor in England, could usually secure the election of their own candidates by revealing their choices to the electorate.[150] Byrd's next advancement, however, came quickly and was won by his own ability. He was sent to London as "Agent for the Virginia Assembly," and there served until 1702, when his criticisms of royal authority where the colony's interests were concerned became unendurable to his Majesty's government.[151] The Assembly was not going to oust Byrd from his diplomatic post, so the crown abandoned the office. Still he remained in London until 1705.[152]

These London years were a postgraduate course for Byrd. Noblemen, famous scholars, noted writers, great ladies and the actresses at Covent Garden—all added to his education. When he returned to Virginia following his father's death, he became the colony's most polished and versatile resident.[153] He made his home in the frame house that his father had built at Westover, not far from the falls of the James and close to the frontier. Most Virginia planters—finding land plentiful in Virginia—ignored the old English law of primogeniture. But the first William Byrd had left substantially all of his property to his eldest son. William Byrd II, therefore, was now the master of about twenty-six thousand acres.[154]

He succeeded his father as Receiver General of revenues. In 1706 he married a daughter of Colonel Daniel Parke, a prominent if notorious member of Virginia's landed aristocracy.[155] In 1708, he became a Councillor.

Not without reason, he regarded himself as a true aristocrat by any eighteenth century standard. He was indisputably one of the greatest of the river barons. His father had been a goldsmith's apprentice and the son of a goldsmith, but was descended from gentry and had become a great planter and political leader in the colony.

And the second William Byrd could take pride in the fact that his mother was supposed to be descended from Charlemagne.[156]

His private library, well on the way toward becoming the largest in Virginia, reflected his cultivated tastes in literature, history, science, art and music.[157] He was a shrewd businessman intent upon profit, but generally his concept of honor was high. His personal correspondence and even his secret notebooks indicate that his word could be relied upon in a business deal.[158] Moreover, he never let business interfere with the cultivation of his mind. Nearly every day he read one or more selections from the classics. All the while, he was developing a polished and flexible writing style that might have made him a famous author had he concentrated upon becoming one.[159]

Though a sorely tempted man, he was devoutly religious. If he failed to say his prayers a single night, it was a matter for confession in his secret diary.[160] Though he had inherited slaves, he disapproved of the institution of slavery and foresaw trouble as a result of its planting in Virginia.[161]

Although written sixteen years later, a letter addressed by Byrd to the Earl of Orrery gives a substantially accurate picture of the life he was leading when Spotswood became Governor.

"I have a large family of my own," he wrote, "and my doors are open to everybody, yet I have no bills to pay, and half a crown will rest undisturbed in my pocket for many moons together. Like one of the patriarchs, I have my flocks and my herds, my bondmen and my bondwomen, and every sort of trade amongst my own servants, so that I live in a kind of independence of everyone but Providence. However this sort of life is without expense, yet it is attended with a great deal of trouble. I must take care to keep all my people to their duty, to set all the springs in motion, and to make everyone draw his equal share to carry the machine forward. But then 'tis an amusement in this silent country and a continual exercise of our patience and economy. Another thing, my lord, that recommends this country very much: we sit securely under our vines and our fig trees without any danger to our property. We have neither public robbers nor private, which your lordship will think very strange when we have often needy Governors and pilfering convicts sent amongst us. . . . Thus, my lord, we are very happy in our Canaans, if we could but forget the onions and fleshpots of Egypt."[162]

Even William Byrd's great estate was dwarfed by the land

holdings of a Northern Neck river baron, Robert Carter of Corotoman, the man to whom Ralph Wormeley II entrusted the education
of his children after his death. His home stood in Lancaster County
at a point where the Corotoman, one of the most beautiful small
rivers in America, flows into the Rappahannock.[163] The second son
of Colonel John Carter, he had succeeded to the Corotoman estate
upon the death of his elder brother.[164] It is interesting to note that,
while Colonel Carter provided handsomely for his elder son and
made provision for a classical education for his second son, he
specified in his will:

"In case my wife put . . . [him] out to apprentice, then so
much of her portion be paid as is thought necessary to bind him out
to a good trade."[165]

This procedure was not unusual even in England. Younger sons
of the aristocracy were frequently apprenticed to merchants or
artisans[166] Thus the English gentleman or Virginia planter of that
day frequently refrained from speaking scornfully of trade, or else
did it in self-conscious snobbishness. To speak so was to disparage
his own relatives.

Colonel John Carter[167] had emigrated to Virginia about the year
1649 and settled in Upper Norfolk County. Apparently a Royalist
of gentle birth and some wealth, he was soon called "Colonel" by his
new neighbors and before long was elected to the House of Burgesses.
He later removed to Lancaster County and was sent to the legislature from that constituency. Here he established the family seat
of Corotoman and, after five marriages and a political career that
carried him to the Council, died and was buried in the Chancel of
Lancaster's Christ Church.

When Robert Carter came into possession of his father's estate,
he automatically became a leader of colonial aristocracy. In addition
to whatever training he had received in the colony, he had acquired
six years of education in England.[168] At the age of twenty-eight, he
was elected to the House of Burgesses and only five years later was
chosen Speaker. Three years after receiving this honor from his
fellow legislators, he was elevated to the Council and thus became a
full-fledged river baron in every respect. In 1699, the very year that
he became a Councillor, he was appointed Treasurer. In 1705, he
became President.[169]

Long before that time, he was conceded to be the richest man in
Virginia.[170] A shrewd, imaginative and energetic businessman, he
had made the most of opportunities afforded him as agent for Lord

Fairfax, the English peer who was Lord Proprietor of the Northern Neck. A study of the records indicates that Robert Carter honestly and loyally served his employer, but he took advantage of his position to patent the choicest lands for himself and his family.[171] Carter was founding a dynasty. His neighbors spoke more truly than they knew when they called him "King."

Carter's way of life made the sobriquet appropriate. Under his ownership, Corotoman became a baronial establishment exceeding in magnificence many a great noble's manor. His holdings comprised a small duchy.[172]

But, despite his avid interest in business, "King" Carter was no mere money grubber. Like other members of his class in Virginia, he served the church and education. At his own cost, he rebuilt Christ Church along lines of simple elegance and was as much the proprietor of that house of worship as Councillor Churchill ever was of its Middlesex namesake. In this interest, pride was joined to piety, for he built a grand avenue between God's house and his own.[173] But all evidence indicates that his piety was as genuine as his pride. Intensely concerned as "King" Carter was with the instruction of his children, his interest in education extended far beyond his own family circle. He was rector of the College of William and Mary and it was claimed that "he sustained that institution in its most trying times."[174] Mindful of those not as wealthy as he, he founded a scholarship.[175]

Carter himself was a man of intellectual interests. His library, though weak in science except for medicine, contained fifty-five religious works; one hundred legal volumes, some of them in Latin or French; forty historical and biographical works; several volumes of philosophy, ancient and modern; and a collection of *belles lettres* in which were represented Horace, Terence, Homer, Ovid, Defoe and Addison. Carter's correspondence indicates that he had a student's knowledge of these works.[176]

The "King" of Corotoman was enough of a philosopher to see himself objectively upon occasion and even to deplore his own acquisitiveness. In a letter to one he had known long, Carter wrote:

"I wish both you and I were more mortified to . . . [the world] than we are. The thoughts of having a little more white and yellow earth than our neighbors would not puff us up with so much vanity and insolence, nor make us so uneasy when we meet with plain dealing. . . . We are but stewards of God's building: the more he lends us, the larger accounts he expects from us, and happy they that make a right use of their Master's talents."[177]

Northern Neck rivals of the Carters were the Lees. The second Richard Lee was the second of his line in Virginia, and was sixty-three years of age and full of honors when Spotswood became Governor.[178] His epitaph described him as "descended of an ancient family of Merton-Regis, in Shropshire," and later research tends to support his claims to aristocratic lineage.[179] His father became a great planter shortly after arriving in the colony and increased his wealth by activity in the tobacco trade. In 1651, the elder Richard was admitted to the Council and later became Secretary. A clause in his will provided for the equal education of his sons John and Richard. John, who died young, was educated at Oxford.[179] Richard may have received comparable advantages.

Mount Pleasant, in Westmoreland County, was Lee's baronial seat and the center of one of Virginia's greatest estates. He parted with none of his ancestral acres; neither did he increase them.[180] Opportunities for expansion were numerous, but Richard Lee II was wealthy enough to live in elegance and felt free to spend his time in more interesting pursuits than the making of money. He was naval officer and collector of duties on the Potomac River and colonel of the Westmoreland militia.[181] After service in the House of Burgesses, he was appointed to the Council. Letters of his contemporaries contain many references to the conscientiousness with which he performed these duties.[182]

His conscience even cost him office when he refused to recognize the sovereignty of William and Mary, believing that they had usurped the throne of the Stuarts.[183] He did not acknowledge the new rulers until convinced that their reign was beneficial to Virginia, preferring to be at peace with his conscience even if at odds with the Crown.

If Ralph Wormeley approached Plato's ideal of the philosopher-king, Richard Lee was its realization. His life struck a fine balance between activity and contemplation. A richly intellectual library[184] fed his voracious mind. Small by modern standards but large by those of his day, it contained three hundred volumes embracing the works of some of the greatest thinkers from ancient Greece to seventeenth century England. Five languages—English, French, Latin, Greek and Hebrew—were represented. Fifty-eight of the volumes were religious works. Quaker and Presbyterian as well as

Anglican treatises were present, and concordances and commentaries indicated serious Biblical scholarship.

Many textbooks were on Lee's shelves. Particularly noteworthy were manuals in rhetoric, logic and oratory.

Thirty-six Greek and Roman classics, twenty volumes of history and biography, twenty-four law books and works on government, science and philosophy, and several humorous books were included.

Without leaving his library, Lee could tap the minds of Aristotle, Aphthonius Sophista, Xenophon, Plutarch, Epictetus, Livy, Seneca, Demosthenes, Cicero, Sallust, Tacitus, Caesar, Quintus Curtius, Velleius Paterculus, Suetonius, Homer, Hesiod, Lucien, Heliodorus, Virgil, Horace, Ovid, Lucan, Martial, Terence, Claudianus, Juvenal, Persius, Flavius Arrianus, Lorenzo Valla, Erasmus, Thomas a Kempis, Descartes, Montaigne, Sir Francis Bacon, Sir Walter Raleigh, and many others.

Richard Lee strengthened his position as a member of Virginia's ruling class by his marriage to Lettice Corbin.[185]

Few river barons in Virginia were so closely allied with the nobles and great leaders of England as were the Littletons of Nandua. on the Eastern Shore. First of the line in Virginia was Colonel Nathaniel Littleton, who emigrated to the colony in 1635 and established the family seat. Described as "a gentleman of the Earl of Southampton's Company in the Low Countries, 1625," he was the brother of Edward, Baron Littleton of Mounsloe, Chief Justice of the Common Pleas and Lord Keeper, and of John Littleton, master of the Temple at All Souls College, Oxford.[186] Colonel Littleton was also the son of Sir Edward Littleton, Chief Justice of North Wales, and the grandson of Sir Edward Walter, Chief Justice of South Wales. His great-great-grandfather was Sir Thomas Littleton, K.B., whose famous *Tenures* was a law book much in favor among Virginia's great planters.[187]

Colonel Littleton's ancestral credentials were impressive, but he was the sixth of eight sons,[188] so it is easy to see why he looked for greater opportunity in Virginia than in his homeland. He found it. In 1640, he was appointed Commander and Chief Magistrate of Northampton County.[189] The following year, he was appointed to the Council.[190] Thus, six years after his arrival in Virginia, he entered the inner circle of its rulers. From that time until his death in 1644, he was the Eastern Shore's leading citizen.[191] In a deed recorded in Northampton County in 1652, he had been referred to as "Governor of Accomacke."[192]

The next lord of Nandua was Colonel Nathaniel Littleton's elder son, Colonel Edward Littleton, who became a justice of Northampton County in 1657, and apparently died about 1663.[193]

Next in succession was Southey Littleton, who was then about eighteen years of age. He too became Colonel Littleton. In 1679 he undertook a diplomatic mission, being one of two representatives appointed by Governor Chicheley to confer on Indian affairs with New York colonial officials. He died in Albany while in the service of Virginia.[194] Besides his ancestral acres on the Eastern Shore, he left land in Maryland.[195] His library included such varied fare as Edmund Wingates' *Body of the Common Law of England*, Norwood's *Trigonometry*, Aesop's *Fables*, Corderius' *Colloquies*, a volume of selections from Plautus, Lucian's *Dialogues*, a *History of the New England War*, and the usual medical and religious works.[196]

When Spotswood became Governor in 1710, the Littletons were in their third generation in Virginia and also their third generation as river barons. Back of their immigrant ancestor were at least eleven generations of leadership in England and descent from King Alfred.[197]

The famous ancestry of a Littleton or the genteel background of a Churchill was helpful to the colonist ambitious to become a river baron, but it was not essential. Witness, for instance, the Bollings and the Carys who took their places as equals beside the Littletons, Churchills, Lees, Byrds, Wormeleys and Carters. Their English background was one of trade, but wealth, education, good manners and qualities of leadership won them high position in Virginia.[198]

Most of Virginia's leading families, however, were descended from the English country gentry. Most were above average in prosperity upon arrival and thus gained a head start in the accumulation of estates. In 1663, Sir William Berkeley, in his *Discourse and View of Virginia*, reported, "Men of as good families as any subjects in England have resided there, as the Percies, the Berkeleys, the Wests, the Gages, the Throgmortons, Wyatts, Digges, Chicheleys, Moldsworths, Morrisons, Kemps, and hundred others, which I forbear to name, lest I should misherald them in the catalogue."[199]

The river barons, who dominated Virginia's social, economic and political life, constituted one of the best qualified and most responsible oligarchies that the world has ever known. They sought to reproduce in Virginia the way of life followed by English lords. Actually, they created something superior. Their concept of an English lord was derived from etiquette books (found in the library of virtually every great gentleman of Virginia) which set forth the ideal of the class.[200] This academic concept of an intelligent, well-educated, and habitually courteous man who accepted responsibility as the price of leadership was reinforced by nostalgic memories of the homeland and the sentiment-suffused recollections of parents and grandparents.

Some English nobles were representative of the ideal, but as a class the lords of England did not approach so near to this exalted standard as did their Virginia counterparts or even their own Elizabethan ancestors. Few English barons had the learning of a Richard Lee, a William Byrd, a Commissary Blair, a Robert Beverley or even of Ralph Wormeley II, a man of broad intellectual interests but apparently not a prodigious scholar in the eyes of his Virginia contemporaries. Too few of the English nobles had the sense of responsibility that prodded and checked even the land-hungry Carters, Byrds and Fitzhughs in Virginia. Though stronger in polish than in learning, the English lords as a whole probably were not as attentive to etiquette as were the first families of Virginia. Surer of their position than the colonials, the English aristocrats sometimes displayed a lordly disdain for courtesy except when dealing with their social inferiors or determined to prove that they were gentlemen even under duress.[201]

The relation of the great planters to the general population of Virginia had undergone several changes since emergence of the class about the middle of the seventeenth century. At first, when uncounted acres of good land east of the mountains were still unclaimed, small planters looked toward the great ones as representatives of the estate to which they themselves might aspire. In succeeding years, taxes weighed heavily on the small planters and the grand manner of the great aristocrats aroused their ire. The best lands had been preempted and the economic system almost precluded the advancement of the man with small capital, so that his resentment of the ruling class was no longer mitigated by the hope of a higher status. He automatically began to think of the government in London as the ultimate source of his troubles, since the Governor was both the representative of the crown and the leader of Virginia's oligarchy. The conflict between the chivalric class of great planters determined to be gentlemen in the highest English tradition and the liberty-loving yeomanry resentful of royal interference in colonial affairs reached its climax in the rebellion of 1676 and was epitomized in the persons of Governor Berkeley and Nathaniel Bacon.[202]

The alternately tyrannical and negligent royal Governors who succeeded Sir William alienated the increasingly proud aristocracy as represented in the Council. The great planters came to feel as keenly as the small that they were misunderstood by authorities in the mother country. Thus, by the dawn of the eighteenth century, the river barons of Virginia were the champions of the colony in its fight for liberty against royal restrictions. The small, and particularly the middle, planters once again imitated the lords of the new land. The separate ideals symbolized by Berkeley and Bacon had merged into one shared by all substantial elements of the population. The ideal was that of a gentleman in the best English chivalric tradition who nevertheless was first of all a Virginian and was prepared to fight for the defense of colonial prerogatives.

Despite the supremacy of the river barons, they were not socially isolated from other Virginians. The large class of middle planters had come to correspond roughly to England's gentry. They mingled freely with the barons and occasionally married their sons or daughters,[203] though the lords of Virginia preferred to strengthen the fortunes and prestige of their clans by advantageous alliances. There were many families of genteel background—the Washingtons, for instance—who were difficult to assign to any stratum. They could boast sheriffs, justices and burgesses, and some of them were quite substantial property owners.[204] The fortunes of the next generation would determine whether the sons of Augustine Washington would descend to the level of small farmers or take their places undisputed beside the great leaders of the colony.[205]

Even members of the poorer classes sometimes enjoyed the hospitality of Virginia's greatest baronial establishments. Virginia courtesy was according to the code of Sir Philip Sidney, and prescribed civility to men and women of every condition. Great planters took pride in the fact that no traveler, whatever his degree, was turned away from their doors. It was said that a man might travel the length of Virginia without any expense except ferriage.[206]

This entire social and economic system rested on the sweating back of the Negro. Brought to the colony as an indentured servant in 1619, he had by the latter part of the seventeenth century become a slave.[207] The Negro indentured servant was frequently persuaded to sign for a new period of indenture. Often, unaccustomed to the responsibility of fending for himself in civilized society, the Negro was glad to recommit himself to a planter's care. Sometimes, though, the planter took advantage of his servant's ignorance. The first Virginia planter to make a slave of his indentured servant was

Anthony Johnson of Northampton County. Interestingly enough, Johnson himself was a Negro.[208]

Although Colonel William Byrd at a much later date observed in his *Natural History of Virginia*, "The government of Virginia agrees wholly and in all things with the English government . . .,"[209] there are abundant evidences that even by 1700 the Old Dominion's government differed in many important respects from its English model. Certainly, it would be hard to support Byrd's assertion that the Governor was "accepted by the native Virginians as well as the English [there] as no different from the King."[210] The lord of Westover may have permitted his love of tradition and devotion to English institutions to blind him to the importance of differences between the conduct of political affairs in London and in Williamsburg. In the same paragraph in which he pictured the Governor as a colonial monarch, he conceded that "the opinion of each member [of the Council was] of as much importance as that of the Governor, and they [could] therefore contradict him freely and in an unhampered fashion, whenever he desire[d] to overstep his prescribed duty."[211]

Technically, indeed, the Governor was a fully-empowered Viceroy. Legally, he possessed legislative and judicial as well as executive powers. The executive functions were well summarized in 1697 by Hartwell, Blair and Chilton in their *Present State of Virginia:*

"[The Governor] represents the King, in granting his Lands, naming of several Officers to all Places of Trust in the Government, in calling, proroguing and dissolving of Assemblies, . . . in giving or denying his Assent to their Laws, in making Peace or War, and in the whole Grandeur, State and Ceremony of the Government.

"As his Majesty's Lieutenant-General and Commander in Chief, he raises and commands all the Militia and Land-Forces, and appoints all military Officers, by Commission, during his Pleasure . . .

"As Vice-Admiral of the Virginia Seas, he takes Account of all Prizes, commands all Ships and Seamen, lays on and takes off Embargoes, and does all other Things that belong to the Admiralty Office."[212]

Robert Beverley's summary of the Governor's executive powers in 1705 was essentially the same as that given by Hartwell, Blair and Chilton eight years before.

His legislative duties included presiding over the Council. When that body performed judicial functions, the Governor perforce became the colony's chief judicial officer.[213]

Virginia's government resembled that of the mother country in no respect more closely than in the fact that its official records conveyed a most inadequate idea of the system. As we have seen, a Governor would sometimes confess that the opposition of the Council prevented him from carrying out royal instructions. Confronting an organized body representing the economic, political and social power of the colony—moreover a cohesive and caste-conscious group united by ties of blood and marriage—the Governor sometimes found that he could exercise the powers of his office only according to the will of his Council.[214]

Robert Beverley in 1705 concisely set forth the duties of the Council:

"The Gentlemen of the Council are appointed by Letter or Instruction from her Majesty, which says no more, but that they be sworn of the Council.

"The number of the Councellors when compleat, is Twelve; and if at any time by Death or Removal, there happen to be fewer than nine residing in the Country, then the Governor has Power to appoint and swear into the Council, such of the Gentlemen of the Country, as he shall think fit, to make up that number, without expecting any direction from England.

"The business of the Council is to advise and assist the Governor in all Important Matters of Government, and to be a restraint upon him, if he should attempt to exceed the bounds of his Commission: They are enabled to do this, by having each of them an equal Vote with the Governor, in most things of Consequence, viz.

"In calling Assemblies.

"In disposing of the Publick Revenue, and inspecting the Accounts thereof.

"In placing, and displacing Naval Officers, and Collectors of all publick Duties.

"In all Votes and Orders of Council.

"In the nomination of all Commission-Officers, either of honorary or profitable Places.

"In publishing Proclamations.

"In making Grants, and passing all the Patents for Land.

"In the General Assembly, the Council make the Upper-House, and claim an intire Negative Voice to all Laws, as the House of Lords in England."[215]

The power of the Council to "be a restraint upon" the Governor might seem to be limited by the fact that Councillors were royally appointed and the Governor had the power to name men to that body if the number of members fell below nine. Actually, however, the Governor's choice was restricted in practice to representatives of the baron class. In effect, the incumbent Councillors determined the list of acceptable men from whom his Majesty's representative might make a choice.[216]

As early as 1697, Hartwell, Blair and Chilton noted the multiplicity of offices to which a Councillor fell heir. "They are the Colonels or Commanders in chief of the several Counties, in the Nature of the Lords Lieutenants in England. They are the Naval Officers, that is, they are entrusted with the Execution of all the Acts of Parliament, and General Assembly about Trade and Navigation, tho' generally great Traders themselves: And in this capacity they enter, and clear all Ships and Vessels, and exact great Fees of them. . . . They are collectors of the standing Revenue . . ., Fort-Duties . . . likewise Collectors of the Penny per Pound upon all Tobacco exported from Virginia to the other English Plantations, and are allow'd for this, 20 per Cent. . . . They are the Farmers of the King's Quit-Rents in their several Counties, which are commonly sold to them by the Auditor, with Advice of the Governor. . . . Out of them are chosen the Secretary, Auditor, and Escheators. . . ."[217]

While chosen from the Council, the Auditor and Secretary received their commissions directly from the Crown.[218]

The Auditor's duties, as his title would suggest, were to "audit the accounts of the public money of the government, and duly to transmit the state of them to England; such as the quit-rents, the money arising by the two shillings per hogshead, fort-duties, the fines and forfeitures, and the profits of escheats." His salary was "7½ per Cent, of all the publick Money."[219]

The Secretary's duties were "to keep the public records of the [colony], and to take care that they be regularly and fairly made up; namely, all judgments of the General Court, as likewise all deeds and other writings there proved; and further to issue all writs, both ministerial and judicial, relating thereto; to make out and record all patents for land, to file the rights by which they issued, and to take the return of all inquests of escheat."[220]

The Secretary's office was also a bureau of vital statistics. In it were kept not only a register of all commissions of administration and probates of wills granted throughout the colony, but also records of "all births, burials, marriages, and persons that go out of the country: of all houses of public entertainment, and of all public officers in the country."[221]

"From this office," added Beverley in his account "are likewise issued all writs for choosing of Burgesses, and in it are filed authentic copies of all proclamations."[222]

The Secretary's salary, like the auditor's, was derived from the fee system. He received not only a percentage of the charges for all business done in his office (out of which sum he paid his clerks), but also "acknowledgements paid him annually by the county clerks, and besides about forty thoussand pounds a year of tobacco, and cask."[223]

Hartwell, Blair and Chilton observed in their *Present State of Virginia:*

"The multitude of places held by the Council occasions great confusion, especially in such things wherein the . . . places are incompatible: as when their Collector's office obliges them to inform their Judge's office against an unfree bottom: or when their honors, as Counselors, sit upon and pass their own accounts as Collectors: Or when they in different capacities do both sell and buy the King's Quitrents: Or when the same man who as ministerial officer takes and returns the inquisitions of escheats, as judicial officer gives sentence in point of law upon the same office, and many other cases of that nature."[224]

Nowhere was this exercise of authority by a few more evident than in the administration of justice. Each County Court was composed of eight to ten gentlemen Justices of the Peace commissioned by the Governor. As explained by Hartwell, Blair and Chilton:

"The courts of justice are not distinct as in England, but causes belonging to Chancery, King's Bench, Common Pleas, Exchequer, Admiralty and Spirituality are decided altogether in one and the same court. And if anyone that apprehends himself to be injured at Common Law would appeal to Chancery, he only desires an injunction in Chancery, and has another hearing, but before the same men still."[225]

If he appealed his case to the General Court, held twice a year when the Governor and Council sat as judges, he might see some of the same faces or at least the faces of the men to whom his original judges owed their offices.[226]

* * *

Colonel Alexander Spotswood, therefore, did not find a pliant government or people when—full of energy and new ideas—he arrived in Virginia in 1710 as Lieutenant Governor and acting Chief

Executive. Born in the year of Bacon's Rebellion, he was now thirty-four years of age, keen-eyed and heavy-browed, but withal pleasant faced—a solid, but not stolid, representative of his Majesty's government.[227]

Probably most Virginians would have been surprised to learn that their new Governor was a native of Africa. He had been born in Tangier when his father was physician to the English garrison there. His ancestors, however, had played important roles in the history of Scotland, and he was the descendant of an Archbishop and a Chief Justice.[228]

His social prestige would help in dealing with class-conscious Virginians. His own personal background of experience was also of the sort to appeal to the colonists. At seventeen, he had become an ensign in the Earl of Bath's regiment of foot and served during the War of the Spanish Succession as Lieutenant-Quartermaster-General under Lord Cadogan, rising to the rank of Lieutenant Colonel. He was wounded at Blenheim in one of history's greatest battles. Later he was captured by the enemy and his exchange was negotiated by Marlborough himself, the first captain of Europe.[229]

He entered upon his new duties with vigor—too much vigor to suit William Byrd and some of the other Councillors who were reluctant to alter a status quo in which they enjoyed unusual advantages.

Spotswood immediately took an interest in Williamsburg and was responsible for much of its architectural improvement. A patron of culture, he helped to bring elegance to the infant capital. He did not spare his own pocketbook. Submitting a plan for a new and graceful Bruton Parish Church, he offered to pay personally for construction of twenty-two feet of one of the walls.[230]

He gave attention to the economy that supported that elegance. Tobacco, however natural a medium of exchange in Virginia, was at best an unsatisfactory one. If the tobacco itself were not held to a standard, the entire monetary system would be a farce. In 1713, he ordered inspection of tobacco before its export or use as legal tender.[231]

He also saw the basic insecurity of an economy dependent upon tobacco and turned to a task that had baffled his predecessors—the promotion of industry. Before 1713, he had received a royal grant of 59,768 acres in the area of the Rapidan River and the upper reaches of the Rappahannock. In that year he sent some of his slaves into this wilderness territory that few settlers dared enter and cleared a plantation near the junction of the two rivers.[232] The discovery of iron deposits near the mouth of the Rapidan must have excited the Governor even though no experienced miners were then available. Spotswood—in the fashion of eighteenth century gentlemen who mixed piety and material interests—probably felt that Providence had come to his rescue when forty-two German Calvinists arrived in Virginia in April 1714. Miners from Prussia's Seig Valley, they had bound themselves to seven years' labor to repay their indenture and arrived in Virginia to find themselves deserted by their sponsor. The Governor promptly accepted responsibility for them, put them to work in his mines, and settled them in a community of their own at what came to be known as Germanna Ford. The Governor pointed out to Virginia leaders the fact that these German immigrants would "serve as a barrier to the people of that part of the country against the incursions . . . of the Indian."[233]

Spotswood's Indian policy, however, was far more enlightened than that advocated by some who believed extermination of the natives to be the only solution for the period's principal racial problem. He looked, instead, to integration of the Indian and colonial economies. In 1714, he founded the Virginia Indian Company, seeking to regulate and stabilize the fur trade.[234]

On August 17, 1716, there was gathered at Germanna as motley and heterogeneous a company as ever assembled at that frontier settlement.[235] Spotswood was in command, and well-known Virginians were with him. Ralph Wormeley had left the urbane comforts of Rosegill to be there. More at home in this rustic setting than the Middlesex river baron was John Washington, who had earned a measure of fame in the wilderness as an Indian fighter. There was also a guest of the colony—handsome young John Fontaine, his ever-present *Journal* probably thrust deep into his waistcoat pocket. Or perhaps it was stuffed into a bulging saddlebag on one of the group of horses nearby, who, sensing the excitement in the air, champed and pawed the red earth impatiently. Noisily making themselves at home within the little stockaded pentagon were laughing young cavaliers who bore such names as Lee, Page, Randolph, Peyton, Harrison, Moore, Dandridge, Carter, Mercer, Wythe and Pendleton.

Closer observation would have revealed brown forms that blended with the logs of the stockade and the pentagon-shaped blockhouse that, rising from the center, brooded protectively over the nine squat houses. These were the bronzed rangers and Indian guides, and they must have been a little contemptuous of the elegant young gentlemen who, dressed more for a picnic than a wilderness expedition, set out as upon a lark. But they too must have felt some excitement.

Certainly the German settlers did. They poured out into the broad street that separated their homes from pens of cackling chickens and squealing pigs to stare as Spotswood gave the signal to mount and the cavaliers sprang to their saddles.

As that merry band rode across the Rapidan and into the wilderness, they rode on into history. John Lederer, a German immigrant whose broken English excited provincial ridicule, had penetrated the mountain areas of Virginia twice in 1670. He had pressed on in each of these expeditions after the men of reputation in his party had abandoned the attempt as hopeless.[236] When he reported his discoveries he was scorned as a liar and, by his own account, "instead of welcome and applause, met nothing but affronts and reproaches."[237] Spotswood's expedition had the prestige of the Governor's leadership and included respresentatives of Virginia's most prominent families. Therefore, their journey had not only the advantage of probing deeper into the West than Lederer's, but also had incomparably greater advertising value. There was more to the Spotswood expedition than the quaffing of an astonishing number of toasts in a great variety of beverages and gazing tourist-like at great herds of stilt-legged elk and shaggy-coated buffalo.[238] It demonstrated that the land west of the Blue Ridge was habitable and suggested that it offered many opportunities for the hardy and persistent. It resulted in creation of the County of Spotsylvania as a buffer against the French and hostile Indians.[239]

Some might sneer at the Knights of the Golden Horseshoe and the little diamond-studded gift emblems from Spotswood that gave them that high-flown sobriquet, but certainly they accomplished far more in practical terms than many knights-errant who suffered more.[240]

The Governor himself, however, did not eschew hardship in the pursuit of his schemes to develop the West. The man who brought unaccustomed elegance to Williamsburg did not disdain to share the ranger's life and the Indian chief's campfire. He stimulated great planters' interest in frontier development and founded the frontier county of Brunswick, a Southern counterpart of the Spotsylvania buffer in the North.[241]

Seeking protection for white settlers and their Indian allies in Brunswick County, Spotswood journeyed to Albany, New York, trade and conference center of the Six Nations, and there negotiated directly with the great chiefs and secured an important treaty. The Governor, like most thoughtful Virginians, was seriously disturbed by the Dutch-Susquehannock-Cherokee fur traffic. When England's quarrel with Holland ended Virginia's profitable trade with the New Netherlands, the Dutch colonists found new "middle-men" in the Susquehannocks. Moreover, the Dutch—in their anxiety to preserve this trading link with the Southern Indians—offered firearms in barter. Fearful of this practice, but aware that they couldn't stop it, the Virginia Assembly concluded that the Old Dominion's merchants might as well share in profits from the lethal transaction, and authorized them to proceed with the exchange of firearms for furs. A North-South trade route running east of the Blue Ridge became well defined and increasingly well traveled, earning the name Shenandoah Hunting Path. A treaty made in Albany in 1684 had restricted the range of the Iroquois in Virginia, but had confirmed their privilege of traveling on either side of the Blue Ridge.[242] In the Albany Treaty of 1722, however, Spotswood obtained from the Iroquois chiefs a promise to keep their tribes west of the mountain barrier. Elated with his success, the Governor presented to the Indian sachems a jeweled, golden emblem like the ones he had conferred on the Knights of the Golden Horseshoe.[243]

But the exploit of Spotswood's which that emblem symbolized had set in motion forces which would make the achievement in Albany less meaningful. Great men of the colony began to patent lands west of the Blue Ridge with a rapidity that must have amazed even the man who initiated the expansion.[244]

That year also saw Spotswood's removal from office. Not surprisingly, Commissary Blair was responsible. The definition of the Governor's power to induct ministers upon the occurrence of a parish vacancy was the issue immediately in dispute, but the whole question of civil versus ecclesiastical authority was involved. As always when his personal prestige was at stake, Blair acted promptly and decisively. Naturally a man of Spotswood's aggressiveness had made influential enemies as well as staunch friends, so that the Commissary easily found allies.[245]

Spotswood was removed from office, but the twelve years of his administration could not be erased. The city of Williamsburg was a monument to Governor Nicholson's energy, but the stamp of elegance it bore was a credit to Spotswood's discrimination.

One structure in the capital was symbolic of Spotswood's contributions in another field—defense. The octagonal powder magazine which he erected on Duke of Gloucester Street across from the Palace Green was a central arsenal for the entire colony. To protect shipping from the incursions of pirates, to thwart smugglers, and possibly to detect the approach of a foreign enemy, he founded a one-ship Coast Guard which patrolled the Chesapeake Bay.[246] The colony's western frontier he sought to protect by treaties with the Indians, creation of the buffer counties of Spotsylvania and Brunswick and the encouragement of outposts of settlement beyond the limits of Virginia's cleared land.

The flood of Virginia settlement, though receding at times under the ill winds of starvation, pestilence and massacre, had flowed westward until reaching the barrier of the Blue Ridge. Spotswood's dramatic exploit had punctured that barrier, and now the tide of settlement burst through the mountain passes like a flood through a cracked dam. Down into the valley flowed the English population, spreading out and threatening to inundate routes used by the Indians and by the colonial representatives of rival European powers. The floodtide of settlement was sweeping Virginia into the vortex of a struggle of empires. Spotswood was well aware of this fact. His trip to Albany to negotiate with the Six Nations was necessitated by expansion of Holland's economic empire in America. Looking southward to another area of conflict, Spotswood foresaw a time when Virginia would have to annex Spanish Florida as a security measure.[247]

Virginia's expansion of settlement was not only bringing the colony into dangerous proximity to rival empires, but also was bringing it into closer association with its sister colonies. In this tightening intercolonial relationship, Governor Spotswood played an important part. His northern trips to negotiate with the Indians intensified his awareness of the common economic and defense interests of the English colonies. Before he stepped down from his gubernatorial post, his reputation and his stature had grown beyond the confines of Virginia. He had intervened when rival candidates for Governor of North Carolina resorted to the sword, and when one of them declared himself adamant against any mediation but the arbitrament of arms, the ambitious fellow was adjudged a rebellious subject and sent to England for trial.[248] South Carolina enjoyed the benefits of another act of intervention when Spotswood sent troops and arms to its aid in a war with the Yamassee Indians.[249] Some years after his retirement from the Governorship, he was appointed

Postmaster General subject to the regulations of Parliament. Establishing an American General Post Office at New Post, near the falls of the Rappahannock, he developed an intercolonial postal service that knit together the colonies from Massachusetts to South Carolina.[250]

Though Spotswood could take pride in the economic, political and cultural progress that he had initiated or accelerated during his residence in Virginia, he did not indulge the dreams of easy optimism. He foresaw the increasing urgency of two vexing problems—defense and racial relations. He sought to postpone as long as possible the colonies' serious involvement in the wars of empire, and his efforts to build up defenses and promote intercolonial cooperation were partly in anticipation of the conflict that seemed inevitable. The racial problem was two-fold—relations between the English and the Indians and relations between the English and the Negroes. Spotswood's approach to the first phase of this problem was well illustrated by his response to an uprising of the Tuscaroras in 1711. He dispatched an expedition against them, but—seeing that continued war would be impractical as well as inhumane—he seized the opportunity to negotiate from strength and make a more secure peace with other tribes. Furthermore, he made the fruit of these negotiations the nucleus for a broader and more enduring peace program. He offered remittances of the annual tribute as an inducement to Tidewater tribes to send their youths to the white man's school at Williamsburg. The offer was accepted by the Nottoways, Nansemonds and Meherrins. To accommodate more students, the Governor founded another Indian school farther west and for awhile supported it out of his own pocket.[251] Thus, while meeting an immediate emergency with force, Spotswood pursued a policy of cultural absorption as the long-term solution to the Indian problem.

The problem of Negro-white relations was not quite so pressing as that of relations between the English and the Indians. But Governor Spotswood and other thoughtful Virginians were aware that it could become an equally dangerous one. The General Assembly of 1710-1711 sought by heavy taxation to curb the importation of Negroes, but the trade-conscious Crown vetoed its efforts.[252] The eighteenth century had its lobbyists and those for the merchants and the slave trade were highly successful. Increase in the number of slaves and in tobacco acreage went hand in hand. Attempts to diversify industry by the production of woolen, cotton and linen cloth were viewed by the mother country as unwelcome competition for home manufactures. Seeking to reconcile the Crown's mercantilism and his administration's plan for diversification, Governor Spotswood tried to stimulate significant production of naval stores and varied raw materials for British factories.[253] Able man though he was, Spotswood could not thwart the designs of an empire and the economic ideology of an age. Like his predecessor, Governor Nicholson, he was deeply concerned about the Negro's place in society and foresaw that the problem was likely to grow with the passing years.[254] Even in the midst of unexampled prosperity and remarkable political and cultural progress, Spotswood and his thoughtful associates could see that the threat of serious conflict loomed. It might result from the schemes of empire or from the related racial problem, but trouble seemed almost certain.

Chapter VIII

"VIRGINIA'S WAR" SHAKES EUROPE

(1722-1763)

Chapter VIII

~~~~~~

(1722-1763)

THE threatening cloud that troubled Spotswood and his thoughtful associates was still no bigger than a man's hand and Virginia, in the years following his administration, continued to bask in the sunshine of its golden age. Great planters prospered and the tenor of life in Williamsburg went on as before while Hugh Drysdale succeeded the colonel as Lieutenant-Governor and quietly served until his death July 22, 1726.[1]

As President of the Council, Robert "King" Carter, of Corotoman, became ex officio acting Governor. By this time Carter, with his vast estates rivaling the great baronies of Europe, was the most conspicuous representative of the planter oligarchy that dominated Virginia life.[2] The titular Governor, the Earl of Orkney, remained resident in England.

William Gooch was appointed Lieutenant-Governor and acting chief executive September 11, 1727.[3] King George I had died some months before, but the Earl of Orkney remained as titular Governor.

In many ways, the new Lieutenant-Governor must have reminded Virginians of Spotswood. Like his great predecessor, he was a Scot and the son of a British officer. He soon revealed that the resemblance was more than superficial. Naturally inclined to the executive role, he promised an energetic administration.[4]

His energy and decisiveness were quickly called into action. The racial problem which Governor Gooch inherited from his predecessors grew rapidly, nurtured by British merchants and those of New England and New York, the northern colonies having found the slave trade highly profitable. As the influx of slaves immediately removed from the jungle state increased, the danger of insurrection became apparent even to the thoughtless. Nevertheless, the Crown had countered the Virginia Assembly's efforts to restrict the traffic in human flesh.[5]

Threat became reality in 1729 when freshly-imported slaves, taking advantage of the sparsity of the white population on the western frontier, made a coordinated break for freedom, taking guns and ammunition with them into the mountains. Obviously, they must have had guidance from some outside source—civilized slaves or perhaps the Indians. They were overcome by the hunting parties that went after them and were led back into captivity.[6] The memory of the massacres of 1622 and 1644 was still strong in Virginia, and fearful planters realized that the slaves had freer access to their homes than had the Indians—indeed, were members of their households.

But some optimists agreed with William Byrd II who, in 1735, expressed confidence that the Negroes were "not so numerous or so enterprising as to give us any apprehension or uneasiness."[7] They stubbornly held to this conviction despite the fact that as early as 1723 the number of slaves imported to Virginia each year was between a thousand and sixteen hundred.[8] Many of the planters were, first and foremost, businessmen, and so long as the trade continued, they would take advantage of it—even though they feared its consequences—and not spend too much time worrying about the future.

Governor Gooch was disturbed by the conditions of slavery. "Some masters," he wrote in 1731, "use their Negroes no better than their cattle and I can see no help for it, though for the greater number the masters here are kinder than those the labourers in England serve."[9] Before mid-century, the Burgesses had adopted no less than nine acts to restrict the traffic, but each attempt was vetoed by an agency of the Crown.[10]

The other aspect of the racial problem—relations with the Indians—was complicated by the colony's increasing implication in world affairs. This involvement was dramatically evidenced when Governor Gooch personally led a Virginia contingent to join forces with the British at Jamaica and then take part in an abortive assault upon the Spanish stronghold at Cartagena. Even had he not been wounded, he would have suffered. "I am a very bad seaman," he wrote, "not to be reconciled to the motion of a ship." As it was, he was wounded in both ankles by a twenty-four pound cannonball, and wrote his brother, "I fear I am quite disabled."[11]

The great American conflict, however, was that shaping up between England and France. The westward expansion of England's coastal colonies and the southward and eastward expansion of France's commercial operations in Canada and the Mississippi Valley had resulted in a number of fierce localized struggles at points of encounter in New England and New York. South Carolina was understandably apprehensive about the French bases of New Orleans and Mobile. North Carolina had suffered fierce raids by the Tuscaroras, Indian allies of France, and Virginia had sent forces to her neighbor's aid.[12] But, so far, Virginia had enjoyed a remoteness from the actual physical conflict between France and England. Its pivotal position among the English colonies made continuation of this favored role impossible. Virginia's own rapid growth hastened the end of its isolation from combat.

During Governor Gooch's administration, settlers poured into the Shenandoah Valley—not only from Eastern Virginia, but also from Pennsylvania.[13] In contrast to the relative homogeneity of Tidewater's predominantly Anglican population, the Valley was being peopled by Palatinate Germans, Lutherans and Mennonites, Scotch-Irish Presbyterians and Quakers. The Scotch-Irish brought with them the traditional Scottish reverence for learning. Like most of the other Valley settlers, though, they brought few material goods to the small acreages which they held under patent from the colony. Virtually all immigrants, however, brought to the fertile and beautiful lands of the Shenandoah a heritage of industry and fierce independence.[14]

Many Virginians found it possible to shove into the backs of their minds the fact that westward expansion brought the colony nearer to conflict with France, and to rejoice in it as a sign of progress that would be reflected in economic prosperity.

They received no encouragement, though, from the Governor, who feared that western settlement "might possibly give umbrage to the French."[15] Besides, the frontier probably did not appeal to this executive who, writing from elegant Williamsburg, boasted to his brother: "The gentlemen and ladies here are perfectly well bred, not an ill dancer in my government."[16]

Gooch dealt more successfully with Commissary Blair than had any of his predecessors.[17] Just a few months after taking office in 1728, the Governor confided to his brother:

"The Commissary is a very vile old fellow, but he does not know that I am sensible of it, being still in appearance good friends; the best policy will be to kill him with kindness, but there is no perplexing device within his reach that he does not throw in my way, purely because he is not my privy Councillor. And yet I have given his nephew a place of 150g. a year, but unless he has all and does all he is not satisfied, and if he did, very few in this country besides himself would be so."[18]

For some months in 1740-41, Blair, now president of the Council, had the pleasure of serving as Acting Governor during Gooch's absence.[19]

On May 14, 1743, Gooch wrote the Bishop of Norwich:

"Old Blair died last month in his eighty-eighth year, and to the great comfort of his nephew, his heir, has left £10,000 behind him. A rupture he has had above forty years, concealed from everybody but one friend, mortified and killed him. If his belly had been as sound as his head and breast, he might have lived many years longer."[20]

In a letter to another correspondent, Gooch reported: "Such was the strength of his constitution, he struggled with the conqueror for ten days, after the doctors had declared he could not live ten hours."[21]

Governor Gooch remained in office more than six years after Commissary Blair's death, ending his service to the colony June 20, 1749. During his remarkably long administration of twenty-two years, the French had all but entrenched themselves along the broad Ohio and had repeatedly stimulated their Indian allies to forays against the English colonies. In 1738 and 1742, the Indians indulged in what were obviously more than sporadic, isolated attacks. Blood was spilled from the Ohio River Valley to Western New York.[22] In 1744, the Treaty of Lancaster deeded the country west of the Ohio to the English, but in that very year the Iroquois invaded the Shenandoah Valley in pursuit of the Cherokees and commandeered the Virginians' horses. The militia was called out. After an indecisive engagement in Rockbridge County, Governor Gooch appealed to Governor Clark of New York to punish the guilty Iroquois. But, since investigation indicated that the actual fighting had been initiated by the Virginia militia, the affair ended somewhat ingloriously with the protesting colony paying indemnity to the Indians.[23]

Undeterred, perhaps even spurred on, by French and Indian activity, planters of the Old Dominion and Maryland, under the leadership of Virginia's Thomas Lee, organized the Ohio Company in 1748 and dedicated it to development of the West.[24] They dispatched on an exploratory expedition Christopher Gist, who went as far west as the present site of Louisville. His glowing reports of great forests and luxuriant grasslands watered by fine streams stimulated commercial interest and increased the determination of many Virginians that this region should not be seized by France.[25]

Gist's report was doubtless Virginia's principal source of information concerning settlement and entrenchment by the French.

Neither Governor Gooch nor a British Ministry had acted on Colonel William Byrd's excellent suggestion. "These inducements to the French," he wrote in 1735, after expressing fears that the French would attempt to seize the entire trans-Allegheny region and control its mountain passes, "make it prudent for a British ministry to be watchful and prevent their seizing this important barrier. In order wherewith it may be proper to employ some fit person to reconnoiter these mountains very diligently, in order to discover what mines may be found there, as likewise to observe what nations of Indians dwell near them, and where lie the most considerable passes, in order to their being secured by proper fortifications."[26]

Following Gooch's departure, John Robinson, president of the Council, served as acting Governor for a period of less than three months.[27] His successor as President and acting chief executive was Thomas Lee, head of the Ohio Company, which was devoted to western expansion, and himself personally dedicated to expulsion of the French from the Ohio Valley.[28] Impressed with Lee's stature, the Crown broke precedent by issuing a resident Governor's commission to a Virginian.[29] The prospects for decisive action against the French threat seemed good. But Colonel Lee died November 14, 1750, little more than a year after assuming office and before his commission could reach him.[30]

Lewis Burwell, Lee's successor as president of the Council, served as chief executive until the arrival November 20, 1751 of the new Governor, Robert Dinwiddie.[31]

A Scotsman nearly sixty years old, a more advanced age by eighteenth century standards than by our own, Dinwiddie had behind him more than two decades of successful experience in colonial administration. He had a reputation for voluminous correspondence and a tireless search for facts.[32] Heavy-jowled, double-chinned, large nosed and large paunched, he did not look like a man who would personally lead a transmontane expedition in the manner of Spotswood, but he did not look like a dreamer either.[33] Some Virginians remembered Dinwiddie's residence in the colony during his term as surveyor-general of customs for the Southern District of America, and recalled his protracted but successful contest to obtain an ex officio seat on the Council with all privileges of membership. They knew he was not one to abdicate his authority.[34]

Governor Dinwiddie inherited from his predecessor a strong government. The skill that Gooch had displayed in avoiding open conflict with Commissary Blair had enabled him to keep internal conflict at a minimum.

The Governor's powers remained essentially what they had been at the start of the century. The government of the colony, however, had become increasingly far removed from London's domination. This fact was clearly indicated by a letter which Governor Gooch, technically Lieutenant Governor, had addressed to the absentee titular Governor, Lord George Hamilton Douglas, Earl of Orkney, September 3, 1739. Expressing surprise that he should be "taxed with lack of respect to your Lordship as Governour, in appointing Mr. Randolph to execute the office [of Lieutenant Governor during Gooch's absence] without notifying to your Lordship either the vacancy or appointment," he wrote:

"I am so well acquainted with the practice of this government for sixty years past, that I can assure your Lordship there is not one instance in all that time of a Lt. Governour being controlled by the Chief Governour in the disposal of any Office of Trust or Profit, whenever such become vacant; tho' some of those Chief Governours, as Lord Culpeper and Lord Effingham, had been in Va., knew the offices, and had friends and acquaintances in the country to gratify; and the reason, My Lord, is very evident, because the letters patents, by which they were constituted devolve the whole power of government upon the person who is Commander in Chief on the place, as well in their absence as on their death. And if your Lordship will be pleased to recollect, you will find no power given you by your commission to exercise any act of government in this colony, during your residence elsewhere; and consequently, that upon the vacancy of any office, your lordship cannot, while you remain out of the government, give a commission to anyone to execute any office of trust or profit here.

"But there is another obstacle to be surmounted before your lordship can dispose of any place in the government, which is, that by the King's instructions, and the laws of the country, the advice and consent of the Council must be first obtained; who have always a large share in the application, and with whom the appointment is debated and approved before it is fixt: And how such consent can be had at a thousand leagues distance, and how unlikely it is to succeed, when every member of that Board hath a possibility of being President, on whom the same powers devolve on the death or absence of Lt. Governour, is worth considering. Nor will your lordship hesitate in believing that whoever is Commander in Chief, will certainly insist, as it is his duty, on the King's Letters Patents under the great seal, as a superior authority to any other command."[35]

Despite Gooch's citation of precedents extending back sixty years, it is hard to imagine that one of his predecessors would have addressed such a letter to the titular Governor. The Lieutenant-Governor had told volumes about the power of the colonial Council and about Virginians' impatience with attempts to dictate colonial policies from "a thousand leagues' distance."

During Gooch's administration, the Governor had ceased to sit with the Council, thus effecting a physical separation of the legislative and executive departments. But the twelve Councillors, being the "principal gentlemen of the Colony," continued to exert an influence that reduced the chief executive's independence. Besides, certain legal restrictions curbed his powers. For example, the Governor was Commander-in-Chief and Vice Admiral and he could provoke enemy attack by his executive policies, but he did not have the power to declare war. Nevertheless, the conservative character of the Council predisposed it toward most imperial policies advocated by his Majesty's representative.[36]

The House of Burgesses, on the other hand, being a more numerous and more popular body, sometimes required more diplomacy from a Governor. By 1755, the House of Burgesses had one hundred four members—two for each county, one each for the towns of Jamestown, Williamsburg and Norfolk and, in the English tradition, one for the College of William and Mary.[37] The voting privilege was enjoyed by all freeholders, they being defined as male persons possessing at least one hundred acres of unsettled land, or twenty-five acres with house and plantation or leasing such property to tenants or owning a house and at least part of a lot in town. Exercise of the franchise was denied to Indians, free Negroes and mulattoes.[38]

Virginia's population in the middle seventeen-fifties probably was between 290,000 and 300,000.[39] Gooch, estimating with excessive conservatism and with few facts to guide him, had guessed that the colony's residents numbered 135,000 in 1749.[40] Thomas Lee, in 1750, had accepted his predecessor's figure. Dinwiddie, in 1756, computed Virginia's population at 293,742, figuring that whites accounted for 173,316 of that number.[41] A check on the accuracy of these computations is impossible, but it is obvious that Virginia's Negro populace had increased greatly, not only in number but also in proportion to total population.

This population was still widely dispersed. Even Tidewater Virginia was almost completely rural, but there were now a number of urban centers. Williamsburg had grown by the 1750's to the point where it could look forward to a population of a thousand before the end of the decade.[42] On the banks of the beautiful and commercially important York River, just twelve miles from the capital, was the port of Yorktown.

At the tip of the same peninsula that claimed these two towns was Hampton, formally incorporated in 1705 but a point of settlement since soon after the founding of Jamestown. Its mid-century population may have approached three thousand. Certainly this assembly point for British convoys was the commercial metropolis of Virginia.[43]

On the southern shores of Hampton Roads was Norfolk, founded in 1682.[44] This community stood high in Governor Dinwiddie's favor. For some unexplained reason it had made him an honorary burgher by 1741, ten years before he became Governor. In 1754, he presented the town a royal mace.[45]

Portsmouth, across the Elizabeth River from Norfolk, was laid off by Colonel William Craford in 1752.[46]

At the falls of the James, fifty miles from Williamsburg, was Richmond, laid out by Colonel William Byrd II in 1737[47] and incorporated five years later. Its population may have reached the three hundred mark in the 1750's.[48]

Fredericksburg, established at the falls of the Rappahannock in 1727, boasted a wharf, a quarry and tobacco warehouses. Nearby Falmouth was founded as a rival.[49]

Dumfries, on the Potomac, had been chartered in 1749. Colchester, eight miles to the north, was founded in 1753.[50]

Development of Alexandria, a Potomac River town laid off in 1749, claimed the interest of prominent Virginians.[51]

The village of Petersburg, planned by Colonel William Byrd,[52] stood at the fall line of the Appomattox.

There were in Eastern Virginia seven villages of notable size that gave promise of developing into cities. The Rappahannock area could boast such river communities as Urbanna, Hobbs Hole or Tappahannock, Leedstown and Port Royal.[53] The community of Delaware, or West Point, was growing up where the Mattaponi and the Pamunkey joined to form the York. [54] Hanovertown and Newcastle were also on the Pamunkey.[55]

West of the Blue Ridge, Virginia was a different country. One might ride in the Shenandoah Valley for a distance of eighty-five miles or more southwest of Winchester before encountering a village. Then the traveler would come upon Augusta Court House, or Staunton, with its twenty homes. West of the Valley lay the wilderness with its scattered English cabins, Indian huts and, at various undisclosed points, French outposts.[56]

England had recently been officially at war with France. The trouble had started with Spain, and the English themselves were responsible for beginning it. British traders had ignored the limit of one English slave ship a year to Portobello on Spain's Isthmus of Panama.[57] Spain sent out against the English merchant fleets her dread *guarda costas*, manned principally by pirates who now had the chance to pursue their brutal tactics under the guise of legality. Grievances on both sides led to war. England struck repeatedly but unsuccessfully at Spanish America. Admiral Vernon, in 1741, had attacked Cartagena in an abortive expedition that included thousands of volunteers from England's thirteen American colonies, Virginia's Governor Gooch among them.[58] In 1742, a Spanish fleet of thirty-six vessels had struck at Georgia. But a stout body of transplanted Scots, fighting in their traditional kilts and under the command of the redoubtable Oglethorpe, had put the Spaniards to flight.[59] Tension in the colonies had continued. Virginians on the coast feared Spanish attack at any moment. Norfolk citizens for months had carried guns to church and the Anglican rector had preached with a pistol on the pulpit.[60]

After the defeat by Oglethorpe, however, the Spanish seemed to lose their ambition and there were no more notable clashes on the southern frontier.[61]

In 1744, though, the war between England and Spain had been caught up in the vortex of the War of the Austrian Succession. England was thus at war with France. The war was concluded by the Treaty of Aachen in 1748. Its only notable incident in North America had been the dramatic seizure of Louisbourg by a New England expedition, and this Canadian fortress was returned to France under terms of the treaty.[62]

The treaty actually established an armed truce between France and England. It did not bring peace. In no theater was undercover continuation of the conflict more evident than in North America. The diplomats had drawn no boundary on the watershed of the Ohio.[63]

In 1749 the French Governor of Canada sent the Chevalier Céloron de Bienville to the disputed region to reinforce French claims. Traveling from Lake Erie to Lake Chautauqua and down the Allegheny River and into and down the Ohio, he then proceeded up the Miami, returning to Canada by the Maunce River and Lake Erie.[64] He had visited many Indian tribes, and told them in his Governor's name:

"The English intend to rob you of your country; and that they may succeed, they begin by corrupting your minds. As they mean to seize the Ohio which belongs to me, I send to warn them to retire."[65]

Céloron gave force to his words by ordering a number of English traders to cease their trespassing on what he asserted was French territory.[66]

Governor Dinwiddie was well aware that the French were not making idle threats. He had invested in the Ohio Company, and his official interest in defending English rights to the territory the company sought to develop was thus bolstered by a strong personal one.[67]

He first sought to strengthen English legal rights to the territory formerly claimed by the Indians. The treaty made at Lancaster in 1744 had never been ratified in a binding manner. Governor Dinwiddie dispatched three men—Joshua Fry, college professor and wilderness surveyor, Lunsford Lomax and James Patton—to secure ratification and establish amicable relations with the Six Nations in conference at Logstown.[68] Ratification was obtained June 13, 1752, and with it confirmation of the English right to build two trading posts on the Ohio and settlements south of the river.[69]

In the same month, the French scored a blow when Charles Langlale, a French trader, with the aid of two hundred fifty Ojibwas, defeated and killed in a battle on the Miami an Indian chief so famed for friendship to the English that he was known as Old Britain.[70]

With winter came the frightening news that the Miami Indians, supposedly friendly with the English, had aligned themselves with the French and that fifteen or sixteen Frenchmen had settled at Logstown. "It is to be feared," said Dinwiddie, "they [the French] will take possession of the river Ohio, oppress our trade and take our traders prisoners."[71]

Voicing his fears as he stated his hopes, he said:

"We would fain hope these people are only French traders, and they have no other view but trade. I hope there is no great army of French among the lakes."[72]

When the Adjutant of the colony, Lawrence Washington,[73] met his death in 1752 while still in his mid-thirties, Governor Dinwiddie divided the Adjutancy among three men. The defense needs of Virginia, Dinwiddie believed, demanded its division into three military districts.[74] A conference between Governor and Council resulted in the creation of four such districts—the frontier, the Northern Neck, the Middle Neck or York-Rappahannock Peninsula, and the Southern District which embraced all of Virginia south of the James and east of the Frontier.[75]

Each adjutant had the title of Major and was charged with instructing "the officers and soldiers in the use and exercise of their arms, in bringing the militia to a more regular discipline, and fitting it for service, besides polishing and improving the meaner people" in his district.[76]

The Adjutant of the Southern district was Lawrence Washington's half-brother, George. This grandson of John Washington, the famous Virginia Indian fighter, was a remarkable young man and an ambitious one. Reared in modest financial circumstances but among the aristocracy of the Northern Neck, he had not had the advantage of education abroad, enjoyed by his brother and other friends, or even at the College of William and Mary. But he had learned many lessons of character and worldly wisdom from his brother and from George William Fairfax. His surveying experience in the employ of George William's father, Lord Fairfax, had taught him much about the frontier and the making of maps and accurate reports. The friendship of influential men had aided his advancement, but these sponsors were principally individuals impressed with his personal qualities rather than allied with his family by blood or marriage. It is therefore remarkable that this young man, who had never had any actual military experience, was made one of Virginia's four Adjutants and thus automatically a major some days before his twenty-first birthday.[77] He was county surveyor, an office much sought after, and he had added to his ancestral lands two thousand acres in the Shenandoah Valley.[78] Lawrence Washington, before his early death, had given promise of becoming one of Virginia's great men. Some shrewd Virginians now thought that the younger Washington might equal the promise of his departed brother.

Major Washington, charged with the defense of Southern Virginia, was interested to learn in 1753 that fifteen hundred French troops had been landed in the spring on the southern shore of Lake Erie and there had built forts and roads.[79] With even greater interest he learned that Governor Dinwiddie purposed to send the French commander warning that he must leave English territory. Being ambitious and possessing a great deal of initiative, young Washington rode to Williamsburg to offer his services as envoy.[80]

Arriving in the capital near the end of October, he presented himself to the Governor at the Palace. Dinwiddie had urgently requested the Crown the previous June to authorize construction of forts to prevent French seizure of the Ohio country. Authorization with the sign manual of the King himself had arrived August 28.[81] Just a few days before young Washington's arrival, a sloop of war had brought special dispatches to the Governor that empowered him to seek the cooperation of other colonies in dealing with the French threat. Dinwiddie had dispatched letters under the King's seal to his fellow English Governors in colonial America, and had called the General Assembly of Virginia into special session slated to convene November 1.[82]

He now desired to acquaint the French at once with the fact that the English regarded them as trespassers and would not continue to suffer their encroachment. His messenger would also have to determine the strength and position of French garrisons and make an accurate report upon his return. The tall, long-limbed young Virginian who stood before the Governor looked capable. He was not mature in years, but there was an appraising look in the steady blue eyes and sobriety in the set of the mouth.[83] If the boy was nearly so good a man as his late brother, he was capable enough for the mission. Besides, he had been well recommended for the highly responsible post of Adjutant, and his surveying experience would stand him in good stead as an observer and reporter. Moreover, there must be no delay in the mission, and here was a man ready for immediate service. Governor Dinwiddie commissioned the youthful major to proceed to Logstown, pay his respects to friendly Indian chiefs and ask them to provide him with a guard as far as the vicinity of the French commander's headquarters. Upon presenting the Governor's letter to the commander, Major Washington was to demand a reply. He was to wait not more than a week for the Frenchman's response, and to ask for a French escort back to the English settlements.[84] So much for the Major's formal instructions. His verbal instructions required him to demand that the French explain why they had made prisoners of English traders dealing with the Indians and why they had driven the Englishman John Frazier from his frontier home of twelve years.[85]

Leaving Williamsburg the very day he received his commission,

Major Washington rode to Fredericksburg, where on November 1 he engaged the services of Jacob van Braam, a young Dutch veteran of military service on the Continent whose knowledge of French should make him valuable as an interpreter. Near Wills Creek on the upper Potomac, the Major visited the veteran frontiersman Christopher Gist and delivered to him an official request from Governor and Council that he accompany the Adjutant on the mission to the French. The addition of four "servitors" completed the Major's party.[86]

After traversing rugged mountains and streams swollen by the cold November rains, the expedition arrived on the twenty-third of the month at a windswept plain overlooking the junction of the Allegheny and Monongahela rivers.[87] At or near this strategic site, Governor Dinwiddie proposed to erect a fort.[88]

The military advantages of the location were not lost on young Washington. "The land in the forks . . .," he noted, "I think extremely well situated for a fort, as it has the absolute command of both rivers. The land at the point is twenty or twenty-five feet above the common surface of the water; and a considerable bottom of flat, well-timbered land all around it, very convenient for building. The rivers are each a quarter of a mile or more across and run here very near at right angles, Allegheny bearing northeast and Monongahela southeast. The former of these two is a very rapid and swift running water; the other deep and still, without any perceptible fall."[89]

After visiting an Indian village where the Ohio Company proposed to erect a fort and pronouncing it "greatly inferior either for defense or advantages" to the site at the forks, the major proceeded to Logstown, an undistinguished-looking assortment of huts with a long house, but famed as the capital of the powerful Chief Half-King and the scene of many Indian conferences.[90]

On November 25, while Washington awaited Half-King's return from a point some fifteen miles distant, a group of deserters from the French army walked into the town. Through Van Braam as interpreter, they told the major that they had been members of a force of one hundred sent up the Mississippi to meet at Logstown another French force, this one from garrisons on the south shore of Lake Erie. They had deserted at Great Beaver Creek, but believed that it had been intended for them to proceed farther up the Ohio after meeting their compatriots at Logstown. The French had erected four small forts between New Orleans and the Illinois (the latter reference puzzled the Virginians). This talk of proceeding farther up the river might indicate French plans to erect a fort at the junction of the Allegheny and the Monongahela.[91]

Upon his return, Half-King orated upon his hatred of the French who, he claimed, had killed, boiled and eaten his father and more recently had insulted him and his people. "I am not afraid of flies or mosquitoes," the chief quoted the French commandant as saying, "for Indians are such as those . . . It is my land and I will have it, let who will stand-up for, or say against it. If people will be ruled by me, they may expect kindness, but not else."[92]

The fiery chief said that he would send a third and last warning to the French to leave the lands of the Six Nations. If the warning was spurned, all pretense of friendly relations between Half-King's subjects and the arrogant trespassers would be at an end. His influence with his fellow sachems made this declaration far more significant than if it had had no effect other than aligning Half-King's own subjects against the French.[93]

Major Washington soon had cause to wonder whether the extent of this influence, while important, had been exaggerated. Not until November 30 did the sachem assemble an honor guard for the Virginia adjutant, and then instead of being a great body representative of many tribes, it was a party of four—Half-King himself, an old chief named Heskake, a Chief White Thunder, and a young hunter to keep them provided with meat. A council of sachems, Half-King told Washington, had decided the night before that a large escort might provoke the French.[94]

On December 4, the party emerged from rain-drenched woods at the point of land where French Creek emptied into the Allegheny. It was now *French* creek indeed. Here, over the log house that had been John Frazier's trading post, floated the white and gold banner of France. The French doubtless were converting this village of Venango into a defense post.[95]

Here the young major was received by Captain Philippe Thomas Joincare, Sieur de Chabert, one of the most remarkable men in the colonial service of the French monarch. The son of a Seneca squaw and a French officer, this forty-six-year-old Chief Interpreter for the Six Nations (a royally conferred title) moved with equal ease among His Christian Majesty's subjects and the Indians who inhabited the Ohio country. Presiding over a profitable trading post and portage at Niagara, he was chief adviser to France's Indian allies in Canada.[96]

Joincare was a courteous host and insisted that Washington and his companions be his dinner guests, but suggested that Washington deliver any official communication to the general officer at Fort Le Boeuf, some forty or fifty miles up the creek. He, Joincare, was in charge only on the Ohio.[97] That night Major Washington, Gist and Van Braam dined with Joincare, Commissary La Force and other French officers, exchanging amenities with men against whom they might very well be fighting in a matter of a few years or perhaps even months. Wine flowed freely, but the Virginia major remained sober and listened attentively as the French rattled on with surprising volubility. They swore that they would gain the Ohio. They realized that it could not be taken without a struggle, and were well aware that the English could oppose two men to every one of theirs. But they were confident that the English would realize their peril too late and act too slowly.[98] La Salle had staked out France's claim to the Ohio and his countrymen would not tolerate English settlement on the great river or any of its tributaries.

By skillful questioning, Major Washington was even able to obtain valuable information concerning the French troops, forts and lines of supply.[99]

The next day Joincare met with Half-King and the other chiefs in the Virginian's party. What ensued amply justified the major's precaution in keeping his Indian allies away from Joincare's table the night before. The wily Frenchman plied them with brandy until even Half-King was too drunk to make his magnificent gesture of defiance.[100] The following day had been appointed for the journey to Fort Le Boeuf, but Half-King insisted upon remaining to deliver his carefully rehearsed warning to the French commander. So Washington anxiously waited another day in Venango while his susceptible allies were exposed to Joincare's influence. This time Half-King spoke at length and climaxed his fiery oration by returning to the Frenchman the belt symbolic of understanding between their two peoples. Joincare politely refused it, saying that the belt should be delivered at Fort Le Boeuf.[101]

On the next day, December 7, Commissary La Force presented himself with three soldiers at Washington's tent and offered to escort the adjutant's party to Le Boeuf. Christopher Gist recorded in his diary: "Joincare did everything he could to prevail on our Indians to stay behind us, and I took all care to have them along with us." Gist won, but not easily.[102]

At the close of the fourth day of travel, the Virginians and their escorts stood on the East bank of the creek and strained their eyes in a vain attempt to pierce the thickening twilight that obscured Fort Le Boeuf on the opposite shore. Van Braam crossed the creek to notify the commandant that an emissary of His Majesty's government had arrived, and several French officers soon pushed out in a canoe. They bore an invitation to Major Washington and his associates to visit the fort.[103]

After spending the night as guests of the French, Washington, Gist and Van Braam presented themselves to the senior officer of the post, the Sieur Legardeur de St. Pierre de Repentigny, Knight of St. Louis. The one-eyed old soldier welcomed the Virginians with the same courtesy his counterpart had shown at Venango but, like Joincare, declined to receive the letter from Governor Dinwiddie. Major Washington was asked to await the arrival from the next fort of Monsieur Repentigny, perhaps a kinsman of St. Pierre.[104]

Captain Repentigny arrived that afternoon and translated the Virginia Governor's letter for St. Pierre.[105]

After delays, the French commandant, on December 14, proposed that Major Washington journey to Quebec with the letter and there present it to the Governor of Canada. The young adjutant refused to be made the dupe of bland attempts to delay still further his return to Virginia. He had fulfilled his commission to deliver a communication to the French commander on the frontier, and having done so he would report to his Governor at once.[106]

That night Washington received St. Pierre's formal written reply to Governor Dinwiddie's letter. The next morning the major's party took their leave of Fort Le Boeuf in two canoes provided by the French and filled by them with food and liquor.[107] "I persuade myself," Dinwiddie had said in his letter, "you will receive and entertain Major Washington with the candour and politeness natural to your nation."[108] On the score of politeness, at least, St. Pierre had given him no reason for disillusionment.

The young adjutant may not have known the wording of the message which he was bearing back to Williamsburg, but he must have been familiar with its substance. When he had asked St. Pierre by what authority British subjects had been seized as prisoners of war, the commander had replied "that the country belonged to [the French]; that no Englishman had a right to trade upon those waters; and that he had orders to make every person prisoner who attempted it on the Ohio, or the waters of it."[109]

Washington had learned some other things without asking questions. The delays occasioned by the French and by his own Indian allies (whom the officers at Le Boeuf had courted as assiduously as had those at Venango) had given him the opportunity to examine the fort at leisure. He learned that eight six-pounders were mounted on each of the corner bastions of the twelve-foot high stockade, and he made observations on the barracks inside the enclosure and the stables, smith's shop and other buildings that stood outside its protection.[110] He discovered that the French had at Le Boeuf fifty birch canoes and one hundred seventy of pine. Other boats were being built.[111] These signs of preparation, coupled with St. Pierre's assertions about French claims to the entire Ohio basin, made inescapable the fact that the French were almost ready to move in force against English outposts and subdue the whole frontier country.[112] The drunken boasts of the officers at Venango had revealed that they were counting on English slowness to act. Major Washington must have wished that he could ride straight to Williamsburg without pausing to eat, sleep or rest his horses.

The return journey was arduous. Christmas Day, following a full day of constant snow, was not merry. In Major Washington's words: "The horses grew less able to travel every day; the cold increased very fast; and the roads were becoming much worse by a deep snow, continually freezing."[113] The next day three of the men were disabled by frostbite. Tortured by the urgency of his report to Governor Dinwiddie, Washington pushed on afoot with Gist, leaving their companions encamped with the horses.[114]

After escaping assassination by a treacherous Indian guide who had volunteered his services, fording cold streams, and tramping through icy woods (exhausting work for a young Virginia gentleman whose chief outdoor exercise was on horseback), Washington arrived in Williamsburg January 16, 1754 and delivered St. Pierre's letter and his own report to the Governor. The Frenchman's letter was evasive in all particulars except its expression of "the evidence and reality of the rights of the King, my Master, upon the lands situated along the River Ohio" and its tribute to Major Washington's "quality and great merit."[115]

Dinwiddie asked the Adjutant to prepare a written report for presentation to the Council the next day. Here the major's daily journal stood him in good stead. When the Council convened to consider his report, young Washington had ready for them a seven thousand word document.[116]

Whatever action the Governor took would be without the authorization of the Burgesses. He had just been engaged with them in the bitter "pistole fee dispute" over taxation of land patents and had prorogued them on December 19, by his own admission "with some marks of anger."[117] He now felt it necessary to call a special session of the Burgesses for February 14, 1754, but that date was nearly a month distant and there was no telling what their response would be when they assembled. (They had recently disregarded Dinwiddie's recommendations for defense appropriations.) In the meantime, he must plan with his Council to meet the French threat.[118]

The French officers who drunkenly boasted to Washington that they would gain the Ohio country because of British slowness knew nothing of Dinwiddie's energy and initiative. To Lord Fairfax, County Lieutenant for Frederick and the most powerful man in the colony, the Governor confided his appraisal of the threat and plans to meet it.

"The French forces on the Ohio," he wrote, "intend to come down as far as Logstown early in the spring. . . . I think it is for his majesty's service and the protection of the settlements of this dominion to do all in our power to prevent their building any forts or making any settlements on that river, and more particularly so nigh us as that of the Logstown. . . . I therefore, with advice of the Council, think proper to send immediately out 200 men to protect those already sent by the Ohio Company to build a fort, and to resist any attempts on them."[119]

A less bold or resourceful man than Dinwiddie would have despaired of executing any of these plans before the Burgesses convened. The law did not empower the chief executive to pay volunteer troops. The Governor determined to secure two hundred enlistments at once from Indian traders and frontier militia and trust to the Burgesses to provide the necessary funds upon assembling in February. He planned to send four hundred more men after that date to join the first volunteers dispatched to the Ohio. He would call upon governors of the other colonies to assist Virginia in this enterprise.[120]

On January 21, Major Washington, now adjutant of the Northern Neck District, was directed to enlist a hundred men from the militia of Augusta and Frederick counties. Captain William Trent, a successful Indian trader, was directed to raise another hundred from the approximately three hundred Virginians who followed his occupation. If Major Washington did not obtain a sufficient number of volunteers from Augusta and Frederick, draft by lot would be resorted to.[121]

Lord Fairfax, county lieutenant for Frederick, was the commander of a ghost militia—not even a paper force, for there was no official roster. He could offer Major Washington not one volunteer. Even his draft order was defied. "You may," Washington commented, "with almost equal success, attempt to raise the dead to life again, as the force of this county."[122] Augusta, even though it had known the terror of an Indian raid the summer before, was almost as sullenly defiant as Frederick.[123]

As might be expected, Dinwiddie had no intention of tolerating such insubordination. Punishment should be meted out against recalcitrant militiamen, and any Frederick County officer who had failed to do his duty should forfeit his commission.[124] Unexpected opposition came from the Council. Several of its members were disturbed about the possible limitations on gubernatorial authority incidentally imposed by legislation intended to enlarge the Governor's emergency powers. The act for repelling invasion, renewed last November, had empowered the Chief Executive to authorize officers commanding men from several counties to exercise their authority within any county from which any of their men came exactly as they would in "any other Counties and places within this Dominion." Though evidently designed to guarantee the Commander-in-Chief or his lieutenants the right to supersede commands by officers of a county's militia even while the men remained within the county in which such an officer enjoyed command, the phrase "within this Dominion" might be interpreted as a restricting one. The militia, according to this probable interpretation, could not be employed beyond the borders of Virginia. Virginians, therefore, could not be drafted by gubernatorial authority to serve outside the colony. Though the Old Dominion claimed the land about the forks of the Ohio, Pennsylvania asserted a like claim. The Councillors thought it unwise to send drafted men into territory not incontestably Virginia's. If the Governor's orders were defied, their legality might not be sustained by the Crown.[125] Dinwiddie was already at war with the Burgesses and possibly soon would be engaged in a struggle with the French. He had no desire to antagonize the Council and incur the Crown's displeasure.

Further action must await the convention February 14 of the Burgesses. On that very date, the Governor addressed the House, warning that fifteen hundred French and unnumbered Indian allies were preparing for an early spring advance, a rendezvous at Logstown, and the erection of "many more fortresses" on the Ohio. Emphasizing the terrors to which the frontier was exposed, he reported that he had already ordered "some part of the militia" to the

Ohio and asked the Burgesses to vote a "proper supply."[126] The next day he placed in the legislators' hands St. Pierre's answer and Major Washington's account of his mission.[127]

Sitting as a Committee of the Whole, the Burgesses debated action on the Governor's appeal for funds. Even with France all but breathing down their necks, some legislators were convinced that Virginia and her sister colonies could remain almost indefinitely isolated from the major theater of conflict. Some branded Major Washington's report "a fiction and a scheme to promote the interest of a private company."[128]

Many refused to believe that the danger was real. At least one declared that the Ohio territory belonged to France. These Virginia lawmakers who, in their determined opposition to tax increases for armed defense, claimed that isolation was practicable and that selfish financial interests were trying to promote war where no threat existed, were not unique among legislators.

Eventually, administration supporters prevailed upon their colleagues to vote ten thousand pounds for the protection of Virginia's frontiers, but only with the humiliating proviso that a committee of fourteen (any nine constituting a quorum) decide with gubernatorial consent how the funds should be spent. Four Councillors were named to the Committee.[129]

One may well imagine the emotions with which Governor Dinwiddie, accustomed to exercising all powers of any office he ever held, received notification of the Burgesses' action. He fumed that they had "clogged this bill with many things unconstitutional and derogatory to the prerogatives of the Crown." They were, he vowed, "very much in a republican way of thinking."[130] But the money was badly needed for the colony's defense, so he swallowed his fury and signed the offensive measure into law. With no reluctance whatsoever, he prorogued the General Assembly that very day—February 23.[131]

The Governor now began to recruit six companies of fifty men each to "erect and support" a fort at the mouth of the Monongahela River. A special inducement—a most attractive one in that land hungry age—was offered each prospective volunteer. Two hundred thousand acres of land, it was announced, would be set aside—half of them adjacent to the fort and half on or near the Ohio. This acreage would be apportioned among the enlisted men according to merit upon completion of their term of service. The land would be free of quit-rents for fifteen years. While they were earning their property, the volunteers would receive regular infantryman's pay.[132] Dinwiddie's offer would not only accelerate recruiting, but also would help to populate with Englishmen the territory which France sought to make her own.

Even these inducements, however, were not enough to arouse enthusiasm for service in the Ohio country, as Major Washington, temporarily turned recruiting officer, learned. Operating from headquarters in Alexandria, he was able to enlist only about twenty-five men, most of whom, according to his own description, were "loose, idle persons." Once they were enlisted, new troubles began. "They are perpetually teasing me," the youthful major complained to the Governor, "to [provide them clothing and to deduct the cost from their pay], but I am not able to advance the money, provided there was no risk in it, which there certainly is, and too great for me to run, though it would be nothing to the country. . . ."[133] Since most of them had no shoes or shirts when they signed up,[134] they may have enlisted in hopes of acquiring those garments.

Meanwhile William Trent was making progress, though not enough, in his efforts to recruit a hundred men among the traders.[135]

Governor Dinwiddie was heartened by faith that one thousand Cherokee and Catawba allies would spring to the aid of the English, and by assurance of reinforcements from South Carolina and New York.[136]

Estimates of the potential enemy force grew far faster than Virginia's army of recruits. There was one report that a force of four hundred Frenchmen was expected on the Ohio.[137] Other troop movements and concentrations were reported. William Trent, on the scene of threatened conflict, sent urgent appeals for help in a hurry. He feared that a mighty French army of invasion would be met by only a handful of ill-trained colonials.[138]

At length Washington had recruited fifty men and, with the aid of fellow officers, assembled a total of seventy-five.[139] Governor Dinwiddie kept up a voluminous correspondence with his fellow American governors, keeping them informed concerning the French, and urging them to appeal to their legislatures for funds that they might send troops to the Ohio.[140] He made it clear that he thought "the command should be undivided" and since Virginia had taken the initiative, should be under command of the Old Dominion's "general officers."[141]

Dinwiddie had to select these "general officers" from a small field. In the deaths of Governor Gooch and Lawrence Washington, the colony had lost its ablest military leaders. Although Dinwiddie secretly had ordered a uniform to clothe his portly figure,[142] the elderly chief executive must have realized in moments of utter frankness with himself that he was not cast in the mold of such active commanders-in-chief as Gooch and Spotswood. Only one of Virginia's adjutants, it is believed, had had experience in the field.[143]

To Joshua Fry, that rare combination of scholar and frontiersman, the Governor awarded a colonel's commission and command of the expedition.[144] Young Major Washington, who had executed so well his mission to Fort Le Boeuf, was rewarded with a lieutenant-colonel's commission and the post of second in command.[145]

Washington's new responsibilities would be even greater than his rank implied. There were signs that the French were preparing to move in force to the Ohio earlier than had been anticipated by the English. This intelligence, Dinwiddie wrote Washington March 15, "makes it necessary for you to march what soldiers you have to the Ohio, . . . [escorting] wagons with the necessary provisions," there to wait the arrival of Colonel Fry with additional recruits.[146]

The lieutenant-colonel's responsibilities were further increased by the considerable initiative allowed him. "You are to act on the defensive," the Governor said, "but in case any attempts are made to obstruct the works or interrupt our settlements by any persons whatsoever you are to restrain all such offenders, and in case of resistance to make prisoners of or kill and destroy them. For the rest, you are to conduct yourself as the circumstances of the service shall require and to *act as you shall find best for the furtherance of His Majesty's service and the good of his dominion.*"[147]

For wagons and supplies, Washington was dependent mainly upon the exertions of Major Carlyle who, perhaps partly through the influence of his Fairfax in-laws, had been appointed commissary for the expedition to the Ohio.[148] Dinwiddie had authorized county lieutenants to impress wagons into service if an insufficient number of owners were willing to sell them.[149] Even so, the supply master had a difficult time. Lieutenant-Colonel Washington believed that, if enough wagons were assembled to go as far as Wills Creek, pack animals could be used to carry sufficient supplies from that point to accompany the vanguard. William Trent assured him that the horses would be available.[150]

On the morning of April 2, 1754, Lieutenant-Colonel Washington rode forth from Alexandria at the head of a column of about one hundred twenty troops and two wagons loaded with food, tents and ammunition.[151] At Winchester, by the addition of Captain Adam Stephens' company and his own dogged, week-long effort to impress vehicles, he raised his force to one hundred fifty-nine men and twelve wagons.[152]

When he left Winchester about the eighteenth of April, he was about two hundred miles from his destination. Shortly after crossing a mountain ridge known as the Devil's Backbone and fording the Cacapon River, Washington saw a man riding toward him with the haste of one pursued by the fiend himself. He bore Captain Trent's desperate plea for immediate reinforcement at the forks of the Ohio. Eight hundred French troops were on the march and might strike at any hour.[153]

North Carolina, in answer to Dinwiddie's appeals, was preparing to send a force of seven hundred fifty.[154] Colonel Fry, presumably in Alexandria, would lead another column. But Trent must have immediate reinforcements and Washington was the only officer near enough to provide them.[155] The young lieutenant-colonel must have been acutely aware that destiny rode with his motley troops and creaking wagons, and he must have been uncomfortably cognizant of the fact that destiny was dependent on a very poor equipage.

Things could still be worse. They soon were. Upon arriving at Wills Creek, Washington found that Trent had provided not one of the horses he had promised. The young officer's only recourse was to secure more wagons by impressment. The nearest post at which they were available lay forty miles behind him.[156]

Meanwhile, on April 22, Ensign Edward Ward, who had commanded the fort under construction at the mouth of the Monongahela, rode into Wills Creek with the news that the structure had been captured by the French.[157] Instead of a small friendly force of Englishmen, there now awaited Washington's band of one hundred fifty-nine men a French army more than one thousand strong.[158]

War had not broken out yet. No shot had been fired when the French took over the fort. Ensign Ward would have been guilty of a tragic act of folly if he had wasted the lives of his men in a futile defense against an enemy outnumbering them more than twenty to one.[159]

Thus the new fort at a strategic site had been turned over to the French just as the last strokes of work were being put on its only unfinished gate.[160] The French had won an important advantage at no immediate cost. A summons which the enemy commander had served on Ensign Ward made it clear that the incident was part of a determined French policy of securing the Ohio Valley.[161]

Some comfort could be salvaged from the wreck of English hopes. One phase of the incident seemed to indicate that the Virginians had a firm ally in Half-King. The chief had been with Ensign Ward's force that marched out of the fort to surrender on the morning of April 18. As he passed the French officers, he hurled at them the defiant boast that he had ordered the fort built and had laid the first log of it.[162]

But the intensity of Half-King's hatred could be a liability as well as an asset. By Ensign Ward, the chief sent an emotion-charged message to the Governors of Virginia and Pennsylvania:

"Have good courage and come as soon as possible; you will find us as ready to fight as you are yourselves. . . . If you do not come to our assistance now, we are entirely undone, and I think we shall never meet together again. I speak with a heart full of grief."[163]

Lieutenant-Colonel Washington, on reading this message, which he was expected to transmit to the Governors, realized that Half-King's insistent demands for reinforcements, in view of the meager English forces within marching distance, could pose a grave problem.

An older man than Washington, or one less animated by thirst for glory, would not have felt the "glowing zeal"[164] which he said was his at this moment. That zeal, tempered by prudence, governed the lieutenant-colonel's decision about the next step. He would advance as far as he could with his small force. He would then hold his advanced position until the arrival of sufficient reinforcements to warrant a march to the forks and attack on the fort.[165]

The next five days were crowded with activity as Washington set his plans in motion, giving the broadest possible interpretation to Dinwiddie's admonition to "act as you shall find best for the furtherance of His Majesty's service and the good of his dominion."

For his advanced position, he chose the junction of Red Stone Creek with the Monongahela. At that point, across Chestnut Ridge and thirty-seven miles above the fork, the Ohio Company had erected storehouses. Washington ordered his men to begin widening the narrow trail to Red Stone Creek so that his wagons and heavy guns could roll.[166]

He not only sent a message of his own to Dinwiddie by Ensign Ward, who was bearing Half-King's message to the Governor, but took on himself the responsibility of sending messages to the governors of Maryland and Pennsylvania instead of waiting for Colonel

Fry or Dinwiddie to do so after receiving the adjutant's reports.[167]

To Governor Sharpe, he wrote:

"I know you are solicitous for the public weal and warm in this interesting cause, that should rouse from the lethargy we have fallen into, the heroic spirit of every free-born English man to attest the rights and privileges of our King (if we don't consult the benefit of ourselves) and rescue from the invasions of a usurping enemy, our Majesty's property, his dignity and land."[168]

Governor Sharpe might consider this exhortation bumptious, coming as it did from a twenty-two-year-old adjutant. But he could take comfort in the fact that this fellow Washington was untainted by any of that "republican way of thinking" which Dinwiddie had found among some Virginians.

Washington was confident that his requests would be quickly met. Sending a message to Half-King by means of a young Indian who had accompanied Ensign Ward, he wrote:

"We return you our greatest thanks and our hearts burn with love and affection for you, in gratitude for your steadfast attachment to us, as also your friendly speech and your wise counsels. This young man will inform you where he found a small part of our army, making towards you, clearing the roads for a great number of our warriors, who are ready to follow us, with our great guns, our ammunition and provisions."[169]

The patronizing reference to "this young man" was excusable. George Washington had rapidly grown older in the ways of diplomacy in the few months since he first set out for Fort Le Boeuf. He showed this growth when he included in his letter to Half-King a request that he or a deputy "come as soon as possible to meet us on the road, and to assist us in council," and when he signed it with his Indian cognomen as well as his English name.[170]

April passed into May, and Washington's troubles multiplied. The arrival of Ward's men who had been forced to leave the fort at the forks added troublemakers to Washington's troops. Their eventual desertion must have been welcome. Even at best, the widening of the road was a heartbreaking task. In some places, detours had to be cut. Day after day, the rain fell, turning the road to mud, swelling streams that lay across the trail. More than two days were spent in bridging one watercourse.[171] Two traders, the most recent arrivals of a whole series of refugees from French marauders, came into camp on May 16 and expressed their astonishment at Washington's plan to build a road over Chestnut Ridge to Red Stone Creek.

Familiar with the height and rugged character of the mountain barrier, they emphatically declared that it was impossible to put a road across it.[172]

Reports of French movements may have stimulated Washington's high resolve, but they had an opposite effect on most of his men. They were not inspired by news that eight hundred French reinforcements had reached the Ohio. Danger seemed especially imminent when a reliable trader reported encountering a party of five Frenchmen under Commissary La Force, a party that might well be a reconnaissance force, no farther from Washington's camp than Gist's new settlement.[173]

There was, however, much good news to offset the fearful rumors. Despite Washington's isolated position, news from the outside world flowed in almost continuously, and it was so varied in character that either an optimist or a pessimist could have a field day. Among the cheering items were reports that North Carolina would send three hundred fifty men to fight at the side of the Virginians and Maryland would send two hundred. Though Philadelphians were kept in painful suspense by rumors of approaching war, Pennsylvania still was not sufficiently moved to put men in the field; it did, however, contribute ten thousand pounds to finance the English expedition. Governor Shirley of Massachusetts would lead six hundred men in a diversionary attack on French Canada.[174] The incipient struggle that had seemed to be Virginia's private war now was the common cause of the English colonies.

For this development, Governor Dinwiddie, above all other men, was responsible. He had prodded and scolded other colonial governors into taking action. On April 27, 1754, he had written Governor De Lancey of New York in the manner of a schoolmaster admonishing a lethargic pupil.

"I am in great pain," he wrote, "for the arrival of your independent companies, as our forces and those from North Carolina are now on their march for the Ohio to the number of 700 men, and I daily expect an independent company from South Carolina which, when all joined together, may make near 1000 men. I therefore, hope [that] long before this your two companies are embarked, for the season of the year will not admit of any delay. I need say no more to you of the necessity of their being soon here."[175]

Governor Dinwiddie was sterner still in a letter of later date to Governor Sharpe of Maryland. Directness itself, he wrote:

"Sir: I have waited with impatience to hear what your Assembly and that of Pennsylvania have done in regard to their granting proper supplies of men and ordnance stores."[176]

Dinwiddie not only goaded his fellow governors into action, but prodded his Majesty's government in London as well.[177]

Besides being cheered by reports of aid from other colonies being sent in response to Dinwiddie's appeals and demands, Washington found additional encouragement in the news that Colonel Fry, though he had been able to secure only five wagons and a cart for transport, had advanced to Winchester.[178]

Some of Washington's fellow officers and their men doubtless were more skeptical than he about the promises from other colonies. The food was bad even by army standards, road building in the wilderness was back breaking labor that promised to grow harder, and the rain fell incessantly. The ground was sodden. The air was heavy and palpable in its wetness. Clothing, rations, men's spirits—all were dampened.[179]

In these circumstances, even the news that an independent company had arrived in Virginia from South Carolina and that two more such companies were expected from New York was cause for increased dissatisfaction. These independent companies, Washington's subordinate officers knew, consisted of soldiers unattached to any regiment but commanded by British regular officers directly commissioned by the King. Captains, lieutenants and ensigns of these companies would receive higher pay than their colonial counterparts. In a signed document which they asked Washington to transmit to Governor Dinwiddie, the Virginia officers protested that they were discriminated against, particularly in view of the extraordinary hardships which they had been forced to endure, and threatened to resign unless adequately compensated.[180]

On May 18 Washington wrote Governor Dinwiddie a diplomatic, but far from mincing, letter in which he skilfully expressed his own recognition of the justice of his subordinate officers' complaints and utter sympathy with them, while confirming his determination to remain a part of the Ohio expedition. Virginia officers, he insisted, should be paid the same amount as British regulars of corresponding rank. "Let me serve voluntarily," he said, "then I will, with the greatest pleasure in life, devote my services to the expedition without any other reward than the satisfaction of serving my country; but to be slaving dangerously for the shadow of pay, through woods, rocks, mountains—I would rather prefer the toil of a day laborer, and dig for a maintenance, provided I were reduced to the necessity, than serve upon such ignoble terms; for I really do not see why the lives of his Majesty's subjects in Virginia should be of less value than . . . those in other parts of his American dominions, especially when it is well known that we must undergo double that hardship."[181]

Even Washington's optimism, which had seemed almost as strong as his pride, was nearly dead. "Upon the whole," he wrote, "I find so many clogs upon the expedition that I quite despair of success; nevertheless, I humbly beg it, as a particular favor, that your Honor will continue me in the post I now employ, the duty whereof I will most cheerfully execute as a volunteer, but by no means upon the present pay. I hope what I have said will not be taken amiss; for I really believe, were it as much in your power as it is in your incli- nation, we should be treated as gentlemen and officers, and not have annexed to the most trifling pay that ever was given to English officers, the glorious allowance of soldier's diet—a pound of pork, with bread in proportion, every day. Be the consequence what it will, I am determined not to leave the Regiment, but to be amongst the last men that quit the Ohio, even if I serve as a private volun- teer, which I greatly prefer to the establishment we are now upon."[182]

The necessity for faster progress toward Red Stone Creek was emphasized by a report from two friendly Indians that a French reconnaissance force had been within six or seven miles of Wash- ington's own camp.[183]

On the twentieth of May, the young Virginian, accompanied by a lieutenant, three soldiers and an Indian guide, began the arduous task of exploring the possibilities of using the Youghiogheny as a water route to Red Stone Creek.[184] They found that "a fall, which continued rough, rocky and scarcely passable, for two miles, and then fell, within the space of fifty yards, nearly forty feet perpen- dicular" denied them the use of a water route.[185]

Returning to the Great Crossing of the Youghiogheny on the twenty-third, Washington slogged along the bad road over Laurel Hill, spurred on by news that the French had been reconnoitering along the Monongahela, confused by conflicting rumors and faulty reconnaissance reports, and heartened by a message from Half-King that the great sachem and his brother chief would counsel with the Virginia adjutant within five days in order that they might defeat a French force now advancing to attack.[186]

Washington's very reflexes must have told him there was more bad news when, on the twenty-fourth, as on so many days before, a trader arrived with information for the commander. This man was from Gist's settlement and he reported that two Frenchmen had been there the night before. He confirmed Half-King's information that an enemy force was on the march.[187]

In view of the weakness of his column, Washington deemed it folly to push on. The Virginians must brace themselves for attack. They were now at Great Meadows, a point about eleven miles beyond the Great Crossing of the Youghiogheny, and by the trail about fifteen miles from Gist's new settlement. It seemed to Washington's inexperienced military eye that news of the French advance had reached him at a spot admirably constituted for defense. Two gulleys not far apart he viewed as "natural entrenchments," manning them and placing his wagons between them.[188]

The next day he sent out reconnaissance parties, some riding bareback on the wagon horses, others proceeding on foot. The men remaining behind were kept busy cutting down undergrowth that would afford cover for the enemy. Washington's optimism had returned. He pronounced his camp site "a charming field for an encounter."[189]

That day and the next, the reconnaissance reports which he received were consistently negative. If enemies were nearby, they were concealing themselves with perfect effectiveness.[190]

Several hours before dawn of the next day, a sentry's cry brought the camp to its feet with guns firing. The discovery that six men were missing indicated that the guard had been alarmed by the sound of deserters creeping away from the camp.[191]

The next day brought definite news of the enemy from a trusted informant. Gist himself appeared at the camp to report that Commissary La Force and fifty soldiers had entered his new settlement the day before while two Indians were taking charge of the trading post in his absence. Only the Indians' fervent pleas had prevented the Frenchmen from destroying his property. On his way to warn Washington, Gist had found just five miles from the Virginians' camp the tracks of many white men, presumably the Frenchmen who had called when he was not at home. This vanguard's canoes were at Red Stone Creek.[192]

Washington now conceived a plan to cut the French off from their boats. Gambling on his opportunity, he sent out seventy-five men, nearly half his force, on reconnaissance under Captain Peter Hog, instructing him to find the French. The implication must have been that he must not return until he succeeded.[193]

Washington received no reports from anyone until about nine

o'clock, when an Indian runner materialized out of the rainy night. From Half-King, encamped just six miles away, he brought news that the chief had seen two sets of footprints crossing the trail, and believed that they were made by members of the party of fifty who had visited Gist's settlement. The enemy troops, he concluded, were near.[194]

Washington was as audacious as he had been the day before. With nearly half of his men off somewhere on reconnaissance duty and only eighty or so men at his immediate disposal, he resolved to march through the rain and the dark with forty of them to join Half-King and surprise the French.[195] None of the forty would forget that nightmare march. No clear thoroughfare was this wilderness road winding through specterlike trees and the blackness of a moonless night. Sometimes even the Indian guide lost his way, and the men were forced to get down on the rain-soaked earth and feel their way along. Water rendered their guns useless, and a Frenchman might be lurking behind any tree or large bush.[196]

Arriving at Half-King's camp at daybreak, they found that the chief's immediately available force consisted of another sachem and about nine warriors. Their greatest contribution would be in their forest skills rather than in their numbers. After a brief council between Indians and Virginians, Half-King sent two of his scouts to follow the tracks left by the white strangers whose footprints had excited him and strengthened his belief that the French were nearby.[197]

The scouts returned with the report that they had found the enemy concealed among rocks and trees about half a mile from the trail. Washington determined to surround the French and attack from all sides.[198]

Deployment was completed before eight o'clock that morning, with Captain Stephen's troops on the left and Washington himself in command on the right. Until he was about one hundred yards from the French, Washington, like Stephen, would enjoy the shelter of trees. From the moment that he stepped beyond that point he would be in a clearing, and he and his men, unlike Stephen's troops, would be standing targets clearly exposed to enemy marksmen.[199]

He stepped into the open and gave his command. The surprised French grabbed for their rifles. Shots cracked the air. There was no telling which side fired first, but it was almost a draw.[200] Bullets whistled past Washington's ears. Men fell on both sides. The French gave ground, but finding implacable Indians in their rear, ran back to the English with arms upraised in token of surrender.[201]

Within fifteen minutes, the Virginians had surprised and completely vanquished the foe. Washington counted one dead and two or three wounded among his men. Ten of the Frenchmen lay dead. The Indians had begun an orgy of scalping and skull smashing among the wounded. Only Washington's earnest efforts prevented Half-King from wreaking vengeance on the unwounded prisoners for the "boiling and eating" of his father.[202]

Among the slain Frenchmen was Joseph Coulon, Sieur de Jumonville, their commander. The captives included Druillon, second in command, and Commissary La Force, one of the wiliest agents of French imperialism.[203]

After reluctantly redividing his force to provide Half-King with a guard to Gist's settlement, where the chief hoped to rally his tribal allies, Washington marched his men and the prisoners to his camp at the Meadows. The march may have been "without incident," but it was not silent. With eloquent gestures and Gallic phrases, the French officers protested that they could not properly be made prisoners of war. They had come on a diplomatic mission to warn the English to leave the domain of His Most Christian Majesty of France.[204]

Certain documents had been found on Jumonville's person at the time of his capture. When translated by Van Braam, two were seen to be official papers prepared at Fort Du Quesne and dated May 23, 1754. One, signed by the Sieur de Contrecoeur and addressed to the English commander, reiterated the French desire for peace, but warned the English to quit the Ohio country or be driven out. The other included Contrecoeur's instructions to Jumonville. The subordinate officer had been directed to take with him on his mission other officers, an interpreter and twenty-eight men. He was to find the road connecting with the one opened by the English, determine the validity of Indian reports that the British contemplated aggression, notify Contrecoeur of any hostile movements observed, and after such notification deliver to the "trespassing" English the summons to retire. Jumonville was instructed to leave undisturbed any peaceful English forces that remained east of the Great Mountain.[205]

Several interpretations of the intent of these instructions were possible. But only one was conceivable to a twenty-two-year-old English officer thirsting for glory in that tense year of 1754 when the menace of France threatened the British dream of New World empire. Washington treated his unwilling guests with punctilious regard for diplomatic niceties, even giving some of his own clothes to La Force and Druillon to replace those claimed by the Indians.[206] But he wrote to Governor Dinwiddie:

"Loosing [La Force] would tend more to our disservice than [releasing] 50 other men. . . . In strict justice [these Frenchmen] ought to be hanged as spies of the worst sort."[207]

* * *

Not even the receipt of a letter from Dinwiddie chastising him for championing his subordinates' "ill-founded"[208] complaints about pay dampened Washington's spirits. He proceeded to argue the question with "his Honor."[209]

His easily won victory had lowered his estimate of the enemy as much as it had raised his self esteem. "If the whole detachment of the French," he wrote the Governor, "behave with no more resolution than this chosen party did, I flatter myself we shall have no great trouble in driving them to . . . Montreal."[210] He *flattered himself* indeed!

He retained enough of his usual prudence to appeal to Colonel Fry for immediate reinforcements, but declared in heroic vein:

"If there does not come a sufficient reenforcement, we must either quit our ground and retreat to you, or fight very unequal numbers, which I will do before I will give up one inch of what we have gained."[211]

The next day Washington's high spirits still had not evaporated. To his brother "Jack" he wrote:

"We expect every hour to be attacked by superior force, but, if they forbear one day longer, we shall be prepared for them. . . The Mingoes have struck the French and I hope will give a good blow before they have done. I expect forty odd of them here tonight, which, with our fort and some reenforcement from Colonel Fry, will enable us to exercise our noble courage with spirit."[212]

Those lines were written May 30. In the ensuing days, the eager young commander found more occasions to exercise his rhetoric and exercise the men at strengthening his "natural entrenchments" than to exercise his "noble courage."

On the second of June the escort which he had granted Half-King returned with eighty or more Indians. This event did not add eighty warriors to Washington's force; some of the new arrivals were women and children. It did greatly increase the number of mouths to be fed from his dwindling food supplies.[213]

Work on the fort was completed the next day, and the food problem became the most pressing one. Only the fortuitous arrival of a trader from the Ohio had saved the camp from going without flour for four days. On June 6, there was none left. The soldiers were grumbling and Washington feared the defection of his Indian allies.[214]

The same day, Christopher Gist rode into camp and informed the harried commander that Colonel Fry had died on the thirty-first, several days after falling from his horse.[215] The twenty-two-year-old Washington, who had served under fire for the first time a few days before, was now the top-ranking field officer in the colony's service.

Reinforcements to the number of one hundred eighty-one—three Virginia companies under the command of Captain Robert Stobo, Captain Andrew Lewis and Lieutenant George Mercer—arrived June 9. Stobo was a twenty-seven-year-old, socially charming wine bibber who found Williamsburg with its gay and elegant life more fascinating than his native Scotland—at least for a time.[216] Lewis and Mercer were Virginians lacking military experience but possessing much native ability.[217] Scarcely any of the men under them had ever been under fire. These reinforcements brought with them nine swivel guns. They were accompanied by Andrew Montour, an interpreter versed in English, French and several Indian tongues. This son of an Oneida chief and his half-breed wife looked like a European, but painted his face and wore brass pendants in his ears. His exotic appearance was enhanced by his habit of letting his shirt hang down underneath his scarlet waistcoat and over his breeches.[218]

Washington was now promoted to the rank of colonel. Major George Muse assumed Washington's old post of lieutenant-colonel, and Adam Stephen, the senior captain, became a major.[219]

Dinwiddie informed the new colonel, though, that Colonel James Innes, "an old, experienced officer" and captain in the British regular establishment, was "appointed Commander-in-Chief of all the forces." His arrival in Virginia was expected daily.[220]

Washington had no objection to serving under an older man who held the rank of colonel, but his pride smarted when Captain Mackay arrived in the middle of June with the independent company of one hundred from South Carolina and politely made it clear that he did not consider himself subordinate to a colonial colonel.[221]

Governor Dinwiddie had tried to prepare the Virginian's sensitive spirit for this relationship. Earlier that month he had written:

"The captains and officers of the independent companies having their commissions signed by His Majesty imagine they claim a distinguished rank, and, being long trained in arms, expect a suitable regard. You will therefore consult and agree with your officers to show them particular marks of esteem, which will avoid such causes of uneasiness as otherwise might obstruct His Majesty's service, wherein all are alike engaged, and must answer for any ill consequences of an unhappy disagreement."[222]

In reply, Washington had pledged show of due respect to Captain Mackay, but had challenged the Governor to end his equivocation. "[I] should have been particularly obliged if your Honor had declared whether he was under my command or independent of it. . . . I hope Captain Mackay will have more sense than to insist upon any unreasonable distinction, though he and his have commissions from His Majesty. . . . I must say that this will be a cancer that will grate some officers of this regiment beyond all measure to serve upon such different terms when their lives, their fortunes and their characters are equally, and I dare say as effectually, exposed as those who are happy enough to have King's Commissions."[223]

On the day after Mackay's arrival, Washington declared in a letter[224] to Dinwiddie that "two commanders are . . . incompatible" and said of the resulting situation, "Its absurdity is obvious." The young Virginian reported with some bitterness that Mackay refused to let the regulars work on the road without extra compensation, and declared with a martyr's anguish:

"I, therefore, shall continue to complete the worke we have begun with my poor fellows; we shall have the whole credit as none others have assisted. I hope from what has been said your Honor will see the necessity of giving your speedy orders on this head." In conclusion, he explained what Dinwiddie might have guessed from previous correspondence, "Rank, . . . to me, sir, is much dearer than . . . pay."[225]

The problem of command remained unresolved and the food problem grew worse.[226] A few chiefs and braves remained loyal, but the prospects of large-scale support from the Indians faded away with the realization that Washington had few gifts to offer them.[227] After advancing along the road to Red Stone Creek in the face of obstacles that would have caused many men to turn back, Washington, Mackay and the other officers decided that intelligence reports of overwhelming French reinforcements made it prudent for the English to retire to the fort at Great Meadows. There they would be nearer their supplies, whereas an attacking French force would find its supply problem complicated. The decision to "return to the fort . . . and wait there until supplied with a stock of provisions sufficient to serve us for some months" was reached unanimously at a council of war following the refusal of the Indian allies to continue with the English unless that step was taken.[228]

Subsisting on a diet of parched corn and lean beef, the Virginians dragged their swivels and ordnance back over the hills, cursing the British regulars who refused to touch the heavy equipment because they were not hired laborers.[229] Arriving on the first of July, they found the cupboards almost bare at Great Meadows. A small convoy arrived with just enough food to keep them and their hunger alive a little longer. Washington had to stand firm against those who wished to retreat to the settlements.[230] The colonel did not know what would develop, but he knew of the disembarkation at Alexandria of the Independent Companies from New York and supposed that they, having arrived three weeks before, would reach him soon.[231]

Weary men went to work felling trees to lengthen the field of fire. What Washington, at the height of his optimism, had pronounced a "charming field for an encounter" was in reality a marshy amphitheater with surrounding heights that would make excellent musket ranges for an enemy. Fortunately, the sodden ground probably precluded a direct assault from any direction but the South.[232]

Making the best of a bad location, Washington, by the night of July 2, had completed a fortified quadrilateral about one hundred feet on its longest side and sixty on its shortest. Trenches, embankments, and an unfinished stockade comprised the defenses.[233] Necessity had dictated its building, and Necessity it was named. The Indians' evaluation of it was evidenced by Washington's discovery that they had silently deserted camp. This loss deprived the colonel of his forest-wise reconnaissance contingent and, with a hundred or more of the remaining men sick or exhausted, reduced his effective fighting force to two hundred eighty-four.[234]

A shot woke the camp at dawn. A sentry had been shot in the heel. Maybe a marauding Indian was responsible. The chance could not be taken, though. Every man able to shoulder arms was ordered to be ready for action. But the only enemy apparent was the rain that began almost at the hour the alarm was given. For five hours it came down, drenching the men and their supplies and collecting in great puddles within the fortifications. The trenches threatened to become canals.[235]

About nine o'clock, the colonel received a reconnaissance report that a great force of naked French and Indians were only four miles away. Another report was that nine hundred French were on the march from the Monongahela.[236] There was nothing to do but wait and listen, straining to separate from the steady monotone of the rain any sound that might mean the approach of the enemy.

At eleven o'clock, a nervous sentinel caught sight of armed men and fired his musket. Three columns of French sprang forward from cover. Their shouts merged with the whoops of Indians.[237]

At once Washington led his men into the open, forming them to repel a charge and commanding them to hold fire. At six hundred yards, the French opened fire. Washington's line stood firm and suffered no losses.

As the French continued to advance, he ordered his men to drop back into the trenches. Here they were wet, but partially covered. Suddenly the French—some of them were only sixty yards away—dropped to the ground and seemed almost to vanish. Just as suddenly they disclosed their presence by a "constant, galling fire" from "every little rising, tree, stump, stone and bush."[238]

The young colonel did not lose his head. He ordered his men to shoot only when they saw a Frenchman. But his efforts to conserve ammunition were being thwarted by the rain and rising water in the trenches.

Horses, cows and dogs about the Virginians' camp became targets. Thus Washington's transport and a considerable portion of his potential food supply were destroyed.

The French enjoyed every advantage of cover. Late in the afternoon they found a new ally—fresh rain, "the most tremendous rain that [could] be conceived,"[239] said Washington. The men were already wet from crouching in the water of the trenches, but they had managed to keep their firelocks and part of their powder dry. Now the water permeated even the cartridge boxes. The falling off of the defenders' fire told the story of their plight to the enemy.

Fire from the attacking forces began to decline too. About eight o'clock, as the late twilight of summer began to dissolve the outlines of familiar landmarks, a shout came from the French: "Voulez-vous parler?" Told that the foreign words were an invitation to parley, Washington refused. This defiance was voiced by a commander who had only three days' rations to feed his men, less than two hundred of whom remained alive and unwounded from two hundred eighty-four who had been in fighting condition at the start of battle. Moreover, these men's muskets were useless, except for their bayonets, until the powder dried.

After a brief silence, the French shouted another proposal, that the commander of Fort Necessity send out a French-speaking officer to receive further propositions. In this way, Washington could communicate with the enemy without admitting any of them to the fort where they might appraise his defenses. The French pledged that any messenger sent by him would be permitted to return unharmed to the fort.

Washington assented, sending two French-speaking officers—William Peyroney and the always dependable Jacob van Braam—who returned with news that the French would permit the English to vacate the fort and return to Virginia as free men. The Virginia colonel refused the terms and sent Van Braam back to continue the negotiations.[240]

On his return to the fort, Van Braam—handicapped by his imperfect knowledge of both French and English—began the task of translating by flickering candlelight the terms of surrender which the French commander had scrawled on two damp sheets of paper. The Dutchman interpreted the terms as saying that the French had merely intended "to avenge" the death of one of their leaders (undoubtedly Jumonville), not to disturb the "bonne harmonie" between the King of England and His Most Christian Majesty of France.[241]

The commander of Fort Necessity and his entire garrison would be permitted to return, without insult or injury from the French, to their own country. The French would also make every attempt to restrain their Indian allies. The English could march out with the honors of war, leaving their artillery and munitions to the victorious attackers and leaving a guard of their own to protect their effects until draft animals could be sent for them. The English must free the Frenchmen taken prisoner after the engagement with Jumonville, returning them under escort to Fort Du Quesne. Two captains from the English forces were to remain as hostages under protective guard to insure return of the prisoners within two and a half months.[242]

By this time, some of Washington's men had broken into the rum supply and a considerable portion of his supposedly "effective fighting force" either was, or soon would be, disabled.[243]

The colonel sent Van Braam back to point out that surrender of their ammunition would leave the English at the mercy of hostile Indians on the hard march back to Wills Creek. The French commander struck out the offending words. Near midnight both Washington and Mackay signed. Captain Stobo and the faithful Van Braam would be the English hostages.[244]

That very night, standing on the muddy field of his defeat with the rain still falling, feeling unheroic in his sodden uniform, young Colonel Washington thanked Providence for his deliverance.[245]

About ten o'clock of the next morning, the fourth of July, the defeated garrison marched out with drums beating and colors flying. Out of sight of the French, their feet dragged as they slogged along the road to home and those who eagerly awaited news of victory.[246] Colonel Washington, unaccustomed to defeat, must then have been gloomy with the assurance that the fourth of July would ever be engraved on his memory with an inglorious significance that no subsequent event could ever erase.

* * *

The mood of the French was quite different. Coulon de Villiers, commander of the forces that took Fort Necessity and brother to the slain Jumonville, wrote in jubilation:

"We made them consent to sign that they had assassinated my brother in his camp; we had hostages for the security of the French who were in their power; we made them abandon the King's country; we obliged them to leave their cannon, nine pieces; we destroyed their horses and cattle and made them sign that the favors granted were evidence that we wanted to use them as friends."[247]

De Villiers' boast was substantially valid. Washington and Mackay had unwittingly signed terms that included a confession that the English had assassinated Jumonville. Of this fact, they were now aware. Virginians, and virtually all Englishmen, however, would dispute the statement that they had agreed to abandon the Ohio country. The English understood that they had agreed that the guard left to protect their goods near Fort Necessity would not work on any establishment west of the mountains within a year following the surrender, but did not admit that this same restriction applied to any men whom the English might send into that region.[248]

There was much bitterness over surrender on the terms signed, especially since defeat had so quickly followed an intoxicating taste of victory. As usual in such cases, the public had to have a scapegoat. Who more appropriate for the role than that confounded Dutchman? Was he not responsible for our Virginians' signing a document that, unbeknown to them, was a confession of murder? Van Braam was not present to defend himself, and few were willing to believe that he had translated incorrectly from ignorance rather than malevolence.[249]

There was some criticism of Washington, from Dinwiddie, William Johnson and others, for exposing his forces to attack by moving on to Red Stone Creek without awaiting reinforcements. Johnson attributed this imprudence to Washington's "being too ambitious of acquiring all the honor, or as much as he could, before the rest joined him."[250]

But Washington was a Virginian born and bred, and most Virginians were inclined to blame Van Braam and men from neighboring colonies for the defeat which they had suffered. Dinwiddie spoke justly when he attributed much of the difficulty to the failure of Virginia's neighbors to contribute their share to the expedition to secure the Ohio.[251] There could be little doubt that the General Assembly spoke for most Virginians when they voted thanks to Washington, Mackay and some of their fellow officers "for their late gallant and brave behavior in the defense of their country."[252]

With bitter irony, Governor Dinwiddie appraised the crisis:

"What a glorious situation is His Majesty's most ancient dominion in! There is nothing more certain than that the French could have cut off every one of our men and might have marched to Hampton without the least danger[;] and within these eight months not three men in Virginia would believe a syllable of the danger that threatened them if ever [the French] got a foot of land there. Again they must purchase it with blood. What a prospect of freedom appears to the slaves and servants on the frontier! It is not to be doubted they will meet with proper encouragement from the French whenever they choose to visit them; and how readily might all these evils have been remedied had our neighbors done their duty in lending their assistance."[253]

Under these circumstances, his Majesty's government was not inclined to remain aloof to events west of the mountains. Dinwiddie saw to it that complacency did not set in after the first shock. On July 24, he wrote:

"It's of great consequence to the nation and these colonies that . . . no time be lost, for if [the French] have a quiet settlement for two years, we shall never be able to root them out."[254]

Earlier he had recounted his disappointment in dealing with the other colonies, saying, "Every government except North Carolina has amused me with expectations that proved fruitless."[255] He now proposed that troops from England be used in the Ohio country and that they be supported by a poll tax levied on all the colonists.[256]

On September 11, the Earl of Albemarle, titular Governor of Virginia, expressed a similar thought in stronger terms. "Washington and many such," he wrote, "may have courage and resolution, but they have no knowledge or experience in our profession; consequently there can be no dependence on them. Officers, and good ones, must be sent to discipline the militia and to lead them on as this nation; we may then (and not before) drive the French back to their settlements and encroach on them as they do at present upon us."[257]

Governor Dinwiddie and the Council had entertained hopes for an autumn offensive, arguing that the French probably would be stronger in the spring of 1755. The Governor bitterly blamed the "obstinacy" of the Burgesses for the thwarting of this scheme.[258] But, with Virginia troops under Colonel Innes and Colonel Washington deserting and all the colonies in a state of unreadiness, the move—as Washington saw—would have been unwise.[259]

Washington had quarreled with the Governor in a rigidly polite manner several times—over the impractical plans for an autumn offensive, the Governor's penny-pinching while the men grumbled for pay, and other grievances—when he rode into Williamsburg October 21. There he learned that money for colonial defense had arrived from England, and more money and arms would be sent later. The General Assembly was moving toward appropriations "for the protection of His Majesty's subjects against the insults and encroachments of the French."[260]

Governor Dinwiddie, acting as His Majesty's agent, had summoned Governor Sharpe of Maryland to the Virginia capital for a conference with him and Governor Dobbs of North Carolina. Sharpe had just been commissioned a Lieutenant Colonel and, by royal order, assigned command of the forces to "be raised on this part of the continent to protect His Majesty's dominions from the encroachments and devastations of his presumptuous enemies."[261] Thus even Colonel Innes, Dinwiddie's choice to command Virginia's troops, would be subordinate to the Maryland Governor.

The three governors, encouraged by reports of reduction of French forces on the Ohio, were agreed upon a fuzzily defined plan to march to Fort Du Quesne as soon as Sharpe could raise a force of seven hundred to be augmented by the independent companies. Blank commissions of the rank of captain and lieutenant would be sent from England to Dinwiddie, who would fill in the names of colonials whom he deemed capable.[262] In this way, provincial officers could become part of the regular forces. Washington disapproved the campaign plan as rash and ill-timed, but he struck out at the greatest flagellant to his indignation when he exclaimed:

"Every captain bearing the King's commission, every half-pay officer, or other, appearing with such a commission would rank before me." Accordingly, declaring, "I think the disparity between the present offer of a company and my former rank too great to expect any real satisfaction or enjoyment in a corps where I once did, or thought I had a right to, command," he tendered his resignation as colonel of the Virginia regiment and had it accepted.[263]

Washington's resignation provided a topic of conversation in Williamsburg and elsewhere in Virginia, as did almost every phase of military organization to meet the French threat. But it could have been a matter of only passing interest in England, and that to few persons. The *London Magazine* had quoted Washington as saying after his first military engagement that there was "something charming in the sound" of bullets, and the King had commented, "He would not say so if he had been used to hear many."[264] But the ruler must soon have forgotten the officer's name. It did not seem likely that a King George of England would have occasion to remember a raw young provincial named George Washington.

PART II (OF CHAPTER VIII)

Though Governor Sharpe was acting commander-in-chief of the military forces being assembled in the colonies, he consulted with Dinwiddie on major matters and the Virginia Governor continued to be the civilian coordinator of intercolonial preparations. Inasmuch as Dinwiddie's initiative had prompted the home government's action and had first roused the other colonies to a semblance of cooperation in the common defense, this respect was due him.

Both Sharpe and Dinwiddie were determined to wrest from the French in 1755 the territory lost to them in 1754. The Maryland Governor agreed with his Virginia colleague that officers and troops from England were needed. Both, however, were fully aware of the necessity of raising colonial troops as well.[265] Sharpe shared Dinwiddie's long-time belief that the Indian allies must be secured as an important part of any large-scale campaign in the Ohio country. The two Governors agreed upon the necessity of building a fort at Wills Creek for the protection of the vast store of provisions that would have to be accumulated to supply both the colonial troops and the soldiers sent from England.[266]

Dinwiddie and Sharpe were learning about some of the supply problems which had vexed Washington. Visiting Wills Creek in November, the Maryland Governor was chagrined to find both the fort under construction and the stockpile far from adequate. Wagons were scarce and farmers were reluctant to part with their horses.[267]

More in duty than in hope, Dinwiddie, on November 8, had appealed to his fellow Governors for men or money to prosecute the war. Before the month was over, he cried in exasperation:

"It's a monstrous thing to think of the supineness and backwardness of our neighboring colonies in granting supplies. South Carolina, Pennsylvania and the Jerseys have granted none."[268] Pennsylvania was a rich colony and would stand to gain or lose as much as any of her neighbors in a full-fledged North American struggle between England and France, but her Assembly announced its intentions of remaining aloof because no French forts had been built within her boundaries.[269] The conflict had begun as Virginia's war, and some of the other colonies were quite willing for it to remain just that.

Dinwiddie was having a serious recruitment problem within his own colony. In October, he had determined to raise a force of two thousand men.[270] His lack of success could be measured by the downward revision of his goal, first to one thousand, and finally to eight hundred in the hope that the latter number might be reached by February 1755.[271] He continued efforts to augment this force with Indian warriors, renewing his overtures to the Catawbas and Cherokees in the face of Governor Glen's mounting irritation over the Virginia Governor's interference with tribesmen within South Carolina's borders.[272]

Dinwiddie's greatest consolation, though, was his hope that British regulars would be sent in sufficient numbers. On November 16, he had written the Lords of Trade:

"Without two regiments of men from Britain, we shall not be able effectually to defeat the unjust invasion of the French."[273]

Before the end of 1754, he learned that "troops from home" would be convoyed to Virginia by a fifty-gun ship and that two more regiments would be raised in New England and commanded by Governor William Shirley of Massachusetts and Sir William Pepperell.[274]

On January 9 of the new year, Sir John St. Clair, Scottish baronet and former major of the Twenty-second Foot, arrived in Virginia to assume the duties connected with his newly assigned local rank of lieutenant colonel and post of Deputy Quartermaster General of forces in America. He soon made it apparent that he was a master of that efficiency which Dinwiddie so much admired in the trained British soldier. Before long, he had contracted for a hundred pack horses, arranged for hospital facilities at Hampton, and ridden to Winchester and from there (over what he pronounced the worst road he had ever traveled) to Wills Creek, renamed Fort Cumberland. There he reviewed the independent companies and, finding more than forty of the men inferior by his standards, discharged them.[275] How long it took to recruit forty men in Virginia!

Meanwhile Virginians learned that two British regiments, commanded by Colonel Sir Peter Halkett and Colonel Thomas Dunbar, were already on their way to the colony. On the night of February 19, the ships *Centurion, Syren* and *Norwich* dropped anchor off Hampton. The *Centurion* was Commodore Keppel's flagship, but the *Norwich* was more interesting to Virginians, because aboard it was Major General Edward Braddock, newly appointed His Majesty's Commander-in-Chief of the forces in North America.[276]

The same issue of the *Virginia Gazette*, published in Williamsburg, that carried the news of the general's arrival bore a front page editorial that showed awareness in the colonies that Virginia's war was now of global significance. Captioned "Extract from McKennedy's consideration on the present state of the affairs of the Northern colonies, published at New York,"[277] it declared:

"As France has hitherto, by the means of Great Britain chiefly, been prevented from enslaving mankind, they are become of course our implacable and most inveterate enemies, and of late everywhere our competitors in trade and encroachers upon our territories; regardless of all faith, oaths or treaties, their national policy being one continued train of chicane and deceit.

"Their late encroachments upon His Majesty's rights and territories in the East and West Indies, in Africa, and in Hudson's Bay, with the most provoking circumstances, are so well known that I believe I need not mention them. And now they seem avowedly, and with much assurance to open the same shameful scheme upon this continent, which they have indeed been long practicing under-hand . . ."

Another paragraph of the same editorial must have infuriated General Braddock when he read it, as he almost surely did. (The *Gazette* was the only journal in the colony, and each issue consisted of only four small pages.) "Regular troops," the writer declared, "are of little use here, farther than to fight behind walls; it is by means of the Indians, and by them only, that any stop can be put to those wicked encroachments."

General Braddock could not be expected to agree. The son of a lieutenant colonel of the Coldstream Guards and himself a veteran of forty-five years in the British Army, the sixty-year-old[278] Major General had the respect for formal military training of a man who had seen long service with much experience in administration, but little in fighting. This short, stout officer who had labored through forty-four years of routine before being promoted above the rank of colonel had a regard for form equal to that of the Deputy Quarter-master General who had preceded him.[279]

Edmund Randolph, a small boy at the time of Braddock's arrival, wrote of the general in later years:

"It was said that the Duke of Cumberland, the generalissimo of Great Britain, had selected him as a man who could fight the devil; misapprehending the nature of this service so as to conceive that undauntedly to face death was, of itself, competency against an enemy trained in the stratagems and retreats suggested by a wilderness uncleared and almost untrodden by a European foot."[280]

Most of those who accompanied Braddock seemed to share a confidence in the ability of regular forces to take effective command of the North American situation. Certainly Captain Robert Orme, the general's aide-de-camp, was not one to question the adequacy of British regulars. A socially charming young man, almost completely ignorant about America, he had been reared in the army.[281]

If we may judge from the evidence of a single diary, even greater confidence was felt by those aboard the transports from Ireland which arrived in March with Braddock's rear companies and stores.

One Mrs. Charlotte Browne, who came along with her brother for the trip, wrote in her journal[282] on March 10:

"At 4 in the afternoon made Cape Henry a fair wind & at 7 cast anchor in Hamton Road. All in great spirits. 4 officers came on board. Drank out 15 bottles of port all in the cabbin drunk (but Mr. Charrington) to be free of Hamton."

The abstemious Mr. Charrington was not otherwise identified. The heavy drinking was to celebrate the clearing of the port of Hampton, because the vessels were proceeding thence to Alexandria, where the expedition was being organized. Clearly there was no reluctance to meet the enemy.

Mrs. Browne seems to have expected that the amenities of life as known in the officers' quarters of European garrisons would be observed along the line of march. There was little to disillusion her, even during the first few days after leaving Alexandria. The June 4 entry in her journal reads:

"At break of day my coachman came and tapped at my chamber door and said Madam all is ready."

She later pursued her journey separate from the armed forces, all the while eagerly awaiting news of the anticipated British victory. By July 17, she had begun "roughing it," but the trip was still a lark. "I received an invitation," Mrs. Browne recorded, "to go to General Johnson's to see the Indians dance."

September 20, she found herself in what she regarded as undesirable society as she paused at "Frederick's Town," Maryland in the course of the western jaunt. "I had an invitation to go to a ball which was composed of Romans, Jews and heretics who in this town flock together." Mrs. Browne had gone far enough along the road to the field of conflict between empires to realize that she could not have the amenities all the way. Critically, she observed: "The ladies danced without stays or hoops."

By that time, the expedition against the French had passed its climax. Much planning and labor had gone into the venture—also much optimism and easy assumption of a sort akin to Mrs. Browne's.

General Braddock's "military family" included, besides Captain Orme, another aide-de-camp—Roger Morris of Pennsylvania, and a secretary—William Shirley, son of the Governor of Massachusetts. George Washington, unwilling to serve with a captain's rank but covetous of opportunities for learning and glory, had left the delights of his newly acquired Mount Vernon estate to serve as a voluntary aide to the General.[283] A man of insular views, Braddock was seeing the world through two pairs of prejudiced eyes—his own and St. Clair's.[284] Frustrated by delay as he sought to execute his instructions to help the Governors "to prevail upon the Assemblies" for financial support of the campaign, he had written as early as March 18:

"I am almost in despair of the [Assemblies'] complying . . ., from the jealousy of the people and the disunion of the several colonies, as well among themselves as with one another."[285]

He was "impatient" with the Governor of Massachusetts and convinced that Pennsylvania was guilty of "pusillanimous and improper behavior,"[286] and probably accepted St. Clair's attribution of "sloth and ignorance"[287] to the Virginians. Two of the few exceptions to his blanket contempt for everything in America were Governor Dinwiddie, whose zeal and energy he admired,[288] and George Washington, who had won the general's respect at first meeting.[289]

Braddock's plans were unfolded at a Governors' conference which convened April 14 in Alexandria, Virginia with Governors Dinwiddie, Sharpe of Maryland, Morris of Pennsylvania and Shirley of Massachusetts in attendance, besides Commodore Keppel and the general himself.[290] In all essential respects, the plans had been formulated in England, principally by the Duke of Cumberland.

Wills Creek was to be the assembly point of the expedition which Braddock would lead against Fort Du Quesne. Having captured that objective, he was to proceed to Fort Niagara, a French stronghold and portage near the western shores of Lake Ontario, arriving in time to assist regiments under Shirley and Pepperell in giving the *coup de grace*.[291] Another assault was to be made on Fort Frédéric, a fortress on the southern shores of Lake Champlain at Crown Point, from which the French not only could imperil the Hudson Valley but might be able to send forth an expedition to separate New England from the colonies to the South. This attack would be commanded by the famous Indian agent William Johnson. This shrewd man was also entrusted with responsibility for the conduct of all relations with the tribes.[292]

The Governors pledged their colonies to aid him in this diplomatic task by providing a fund for the presents so essential in negotiations with Indians. They also promised to provide a garrison for Fort Du Quesne, so that Braddock, after capturing it, could safely move on to Fort Niagara. They did not, however, pledge to provide a common fund to finance the campaign.[293]

To Braddock's disappointment over the conference was added the shock of learning that sixty to seventy miles of mountainous country —not the mere fifteen he had supposed—lay between him and Fort Du Quesne. He was in a black mood when, on April 19, he wrote back to England:

"I have been greatly disappointed by the neglect and supineness of the Assemblies of the provinces with which I am concerned; they promised great matters and have done nothing, whereby instead of forwarding they have obstructed the service. When I get to Wills Creek, I will send you . . . what other information or intelligence I shall get there, it being impracticable to get any here, the people of this part of the country laying it down for a maxim, never to speak truth upon any account."[294]

Still an exception to his condemnation of colonials, though, was George Washington who was appointed "aid de camp to His Excellency General Braddock" on May 10.[295] Four days later, the ambitious young Virginian revealed his reaction to the appointment, confiding in a letter to his brother:

"I shall serve this campaign agreeably enough, as I am thereby freed from all commands but his [General Braddock's], and give orders to all, which must be implicitly obeyed."[296]

He never mailed the note. Perhaps, after reading it over, he concluded that it was too naively self-revealing.

Braddock's distrust of colonials was almost matched by their distrust of him. Many, of course, were overawed by his military rank, but others were shocked by his failure to acquire greater familiarity with conditions of warfare in North America. Some of these trusted to the general's subordinates to compensate for his defects.[297]

Even among those who had full confidence in the force of British arms, there were criticisms of the organization of the campaign. Many of the troops themselves were demoralized during long periods of idleness and waiting by hard liquor and the availability of Indian girls willing to ease their loneliness.[298]

Braddock proposed to march the one hundred ten miles from Wills Creek to Fort Du Quesne in six stages.[299] By May 30 the advance force had begun the march and been quickly disillusioned about the ease of their task. Captain Orme reported:

"Major Chapman marched . . . at daybreak, and it was night before the whole baggage had got over a mountain about two miles from the camp. The ascent and descent were almost a perpendicular rock; three wagons were entirely destroyed . . . and many more were extremely shattered."[300]

The shattered wagons were a serious loss. The expedition already was crippled by inadequate transport. Movement was further complicated by the fact that the general's artillery was too heavy for the rocky wilderness road over the mountains. Braddock spoke truly when he said that colonial leaders had misled him about the number of vehicles that would be available, but he wrongly ascribed their motivation when he accused them of deliberate deceit. They were inclined to the generous estimates of a new land where most things seemed boundless, and they had had little experience in obtaining transport from rugged individualists in whom the love of property was preternaturally strong. Nevertheless, Braddock's march was not delayed more than about two weeks by the inadequacy of his transport.[301]

A more serious loss was that of Indian allies whose defection dated from the English defeat at Fort Necessity. Braddock, though appreciative of Indian usefulness in reconnaissance, was not cognizant of the natives' value in actual fighting. Even had he been, though, it is doubtful that he could have rallied many tribes for a war against the French, whose show of strength at Necessity had left a strong impression.[302]

Progress was made both difficult and hazardous by Braddock's ignorance of the terrain and even of the distances to be traversed. The general, however, was undismayed. To Benjamin Franklin, a Pennsylvanian who had risen in the old soldier's estimation as Dinwiddie fell, he had written:

"Fort Du Quesne can hardly detain me three or four days; and then I see nothing that can obstruct my march to Niagara. . . . These savages may, indeed, be a formidable enemy to your raw American militia; but upon the king's regular and disciplined troops, sir, it is impossible they should make any impression."[303]

The general advanced from Fort Cumberland toward Fort Du Quesne without pausing to establish depots or magazines at the several stages of his progress.[304]

On July 8, Braddock and the main force were encamped at a spot about two miles from the East bank of the Monongahela River and ten to twelve miles from Du Quesne.[305] Five days before, Sir John St. Clair had proposed that this body halt to await the arrival of Colonel Dunbar with the rest of the troops. The suggestion was rejected by fellow officers who argued that delay would reduce the store of provisions and increase French opportunities for preparation.[306] And so, on the eighth, the British found themselves just twelve miles or less from their objective. But the river, a stream, and an abrupt ascent and descent lay between in the difficult area known as the Narrows. Therefore an advance under cover of darkness to surround the fort was ruled out in favor of one more day's march before attempting the surprise march by night.[307]

Though the camp was astir at two o'clock the next morning and excited over the prospect of victory, it was not till eight o'clock that General Braddock reached the first crossing. The two crossings were made with ease. If the enemy had been aware of the approach and prepared to attack the British, they surely would have done so by now. One of those present reported, "Men hugged themselves with joy at our good luck in having surmounted our greatest difficulties."[308]

Before two o'clock in the afternoon, St. Clair's men had made a passageway through a bluff that seemed to be the principal remaining natural obstacle.[309] The bright sunlight shone on a long file of redcoats that moved down the incline and across the ford. To Washington, who had just rejoined the campaign after serious illness and even now sat with cushions tied into his saddle, the sight was "the most beautiful spectacle [he had] ever beheld."[310]

Here Braddock's spit-and-polish efficiency showed to best advantage. Here in a wilderness were the order and organization of a British parade ground—about fifteen hundred men forming a column of about nineteen hundred yards[311] that moved along with the precision of a scarlet caterpillar. Now they were safely across.

Suddenly shots rang out! Volley after volley echoed in the forest. About three hundred French and Indians—scarcely distinguishable one from another in their near nudity—were rushing toward the British. Quickly they divided and began to encircle the head and flanks of Braddock's column. War whoops rang out all around. Some French and Indians dropped before the British bullets. Braddock's advance force fell back fifty to sixty yards. Red-coated officers, sitting properly erect in their saddles, were easy targets.

St. Clair, with his life's blood flowing away, rallied his men—but only for a moment. Panic seized Gage's troops, then St. Clair's. Soon all was confused flight, with fleeing men running smack into those, almost as confused, attempting to advance.

Braddock rode to the front where a huddled mass of British soldiers fired wildly, part of the time shooting each other. But the old general's wits were not the equal of his courage. Arrived on the scene, he did not know what order to give.

St. Clair pressed his way through the milling mass to shout to his commander, "For God's sake, take the northern hill before we're surrounded!"[312] Then he collapsed.

Braddock charged Washington with the duty of rounding up

officers to lead a party of 150 up the hill. The Virginian tried manfully, even after two horses were shot under him, and three bullets
had passed through his hat and a fourth through his uniform.
Meanwhile, Braddock was attempting to carry out the same assignment he had given Washington. Five bullets had hit his mounts. A
sixth pierced his right arm and lodged in his lung. Frenchmen and
Indians continued to fire from every kind of natural cover.

At sunset, heavier fire was heard. Whatever nerve the men had,
cracked then. In Washington's words, "they broke and ran as sheep
pursued by dogs," some discarding arms and clothing in their mad
flight. Washington and others attempted to halt the stampede but,
by his own admission, "met with as much success as if we had
attempted [to stop] the wild boars of the mountains."[313]

Washington placed Braddock in a small cart and got him across
the river. Three hundred wounded and helpless were left on the
battlefield to the mercy of the Indians.[314]

The British general now asked Washington to ride through the
night to Dunbar, who was advancing toward Du Quesne, to warn
him of what had happened. Weak from fever, battle and twelve
hours in the saddle, the Virginian nevertheless undertook the mission
without complaint.[315]

Late on the morning of the tenth, after a nightmare ride over
corpses and past dying men whose cries of help must be disregarded
to save the lives of many more, Washington reached Dunbar's
camp.[316] Braddock arrived on the evening of the same day, having
been forced to ride horseback in the agony of death after soldiers
refused to carry him. On the night of the thirteenth of July, the
general instructed Orme to report promptly to Keppel, telling him
that "nothing could equal the gallantry and good conduct of the
officers nor the bad behavior of the men."[317] About nine o'clock, he
breathed his last. It was the general's recently acquired young
friend, George Washington, who directed his burial in this strange
country.[318].

Arrived safely at Wills Creek about two days later, the Virginian
took occasion to contradict to his brother reports of his own death
and dying speech.[319] But six of the twelve Virginia company officers
in the battle had been killed. Casualties, dead or wounded, numbered
977 in a force of 1,459.[320] Colonel Dunbar, convinced of the hopeless-
ness of the situation, proposed abandonment of Fort Cumberland and
withdrawal to winter quarters in Philadelphia.[321]

Such a move would leave the frontier exposed. Therefore, announcement of the decision struck terror in the hearts of Virginians in the Shenandoah Valley and even in the Piedmont section. They still reeled from the shock of Braddock's defeat, and the general withdrawal that followed stimulated visions of thousands of French soldiers and bloodthirsty savages swooping down on almost defenseless farms. The task of raising a volunteer army to repel invaders seemed almost impossible. Nearly every family man felt that his first duty was to protect his own wife and children by remaining with them.[322] Besides, the sturdy English, Scotch-Irish and Palatinate Germans who made their home on or near the frontier were an independent people hostile to regimentation.

Those colonists intent upon blaming someone for the defeat at the Monongahela heaped censure upon the British regulars. By contrast, Washington, who had conducted himself with a gallantry equal to that of the British officers and had respectfully but fecklessly pointed out to his superiors the differences between continental and frontier warfare, emerged a hero. He was recommissioned colonel and made commander-in-chief of Virginia forces,[323] and thus fell heir to a defense problem that might well have vexed history's greatest commanders.

Operating from headquarters at Winchester, he issued commands to a people to whom any discipline except self-discipline was only a word. When he issued a call to arms, not only apathy, but firm-spoken defiance, was the response. One captain of militia answered that it was "impossible for him to come" inasmuch as his "wife, family and corn" and those of his soldiers "were all at stake."[324] Later another militia officer reported that his men had "absolutely refused to stir, choosing, as they say, to die with their wives and families."[325] No wonder Washington cried in desperation:

"Such is the example of the officers; such the behavior of the men; and upon such circumstances depends the safety of our country!"[326]

Colonel Washington, early in 1756, called for legislation that would empower him "to enforce military law in all its parts."[327] Indian forays and the threat of more and larger incursions give force to the colonel's insistence. The Assembly did not comply with his request for martial law patterned "after our Mother Country," but it did authorize the raising, equipping and drilling of a substantial quota of Virginia troops and appropriated the equivalent of three million dollars for defense. Preparations were made for the erection of forts.[328]

If frontiersmen were too ruggedly independent to be well-disciplined soldiers, most of the Tidewater militiamen were familiar with Indian fighting only by hearsay. Commissions as militia officers were notable mainly for the social distinction that they conferred or confirmed. Trying to rouse the spirit of a group of volunteers, Samuel Davies, prominent Presbyterian divine, expressed a hope that ventured on prophecy. "I cannot but hope," he said, "that Providence has raised up the heroic youth, Colonel Washington, whom hitherto Providence has preserved in so signal a manner, for some important service to his country."[329]

Nevertheless, one man—however remarkable—could do only so much. He could and did train his men in bush fighting. But he could not prevent frontier raids in which Indians smashed the skulls of the men, scalped the children and bore off the women to provide amusement in camp.[330] Washington was not given to emotional comment, but in the spring of 1756, he wrote Governor Dinwiddie:

"The supplicating tears of the women, and moving petitions of the men, melt me into such deadly sorrow, that I solemnly declare, if I know my own mind, I could offer myself a willing sacrifice to the butchering enemy, provided that would contribute to the people's ease."[331]

Governor Dinwiddie had dispatched Peter Randolph and William Byrd envoys to gain the support of three important Southern tribes—the Cherokees, Catawbas and Tuscaroras. They induced the Indians to come to Virginia, but these new-found allies plundered on the way up and soon headed back, still pillaging as they went. Fighting broke out between them and the frontier settlers, thus adding Indian enemies in the South to those already giving so much trouble in the North and West.[332] An expedition led against one of the latter tribes —the Shawnees—turned back before reaching its objective when even so strong a leader as Andrew Lewis lost control of his ill-fed men.[333]

Dumas, architect of the victory over Braddock and commandant at Fort Du Quesne, was exultant:

"I have succeeded in ruining the three adjacent provinces, Pennsylvania, Maryland, and Virginia, driving off the inhabitants, and totally destroying a tract of country thirty miles wide, reckoning from the line of Fort Cumberland. M. de Contrecoeur had not been gone a week before I had six or seven different war parties in the field at once, always accompanied by Frenchmen. Thus far we have lost only two officers and a few soldiers; but the Indian villages are full of prisoners of every age and sex."[334]

The year 1755, with Braddock's defeat and Governor Shirley's failure to take Fort Niagara, had been so disastrous for British arms in America that William Johnson was rewarded with a knighthood for a small victory over the French on Lake George, even though he was unable to capture Crown Point on Lake Champlain.[335] The success on Lake George was the only British triumph in North America that year.[336] The two succeeding years were even worse. Through the whole tragedy of Braddock's defeat and frontier slaughter, the kingdoms of George II and Louis XV had been officially at peace.

Under the Earl of Loudoun as his Majesty's Commander-in-Chief in North America, the British suffered so many reverses that the brightest spot in the entire picture was the feat of Washington's militia in holding the Shenandoah Valley line against repeated onslaughts by France's Indian allies.[337] The brilliant young French General Montcalm took Oswego, the English fort on Lake Ontario, then moved down Lake Champlain to Lake George. Near the scene of Johnson's brief triumph, he captured Fort William Henry. Britain's Admiral Newcastle reluctantly allowed a Canadian-bound French convoy of three thousand troops to escape because he respected the "peace" officially existing between his country and France. Admiral Boscawen did not succeed in turning them away at the mouth of the St. Lawrence.[338]

Before the end of 1756, the war became official. Soon it extended to all parts of the world. Old alliances were abandoned for new ones. Austria came to the support of France. Frederick the Great, of Prussia, invaded Saxony and fought at England's side. Most of the other German states allied themselves with France. Russia and Sweden also came to Louis' aid.[339] By 1761, France, Austria, Russia, Sweden, Spain, and most of the German states stood opposed to England, Portugal and Prussia.

England was supposed to have the strongest navy in the world and Prussia the strongest army. Nevertheless, the issue was long in doubt, and in the early stages the odds favored Louis' alliance.[340] By the end of 1757, Britain's Admiral Byng had been courtmartialed and shot on the deck of his ship for his conduct of the Battle of Minorca, which he lost to the French. This Mediterranean disaster was matched by a continental one. King Frederick, despite his brilliance, was beaten by the French and Austrians; and King George's son, the Duke of Cumberland, was forced to surrender his English and Hanoverian troops to Louis' officers. The war was being waged in Asia as well as America and Europe, and with uniformly disappointing results for the British. English hopes in India fell with Calcutta.[341]

By 1758, England's position was so desperate that his Majesty's ministers turned for leadership to William Pitt, obnoxious both to the King and the dominant Whigs by reason of his bluntness and independence and hitherto tolerated in the councils of government only because his fiery genius, searing eloquence and glowing integrity were feared as an avenging flame. The formal title of Prime Minister was withheld from him, but his powers were such that George II soon complained that he did not rule in his own kingdom.[342]

By a boldly dramatic gesture, Pitt quickly fired the English people—military, naval and civil—with his own burning enthusiasm and confidence. He informed the Dutch and German troops who had been brought to Britain to man the island kingdom's defenses that their services were no longer needed. Much to the alarm of some of his countrymen, who feared another Jacobite rebellion,[343] he began recruiting regiments of Scotch Highlanders and thus added to the Army some of the world's finest warriors. Not only did he refuse continental aid for England's defense, but soon was sending more English troops to the defense of the Continent. He also induced Parliament to appropriate large sums to subsidize Frederick's armies.[344]

Perhaps the greatest of Pitt's many contributions in the hour of crisis was his recognition of the fact that the struggle was a world war and his capacity to conceive its strategy on a global scale. Coupled with this factor was his perception that North America, the territory where the war had begun, should be its principal theater.[345] With Prussia's subsidized soldiers fighting under Frederick's brilliant generalship in Europe and a rejuvenated British navy keeping French ships in port, the strength of England's armies could be concentrated in America.

To command these troops he named able and dynamic generals. Ignoring the sputtering indignation of older officers hitherto complacent in their seniority, Pitt thrust aside their claims to name General Jeffrey Amherst commander-in-chief of his Majesty's forces in North America. He gave a brigadier general's commission to James Wolfe, a thirty-one-year-old imaginative genius, thereby affrighting a number of stolid citizens who distrusted both imagination and genius.

The results of Pitt's policies were soon manifest. Louisbourg, the fortress returned to the French by the Treaty of Aachen in 1748 after its capture in 1745 by the New Englanders, was rewon while at its greatest strength in July 1758 by the good generalship of Amherst and Wolfe. New England could rejoice, too, over the capture of Fort Frontenac at the junction of the St. Lawrence and Lake Ontario, a feat accomplished by a provincial force under Massachusetts' Colonel Dudley Bradstreet.[346]

The defeat at the Monongahela still rankled in the colonial mind, however; and in the Middle and Southern colonies, Du Quesne was an ego-piercing name. General Forbes, in command of English regular and colonial forces in this territory, moved against the fort. He was better prepared than Braddock had been and benefited from Washington's advice.

These advantages, however, were almost thrown away. A vanguard action, undertaken by a subordinate during Forbes' inopportune illness and involving eight hundred men, nearly ended in a disaster reminiscent of Braddock's defeat. The panic of the British militia, thrown into wild alarm by their first experience with Indians and French ambush by Indian methods, was offset only by the Virginia militia, which fought a valiant and effective rear-guard action. Hero of the day, and rightly so, was Colonel Washington.[347]

Before winter, the Indians—perceiving the turn of battle—deserted the French, and the French thereupon abandoned and destroyed the fort. Thus, some weeks after the abortive and costly action undertaken by a too hasty subordinate, Forbes was enabled to celebrate a bloodless triumph. Preparations were quickly made for the erection of a new fort bearing Pitt's name.[348]

The victories in America were matched by triumphs in Europe and Asia. Frederick had burst through the encircling French, Russian and Austrian forces, and added his name to the list of history's great captains by his shining successes at Rossbach, Leuthen and Crefeld.[349] In India, Clive, the civilian clerk who had become one of his century's most unorthodox commanders, proved himself one of its most brilliant.[350]

The year was one of spectacular triumphs engineered by extraordinary men. But its successor was even more remarkable. On the Continent, Frederick crowned earlier victories with dramatic success at Minden. More immediately significant to the American colonists was the British Navy's success at Quiberon Bay on the coast of France, an accomplishment which made it impossible for the French to reinforce their troops in Canada. The Army and the Navy shared glory in the conquest of Guadeloupe in the West Indies. On the mainland of North America, Sir William Johnson took Fort Niagara, guardian of the western lands.

Even this achievement, however, was dwarfed by the climactic battle of the year—Wolfe's assault on Quebec. The fortress had thrice successfully resisted the power of British arms, and now was commanded by General Montcalm, an officer of considerable reputation. Wolfe had only four thousand men, but he counted upon the cooperation of a force personally led by Amherst. Amherst, though he succeeded in taking Crown Point and Ticonderoga, failed to arrive in time. Older heads might have been deterred by this misfortune, but the thirty-two-year-old general and his chief lieutenants, Robert Monckton and George Townshend, thirty-three and thirty-five years old respectively, pressed on.

Following the failure of two assaults on the citadel, Wolfe devised a scheme which enabled him secretly to gain the Plains of Abraham, from which elevation his concentrated musketry could command the city. Only one volley from the English guns was necessary on that fateful day of September 13 when Quebec changed hands. As he had advanced by boat up the St. Lawrence River toward his goal, the tall, gaunt young general had quoted aloud Gray's famous verse:

> "The boast of heraldry, the pomp of power,
>   "And all that beauty, all that wealth e'er gave,
> "Awaits alike the inevitable hour:—
>   "The paths of glory lead but to the grave."[351]

In moving forward to his objective, he had set his feet in the path of glory. On his day of triumph, that path had led him to his grave. For he died on the Plains of Abraham after learning that he had won. Montcalm died on the same day.[352]

Clearly, the course of the war in America was decided, and Pitt knew that America was the decisive theater. Small wonder that Horace Walpole reported that the bells of London were worn with the pealing of victories in 1759;[353] and that David Garrick spoke for many Englishmen when, in a song celebrating "this wonderful year," he wrote, "We'll fight and we'll conquer again and again."[354]

The next year Montreal surrendered, and the realistic French knew that they were beaten. Surprisingly enough, many of France's Indian allies chose to continue the struggle.[355]

The European phase of the war was not cleanly concluded.

Spain entered the fight against England and in 1762 repented her rashness when both Havana and Manila fell to the English. George III, who had come to the throne in times less perilous than some his predecessor had known, decided he had rather dispense with Pitt's genius than endure his proud independence. Accordingly this remarkable man, the only English statesman "who carried the map of the empire in his head and in his heart"[356] and for nearly half a decade the dictator of its war effort, was dismissed from office. Little men sought to buy peace at the price of some of Pitt's hard-won conquests. There was even talk of returning Canada to France in exchange for the island of Guadeloupe. But this particular folly was not committed. The Peace of Paris, concluded in 1763, confirmed England's possession of French Canada and indeed of all of North America east of the Mississippi, for Spanish Florida was ceded to the British. England also gained four of the islands of the West Indies and some possessions in Africa. India, an empire in itself, became a British dominion. England's triumph was even greater than the land transfers would indicate, for the island kingdom had secured domination of the seas. Between 1758 and 1762, England had captured or destroyed nine-tenths of all warships flying the flag of France.[357]

The hostilities ended by the Peace of Paris were known in America as the French and Indian War and in Europe as the Seven Years' War. "Virginia's war" had become a global conflict.

Yet the label "Virginia's war" was not entirely inappropriate. As Louis Koontz said of the contest, in describing Dinwiddie's role: "It was begun in his attempt to protect Virginia territory. The first hostile forces sent out were Virginians; and the first blood was shed by Virginians."[358] Moreover, Virginia's Governor was responsible for interesting the Crown in extensive operations to combat the French threat in North America. It was also he who initiated and coordinated communication among the colonies in preparation for large-scale conflict. Even when the struggle had become a world war, North America remained its principal theater and it was the Virginia militia under Colonel Washington's command that prevented one of the principal British expeditions in that arena from terminating in disaster instead of success. Virginia, together with New England, bore the brunt of the colonial struggle, while other colonies hesitated, quibbled and, generally speaking, made only a half-hearted contribution. When the French withdrew from North America and most of the British regulars sailed for home, to Virginia principally fell the task of finishing the war with France's Indian allies—a wearing, daily effort, long on hardship and short on glory.

Voltaire, sixty years old when a young Virginia officer named Washington fought a losing battle at Fort Necessity, wrote:

"Such was the complication of political interests that a cannon shot fired in America could give the signal that set Europe in a blaze."[359]

More than a century after the Treaty of Paris, Thackeray wrote:

"It was strange that in a savage forest of Pennsylvania a young Virginia officer should fire a shot and waken up a war which was to last for sixty years, which was to cover his own country and pass into Europe, to cost France her American Colonies, to sever ours from us and create the Western Republic; to rage over the Old World when extinguished in the New, and of all the myriads engaged in the vast contest, to leave the prize of the greatest fame with him who struck the first blow."[360]

John Richard Green, in his monumental *History of the English People*, saw the war and its effects in even broader scope. He proclaimed it "no exaggeration to say that three of the many victories of the Seven Years War determined for ages to come the destinies of mankind. With that of Rossbach began the recreation of Germany; with that of Plassey the influence of Europe told for the first time since the days of Alexander on the nations of the East; with the triumph of Wolfe on the Heights of Abraham began the history of the United States."[361]

No war is ever caused solely by the events of a single week or even a single year. The struggle between England and France was rooted in ancient rivalries and antagonisms. But the fact that the war actually began in North America because of Virginia's economic interests and her action to protect them, and that Pitt made America the principal theater of conflict, shaped the careers of nations in a way that altered the course of world history. Pitt's policy of concentrating British military might in America while subsidizing Frederick's armies in Europe enabled the shrewd monarch to build Prussia into the strongest kingdom in Europe and thus profoundly affect the future history of that continent. The success of British operations in North America complemented those in India and helped England, by the Treaty of Paris, to secure domination of that great sub-continent.

The events leading up to the settlement of 1763 proved that the New World was not simply raw material to receive the impress of

European cultures, but could itself strongly influence events in Europe and other portions of the globe. That lesson was written boldly across the face of Europe and Asia. It could be read as clearly in Bombay and Manila as in Paris or Potsdam. And it was written in English. England had emerged from the war as mistress of the seas and of all of North America east of the Mississippi, besides being an important force in the Orient. A great deal of history would be written in English for some time to come.

Chapter IX

AMERICA LOOKS TO VIRGINIA

(1763-1774)

Chapter IX

(1763-1774)

THE Treaty of Paris in 1763 did not immediately bring peace to the Virginia frontier. On April 27 of that year, Pontiac, an Ottawa chief with a formidable ability for organization, addressed a great conclave of tribal leaders, eloquently reciting the injuries visited upon the aborigines by the white invaders and calling for a unified offensive against the despoilers of their traditional hunting grounds. As had Opecancanough one hundred forty-one years before, Pontiac planned a concerted attack upon outposts many miles apart.

His proposed line of attack was even longer than that of the seventeenth century werowance, for he envisioned simultaneous assaults upon all Western forts. The task was far greater than that attempted by Opecancanough, but Pontiac's resources were comparably greater. He had succeeded in forging the largest alliance of Indian tribes in American history. Tribes from both the North and the Deep South were poised for attack.[1]

But, as in 1622, a timely warning—received this time at Detroit —frustrated the offensive strategy. Even so, eight of the twelve forts fell. Detroit, however, was the rock that broke the wave of attack. Pontiac signed peace terms at that frontier post in 1764, and again in 1766 at Oswego.[2]

Three years later, the chief was murdered by an Indian bribed by an English trader. But his death did not end the Indian threat. The Shawnees nursed their resentment with ominous assiduity.

In 1763, Francis Fauquier was in his fifth year as Governor of Virginia, having succeeded to that office upon Dinwiddie's retirement during the French and Indian War. He had to vex him, besides the Indian problem, an even more troubling matter closely related to it. In that very year, England's armed forces having compelled the formal capitulation at Paris, George III issued a proclamation forbidding trade with the Indians and prohibiting the issuance of grants for land west of the Alleghenies.[3] His Majesty's ministers may have considered this proclamation's effect on colonial economy a matter of trifling significance amid the grand schemes of empire following triumph upon three continents and seven seas. But to the Virginians it was a ukase designed to deprive them of the very thing for which they had initiated the struggle culminating in global strife. It was to protect the western lands that Governor Dinwiddie had dispatched George Washington on his mission to the French, and it was Virginia land speculators who had roused the Governor's interest in protection. His personal investment in Virginia's Ohio Company guaranteed his zeal in a cause which he was convinced served the interest of colony and Crown.

The royal proclamation was counter, not only to the aspirations of Virginians, but also to a partly accomplished fact. Grants had been issued west of the Alleghenies years before the King's edict. Though earlier charters had been abrogated by James I in 1624, the western boundary of Virginia was not redefined. Virginians continued to regard the Pacific Ocean as the natural western border of their domain. A trans-Allegheny grant to the Ohio Company, issued in 1749, with the sign manual of the King, defined the designated tract as lying "within the dominion of Virginia." Representatives of the Loyal Company, under authorization of the Virginia Council, had surveyed eight hundred thousand acres west of what royal proclamation now sought to make the demarcation line of settlement. One hundred thousand acres in the forbidden region had been granted to the Greenbrier Company in 1751. The following year the General Assembly declared the banks of the Mississippi to be within the bounds of Augusta County, Virginia. By the time of George III's decree following the Treaty of Paris, many settlers were already living in the region west of the Alleghenies. Some of them were veterans who occupied the land as compensation for their service in its defense, and they did not propose to be moved.[4]

Virginians considered it their right to ignore a proclamation so contrary to established precedents and interpretations, so inimical to their interests and apparently dictated with such ignorance or disdain for the colony's welfare. Even so scrupulous a man as George Washington confided his intention to "secure some of the most valuable lands" in the forbidden territory, expressing confidence that acquisition would be possible "after awhile, notwithstanding the proclamation that restrains it at present, and prohibits the settling of them at all; for I can never look upon that proclamation in any other light . . . than as a temporary expedient to quiet the minds of Indians."[5] He went so far as to suggest that the desired lands be "immediately surveyed, to keep others off." Averring that "the rest" might safely be left to time, he cautioned his correspondent not to quote him, because he might be "censured for the opinion . . . given in respect to the King's proclamation." Few, if any, Virginians would have censured him.

Their accomplishments in the French and Indian War had given them new confidence, and their observation of British regulars' inadequacy in bush warfare had reduced their awe of all things from the home country. James Otis, of Massachusetts, might declare that it was the "duty of all humbly . . . to acquiesce in the decision of the supreme legislature (Parliament)."[6] But Richard Bland, of Virginia, asserted in a pamphlet in 1764 that England and the American colonies were "coordinate kingdoms under a common Crown."[7]

The war had opened new roads to the West. Great planters were taking out large patents and many small farmers were using the new routes to the lands being developed. News of competition from the North spurred Virginians on in the westward movement. Benjamin Franklin, of Pennsylvania, and partners in America, England and France, operating as the Walpole Company, had petitioned the Lords of the Treasury for a grant of millions of acres in the West.[8]

Another incentive to accelerated settlement of western lands was competition among Virginians themselves—a commercial rivalry that expressed itself in political contests within the Old Dominion. Conclusion of the Treaty of Lancaster in 1744 had inspired James Patton, John Robinson and other Virginia planters to obtain large grants for development of the trans-Allegheny region. But their plans were dwarfed by the bolder schemes of Thomas Lee, Lawrence Washington and other gentlemen of the Northern Neck who conceived the idea of the great Ohio Company. Aided by the Duke of Bedford and John Hanbury, a wealthy London merchant, this company received on February 23, 1749 a royal authorization for a grant of 200,000 acres with the proviso that an additional 300,000 acres would be allotted if the terms attached to the grant were executed.[9]

The actual grant was made by Governor Gooch on July 12, 1749. But what was to have been a day of triumph became one of disappointment for directors of the Ohio Company. On that very day, Governor and Council allotted 800,000 acres to a newly-formed rival enterprise, the Loyal Company.[10]

Strong political pressure had enabled the Loyal Company to obtain its grant at the same time that the Ohio Company received title to Western acres. The organizer of the Loyal was none other than John Robinson, Speaker of the House of Burgesses, well on his way to becoming the most powerful and popular political figure in Virginia.[11] Associated with Robinson in the great land operation were prominent planters from Tidewater south of the Rappahannock and from Albemarle County.[12]

The intense rivalry between the two companies oftentimes amounted to enmity. In each camp were men who would not scruple to deal a surreptitious blow to the other's fortunes. This hostility was antedated and heightened by a political rivalry between forces captained by Speaker Robinson and those led by the Lees.[13]

In 1751, the Ohio Company gained a great advantage when one of its members, Robert Dinwiddie, became Governor. A more permanent advantage was the active interest of Richard Henry Lee and George Washington.

The Loyal Company in 1753 attracted the interest of an exceptionally promising young man—Edmund Pendleton, a new Burgess and protégé of the Robinsons.[14]

The rapid rate at which Virginians moved into the region beyond the mountains might lead one to believe that the Proclamation of 1763 was a negligible factor in the life of the colony. Such was by no means the case. Virginians ignored it, but it generated resentment. Uncertainty regarding the validity of land grants bred an atmosphere of insecurity that generated still more resentment.

Umbrage was heightened by a growing sense of colonial patriotism. About the time that the French and Indian Wars ended, one Lieutenant Timberlake, who had brought three Cherokee chiefs to London by order of the Governor of Virginia, petitioned the Earl of Bute for money to return to "my native country Virginia."[15] The Reverend Andrew Burnaby, who published his account of *Travels Through the Middle Settlements in North America in the Years 1759 and 1760*, wrote of the Virginians:

"Many of them consider the colonies as independent states, unconnected with Great Britain, otherwise than by having the same king, and being bound to her with natural affection."[16]

The "natural affection" was sometimes strained. Burnaby also wrote:

"The public or political character of the Virginians corresponds with their private one: they are haughty and jealous of their liberties, impatient of restraint, and can scarcely bear the thought of being controlled by any superior power."[17]

Discontent was aggravated by economic misfortune. In 1759, the very year that Burnaby made his observations of the colony, Tidewater planters looked forward to prosperous times. A tobacco shortage the year before had raised tobacco prices, and growers anticipated even higher returns for succeeding seasons.[18] In the enthusiasm of their hopes, a number of planters "plunged into a frenzy of slave-buying at extravagant prices."[19] But they paid dearly for their unreined optimism and extravagance when tobacco prices dipped sharply. Partly responsible for the drop was the aggressive unanimity of buyers who, deeply concerned over their own narrowing margin of profit, agreed to drive leaf prices down. Prices were also brought down by the extensive planting of tobacco in anticipation of large profits.[20]

The small returns from sale of their crops left many Tidewater planters unable to pay their old debts, much less those contracted in the orgy of extravagance into which they had been lured by intoxicating hopes. Merchants foresaw that several seasons of low prices would eliminate the necessity for paying cash to the growers "as it will then take the most of their tobacco to provide clothes and necessaries for their families."[21]

By April 1763, there was no market for tobacco. The following year merchants made huge profits, but the prices paid the growers were so low that Tidewater planters had to maintain their families and plantations on one-fourth of the cash income they had received in 1760.[22]

A weakness of the planters themselves contributed to their difficulties. The caustically shrewd Burnaby had observed: "There are but few of them that have a turn for business, and even those are by no means adroit at it."[23] He had also reported, "Virginians outrun their incomes. . . ."[24]

"Not a tenth of the land," Burnaby wrote, "is yet cultivated: and that which is cultivated, is far from being so in the most advantageous manner."[25] Signs of the decline of the plantation system had been apparent even as early as 1759, for the traveling minister declared:

"It is hard to determine, whether the colony can be called flourishing, or not: because though it produces great quantities of tobacco and grain yet there seem to be very few improvements carrying on in it."[26]

Men accustomed to dominating everything around them found themselves hounded by creditors. Signatures that carried the force of law in some parts of the colony could not command respect on a bill of exchange. Proud planters who bore such names as Carter, Byrd, Lee and Page had the mortification of having their bills dishonored and protested, even when the sums were of a size that they had once deemed almost insignificant. William Byrd III, though perhaps the most conspicuous, was by no means alone among once-wealthy Virginians in finding his entire estate insufficient to pay his debts.[27]

So many creditors sought judgment in the General Court that the congested mills of justice almost ground to a halt. A creditor who obtained judgment for a debt within less than three years' time could congratulate himself and his lawyer. Following issuance of an execution, the unhappy plaintiff might have to wait as long as two years for action from the sheriff. As an increasingly large number of honest men were threatened with imprisonment for debt, many of them united in agreement "to defend one another against the officers." Prudent merchants began to carry pistols when they ventured far from home.[28]

Virginia's economic plight was worsened by the heavy financial burden of war. Since the colony had no money to support forces fighting the French and Indians, the Assembly repeatedly issued paper money to be redeemed through returns from future tax collections. Prompted by London, the legislators provided more troops in 1759 at an expense of £52,000. Treasury notes were issued in that amount, maturing on April 20, 1768, to be redeemed from new poll taxes and a tobacco tax which were projected into 1767. The tax burden became even more onerous when Virginia's lands were no longer threatened and Virginians were fighting for the defense of the Carolinas.[29]

Two military appropriation acts were passed by the Assembly in 1761, but by this time Parliament had appropriated the sum of £200,000 for Virginia's use in prosecuting the war, and there was no necessity for new issues of paper money.[30]

The situation was quite different in 1762. On March 30, Governor Fauquier transmitted to the Assembly a request by his Majesty's government that Virginia troops be kept in service despite the making of peace with the Cherokees. The House quickly agreed to new appropriations, passing, sixty-six to three, a bill calling for the issuance of £30,000 in paper money to be redeemed through the collection of a one shilling tax on every tithable during the years 1764 through 1769. So different were the sentiments of House and

Council that the Governor's strongest powers of persuasion were necessary to obtain a five to four vote of approval by the more exclusive body. The four defeated members of the Council argued that continued issuance of paper money was unsound, but they were swamped by the popular will and the Governor dismissed their reasoning as pretense.[31]

Only £20 of the first one-fourth of quitrents paid in Virginia in 1763 was in hard money, and the collectors swore that no more could be gotten. In May of that year, the Governor himself, probably in accordance with instructions from London, warned the Assembly that sound credit was "of most urgent importance to a trading country" and that paper money must therefore be redeemed as it matured. Merchants, he said, would "call upon a higher power" if their contract-supported demands for sterling were not met.[32]

The Burgesses were incensed at the Governor's about-face. What alternative to the issuance of paper money had there been if royal appeals for funds, requests transmitted by the Governor himself, were to be met?[33] Following Fauquier's address, the House appointed a committee to draft a reply and named to it Charles Carter, member of a powerful clan and one of Virginia's foremost parliamentary leaders; Edmund Pendleton, who had attained the position of legislative influence forecast for him a decade before; and George Wythe, a brilliant young lawyer who was perhaps the most learned member of the Virginia bar.[34]

The reply which they wrote was presented and approved the following day. It declared:

"Emissions of Treasury notes, so loudly complained of, were made in consequence of his Majesty's requisitions when it was impossible to procure specie for these exigencies; and, there being no other succedaneum than paper within our knowledge, we could not expect what we then did would be considered otherwise than as acts of duty to our Sovereign; and we hope that expedient, not indeed in itself always eligible, was justified by necessity."[35]

The Burgesses said that they had not deemed it "equal or just to circulate such notes without giving them the essential quality of money by making them a legal tender in payment of all debts, except for his Majesty's quitrents, and [the Assembly] would not have emitted them at all upon any other conditions."[36]

Answering the threat that merchants would "call upon a higher power" if not satisfied in demands for payment in sterling as provided by contract, the Burgesses said that, since "the courts were empowered to direct at what difference of exchange judgments for sterling debts should be discharged, . . . none of [the merchants] could suffer, except from the fluctuating nature of exchange." Furthermore, the losses occasioned by a sharp rise of exchange would be "sufficiently balanced by the advantage they must inevitably receive from its present declining state."[37]

While reiterating their loyalty to the crown, the Burgesses were already at war with British merchants. Eight days after formally approving the reply to Governor Fauquier prepared by Carter, Pendleton and Wythe, the House appointed the same committee, with the addition of the scholarly and eloquent Richard Henry Lee, to draft an address expressing its firm opposition to any proposed concessions to the merchants which would favor them above other creditors. The document, a fine combination of diplomacy and forthrightness, called colonial dependence upon Great Britain "our greatest happiness and only security," but served notice:

"This is not the dependence of a people subjugated by the arms of a conqueror, but of sons sent out to explore and settle a new world, for the mutual benefit of themselves and their common parent: It is the dependence of a part upon one great whole, which, by its admirable Constitution, diffuses a spirit of patriotism that makes every citizen, however distant from the Mother Kingdom, zealous to promote its Majesty and the public good."[38]

The Assembly reserved the right to decide what was for "the public good" in Virginia. This reservation was made clear January 12, 1764 when the legislature convened in response to a special call from Governor Fauquier, who relayed and endorsed General Amherst's appeal for five hundred troops as a defense against the Indians. The reply on behalf of the House was the work of Edmund Pendleton and Peyton Randolph, popular scion of a powerful family. In most courteous terms, and with due regard to all proper sentiments, the reply congratulated the Governor upon his safe return to the colony and lamented the destruction wrought by the Indians. A perceptive man might have detected the Burgesses' intentions of relying on "the militia, whose conduct and bravery . . . prevented the barbarians from extending the dismal scenes of outrage and murder,"[39] rather than trying to raise the troops requested by Amherst. Even before approval of this reply, its two authors, together with Richard Henry Lee and Richard Bland, perhaps the House's foremost expert on constitutional law, were instructed to prepare "an humble address" to the Governor explaining why troops could not be raised. The Burgesses had not surrendered on the paper money issue. They explained that they could not appropriate funds for troops without printing more paper money, a condition which they knew would be offensive to British merchants.[40]

Britain's Parliament, too, had been concerned with the paper money problem. Much importuned by the merchants, it had passed in 1763 an act which forbade the use, as legal tender for the payment of debts, of any colonial currency issued after September 1, 1764. It guarded against colonial use of an escape stratagem by forbidding any extension of time for the circulation of paper money already in use as legal tender. A fine of £1,000 and dismissal from office would be the punishment for any colonial Governor who assented to a legislative act contrary to provisions of the act of Parliament. Though applicable to all the colonies, the Parliamentary measure was framed primarily because of conditions in Virginia. A similar prohibition had been operative in New England since 1751.[41]

This victory was not sufficient for the merchants, who appealed to the Lords of Trade and Plantations to force the colonial legislatures to recognize their right to collect debts in sterling as specified by contract. Avoiding direct action themselves, these officials referred the complaint, as regarded Virginia, to Governor Fauquier who in turn presented it to the Assembly October 30, 1764. The Committee of the Whole House resolved not to comply with the request.[42]

When the Assembly convened again in May 1765, the House adopted resolutions advancing a naive plan of recalling outstanding paper currency and replacing it with gold-based currency, the whole to be accomplished by borrowing from the already exasperated British merchants. The Council killed the plan because, wrote wealthy Richard Corbin, "they considered it as a tax upon the frugal and industrious."[43]

Other taxes were falling heavily upon frugal and profligate alike in Virginia and her sister colonies. On the fifth of April 1764, Parliament passed an American Revenue Act, which was the first law ever passed in London for the specific purpose of raising money in the colonies for the Crown.[44] Known as the Sugar Act, the measure continued the old duty on raw sugar and increased that on foreign refined sugar; while cutting in half the duty on foreign molasses. Many of the most important provisions, however, had nothing to do with sugar. The Act placed new or higher import duties on non-British textiles, coffee, indigo and directly imported Madeira and Canary wines, while prohibiting colonial importation of French wines and foreign rum. Duties on foreign goods reshipped through England to the colonies were doubled, and iron, hides, whale fins, raw silk, potash and pearl ash were added to the duty list.[45]

Chancellor of the Exchequer George Grenville, who had introduced the Revenue Act, pushed another measure that hit the colonists harder. This one put teeth in the American customs service, which had been returning to Britain only a little more than one-fourth the cost of collection. The new Act established at Halifax a vice-admiralty court with original jurisdiction over all admiralty cases in all the colonies which the prosecutors or informers chose to bring there rather than to a local court. The measure also shifted the burden of proof to the accused, and annulled his right to sue for illegal seizure. Stricter registration and bonding procedures for ships were established. Grenville required that customs officials for the colonies reside in the territory where they served, rather than remain in England and depend upon deputies.[46] British men-of-war, no longer needed against the French, patrolled coastal waters, exerting an inhibiting influence on the private enterprise of smugglers. Thus the colonists could no longer obtain appreciable quantities of goods from the West Indies without paying duty.[47]

On paper, Grenville's program seemed admirable. Who could deny that efficiency in any operation of government was preferable to inefficiency?

Such efficiency, however, had been eschewed by government leaders more astute than Grenville. England's first real Prime Minister, Robert Walpole, had brushed aside suggestions for taxing America, saying: "I will leave that for some of my successors, who may have more courage than I have, and be less a friend to commerce than I am."[48] Walpole had even winked at colonial smuggling, saying, "By encouraging them to an extensive, growing foreign commerce, if they gain 500,000 *l.*, I am convinced that in two years afterwards full 250,000 *l.* of their gains will be in his Majesty's exchequer," and adding that thus England would be taxing the colonists "more agreeably both to their own constitution, and to ours."[49]

George Washington, though probably unacquainted with Walpole's words, reasoned in much the same way two decades later. "The advantage accruing to the mother country," he wrote, "will fall greatly short of the expectation of the ministry; for certain it is, our whole substance does already in a manner flow to Great Britain and that whatsoever contributes to lessen our importations must be hurtful to their manufactures."[50]

Benjamin Franklin, of Pennsylvania, pithily wrote an Englishman: "What you get from us in taxes you must lose in trade. The cat can yield but her skin. And as you must have the whole hide, if you first cut thongs out of it, 'tis at your own expense."[51]

In the course of his address to Commons March 9, 1764, in which he had presented the American Revenue Act, Grenville had observed that it might be "proper to charge certain stamp duties in the . . . colonies and plantations."[52] Though no effort was made to translate the thought into action, members of Parliament had assented and the general impression was that Parliament was prepared to act whenever the ministry should present a stamp act bill. News of Grenville's speech and its reception reached Virginia in May.[53]

The colonists, already financially distressed, were alarmed at the prospect of utter ruin. Furthermore, they believed that even the consideration of a stamp act bill was rank injustice. Never before had the Virginians been taxed directly for revenue except by their own elected representatives. As early as 1652, the citizens of the Eastern Shore had formally protested against taxation without representation. Idealism and cherished traditions of liberty reinforced economic interest. Richard Henry Lee asked a Londoner:

"Can it be supposed that those brave adventurous Britons, who originally conquered and settled these countries . . ., meant thereby to deprive themselves of that free government of which they were members, and to which they had an unquestionable right?"[54]

Lee soon had the opportunity to address his sentiments to a large company of gentlemen in the mother country. With Pendleton, Landon Carter, Wythe, Benjamin Harrison, Archibald Cary and John Fleming, he was appointed November 14 to a committee headed by Peyton Randolph which was instructed to frame an address to the Throne and separate protests to Lords and Commons regarding the proposed stamp act.[55]

The three documents were presented to the Committee of the Whole December 13 and, after two conferences with the Council and resultant amendments, were accepted by both houses.[56]

His Majesty was appealed to for protection of Virginians "in the enjoyment of their ancient and inestimable right of being governed by such laws respecting their internal polity and taxation as are derived from their own consent, with the approbation of their sovereign or his substitute."[57]

The Memorial to the Lords declared:

"Your memorialists conceive it to be a fundamental principle of the British constitution, without which freedom can nowhere exist, that the people are not subject to any taxes but such as are laid on them by their own consent, or by those who are legally appointed to represent them."[58]

The Virginians spoke for citizens of the other colonies as well as themselves. Taxation of the American colonists by a legislative body in which they were not represented, said the Memorial, "must necessarily establish this melancholy truth, that the inhabitants of the Colonies are slaves of Britons from whom they are descended and from whom they might expect every indulgence that the obligations of interest and affection can entitle them to."[59]

The Remonstrance to the House of Commons used some of the same arguments employed in the Address and Memorial, and added another one calculated to appeal to the trade-minded middle classes represented in Commons. The colonists, already staggering under a burden of debt greatly increased by war with the French, would, by a stamp act, be "reduced to extreme poverty . . . [and] compelled to manufacture those articles" which they had been importing from Britain.[60]

In the context of the times, protests to the Lords and Commons were strongly worded, but many of the Burgesses must have thought they had been vitiated in conferences with the Council. In writing to the Lords of Trade that Christmas Eve, Governor Fauquier said:

"In the resolutions of the House of Burgesses, the terms are very warm and indecent as your lordships will observe in their journals; but I have been told by some men appointed to draw them up that their whole study has been to endeavor to mollify them, and they have reason to hope there is nothing now in them which will give the least offense."[61]

The hopes of the colonists were dashed in the spring. Word was received that in February Grenville had presented in Commons fifty-five resolutions providing for stamp taxes on virtually every type of document used in the colonies. The House of Lords did not even bother to read the eloquent and persuasive Memorial on which some of Virginia's keenest minds had worked so hard. As an historian later wrote, the Stamp Act passed both Lords and Commons "with less opposition than a turnpike bill."[62] The taxes would become effective November 1. Stamps would be required for every kind of legal paper imaginable, bills of lading, bills of sale, contracts, newspapers and individual advertisements in newspapers, pamphlets, almanacs, calendars, packs of cards, land survey orders, college diplomas and "every skin or piece of vellum or parchment, or sheet, on which shall be engrossed or printed an declaration."[63]

"Poor America!"[64] wrote Pendleton, who had helped to phrase the protests to Parliament. He was only one of many Virginia leaders who foresaw great travail, only one of a number who keenly felt a sympathetic unity with the other American colonies. As early as 1750, Thomas Lee, then President of the Council and acting Governor, had surveyed intercolonial problems and concluded: "We are all one people and should have no selfish ends."[65] In 1765, few Virginians were prepared to accept the second part of that statement, but the major premise would now provoke no argument from some who would have scoffed at it fifteen years earlier.

The Currency Act, aimed principally at Virginia, had aroused resentment up and down the Atlantic seaboard. The Grenville Program, of which the deflationary Currency Act was one leg and strictly enforced higher imposts the other, was nowhere more strongly denounced than in Massachusetts where British manufactures were being boycotted. The Stamp Act threatened to work an even greater hardship on commercially dominated Massachusetts than on agricultural Virginia, and leaders of the two colonies corresponded concerning the common danger. Virginia's protests to Parliament were not read by those to whom they were addressed, but they found eager and responsive readers in America.

*　*　*

On the 26th of May 1765, the House of Burgesses had quietly concluded what it believed to be its business for the session and many members, taking little interest in the concluding ceremonies, had already left when a missive from the Burgesses' agent in Britain was opened.[66] It contained a copy of the Stamp Act resolutions passed by Parliament. The excitement could not have been greater if a cannon ball had shattered one of the windows of the legislative chamber, nor could the threat have seemed more palpable. Immediately, the thirty-nine members present convened as a Committee of the Whole.[67]

The fewer than two score Burgesses over whom John Robinson presided as committee chairman after technically leaving the Speaker's chair were representative of a house of one hundred sixteen[68] legislators that differed markedly from its predecessors of previous decades.

When Robinson had first been elected Speaker, he had served a body composed of men much like himself. Few were as astute as he or as wealthy, and none was so popular. But most were products of the same plantation society which had produced him, a society which took the English gentry as its archetype. One instructed to divide the House, as then constituted, into social classes would have erred little if he had effected a simple dichotomy between those who were aristocrats and those who wanted to be.

By 1765, the House had lost its cohesiveness. Members of Speaker Robinson's class were still numerous and held virtually all committee chairmanships. But men of another class were present as representatives of the hill country west of Tidewater. They were not an organized bloc, but on many measures they were united by common interests. As Edmund Randolph later wrote:

"When intelligence arrived of the parliamentary resolutions preparatory to the Stamp Act, a corps of members in the House of Burgesses whose habits and expectations had no relation to men in power had increased without being discovered by the aristocratic part of the House, or by those members themselves. From the lower [or Tidewater] counties, fortune, rank, and perhaps fashion, had often sent representatives; but the repeated divisions of the upper [or hill country] counties drew representatives from humble walks. A collision between these two classes caused them to diverge from each other as widely in their sentiments in granting public money as in their incomes and expenses. While one would pay a public servant upon a strict calculation of the labor to be performed, the other would augment the stipend for the sake of dignity. A rivalship was the consequence; but the new party had hitherto not been able to vote and to be counted. They wanted a leader."[69]

They soon found one in the person of one of their newest recruits—Patrick Henry, who had been a member of the House about a week when the Committee of the Whole began a study of the Stamp Act Resolutions.[70] Just a few days before his twenty-ninth birthday, the Hanover lawyer had subscribed to the oath of office, having been elected from Louisa County to fill the vacancy created by retirement of William Johnston.

Henry was then neither resident nor property holder of Louisa,[71] but his fame had spread far beyond his native county. In December 1763, he had leaped into prominence as attorney for the defense in the Parsons' Cause, a suit brought by the Reverend James Maury, Anglican minister of Hanover County, against officials responsible for tax collection. The suit had grown out of an act of the General Assembly of 1758 authorizing payment in cash of ministers' salaries and other fees and levies which existing law provided be paid in tobacco at an average of two pence a pound. An anticipated increase in tobacco prices would make it cheaper for planters to pay in cash the tax exacted for support of the Established Church's ministers. The clergy felt cheated, since they had accepted payment in tobacco at times when it brought less than two pence a pound. An appeal to the throne for "disallowance" of the Act of Assembly brought nullification of the law August 10, 1759 by action of the Privy Council. Reverend James Maury, in 1763, brought suit for back pay on the grounds that the "two-penny bill," as the Act of Assembly was called, had not been operative during the ten months between the Governor's signing of it and its disallowance by the Privy Council. The judge ruled that damages were due the minister, but Henry's eloquence so swayed the jury that the twelve men returned quickly with a verdict of one penny for the plaintiff.[72]

In pleading his case, Henry had charged that the Crown was guilty of misrule or tyranny if it nullified a law passed by the General Assembly. "After the court adjourned," Maury wrote, "[Henry] apologized to me for what he had said, alleging that his sole view in engaging in the cause, and in saying what he had, was to render himself popular. You see, then, it is so clear a point in this person's opinion that the ready road to popularity here is to trample under foot the interests of religion, the rights of the church, and the prerogatives of the Crown."[73]

Mr. Henry, therefore, excited considerable interest when he took his seat in the General Assembly in May 1765. Many, probably most, of the Tidewater Burgesses considered him a threat to the established order. Legislators from the hill country, whose constituents were mostly small farmers and included many religious dissenters, looked to him as their champion. Both groups united in regarding him as a young man of great potentialities.

Some of the Tidewater planters soon discovered that Henry was not the devil incarnate. They found him "amiable" and were impressed with the "mildness of his temper" in conversation. They even decided that, far from being an enemy of religion, he had "imbibed a disposition to religion and virtue."[74] Though some of his underprivileged constituents may have felt a kinship with him because he was "not always grammatical and sometimes coarse in his language,"[75] Henry was not born of the mob. His father was presiding justice of the Hanover County Court, a militia colonel and a vestryman. His uncle was a clergyman of the Established Church, and hence one of those privileged ecclesiastics against whom Henry had inveighed in the Parsons' Cause.[76]

Two days before the House of Burgesses convened as a Committee of the Whole, Henry had demonstrated that he was not always "amiable." With a boldness reminiscent of his speech in the case that won him fame, Henry, though a rank newcomer to the legislature, had vigorously assailed the House leaders' scheme to borrow money from English merchants to enable the colony to retire its outstanding currency and advance funds to individual planters on the security of their property. The authors of this plan must have squirmed when the Hanover lawyer asked: "What, sir, is it proposed then to reclaim the spendthrift from his dissipation and extravagance, by filling his pockets with money?"[77]

Great then was the excitement on May 26 when Patrick Henry seconded George Johnston's motion that the House go into Committee of the Whole to consider "steps necessary to be taken in consequence of the Resolutions of the House of Commons of Great Britain relative to the charging certain Stamp duties in the Colonies and Plantations in America."[78] Excitement mounted still higher when, with the committee session begun, Johnston deferred to Henry and the lean young man rose from his seat, drawing forth a sheet of paper as he unfolded his long frame. He announced his intention of presenting a series of resolutions, and began reading in a manly and melodious voice.[79]

"Resolved," he read, "that the first Adventurers and settlers of this his Majesty's Colony and Dominion brought with them and transmitted to their Posterity and all other his Majesty's Subjects since inhabiting in this his Majesty's said Colony, all the Privileges, Franchises and Immunities that have at any Time been held, enjoyed, and possessed by the People of Great Britain."[80]

The attitude of the House was still one of expectancy. Henry was saying no more than Bland and Richard Henry Lee and others had said. But how far would he go?

"That by two royal Charters, granted by King James the first," the rich, clear voice read on, "the Colonists aforesaid are declared entitled to all the Privileges, Liberties and Immunities of Denizens and natural-born Subjects, to all Intents and Purposes as if they had been abiding and born within the Realm of England."

So far Henry's resolutions sounded like a paraphrase of the earlier protests sent to Parliament by the Burgesses. No undue radicalism here.

"Resolved," Henry read next, "that the taxation of the people by themselves or by Persons chosen by themselves to represent them, who can only know what Taxes the People are able to bear, and the easiest Mode of raising them, *and are equally affected by such Taxes themselves*, is the distinguishing Characteristic of British Freedom and without which the ancient Constitution cannot subsist."

"Resolved," Henry went on, "that his Majesty's liege People of this most ancient Colony have uninterruptedly enjoyed the Right of being governed by their own Assembly in the article of their Taxes and internal police. . . ." Here some of the Tidewater members frowned in disapproval. The Assembly's power was ultimately derived from the sovereign.[81] If Henry noticed the disapproving looks, he did not show it. "And that the same," he said, referring to the people's "right of being governed by their own Assembly," "hath never been forfeited or in any other way given up, but hath been constantly recognized by the Kings and People of Great Britain."

"Resolved, therefore," he continued, and the "therefore" hinted to alert listeners that this was the main resolution, to which the others had been prologue. "Resolved, therefore, that the General Assembly of this Colony have the only and exclusive Right and Power to lay Taxes and Impositions upon the inhabitants of this colony," (Henry's voice was strong and resonant), "and that every Attempt to vest such Power in any Person or Persons whatsoever, other than the General Assembly aforesaid, has a manifest Tendency to destroy British as well as American Freedom."

When the young legislator sat down, conservative leaders sprang to their feet to oppose his resolutions. A motion that they be considered seriatim was passed. Henry listened with the sensitive and jealous pride of authorship. "Alone, unadvised, and unassisted," he had written the resolutions on a blank page of an old law book.[82]

The first resolution passed after amendment that did not weaken it and, if anything, strengthened it. The second was adopted. The third passed after a minor change in phraseology.

The fourth resolution was re-read for consideration. Those who had shaken their heads during its first reading could now shake their fingers. One after the other, Tidewater leaders rose to oppose it, disputing its assertion that the people of Virginia were "governed by their own Assembly." Supporting their arguments with learned references to English constitutional law, they insisted that legislative authority, though wielded with the consent of the people, was ultimately derived from the Crown. Peyton Randolph, George Wythe, Richard Bland and Robert Carter Nicholas—men of the highest ability and prestige—assailed the resolution.[83] Henry, more dependent upon eloquence or reason than on legal knowledge for the winning of his court room battles, was at a loss to deal with involved constitutional questions. But George Johnston came to his rescue, and some of the newer members—those whom the Governor called "young, hot and giddy"—rallied to Henry's support. When the vote was taken, both advocates and opponents held their breath. By a margin of two or three votes, it passed.[84]

Now the fifth resolution was reread. This was the keystone of the entire structure of resolutions. If this was defeated, the passage of the first four would count for nothing, for they were little more than a reiteration of principles already stated in earlier appeals to Parliament. This resolution, with its bold declaration that "the General Assembly of this Colony have the only and exclusive Right and Power to lay Taxes and Impositions upon the Inhabitants of this Colony," made some conservatives swell with rage.

None of the resolutions had passed by a margin of more than three votes.[85] Could the fifth, most controversial of all, possibly survive?

Stung by criticism and impelled by desperation, Patrick Henry took the floor. His face was flushed and he breathed heavily with anger and excitement. Gaunt and plain-garbed, like a figure in a morality play, he swept the house with his flaming glance and hurled his words like avenging bolts. Self-taxation, he thundered, was essential to freedom. As his voice now rose to a roar, now sank to a whisper, it was almost like a multitude of immortal voices rushing down the winds of time. Here and there a listener sat taller in his seat as he saw himself an actor in a universal drama.[86]

The excitement was already almost unbearable when Henry shouted that the Stamp Act was tyrannical and then, with mounting emphasis, cried out:

"Caesar had his Brutus, Charles the First his Cromwell, and George the Third—"

"Treason!" shouted Speaker Robinson, his full face swollen with anger.

"And George the Third," finished Henry, "may he never have either."[87]

He had adroitly freed himself from the charge of treason without leaving any doubt as to the import of his warning. When he took his seat, the House still vibrated with excitement.

Some of the members were visibly agitated as they stood for the vote on the fifth resolution. Twenty voted for it, nineteen against.[88] By a margin of one vote, Henry and his supporters had carried the day!

Peyton Randolph, besides being one of the foremost representatives of Tidewater aristocracy, was famed for his affability in conversation and equanimity in debate. [89] Some acquaintances might have had difficulty in recognizing his usually placid countenance as he lumbered from the chamber, for it was distorted with the pain of frustration. His multiple chins bobbed furiously as his corpulent frame hurtled through the door. A William and Mary college student standing by the exit heard Randolph exclaim, "By God, I would have given five hundred guineas for a single vote!"[90]

The student greatly admired Randolph and he was a protégé of such substantial conservatives as George Wythe, his law professor, and Governor Fauquier, who liked both the young man and his fiddle. Nevertheless, the student had been captivated by the eloquence of the radical orator who, though just seven years his senior, had held enthralled a majority of the Burgesses. Afterwards, the student wrote of Henry as he seemed that day: "He appeared to me to speak as Homer wrote."[91]

The college boy whose heart had leaped high at Henry's words was a red-headed young man from Albemarle County named Thomas Jefferson.

* * *

On the following day the House, as a legislative body, was scheduled to vote on the resolutions which it had adopted as a Committee of the Whole. But something delayed action. The Committee on Privileges and Elections reported on the return of writs from counties which had named Burgesses to fill vacancies. All writs were acceptable or could be easily amended to make them so except one—the certificate of election for Mr. Patrick Henry as Burgess from Louisa. The House voted to summon the sheriff of that county "in custody to amend his said return."[92] Was the move intended to discredit Henry before a crucial vote? Perhaps not.

Henry himself had the preceding year appeared before the Committee of Privileges and Elections as counsel for a defeated candidate in a contested election result for his own native Hanover County, a case reminiscent of the present one.[93] In any event, it was easy for some of Henry's more passionate followers to interpret coincidence as malevolence, and it was equally easy for some conservatives to enjoy any embarrassment that might come to the brash young legislator who had challenged their leadership a few days after taking his seat.

Now came the formal vote on the resolutions, and the effect of any discrediting of their sponsor should soon be evident. The vote was twenty for, nineteen against.[94] The House, sitting as a legislature, had duplicated its voice as a committee. The effect of Henry's oratory had outlasted a good night's sleep. Believing his victory secure, Henry rode back to Hanover County with dreams of glory in his head.

But the young lawyer, wise in the motives of the human heart and shrewd in his appeal to them, was naive in the ways of legislatures. On the morning of May 31, the day after the Burgess from Louisa and many of his supporters left Williamsburg, the usually dominant conservatives sought to recoup their losses of the day before. Peyton Randolph, his composure regained, rose in ponderous dignity to move that the resolutions be expunged. But, since they had been voted seriatim, it was necessary that a separate vote on expunging be taken for each resolution. Motions to expunge the first four were defeated. But the fifth, the one that gave force to the others, was wiped off the records.[95]

Governor Fauquier considered even the four surviving resolutions too strong and took comfort in the possibility that the result would have been different "if more of the representatives had done their duty by attending to the end of the session."[96] At least, he would make this statement in his report to the Lords of Trade, either by way of apology for events in his bailiwick or as a defense of the colonists. Probably, he had not definitely determined what his attitude should be. On the first day of June, he summoned the Burgesses to the Council Chamber and, after signing the completed bills and joint resolutions, dissolved the House. Not one word of praise or censure did he speak.[97]

When news of these events reached Hanover County, a very cocksure young man learned a political lesson the hard way. His fifth resolution, which he had carried to victory against the most disheartening odds, had been expunged, and future readers of the House Journal would not even know that it had been adopted.

Before the end of June, though, Henry and all Virginia knew that his fifth resolution was not destined for oblivion. Feeling against Parliament ran even stronger in New England than in the Old Dominion, and the Hanover lawyer's resolutions expressed the feeling of many merchant leaders in the Boston area. The four resolutions remaining on the Journal of the House of Burgesses, the fifth (or expunged) resolution, and a sixth which had been introduced but rejected the day after Henry's dramatic speech, all were printed in *The Newport Mercury* of June 24. The first day of July they must have been the major topic of conversation in Boston, for on that date they appeared in *The Boston Post-Boy and Advertiser* and *The Boston Evening Post*. On the fourth of July, then a date of no special significance in the struggle for liberty, the resolutions were carried by *The Massachusetts Gazette and Boston News-Letter*.[98]

On September 25, General Thomas Gage, commander of his Majesty's forces in North America, ruefully paid tribute to the effectiveness of Henry's resolves when he reported to his government that they "gave the signal for a general outcry over the continent."[99] A New Englander, Ezra Stiles, turned away from his telescope and the observation of astral fires long enough to take note of a nearer conflagration. The Virginia resolves, he wrote, "came abroad and gave fire to the Continent."[100]

On September 20, in that same brooding month of threat when General Gage wrote to London about the "general outcry" in the colonies, George Washington, Burgess for Fairfax County, summarized the situation in a letter to a friend. "The Stamp Act imposed on the Colonies by the Parliament of Great Britain," he reported, "engrosses the conversation of the speculative part of the colonists, who look upon this unconstitutional method of taxation as a direful attack upon their liberties, and loudly exclaim against the violation. What may be the result of this and some other (I think I may add) ill-judged measures, I will not undertake to determine."[101]

But Washington said he would "venture to affirm" that the mother country would gain far less from the Stamp Act than the government expected, since the colonists had begun to realize that many of the things they had imported from England were not essential to their welfare or happiness. The real "necessaries of life" were, for the most part, available in America. The Stamp Act would, therefore, "introduce frugality and be a necessary stimulation to [colonial] industry." Even if the people were willing to buy stamps, said the master of Mount Vernon, they would not have the money to do so. He foresaw that the requirement of stamps for legal documents might bring colonial judicial machinery to a halt but, mindful of the many suits brought by English creditors, he wrote: "If a stop be put to our judicial proceedings, I fancy the merchants of Great Britain trading to the colonies will not be among the last to wish for a repeal of it."

Washington himself was plagued by debts to British merchants, but was nevertheless far better off financially than many of his fellow planters, and hence the harassed recipient of many requests for aid. Indebtedness, however, did not deter the Fairfax Burgess or many other prominent planters from land speculation, for land was still regarded as the source of fortune.[102]

A melancholy story had been told in the "Virginia and Maryland News" column of the *Providence Gazette* of January 19, 1765 and reprinted in the *Boston Post-Boy* of July 29, for a Virginia correspondent had written:

"The courts are filled with lawsuits, and many people are obliged to sell their estates."[103]

Richard Corbin, of Middlesex County, was considered so wealthy that his neighbors said "rich as Corbin" instead of "rich as Croesus." But he considered himself and the whole colony poor. Being Receiver General of Virginia, he was in an excellent position to know. On July 25, 1763, he had written:

"The precarious situation of credit in this country is such that I find it will be extremely difficult for me to observe that punctuality in the remittance of the quitrents as will be satisfactory to myself."[104]

In a letter the following month to Robert Cary Esq. and Company, merchants, he complained: "Good bills are so extremely scarce that [it] renders it difficult for me to make the revenue remittances." Deploring the "evil" of inflation, he lamented, "No one can say where it will end."[105]

By 1765 conditions had grown even worse. Men threatened with financial ruin were not inclined to temporize in the matter of an additional tax which they believed to be unconstitutional. The common threat was drawing Virginia, New England, and the middle colonies closer together. The Virginia Resolves were hailed in the North, and Virginians read eagerly the stories of growing Northern resistance to the Stamp Act. The October 25 issue of Royle's *Virginia Gazette*, published in Williamsburg, devoted most of the front page to news from Boston. There was more news from Boston inside the four-page newspaper, besides stamp tax news from Newport, New York and Philadelphia.[106] Quite a change in fare for readers of a publication that usually concentrated on Virginia and overseas news to the near exclusion of intelligence from other sources!

The Massachusetts legislature had issued invitations to the assemblies of all the other colonies for a meeting in New York on October 7. Virginia leaders, however, were unable to participate for there was no active General Assembly to name delegates and none could be convened. During the summer, almost on the eve of distant Burgesses' departure for a new session in Williamsburg, the Virginia legislators learned that Governor Fauquier had prorogued the session. George Washington wrote: "I am convinced . . . that the Governor had no inclination to meet an Assembly at this juncture."[107]

Ironically enough, because of the Governor's action, Virginians were absent when twenty-seven representatives of nine colonies met in New York City and formulated a "Declaration of Rights and Grievances" which drew considerable inspiration from the Virginia Resolves.[108]

By this time, late in October, Virginians knew that the Stamp Act threat would soon materialize in the person of a Distributor of Stamps, whose arrival from England was expected by the end of the month.

This officer was a man already well known to Virginians, for he was none other than Colonel George Mercer, aide to Washington in the French and Indian War and later his colleague from Frederick County in the House of Burgesses.[109]

Mercer had left the Old Dominion in 1763, hoping to receive a government appointment as a reward for his services in the American theater of what Englishmen chose to call the Seven Years War. He was armed with highest testimonials of the esteem in which he was held by fellow Virginians. He carried a letter to Edward Montagu, agent for the colony, from the Committee of Correspondence established by act of the General Assembly. In this communication, the committee related that Mercer, on entering the Virginia Regiment, was "at first appointed a captain but, as he soon distinguished himself by his gallant behavior, was promoted to the rank of a lieutenant-colonel, in which character he gained universal applause." In a letter of recommendation that was all any young man could ask, the committee said:

"This gentleman goes home to endeavor to be in some manner

rewarded for his faithful services, and you are desired to introduce him properly, and at the same time to use all your interest and influence in his favor. Besides this our recommendation, we doubt not but that his conduct and behavior will be such as to entitle him to your favor and protection."[110]

The recommendation was vastly increased in value by the attesting signatures: Peyton Randolph, Richard Bland, George Wythe, Robert Carter Nicholas, Lewis Burwell, John Blair, Peter Randolph and John Robinson.

The generous praise which filled this document was rivaled by the testimonial of the Governor and Council of Virginia. "We the Lieutenant-Governor and Council," it said, "do, with the highest satisfaction and the most religious regard to truth, hereby testify that the said George Mercer has for many years served in the troops of this colony, was lieutenant-colonel of a regiment, and always behaved as a brave and gallant officer—That he has often been employed by the government in many important services, and ever discharged the trusts reposed in him with the greatest expedition, exactness and fidelity: That his conduct in every station and upon all occasions, as well in a private as public capacity, has been such as we have observed with pleasure and can commend with justice: And judging him entitled to all the favor, countenance and protection due to honor, virtue and merit, we most willingly give him this testimonial. . . ."[111]

Despite the prodigal praise of Virginia leaders, Mercer did not secure a government appointment in England until 1765 when Grenville, perhaps seeking an agent whose popularity would compensate for the unpopularity of a hated Act of Pariament, asked him to serve as Distributor of Stamps for Virginia. Mercer accepted reluctantly.

"From the beginning," he later said, "I was convinced it would be an unpopular office, and took the liberty to mention it often to Mr. Grenville; although I was of opinion, from the necessity an opposition to the law would reduce the colonists to, and the absurdity (as I really conceived it) of their union in any particular point, the act would enforce itself."[112] Whatever reassurance Colonel Mercer had gained from his own sophistry and from conversations with Grenville was badly shaken when, before leaving London, he read the Virginia Resolves on the Stamp Act. At that moment, Mercer later confessed, "I was alarmed and still more convinced of the difficulties I must encounter on my arrival in Virginia. . . . I then expressed, in strong terms, my concern, and would not have proceeded farther in the office but for the consideration of the method in which I was appointed, and knowing it was then too late to appoint another. Having accepted, too, when all was calm and quiet, I thought I could not be justified in quitting the charge when there were appearances of a storm."

Though commissioned August 2, Mercer was left to agonize in London until September 12 when, after delays occasioned by contrary winds and difficulties regarding his ship, he sailed to Virginia with stamps for the Old Dominion, Maryland and North Carolina.[113]

The colonel's apprehension must have been very nearly matched by that of the Governor who awaited his arrival. Fauquier had not even been favored with instructions from London regarding reception of a Stamp Act Distributor and had learned about Mercer's appointment only through the public prints.[114] But he was responsible for maintaining order and the dignity of his Majesty's government in Virginia, and this duty would be greatly complicated by Mercer's arrival.

Use of the stamps would be required beginning November 1. There were rumblings of revolt from the colony's ruling class. Justices of two counties had filed petitions for appointment of their successors, for they had sworn not to serve in any public capacity requiring use of the hated stamps.[115]

Apart from the context of the times, these petitions might not have seemed ominous. In 1744, seven gentlemen justices of Spotsylvania County had paralyzed local government by refusing to continue in office because the Governor had filled a vacancy on the court without consulting them.[116] But the Spotsylvania instance, as in similar cases, had been an isolated occurrence. The justices of individual counties occasionally took umbrage at a real or imagined slight from the Governor. Attempts to enforce the Stamp Act might be regarded as a threat by the justices of many counties, and these officials from all parts of Virginia might unite in passive destruction of the colony's local government.

The thought of such a possibility was enough to keep any Royal Governor awake through nights of painful cogitation. The justices were the key men in each county. Individually they exercised authority in a number of matters ranging from the issuance of peace bonds and summonses to the settlement of suits for small debts.[117] Collectively, of course, they comprised the county court, a body exercising executive as well as judicial functions and empowered to fix the rate of local taxation.[118] Without the advantage of any such legal guarantee, many of the justices enjoyed life tenure. They had established the custom of nominating any justices to be added to the court and, as the Spotsylvania incident of 1744 showed, were quick to express their indignation when a Governor transgressed the unwritten law.[119] If they chose to express that feeling by resigning, their action not only suspended the court, but exercised a powerful influence on other officers. The clerk of the county owed his job to direct vote of the justices. The sheriff, the coroner, tobacco inspectors and militia officials below the rank of brigadier were all commissioned by the Governor on recommendation of the justices.[120] If the justices should simply suspend operation of the courts, and months of judicial inactivity should stretch into years, the citizens had no power to discharge them from office.[121] It is no exaggeration to say, as one historian has, that "Neither Williamsburg nor London controlled the government of the Virginia counties."[122]

There was dramatic evidence that popular hatred of the Stamp Act was far stronger in Virginia than the hitherto general admiration of the man appointed Distributor. Mercer had been burned in effigy in the Northern Neck.[123] There were rumors that angry men would march on Williamsburg and destroy the consignment of stamps when it arrived.[124]

In the last days of October, with planters and merchants crowding into Williamsburg for the customary settlement of accounts at the General Court, which would convene November 1, there was an exchange of inflammatory prejudices and a collective generation of indignation. On Wednesday, the thirtieth of October, the ship *Leeds* arrived in the York River with Colonel Mercer and the stamps.

Prudently leaving the stamps on board, Mercer disembarked at a York landing, rode to Williamsburg, and quietly took up private lodgings.[125]

Word of his arrival may have been welcomed by Fauquier as relief from suspense, but the Governor was sorely troubled by the conjunction of events that brought the Stamp Act Distributor to Williamsburg two days before the General Court. "Very unluckily," he said, "Colonel Mercer arrived at the time this town was the fullest of strangers."[126]

"I then thought proper," the Governor later reported, "to go to the Coffee House (where I occasionally . . . go) which is situated in that part of the town which is called the Exchange, though an open street where all money business is transacted. My particular reason for going then was that I might be an eyewitness of what did really pass, and not receive it by relation from others. The mercantile people were all assembled as usual. The first word I heard was 'One and all!' upon which, as at a word agreed on before between themselves, they all quitted the place to find Colonel Mercer at his father's lodgings, where it was known he was."

Governor Fauquier was astonished at some of the faces he recognized among the jostling throng that pressed on with a sort of primitive fury to the quarters of a respected attorney and his soldier son whom they had once hailed as a hero. "This concourse of people," he said, "I should call a mob, did I not know that it was chiefly, if not altogether, composed of gentlemen of property."[127]

When the surging mass got as far as the capitol, it came to an abrupt halt, for walking toward them was the man they sought.[128] Colonel Mercer quickly found himself surrounded by what seemed to be more than two thousand hostile faces.[129]

Someone voiced the demand of the crowd:

"Will you resign or act in this office as Distributor of the Stamps?"[130]

"The issue means a great deal to me," Mercer replied, and his control must have elicited grudging admiration. "I cannot attempt to answer your question at once. I shall have to give it thought. I shall make my answer Friday at ten o'clock in the morning, here in front of the capitol."[131]

With the air of a man who had said his say, Mercer resumed his walk toward the Coffee House. But the crowd would not be so summarily put off. Friday was the day the stamps were supposed to go into circulation. An answer then would be too late. The mob— surely Mercer did not suffer Fauquier's compunctions about using this name—followed him and all but surrounded him like a guard as he walked. All the while excited planters argued and expostulated, clenching their fists and waving their arms.

Thus was the unhappy colonel escorted to the Coffee House, and it must have been with great relief that he saw sitting on its porch, the Governor, most of the Councillors and Speaker Robinson. Eagerly he strode toward these stout symbols of law and order. Fauquier and his associates immediately received him "with the greatest marks of welcome," taking care that none of their warm smiles and ostentatious gestures of friendship escaped general notice.[132]

When Mercer turned to face the crowd, he saw it wore a single expression—a look of frowning savagery. On the porch, he had the advantage of elevation above the seething mass. Appeals for him to resign and declare himself for the people's cause, pleas signed by his friends, were passed up to him. Mercer started to speak, and the mutterings of the crowd subsided. He reminded the people that he had promised to announce his decision on Friday.

"Friday is too late," one or more voices yelled amid the general agitation. The cry might have become a chant, but someone else called out, "Promise to give your answer tomorrow."

"Tomorrow!" came the discordant chorus. But Mercer stood firm.

A voice cut through the confusion: "Let's rush in." The words had the force of a command. Forward the crowd surged with a fury that threatened to overrun those in front unless they charged up the steps. Instantly, Fauquier and the Councillors sprang from their seats and formed a living wall at the head of the stairs.

"See the Governor!" someone shouted. "Take care of him." Fauquier was the embodiment of British majesty in Virginia, and he looked it. The leaders of the mob faltered, then backed down the steps. Gradually the crowd withdrew a short distance from the porch. Messages passed back and forth between the two groups as between negotiating armies. Eventually Mercer promised to give his answer at five o'clock in the afternoon of the next day.

Fauquier and Mercer now waited for the crowd to disperse, and waited in vain. Twilight was thickening, and savagery lurked in the shadows. Mercer's life would be at stake if he remained at the Coffee House. But the alternative was walking through the crowd to his lodgings. The Governor grasped the situation and suggested to the colonel that they walk away together to the Governor's Palace.

A show of confidence was essential if the two men were to carry off this bold scheme. Down the steps they walked with firm and deliberate tread. Through the crowd they strode. A low cacophony of ominous muttering increased the nightmare quality of their un-hurried walk through the deepening shadows. The prudence-enforced slowness of their pace increased the air of unreality. When the mob thinned, Mercer and his distinguished escort were still not secure. Silent death might spring upon them from the dark. How indescrib-able their relief must have been when they passed through the palace gate, heard a ponderous door turn on its heavy hinges, and saw a rectangle of warm yellow light leap out from the gloom!

That night and the next morning Mercer was "assured [by] all the chief gentlemen of the place, not only of the danger of an attempt, but of the impossibility, to execute the act." He became convinced that there was not "a single person in the whole colony who dared openly to assist" him.[133]

What would he do under these circumstances? Precisely that question was in the minds of virtually all the citizens of Williamsburg and the other Virginians who, in town for the General Court, swelled the population till the capital could not contain them in comfort. Fever pitch curiosity had brought a large and expectant crowd to the capitol building long before 5 o'clock Thursday afternoon, the hour at which Mercer had promised to give his answer. By the time the colonel arrived, he was facing a host even larger than that which had threatened him the evening before.

The excitement of the mob was unmistakable. Some of the men who faced him might be mad enough to kill. Would they even listen to him? This was no time to risk the possibility of an ill-chosen word that might bring death before the speaker could clarify his statement. Mercer began reading from a prepared statement.

"Gentlemen," he read, "I now have met you agreeable to yesterday's promise to give my country—." He had called Virginia his country. Some members of the crowd were quick to note the reference. They listened respectfully. "To give my country," he said, "some assurance, which I would have been glad to do . . ., with any propriety, sooner."[134]

It was clear by this time that the mob was willing to listen. A misunderstood word, though, could still provoke the crowd to violence.

"I flatter myself no judicious man could blame me for accepting an office under an authority that never was disputed by anyone [by] whom I could have been advised of the propriety or right of the objections."

Mercer now became disarmingly frank:

"I do acknowledge that, some little time before, I heard of and saw some resolves which were said to be made by the House of Burgesses of Virginia, but as the authority of them was disputed, they never appearing but in private hands, and so often and differently reported to me, I determined to know the real sentiments of my countrymen from themselves. And I am compelled to say"— Was that a wry smile twisting the corners of Mercer's lips?—"that those sentiments were so suddenly and unexpectedly communicated to me that I was altogether unable to give an immediate answer upon so important a point."

The colonel must have drawn confidence from his sense of the crowd's emotions as he went on:

"In however an unpopular light I may lately have been viewed, and notwithstanding the many insults I have from this day's conversation been informed have been offered me in effigy in many parts of this colony, yet I still flatter myself that time will justify me and that my conduct may not be condemned after having been cooly inquired into."

There was no mistaking the eager interest on the faces before him. They were ready to give rapt attention to the colonel's story.

"This commission so very disagreeable to my countrymen," he said, "was obtained by the genteel recommendation of their representatives in the General Assembly, *unasked for*. And, though this is contrary to public report, which I am told charges me with assisting in the passage of the Stamp Act upon the promise of a commission in this colony, yet I hope it will meet with credit when I assure you that I was so far from assisting it or having any previous promise from the Ministry that *I did not know of my appointment until some time after my return from Ireland, where I was at the commencement of the session of Parliament and for a long time after the act had been passed.*

"Thus, gentlemen, am I circumstanced." Now he would reveal his intentions.

"I should be glad to act now in such a manner as would justify me to my friends and countrymen here and the authority which appointed me. But the time you have all allotted me is so very short that I have not yet been able to discover that happy medium and therefore must entreat you to be referred to my future conduct with this assurance in the meantime, that *I will not, directly or indirectly, by my deputies or myself, proceed further with the Act until I receive further orders from England, and not then without the assent of the General Assembly of this Colony [whom] no man can more ardently or sincerely wish the prosperity of than myself . . ., your sincere friend and humble servant. . . ."*

Mercer made a motion as though to leave. But men dashed forth from the crowd to seize him and lift him off his feet. They were wild with excitement—but not with anger. On their shoulders, they bore the colonel in triumph to the Coffee House. And there, in the very place where they had threatened his life the day before, they plied him with food and drink in an orgy of hero worship.

The next day Mercer was the central figure in a tense drama enacted on a smaller stage.[135] The General Court convened and the crier shouted the usual proclamation to open court, but no litigants appeared. No lawyers presented themselves except the King's Attorney, who sat "at his place at the table within the bar." An acute observer, though, might have been able to spot some members of the bar among the throng that packed the room. The Governor had the proclamation repeated and, when silence ensued, addressed Colonel Mercer, asking whether he could supply the Court with proper stamps so that its business might be conducted according to the law. The colonel said he could not, and explained in a vein similar to that of his speech the night before.

Fauquier then asked the clerk whether he could carry on the business of the Court without the stamps. "I cannot," was the answer, "without subjecting myself to such penalties as I would not expose myself to."

As Governor, Fauquier was ex officio President of the Court. He now asked each of his "brother judges" separately: "May we not legally adjourn to the tenth of April next, as there is no business before us?"

One of the justices, turning to the Governor, asked, "Have you received any particular instructions or directions how to act on this occasion?"

"I have not," the Governor answered, and there was unanimous agreement the Court might adjourn until the April term.

At this moment, Mercer rose and offered his resignation to the Governor, who said he had no authority to accept it.

The colonel had one remaining obligation, to protect the stamps which had been entrusted to him. He had tried, without the slightest success, to bribe men to bring the stamps from his ship, and he was now convinced that the hated seals "would be immediately destroyed if they were landed."[136] Accordingly, he applied to Captain Stirling, commander of the Royal warship *Rainbow*, to take the stamps aboard for safekeeping, as Fauquier said, "till the madness of the people" subsided.[137]

A week later, the Governor reported to the Lords of Trade in great detail concerning the events surrounding Mercer's arrival. "The first and most obvious consequences of all this," he wrote, "must be the shutting up [of] all the ports and stopping [of] all proceedings in the courts of justice." But in these very conditions he found food for optimism. "I am not without hopes," he said, "that the distress the country will feel on a total stagnation of business will open their eyes and pave the way for the act's executing itself. For I am very credibly informed that some of the busy men in opposing the reception of the stamps are already alarmed at the consequences of the imprudent steps they have taken."[138]

Fauquier had correctly stated "the first and most obvious consequences." He could not give stamped clearances to vessels since no stamps were available. Like his fellow governors in the American colonies, he could only issue "certificates of impossibility" to outward-bound vessels, and hope that these papers would prevent seizure of the ships by British men-of-war. English shipmasters heard rumors that, if they attempted to carry stamps to Virginia, their vessels might be burned and they themselves might meet death at the end of a rope. They concluded that discretion was the better part of valor.[139]

Fauquier was soon proved right in his prediction that proceedings would be halted in the courts of justice. From Caroline County, William Allason wrote on December 8:

"We are now entirely without a law, and have been since the first [of] November. The Stamp Officer, immediately on his arrival, was under a necessity of giving a formal resignation from under his hand. There is none other qualified for that purpose, nor dare take it upon them at the peril of their lives and everything that is dear to them, from the enraged mob. And so it is in all the other governments on the Continent. No judgment can be formed of the consequences . . . by which we shall have nothing but anarchy and confusion in every part of this extensive country."[139]

Governor Fauquier did not share Allason's alarm. He hoped to call another session of the General Assembly and, with Tidewater Burgesses in full attendance, secure the passage of resolutions repudiating the Virginia Resolves introduced by Patrick Henry.[140]

* * *

Early in 1766 many Virginia counties were approaching the anarchy which Allason had envisioned. Some county courts closed altogether, thus depriving the districts which they served not only of the judicial operations of government, but also of the legislative and executive. Others convened only to fix county-tax levies and conduct the few types of business legal without the use of stamps. But, even in operating on such a limited scale, they performed a valuable function.[141]

Some judicious men were of the same mind as Edmund Pendleton, now presiding justice of Caroline County, who, explaining why he kept his court in session even when little could be done without stamps, said:

"Our distributor of stamps having resigned, a great part of the business of this colony must stop and some courts decline to sit altogether. But I don't think that prudent. As the appearance of courts may convince the people that there is not a total end of laws, though they are disabled to act in some instances, I think they should be held for that purpose and as many things done as can be without stamps, particularly wills, which may be proved and ordered to be recorded, though they can't be recorded, nor any order made for the appraisement. Administration can't be granted because the bond can't be taken. Grand juries may be sworn and all proceedings had on their presentments and all criminal matters or breaches of the peace. Justices may issue and try any warrants or attachments . . . [returnable to them as individual officers] but not attachments returnable to Court."[142]

When the court met in February, Pendleton proposed that it take up any matters normally within its jurisdiction, ignoring the Stamp Act on the grounds that it violated the British constitution.[143] "It appears to me," he argued, "we must resolve either to admit the stamps or to proceed without them, for to stop all business must be a greater evil than either. And who is there that will admit them? Not one in 1000, I believe. For my own part, I never have or will enter into noisy and riotous companies on the subject; my sentiments I shall be always ready to communicate to serious men. As a magistrate, I thought it my duty to sit, and we have constantly opened court, and I shall not hesitate to determine what people desire me to, and run the risk of themselves; and, having taken an oath to decide according to law, shall never consider that act as such for want of power (I mean constitutional authority) in the Parliament to pass it. . . . Were I applied to for an attachment, or any other thing within my office out of court, I would grant it at the party's risk as to the validity of it, for I am not afraid of the penalty, at least so much as breaking my oath."[144]

When Pendleton proposed that the county court ignore the Stamp Act, some of his fellow justices assented, but others disagreed. They opposed the Act as strongly as Pendleton himself, but they argued that to proceed without stamps would be injurious to innocent litigants. The General Court, these justices reasoned, would not sanction operation without stamps and, when appealed to by a losing defendant, would "reverse, for want of stamps, all the county courts do, to the ruin and vexation of the suitors."[145]

"Others say," Pendleton explained in recording the views of those who disagreed with him, "that the Governor, being enjoined by oath and the duty of his station to endeavour to enforce the law, as soon as he is informed the courts are proceeding, must issue new commissions to turn the magistrates out of office; and as none that are fit for it will, and others dare not, succeed them, a total privation of magistracy must follow."[146]

Pendleton did not attempt to force his views upon his fellow justices, and their objections prevailed. But opposition to the Stamp Act burned hot in Virginia when a leader enjoying Pendleton's prestige with conservative Tidewater Burgesses urged a Virginia county court to declare unconstitutional an act of the British Parliament. Some counties were bolder than Caroline. The justices of Northampton, whose citizens had formally protested against taxation without representation as early as 1651, instructed their clerk to disregard the Stamp Act, as it was void. Two weeks later Accomack took the same action.[147]

Pendleton's brother magistrates had correctly evaluated the problem facing the Governor if he should attempt to replace recalcitrant justices. Fauquier himself had anticipated the problem. Just two days after the Stamp Act officially went into effect he informed the Lords of Trade that the result of gubernatorial removal of incumbent justices would be either "that the courts must have been filled with a meaner sort of people, or there could have been no courts at all, the last of which was to be expected. For, if the first gentlemen of the counties refused to act, it would have become a fashion for the others to follow their examples. Indeed, they would hardly have dared to have done other. And, if these gentlemen had been removed, without a proper submission they could never have been reinstated."[148]

Pendleton, who said that he would never "enter into noisy and riotous companies" as an expression of opposition to the Stamp Act, must have been indignant with scorn when he learned of events at Leedstown February 27 and of what happened at Hobbs Hole the next day.[149]

The sequence of violent events was touched off when Archibald Ritchie, a merchant of Hobbs Hole on the south bank of the Rappahannock in Essex County, made a bold declaration at the February Court across the river in Richmond County. He said he knew where he could get stamps and that he would clear his vessels with "stamped paper" in compliance with the Act of Parliament. Richard Henry Lee had already used his brilliant oratorical gifts to nurse the wrath of Northern Neck residents into a flaming fury against all who would comply with the act. The planters of that peninsula were quick to perceive that submission by the merchants would permit partial enforcement of the despised legislation. If one merchant used the stamps with impunity, others would do likewise, and the whole battle in defense of self-taxation would be lost.

On February 27, some of the leading Northern Neck planters met at Leedstown, in Richard Henry Lee's county of Westmoreland, to discuss the problem posed by Ritchie's announcement. They adopted articles of association declaring that they bound themselves "to each other, to God, and to our country, by the firmest ties that religion and virtue can frame, most sacredly and punctually to stand by, and with our lives and fortunes to support, maintain, defend each other in the observance and execution" of the articles to which they subscribed. In the preamble, they said that they were "roused by danger and alarmed at attempts, foreign and domestic, to reduce the people of this country to a state of abject and detestable slavery by destroying that free and happy constitution of government under which they have hitherto lived . . . ."

After declaring "due allegiance and obedience" to the King and determination "to preserve the laws, the peace and good order of the colony, as far as is consistent with the preservation of our constitutional rights and liberty," the associators stated that a Virginian, being a British citizen, could not legally be tried except by a jury of his peers nor taxed except by a legislature in which he was represented. "If, therefore, any person or persons," the resolutions read, "shall attempt by any action or proceeding to deprive this colony of those fundamental rights, we will immediately regard him or them as the most dangerous enemy of the community; and we will go to any extremity not only to prevent the success of such attempts, but to stigmatize and punish the offender."

In the third article of their declaration, the associators stated:

"As the Stamp Act does absolutely direct the property of the people to be taken from them without their consent expressed by their representatives, and as in many cases it deprives the British American subject of his right to trial by jury; we do determine, at every hazard and paying no regard to danger or to death, we will exert every faculty to prevent the execution of the said Stamp Act in every instance whatsoever within this colony. And every abandoned wretch who shall be so lost to virtue and public good as wickedly to contribute to the introduction or fixture of the Stamp Act in this colony, by using stamp paper, or by any other means, we will, with the utmost expedition, convince all such profligates that immediate danger and disgrace shall attend their profligate purposes."

Next the resolutions provided:

"That the last article may most surely and effectually be executed, we engage to each other that, whenever it shall be known to any of this association that any person is so conducting himself as to favor the introduction of the Stamp Act, that immediate notice shall be given to as many of the association as possible; and that every individual so informed shall, with expedition, repair to a place of meeting to be appointed as near the scene of action as may be."

Each associator was pledged to obtain as many new signers as possible and to risk his "life and fortune" in defense of any member who suffered assaults on "liberty or property" as a "consequence of this agreement."

It took no seer to determine the identity of the first "abandoned wretch" whom the associators would "convince . . . that immediate danger and disgrace [attended his] profligate purposes."

The day following the meeting four hundred men gathered in the little town of Hobbs Hole. Like other groups that had appeared in Boston and New York, they called themselves "Friends of Liberty" or "Sons of Liberty," thus assuming in pride a name that had been scornfully applied to colonials in the course of Parliamentary debate. Most members of the crowd aligned themselves on either side of the little street, and a committee went to Ritchie's door to demand that he sign a paper drafted the day before at Leedstown.

Ritchie asked that a committee be named to "reason with him on the subject." His visitors assured him the Sons of Liberty were not in a bargaining mood. He must either sign the paper or submit to his punishment, already prescribed by resolution, which was to be "stripped naked to his waist, tied to the tail of a cart, and drawn to the public pillory, where he should be fixed for one hour; and if in that time he did not comply, that he should be brought up by the whole company to Leedstown, there to be further determined on, as should seem expedient to the Friends of Liberty." Ritchie was then invited to step outside where the "Friends of Liberty" from both sides of the Rappahannock awaited him in grimly solemn files. He knew the invitation was a command, and he obeyed it. Ritchie stood while one of the men read to him the declaration which he was ordered to sign. "Sensible now of the high insult I offered this county," read the statement, "by my declaration at Richmond Court lately of my determination to make use of stamped paper for clearing out vessels; and having been convinced such proceedings will establish a precedent by which the hateful Stamp Act might be introduced into this colony to the utter destruction of the public liberty, I do most submissively in the presence of the public sign the paper meaning to show my remorse for having formed so execrable a declaration, and I do hereby solemnly promise and swear on the Holy Evangelist that no vessel of mine shall clear on stamped paper; that I never will on any pretense make use of stamped paper unless that use be authorized by the General Assembly of this colony."

What galling phrases. Every element of pride in Ritchie rebelled against the idea of signing such a declaration. "Is the statement just?" one of the leaders asked. The merchant saw two long lines of faces as grim as death's heads. He murmured that the declaration was just, took the quill handed him, and signed his name.

* * *

By March, hopes were high in Virginia that the Stamp Act would be repealed. Royle's *Virginia Gazette* fed those hopes. The March 7 issue of the Williamsburg newspaper carried under a Philadelphia dateline of January 30 the "Extract of a letter from a Gentleman in London to his friend here," in which the anonymous Englishman reported:

"I have the pleasure to assure you there is a plan formed for your relief by the new ministry, who are really friends to America. It is not your mother country, it is not your King, oppresses you, but it was a bad ministry, who carried things so far as to bring universal odium on themselves."[150]

In the same issue was a correspondent's report of February 6:

"Our advices, by private letters from Cork, are that the people of Ireland highly commend the opposition the North Americans have given to the Stamp Act; and that it was the general opinion there that that law would be repealed, or at least suspended, on the meeting of the Parliament."

Optimism undimmed on the eve of the Ides of March, next week's issue of the Gazette featured a dispatch from New York which said:

"We are favored with copies of many other letters, dated from the 14th to the 19th of December last, to gentlemen in this city, from several members of Parliament, eminent merchants and gentlemen of distinction in London, from which we have made the following extracts:

"That, in general, our opposition to the Stamp Act has been highly approved in England, except the acts of violence . . . which, though generally disapproved among us, and executed by men not at all concerned in our cause, . . . furnish the enemies of the colonies . . . with arguments which they are glad to improve against them. . . . These disorders are generally blamed in England, but they are even there commonly imputed to the right authors; that is, to the contrivers and promoters of the late oppressive acts, and especially the Stamp Act, calculated to strip us of all our most valuable inherent rights, liberty and property, to overturn the English Constitution and reduce us to the condition of slaves. . . . It was the general opinion, especially among the most intelligent people, that the Stamp Act in particular ought to be, and would be, immediately repealed or suspended as soon as the Parliament met, as also some other oppressive acts and measures, which were thought to be injudicious, impolitic and attended with extreme bad consequences to Great Britain.

"That many gentlemen in London had so nobly exerted themselves, both by speaking and writing, in favor of the colonies that they had convinced and brought over many who had formerly opposed them to espouse their cause (which is indeed the cause of Great Britain also) and become their powerful friends and advocates . . .; and that their cause was becoming more and more popular."[151]

Encouraging news indeed for those who longed for an end to the Stamp Act and a reconciliation with the government in London! But some skeptical readers of the *Virginia Gazette* must have recalled that the November 4, 1763 issue had carried a similar dispatch from a New York correspondent who said that in Britain "taxes were continued very high and paid unwillingly" to support the military establishment. "From private letters by the packet," this correspondent had said, "we learn that the national discontent seemed rather to increase than abate, and it was thought the ministry would soon be changed."[152]

Some radicals probably enjoyed their skepticism, for the fight against Parliament had lifted them from obscurity. The Leedstown Association had inspired imitation. On March 31, Norfolk Sons of Liberty resolved to use all "lawful ways and means" to protect their right "of being taxed by none but representatives of their own choosing and of being tried only by a jury of their own peers." Most Virginians were prepared for a long struggle, if it proved necessary. Reconciliation, though, was undoubtedly the earnest desire of virtually all responsible leaders and the masses of the people.

Washington's prediction that passage of the Stamp Act would bring a closing of the courts and a decline in trade that would make British merchants advocates of repeal had proved true. One Englishman wrote:

"You must know that the Stamp Affair has been the only topic for some time over all Britain, and in short seemed to be the whole cause of the Parliament's meeting, [judging] by the King's speech. The trading part of the country and manufacturers seem all to be keen for a repeal or a mitigation, though at the same time [they] condemn the behavior of the colonies."[153]

The April 11 issue of Purdie and Dixon's *Virginia Gazette* carried the letter of a Bristol merchant, who declared:

"Of late, there has been a total stagnation of all business; thousands of poor manufacturers at Birmingham, Sheffield, Yorkshire, etc., have been turned off, and are now starving for want of employ. And what the consequences will be, unless the Stamp Act is repealed, God only knows, as all the orders for goods to be sent to North America are conditional and not to be sent until the act is repealed."[154]

On the second day of May, the ship *Lady Baltimore* sailed into the York River with the most welcome cargo to arrive in Virginia in many days—news that the Stamp Act had been repealed.[155] There was rejoicing in England among merchants and manufacturers,[156] but their pleasure did not exceed that of William Pitt who had led the fight against the tax and who now declared that he had "never had greater satisfaction than in the repeal of this Act."[157] Formal proclamation of repeal in Virginia, June 9, touched off a series of celebrations. Rejoicing reached its climax amid a glitter and cacophony of "general illuminations, bells, bonfires, guns [and] fireworks"[158] with a great party led by the Governor which, according to the seemingly contradictory statements of a Williamsburg editor, "spent the evening with much mirth and decorum, and drank all the loyal and patriotic toasts."[159] Only a man of prodigious capacity could maintain his decorum while drinking "all the loyal and patriotic toasts." For there were tributes to the King, to Mr. Pitt, to other Parliamentary leaders and even to Parliament as a whole. The erstwhile villains of Whitehall were now heroes.[160]

In the frenzy of their rejoicing, Virginians and other American colonists overlooked the fact that, on the very day the repeal measure had been enacted into law, there had also been enacted a Declaratory Act asserting that Parliament had full authority to make laws for the American colonists "in all cases whatsoever."

*　*　*

Tragedy struck in Virginia just nine days after the good news of Stamp Act repeal. John Robinson, Speaker of the House and Treasurer of the colony, died. For nearly forty years he had helped to govern Virginia, and for more than half that period he had been its most powerful citizen.[161] United in him were the aristocracy, wealth, intelligence, generosity and capacity for leadership that the Old Dominion's ruling class liked to regard as its own peculiar attributes. Almost exactly five years before Robinson's death, Governor Fauquier, himself an able and popular man, had reported to the Lords of Trade that the Speaker was "the darling of the Country," and deservedly so because of his "great integrity, assiduity and ability in business."[162]

Edmund Randolph both recorded and explained in part the extent of Robinson's influence when he wrote:

"When he presided, the decorum of the House outshone that of the British House of Commons . . . When he propounded a question, his comprehension and perspicuity brought it equally to the most humble and the most polished understanding. To committees he nominated the members best qualified. He stated to the House the contents of every bill, and showed himself to be a perfect master of the subject. When he pronounced the rules of order, he convinced the reluctant. When on the floor of a committee of the whole house he opened the debate, he submitted resolutions and enforced them with simplicity and might. In the limited sphere of colonial politics, he was a column.

"Hence he was, for a long time, elevated above the criticism of his faults. The thousand little flattering attentions, which can be scattered from the chair, operated as a delicious incense."[163]

Purdie's *Virginia Gazette*, after eulogizing Robinson's public career, said:

"The many amiable virtues which adorned his private station, whilst they consecrate his memory among his friends, dependents and acquaintance mark his death as a calamity to be lamented by the unfortunate and indigent who were wont to be relieved and cherished by his humanity and liberality."[164]

The writer of that obituary did not suspect how many planters not generally regarded as "indigent" had been "relieved and cherished" by the Treasurer's "humanity and liberality." Soon all Virginia knew.

The Receiver-General was charged with responsibility for collection of royal revenues,[165] but the Treasurer—who operated independently of that officer—was appointed by the General Assembly to be custodian and disburser of revenues.[166] As Governor Fauquier himself once explained to the Lords of Trade, the office of Treasurer had been conferred upon Robinson "as a recompense for his service as . . . [Speaker], the advantages and profits arising from the Speakership being very inconsiderable, and inadequate to the great trouble and attendance of that office."[167] The Treasurer received in payment for his services 2½ percent of all money granted and raised by the General Assembly.[168] Among his duties was the burning of all Treasury notes received in payment for taxes so as to remove the emergency currency from circulation.[169]

In June 1765, Fauquier had explained the hardship that burning worked upon the people. "Circulating currency," he wrote, "is grown very scarce so that people are really distressed for money of any kind to satisfy their creditors. And this evil is daily increasing; for the Treasury notes are annually diminished by the burning and sinking [of] all that are received for taxes; and gold or silver cannot pass in common circulation, as by the laws in force they cannot pass as their real value at the present high exchange, so that there is no appearance of either in the colony."[170]

Under such conditions, the burning of paper money seemed criminal to many Virginians. Some reasoned that obedience to the law was not necessary when it would send good men to ruin. Besides, these were times when some men earned the title of "patriot" by resisting unjust laws. It is not surprising that some of Robinson's friends, faced with the loss of their estates, pressured him to lend them some of the paper money. Surely, events would soon take a turn for the better and then they would, on their honor as gentlemen, make due restitution.

A year before Robinson's death, rumors were rife that money supposed to have been burned was still in circulation because the Treasurer had "not been sufficiently strict with the sheriffs and inspectors" to prevent them from lending out "considerable sums."[171] As early as January 10, 1764, "The Merchants in Glasgow Trading to Virginia" had, in a memorial to the Lords of Trade and Plantations, urged "that such notes as are brought into the Treasury be duly burnt at the oyer and terminer courts in June and December at the sight of a committee of the Council and Burgesses, whereby all possibility of issuing them out again would be prevented."[172]

Legislative committees had several times investigated the state of the Treasury notes and had found no irregularities.[173]

On reading the June 13 issue of Purdie and Dixon's *Virginia Gazette*, Virginians learned of the anxiety in which some of their prominent neighbors had been living since Robinson's death. There was a notice in which Edmund Pendleton, an administrator of the late Treasurer's estate, said that all of its debtors "must make immediate payment," and then, shifting from the imperative to a note of appeal, added:

"As the deceased gentleman, in his lifetime, from a goodness of heart and benevolent disposition peculiar to himself, could not resist the importunities of the distressed, but advanced large sums of money to assist and relieve his friends, and others in that situation that applied to him, and was always ready to advance his credit and fortune to assist such as really stood in need of it, his administrators now hope that all those that have received favors from him will, in honor and gratitude to the memory of so kind a friend and benefactor, pay immediately what they owe, without further trouble or application; and even cheerfully sell their own estates to discharge it, rather than suffer the estate of their friend to be distressed for the payment of their debts."[174]

It soon became known that Robinson's friends owed his estate more than £130,000, nearly £30,000 of which the generous man had lent from his own substance, but the remainder of which—more than £100,000—had come from the Treasury. Moreover, the list of debtors read almost like an Almanac de Gotha of Virginia. Some of these debtors—like Henry Fitzhugh, John Randolph, Lewis Burwell, Carter Braxton, the Lees of the Northern Neck and the Churchills of Middlesex—had borrowed so little or were so wealthy that reasonably prompt payment could be expected from them. But, in the cases of some gentlemen who bore the proud names of Byrd, Carter, Mercer, Moore and Grymes, their good intentions did not match their resources. Famous names were, of course, most conspicuous in the list of debtors, but shopkeepers and other tradesmen had also been the beneficiaries of Robinson's generosity with personal and public funds. In most cases, he had not required security from the borrowers. The Treasury records were almost hopelessly confused.[175]

As administrator of Robinson's estate, Edmund Pendleton was in a dilemma. If he did not act quickly to collect debts due the estate, he could not for a long time satisfy the demands of the Colony as creditor. If he did proceed promptly to collect what was due the estate, so many debtor families would be ruined that the economic structure of Tidewater would fall with them.[176] Pendleton resolved to give debtors to the estate a reasonable length of time to meet their obligations. Full payment of the estate's indebtedness to the Colony would not be possible for a number of years,[177] but the immediate threat to Tidewater economy was removed.

Many members of the ruling class were prepared to defend Robinson's honor. Governor Fauquier explained to the Earl of Shelburne that the late Treasurer had "illegally remitted" funds only "to supply the necessities of his distressed friends, to whom he could never give a denial." The Governor added, "Such was the sensibility of his too benevolent heart."[178]

Robert Carter Nicholas, who succeeded Robinson as Treasurer, afterwards said he "had abundant reason to believe" that his predecessor had lent money from public funds "more owing to a mistaken kind of humanity and compassion for persons in distress than any view to his own private emolument."[179]

Robinson's actions were not so kindly interpreted, however, by some political enemies within the ruling class, nor by a great many men outside it. The scandal weakened the prestige of the Tidewater oligarchy at a time when it was being challenged by the mountaineers who rallied around Patrick Henry.[180]

* * *

Hope burgeoned in Virginia when news arrived that a ministry headed by William Pitt, Lord Chatham, had come into power in August. Pitt had proved himself a strong defender of the colonial spirit of freedom. It soon became apparent, though, that he was a sick man. By the beginning of 1767, the Chancellor of the Exchequer, Charles Townshend, was Prime Minister in all but name.[181]

Publicly inveighing against Chatham's distinction between external and internal taxation, Townshend soon announced that he was preparing new revenue measures. Reducing the British land tax and thus cutting home revenue, he sought to compensate for this loss by taxation of the American colonists. On June 29, 1767, the Townshend Acts received the royal assent. They would become effective November 20.[182]

These measures imposed new import duties on glass, lead, paints, paper and tea. A preamble declared that the funds derived from this taxation could be used for the defense of the colonies, and also for "defraying the charge of the administration of justice and the support of civil government" in America.

To facilitate collection of the duties, the Townshend Acts provided for establishment of new vice-admiralty courts and an American Board of Commissioners of the Customs, resident in Boston and directly responsible to the British Treasury Board. In positive terms, the Townshend Act affirmed the right of superior court judges to issue writs of assistance as an aid to customs officials. "Champagne Charlie," as Townshend was called, congratulated himself upon having raised taxes in the colonies to compensate for reductions at home, at the same time keeping the new taxes well within the realm of external taxation, a distinction upon which the colonials insisted.

Thoughtful men in all the colonies were alarmed by the prospect of royal governors independent of the legislatures. Such an intolerable situation would exist if funds derived from a tax levied by Parliament were used for "defraying the charge of the administration of justice and the support of civil government" in America. Legislative control of the purse strings, in the colonies as in England itself, had been a chief deterrent to tyranny.

Colonial fears were justified when Townshend, angered by the New York Assembly's refusal to appropriate beer and cider money for General Gage's troops, rammed through Parliament a measure suspending the colonial legislature's powers, effective October 1, 1767, until its compliance with all requirements set forth by the general for the billeting of his men.

The suspension was not carried out by the governor since, unknown to Parliament, the Assembly had made an appropriation the preceding June.[183] Nevertheless, the danger to colonial liberties had been effectively demonstrated. What had happened in New York might happen anywhere in America—even in Virginia.

Yet royal governors were not everywhere hated. Governor Fauquier died on the third day of March 1768, and was laid to rest in Williamsburg with all the pomp and ceremony of which the little capital was capable. The *Virginia Gazette* apparently voiced the popular as well as the official estimate when it described him as "a gentleman of a most amiable disposition—generous, just and mild, and possessed in an eminent degree of all the social virtues."[184]

While in the grip of his fatal illness, Fauquier had issued a call for a General Assembly session the last of March to deal with a threat to frontier settlements posed by white encroachment on Indian lands along Red Stone Creek and Cheat River.

Having met and resolved that both Indians and settlers be adjured from fighting, and having also canceled the land tax and poll tax for two years, the Assembly began consideration of what was uppermost in the minds of the legislators and their constituents —the dangers to freedom implicit in the Townshend Acts.

Freeholders in some Virginia counties had petitioned the Assembly to support the proposals advanced in the Massachusetts Circular Letter of February 11.[185] This document, drafted by Samuel Adams and approved by the Massachusetts House of Representatives, voiced the old protest against taxation without representation, assailed action by Parliament to make colonial officials independent of the people, and appealed to all the colonies for united action in defense of liberty.

The House, sitting as Committee of the Whole, voted to address a petition to their sovereign, a memorial to the Lords, and a remonstrance to Commons. Richard Bland, Robert Carter Nicholas, Edmund Pendleton and Archibald Cary were named to a committee to prepare these papers.[186]

The appeal to His Majesty was a most respectful solicitation of his "fatherly goodness and protection."

The memorial to the Lords and remonstrance to Commons were logical, specific and argumentative. They restated a proposition that the Virginia legislators called the basic principle of British government: "No power on earth has a right to impose taxes upon the people or to take the smallest portion of their property without their consent, given by their representatives in Parliament." Since the colonies could not be represented in that body, the right of self taxation necessarily resided in the colonial legislatures. Parliament might rightly and lawfully regulate colonial trade for "the general welfare, . . . but a tax imposed upon such of the British exports as are necessities of life, to be paid by the colonials upon importation, and this not with the most distant view to the interests of commerce, but merely to raise a revenue, or in plainer words to compel the colonials to part with their money against their inclinations, your memorialists conceive to be a tax internal to all intents and purposes." Here was an adroit thrust at Charles Townshend's sophistic distinctions between internal and external taxation.

The Virginia legislators cited the "Suspending Act" directed at New York as an example of the threat to American liberties. They called it "more alarming" than measures restricting "to the colonies in general, though it has that single province in view as its immediate object." They asked: "What advantage could the people of the colonies derive from their right of choosing their own representatives [if], when chosen, [they were] not permitted to exercise their own judgments, [but] were under a necessity (on pain of being deprived of their legislative authority) of enforcing the mandates of a British Parliament, though ever so injurious to the interests of the Colony they represented?"[187]

In the remonstrance to Commons, the Virginians advanced the enlightened argument that the "exercise of anti-constitutional powers" anywhere in the Empire, even in so remote a part as Virginia, might set a dangerous example for the island kingdom itself. Expressing hopes that the soundness of this argument would be accepted in Westminster, the memorialists threatened:

"Should the remonstrants be disappointed in these hopes, the necessary result will be that the Colonists, reduced to extreme poverty, will be compelled to contract themselves within their little spheres and obliged to content themselves with their homespun manufactures."[188]

Richard Bland's committee had done its job well. The three documents that it had prepared were unanimously approved by the Burgesses and concurred in by the Council.

The House of Burgesses took additional action that ranged Virginia with Massachusetts in the building of American unity for defense of cherished liberties. By unanimous vote, the House instructed the Speaker, Peyton Randolph, to answer the Massachusetts Circular Letter with a declaration to its authors that Virginia legislators "could not but applaud them for their attention to American liberty," together with an expression of confidence that the steps taken by the Burgesses would convince their Massachusetts counterparts of Virginia's "fixed resolution to concur with the other colonies in their application for redress." Taking action appropriate to leaders of the colony that had rallied sister colonies on the eve of the French and Indian Wars, the Burgesses also instructed their speaker "to write to the respective speakers of the assemblies and representatives on this continent to make known to them our proceedings on this subject and to intimate how necessary we think it is that the colonies should unite in a firm but decent opposition to every measure which may affect the rights and liberties of the British colonies in America."[189]

Because the royal Governor had died just before this spring session of the Assembly of 1768, and the duties of his office had automatically devolved for the time upon the President of the Council, the aged John Blair, the Burgesses were able to take action with an impunity which they would not otherwise have enjoyed. Not only could they get by with moves which, under ordinary circumstances, would have insured their prompt dissolution, but they were allowed to gain extra time for their deliberations by running the session through the first full week of General Court.[190] In his report to Lord Hillsborough, Secretary for the Colonies, Blair wrote of the Burgesses:

"Though their reasons are delivered in strong terms, I hope your lordship will think them expressed with great modesty and dutiful submission, and as such I cannot but recommend them to your Lordship's favor."[191]

Toward the end of October 1768, Norbonne Berkeley, Baron de Botetourt, arrived in Virginia with a commission as royal Governor. Stocky and tending to portliness, he had an intelligent, pleasant face and a warm personality.[192] Moreover, he had arrived in the Old Dominion in an especially good humor. His voyage had been so pleasant that his lordship declared it was "impossible for people to live better together than the crew of His Majesty's Ship Rippon."[193] The king could scarcely have sent a more likeable representative to his discontented subjects in Virginia.

Botetourt found the Virginians as attractive as they found him. He discovered bare cupboards and empty larders in the Governor's Palace, but his diet did not suffer. Night after night, Williamsburg's most elegant households vied for the privilege of having him to dinner. The legislative leaders of the colony were in town for the General Court and they helped to impress the newcomer with the quality of Virginia hospitality. A few days after his arrival, Botetourt wrote Lord Hillsborough that he had met many Virginians and liked "their style exceedingly."[194]

The baron knew that this happy relationship, so quickly established, between Governor and people, was not an altogether dependable augury of his administration. He had been wined and dined by the colony's elder statesmen. These were the men whom Fauquier had called "the cool old members" of the General Assembly. But Fauquier had also lamented their loss of control in the legislature as a result of maneuvers by some of "the young, hot-headed, inexperienced members."[195]

Botetourt bore instructions from his Majesty to dissolve the Assembly and order their successors "to desist from their unwarrantable claims and pretensions, and yield due submission to the supreme authority of Parliament."[196]

Accordingly, the Governor prorogued the legislature, and elections were held in December.

But the Crown was aware that diplomacy as well as force would be necessary in dealing with the increasingly independent Virginians. Botetourt's instructions from his Majesty included directions "to make particular inquiry into the characters, views and connections of, and to hold converse with, the members of our said Council, separately and personally, as also with the principal persons of influence and credit in our said colony, and endeavor to lead them by every just argument that can be urged, to disclaim the erroneous and dangerous principles which they appear to have adopted, and to return to a becoming sense of their duty, founded upon just ideas of the Constitution."

The Crown's realization that Virginia could not be held by force alone was made evident Monday, May 8, 1769, when the newly elected Assembly convened. There was such pomp and pageantry as must have convinced the most skeptical Virginian that his sovereign attached importance to events in the Old Dominion.

The Governor rode down Duke of Gloucester Street to the capitol in a glittering coach drawn by six cream-white Hanoverian horses whose silver-mounted harness sparkled in the sun. The cheering crowds were dazzled by the splendor of the magnificent vehicle and its equipage. The procession was positively regal, and well it might be, for where the arms of Virginia were boldly blazoned on the coach's sides, the Royal Arms had once appeared. Originally built for the King, the imposing carriage had been presented to Botetourt by his Majesty's nephew, the Duke of Cumberland.[197] When had such elegance been seen in Virginia?

Arriving at the capitol, the Governor emerged in a red coat resplendent with gold braid that rivaled the sparkle of his coach.[198]

Later, seated amid the Council Chamber's dark furnishings, a fitting foil for his own glittering magnificence, he received the newly-organized House of Burgesses. The legislators presented their speaker, Peyton Randolph, who then reminded the Governor of the House's "ancient rights and privilege." This procedure was in accordance with time-honored ritual except that, whereas it had once been the custom to "petition" his Majesty's representative for the enjoyment of these "prerogatives," the speaker now "laid claim" to them.[199]

Sophisticated Virginians said that the Governor's manner in delivering his speech was like that of George III in reading the address from the throne. The effort to be ingratiating was obvious, but nonetheless flattering, when Botetourt said:

"It is a peculiar felicity to me, and a great addition to the many honors I have received from my Royal Master, that I have it in command from his Majesty to declare and communicate what will be so honorable to this colony and must therefore be so agreeable to you, his gracious intention that, for the future, his Chief Governors of Virginia shall reside within their government."[200]

The Governor's instructions were simply stated. "I have nothing to ask," he said, "but that you consider well and follow exactly, without passion or prejudice, the real interests of those you have the honor to represent; they are most certainly consistent with the prosperity of Great Britain, and so they will ever be found when pursued with temper and moderation."

The Burgesses were in complete agreement with this advice, but their definition of the "real interests" of their constituents was quite different from the Governor's.

Edmund Pendleton maneuvered the naming of a newcomer to the House, Thomas Jefferson, to the committee appointed to draft a reply to the Governor's speech.[201] This twenty-six-year-old Burgess was the same man who, as a college student four years before, had stood by the door of the legislative chamber and thrilled to Patrick Henry's eloquence.

When the committee met, Pendleton again exerted his influence in Jefferson's behalf—this time to see that the Albemarle legislator was assigned the duty of composing the reply to the Governor. The young man eagerly complied, but his prose was too simple to satisfy Robert Carter Nicholas who, besides being Burgess from James City County, was Treasurer of Virginia. Jefferson's composition, therefore, was rejected, and Nicholas prepared one which no one ventured to challenge.

Thomas Jefferson was crestfallen. He had muffed his first opportunity to gain prominence in the Assembly. Perhaps he would never again be entrusted with the writing of an important public document.[202]

On May 16, the House sat as Committee of the Whole to consider two threats to freedom. One was the citation in Parliament of a treason statute, dating from Henry VIII's reign, as legal authority for making colonials accused of treason stand trial in England. The second threat was the old one of "taxation without representation."[203]

There was no violent debate like the one over Patrick Henry's resolutions four years earlier, because this time the House was united in sentiment: There were resolutions reasserting the principle that the right of taxing Virginians had always been "legally and constitutionally vested in the House of Burgesses" and reiterating the propriety of petition to the throne. But the legislators were not content merely to affirm the right of petition, as in the past. They declared: "It is lawful and expedient to procure the concurrence of his Majesty's other colonies, in dutiful addresses, praying royal interposition in favor of the violated rights of America."[204]

In another resolution, the Burgesses dealt with a threat which had been raised in Parliament with the idea of making the colonists submissive, but which had had the opposite effect. They protested:

"The seizing any person or persons residing in this colony, suspected of any crime whatsoever committed therein, and sending such person or persons to places beyond the sea to be tried, is highly derogatory of the rights of British subjects; as thereby the inestimable privilege of being tried by a jury from the vicinage, as well as the liberty of summoning and producing witnesses on such trial, will be taken away from the party accused."[205]

The Committee of the Whole voted that the King be petitioned to end, by "his royal interposition," the "dangers and miseries" occasioned among his colonial subjects by the threat of removal for trial "in any other manner than by the ancient and long established course of proceedings." By unanimous vote, the Burgesses approved in regular session what they had done in Committee of the Whole and directed the Speaker to send a copy of their address to the King to the presiding officer of every legislature in America.[206]

John Blair was appointed chairman of a committee to draft the address, and Patrick Henry and Richard Henry Lee were named to serve with him. The document which they produced recited the catalogue of colonial apprehensions, then concluded in a paragraph that was part bold assertion and part oriental obsequiousness:

"Truly alarmed at the fatal tendency of these pernicious counsels, and with hearts filled with anguish by such dangerous invasions of our dearest privileges, we presume to prostrate ourselves at the foot of your royal throne, beseeching your Majesty, as our King and Father, to avert from your faithful and loyal subjects of America, those miseries which must necessarily be the consequence of such measures. After expressing our firm confidence in your royal wisdom and goodness, permit us to assure your Majesty that the most fervent prayers of your people of this colony are daily addressed to the Almighty, that your Majesty's reign may be long and prosperous over Great Britain and all your dominions; and that, after death, your Majesty may taste the fullest fruition of eternal bliss, and that a descendant of your illustrious house may reign over the extended British Empire till time shall be no more."[207]

The House was so pleased with this document—untainted with a scintilla of Jefferson's "simplicity"—that it adopted it unanimously without changing a word and ordered that it be presented to the King and published in English newspapers.[208]

From the rarefied atmosphere of political philosophy, the House descended to the consideration of local grievances. The morning had worn on to an end and a petition of certain planters in Brunswick County had just been referred to the proper committee, when the Sergeant at Arms called out: "Mr. Speaker, a message from the Governor."

The clerk of the General Assembly read out the message: "Mr. Speaker, the Governor commands the immediate attendance of your House in the Council Chamber."

Obediently, the Burgesses marched upstairs. There, in the Council Chamber, in the high-backed chair of state, sat Governor Botetourt. "Mr. Speaker, and Gentlemen of the House of Burgesses," he said, "I have heard of your resolves, and augur ill of their effect. You have made it my duty to dissolve you, and you are dissolved accordingly."[209]

There was to be no tirade, no further explanation. Stunned, the Burgesses filed downstairs, collected papers and personal belongings from the chamber in which they no longer had a right to meet, and then walked out onto the streets of Williamsburg.

A little later they reconvened in the handsome Apollo Room of the Raleigh Tavern, on Duke of Gloucester Street. The gilded motto, "Hilaritas Sapientiae et Bonae Vitae Proles," [Jollity, the offspring of wisdom and good living], shining against the lead-blue paneling over the fireplace, provided an ironic legend for the scene when the deadly grim Burgesses crowded around the mahogany tables in the long chamber.[210]

Peyton Randolph was unanimously elected moderator. Then one man after another rose to vent his indignation over the threat to colonial liberties. The first constructive proposal was made by a young member with no pretensions to oratorical ability. It was George Washington who gave focus to the discussion by presenting a plan entrusted to him, perhaps by Richard Henry Lee, and edited by George Mason.[211]

The plan advocated the organization of associations whose members were pledged not to import any British goods except a few necessities. Such groups had been formed in the Northern colonies. Both Mason and Washington recognized the fact that Virginia, with its plantation economy, was far more dependent on the mother country than were the Northern colonies with their manufactures. Accordingly, they held that the importation of cloth and sewing thread should be permitted.[212]

A motion that a non-importation association be formed was carried, and a committee was named to draft plans. By ten o'clock that night, the committee had completed its work. The list of prohibited articles was accepted almost without change. No taxed article would be imported, and even taxed articles already in the Colony should not be bought after September 1, 1769, so long as the tax on them remained. A great many untaxed items classified as luxuries were also placed on the non-importation list.

The importation of slaves after November 1 would be forbidden, and the slaughtering of lambs would be restricted in the interest of obtaining more wool for native manufacture of clothing.

Termination of the hated taxes would automatically end the association. Otherwise, it could be dissolved only at a general meeting of subscribers after a month's notice. Even dissolution of the organization would not free the members from their non-importation pledge.[213]

The plan drafted by the committee was adopted next morning, May 18, 1769, and signed by ninety-four former Burgesses. There had been 116 members of the House, but some had already returned home and others were unwilling to commit themselves wholeheartedly to the association.[214]

But there was enthusiasm, even exuberance, on the part of many signers, and a succession of toasts followed the signing. Eleven toasts were drunk, and tribute was paid to King, Queen and Governor, as well as to "The constitutional British liberty in America and all true patriots."[215] Before adjournment, the Apollo Room's gilded motto, with its reference to jollity and good living, did not seem at all ironic.

The next night many of these same former Burgesses were guests of the Governor who had dissolved their house. Botetourt was host at a party in celebration of the Queen's birthday.[216] If revolution was afoot in Virginia, it was certainly an urbane rebellion.

Soon after the legislators returned to their plantations, it became apparent that the rules of their association would not be easy to follow. Even Washington, a member of the committee that framed them and a man scrupulous in his efforts to obey them, found himself confused by the ambiguity of some clauses.[217] There were at least a few deliberate violations. Yet Virginians reduced their imports from England sufficiently to make their temper clear to his Majesty's ministers.[218]

Furthermore, the Virginia action influenced other colonies. A Maryland association, formed June 22 at Annapolis, took the Virginia Association as its model. South Carolinians were inspired to take similar action July 22. Next citizens of Savannah, Georgia copied the example of the South Carolinians. Making no bones of their imitation, North Carolina Assemblymen endorsed the Virginia Association November 7.[219]

When a new House of Burgesses convened November 7, its membership was almost the same as that of the House which Botetourt had dissolved. In his speech, the Governor showed himself the diplomatic representative of a conciliatory government.

Botetourt said that his Majesty had approved westward extension of the boundary between the Colony and the Cherokees, a move which interested land-hungry Virginians.

Now came a greater concession. "His Majesty's present administration," said the Governor, "have at no time entertained a design to propose to Parliament to lay any further taxes upon America for the purpose of raising a revenue, and . . . it is their intention to propose in the next session of Parliament to take off the duties upon glass, paper and colors, upon consideration of such duties having been laid contrary to the true principles of commerce."

Botetourt declared his "firm opinion" that this policy of respecting the "true principles of commerce" would "never be departed from."

Then the Governor put the force of his personality behind strong words of assurance:

"So determined am I to abide by [this policy] that I will be content to be declared infamous If I do not, to the last hour of my life, at all times, in all places, and upon all occasions, exert every power with which I either am or ever shall be legally invested, in order to obtain and to maintain for the Continent of America that satisfaction which I have been authorized to promise this day, by the confidential servants of our gracious Sovereign who, to my certain knowledge, rates his honor so high that he had rather part with his crown than preserve it by deceit."[220]

The Governor had exerted the magnetism that made it impossible for most Virginians to hate him, regardless of their opinion of the ministry he served. He had promised that certain offensive taxes would be removed, but the despised tax on tea was not one of these. Moreover, there was no admission that Parliament did not have the constitutional right to impose internal taxes on the colonies. Botetourt had stated his "firm opinion" that the taxes just removed would never be reimposed, but his assurance remained only an "opinion." He might speak authoritatively regarding the present ministry, but he could not commit future ministries.

The Burgesses' reply to the Governor, therefore, was phrased with cautious courtesy. After expressing thanks for the prospective repeal of duties on glass, paper and colors, the legislators said they did so "especially as we cannot doubt but the same wisdom and goodness which have already induced his Majesty favorably to regard the humble entreaties of his faithful subjects in America will still farther incline the royal breast to an exertion of his Majesty's gracious and benign influence toward perfecting the happiness of all his people."[221]

The legislative session was a busy one. Considerable interest centered upon a petition to the King and memorial to the Governor, seeking confirmation of Virginia's claims to Western lands on which newly organized English companies were rumored to have designs. Veterans' claims to Western lands promised to them as a reward for service in the campaign of 1754 also occupied Burgesses and Council. The Assembly did not adjourn until December 21.

The great social event of the holiday season was a ball given in the Governor's honor by the Speaker and the Burgesses. Nearly a hundred of the colony's ladies were present, but the assemblage was not a glittering one. They were clad in homespun from Virginia looms, not in silks and satins of English manufacture.[222] More eloquently than the Burgesses' formal reply to the Governor's message, the dress of their wives warned Botetourt that his Majesty's government still had a long way to go "toward perfecting the happiness of all his people."

The Burgesses' policy of friendly social relations with the Governor and determined resistance to his government continued into the spring session of 1770. It was well illustrated in the case of George Washington, who dined with Botetourt at the Palace on May 25 and took leave of his host to attend a meeting of the Non-importation Association, where he was named to a committee of twenty to make plans for a new association superseding the existing organization.[223]

Some leaders, like Edmund Pendleton, believed that Parliament's removal of all the disputed taxes except that on tea was enough of a concession to justify abandonment of the Association, or at least the substitution of less stringent requirements for those then in effect.[224] Others had no patience with this view. Landon Carter exclaimed: "Fine language this, as if there could be any half way between slavery and freedom. Certainly one link of the former preserved must be the hold to which the rest of the chain might at any time be joined when the forging smiths thought proper to add it."[225]

Repeated meetings of the Association were necessary before a compromise plan was accepted June 22, 1770. Though the new instrument was milder in tone than its predecessor, it was also designed to be more effective. It wasted few words in denunciation, but provided for enforcement by pressure of public opinion.

The Association resolved:

"That a committee of five be chosen in every county, by the majority of associators in each county, who, or any three of them, are hereby authorized to publish the names of such signers of the association as shall violate their agreement."[226]

It also provided:

"When there shall be an importation of goods into any county, such committee, or any three of them, are empowered to convene themselves, and in a civil manner apply to the merchant and importers concerned and desire to see the invoices and papers respecting such importation, and if they find any goods therein contrary to the association to let the importers know that it is the opinion and request of the country that such goods shall not be opened or stored, but reshipped to the place from whence it came: And in case of refusal, without any manner of violence, inform them of the consequences, and proceed to publish an account of their conduct."

Washington wished that the provisions were "ten times as strict."

He was afraid that Virginia's sacrifices would not approach those of the Northern colonies.[227] Many Virginians felt a particularly strong sympathy for Boston. On March 5, a British sentry in that city, finding himself surrounded by a threatening mob, had called for help. The main guard had come to his rescue, but were themselves threatened with violence. When a civilian started clubbing a soldier, shots rang out and three of the mob fell dead while two others were mortally wounded. Though the captain of the guard was acquitted in a local court after a defense by John Adams and Josiah Quincy, New England ministers preached about the "Boston Massacre" until colonists up and down the Atlantic Coast believed that British soldiers had made a cold-blooded attack upon the citizens of Boston.[228]

Sympathy for the Northern colonies began evaporating rapidly, however, when word spread that they were importing British manufactures almost without restriction. Under such conditions, Virginians felt that their sacrifices were futile. A meeting of Virginia Associators on December 14 was adjourned because of the small attendance.[229]

Virginia's leaders were planters, and problems besetting them in 1771 made even the grievances against Parliament fade into the background.

Though the clouds seemed to empty above the Blue Ridge mountains without ceasing for so many days that the pious were reminded of Noah's world, the middle of May, 1771, brought cloudless skies to Tidewater. Planters took advantage of the good weather to haul their tobacco to the warehouses.

But the James, the Rappahannock and the Roanoke Rivers, fed by the mountain torrents, were rising steadily and, at last, ominously. For sixty hours the James River rose continuously. Anxious eyes saw the flood waters mount sixteen inches within an hour. The crew of a ship anchored below Richmond were amazed to find themselves, on May 27, borne by a flood "forty feet higher than the common tides."[230] A prodigious roar brought frightened householders onto their porches in time to see a forty foot wall of water rushing toward them. Then their own homes were caught up in the tide and swept along like rudderless craft. Desperately the people crawled onto the roofs and vainly they shouted for help.

When the waters receded, some islands had become little more than sand bars, and hills of sand rose in many places. In other places, there were mounds twelve to twenty feet high built of trees, building wreckage, dead livestock and human carcasses. Within a few days, they were reeking with the odor of rotting flesh.

Tobacco warehouses on the James had been swept away. Warehouses of tobacco along the Rappahannock and Potomac were spoiled. The loss to the colony as a whole was incalculable. Along the James River alone, 2,300,000 pounds of tobacco had been destroyed or damaged. A conservative man who ventured an estimate of the financial loss placed it at £2,000,000.[231]

William Nelson, President of the Council and acting Governor since the death of Botetourt, called a meeting of the legislature for July 11, three months before the regularly appointed time. The Burgesses required no urging to move swiftly for the relief of "Sharers in [the] Melancholy Catastrophe." Commissioners were appointed to determine the extent of losses in public warehouses and certify compensation at a stated rate from a fund of £30,000 to be provided by the emission of treasury notes.[232]

Since most of the Burgesses were Associators, the special session brought together a quorum of the group that had failed to attend the Association meeting the previous December. A group including George Washington and George Mason had petitioned Peyton Randolph, as Moderator, to call a meeting of the Association to consider "how far it may or may not be consistent with good policy to attempt keeping up a plan here which is now being dropped by all our sister Colonies, except refusing to import tea and such other articles as are or may be taxed for the purpose of raising revenue in America."[233]

The petitioners explained:

"At present those who faithfully adhere to their engagements have the mortification not only of seeing their own good intentions frustrated by the negligence, the insincerity, and the malpractice of others, but many of them find themselves from the same causes greatly embarrassed in their business, and their trade daily falling into the hands of men who have not acted upon the same honorable principles, and who have very little title to the countenance, or even the connivance of the public."

On July 18, the *Virginia Gazette* printed a public notice that, three days before, at "a general meeting of the gentlemen of the Association at the Capitol, it was agreed upon to dissolve the same, except as to tea, paper, glass and painters' colors of foreign manufacture upon which a duty is laid for the purpose of raising a revenue for America."[234]

Botetourt's successor as Governor arrived in September.[235] A Scotsman, he had been Governor of New York for eleven months. His social prestige left nothing to be desired for he was John Murray, Earl of Dunmore, Viscount Fincastle, Baron of Blair, of Moulin and of Tillymont, and a descendant of the royal Stuarts. The Governor's auburn hair and flashing brown eyes might have suggested temper to those who believed physical features an index to character. A weak chin and petulant mouth did not rob his face of a certain forcefulness, and when he looked down his long, sharp nose he seemed to be a man fully conscious of the weight of his ancient titles.[236]

Virginia gentlemen and their ladies learned that Dunmore could be charming. He shared their love of gracious living and, as scholars soon discovered, took great pleasure in good literature.[237]

Shortly after his arrival, the new Governor dissolved the Assembly, which had been prorogued to October 23, and issued writs of election.

The new Assembly convened February 10, 1772. The session was a quiet one. Some legislators spent a great deal of time at the theater. Certainly there was more action there than in the House of Burgesses.[238] Nothing that happened in the capitol was half so notable as the January blizzard which, first with its piled drifts, and then with their melting and swelling the streams, delayed the arrival of a number of Burgesses. One of the latest, George Washington, who reached Williamsburg March 2, said the snow was "the deepest . . ., I suppose, the oldest man living ever remembers to have seen in this country." Everywhere on his Mount Vernon plantation, the snow had been "up to the breast of a tall horse." An open boat had not been able to cross the Potomac until February 21.[239] The spirit of rebellion seemed just as cold as the land and the process of revolution as frozen as the rivers.

In January 1773, scandal erupted on the quiet scene. The Treasurer discovered that counterfeit notes, most ingeniously executed, were circulating in the colony. It was soon reported that coins had also been counterfeited. Such was the fear of accepting bad currency, that commerce was almost strangled.[240]

The Governor summoned his Council for advice. They suggested that he call the General Assembly to enact legislation fitting the problem, and that he offer substantial rewards for apprehension of the counterfeiters and of any person who, in full knowledge of what he was doing, attempted to circulate the false currency.[241]

Sometime afterward, one John Short, said to have been at one time an officer of the law, arrived in Williamssburg and poured forth a tale of major counterfeiting operations centered in Pittsylvania County and presided over by some fifteen or sixteen Virginians, some of them prominent, who acknowledged the leadership of a North Carolinian.

Dunmore quickly conferred with Speaker Peyton Randolph, Attorney General John Randolph and Treasurer Robert Carter Nicholas, who advised him that, as ex officio Chief Justice of the General Court, he could issue a warrant under which, when served through local officers, suspected persons could be brought to the capital for examination. On February 23, five suspects were brought into Williamsburg under heavy guard. After examination by Speaker Randolph in the Governor's presence, one prisoner was released. The others were given a hearing before the Court of York County and then remanded to the Williamsburg gaol.

On March 4, 1773, the Assembly convened. The Burgesses pouring into town were relieved that the counterfeiting ring had been broken, but they were not disposed to congratulate the Governor wholeheartedly for his swift and effective methods. Was not his action in bypassing the Pittsylvania County Court to bring the accused to York County for trial comparable to the Parliamentary proposal to transport American colonists to London for trial on treason charges? Was not the same right of vicinage violated in both cases?

The Burgesses raised this question in a formal address to the Governor early in the legislative session. After thanking him for his efforts to protect the colony from counterfeiters, they protested:

"But the proceedings in this case, my Lord, though rendered necessary by the particular nature of it, are nevertheless different from the usual mode, it being regular that an examining court on criminals should be held, either in the county where the act was committed or the arrest made. . . . The duty we owe our constituents obliges us, my Lord, to be as attentive to the safety of the innocent as we are desirous of punishing the guilty; and we apprehend that a doubtful construction and various execution of criminal law does greatly endanger the safety of innocent men. We do therefore most humbly pray your Excellency that the proceedings in this case may not in future be drawn into consequence or example."[242]

Dunmore was pointedly incredulous that his efforts to punish the guilty "could by any means be thought to endanger the safety of the innocent." He added, with the strained and emphatic politeness of an angry man:

"Permit me to say that all laws doubtful in their construction must be interpreted by the courts of justice. If I have done amiss, the same method will not be repeated; but, if it should be determined to be regular, I shall continue to exercise the powers I am invested with, whensoever the exigencies of government and the good of the country require such exertion. And, under such circumstances, I am persuaded that no one (not even the most timid) will be under the least apprehension that this proceeding may in future be drawn into consequence or example."[243]

The legality of the Governor's actions was upheld by a majority of the General Court.[244]

On March 12, the House resolved itself into a Committee of the Whole on the State of the Colony. The Chair recognized Dabney Carr, the thirty-year-old brother-in-law and political protégé of Thomas Jefferson.[245] Speaking convincingly, but with moderation,[246] Carr said that "his Majesty's faithful subjects" had been so "much disturbed by various rumors and reports tending to deprive them of their ancient, legal and constitutional rights" as to make necessary a "communication of sentiments" between Great Britain and the American colonies and among the colonies themselves. He called for the naming of eleven Burgesses to a Committee of Correspondence "in order . . . to remove the uneasiness and to quiet the minds of the people." The committee would be instructed "to obtain the most early and authentic intelligence of all such acts and resolutions of the British Parliament, or proceedings of administration, as may relate to or affect the British colonies in America, and to keep up and maintain a correspondence and communication with our sister colonies respecting these important considerations; and the result of such their proceedings, from time to time, to lay before this house."[247]

The committee would be directed specifically to examine the proceedings of the Rhode Island Court of Inquiry into the burning of the British schooner *Gaspee*, the court reportedly being empowered to transport "persons accused of offences committed in America to places beyond the seas to be tried."

Carr's proposals won ready acceptance in Committee of the Whole and were unanimously adopted by the House.[248]

This legislative action, so quickly taken, was the result of many private meetings in the Raleigh Tavern, where the "young Turks" deplored the conservatism of elder leadership. Prominent in these meetings, besides Carr and Jefferson, had been Paatrick Henry, Richard Henry Lee and Francis Lightfoot Lee.[249]

If any one man was the author of the idea that Virginia should have a committee of correspondence, Richard Henry Lee probably should take the credit.[250] Thomas Jefferson had been asked to introduce the resolutions calling for creation of the committee, but had secured that distinction for Carr instead.[251]

Massachusetts had had local committees of correspondence, but now Virginia would have a far more effective instrument—a committee representative of the entire colony.[252]

As Jefferson and Carr rode back to Albemarle County, they agreed that the resolutions establishing Virginia's committee of correspondence would lead to a meeting of representatives from all the American colonies.[253] In faraway Massachusetts—which no longer seemed quite so far away—Samuel Adams exulted that the "truly patriotic resolves" of the Old Dominion would fire "the hearts of all who are friends of liberty."[254]

His Majesty's Governor attached no such importance to the Virginia Resolutions. Dunmore had written the Earl of Dartmouth: "Your lordship will observe there are some resolves which show a little ill humor in the House of Burgesses, but I thought them so insignificant that I took no matter of notice of them."[255]

After prorogation of the Assembly March 13, Virginia's political leaders returned to the planter's role. They followed events in the public prints, but did not attempt to mold them.

The next event in the conflict between England and the colonies to cause much comment in Virginia was the Boston Tea Party of December 15, 1773.[256] Virginians learned of this event in January. The action had resulted from arrival of a tea consignment in Boston, following an act of the House of Commons authorizing the East India Company to sell tea directly to carefully selected consignees among the American colonists. Hitherto, the company had been required to sell its tea at public auction in England, and English purchasers in turn had resold to Americans. Authorization of direct sales to the colonists made it possible for the company to undersell both the smugglers of tea from Holland and colonial merchants who had purchased from English middlemen. Even with the three pence per pound import tax on the tea, it was still cheaper than that offered by the smuggler. Parliamentary authorization of direct sales, therefore, was regarded both as a means of rescuing the East India

Company from bankruptcy and of getting the colonists to accept the tea tax.

The arrival of the tea ship *Dartmouth* in Boston Harbor had alarmed local tea merchants who feared the complete loss of their investment in tea stocks and disruption of the commercial system on which their prosperity was based. The merchants agitated the Sons of Liberty. On the night of December 16, Boston men thinly disguised as Indians swarmed over three tea ships in the harbor, and dumped overboard three hundred forty-two chests of tea that were the property of the East India Company. The crews made no resistance, and the English soldiers and warships held their fire.

The Boston Tea Party did not cause great excitement in Virginia, but it was disapproved by such Virginians as Washington, who thought the destruction of private property unjustifiable and was mindful of the possibility of retaliation by his Majesty's government.[257] Some sober Americans in other colonies shared Washington's views. On December 1, New York City Sons of Liberty, without resorting to violence, had secured the resignation of commissions held by tea consignees.[258] Similar action was successfully taken December 22 by the citizens of Charleston, South Carolina.[259] Discussion of the raid by Boston's masquerade Indians had faded by the time the Assembly convened in May, but the threat of frontier raids by real Indians was a consuming topic of conversation. Governor Dunmore had authorized John Connolly to seize Fort Pitt in the name of the colony of Virginia—a highly provocative act on Pennsylvania's doorstep. Having accomplished this mission, Connolly was prepared to make a punitive march against the Shawnees.

A few days later, though, Boston became the subject of earnest and anxious argument. A copy of the Boston Port Bill, passed by Parliament with the idea of closing the harbor in punishment for the "Tea Party," reached the Assembly. Burgesses like Edmund Pendleton were convinced "that the Bostonians did wrong in destroying the tea," but were equally sure that "the Parliament's giving judgment and sending ships and troops to do execution in a case of private property [was an] attack upon constitutional rights." Pendleton, known among his colleagues as a man of moderation, considered the action against Boston "a common attack upon American rights."[260]

The Burgesses believed "it was a preconcerted scheme between the Ministry and East India Company to send the tea for the very purpose of producing the consequences which happened."[261]

"We were in a flame and intended some spirited resolves," Pendleton later reported, "but postponed them till we should have finished the public business, lest an expected dissolution should leave that undone."[262]

On the night of May 23, a group of bold Burgesses led by Patrick Henry met privately in the Council Chamber to consider means of showing their sympathy with Boston and arousing Virginians to the danger implicit for all Americans in the fate of that port.[263] There were Richard Henry Lee, Francis Lightfoot Lee, Thomas Jefferson, and one who was not a burgess—George Mason, the stout, ailing and unhappy philosopher-lawyer-farmer of Gunston Hall. Mason just happened to be in Williamsburg at the time, but he was a welcome addition to the company. It was he who had fathered the scheme of Virginia's Association, which had been so widely copied in other colonies.

The plan eventually adopted by this group of Henry's followers, however, apparently came from young Jefferson. Why not, he proposed, observe a day of fasting and prayer because of what was happening in Boston and might happen elsewhere in the colonies? The conferees had gathered in the Council Chamber rather than a tavern room so that they might have access to the legislative library. They may have hunted eagerly through a number of volumes. In any event, they settled upon John Rushworth's *Historical Collections*. Surely the Puritan historian would provide precedents for fast days. "No example of such a solemnity," Jefferson afterwards explained, "had existed since the days of our distresses in the war of '55, since which a new generation had grown up. With the help, therefore, of Rushworth, whom we rummaged over for the revolutionary precedents and forms of the Puritans of that day, preserved by him, we cooked up a resolution. . . ."

With great discretion, the group did not claim for any of its number the privilege of presenting the resolution. Instead it approached a high official from the old faction of the House who also had a strong reputation for genuine piety. It was, therefore, Mr. Treasurer, Robert Carter Nicholas, who rose in the House the next day and read aloud:

"This House, being deeply impressed with apprehension of the great dangers to be derived to British America from the hostile invasion of the City of Boston in our sister colony of Massachusetts Bay, whose commerce and harbor are, on the first day of June next, to be stopped by an armed force, deem it highly necessary that the first day of June be set apart by the members of this House as a day of fasting, humiliation and prayer, devoutly to implore the divine interposition for averting the heavy calamity which threatens destruction to our civil rights and the evils of civil war; to give us one heart and one mind firmly to oppose, by all just and proper means, every injury to American rights; and that the minds of his Majesty and his Parliament may be inspired from above with wisdom, moderation and justice to remove from the loyal people of America all cause of danger from a continued pursuit of measures pregnant with their ruin."[264]

The resolution also provided that members of the House should, on the appointed day, march in a body with the Speaker and mace to church, there to hear a sermon by a minister chosen especially for the occasion.

The House approved without a dissenting vote.

Two days later, the Burgesses were engaged in routine business when, a little after three o'clock, a message arrived: "The Governor commands the House to attend his Excellency immediately in the Council Chamber."[265]

Minutes later the Burgesses stood before the Governor who, his dark eyes flashing, told them:

"Mr. Speaker and Gentlemen of the House of Burgesses, I have in my hand a paper published by order of your House, conceived in such terms as reflect highly upon his Majesty and the Parliament of Great Britain, which makes it necessary for me to dissolve you; and you are dissolved accordingly."[266]

There was no question in the Burgesses' minds about what to do. They had the precedent of May 1769. Quickly they reassembled in the Apollo Room of the Raleigh Tavern.[267]

Resolutions which Richard Henry Lee had prepared before dissolution of the House provided a basis for action. The conferees approved a paper warning that continuation of unconstitutional taxation might "compel us against our will to avoid all commercial intercourse with Britain." But another part of the document might have given thoughtful members of Parliament more to think about than the threat. "We are . . . clearly of opinion," it said, "that an attack made on one of our sister colonies to compel submission to arbitrary taxes is an attack made on all British America, and threatens ruin to the rights of all unless the united wisdom of the whole be applied. And for this purpose it is recommended to the Committee of Correspondence that they communicate with their several corresponding committees on the expediency of appointing deputies from the several Colonies of British America to meet in general congress at such place annually as shall be thought most convenient, there to deliberate on those general measures which the united interests of America may from time to time require."[268]

Two colonial congresses had already been held and a third was proposed by leaders in Rhode Island, Pennsylvania and New York. But the Virginians had gone a step farther in proposing that there be an annual congress to consider colonial affairs.

The revolution in Virginia was still urbane. On the evening of the very day the proposals were adopted at the meeting in the Apollo Room, the Burgesses were hosts at a ball which they had planned in honor of Lady Dunmore.[269] Some of Patrick Henry's constituents would doubtless have suspected hypocrisy in the gallantries with which leading Burgesses honored the Governor's wife that night. Tidewater planters would have been incensed at any suggestion of insincerity on their part. The ball had been arranged before dissolution of the House. A lady was their guest, and they would not demean themselves to be anything but gentlemen.

The next day, the Committee of Correspondence approved a circular letter proposing an annual congress as "a measure extremely important and extensively useful," and soliciting "sentiments on this subject" from the other colonies.[270]

Two days later, twenty-five erstwhile Burgesses who remained in Williamsburg met at the call of Peyton Randolph. He had received dispatches from Maryland, together with other messages emanating from Boston and Philadelphia. Bostonians had advocated a general colonial suspension of trade with Britain and the West Indies for the duration of the Port Act. Philadelphians had responded to the Bostonian exhortation with a highly generalized pledge of "firm adherence to the cause of American liberty." Maryland's Committee of Correspondence had been as specific as Philadelphia's had been indefinite. The group at Annapolis sought colonial opinions on the suspension of commercial intercourse with Britain, the pledging of lawyers to a policy of not entering suits for debts due in the mother country and the boycotting of any colony that refused to join with a majority of others in such a plan.[271]

Most moving of all the appeals was the one written by Samuel Adams of Boston. He wrote that it was feared his city could not long hold out alone. Describing Boston's ordeal, he said, "As the very being of each colony, considered as a free people, depends upon the event, a thought so dishonorable to our brethren cannot be entertained as that this town will now be left to struggle alone."[722]

Many of the assembled Virginians opposed the idea of refusing to pay debts owed in Britain, and held that planters must be free to export if they were to be financially able to pay. Most agreed, however, that the "late association" for non-importation should be enlarged. It was agreed also that any scheme adopted should have large backing. By unanimous consent, an invitation was issued to all former members of the House of Burgesses to assemble in Williamsburg August 1. Those to participate in the convention were expected to determine "the sense of their respective counties" in the meantime. The invitation, signed by the twenty-five former Burgesses concluded with the statement, "Things seem to be hurrying to an alarming crisis, and demand the speedy, united council of all those who have a regard for the common cause."[273]

The next day was Sunday and the appointed fast day. A Northern Neck rector did something that Virginians could not have imagined an Anglican minister doing a generation before. Instead of concluding with the words "God save the King," he had exclaimed, "God preserve all the just rights and liberties of America."[274]

When the convention met in Williamsburg August 1, 1774, the former Burgesses had had ample opportunity to determine the sentiments of their constituents. Groups in a number of counties had adopted resolutions of their own. Non-importation was urged by residents of Prince George, Surry, Hanover, Elizabeth City County, Caroline, Henrico and Princess Anne. Groups in Prince William, Frederick, Westmoreland, Spotsylvania, James City and Albemarle counties went so far as to call for non-intercourse with Britain. The Prince George resolutions proposed a colonial Congress "to consult and agree upon a firm and indissoluble union and association for preserving by the best and most proper means their common rights and liberties."[275]

Before July, Virginians learned that Parliament had passed a "bill for the better regulating the government of the Province of Massachusetts Bay," a measure which abolished the elective nature of the Council of the colony and empowered the Royal Governor to name nearly all officials. Even more feared were the effects of a bill, long threatened and now actually passed, authorizing the Governor to transfer to Britain the trial of an official or citizen charged with a capital offense committed in the suppression of a riot or collection of revenue. The fact that part of these oppressive measures became effective August 1, the very day on which the Williamsburg meeting convened, must have underlined the seriousness of the common threat.[276]

The sentiments of most of the delegates had already been well summarized in the Hanover County resolutions, which stated:

"Whether the people there [in Boston], were warranted by justice when they destroyed the tea we know not; but this we know, that the Parliament, by their proceedings, have made us and all North America parties in the present dispute . . . insomuch that, if our sister colony of Massachusetts Bay is enslaved, we cannot long remain free."[277]

Events had tended to confirm the validity of warnings which Arthur Lee had expressed to Richard Henry Lee in a letter written from London just before passage of the Boston Port Act. "The affairs of America," he said, "are now become very serious; the Ministry are determined to put your spirit to the proof. Boston is their first object . . . There is a persuasion here that America will see, without interposition, the ruin of Boston. It is of the last importance to the general cause that your conduct should prove this opinion erroneous. If once it is perceived that you may be attacked and destroyed by piecemeal, . . . every part will in its turn feel the vengeance which it would not unite to repel, and a general slavery or ruin must ensue. The colonies should never forget Lord North's declaration in the House of Commons that he would not listen to the complaints of America until she was at his feet. The character of Lord North, and the consideration of what surprising things he has effected towards enslaving his own country makes me, I own, tremble for ours."[278]

A sensation was caused at the convention by a delegate who never arrived. Thomas Jefferson, taken sick on the road, sent on to Peyton Randolph some resolutions which he had composed "for the inspection of the Present Delegates of the People of Virginia, now in Convention."[279]

The paper, which was laid on the table for examination and was read once before a great number of the delegates, was a strange mixture of rashness and mature wisdom. Jefferson admonished the King: "Open your breast, sire, to liberal and expanded thought. Let not the name of George the third be a blot in the page of history." He reminded the King that Virginia's attempts to stop the importation of Negro slaves had been nullified by the Royal veto, and cited this fact as evidence of his Majesty's preference for commercial advantages to "the lasting interests of the American States, and to the rights of human nature." Nevertheless he denied a desire for independence from the Mother Country. "It is neither our wish nor our interest," he said, "to separate from her. We are willing, on our part, to sacrifice everything which reason can ask to the restoration of that tranquility which all must wish."

Parliament he saw as the real villain. "Single acts of tyranny may be ascribed to the accidental opinion of a day; but a series of oppressions, begun at a distinguished period and pursued unalterably through every change of ministers, too plainly prove a deliberate and systematical plan of reducing us to slavery."

He then proclaimed: "The true ground on which we declare these acts void is that the British parliament has no right to exercise its authority over us."

Jefferson was actually declaring American independence of Parliament. He saw the colonies and Britain as separate states, and the King as the "mediatory power between the several states of the British Empire."

No wonder the Virginian's contemporaries were astonished. His concept of the empire as a Commonwealth of nations did not gain full acceptance until the twentieth century.

Jefferson's resolutions were, of course, too radical for the planters assembled in Williamsburg. But they were moved by his paper. Its eloquence drew their applause, and it started them thinking about independence from Parliament, even though most of them considered it a rash idea. Without the author's knowledge, his resolutions were printed in pamphlet form in Williamsburg, then in Philadelphia and even in England.[280] Men read and remembered the statement: "The God who gave us life gave us liberty at the same time; the hand of force may destroy, but cannot disjoin them."

While the delegates did not go nearly so far as Jefferson wished, they did take decisive steps. By August 5, they had agreed to accept Philadelphia's invitation to a General Congress September 5. The next day, the delegates unanimously approved declaratory resolutions and instructions for seven representatives to be sent to Philadelphia. It was declared that the importation of British goods must end in November, and that the export to Britain of tobacco and all other American products would be halted by August 10, 1775 unless "American grievances" were remedied before that date. It was also proclaimed that, if Boston were forced to pay for cargoes destroyed in the now famous "tea party," the Massachusetts city must be recompensed before Virginians, to whatever extent their own grievances might be redressed, would ever import or use any tea of the East India Company.[281]

Most of the delegates shared George Washington's anxiety that Virginia's moral indignation be supported by soundly moral conduct. They expressed "the earnest desire . . . to make as quick and full payment as possible of our debts to Great Britain."[282]

The delegates modestly admitted to "being fully persuaded that the united wisdom of the General Congress" might improve the Virginia instructions and accordingly resolved that they would "conform to and strictly observe all such alterations and additions assented to by the Delegates for this Colony, as they may judge it necessary to adopt, after the same shall be published and made known to us."[283]

Next came the business of electing the seven delegates. Those chosen were Peyton Randolph, Richard Henry Lee, George Washington, Patrick Henry, Richard Bland, Benjamin Harrison and Edmund Pendleton.[284]

*   *   *

On August 30, Edmund Pendleton and Patrick Henry arrived at Mount Vernon in the course of their journey to Philadelphia. Colonel Washington was a good host and a good listener. George Mason came over and he and the two attorneys talked far into the night. Plump, pleasant-faced Martha Washington was excited about the convention to be held in Philadelphia and proud that her husband would have a part in it. Pendleton thought she talked "like a Spartan to her son on his going to battle."[285]

After dinner the next day, Washington, Pendleton and Henry, according to plan, mounted their horses for the journey to Philadelphia. Mrs. Washington looked at them—the dark, lean, gangling Henry; the blondly handsome, compact Pendleton; and her own husband, a noble figure in the saddle and obviously the best horseman of them all. "God be with you gentlemen," she said with quiet dignity. And then could not resist adding: "I hope you will stand firm. I know George will."[286]

*   *   *

The three horsemen were not of so philosophical a mind as George Mason, their companion of the night before. But, on the long road to Philadelphia, they must have thought often of the events which caused them, and the delegates from other colonies, to be traveling now to a continental congress. The history of what they regarded as increasing Parliamentary usurpation of power was painfully etched on their memories. But the actual growth of the conflict, and above all the growth of the consciousness of Americanism, was something which they could not see in perspective.

As an English colony in territory coveted by France and Spain, Virginia had from its inception been involved in international affairs. It had also had commercial, military and political relations with other colonies. A Virginia expedition had routed the French from New England and made that rugged land safe for the Puritan brand of democracy. Virginia had later furnished grain to starving New Englanders. Under protest, it had aided Lord Baltimore in the colonization of Maryland, and then had quarreled with Maryland over the possession of Kent's Island. Virginia had helped to populate North Carolina.

Not until the French and Indian War, however, had the Old Dominion come to be a force for unity among the American colonies and an actor rather than a pawn in international affairs. That struggle, though its origins were complex and centuries old, began as a result of action by Virginia's governor to protect Virginia's territory. It was Virginia that took the lead in uniting the colonies for the conflict which, though it became celebrated in world history as the Seven Years' War, was once known as Virginia's War.

That same struggle had shattered American awe of British arms and built Americans' confidence in their own prowess. The Stamp Act galvanized American resistance. Patrick Henry's Stamp Act Resolves spread up and down the Atlantic Seaboard in 1765 and "set fire to a continent." A Stamp Act Congress, called at the instigation of Massachusetts, met in New York City. Because of a royal governor's action in dissolving the Virginia Assembly, the Old Dominion was not one of the six colonies officially represented, but the Virginia Resolves were in large part the inspiration of action taken.

In 1768, Virginia and Massachusetts issued circular letters to the other American colonies saying that Americans faced a common danger and should take common action. Late in 1772, Boston established a Committee of Correspondence to communicate with other towns in the interest of the common defense. In March of the next year Virginia became the first colony to establish an intercolonial Committee of Correspondence.

Virginia took the lead in organizing non-importation associations to boycott British goods. The pattern of the Virginia Association was copied in sister colonies. Charles Thomson, writing in his official capacity as secretary to the Philadelphia Committee of Correspondence, had said: "All America look up to Virginia to take the lead on the present occasion . . . None is so fit as Virginia. You are ancient, you are respected; you are animated in the cause."[287]

Now, late in the summer of 1774, and in response to demands from Rhode Island, Pennsylvania, New York and Virginia, men were riding to Philadelphia to frame defense measures binding the American colonies. From the rice fields of South Carolina, from the prim towns of New England, from the tobacco plantations of Virginia—from twelve colonies came more than fifty men impelled by concern for American liberties.

The three Virginia horsemen, Washington, Henry and Pendleton, and their four colleagues, who had gotten a head start, would be respected figures at the Congress, even apart from their abilities. They represented the most populous of the colonies and the one which, together with Massachusetts, had led the way toward colonial unity in defense of liberty. Virginians were bringing to the Congress the spirit that expelled Sir John Harvey and rose in rebellion under Bacon. Virginia was prepared to move in concert with her sister colonies. Virginia's fortunes would be part of the American destiny.

Chapter X

LEAGUE OF REBELS

(1774)

Chapter X

~~~~~~

(1774)

FOUR Virginians rode into Philadelphia September 2, 1774, and created a sensation.

Their mere arrival raised to fever pitch the excitement that had been mounting in the city ever since the scheduling of the first Continental Congress. For these men were members of the Virginia delegation to that great meeting of twelve colonies. The Massachusetts representatives had arrived several days before. They had come from the colony which had borne the brunt of Parliament's vengeance, and resentment would insure the strength of their resolve. But the colonies could not be strong in the defense of liberty unless Virginia, the oldest and most populous of all, matched the resolution of Massachusetts. There was, therefore, great eagerness to meet the Virginians, to learn what they were thinking, and to form an estimate of their character.

Of all the excited and inquisitive people who crowded around the men from the Old Dominion, none excelled in animation or curiosity a short, plump, bouncy little man of early middle age—John Adams, a delegate from Massachusetts.[1]

One in the group of Virginians had the air of a man accustomed to the place of honor. Well he might, for he was Peyton Randolph— Speaker of the House when there was a House of Burgesses and moderator of the convention after the Assembly's dissolution. Cleareyed, smooth-faced, multiple-chinned, he seemed a symbol of security and good living.[2]

Also obviously no stranger to good living was Benjamin Harrison, fully as portly as Randolph, and with the flushed face and general aspect of a sufferer from the gout—which he was.[3] Yet Harrison was no sybarite. He vowed that he would have walked to Philadelphia on his gouty feet rather than remain at home.[4]

A vow that he would not have missed the Congress if it had been held "in Jericho" was made by a third member of the party, a tall, lean, aged man, whose failing sight and studious cast of countenance suggested the serious scholar. This was Richard Bland, reputed to know more history than any other man in Virginia.[5]

But he probably did not get any opportunity for extended discourse on the subject so long as he remained in the company of his fellow delegate Richard Henry Lee. The Westmoreland planter possessed a gift for eloquence which he fully appreciated, and he carefully saw that it did not diminish for want of exercise. In private discourse, as in public assembly, his speech was spirited, rich in classical allusion and seemingly endless in its flow.[6] He was "a tall, spare man." His eyes were commanding, his proud-nosed profile was that of a Roman senator, and his patrician features glowed with animation.[7] One need not be told that here was an orator.

These four Virginians were all aristocrats, all men of property. They were certainly not cast in the tradition of revolutionaries, yet they were zealots in the cause of liberty. John Adams was impressed. "These gentlemen from Virginia," he said, "appear to be the most spirited and consistent of any."[8]

The next day saw the arrival of the three remaining members of that delegation. Adams was especially eager to meet them, for among them was Colonel George Washington. Not only was this officer's valor well known, but Adams had heard a most exciting report concerning his interest in the "patriot cause." Since arriving in Philadelphia, the Massachusetts delegate had been told by a "solid, firm, judicious man" that "Colonel Washington made the most eloquent speech at the Virginia Convention that ever was made. Says he, 'I will raise one thousand men, subsist them at my own expense, and march myself at their head for the relief of Boston.'"[9]

The report, of course, was false. Even Washington's resourcefulness and wealth were not equal to such an undertaking. Furthermore, the Virginian, always embarrassed when called on to speak in public, had never delivered an eloquent oration in any assembly.

When Adams met Washington, he was impressed with the dignity and poise of the tall, blue-eyed Virginian, but he must have been puzzled by the colonel's taciturnity. Perhaps the Massachusetts delegate concluded that Washington was one of those flaming orators who bank the fires of their eloquence until the occasion and the audience demand burning words.

In any event, one of Washington's colleagues was capable of doing enough talking for both. This was Patrick Henry, agog over seeing a large city for the first time in his life[10] but not overawed at the prospect of matching wits with its inhabitants. Tall, lean, coarse-featured except for a noble brow and eyes,[11] Henry had an awkward majesty and an arresting voice.[12] He also had the ability to captivate. Conversations with Henry had convinced George Mason that the Hanover lawyer was "the first man upon this continent."[13] No wonder Adams was impressed.

The last of the Virginia delegates was Edmund Pendleton, fifty-four years old, a tall, graceful, handsome, bright-eyed man dressed with unostentatious elegance.[14]

Having met them all, Caesar Rodney, of Delaware, wrote: "All the seven delegates . . . are here and more sensible, fine fellows you would never wish to see . . . and the Bostonians who (we know) have been condemned by many for their violence are moderate men when compared [with] Virginia. . . ."[15]

Silas Deane, of Connecticut, was soon writing his wife a description of his fellow delegates.[16] Though he dismissed Harrison as "uncommonly large" and "rather rough in his address and speech," Deane was full of praise for the other delegates from the Old Dominion. He admired Randolph's "noble appearance" and "dignity." Pendleton's legal mind, "easy and cheerful countenance," graceful manners and elegant speech also captured his admiration. After hearing a speech by Patrick Henry, the Connecticut man was rhapsodic. "Mr. Henry," he wrote, "is . . . the completest speaker I ever heard . . . I can give you no idea of the music of his voice, of the highwrought yet natural elegance of his style and manner." Deane added, in awe, "Colonel Lee is said to be his rival in eloquence, and in Virginia and to the southward they are styled the Demosthenes and Cicero of America." He had not yet been able to take the measure of Washington, whose countenance he thought hard, and was chiefly impressed with such superficialities as the Virginian's height, "very young look" and "easy, soldier-like air." The delegation, as a whole, he thought "sociable, sensible and spirited."[17]

"Sensible" and "spirited"—John Adams had used the same words.

More tangible evidence of the prestige enjoyed by the Virginians and their colony came when the delegates from all the colonies, assembled in Carpenters' Hall, unanimously elected Peyton Randolph as chairman.[18]

The Congress had been offered the State House by the Pennsylvania Assembly and Carpenters' Hall by the Carpenters' Guild. Selection of the latter as a meeting place had been a defeat for the conservative element in Pennsylvania which acknowledged the leadership of Joseph Galloway.[19]

The delegates had been so pleased with Carpenters' Hall that they had not even bothered to examine alternative quarters.[20] Sunlight poured inside the hall through the large fanlight over the great double doors and through the large multipaned windows on either side, revealing the excellencies of cabinet work that must have made the carpenters proud. The interior had the clean-lined, substantial look popular in public buildings of the period, and some of the delegates must have been reminded of statehouses in their colonies. The Virginians doubtless felt most at home for, from their chairs on the floor, they looked up into the placid face of the same presiding officer they had known for so many years in Williamsburg.

It quickly became evident that the Congress itself would be far from placid. There was a motion by New York delegate James Duane that a committee be named to draw up "regulations" for the Congress.[21] Other delegates asked why the rules of Parliament would not suffice, and John Adams demanded to know what sort of regulations the New Yorker was talking about. "The method of voting," was the reply. "Whether it should be by colonies, or by the poll, or by interests."[22]

Patrick Henry, clad in "parson's gray,"[23] rose with fire in his eyes. His fellow Virginians knew what to expect. The other delegates did not, but they were fascinated.

Virginia was Henry's native land. It was the object of his patriotism and the center of his political aspirations. Virginia, he felt strongly, must not be denied the strength of representation to which the size of its population entitled it. Henry had said as much many times in the Old Dominion. But he was too wise to say such things in Philadelphia before the delegates of twelve colonies.[24]

Instead, he began to discuss impressive generalities that made his listeners mindful of their place in history. The rich music of his voice enchanted the Congress as he reminded its members that they constituted the first body of the kind to sit in North America. They, he told them, would set precedents by their actions. They should consider the fact that they might be deciding questions not only for themselves, but for their successors also.[25]

"It would be a great injustice," Henry declared, "if a little colony should have the same weight in the councils of America as a great one."[26]

This argument could expose Henry to the charge that he selfishly sought special advantage for his own colony. But his oratorical genius quickly decked provincialism in the gleaming armor of altruism. "Fleets and armies and the present state of things," he argued, "show that government is dissolved." Then, his voice throbbing with emotion, Henry demanded: "Where are your landmarks, your boundaries of colonies? We are in a state of nature, sir. . . . The distinctions between Virginians, Pennsylvanians, New Yorkers and New Englanders are no more. I am not a Virginian, but an American."[27]

Such argument was more than a delegate from little New Hampshire could endure; Major John Sullivan, his Irish blood aboil, sprang to his feet to assert that, since sacrifice and risk would presumably be the same for all colonies, large and small, representation should likewise be the same. "A little colony," he said, "has its all at stake as well as a great one."[28]

Placing Virginia on a plane of equality with all the other colonies seemed insufferably bumptious to Benjamin Harrison, and he restlessly shifted his great bulk in his chair until he got a chance to reply. His fellow Virginians, he told the Congress, would think him unfaithful to duty if he did not demand that "his country" be accorded representation commensurate with its population. If any other scheme were "put upon" the Old Dominion, the other delegates might never see Virginians at another convention.[29]

Thomas Lynch, of South Carolina, took the floor to express partial agreement with Henry and Harrison's position. Population should be a factor in determining representation, he said, but wealth should also enter into the equation. ". . . A compound of numbers and property should determine the weight of the colonies."[30]

Governor Samuel Ward, of Rhode Island, charged the Virginia delegates with inconsistency. "There are," he said, "a great number of counties, in Virginia, very unequal in point of wealth and numbers, yet each has a right to send two members" to the House of Burgesses.[31]

With the exception of Patrick Henry, Virginia's delegates were Burgesses from Tidewater counties which had long controlled the legislature by virtue of an apportionment that had never changed in recognition of the growing western constituencies. Ward's thrust drove home.

Opposition to Henry's plan showed next within the Virginia delegation. Richard Henry Lee raised the objection that there was no basis for determining representation according to population, since accurate statistics for the several colonies were not available.[32]

John Adams agreed with Lee. He said, "I question whether it is possible to ascertain at this time the numbers of our people or the value of our trade."[33]

Undaunted, Henry was up again to argue for a committee to determine representation according to population. "I agree," he said, "that authentic counts cannot be had, if by authenticity is meant attestations of officers of the Crown. I go upon the supposition that all government is at an end. All distinctions are thrown down. All America is thrown into one mass. We must aim at the minutiae of rectitude."[34]

The chair recognized John Jay,[35] brilliant young lawyer from New York. His height and calm demeanor, even his arched eyebrows, gave him a look of detachment as he surveyed his audience. He applied the scalpel of cold reason to Henry's argument. Like a good surgeon, he spoke soothingly before beginning the operation.

"To the virtue, spirit and abilities of Virginia, we owe much," he said. "I would always, therefore, from inclination as well as justice, be for giving Virginia its full weight." He quietly pointed out the fact that all government had not ended, and that the congress therefore was not faced with the necessity for creating government out of chaos. "The measure of arbitrary power is not full, and I think it must run over before we undertake to frame a new constitution."[36]

When the vote was taken, it was determined that each colony should "have one voice." Thus, Virginia and New Hampshire would each have a single vote, and this vote would be determined by the will of a majority in each delegation. But Henry and some of his supporters had won a minor concession. As the Connecticut delegates reported to Governor Trumbull:

"As this . . . [system of one vote for each colony] was objected to as unequal, an entry was made on the journals to prevent its being drawn into precedent."[37]

Neither Henry nor the Virginia delegation lost any prestige as a result of the vote on Duane's motion. Several days after the debate, Silas Deane wrote his wife, concerning Henry: "If his future speeches are equal to the small samples he has hitherto given us, they will be worth preserving." He was convinced that both Henry and Lee had "made the Constitution and history of Great Britain and America their capital study ever since the late troubles between them [had] arisen."[38]

The day after Henry had launched his oratorical assault on Duane's motion, Deane had written home:

"You may tell our friends that I never met, nor scarcely had an idea of meeting, with men of such firmness, sensibility, spirit, and thorough knowledge of the interests of America, as the Gentlemen from the Southern Provinces appear to be."[39]

Caesar Rodney was still convinced that the Virginia delegates were "sensible, fine fellows."[40]

In general, most of the delegates seemed to have respect for their counterparts from other colonies. Most were ready to emphasize the bonds that united, rather than the issues that divided, them.

Their spirit was illustrated by Sam Adams, the stormy petrel of Boston, who though a Puritan, seconded the motion that an Anglican clergyman be invited to serve as chaplain for the Congress since "many of our warmest friends are members of the Church of England."[41]

On the afternoon of September 6, a report arrived that Boston had been bombarded by the British garrisoned there. Muffled bells tolled in Philadelphia, crowds milled back and forth in confusion, and the word "war" was repeated over and over in a multitude of accents, sometimes gasped in fear, sometimes shouted in exultation.[42]

The next morning, the Rev. Jacob Duché opened the Congress by reading from the Psalter: "Plead my cause, O Lord, with them that strive with me; fight against them that fight against me. . . ."[43]

Virtually all the delegates now knew in their hearts what they had before perceived intellectually. Boston's fight was theirs.[44]

Two days later, the delegates learned that the report of a bombardment was false. Nerve strain was released in a celebration which John Adams, a Puritan on a holiday, faithfully described to Abigail as "a most sinful feast . . . everything which could delight the eye or allure the taste."[45]

But Adams also wrote, if the report of Boston's fate "had proved true, you would have heard the thunder of an American Congress." The delegates had learned that they could rely on each other in a genuine crisis.

On September 8, there was a meeting of the committee appointed two days before to state the rights of the colonies and recommend measures for their preservation. There were two members from each colony, and Virginia was represented by Richard Henry Lee and Edmund Pendleton. The cold minutes say that the committee "entered into the [assigned] subject and adjourned." But John Adams reported that the group met all day, "and a most ingenious, entertaining debate we had."[46]

After a festive night, the committee resumed the debate the next day. Argument revolved around the origin of the colonists' rights. Richard Henry Lee declared that they were "built on a fourfold foundation: on nature, on the British constitution, on charters and on immemorial usage."[47]

Galloway and Duane maintained that political rights were not founded in the law of nature. John Adams supported Lee in the contention that they were.[48] William Livingston, of New Jersey, and John Jay were also insistent on natural law.[49] A compromise between the adherents of natural law and the constitutionalists resulted in the formal statement of a position essentially the same as that originally taken by Lee. It was "Agreed to found our rights upon the laws of Nature, the principles of the English Constitution, and charters and compacts."[50]

Meanwhile, another committee appointed by the Congress, and consisting of one representative from each colony, was at work on a study of "the several statutes that affected the trade and manufactures of the colonies."

The major business of the Congress proceeded for many days in the two committees—so much so, that some of the delegates felt "left out."[51]

On September 17, a major concession was made to the three most populous colonies when Virginia's Patrick Henry, Massachusetts' Thomas Cushing and Pennsylvania's Thomas Mifflin were added to the Committee on Rights, thus ending equality of representation in that group.[52]

On that same day, Paul Revere galloped into Philadelphia with a copy of the Suffolk Resolves. These resolutions, adopted by citizens of Suffolk County, Massachusetts, in opposition to General Gage's efforts to fortify Boston, cited offensive acts of Parliament and declared "no obedience is due from this province to . . . any part of the acts."[53] The resolves also recommended that tax collectors withhold their funds from the royal treasuries "until the civil government is placed upon a constitutional foundation," urged the people to form a militia, and proposed the near-cessation of trade with Great Britain.

The signers asserted that they were "determined to act merely upon the defensive, so long as such conduct may be vindicated by reason and the principles of self-preservation, but no longer." They expressed confidence "in the wisdom and integrity of the Continental Congress," and declared their willingness to "pay all due respect and submission" to plans which that body might devise "for the restoration and establishment of our just rights, civil and religious, and for renewing that harmony and union between Great Britain and the colonies, so earnestly wished for by all good men."

The Suffolk Resolves were the catalyst that brought to a boil a fight that had been brewing even before the Congress convened. The radicals, pressing for prompt resistance to Parliament at any cost, and the conservatives, eager to heal the breach between Britain and her American colonies, had jockeyed for control when some delegations were being selected. The choice of Carpenter's Hall as a meeting place, though determined in large part by non-political considerations, was relished by some of the radicals as a slap at Joseph Galloway, leader of Pennsylvania's conservative faction, who had offered the use of the State House.[54]

The unanimous election of Peyton Randolph as chairman had revealed the basic unity of the Congress in its concern for American liberties and the desire to insure Virginia's support of organized moves for their preservation. But factional warfare played a big part in the election of Charles Thomson as secretary. Thomson, leader of the radical movement in Pennsylvania, was anathema to Galloway, who had maneuvered the election of his colony's delegates to exclude the man. The conservatives proposed the name of Silas Deane, but the Connecticut delegate was defeated by so large a majority that support for him was withdrawn and Thomson's election was recorded as unanimous.[55]

Galloway was an unhappy delegate. The hall in which he sat was a reminder of one defeat, and the face of the secretary, who sat, quill in hand, at a table up front, was the reminder of another. Many of his fellow conservatives were almost equally chagrined at the turn of events. Their strength had not yet been put to a decisive test, but they had reason to be apprehensive of the results when it should be.

The radicals, on the other hand, were encouraged by the two reverses handed the Galloway faction, as well as by the sympathy for Massachusetts which they found among the Virginia delegates. Sam Adams, the perpetual agitator, was yearning for a trial of strength, and his Cousin John was almost as avid. Sam Adams is credited with a large role in seeing that the Suffolk Resolves, penned by Joseph Warren, were dropped in Congress' lap at the proper psychological moment.[56]

These resolutions really resulted in a demonstration, rather than a trial, of strength. There was no battle on the floor between drawn lines of conservatives and radicals. Instead, emotion ran so high that John Adams, scarcely able to contain his excitement, "saw tears gush into the eyes of the old, grave, pacific Quakers of Pennsylvania"[57] as Congress

"Resolved, unanimously, That this Assembly deeply feels the sufferings of their countrymen in the Massachusetts-Bay . . . that they most thoroughly approve the wisdom and fortitude with which opposition to these wicked ministerial measures has hitherto been conducted, and they earnestly recommend to their brethren a perseverance in the same firm and temperate conduct as expressed in the resolutions determined upon . . ., trusting that the effects of the united efforts of North America in their behalf will carry such conviction to the British nation, of the unwise, unjust and ruinous policy of the present administration as quickly to introduce better men and wiser measures."

The Congress ordered the printing of this resolution and of the Suffolk Resolves. That night John Adams confided to his diary:

"This was one of the happiest days of my life. In Congress, we had generous, noble sentiments, and manly eloquence. This day convinced me that America will support . . . Massachusetts or perish with her."[58]

By September 22, the delegates had agreed that the colonies they represented should enter into a non-importation pact, a continental version of the Virginia Association.[59] Further deliberation would be required before these representatives of twelve units of varying commercial interests and needs could agree on the specific terms of such a pact. Would some items have to be excluded from its provisions? If so, which? Meanwhile, it was "Resolved unanimously, that the Congress request the merchants and others in the several colonies not to send to Great Britain any orders for goods, and to direct the execution of all orders already sent to be delayed or suspended until the sense of the Congress, on the means to be taken for the preservation of the liberties of America, is made public."[60]

Tedious though it seemed (John Adams called it "tedious beyond expression"),[61] the pace of business was quickening. That very day the Committee to State the Rights of the Colonies brought in its report. A copy was ordered for each delegation, and formal consideration was scheduled for the twenty-fourth.[62]

When the time arrived, agreement was threatened by the desire of many delegates to discuss a multitude of historical grievances against Britain, some of which, while of great importance to one or more colonies, were unfamiliar to the majority. The day was saved by Edmund Pendleton and Patrick Henry, who, having already won their point in committee, persuaded the Congress to limit the discussion of grievances to events since 1763, the year that marked the end of the French and Indian War.[63]

While Congress was at work on the problems of stating the colonies' rights and of framing a non-importation agreement as an instrument of their preservation, Joseph Galloway, like a challenger throwing down the gauntlet, tossed into the assembly "A Plan of a Proposed Union Between Great Britain and the Colonies."[64]

Conceived as a counter blow to the Suffolk Resolves, the Galloway Plan called for a Grand Council of the colonies, whose members would be chosen for three-year terms by the colonial assemblies. Acts of the Council would be subject to the veto of a President-General appointed by the King and holding office at royal pleasure. Together, Council and President-General would constitute an "inferior and distinct branch of the British legislature." Each colony would continue to manage its own internal affairs, but measures affecting the general welfare of all the colonies might originate in either the British Parliament or the colonial Council. Any measure applicable to the American colonies would have to have the consent of both legislatures in order to become law.

Galloway told the Congress: "I am as much a friend of liberty as exists; and no man shall go further in point of fortune, or in point of blood, than the man who now addresses you." But the security of American liberties, he argued, demanded protection within the framework of the British Empire. His plan would give the colonies a considerable measure of autonomy while preserving the union with the mother country.

If the colonies should be severed from Parliamentary authority, they would be beset with quarrels arising from the fact that "the seeds of discord are plentifully sowed in [their] constitution." These quarrels, he feared, would probably "only be settled by an appeal to the sword." The American provinces, he asserted, were only "so many inferior societies, destitute of any supreme direction or decision." They were, (and here he delighted in turning against Patrick Henry the sword of the Virginian's own eloquence), "in respect to each other, in a perfect *state of nature*."[65]

Duane, still the cool logician, praised the reasonableness of Galloway's plan. John Jay brought his lawyer's logic to the Pennsylvanian's support. Delegates from the Middle Colonies were not hot for revolution, and they were prepared to give respectful attention to Galloway's proposal.[66]

Sam Adams quickly objected to the plan, saying that the delegates had no authority to enact it, and that, if enacted, the scheme would rob the individual colonial legislatures of some of their "rights."[67]

Support for Galloway came from the South. Edward Rutledge, of South Carolina, was on his feet. Speaking rapidly in a nasal twang (some people said he sounded like a "Yankee"), he argued for the plan of union.[68]

Lee stood up, tall and straight, to say that the Galloway Plan "would make such changes in the Legislature of the Colonies" that he could not vote for it without consulting his constituents.[69] This distinguished Virginian was respected as a student of constitutional government, and his words raised doubts about a proceeding that had seemed to offer great hope.

Doubts grew into fears as the delegates listened next to Patrick Henry, who, picturing the effects of the Galloway Plan, roared: "We shall liberate our constituents from a corrupt House of Commons, but throw them into the arms of an American Legislature that may be bribed by that nation which avows, in the face of the world, that bribery is a part of her system of government."[70]

A motion to lay the plan aside for future consideration was carried by a vote of six to five. Massachusetts and Virginia had defeated the conservatives. The radicals and near-radicals were masters of the Congress.

Congress, in its next important action, named a committee "to bring in a plan for carrying into effect the non-importation, non-consumption and non-exportation resolved on."[71] The appointees could have no doubt about the temper of the legislature they served.

Not so much in hope as in the attitude of men clearing their record for history, Congress voted October 1 to send a "loyal address" to the King. October 2, perhaps in more hope, they voted to send an address to the people of Great Britain. The colonists had friends in high places in the mother country.[72]

Two Virginians—Lee and Henry—were named to the committee of five which would prepare the petition to his Majesty. Their working partners were Thomas Johnson, of Maryland, John Adams and John Rutledge. Lee was chairman. Henry, whose oratorical eloquence had made a vivid impression, was chosen to draft the document.[73]

Perhaps the Virginian, who had once reminded his Majesty's government that "Caesar had his Brutus," wrote an address too blunt or too fiery for a majority of the Congress. In any event, the delegates asked that the petition be rewritten. John Dickinson, the "Pennsylvania Farmer," a journalist and able pamphleteer for the American cause, was added to the committee.[74]

The task of preparing the Address to the People was assigned to Lee, Jay and William Livingston. The actual drafting was done by Lee, whose scholarship and eloquence were much admired.

Lee was accustomed to applause. Many of the delegates shared John Adams' opinion that the Virginian was "a masterful man." His patrician poise must have received a severe jolt when a dead silence followed the reading of his work to the Congress. Being an orator, he must have wondered for a moment if his eloquence had produced the hypnotic effect that sometimes holds an audience entranced for a moment before registering vociferous approval. But the silence dragged on and Lee's friends began to look uncomfortable. Someone proposed that consideration of the document be postponed until the following day.[75]

When the Congress convened again, Jay happened to have an Address to the People which he had prepared, and Livingston begged that it be read. Jay's draft was approved.

But victories had been won by the Virginians, triumphs that could assuage hurt egos, and that were really of far greater significance than the two addresses to the King and the people. On October 14, the Congress approved a Declaration of Rights that, as advocated by Lee, was based on "the immutable laws of nature, the principles of the English Constitution, and the several charters or compacts." Galloway and Duane had opposed citations of natural law.[76]

In the ten resolutions comprising the Declaration, Congress asserted the right of the colonists to life, liberty and property. It declared that the Americans had never forfeited any of the "rights, liberties and immunities of free and natural born subjects within the realm of England." One of these, "a right in the people to participate in their own legislative council," was termed "the foundation of English liberty and of all free government."

The document acknowledged that the colonies could not practicably be represented in the Parliament in London, and asserted that they were therefore "entitled to a free and exclusive power of legislation in their several provincial legislatures . . . subject only to the negative of their sovereign. . . ."

But, from "a regard to the mutual interest of both countries," the resolutions said, "we cheerfully consent to . . . such acts of the British Parliament as are . . . restrained to the regulation of our external commerce. . . ."

The document stated the colonists' determination to hold to the "inestimable privilege of being tried by their peers of the vicinage" and to the right of Assembly and petition. They were convinced that rights were violated when a standing army was kept among them in peacetime "except by the consent of the legislature in that colony in which such army is kept."

The tenth resolution was another nail driven in the coffin of the Galloway Plan of Union. It declared, "The exercise of legislative power in the several colonies by a council appointed, during pleasure, by the Crown, is unconstitutional, dangerous and destructive of the freedom of American legislation."

Congress heard the report of the committee to frame a plan for non-importation, non-consumption and non-exportation of British goods. The plan was already generally known as the Association, a name reminiscent of the Virginia Association of August 1774. The resemblance was more than a matter of nomenclature.

After such compromises as the exclusion of rice from the list of restricted exports to woo the disgruntled South Carolina delegation back to the meeting hall, the Association was still a continental version of the Virginia Association. Moreover, the copy was remarkably faithful to the original.[77]

As finally adopted by the Congress, the Association was a pledge that the colonies would end all importations from Britain by December 1, and put a stop to the slave trade by the same date. Consumption of British products was to cease by March 1, 1775. An embargo on all exports to Britain, Ireland and the West Indies would be clamped down September 1, 1775.

As with the Virginia Association, a committee of enforcement was to be elected in each county and town. Boycott and ridicule would be their weapons against those who did not conform. The scope of boycott would be extended to include any colony which violated its pledge to support the Association.

The delegates were well aware that their proceedings might be branded treasonable, and that their arrest as traitors might be ordered by agents of the crown. On October 21, they resolved "that the seizing, or attempting to seize, any person in America, in order to transport such person beyond the sea, for trial of offences committed within the body of a county in America, being against law, will justify and ought to meet with resistance and reprisal."[78]

Yet some of the conservative delegates feared the reprisals of their colleagues and neighbors more than threats that might issue from distant London. Accordingly, Galloway, though inwardly seething, was among the solemn signers of the Association. He confided to friends that he had signed in the hope of "preventing the Congress from proceeding to more violent measures."[79]

The next day, a majority of the delegates, undaunted by threats of any kind, voted a recommendation that the colonies name delegates to a new Congress, to convene May 10, 1775, in Philadelphia.

On October 26, 1774, the first Continental Congress was dissolved, following the signing of the Address to the King. Washington signed for himself, and for Pendleton, Bland and Harrison, who had left the city three days before. Lee signed for Patrick Henry, who was also on the road home.[80]

Nine years before, Henry had started for home before the end of a legislative session and had later been chagrined to learn that his boldly defiant Stamp Act resolutions had been mutilated in his absence by a greatly reduced House of Burgesses. But there was no danger now in leaving Philadelphia. The men of Virginia and Massachusetts were securely in control. There seemed to be soundness in John Dickinson's prediction:

"The first act of violence on the part of the administration in America, or the attempt to reinforce General Gage this winter or next year will put the whole continent in arms, from Nova Scotia to Georgia."[81]

The Virginians were eager to return to a more familiar legislative arena, the House of Burgesses, which was slated to convene on the first Thursday in November. These veterans of the Philadelphia Congress would be needed in Williamsburg.

Besides, another incentive quickened the pace of their homeward journey. They had been participants in the greatest assembly of talents in the history of North America. Their activities had been the subject of excited speculation from Georgia to New England. Most had not written home so copiously and exhaustively as John Adams. There was much to tell.

*   *   *

The Virginians had played a major role in the First Continental

Congress. Only the men of Massachusetts had exercised comparable influence.

The Old Dominion's delegates probably excited more admiration in Philadelphia than those of any other colony. The New England representatives, even in their private letters and journals, waxed rhapsodic over the Virginians. Conservative leaders of the middle colonies frequently were at odds with the Southerners, as they were with the New Englanders. But they respected Lee's and Henry's gifts of persuasion as well as the less spectacular, but no less formidable, talents of some of the other Virginians.

Peyton Randolph, veteran speaker of the Virginia House of Burgesses, was unanimously elected chairman of the Congress.

The two most important committees of the Congress were one named "to state the rights of the colonies" and another appointed to make recommendations concerning their "trade and manufactures."

On the first of these, Virginia had three representatives—a distinction enjoyed by only two other colonies, Massachusetts and Pennsylvania. Great influence was wielded by the Virginia members—Richard Henry Lee, Edmund Pendleton and Patrick Henry. As a result of the committee's reports, the Congress made two important decisions about the statement of American rights. The first was to "found our rights upon the laws of Nature, the principles of the English Constitution, and charters and compacts." This agreement was a great personal triumph for Lee. The second important decision was the determination to base the colonial bill of complaints on the actions of Parliament since 1763. For this agreement, which eliminated much fruitless and potentially dangerous debate, thanks are due chiefly to Lee and Pendleton and to the Virginia Convention on whose instructions they acted.

Consideration of the problems of commerce and manufacture and of "the means most proper to be pursued for a restoration of our rights" merged in the Congress' decision to enter into an Association for the enforcement of a non-exportation, non-consumption and non-importation agreement. This Association was a continental model of the Virginia organization of the same name. Thus Virginia furnished the prototype for the one practical instrument forged by the Congress.

The spirit of revolution was growing in the land, and it found expression in the actions of the Congress. At one time it seemed that that spirit might be dampened by compromise in the form of the Galloway Plan. But this proposal for an inter-colonial legislature inferior to the Parliament in London was defeated, principally through the united efforts of the Virginia and Massachusetts delegations.

By example and by cooperation, Virginia was in the forefront of the colonial struggle for liberty. Her leaders were hailed as heroes in New England and the South, and feared as dangerous men by influential groups in the Middle Colonies. On one fact, though, thoughtful men in all the colonies could agree. Virginia's leaders were towering figures on the American stage.

Chapter XI

SWORD OF UNITY

(1774-1775)

Chapter XI

(1774-1775)

STREET corner orators and coffee house oracles were busy in Williamsburg November 3, 1774.[1] Wherever they could find an audience of two or three, they held forth. Some were elegant young gentlemen with ruffled tempers and ruffled shirts, satin-clad gallants whose arguments waxed hot while their coffee grew cold. Others were plain men moved to colorful language, a brown-garbed blacksmith who made the sparks fly as he hammered out a horseshoe while he pounded out his arguments for the benefit of his apprentice; a rotund shopkeeper in shirtsleeves and leathern apron arguing with one customer while another drummed on the counter in impatience. While ruddy firelight chased shadows on the walls of the Raleigh Tavern tap room, others, intoxicated with liberty and the grog in which they had toasted it, banged their pewter tankards on stained table tops to drive home their eloquence.

However widely the speakers might differ in appearance, they had at least one thing in common. The text of their discourse was provided by that day's issue of the *Virginia Gazette*. Before the next day dawned, many copies of the four-page journal would have suffered rough treatment. They would have been waved in exuberance, snatched at in rude eagerness, and splashed with coffee and liquor by gesticulating debaters. But they would have been read and reread, both silently and aloud, and with degrees of comprehension as various as the accents and the pronunciations—some of them remarkably original—that were heard in Williamsburg that day.

Mr. Purdie and Mr. Dixon had had little trouble in compiling this sensationally successful issue of their paper. They had filled nearly the whole front page with verbatim printings of selections from the proceedings of the Continental Congress, including the Address to the People of Great Britain, the Memorial to the Inhabitants of the Colonies and, above all, "the Association entered into by that august Body in Behalf of all North America."[2]

Some citizens of Williamsburg had heard first-hand about the Congress's proceedings from Peyton Randolph, Richard Bland and

Benjamin Harrison, who had ridden into town from Philadelphia the Sunday before. The Sabbath was a social day that drew to Bruton Parish Church planters who otherwise were seldom seen in the city unless brought by a political or commercial mission. It is safe to assume that most of the conversation after divine services that day was not devoted to comment on the sermon.

But only a minority had the privilege of discussing the acts of the Congress with the returned delegates. The rumors that spread through the entire population of Williamsburg and the surrounding country only whetted the appetite for news. No wonder the *Virginia Gazette* had so many eager readers!

Many were surprised to learn that the Association not only was a "non-importation, non-consumption and non-exportation agreement," but also included provisions that seemed to exalt austerity for austerity's sake. There could be no quarrel with the pledge, "We will use our utmost endeavors to improve the breed of sheep, and increase their number to the greatest extent . . . and those of us who are or may become overstocked with, or can conveniently spare any sheep, will dispose of them to our neighbors, especially to the poorer sort, on moderate terms."[3] If the colonists must not import textiles from Britain, prudence dictated that they should build up their own reserves of wool.

But article eight of the pledges was quite another thing. It must have been written by New England Yankees or Pennsylvania Quakers. "We will, in our several stations, encourage frugality, economy and industry, and promote agriculture, arts and the manufactures of this country, especially of wool," it said. So far so good, but what followed was excruciating. "—and will discountenance and discourage every species of extravagance and dissipation, especially all horse-racing, and all kinds of gaming, cock fighting, exhibitions of shows, plays and other expensive diversions and entertainments; and on death of any relation or friend, none of us, or any of our families will go into any further mourning-dress than a black crepe or ribbon on the arm or hat for gentlemen, and a black ribbon and necklace for ladies and we will discontinue the giving of gloves and scarves at funerals."[4]

Horse racing was a proper diversion for gentlemen. There might be sound arguments for abolishing the prizes, but how could a contest between Virginia horses affect the struggle between the colonies and the Mother Country over American rights?

Giving up the theater would go hard with the people of Williamsburg, the first regular theater patrons in America.[5]

The pledge to reduce mourning dress to the minimum and abolish the giving of remembrances to friends of the deceased represented an abrupt departure from Tidewater mores. Visible honor to the dead was important to the planter society which buried its great men under marble tablets with eulogistic epitaphs of prodigious length. Many gentlemen provided in their wills for the purchase of mourning rings to be worn by friends as well as relatives.[6]

It was plain that some Puritans had written their ethical prejudices into the continental Association, but the plan was essentially the same as the Virginia Association. Virginia's delegates had had to make some concessions to get their ideas adopted. The colonies would have to learn to live together if they were ever to command Parliament's respect.

Some Virginians did not reason that deeply in the matter. To a small farmer in Westmoreland County, the fact that Mr. Richard Henry Lee had signed the Association was argument enough. An unlettered man in Caroline County was willing to go along with anything that Mr. Pendleton said. The mountaineers knew that Patrick Henry would not lead them astray. And so it was with other delegates and their neighbors.[7]

The November 17 issue of the *Virginia Gazette* carried a notice to the freeholders of James City County to assemble for the election of a committee to enforce the Association. In the same column appeared an advertisement illustrative of the fact that Virginians were determined to comply even with the pledges that seemed senseless. Moreover, though they might forego some fun, they would not part with their sense of humor. The notice, dated November 8, read:

"At a meeting of the Jockey Club this Day, resolved, that in conformity to the 8th Article of the Resolves of the General Congress, the Dumfries Races, that were advertised to be run the 29th of this Month, be postponed.—The Gentlemen Farmers that are fattening Beeves, Muttons and Veals for our Premiums must, for the present, put up with Honour and Glory in place of the guineas that were intended for them."[8]

Next week's issue of the *Virginia Gazette* revealed that some of the county committees had been earnestly at work. Above a citizen's signature appeared the statement:

"It gives me much concern to find that I have incurred the

displeasure of the York and Gloucester committees, and thereby of the public in general, for my omission in not countermanding the order which I sent to Mr. Norton for two half chests of tea; and do with truth declare that I had not the least intention to give offense, nor did I mean an opposition to any measure for the public good. My countrymen, therefore, it is earnestly hoped, will readily forgive me for an act which may be interpreted so much to my discredit; and I again make this public declaration that I had not the least design. . . ."[9]

The statement trailed on in obsequious reiteration of submission, as did statements by other offenders which appeared in successive issues of the *Gazette*. The words varied, but the attitude was always groveling.

Between four hundred and five hundred merchants, gathered in Williamsburg to hear a report on the Association by Peyton Randolph and other Virginia delegates to the Continental Congress, had praised the representatives for their "wisdom and prudence" and had signed the agreement.[10] Having committed themselves to a policy that would cost them dearly, these men were zealous to see that less inhibited competitors did not take advantage of the situation.

Every effort was made to humiliate merchants who violated the Association. Prominent citizens with a reputation for moderation—men like Robert Carter Nicholas[11] and Edmund Pendleton—headed some of the county committees. But popular feeling ran so high that many of the merchants feared violence. After Port Royal merchants failed to appear when summoned before the Caroline County committee, Pendleton had to issue a second call, promising: "I am authorized to engage the faith of the Committee that no kind of injury shall be offered to . . . such of you as may attend tomorrow, during your attendance, coming and returning."[12]

A few days later, some Stafford County offenders listened in anguished suspense while "bystanders" at a committee hearing debated whether to throw them out the windows. Such drastic action was overruled, but the merchants took the hint and, as one of their number reported, signed a statement of submission "not from any conviction, but from motives of self preservation."[13]

Observance of the Association was so strict in Virginia that businessmen suffered grievously. One sign of the times was a letter of December 10 which a boy who had been clerking in a Leedstown store delivered to his father in London. Written by the lad's erstwhile employer, the message said: "This I hope will be delivered by your son who comes passenger with Captain Mitchell. The unhappy disputes between Great Britain and the colonies put it at present out of my power and Mr. Holland['s] to keep him any longer in the store, we having determined to discontinue our business as no importations are or can be made in America from Britain. . . . God send things may soon be mutually settled. The Americans will never submit to be taxed by the British Parliament."[14]

Governor Dunmore's brown eyes must have flashed fire when the auburn-haired scion of the Royal Stuarts penned a report, December 24, to Lord Dartmouth. The Association, he said, was being enforced "with the greatest rigor."[15] Virginians accorded "the laws of Congress . . . marks of reverence which they never bestowed on their legal government or the laws proceeding from it."

Dunmore testified to his own frustration. "I have discovered no instance," he wrote, "where the interposition of government, in the feeble state to which it is reduced, could serve any other purpose than to suffer the disgrace of a disappointment, and thereby afford matter of great exaltation to its enemies and increase their influence over the minds of the people."

The Association was working remarkably well in Virginia, but its record was not one of unstained glory. Some of the merchants publicly branded for "contumacious conduct" in refusing to submit to the examination of their records by officious committees and sub-committees had no violations to conceal, but were simply standing up for what they believed to be their rights. For example, when the Port Royal merchants were finally compelled to submit their books, no offenses were discovered. The Caroline County Committee, to its everlasting credit, was as zealous to publish the exoneration as it was the implied accusation in this case. But not all committees were quite so scrupulous, and too many men not affiliated with committees took it upon themselves to enforce committee mandates.[16]

Lord Dunmore's accuracy was injured by his prejudice when he reported to Dartmouth that "the abolishing [of] the courts of justice was the first step taken" in enforcing the Association. The trial of cases brought by British merchants was largely suspended, but courts continued to sit for the probate of wills, administration of estates and recording of deeds in property-conscious Virginia, as well as for the trial of criminals and the supervision of roads, mills and ordinaries.[17] The governor may not have exaggerated, though, when he said that "There is not a justice of peace in Virginia that acts except as a committee man."

As the year 1774 neared a close, a superficial observer might have concluded that Dunmore had a chance to regain his popularity and prestige in Virginia. A special supplement to the *Virginia Gazette* of December 8 reported:

"Last Saturday morning the Right Honorable the Countess of Dunmore was safely delivered of a daughter, at the Palace [in Williamsburg.] Her ladyship continues in a very favorable situation, and the young Virginian is in perfect health."[18]

But the style of the announcement had nothing to do with the political tensions which gripped the colony. Graceful social statements could mislead only those who forgot that Virginians were urbane revolutionists. Had not the Burgesses, just five years before, honored with a Christmas ball the royal Governor with whom they were contending for their liberties? And had they not the year before that toasted the Queen with the same Governor the very day after he had dissolved their Assembly and they had subscribed to the Virginia Association?

Tidewater Virginians were still congratulating the Governor on his recent success as a military leader.[19] But he could not hope to become a popular hero. In fact, the repercussions of his exploit threatened to shake his prestige.

Dunmore had followed the example of some of his predecessors in leading an expedition against the Indians. The war whoop had not been heard in Tidewater for many years except as an accompaniment to the blood-curdling stories of frontiersmen from the West or of oldsters by a tavern fireside. In the Valley of Virginia, though, a chorus of ululating wails was still the prelude to mass murder.

By the Royal proclamation of 1763, Englishmen had been forbidden to settle in the areas west of the sources of the James, Rappahannock, Potomac and other rivers flowing into the Atlantic. The western lands were expressly reserved as hunting grounds for the Indians.

But, as Dunmore reported to London, no proclamation could restrain men who "forever imagine the lands farther off are still better than those upon which they are already settled," men who "do and will remove as their avidity and restlessness incite them."[20]

Bloody warfare ensued.

Many whites called the Indians "varmints." More fluent spokesmen for the frontier said the natives were "without any kind of sensibility" and "little removed from the brute creation." They sneered at suggestions from Williamsburg that the aboriginal owners of the land had souls.[21]

However much the frontiersman might derogate the Indian by way of rationalizing his own conduct, he paid him the compliment of imitation. Leather skinned, his lean, hard body clad in doeskin, a tomahawk at his side and the dripping scalps of slain enemies dangling from his belt, the pioneer returning from the warpath might well be mistaken for the savage he hated.[22]

As white traders, disobeying orders from Williamsburg, built up a liquor trade with the Indians, frontier attacks increased in number and ferocity. So did white reprisals. Friendly Indians were sometimes the victims of whites who insisted that all red men were alike.[23]

Some officials of the western counties strove valiantly to bring to justice the killers of innocent Indians. But mobs worked against them and, in at least two cases, broke open jails and freed men charged with murder.[24]

By the summer of 1774, the Indians were attempting to form a confederacy of all the Ohio tribes. The frontier militia were called out to protect the white settlements.[25]

In the fall, two divisions marched toward the Ohio. One, from the northern part of the Valley, was led by Dunmore. The other, from the southern part, was led by Andrew Lewis, Washington's stalwart colleague in the campaign against Fort Duquesne and a respected Valley citizen who had tried to halt the killing of friendly Indians.[26] The first division proceeded by way of Fort Pitt. The second advanced through the Great Kanawha Valley.

When Lewis' men arrived at Point Pleasant, the confluence of the Ohio and Great Kanawha rivers, they found a large force of Shawnee warriors under Cornstalk. The Shawnees were the most feared of all the tribes that entered the Valley. Cornstalk was a great chief whose name kindled admiration when spoken in the lodges of the Delawares and the Cherokees and chilled stout hearts when whispered in the cabins of white settlers from Pennsylvania to Virginia. Lewis' Virginians, in their fringed hunting shirts, were the Long Knives, a name which the Indians had given them in awed tribute to the quickness with which they could bring flashing death to the warrior's heart. To the white man's science, they had added Indian artifice.

Both sides knew that they faced what might well be the climactic battle of the disputed frontier. The Indians were the first to attack.

Even above the maddening whoops of his warriors roared the mighty voice of Cornstalk. Like so many glistening, painted devils the Indians appeared from every conceivable cover. Their leader was like Satan himself. Hour after weary hour, he could be heard above the turmoil of battle, shouting orders to his tribesmen in a voice that seemed superhuman in its strength.[27] But when night fell, the Shawnees retreated across the Ohio like fleeing shadows. The Virginians were masters of a field on which two hundred of their own number lay dead or wounded.[28]

Lewis erected a rude fort on the scene and then marched toward the Indian towns north of the Ohio, effecting a juncture with Dunmore's forces. Soon, though, the Governor ordered Lewis' division to return to their home counties, and reluctantly they complied. There was a great deal of grumbling in the ranks, and Lewis, however circumspect his conduct as a commander, must have been strongly in sympathy with his men.

Dunmore had led an expedition into the Ohio country despite the proclamation of 1763 and the new Quebec Act of 1774, which made the contested region part of Canada. As he sat at his desk in the Governor's Palace on Christmas Eve of 1774, he was faced with the necessity of explaining his actions to His Majesty's Secretary of State. Further complicating his task was the knowledge that London would not be pleased over renewal of the contest between Pennsylvania and Virginia for the territory around Fort Pitt, a struggle made inevitable by what was already being called Dunmore's War.

There was no gain for his government to counterbalance official disfavor. The men of the Valley had learned to hate Dunmore. Congratulations from Tidewater and the Piedmont were overshadowed by the growth of martial spirit as a result of the victory of Virginians at Point Pleasant. Young men in the more sheltered counties envied the battle laurels of their counterparts on the frontier. They were organizing independent companies and drilling with zeal.[29]

Word was abroad that the Indians were suing for peace and had given hostages.[30] The young men of Eastern Virginia could not be preparing to fight the redskins. Could it be—the thought was a sobering one for His Majesty's royal Governor on Christmas Eve— could it be that they were preparing to fight red*coats*?

* * *

"If I must be enslaved, let it be by a King at least, and not by a parcel of upstart lawless committeemen. If I must be devoured, let me be devoured by the jaws of a lion, and not gnawed to death by rats and vermin."[31] In those words of anguished contempt, Samuel Seabury, a New York loyalist, protested the activities of committees organized to enforce the Association.

If Seabury had lived in Virginia, he would have had to find another metaphor. Most of the committees in the Old Dominion were headed by men who were lions in their own counties at least, and in some cases by those whose roars were heard with respect in Williamsburg or even Philadelphia.

In the letter that Governor Dunmore penned to the Secretary of State on Christmas Eve, 1774, he said that, in the business of the Association, "men of fortune and preeminence joined equally with the lowest and meanest."[32]

This fact greatly magnified the Governor's problem if rebellion was afoot. Prominent politicians, aristocrats and wealthy men were among the Association's supporters in virtually all the colonies, but probably in none but Virginia was the Association led by so many of those who combined preeminence in political leadership, wealth and social prestige. Virginia had its loyalists who opposed the committees, but they were distinctly in the minority and there was no class cleavage on the issue of restricting imports.[33]

The effectiveness of Virginia's Association was manifest in 1775. Exports from England to Maryland and Virginia plummeted from £528,738 in 1774 to £1,921 in 1775. The importation of British goods was sharply reduced in all the colonies except Georgia, which registered a marked increase, but the reduction in Virginia was on an even more impressive scale than that in New England.[34] This circumstance is especially remarkable in view of the fact that the sufferings of the Port of Boston were the immediate impetus for adoption of a Continental Association.

Governor Dunmore reminded London that nonexportation was a two-edged sword. The colonists had pledged to import from Britain only the necessities that were not obtainable in America. Dunmore was confident the rebels could be brought to their knees if these necessities were denied them through control of exports from the mother country.[35]

Whether his Majesty's government would act on the Governor's proposal was doubtful. Nevertheless, Dunmore may have congratulated himself on eliminating by his own action a problem within his immediate sphere. He had prorogued until May 26, 1775 the Assem-

bly session originally scheduled for 1774. The prospect of this session
had hastened the return from Philadelphia of the Virginia delegates.
If the Governor had not acted decisively, the seven representatives
would have ridden into Williamsburg and, still breathing sedition,
infected virtually the whole House of Burgesses. By proroguing the
Assembly, the Governor had gained a breathing spell until the end
of May. Prompt and forceful action by London might quell rebellion
and ease his problems before then.

Such must have been Dunmore's line of reasoning. Early in 1775,
he received a rude shock. Peyton Randolph, evidently drawing
heavily on "natural law" and the support of public opinion, "requested" the election in each county of delegates to a Virginia
conclave which in turn would name delegates to the second Continental Congress. The Virginia convention would be held March 20
in Richmond.[36]

The little town at the falls of the James could not approach the
accommodations for a large gathering which were available in
Williamsburg. Richmond had grown slowly but surely since its
founding by Colonel William Byrd II in 1733, and it was no longer
a frontier outpost. But it still could not boast elegant hostelries or
superior facilities of any kind for a convention. Nevertheless, the
delegates would be far more comfortable here than in the capital,
where their deliberations would have been conducted in the shadow
of the Governor's Palace.

The actual scene of the convention was outside Richmond and
across shallow Shockoe Creek. Since no building within the town
was large enough for the convocation, St. John's Episcopal Church
was pressed into service. A frame structure of severe dignity, set
among trees on the crest of a hill, it seemed architecturally akin to
the classically simple, sharp-spired Congregational churches which
dotted the hills of New England.

Shocked Tories doubtless thought that the assembled delegates
were adding blasphemy to revolution in the catalogue of their sins.
Some of the delegates themselves may have had qualms about putting
the house of religion to political use. All but the most insensitive
must have been acutely aware that they were in strange surround-
ings for the business at hand.

Soon, however, they forgot that they were not back in the old
House of Burgesses. Their pew mates were their desk mates of
former sessions. Peyton Randolph was acclaimed chairman. That
familiar, placid face—a symbol of good-humored dignity—made

revolution seem like tradition. The rules and orders of the House of Burgesses were adopted *in toto* by the Convention.[37]

For two days the delegates discussed the recommendations of the Continental Congress.[38] Hopes were fed by reports that most of the King's troops would be removed from Boston and that hard-hit English merchants would appeal to the House of Commons to redress the grievances that inspired the Association.[39] It was generally known that bets of three to two "that the American acts will be totally repealed" had been laid in a London coffeehouse.[40] But these encouraging rumors did not throw the Convention into indecision. The proceedings and recommendations of the Congress were unanimously approved.

The next morning a Jamaican petition to the King was laid before the delegates. The document was an appeal in behalf of colonial rights, but was couched in much less forceful terms than similar petitions from the American colonies. The Jamaican petitioners made it clear that their efforts to obtain redress would stop short of armed resistance.

The secretary recorded that the petition was "maturely considered." Internal evidence supports his statement, for the replying resolutions presented by leaders of the Convention revealed considerable adroitness. They expressed appreciation of the Jamaican Assembly's address in a way likely to retain the sympathy of that body, and at the same time did not endorse its cautious terms. The Virginia Convention's reply to the Jamaicans was as follows:

"Resolved, That the most unfeigned thanks, and most grateful acknowledgements of this Convention be presented to that very respectable Assembly, for the exceeding generous and affectionate part they have so nobly taken in the unhappy contest between Great Britain and her colonies, and for their truly patriotic endeavors to fix the just claims of the colonists upon the most permanent constitutional principles.

"That the Assembly be assured, that it is the most ardent wish of this Colony (and, we are persuaded, of the whole continent of North America) to see a speedy return of those halcyon days when we lived a free and happy people."[41]

The leaders of the Convention, judicious men, might well congratulate themselves on so painless an extrication from the horns of a dilemma. But apprehension quickly seized them. Patrick Henry, the giant of the hills, was demanding recognition and the fire of prophecy was in his eyes. He proposed that additional resolutions be adopted. In a deep, melodious voice, he read:

"Resolved, that a well regulated militia, composed of gentlemen and yeomen, is the natural strength, and only security, of a free government; that such a militia in this Colony would forever render it unnecessary for the Mother Country to keep among us, for the purpose of our defense, any standing army; That the establishment of such a militia at this time is peculiarly necessary . . . Resolved, therefore, That this Colony be immediately put into a posture of defense. . . ."[42]

Richard Bland took the floor. There was quiet dignity in the elderly man's tall, stooped figure. Like a courteous schoolmaster addressing his class, he spoke haltingly but with undeviating logic, dealing with Henry's arguments with scholarly precision.[43] He saw no need to talk of arms when there were signs that trade restrictions already adopted might bring Parliament to a realistic reappraisal of the American situation.

Robert Carter Nicholas spoke next. A balding, rather average-looking man, he would have been underestimated by an uninformed observer. He was no orator, but he had the force and business sagacity of his grandfather, Robert "King" Carter.[44] The delegates listened respectfully as he warned of the folly of incendiary talk.

Now a great bear of a man arose to attack Henry's arguments. Benjamin Harrison did not deign to conceal his impatience in a plethora of diplomatic niceties.[45] Talk of arming, except as a last resort, harmed rather than helped the cause of liberty, he maintained.

Edmund Pendleton, who clothed his thoughts as elegantly as he did his handsome frame, was the next speaker. His appearance contrasted markedly with Harrison's, but his arguments were similar.[46] Pendleton knew, as did everyone there, that more and more Virginians were shouldering arms every week without the incitement of an official pronouncement on the subject.

Again Henry got the floor.[47] There was still fire in his eyes, but none in his voice. His manner was deferential and he spoke only a little less haltingly than Bland. His speech quickened as he began to catalogue colonial grievances against the British ministry. The razor's edge of sarcasm crept into his voice as he taunted his listeners with rhetorical questions about the arrogance with which their petitions had been spurned.

Suddenly Henry seemed almost to become a new speaker interrupting his former self. "We must fight!" he shouted. "I repeat it, sir, we must fight; an appeal to arms and to the God of Hosts is all that is left us!"

His voice dropped again, but now throbbed with an emotion more exciting than his exclamation. "They tell us, sir, that we are weak— unable to cope with so formidable an adversary. But when shall we be stronger? Will it be the next week or the next year? . . . Sir, we are not weak if we make the proper use of those forces which the God of nature hath placed in our power. Three millions of people armed in the holy cause of liberty, and in such a country as that which we possess, are invincible by any force which our enemy can send against us.

"Besides, sir, we shall not fight our battles alone. There is a just God who presides over the destinies of nations, and who will raise up friends to fight our battles for us. The battle, sir, is not to the strong alone; it is to the vigilant, the active, the brave.

"Besides, sir, we have no election. If we were base enough to desire it, it is now too late to retire from the contest. There is no retreat but in submission and slavery! Our chains are forged. Their clanking may be heard on the plains of Boston! The war is inevitable —and let it come!! I repeat it, sir, let it come!!!

"It is in vain, sir, to extenuate the matter. Gentlemen may cry, Peace, peace—but there is no peace. The war is actually begun. The next gale that sweeps from the North will bring to our ears the clash of resounding arms! Is life so dear, or peace so sweet, as to be purchased at the price of chains and slavery? Forbid it, Almighty God! I know not what course others may take; but as for me, give me liberty, or give me death!"

Henry sat down. Men gradually became aware of the silence. Some felt a little dizzy, as though they had been standing on the summit of a mountain.

A few delegates rose to speak in opposition to Henry, but what were their rumblings to men who had just heard thunder from Olympus?

Richard Henry Lee sprang up to speak for Henry's resolution. He could not match the Piedmonter's eloquence, but his Ciceronian periods had a majesty of their own and he was urbanely persuasive.[48]

Thomas Jefferson asked for recognition. The delegates were sur- prised. The Albemarle lawyer, now in his mid-thirties, had made a considerable reputation as a writer but was not an accomplished orator, and usually eschewed the speaker's role. Ten years before, Jefferson, then a college student, had stood in a doorway of the

House of Burgesses chamber and thrilled to Henry's eloquent plea for Stamp Act resolutions that "set fire to the continent." The young man had seen his own cousin, Peyton Randolph, who had presided, stride out of the hall growling in anger. Now the same Peyton Randolph, in the chair now as then, had just recognized Jefferson, who rose to speak in Henry's support. The red-haired young giant did not plead smoothly, and he gestured awkwardly with his large hands. But his fervor had a compelling quality.[49]

Nicholas quickly perceived the temper of the Convention, and his good sense told him that, if the delegates were bent on issuing a formal call to arms, the two regiments for which Henry called would be ridiculously inadequate. He, therefore, urged the raising of a force of ten thousand to twenty thousand men.[50]

Henry's resolution was adopted. In its final form, it avoided any specific reference to the number of troops needed, simply calling for "such a number of men as may be sufficient." But there was no equivocation in the decision that the "Colony be immediately put into a posture of defense. . . ."[51]

A committee was appointed to formulate a plan for "embodying, arming and disciplining such a number of men as may be sufficient for that purpose." Appropriately enough, Henry was the first man appointed to the committee, which included three experienced soldiers, Washington, Adam Stephen and Andrew Lewis; three powerful conservatives, Pendleton, Nicholas and Harrison; and several of Henry's radical supporters, of whom Jefferson was the most conspicuous and most promising.[52]

The committee's report was ready by the next day. The day after that, the 25th, it was debated, amended and adopted.[53] The plan called upon Virginians to organize "one or more volunteer companies of infantry and troops of horse in each county, and to be in constant training and readiness to act in any emergency." The Tidewater counties, where riding well was an accomplishment essential to "The Compleat Gentleman," were urged to concentrate on cavalry. The northern and western counties, where moccasined frontiersmen rivaled the Indians in endurance on the trail, were asked to give "particular attention to the forming [of] a good infantry." For the present, these volunteer companies would be responsible only to their own county committees of defense. But they could quickly be welded into a single force under colony-wide command if a sudden threat should make unity necessary.

Complaining that "a proper provision of arms and ammunition

has not been made, to the evident danger of the community in case of invasion or insurrection," the authors of the plan recommended that each county levy a head tax for the purchase of ammunition. Such action had already been taken in Fairfax County. A Virginia committee of three was appointed to act as purchasing agent for counties which felt the need of such a service.[54]

On the same day that it adopted the defense report, the Convention appointed a committee to "prepare a plan for the encouragement of arts and manufactures in this colony."[55] Of course, emphasis would be on the production of munitions and defense materials.

Before that momentous day was over, the Convention re-elected the seven delegates that it had sent to the first Continental Congress and made them fully accredited representatives to the second. Peyton Randolph, of course, garnered the most votes. But many delegates must have been surprised when Washington came in second, and only one vote behind the popular chairman. The poll must have reflected in large part the esteem which had been won by this counselor who spoke seldom but always judiciously. It may have reflected also the general realization that the new Congress' problems might be largely military.

That day Washington wrote to his brother Jack, consenting to review the younger man's independent company, and assuring him that he would "very cheerfully accept the honor of commanding it if occasion requires it to be drawn out, as it is my full intention to devote my life and fortune in the cause we are engaged in, if need be."[56]

The Convention adjourned March 27, and those who had participated in its deliberations returned to their home counties, there to guide the defense preparations which they had urged in Assembly. Meanwhile, there was work to be done on the plantations, and outwardly the tenor of life was little disturbed. Preparations for another crop of tobacco went forward. A Warwick merchant wrote: "The planters, especially the common sort of them, are in high spirits, so that they think little about the political dispute."[57]

Something that happened April 20 changed the picture. In the blackness before dawn, fifteen British Marines and their captain stole ashore from an armed schooner anchored in the James. Stealthily they removed the gunpowder stored in the magazine at Williamsburg and bore it back to the riverbank, where it was loaded aboard another vessel, H.M.S. *Fowey*.[58]

When the removal of the powder was discovered, an angry mob

congregated near the Capitol. Someone shouted "To the Palace!" and the seething, unchanneled mass began turning into an angry procession. Peyton Randolph and Robert Carter Nicholas managed to command the throng's attention. They argued that the excited citizens might defeat their own purpose. Mob action might so infuriate the Governor that he would refuse to listen to the people. Something might be accomplished by a formal protest from the Common Hall, the city's governing body. The crowd acquiesced and dispersed.

The Common Hall drafted a protest and soon appeared in a body at the Palace. Randolph presented the address to the Governor. He respectfully reminded His Excellency that the powder stores in the magazine had been placed there for the colony's security. In the event of a slave uprising, they would be needed immediately. On behalf of the citizens of Williamsburg, the Common Hall requested that his lordship explain why he had removed the powder, and that he return it.[59]

Dunmore replied that he, too, had been concerned over the threat of a slave insurrection, especially in view of disturbing reports from a neighboring county. Under these circumstances, he had thought it best to remove the powder to a location of greater security lest it fall into the hands of rebel blacks.

He vowed that the powder could be brought back within half an hour, and would be if public security should necessitate its return. It had been removed under cover of darkness to avoid exciting the public. Since the removal had been discovered and had caused considerable agitation, the Governor said, it would be imprudent to place gunpowder within reach of men who had already taken up arms.

As Randolph and the other petitioners left the Palace, they confronted an impatient crowd waiting outside. He and Nicholas had to exercise their best persuasive powers to get the excited townspeople to disperse. Both men, though, were too wise to assume that the mob would not assemble again.

There were angry meetings elsewhere in the colony.

The Caroline County Committee authorized the release of powder to volunteers gathered at Bowling Green, but its chairman, Edmund Pendleton, would not permit a march on Williamsburg before receiving word from Randolph.[60]

At least fourteen companies of light horse had congregated in Fredericksburg and were eager to ride to the capital. They were soon augmented by the arrival of men from the frontier counties—

soldiers in fringed hunting shirts, bronzed warriors with tomahawks in their belts, fighters like the "Long Knives" who had defeated Cornstalk.

On the night of April 28, a messenger galloped into town with a letter from Randolph. He wrote:

"If we . . . may be permitted to advise, it is our opinion and most earnest request that matters may be quieted, for the present at least. . . . By pursuing this course, we foresee no hazard, or even inconvenience, that can ensue, whereas we are apprehensive, and this we think upon good grounds, that violence may produce effects which God only knows the effects of."[61]

Randolph's letter bore the marks of hasty composition, but he had taken time to be tactful. If he had not, the angry young men in Fredericksburg probably would not even have listened to the reading of his advice.

Randolph's message raised doubts that led to debate. Messages arrived from Pendleton and Richard Henry Lee, and from Washington, a man who understood a soldier's feelings. All urged moderation, and said that no good could come from a march on Williamsburg at this time.[62]

The counsel of Virginia's leaders was heeded. The men left Fredericksburg and headed back to river plantations and cabins in the hills, but not before unanimously subscribing to a declaration of unity:

"Whilst the least hope of reconciliation remains . . . the several companies now rendezvoused here do return to their respective homes. But, considering the just rights and liberty of America to be greatly endangered by the violent and hostile proceedings of an arbitrary ministry, and being firmly resolved to resist such attempts at the utmost hazard of our lives and fortunes, we do now pledge ourselves to each other to be in readiness, at a moment's warning, to reassemble, and by force of arms, to defend the law, the liberty and rights of this or any sister Colony from unjust and wicked invasion."[63]

This declaration did not conclude with the words, "God save the King." Instead, it said, "God save the liberties of America."

If the decision had been postponed a day, the men would have elected to march on Williamsburg. For the *Virginia Gazette* of April 29 carried news that galvanized Virginia. A British column, it was reported, had "marched to Lexington, [Massachusetts,] where they found a company of our militia in arms, upon which they fired without provocation, and killed six men, and wounded four others."[64]

The account was incomplete, and in some respects inaccurate. What it lost in veracity, it gained in provocativeness.[65]

Patrick Henry was easily provoked, and skilled in provoking others. He made an inflammatory speech to volunteers at New Castle and at Doncastle and marched at the head of the combined forces toward Williamsburg.[66]

Dunmore added sailors, marines, some slaves and a few Indians to his palace guard. On his orders, cannon were rolled out on the Palace Green.

Henry and his troops were met outside the city on the morning of May 2 by an emissary from the Governor who paid £330, in the name of His Majesty's receiver general, to cover the cost of the powder removed from the magazine. Henry said that he would present the bill of exchange to Virginia's delegates to the Continental Congress, so that they might purchase more gunpowder.[67]

Two days later, the Governor issued a proclamation branding as rebels "a certain Patrick Henry, of the county of Hanover, and a number of his deluded followers," and calling upon the people "to oppose them and their designs by every means."[68]

When the Virginia delegates took the road to Philadelphia, the independent companies of Spotsylvania and Caroline counties escorted them to the Potomac landing where they took the ferry to the Maryland shore.

The Governor's proclamation against Henry had aroused fears that officers of the Crown might arrest the Hanover lawyer. For that matter, the other delegates might be in danger. On March 28, Dunmore had issued a proclamation enjoining "all magistrates and other officers to use their utmost endeavors" to prevent the naming of delegates to the Second Continental Congress.[69]

* * *

The delegates were met by another escort when they were six miles from Philadelphia.[70] It was not provided for protection. The only immediate threat to the Virginians was from the dark clouds which hung ominously over the hot earth. They heard muffled thunder, but soon learned that it was the thunder of horses' hooves. First came the officers of all the independent companies in Philadelphia, then a seemingly endless column of ununiformed horsemen. When the Virginians recovered from their astonishment, they learned that no less than five hundred gentlemen had ridden out from the city to welcome them.

They jogged along in this company for four miles, and then were met by a band and a company of riflemen and other infantrymen who joined the procession. The citizens of Philadelphia were treated that day to a parade that would have created a sensation in London or Paris. They lined the streets, stood a-tiptoe on the mounting blocks beside hitching posts and leaned out of windows in mellowed brick façades to see and cheer. Even then, some saw only heads— the passing heads of horsemen in the street if they were lucky, or the white-capped heads of excited matrons and the broad-brimmed, black hats of Quaker gentlemen in the watching crowd if they had the misfortune to be very small and very much in the rear.

Rumbling drums and wheedling fifes signaled the appearance of the cavalcade of gentlemen officers and the Virginians whom they escorted. The delegates had been widely seen in Philadelphia the year before but, with war imminent if not already begun, they now were objects of renewed curiosity. The Virginians were nearly all tall, but one sat in the saddle with an erect, soldierly grace that made him seem even taller. Those in the know pointed him out, explaining that he was Colonel Washington, the military hero. Men like him might be more needed soon than a great many orating lawyers.

Blue coats probably predominated among the escorting horsemen, but many a proud equestrian seemed to be wearing his own personal conception of what constituted a uniform, and the variety of plain and fancy tastes thus exhibited was a spectacle in itself. Soon the band was lost to view somewhere ahead of the long procession, and the sound of fife and drum was drowned in the jingle of spurs and the staccato clack of hooves on cobblestones. Even louder than these, at times, was the roar of the crowd.

At last the infantrymen appeared, marching with the undisciplined zeal of citizen soldiers. Some plodded along purposefully as if they were doing a fast job of plowing.

Now, in long, loose-jointed strides, came the hunting shirt boys with their round wool hats and slender rifles of fabulous length.

Henry had not shared in this enthusiastic reception, which he would have hugely enjoyed. His march on Williamsburg had delayed his departure, and two days would pass before he set out for Philadelphia. He would, however, be accompanied all the way across the Potomac by an armed guard. It was believed that he needed protection even more than the other delegates.[71]

The Virginian was not the only missing delegate. The New Englanders had not yet arrived.

But the morning after Randolph, Washington, Lee, Harrison, Pendleton and Bland were escorted into the city, word came that the delegates from Massachusetts and Connecticut were approaching. Escorting horsemen led them into town and cheering crowds poured out again. But for some reason—perhaps a great deal of enthusiasm had been spent in welcoming the Virginians, or perhaps Quaker decorum had returned to match puritan solemnity—the parade was a much more sedate affair than the one staged for the Old Dominion's delegation. A hundred carriages rolled slowly by to the tolling of bells in scattered steeples.[72]

Later in the day, the Congress convened at the State House. Unlike Carpenter's Hall, this building did not have a gallery "for gentlemen to walk in," but inside the wall surrounding it was a bare yard in which exasperated or cogitating delegates could pace. The Council Chamber, in which the Congress assembled, was a white-paneled room with tall windows. Rows of sturdy Windsor chairs faced the low dais where the presiding officer sat.

Virginia was again honored by the unanimous election of Peyton Randolph as chairman. The possibilities of agreement in other matters seemed good. Richard Henry Lee said, "There never appeared more perfect unanimity among any set of men than among the delegates, and indeed all the old Provinces, not one excepted, are directed by the same firmness of union and determination to resist by all ways and to every extremity."[73]

The very fact that this was the second, not the first, Continental Congress made a great difference. The delegates, guided by precedent, moved swiftly and surely in the routine of a legislature.

The day after formal organization, the new Congress went into secret session. It received a communication from Dr. Joseph Warren, acting president of the Massachusetts Provincial Congress, who reported that that body had unanimously resolved that "thirteen thousand six hundred men . . . be forthwith raised by this colony" and had recommended that New Hampshire, Rhode Island and Connecticut furnish men "in the same proportion." The letter continued: ". . . We beg leave to suggest that a powerful army on the side of America hath been considered by [Massachusetts] as the only means left to stem the rapid progress of a tyrannical ministry."[74]

Soon a request for advice arrived from New York. British troops were headed for New York City. What should be done?

Congress was quick to answer that the troops should not be molested if they gave no sign of hostility, but that they must be

resisted if they violated the rights of private property, raised fortifications or attempted to isolate the city.[75]

But the threat to the town was a threat to the whole colony of
New York—to all the colonies, for that matter—and it called for
major decisions of strategy. How could the colonies deal with the
problem, and how far should they go in unison? Congress named a
committee to seek answers to these questions. Since New York was
most directly concerned, the entire delegation of that colony was
appointed to the group, as were Thomas Lynch of South Carolina
and Sam Adams of Massachusetts. Virginia's Washington was made
chairman.[76]

While the committee was deliberating, word arrived that Ethan
Allen, commissioned by Connecticut, and Benedict Arnold, authorized by Massachusetts, had taken famed Fort Ticonderoga. Possession of this fort, called "the key to the gateway to the continent,"
was vital to control of Lake George and Lake Champlain, and hence
of the principal route from Canada to the thirteen colonies.[77]

Members of the Continental Congress were elated over the success
of the Connecticut and Massachusetts forces. They chuckled over
stories that the British garrison was so caught by surprise that Allen's
demand, "Come out of there, you damned old rat," was answered by
an indignant British officer who found it hard to summon all his
dignity when he had not had time to pull on his breeches.[78]

But congressional joy was alloyed with foreboding. The Congress
hitherto had stressed the fact that all its military measures were
defensive. The expedition led by Allen and Arnold had made that
fact a fiction, but it was a fiction in which many of the delegates
were eager to believe. Congress adopted a resolution declaring that
Ticonderoga had been seized to forestall a projected invasion of the
American colonies by "ministerial forces" operating from Quebec.
Guns captured with the fort were badly needed in Boston, and
Congress recommended to the provincial committees of New York
that the cannon be removed to the southern shores of Lake George,
but with the formal proviso "that an exact inventory be taken of all
such cannon and stores in order that they may be safely returned
when the restoration of the former harmony between Great Britain
and these colonies, so ardently wished for by the latter, shall render
it prudent and consistent with the overruling law of self-preservation."[79]

Congressional prudence contrasted strangely with the rashness
of Allen, who had obtained the surrender of the fort by threatening

to slaughter every man, woman and child within its walls if his terms were not complied with.[80]

Its task greatly complicated by the American offensive on Lake George, Washington's committee worked diligently on plans for the defense of New York and submitted recommendations to the Congress on May 19. The report was vigorously and lengthily debated in Committee of the Whole and finally approved May 25.[81]

Randolph had left the day before to return to Williamsburg for the session of the General Assembly of Virginia. Most of the delegates would doubtless have agreed with him that speaker of the Virginia House of Burgesses was an even more important position than chairman of the Continental Congress.

Randolph's successor as chairman was John Hancock, a slender, rather nervous young man from Boston who displayed his inherited wealth through handsome philanthropies and magnificent equipages. The fact that he was extremely popular despite his obvious vanity is impressive testimony to his charm.[82]

Washington was now named chairman of a committee "to consider ways and means to supply these colonies with ammunition and military stores. . . ." The responsibility would have been a formidable one even without the additional instruction to "report immediately."[83]

By this time Washington was the most conspicuous figure in the Congress, and without benefit of verbal histrionics. He wore the red and blue uniform that he had worn in the French and Indian war.[84] It was a reminder to the delegates of the Virginian's military experience and of his valor in defense of the colonies in former times. It was also more than a hint that he was available for further military service.

Such was Washington's dignity that his fellow delegates do not seem to have imputed to him any flamboyance in the wearing of his uniform. Sam Adams was impressed. He made note of Washington's military dress, and added, "By his great experience and abilities in military matters, [he] is of great service to us."[85]

From Adams' native Massachusetts came an appeal to Congress: "As the Army now collecting from different Colonies is for the general defense of the right[s] by America, we would beg leave to suggest to your consideration the propriety of taking the regulation and general direction of it. . . ."[86]

The urgency of this request was underlined by news from London. Edmund Burke had made an eloquent plea for conciliation of the American colonies, but the ministry and its supporters, far from entertaining thoughts of peaceful overtures, were bent on reprisals.

Washington himself had concluded:

"The once happy and peaceful plains of America are either to be drenched with blood or inhabited by slaves. Sad alternative! But can a virtuous man hesitate in his choice?"[87]

The Virginian submitted his committee's report on plans for procuring ammunition and military stores, and it was approved. He also worked as one of a committee of five to prepare financial estimates for the Congress. But all the while he realized that these measures were not enough. Boston could not be expected to continue its resistance indefinitely without the assurance of united support from the colonies.

Washington heard increasing talk of the need for a continental army, and occasionally heard himself mentioned as a logical choice for its commander. Though he was eager to bring his military qualifications to the delegates' attention and was determined to be an officer in any army of the united colonies, he was loath to consider accepting the top command. Not unreasonably, he believed that his experience was not commensurate with the responsibility.[88]

Of course, Washington's experience probably equaled that of any other American officer still in his prime with the exception of Charles Lee, a professional soldier who had recently made his home in Virginia. This swaggering adventurer was not related to the famous Northern Neck family of Lees, and had spent most of his life in England and on the Continent.[89]

Washington had little reason to think that he would be chosen. New England was the center of conflict, and had its own military heroes. Would the inhabitants of that region be likely to welcome a commander from the South?

At least one New Englander, though, was convinced that a commander should be named at once and that Washington was the man for the job. John Adams was so positive that he was not dissuaded by the coolness with which his suggestion was received in private conversations or even by the opposition of Washington's fellow Virginian, Edmund Pendleton.[90]

On the morning of June 14, John Adams walked with his cousin Sam in the enclosed yard outside the State House. The voluble John was even more excited and earnest than usual, and his intensity, coupled with Sam's obvious seriousness, must have offered a great temptation to eavesdroppers. What were these Massachusetts radicals up to?[91]

A keen-eared listener might have learned that John Adams was reciting the difficulties and dangers that confronted Massachusetts and her sister colonies. Sam readily agreed that his cousin's catalogue was accurate, but halted the recital by asking, "What shall we do?"

John Adams replied that he was "determined to take a step which should compel [the Massachusetts representatives] and all the other members of Congress to declare themselves for or against something."

Looking Sam full in the face, John said, "I am determined this morning to make a direct motion that Congress should adopt the army before Boston, and appoint Colonel Washington commander of it."

Sam looked very serious, but said nothing. Other delegates were going into the hall for the day's session of Congress, and the two cousins joined them.

When the opening formalities had been dispensed with, John Adams got the floor. He pictured "the state of the Colonies, the uncertainty in the minds of the people, their great expectation and anxiety, the distresses of the army, the danger of its dissolution, the difficulty of collecting another."

He warned of the "probability that the British army would take advantage of our delays, march out of Boston, and spread desolation as far as they could go."

He then moved "that Congress . . . adopt the army at Cambridge and appoint a general."

John Hancock coveted military laurels and, as he sat in the president's chair, his face glowed with pleasure. He had let it be known that he would accept command of the forces protecting Boston.

His pleasure increased visibly as Adams said:

"Though this is not the proper time to nominate a general, yet, as I have reason to believe this is a point of the greatest difficulty, I have no hesitation to declare that I have but one gentleman in my mind for that important command."[92]

Hancock was sure that he, a fellow townsman of Adams, was about to be named.

But Adams went on, "A gentleman from Virginia who is among us. . . ."

Immediately, Hancock's countenance was transformed by "mortification and resentment." Washington, who now knew that he was to be named, darted from the room.

Adams concluded his speech, ". . . a gentleman from Virginia who [is] among us and very well known to all of us, a gentleman whose skill and experience as an officer, whose independent fortune, great talents, and excellent universal character would command the approbation of all America, and unite the cordial exertions of all the colonies better than any other person in the Union."

John Adams sat down. His cousin Sam sprang up to second the motion.

In the ensuing debate, Pendleton (perhaps influenced by Washington's own wishes) joined Roger Sherman, of Connecticut, and Cushing, of Massachusetts, in opposing appointment of the Virginian. They all declared that they had no personal objection to the man, but that the army as now constituted was composed of New Englanders who had a commander of their own and "appeared to be satisfied with him."

No decision was reached, and further debate was postponed till the next day. Washington's supporters made good use of the interim. Virginia was the most populous and powerful of the provinces, and delegates from the Middle Colonies had already agreed to acknowledge Virginia's leadership. Some had gone so far as to meet New England delegates at Frankfort, outside Boston, just before the convening of the Congress and exact from them a pledge to acknowledge Virginia's primacy.[93] Some of the patriots, especially those from Pennsylvania, knew that many Americans feared the Massachusetts radicals and suspected them of a largely selfish desire to draw the other colonies into conflict as a solution to the problem of defending Boston. We may be sure that there were many references to what John Adams called "the Frankfort advice."

A strong impression was made on the New Englanders by the argument that the naming of a Virginian as commander would insure the support of Virginia's wealth and manpower in a broadening conflict. It was also argued that, with Virginia in the lead, the other Southern colonies would fall into line.[94]

New Englanders were jealous for their own heroes, particularly Artemas Ward, but most were prepared to admit that Washington was probably the equal of any of their officers in military skill, even though loyal Yankees were not prepared to concede his superiority. One New England delegate was swayed by the fact that the Virginian was "a gentleman highly esteemed by those acquainted with him."[95] He was also influenced by the fact that he had never heard Washington swear.[96] For various reasons, weighty and trivial, most of the delegates respected him. Virtually all seemed to be convinced that he was a man of strong character.

The next day Washington stayed away from Congress. He knew the results of the debate when fellow delegates, joining him for dinner, called him "General."[97]

Thomas Johnson, of Maryland, had nominated him and the vote had been unanimous.

On the following day, Friday, June 16, Washington was formally notified by John Hancock, who must have summoned all the resources of his breeding to perform the task with composure.

Washington read his reply, which had probably been prepared with Pendleton's aid. He expressed his appreciation of the "high honor" and promised to "exert every power" he possessed "for the support of the glorious cause."[98]

But still, as in the days of the French and Indian War, Washington was deeply concerned with his reputation. He did not wish for anyone to misunderstand the conditions under which he accepted the command. He told the Congress:

"Lest some unlucky event should happen unfavorable to my reputation, I beg it may be remembered by every gentleman in the room, that I this day declare with the utmost sincerity, I do not think myself equal to the command I am honored with.

"As to pay, sir, I beg leave to assure the Congress that, as no pecuniary consideration could have tempted me to have accepted this arduous employment at the expense of my domestic ease and happiness I do not wish to make any profit from it. I will keep an exact account of my expenses. Those, I doubt not, they will discharge, and that is all I desire."[99]

Washington's apprehension was unfeigned. Tears were in his eyes when, in private conversation, he told Patrick Henry:

"Remember, Mr. Henry, what I now tell you: from the day I enter upon the command of the American armies, I date my fall, and the ruin of my reputation."[100]

*   *   *

Another Virginian in Philadelphia was worried about his reputation. Thomas Jefferson, as an alternate delegate, had come to the Congress as replacement for Peyton Randolph when "Mr. Speaker" returned to Williamsburg to preside over the House of Burgesses.

Jefferson's fame had preceded him. His pamphlet "Summary View of the Rights of British America" had been widely circulated among the delegates and had exerted an influence equaled by no other colonial literary production with the exception of James Wilson's "Considerations on the Nature and Extent of the Legislative Authority of the British Parliament."[101]

Since his arrival in Philadelphia, nothing had happened to increase Jefferson's reputation. He was a writer, not a speaker, in an assembly that seemed to put a premium on spoken eloquence.

If he were back in Virginia now, he might be playing a commanding role in legislative proceedings. He had delayed the journey to Philadelphia to replace Randolph so that he might sit in the House of Burgesses for the first ten days of the session.[102] Those days had been exciting ones in which he had made his influence felt.

Governor Dunmore had presented to the General Assembly a proposal by the Prime Minister, Lord North, that any colony making a contribution to imperial defense and financial support of its own civil government in an amount deemed adequate by Parliament should thereafter be exempt from taxation for revenue.[103]

Jefferson was one of the principal authors of the reply to the Governor, a document in which the Burgesses not only rejected the proposal, but also declared:

"We consider ourselves as bound in honor, as well as interest, to share one general fate with our sister Colonies; and would hold ourselves base deserters of that union to which we have acceded, were we to agree on any measures distinct and apart from them."[104]

By the time Jefferson left Williamsburg for Philadelphia, Dunmore had already fled the Governor's Palace for the security of the man-of-war *Fowey* and was attempting to administer Virginia from the quarterdeck.[105]

In Philadelphia, things were much duller than in Virginia, and Jefferson was a much less successful man. A few days after taking his seat in Congress, he was added to a committee to prepare a Declaration on the Necessity of Taking up Arms. This group, headed by John Rutledge, had prepared one paper before being joined by Jefferson, but this production had been rejected by the Congress. Jefferson was asked to prepare a second. But, when he presented his paper to the committee, John Dickinson thought it too strong in condemnation. William Livingston, of New Jersey, thought it consisted too much of "fault-finding and declamation," and observed privately that both Rutledge's and Jefferson's compositions had "the faults common to our Southern gentlemen."[106] By the fourth of July, Jefferson knew that his Declaration would not be used. The one finally accepted was prepared by Dickinson, who, with the committee's approval, incorporated some of Jefferson's most eloquent phrases.[107]

For the young Virginian, the whole experience was humiliatingly reminiscent of his first term in the House of Burgesses. He had then been asked to draft an address to the Governor, only to have his work rejected. Then, as now, some of his choicest phrases had been incorporated in an acceptable address prepared by an older man.

But, when Jefferson left a sweltering Philadelphia early in August[108] after a congressional session that had dragged tediously on to an anticlimactic conclusion, he had made a profounder impression than he realized—and on delegates of considerable influence. James Duane was amazed at the Virginian's remarkably vigorous intellect.[109] John Adams, though only eight years older than Jefferson, took an almost fatherly interest in the younger man. He considered him, in many respects, the equal of his own Cousin Samuel—a major concession for an Adams. Furthermore, he believed that Jefferson had "a happy talent for composition" that might prove of value to the united colonies.[110]

Chapter XII

VOICE OF A NATION
(1775-1776)

Chapter XII

(1775-1776)

WHEN the Virginia delegates, freshly returned from the Philadelphia Congress, rode into Richmond in August 1775, a
provincial convention had been sitting in the city for more than
two weeks. "Sitting" was the correct word. By no stretch of the
imagination could it be said that a meeting was "in progress."

The General Assembly had adjourned June 24 without passing a
single act. The entire session had been spent in quarreling with the
Governor. The convention had been called for July 17 to arm the
colony against anticipated invasion by British forces. Dunmore's
removal to H.M.S. *Fowey*, which lay at anchor in the York, lent
credence to reports of threatened attack. Now it seemed probable
that the convention, like the Assembly, would spend its energies in
controversy and adjourn with no achievement to its credit. Moreover, the consequences would be far more serious in the case of the
convention than in that of the Assembly, for the delegates were
quarreling among themselves rather than with the Governor.

In its first days, the convention had suffered from the fact that
Virginia's top leadership was in Philadelphia. Able men were present, but their efforts were not sufficient to compensate for loss of the
stabilizing force provided by the acknowledged masters of statecraft.
George Mason, possessor of one of the keenest intellects in America,
was a delegate, but his influence was confined largely to the use of
delaying tactics to prevent rash action or give hot heads time to cool.
Again and again, when tempers flared in the August heat, Mason
rose to "urge the previous question." His portly figure hid a frail
physique, and his moral courage did not make him immune to
hypochondria.[1] Mason confessed that "mere vexation and disgust"
over the constant babbling and squabbling threw him into "such an
ill state of health" that he "was sometimes near fainting in the
House."[2]

The convention elected military officers before it decided on a
method of raising troops. Virginia's most famous soldier, George
Washington, was in Massachusetts, trying to weld a disciplined

Continental Army out of disparate elements whose principal common characteristic was individualism. Charles Lee, who had made his home in Virginia after winning distinction on European battlefields, was one of four major generals elected by the Congress. The most distinguished soldier remaining in Virginia was Hugh Mercer, of Fredericksburg. A veteran of Culloden, he had been a captain under Braddock, had once commanded all Pennsylvania forces west of the Susquehanna, and had been a leader in the last campaign against Fort Duquesne.[3] Mercer was nominated August 5 for commander of Virginia's first regiment. But the honor went instead to Patrick Henry, an oratorical son of thunder who knew almost nothing about the thunder of guns. Thomas Nelson and William Woodford, respectively, were named commanders of Virginia's second and third regiments. Fortunately, both of these men were better qualified than Henry.

Soon the newly returned delegates to Congress made their influence felt in the convention. It was no longer necessary for a conscientious member to feel frustrated when he went to his lodgings after a daily session beginning at seven in the morning and ending at ten at night.[4] The work of the convention was beginning to go forward.

On August 11, delegates to the next meeting of the Congress were elected. Edmund Pendleton asked to be excused from consideration because of the poor state of his health.[5] His wish was deferred to, but within a week he was given a heavier burden than that of representing the colony in Philadelphia.

The convention decided to name a Committee of Safety to govern the Colony. A committee of the convention went to work August 16 to draft an ordinance for creation of the governing body. The next day an eleven-man Committee of Safety was elected. Pendleton led the ballot, followed by George Mason, John Page, Richard Bland, Thomas Ludwell Lee, Paul Carrington, Dudley Digges, William Cabell, Carter Braxton, James Mercer and John Tabb.[6]

In Edmund Pendleton, the committee had a chairman of acute intellect, judicial temper, prodigious diligence, unusual tact and remarkable powers of persuasion.[7]

Mason, though his reputation had not spread far beyond Virginia, was one of the most thorough students of constitutional law in the American colonies. His influence greatly exceeded his fame. He was the chief author of the Fairfax Plan which was adopted as the Virginia Association—the prototype of the Continental Association, which was the most important instrument of resistance forged by the First Continental Congress.[8]

Probably his only Virginia rival in knowledge of constitutional law was Richard Bland, whose vast erudition would be a rich source of precedents as the committee went about the work of forming a government.[9]

The other members were all men of more than ordinary talents. Besides, they possessed the social prestige which gave to revolution the aura of respectability so important to many Virginians of the middle group. In the persons of Thomas Ludwell Lee, son of Thomas Lee of Stratford, and Carter Braxton, grandson of "King" Carter of Corotoman, two of Virginia's most powerful clans found able representation.

It was a good thing that the committee could command such a roster of talents and a bad thing that its chairman and two of the other members—Bland and Mason—were in poor health. For the ordinance for its creation—presented to the convention two days after the election of committee members—conferred upon the new group executive powers of a scope unknown to the Royal governors.

The Committee of Safety was charged with carrying "into complete and full execution all . . . ordinances and resolutions of the Convention." But its assigned duties were few compared with those that might be undertaken at its own discretion. It was empowered to call into active service volunteer companies and minute men, to control all supplies of arms, "ammunition and warlike stores," to use public funds to meet military expenses, and to control all troop movements, even to the extent of sending soldiers beyond Virginia's borders.[10]

The Committee of Safety convened in Richmond August 26 to begin the work of raising troops and equipping them. On September 18, it reconvened in Hanover Town for the selection and commissioning of officers, as well as contracting for provisions.[11]

By this time, it had been decided to raise two regiments in Virginia, rather than the three originally contemplated. Nelson, who had been named commander of the second regiment, gave up that honor to accept election to the Congress. Woodford, who had been assigned command of the third regiment, then moved up to the second.

The Committee of Safety depended heavily on the county committees as agencies of local government. Still the central body had no power to command these local groups. The situation was aptly illustrated by a public notice which Pendleton's committee had published in the *Virginia Gazette:*

"The Committee of Safety *earnestly recommend* it to the committees of the several counties to lose no time in collecting and forwarding the public arms, according to the order of Convention; and also to elect their militia officers where it is not done, and forward their certificates to this committee, that commissions may be made out, and the militia embodied as soon as possible."[12]

A commissary of provision was appointed for the two regiments, and, in the true spirit of popular government, was directed to make his purchases "as diffusive as possible."[13]

As colonel of the first Virginia regiment, Patrick Henry was styled "commander-in-chief of the Virginia forces." By the end of September, his troops were encamped behind the College of William and Mary. The men furnished their own blankets and some did not enjoy the shelter of a tent. On September 30, the Committee of Safety moved to Williamsburg to facilitate cooperation between civil and military authorities, and that city was once again—in fact as well as name—the capital of Virginia.

By the middle of October, there were camped in and about Williamsburg companies from the counties of Amelia, Prince William, Gloucester, Culpeper, Elizabeth City, Lancaster, Princess Anne and Caroline.[14]

The minute men of King and Queen County had been sent to Hampton, at the mouth of the James. Three hundred fifty minutemen drawn from Culpeper, Orange and Fauquier counties had bivouacked near Fairfax. Of these, the largest, and easily the most colorful, contingent was the one from Culpeper. They were riflemen like those who had defeated Cornstalk. Together with their counterparts elsewhere on the Virginia frontier and in western Maryland and Pennsylvania, they would be the best marksmen fighting in the name of the American colonies. They carried, besides their long rifles and tomahawks, a fearful insignia. In the center of their banner was a striking rattlesnake. This formidable device bore two mottoes—"Don't Tread on Me" and, in the very words of the frontier's own hero, "Liberty or Death." The same quotation from Henry was emblazoned across the front of each rifleman's green hunting jacket.[15]

So savage was the appearance of these minutemen that some Tidewater residents doubtless would have preferred to take their chances with King George's redcoats. But many of the riflemen were not so primitive as they looked. One youngster, for instance, had a Randolph for a mother, and was himself a lad of promising intellect —that tall, rangy youth, John Marshall.[16]

Tidewater apprehension of the men from the hills was aggravated when armed bands of uplanders made forays into the river towns and removed stocks of salt and other commodities which were extremely scarce in Eastern Virginia as well as farther inland.[17]

But there were shortages even more serious—the lack of arms and ammunition.[18] And they might soon be needed, not only for the general defense of the colonies, but in action on Virginia soil.

Another great disadvantage crippling the Virginia forces was the lack of a Navy—a most serious deficiency in Tidewater, where the waterways were the true highways.

The only naval power in the colony was commanded by Governor Dunmore, who now was the guest of Andrew Sprowle at his private shipyard, Gosport, near Portsmouth. Gosport was actually a small village as well as a yard.[19] Sprowle, a Scotsman like the Governor himself, was also intensely loyal to the Crown. He was a British Navy agent and a trustee of Portsmouth.[20] Though it was reported that Dunmore "lived riotously" upon his host's resources, the Governor must have had no illusions about taking over Sprowle's domain, for his lordship is said to have wryly referred to himself as "Lieutenant-Governor of Gosport."[21]

Certainly, the British seamen under the Governor's command were not living on a luxurious scale. Patriots, and merchants intimidated by them, were loath to supply victuals to ships that might any day bombard the coast. Miserable sailors, in fear of their lives, were put ashore to forage and plunder for such provisions as might be obtained.

Dunmore, who long had been infuriated by the "public prints of this dirty little borough of Norfolk," seized one of the town's presses and two printers. Residents of the seaport protested and appealed to the Committee of Safety for protection from the Governor's "illegal and riotous" acts.[22]

Before aid could be sent to Norfolk, word arrived that Dunmore had threatened to burn Hampton, and Woodford was dispatched to the community to discourage the attempt. His men quickly gave Captain Squire's squadron an effective lesson in the potency of the long rifle, and the British seamen lost no time in returning to their commander with their new-found wisdom.[23]

A few days later, one of Dunmore's parties soundly thrashed the Princess Anne militia.[24]

The situation of the Virginians was made still more perilous by an emancipation proclamation which the Governor had issued November 7. He had declared martial law, and had ordered "every person capable of bearing arms to resort to His Majesty's standard, or be looked upon as traitor to His Majesty's crown and government, and thereby become liable to the penalty the law inflicts upon such offenses—such as forfeiture of life. . . ." But the supreme irony in this proclamation, signed by the man who said he had removed the powder from the magazine at Williamsburg as a precaution in case of slave insurrection, was the freeing of all indentured servants and Negroes who were "able and willing to bear arms . . . for the more speedily reducing this Colony to a proper sense of their duty to His Majesty's crown and dignity."[25]

Most miserable of all the colonists were the inhabitants of Norfolk, Norfolk County and Princess Anne, who lived under the shadow of Dunmore's guns and at the same time were in constant fear that the Virginia troops would burn the towns and villages to prevent capture of these communities by the Governor. The Committee of Safety on November 11 issued a reassuring proclamation of its purpose to "support and protect the persons and properties of all friends to America, and not wantonly to damage or destroy the property of any person whatsoever."[26]

But, three weeks before this proclamation, nearly a third of Norfolk's families had already deserted the town,[27] and no piece of paper signed by the leaders of Virginia's provisional government could halt the egress.

In his own way, Dunmore was as desperate as the inhabitants. Having made a bid for the support of slaves, he now even appealed through an Indian intercessor to his old enemy Cornstalk.[28]

Virginia troops were already on the march to Norfolk. The many Loyalists in that city and Portsmouth were alarmed, for they quite naturally assumed that the First Regiment was being dispatched to what promised to be the major area of conflict.[29] And the commander of the First Regiment was Patrick Henry, who seemed not to blanch at the death of kings and certainly could not be expected to have pity on their adherents.

But Henry was not marching toward Norfolk. He was sulking in his tent at Williamsburg. Henry was not only colonel of the First Regiment, but also commander-in-chief of the Virginia forces. It was his expectation, and that of his many enthusiastic followers, that he would personally lead the march on Norfolk, or at least give marching orders to the man who did.

But the Committee of Safety, in a bold assertion of civil authority over the military, had bypassed Henry to direct Colonel Woodford to proceed to Norfolk with his Second Regiment. Also assigned to his command were five companies of Culpeper minutemen, and at Smithfield his force was joined by two more companies of minutemen. Woodford was authorized by the Committee of Safety to add to his forces at his own discretion, "giving notice thereof to the Committee of Safety and the commanding officer at Williamsburg."[30]

The commanding officer was infuriated that he should be left at Williamsburg. He was convinced that he was not being accorded the respect due a commander.

Pendleton informed Henry by note that Woodford would be sent to Norfolk, and wrote the message *the day after the committee reached the decision*, saying, "I have the honor to enclose you the resolution of yesterday for forming an encampment near Norfolk, which you'll please to give the necessary orders for the execution of . . . ."[31]

Pendleton and Henry had frequently been opponents in debate, Pendleton being a leader of the most conservative faction of Virginia revolutionists while Henry was the chief advocate of the fire-eaters. The Piedmonter's followers were quick to accuse Pendleton of base motives in depriving Henry of a chance for military glory. They charged that Pendleton feared the political rivalry of a Henry returned to the forensic arena after triumphs in the field.[32]

But Pendleton was supported in this action by at least six powerful members of the Committee of Safety.[33] There can be little doubt that he also had the approval of a most judicious military observer. Washington, who was having his own troubles in New England, had written to Woodford to tell him he "highly approve[d]" his appointment as commander of the Second Regiment. But Washington had written in another connection, "I think my countrymen made a capital mistake when they took Henry out of the senate to place him in the field; and pity it is that he does not see this and remove every difficulty by a voluntary resignation."[34]

Woodford had no time to ponder the political significance of his appointment. He was too busy with pressing military realities. Reinforcement of the Virginians by 170 men under Colonel Hutchings had been prevented by the landing of a British force at Kemp's.[35]

Dunmore, by this time, had assembled a force of about 1,200, including two hundred to three hundred Negroes.[36] These comprised the Governor's Ethiopian Regiment. Whether or not Dunmore was aware of the irony of his own position in arming slaves after stating his fears of an insurrection, he was cognizant of the irony inherent in a fight by slaveholders for liberty. Apparently in answer to the Culpeper minutemen, with their slogan of "Liberty or Death," his lordship outfitted his Sables in jackets bearing the motto "Liberty to Slaves."

Dunmore sent a detachment to Great Bridge, about twelve miles south of Norfolk, and set up an artillery emplacement of seven guns at the north end of the bridge which gave the place its name. This wooden structure spanned the Southern Branch of the Elizabeth River and was approached on either end by a long narrow causeway over swampy ground.

The last week in November Woodford erected a semicircular breastwork at the south end of the bridge and posted a guard of twenty-five in it, encamping with the main body of his troops at a little distance from the spot.

A stalemate followed. Dunmore's detachment was not large enough to warrant the risk of attacking over the narrow causeway. On the other hand, Woodford's small arms were no match for the British artillery, or for the naval guns that might be brought to bear on them.

The Committee of Safety knew that Dunmore would make a real fight for Great Bridge. If that position were lost by the Governor, Norfolk would be lost too, and with it Dunmore's opportunity to provision his vessels at a Virginia port. It was evident that a major battle was in the making. On December 7, the Committee ordered three companies of Colonel Henry's regiment to go to Woodford's aid. Reinforcements were badly needed by Woodford, but such was the animosity between rival regiments that Henry's men "were neither welcomed, [nor] invited to eat or drink."

The inaction at Great Bridge was misunderstood by many armchair strategists far removed from the scene, and they were bitter in their criticisms of Woodford and speculated on what might have been accomplished if Henry had been in command.

While civilian morale sagged throughout Virginia, Woodford was hard put to keep up his men's spirits. The cold, the damp, and above all the inaction, were oppressive.

There was, however, some encouragement in the knowledge that

Colonel Robert Howe and his Second North Carolina Regiment were moving with artillery to the aid of the Virginians.

Perhaps because he had word of the North Carolinians' approach, perhaps because Woodford planted a false rumor about the inadequacy of his own forces, Dunmore resolved to attack immediately. At dusk, on December 8, the Governor moved his troops out of Norfolk to reinforce his garrison at Great Bridge. He told his men that the Virginians had never faced regular troops and therefore would not stand their ground after receiving the first volley.

In the gray December dawn of the next day, Captain Samuel Leslie ordered Dunmore's artillery to fire. Then the regulars, their coats very red in the half light, marched six abreast along the causeway toward the colonial troops, displaying all of the precision of men drilling on a parade ground. Guns from the British emplacement continued to roar, and there was no answering fire from the Virginians. Now Captain Fordyce's attacking column was only fifty yards from the defending breastworks, moving forward with a mechanical efficiency which seemed inexorable.

Suddenly, Lieutenant Travis, commanding the guard in the breastworks, gave a signal and ninety rifles cracked in unison. Redcoats crumpled to the ground. Fordyce rallied his shattered forces, but a second volley of rifle fire brought death to the British officer, who fell with fourteen bullets in his body, and to many of his grenadiers. All who were alive and not too wounded to run fled back across the bridge.

Leslie again opened fire with the artillery, but by this time Woodford was on hand with the main body of his troops. Colonel Edward Stephens led his Culpeper minutemen over the bridge to the north bank of the river, where they flanked the British and drove them into their fort. The Redcoats were only too glad to abandon their emplacement that night and retreat to Norfolk. They had suffered sixty casualties, killed and wounded. No Virginian had lost his life, and only one had been even slightly wounded.

The active engagement had lasted only half an hour, but during that time, and in the hours that followed, the Americans and British learned a great deal about each other. The Colonists learned that the Redcoats were not mere strutting dandies, but gallant warriors, worthy of their admiration. The British had gained a new appreciation of the shirtmen who they had believed would quickly retreat before regular troops, venting their savagery in the scalping of helpless prisoners. The new-gained respect of gentlemen for gentlemen, of men for men, was expressed when Captain Leslie stepped into range of the shirtmen's rifles to bow to these rugged looking Virginians who were so tenderly nursing the British wounded.

Perhaps the Virginians learned something about their own people, too. Among the Americans most conspicuous for gallantry was William Flora, a free Negro from Portsmouth.

Five days later, Woodford's men marched into a ghost town. Norfolk had been Virginia's largest city a few months before, but its cobblestone streets were now deserted and the houses had the faceless look of vacant buildings. Occupying Norfolk with the Virginians were Colonel Howe and his North Carolinians, who had arrived just in time for this agreeable duty.

Dunmore had disarmed his Ethiopian Corps and had taken his troops and a number of Tory sympathizers aboard his ships. The colonials destroyed the property of some of the Tories who had fled, and in the woods and fields rounded up some who had missed the boat.

Dunmore's vessels continued to ride at anchor offshore. The men on deck provided targets for the American riflemen. Disease was also taking its toll among the Governor's men, and corpses were dumped overboard daily.

Dunmore announced that he would burn Norfolk on New Year's Day, and he kept his promise. At four o'clock in the morning, he trained the seventy guns of his fleet on the hapless town. Parties went ashore and set fire to waterfront structures. The cannonade continued for seven hours. Inspired by the Governor's example, the riflemen put the torch to Tory property. By nightfall, what had been a flourishing town was now the tinder for one of the greatest conflagrations in the history of the North American continent.[37] From the decks of some of the Governor's vessels, the ships nearest shore seemed to be silhouetted against the mouth of a fiery furnace. Far out at sea, the red glow could be seen like some hellish dawn.

By the next night only embers still glowed, and only one-fifth of the town's buildings remained. A few weeks later, remaining buildings were destroyed on orders of the Committee of Safety, after their value had been determined for compensation to the owners. St. Paul's Episcopal Church, with a cannon ball lodged in its thick walls, was one of the few structures spared.

The effects of the action at Great Bridge and Norfolk were far reaching and of first importance. Among the immediate results were the driving of Lord Dunmore from the mainland and the dispersion of his Ethiopian Corps with the attendant threat of slave insurrection. More important still was the fact that the destruction of Norfolk had wrecked a nest of Tories and deprived the British Navy of a valuable base and provisioning center.

The Virginian who commanded the Continental Army saw the events at Norfolk in continental terms. On December 18, 1775, George Washington wrote the President of the Continental Congress:

"I do not mean to dictate; I am sure they will pardon me for giving them my opinion, which is that the fate of America a good deal depends on [Dunmore's] being obliged to evacuate Norfolk this winter or not."[38]

Washington, now convinced that independence from Britain was the only solution to America's troubles, found hope in the news that Dunmore had burned Norfolk. On January 21, he wrote:

"A few more such flaming arguments as were exhibited at . . . Norfolk . . . will not leave numbers at a loss to decide upon the propriety of a separation."[39]

* * *

Other prominent Virginians shared Washington's conviction that independence was essential to America's salvation. The Continental Congress had reconvened in Philadelphia on September 12, 1775. On December 6,' the Congress, angered by King George's proclamation of open rebellion in the colonies, had declared its independence of Parliament but reaffirmed its allegiance to the Crown. Virginia's Richard Henry Lee had worked with James Wilson and William Livingston on the committee that prepared the Congressional statement. But even then Lee did not blanch at talk of independence, and another Virginia delegate, Thomas Jefferson, was impatient with a Congress that moved so slowly and hesitatingly toward separation from Britain. He had been ready a year ago to disavow allegiance to Parliament, saying, "We never owed—we never owned it." On the day that the committee's report was submitted to the delegates, Jefferson wrote to John Randolph, Peyton's brother:

"Believe me, dear sir, there is not in the British Empire a man who more cordially loves a union with Great Britain than I do. But, by the God that made me, I will cease to exist before I yield to a connection on such terms as the British Parliament propose; . . . . We want neither inducement nor power, to declare and assert a separation. It is will, alone, that is wanting, and that is growing apace under the fostering hand of our King. One bloody campaign will probably decide, everlastingly, our future course; and I am sorry to find a bloody campaign is decided on."[40]

Congressional sentiment for independence was bolstered by the growing realization that the riflemen from Virginia, Maryland and Pennsylvania, because of a happy combination of remarkable weapons and forest-bred skills, were the most formidable wielders of small arms in military history.[41] It was bolstered also by the hope that Canada, now being invaded by American troops under Richard Montgomery and Benedict Arnold, would unite with the thirteen colonies in opposition to British tyranny.

There was also the hope that France, and perhaps other continental nations, would come to America's assistance. On December 12, Congress asked Arthur Lee, Richard Henry's brother, who was then in London, to sound out European sentiment on the colonies' struggle. Arthur was as ardent an American patriot as his brother Richard Henry. Indeed, Arthur's patriotism was the passionate loyalty of the American abroad. His messages to the Congress would do much to convince the delegates that reconciliation with Britain would not be possible so long as the colonies remained in a state of dependency.[42]

There was still talk of peace, but it sounded strange against the background of booming cannon. To some, as the year drew to a close, such words seemed utterly fantastic six months after Bunker Hill and at a time when Congress was commissioning officers for a Navy to carry the continental struggle onto the seas.

The only navy Virginia saw these days was the small squadron at Dunmore's disposal. Its harassing operations along the Chesapeake shores inspired considerable apprehension and provoked more and more Tidewater men to call for all-out war.[43]

The problem of defense continued an agonizing one for the Committee of Safety. On December 17, Edmund Pendleton had been re-elected to the Committee. But this time he was fourth on the ballot, and the first place went to Dudley Digges.[44] The controversy with Henry's followers had taken its toll of Pendleton's popularity. Nevertheless, his fellow committeemen re-elected him to the chairmanship.

Upon him, more than any other man, fell the burden of raising troops and procuring supplies within Virginia, of examining the war-connected claims of soldiers and civilians, of interrogating slaves and prisoners, of studying reports from local committees and of evaluating charges and countercharges of Toryism.[45]

The Convention assigned the Committee several formidable tasks for the new year of 1776. One of these was the creation of seven regiments to augment the two already in service. One of the nine regiments was to be stationed on the Eastern Shore. Two regiments would guard the Northern Neck, two the neck between the Rappahannock and York, two the peninsula between the York and the James, and the remaining two the Southside. This Virginia army would be commanded by a major general and two brigadiers who, in accordance with the desire of the Convention and Pendleton's own wish, would be named by the Continental Congress.[46]

The second great responsibility with which the Convention charged the Committee was that of providing a navy of a size "necessary for the protection of the several rivers in this Colony in the best manner the circumstances of the country will admit."[47]

When the Convention adjourned January 20, 1776, the Committee of Safety was left with "full and ample powers, during the recess of Convention, to direct all such measures and military operations as in their judgment shall be necessary for the public security."[48]

During that recess, the Committee had to deal with several grave problems not foreseen by the Convention. One of these was posed by Dunmore's offer to negotiate for peace with representatives of his Majesty's colony of Virginia. The Governor's offer was inspired by a royal address calling for the appointment in each colony of Commissioners chosen from loyal subjects "to restore such Province or Colony . . . to the same protection and security as if such Province or Colony had never revolted."[49]

Richard Corbin, a highly respected Loyalist, was Dunmore's choice as an intermediary. Corbin transmitted the Governor's message to the Committee of Safety, and bore the Committee's reply to Dunmore, who read it aboard ship in the presence of General Henry Clinton. Hopes for peaceful settlement exploded when the Governor learned that Virginia scorned the opportunity for a separate peace. The Committee's letter said:

"The Continental Congress have, in their last petition to the Throne, besought His Majesty to point out some mode for such negotiation; and if [the] Administration are disposed to heal this unnatural wound in the empire, they will embrace that occasion (which, probably, will be the last) of accomplishing it. At all events, any other steps to be taken must proceed from the Representatives of the Continent, and not from us."[50]

Another difficult task for the Committee was that of notifying Patrick Henry that the Continental Congress had recommissioned him colonel of the First Regiment instead of making him a brigadier or major general in Virginia's new army of seven regiments integrated with the Continental Army. When Henry learned that he would no longer be even the titular commander of Virginia forces, he refused his commission and angrily strode from the room.[51]

Henry's troops wore mourning and protested the Committee's action with a passion which must have been flattering to their erstwhile commander. But Henry would not assuage his ego at the expense of patriotism and, when some of the troops threatened to quit the army rather than serve under another commander, he used his great persuasive powers to bring them to a sense of duty.[52]

The Committee of Safety, and especially its chairman, were held responsible for what some regarded as an "insult" to the people's spokesman. The hostility between Henry's followers and Pendleton's adherents became a central fact of Virginia politics.[53]

Andrew Lewis, by Washington's own recommendation, was made commander of the Virginia forces. The hero of Point Pleasant and an old enemy of Governor Dunmore, he was acceptable to virtually all except those who could tolerate no one but Henry in the post.[54]

In the latter part of March, Major General Charles Lee, commander of the Continental Army's newly-created Southern Department, paid an official visit to Virginia and changed the disposition of troops. This action, confined to the military sphere, was considered legal. But another move by Lee was regarded as a violation of the prerogatives of civil government, rights jealously guarded by Virginia's rulers. Accordingly, on April 25, Pendleton sent the general a pedagogic reprimand:

"We wish to continue on terms of the most cordial friendship with you, sir, and that no occasions may be given for uneasiness or jealousy between the civil and military powers in this colony, we feel it an indispensable duty to mention that your quartering soldiers in the college and ordering it to be prepared for an hospital without our previous consent, which might easily have been obtained, was, in our opinion, an improper step. We presume this proceeded from inattention, and are satisfied you are too good a citizen to repeat such acts of power which, though not intended, may produce destructive consequences, as it will convey to the people an idea of our being subjected to an absolute military government whilst we are straining every nerve in defense of our liberty."[55]

On May 4, Lee, having made an acceptable explanation to the Committee, reported a still more drastic act, writing that he considered it his "duty to make a report of every transaction that is not merely and purely military." He had forced all inhabitants of Portsmouth to abandon the city, which had succeeded Norfolk as a capital of Toryism and center of royalist espionage, and had burned the homes of especially notorious confederates of Dunmore. The Committee immediately replied, "When we reflect on the several reasons by you assigned for your proceedings at Portsmouth, we much approve of the whole of your conduct to those people."[56]

But Lee, who had at first been contemptuous of Virginia's Committee, now had a wholesome respect for the colony's political leaders. This fact was evident when the general, who had a reputation for arrogance as well as brilliance, wrote to Robert Morris, of Philadelphia:

"The Convention and Committee of Virginia are certainly a most respectable body. 1 hope I shall not inadvertently run myself into any dispute with 'em—I am sure I shall not intentionally."[57]

On May 6, 1776, the Convention met again, this time as the formal successor to the old House of Burgesses.

The gathering in Williamsburg almost rivaled in distinction the Congress then sitting in Philadelphia, despite the fact that such Virginia luminaries as Jefferson, Wythe and Richard Henry Lee were in the Northern city, where they sat in counsel with Franklin of Pennsylvania, the Adamses of Massachusetts and the foremost men of other colonies.

Not only were Virginia's ablest political leaders, with the exception of those in Congress, gathered in the capitol, but the chief men of neighboring counties had come to witness a session that they knew would be historic. The wives and daughters of delegates sat in the gallery in eager expectancy, and other women collected in the halls after the limited spectator space was filled. Even to be outside the chamber, if near enough to hear voices raised in debate or catch the comments of those issuing from the hall, was an exciting privilege.[58]

The air was charged with a sense of portentousness. There was talk of independence. Would the Convention dare vote for such a course? Even the governing body of Massachusetts had not gone so far as to advocate a complete break with the mother country. And, if the colonies should take such a step, what would be their fate if no European nation came to their aid? And, even if the colonies should receive foreign aid and make independence a reality, how long could they preserve it without the stabilizing influence of a monarchy?

The question of independence could not be sidestepped. Petitions on the subject had poured into Williamsburg from the counties. The Cumberland County Committee of Safety had instructed the delegates from its hill-country constituency to deny allegiance to his "Brittanic Majesty, and bid him a good night forever."[59] This meeting in Williamsburg might be the prelude to tragedy or triumph. In either case, it would be part of the drama of history.

Many an apprehensive conservative must have longed for the guiding hand of Peyton Randolph. But Virginia's perennial "Mr. Speaker" was dead.[60]

Another Randolph, Edmund, the Speaker's nephew, was present as alternate for George Wythe, delegate from Williamsburg. Some predicted that this twenty-three-year-old lawyer would outstrip the accomplishments of his most illustrious ancestors. Tall, dark and somewhat portly, he moved among his fellow delegates with an ease and elegance of manner that commanded admiration. His fluency may have been abetted by his knowledge of the classics.[61] It was said that, for one so young, he had delved deeply into metaphysics. Yet all these attainments—social and intellectual—were no substitute at this juncture for the mature wisdom of his uncle.

Two more striplings could be seen in earnest conversation. One, the same age as Edmund Randolph, was Henry Tazewell, representative from Brunswick County, but a descendant of the powerful Littleton clan of the Eastern Shore. Women admired the classic features of his swarthy face, but his abilities were untested.[62]

The second of the pair was a small, pale, unprepossessing looking man who might have been thought younger than his twenty-five years except for the appearance of frailty which put his age in doubt. He was James Madison, son of the highly respected Colonel Madison, and his external appearance was a poor advertisement of what lay within. Last year, when just four years out of college, he had been elected chairman of the Orange County Committee of Safety. He was said to be a deep thinker.[63]

To those who feared what turn precocity might take in time of crisis, there was comfort in the presence of Edmund Pendleton, the epitome of the urbane lawyer, and a veteran of twenty-five years in Virginia's legislative assemblies.

And there was Robert Carter Nicholas, a living link with the colony's Golden Age. A grandson of Robert "King" Carter, he had sat upon the knee of the fabulous lord of Corotoman. But Nicholas himself was a reassuring symbol, apart from ancestral associations.

From that bald head had come sagacious solutions to many critical problems.[64]

There, too, was Richard Bland, his tall figure bent with age as he moved toward his seat with the uncertain step of a man nearly blind. His skin was yellow now, and called to mind the fact that the blood of Powhatan flowed in his veins. Last year, Bland's conservative approach to revolution had caused some to suspect his loyalty to the patriot cause. Now those who had suspected were ashamed of themselves. They knew that, whether he plunged into revolution as his kinsman Giles Bland had into Bacon's rebellion, or advised caution like the royal councillors who had borne his name, he was moved by sincere conviction. And they knew that those convictions were based upon a scholar's knowledge of precedent and a statesman's experience in government. He had played an important role in Virginia assemblies for thirty years.[65]

There were other experienced men—Dudley Digges, Archibald Cary, Philip Ludwell Lee, James Mercer, Joseph Jones. The list could be extended.

But one of the most experienced politicians, one of the most famous delegates present, was the man most feared by many of the planter aristocrats who had come to Williamsburg. This man was the tall, rawboned Patrick Henry, firebrand of revolution.

By the time the delegates had taken their seats, it was possible to pick out many of his followers in the Convention. The hard core of Henry's following was composed of men from the Western counties. Their homespun clothes contrasted with the elegant, lace-trimmed, satin coats of the Tidewater men, some of whom wore large and heavily powdered wigs. Some of the mountaineers wore buckskin and clutched hunting caps in their hands. More than a few had their shooting irons with them.[66]

These men were obviously followers of Henry, but how many of his adherents were concealed in satin and silk? For example, Thomas Ludwell Lee was an enthusiastic supporter of Henry. What about some of the younger delegates who bore distinguished Tidewater names?

And to what acts would the Henry men be inflamed by the real or fancied insult which their leader had received at the hands of Pendleton and other great gentlemen? If a motion for independence were made and carried in a convention controlled by Henry's faction, there would follow a revolution against much that was traditionally Virginian as well as against all that was British.

The meeting was called to order. Nominations for chairman were called for. The venerable Richard Bland nominated Pendleton, "who had already executed that important trust, and had given undeniable proofs of his abilities and integrity." Archibald Cary seconded the nomination.

Then Thomas Jefferson, a Henry man from the word go, nominated Thomas Ludwell Lee and a quick second came from Bartholomew Dandridge.

The balloting began, and at its conclusion Pendleton was the victor.[67] A sigh escaped the Tidewater planters, who exchanged comradely glances of relief.

In succeeding days of the Convention, these same gentlemen made a surprising discovery. Patrick Henry, who had thundered against the tyranny of kings and shouted "Give me liberty or give me death," was far more cautious in his approach to independence than some of the great planters. Support was gathering among the Tidewater and Piedmont delegates for a flat declaration that "the inhabitants of this colony are discharged from any allegiance to the crown of Great Britain."[68]

Henry counseled caution. What could Virginia accomplish, even in league with the other colonies, if foreign support was wanting? French and Spanish sentiment should be sounded before making a complete break with the mother country.[69]

Robert Carter Nicholas stoutly opposed independence, and no one could ignore a man of his stature. At the other end of the spectrum of opinion were those who clamored for an immediate, unilateral declaration of independence and thought that every day's delay comforted the enemy. The remainder of the one hundred twenty-eight delegates fell into various positions between these two extremes.

But these Virginians were never more British than in moving to sever their ties with Britain. They relied on the fine old English art of compromise. When a resolution written by Pendleton emerged from committee, it had the approval of many men of varying opinions. Even Nicholas' support was won after the proposal was brought before the House. As unanimously approved by the Convention, May 15, 1776, the resolution provided:

"That the delegates appointed to represent this colony in General Congress be instructed to propose to that respectable body to declare the United Colonies free and independent States, absolved from all allegiance to, or dependence upon, the Crown or Parliament of Great Britain; and that they give the assent of this colony to such declaration, and to whatever measures may be thought proper and necessary by the Congress for forming foreign alliances, and a confederation of the colonies, at such time, and in the manner, as to them shall seem best. . . ."[70]

The pedestrian prose of parliamentary usage tended to obscure the significance of the bold action just taken by the Virginians. Coming after days of debate and compromise, it may even have seemed anticlimactic.

In formally calling for a congressional Declaration of Independence, and instructing its delegates in Congress to press for such a declaration, Virginia had taken a step which the other colonies had not dared to take, or at least did not regard as expedient.[71] On April 12, the North Carolina Convention had authorized its delegates in Congress to vote for a declaration of independence if one should be proposed, but stopped short of initiating an independence movement. In some of the other provinces, there were local petitions for independence, but none of the eleven other colonies went so far as North Carolina, and all stopped far short of Virginia's action.[72]

The citizens of Williamsburg, however, seemed to conclude that independence was already a fact. The day after adoption of the resolutions, civilians treated the soldiers encamped in the town. Enjoying the refreshingly new status of heroes, these warriors paraded before General Andrew Lewis and the Committee of Safety, much to the envy of small boys who would far rather have traded places with any unshaven private than with Chairman Pendleton, who occupied the place of honor. The resolutions were read aloud and lustily cheered. There were toasts to "the American independent States," "the Grand Congress of the United States and their respective legislatures," and "General Washington and victory to the American arms." Cannon roared and rifles cracked in salute as a "Union Flag of the American States" fluttered from the flagstaff atop the cupola of the brick capitol. Perhaps the most vociferous demonstrators of all were those whose vocabularies were outdistanced by the words of the resolutions and who assumed that they were listening to a declaration of independence. By nightfall, when torches and bonfires flared as they used to at celebrations of his Majesty's birthday, there was general agreement that the food and drink were good and that Governor Dunmore had been put in his place.[73]

His lordship, formerly his Majesty's symbol of law in Virginia, was now playing a pirate's role in a land where the Committee of Safety was responsible for the orderly processes of government. His vessels raided Chesapeake plantations and penetrated deep into Tidewater by means of the rivers. It was feared that one of his marauding parties might land at Mount Vernon and kidnap Mrs. Washington.[74]

On June 1, 1776, Dunmore anchored his little fleet off Gwynn's Island[75] and determined to make that domain of about 2,000 acres his capital. He threw up breastworks and boasted that from this bastion he would drive back any "crickets" sent against him. At least one rebel saw the Governor as an insect too. Richard Henry Lee reported that Dunmore was living "caterpillar like" on Gwynn's, devouring "everything in that place." Lee did not know that Dunmore's men themselves were preys of disease.

Early in July, Brigadier General Andrew Lewis, who had nursed a grudge against Dunmore since the battle with Cornstalk, took command of militia gathered on a mainland elevation overlooking the island, and personally fired the shot that opened hostilities. It was an eighteen-pound ball that crashed into Dunmore's own cabin. A second shot killed three of the Governor's crew. The third shot ripped into the cabin again, wounding Dunmore in the leg and bringing his china collection crashing about him. Lewis' men then methodically wrecked the fortifications on the island.

The Governor attempted a few more expeditions in Virginia and Maryland and then, perceiving the futility of his efforts, sailed for Britain.

By the time Andrew Lewis' cannon sent the Governor's china collection crashing "about his ears" (as the *Virginia Gazette* gleefully noted), events in Williamsburg and Philadelphia had conspired to send royal government itself crashing about the ears of Loyalists still attempting to execute the King's commissions.

The resolutions for independence adopted May 15 by the Virginia Convention had contained a provision "that a committee be appointed to prepare a Declaration of Rights, and such a plan of government as will be most likely to maintain peace and order in this colony, and secure substantial and equal liberty to the people."

Pendleton promptly appointed Archibald Cary chairman of the committee. But George Mason, who arrived May 17 to serve as a delegate, was quickly added to the group, and the weight of his erudition soon made him its leader.[76]

Mason was almost the sole author of the Declaration of Rights, which was presented to the Convention May 27.[77] After long debate resulting in small changes, it was adopted June 12.

Far more than ten days of thought went into preparation of the document. Mason had been a student of political philosophy since his youth. United with his learning were unusual and highly cultivated gifts of eloquence.[78]

The Declaration of Rights which Mason produced was not simply a document to fit Virginia's needs in a particular emergency. It expressed universal principles in terms universally and timelessly applicable. It was not only one of the great state papers of history, but also one of the noblest expressions of mankind's aspirations toward a free society.

It declared that "all men are by nature equally free and independent, and have certain inherent rights." It boldly stated that "all [political] power is vested in, and consequently derived from, the people," and that "government is, or ought to be, instituted for the common benefit, protection and security of the people."[79]

Among the rights of man, as set forth in this document, was "the enjoyment of life and liberty, with the means of acquiring and possessing property, and pursuing and obtaining happiness and safety."

But the document was not merely a declaration of high-sounding generalities. It set forth the importance of such safeguards of freedom as an independent judiciary, free and regular elections, trial by jury and a free press. It outlawed general warrants, excessive bail, cruel and unusual punishments, hereditary office and taxation without representation.

Mason and his colleagues were consciously writing for countries and generations other than their own. Edmund Randolph, a member of the Convention, testified later that the authors had undertaken the work in order that "a perpetual standard should be erected, around which the people might rally, and by a notorious record be for ever admonished to be watchful, firm, and virtuous" in "all the revolutions of time, human opinion and government."[80]

The triteness today of the phrases which rang with revolution in 1776 is a measure of the success with which their authors wrote for posterity.

A great student of law, Roscoe Pound, has said:

"The Virginia Bill of Rights of 1776 is the first and, indeed, is the model of a long line of politico-legal documents that have become the staple of American constitutional law. . . . Moreover, in actual application in the courts, the Bills of Rights, both in the Federal and in the State constitutions, are the most frequently invoked and constantly applied provisions of those instruments.

"Nor has the Virginia Bill of Rights been conspicuous only as a model. With all allowance for the historical documents that went before it, it must be pronounced a great creative achievement."[81]

George Bancroft, one of the greatest historians of the New England school, wrote:

"Other colonies had framed bills of rights in reference to their relations with Britain; Virginia moved from charters and customs to primal principles, from the altercation about facts to the contemplation of immutable truth. She summoned the eternal laws of man's being to protest against all tyranny. The English petition of rights in 1688 was historic and retrospective; the Virginia declaration came out of the heart of nature, and announced governing principles for all peoples in all time. It was the voice of reason going forth to speak a new political world into being. At the bar of humanity Virginia gave the name and fame of her sons as hostages that her public life should show a likeness to the highest ideas of right and equal freedom among men."[82]

The adoption of a Virginia State Constitution June 29 was overshadowed by the Declaration of Rights which preceded it. The constitution's provisions, unlike those of the greater document, were dictated almost solely by the exigencies and apprehensions of the moment. It was the work of a people in revolt against tyranny and hence wary of executive power in any form. The center of gravity in the new government was to be the House of Delegates, which would consist of two representatives from each county, to be chosen annually. All legislation must originate in this house. A senate of twenty-four members would be elected by districts. Senators would serve four-year terms under a staggered membership plan.

The Governor would be elected annually by joint ballot of House and Senate, and would have no veto power. In the course of debate on the constitution, Patrick Henry argued that the chief executive "would be a mere phantom, unable to defend his office from the usurpation of the legislature."[83] The truth of his own words would be ruefully recalled by Henry many times. On June 30, he was elected Governor.

The Convention met for the last time July 5, 1776. Then the colony became a Commonwealth under "the first written constitution given to the world."[84]

No man in Williamsburg was more interested in the new constitution than a frustrated young Virginian in Philadelphia. Thomas Jefferson had been sitting in Congress since the middle of May, and almost all the while he longed to be back in his "country" instead. Virginia was the place for him when a government was being framed that would transform the Old Dominion into a Commonwealth. Apparently, he thought the work being done in Williamsburg was more important than anything going on in Philadelphia. Certainly it was nearer his heart.[85]

He wrote his friend Thomas Nelson, Jr., who had returned to Virginia from Philadelphia, concerning the framing of a new government in Williamsburg:

"It is a work of the most interesting nature and such as every individual would wish to have his voice in. In truth, it is the whole object of the present controversy; for should a bad government be instituted for us, in future it had been as well to have accepted the bad one offered us from beyond the water without the risk and expense of contest."[86]

Jefferson doubted the authority of the Convention to write a permanent constitution. He believed that such power could properly be vested only in deputies elected for the specific purpose of framing a government.

He longed to be in Williamsburg to voice his objections, but had to depend upon Edmund Randolph to present them. Randolph made a polished presentation, but the delegates were not convinced.[87]

When Jefferson learned that the Convention was going ahead with the work of framing a constitution, he was determined to have a part in it despite the obstacle of absence. He went to work on his own draft of a model constitution, and George Wythe, his old law professor and now a fellow delegate to Congress, carried it with him when he returned to Williamsburg in June. But, when Wythe arrived on the scene of the Convention, Mason's draft of a constitution had already been approved in committee and presented on the floor. There were proposals for changes in the document, but the delegates were hot and tired and eager to go home. He knew that they were in no mood to consider the substitution of a new plan for the one already under consideration. He therefore offered Jefferson's draft as a source of amendments. Jefferson later was chagrined to learn that the only part of his paper to be adopted was the preamble, which had been tacked on to Mason's work.[88]

Jefferson had long been a student of government. He had learned from Governor Fauquier and George Wythe. Through the medium of books, he had learned also from Bacon and Locke. Many men—colleagues, opponents and constituents—had taught him the practical realities of politics. His graceful pen, the disciplined instrument of a cultivated mind, could give fit expression to his ideals. Now there was a crisis, not only in America, but in the life of mankind, that demanded talents and knowledge like his. And he seemed condemned to the role of a spectator.

Jefferson was so discouraged that, even at a later date, Edmund Pendleton thought it necessary to write him, "I hope you'll get cured of your wish to retire so early in life from the memory of man, and exercise your talents for the nurture of our new constitution."[89] Homesick for Virginia, and believing that his future usefulness lay chiefly in service within his native province, Jefferson had already sent word back to Williamsburg that he did not wish to be re-elected to Congress.[90]

Jefferson's congressional service, however, had not been completely devoid of satisfactions. He had creditably performed a great deal of paper work for the Congress and was one of its principal parliamentarians.[91] And he had glowed with pride on June 7, 1776, when Richard Henry Lee, obedient to instructions from the Virginia Convention, had asked for the floor. There was something portentous in the bearing of the tall Virginian.[92] His gaze was at once piercing and withdrawn as he surveyed the assembly. He was called "the American Cicero" and, as he hunched his shoulders and thrust his patrician head forward, his was the classic stance of a Roman senator. His rich voice, controlled as always, had this time a suppressed excitement that vibrated the nerves of his hearers as he explained that he was prepared to present resolutions pursuant to instructions from his constituents. Then, at the climactic moment, he called upon Congress to declare "that these united colonies are, and of right ought to be, free and independent States, that they are absolved from all allegiance to the British Crown, and that all political connection between them and the state of Great Britain is, and ought to be, totally dissolved. . . ."

Many of the delegates must have known the general nature of the proposal from Virginia before Lee presented it. Nevertheless, it was shocking to hear so explicitly stated an idea from which many of them shied even in private conversations.

Debate on the resolution took place two days later. It became evident then that the Middle Colonies and South Carolina were not yet ready for a final break with Britain. Massachusetts was very happy over the Virginia move; there can be no doubt that the Adamses had hoped for it. The other New England provinces would follow Virginia's lead. North Carolina's delegates, of course, had already been authorized to support an independence resolution if it were offered.[93]

Decision on the Virginia proposal was postponed to July 1. Jefferson and other proponents of independence took heart from signs of changing sentiment in the reluctant colonies.[94]

Congress, in preparation for what it might do, appointed a committee consisting of Jefferson, John Adams, Benjamin Franklin, Roger Sherman and Robert R. Livingston to prepare a declaration of independence.

Why the eloquent Richard Henry Lee, who presented the resolution for independence, was not appointed to the committee remains to this day a subject for speculation. He may have asked to be spared the duty, or he may have been kept off by political maneuvering within the Virginia delegation.[95]

In any event, there is little doubt that Jefferson envied Lee when the famous orator left Philadelphia to return to his Westmoreland plantation and his sick wife. Jefferson's own wife was in delicate health and he longed to be with her.[96] Besides, he was very much the junior member of a committee that included John Adams and the sage Benjamin Franklin. What of lasting importance could he hope to accomplish in Philadelphia?

Jefferson seemed not to realize that he would be head of the committee in fact as well as name. He had drafted Congress' reply to the conciliatory proposals of Lord North, but he was aware that his present appointment was due more to his being a Virginian than to his individual merits.[97]

In the beginning, Jefferson suggested that Adams write the first draft.[98] The Bostonian refused in his blunt and positive fashion. "I will not," he vowed.

"Why?" Jefferson demanded.

"Reasons enough," Adams replied with an air of finality and a determined expression on his round face.

When Jefferson insisted on knowing the reasons, Adams ticked them off:

"Reason first, you are a Virginian, and a Virginian ought to appear at the head of this business. Reason second, I am obnoxious, suspected, and unpopular. You are very much otherwise. Reason third, you can write ten times better than I can."

Jefferson gave no further argument and, apparently with the unanimous assent of the committee, accepted the assignment.

Alone in his rented room, he opened his writing box—a sort of portable desk—and commenced the task of writing. Many times the ink dried on his upraised quill, and many a time he dipped his pen into the ink again and crossed out what he had written.[99] His purpose was "not to find out new principles, or new arguments, never before thought of, not merely to say things which had never been said before, but to place before mankind the common sense of the subject in terms so plain and firm as to command their assent and to justify ourselves in the independent stand we are compelled to take."[100] Clarity and conciseness in the statement of great truths are not easily attained.

Jefferson must summon dispassionate truth to defend a position adopted in a time of passionate struggle. Without overindulgence in windy rhetoric, he must make it clear that America's battle for independence was part of man's battle for freedom.

He had a great deal of trouble with the second paragraph. Here he wished to justify secession on the grounds of natural rights and natural law. He must compress within a few simply worded sentences the essence of the philosophy which he himself had expressed in innumerable writings, which George Mason had enunciated in the Virginia Declaration of Rights, which Locke had explained in tortuous statements burdened with innumerable qualifications.

Jefferson began to find words for his ideas. "We hold these truths," he wrote, "to be sacred and undeniable; that all men are created equal and independent. . . ."[101]

The wording was not yet right, but the idea was there. Men were not born equal physically or mentally, nor were they born with equal social opportunities. But they were born with an equal right to life and liberty and to the pursuit of happiness.

After Jefferson finished his draft, there came the painful duty of submitting it to the criticism of his fellow committeemen. The Virginian was more an artist than a politician, and he felt that every excision was a mutilation.

As a ferocious foe of slavery—one no less vehement than the great abolitionist Richard Henry Lee—he agonized when the committee voted to delete his condemnation of the slave system as a "cruel war against human nature itself, violating its most sacred rights of life and liberty."[102] Could his colleagues not see the inconsistency of tacitly approving slavery while asserting man's inviolate right to liberty?

But some of the committeemen thought Jefferson was inconsistent with fact in seeking to lay at the foot of the throne all responsibility for the institution. And they were restrained by more practical considerations. Such Virginians as Jefferson, Lee, Washington and Madison might call for a gradual abolition of slavery, but the provinces of the Deep South would fight tenaciously for the institution that was the foundation of their economy. The men of New England might raise their voices in righteous indignation, but the Southerners would remind them that Yankees had been the masters of traffic in human flesh.

Jefferson's colleagues admired his idealism but, with the exception of Adams, they did not believe a debate on slavery should be provoked in a crisis when unity was essential to survival.[103] There were other changes, a little softening of Jefferson's polemic against the King, a few minor alterations.

Of course, none of these changes seemed small to the suffering author, who could not conceal his misery from Dr. Franklin. That perceptive philosopher leaned his old gray head close to the Virginian's ear and said sympathetically, "I have made it a rule, whenever in my power, to avoid becoming the draftsman of papers to be reviewed by a public body."[104]

When the pruning by the committee and by the Congress was over, the passage about slavery was gone, as were several phrases on other subjects. A few words had been grafted on. But the work was essentially the same as when Jefferson brought it forth from his quiet cell after days of labor.[105]

On July 2, 1776, Congress adopted Virginia's resolution for independence. On July 4, the text of the Declaration was approved in final form.

It has been said of that document:

"The lineage is direct: Jefferson copied Locke and Locke quoted Hooker."[106]

The line of descent is not open to serious question. Jefferson never claimed originality of ideas or sentiment. But the coinage of the document's immortal phrases bore the stamp of Jefferson's mind, and it was a stamp of greatness. The people knew them to be sterling, and they prized them from the first.

Had John Adams been thinking of poetic appropriateness or dramatic fitness instead of political realities, he could not have spoken more truly when he told Jefferson that a Virginian must be the author of the Declaration of Independence.

The drama of representative government in America had begun in Virginia on a day in May of 1607 when an Englishman had opened at once a small sealed box and a new era in world history. The document within the chest had named the members of the London Company's Council in Virginia, but had failed to name a president. A chief executive had been chosen in a free election on American soil.

But representative government wielding legislative power did not come to America until 1619. In that year, the first elective legislature in the New World met in Jamestown under the terms of a charter secured by Sir Edwin Sandys, "the father of self government in America."

Sandys, like Jefferson, was a man of contemplation—a student of philosophy who sought to make his ideals of government live in Virginia. Sandys shocked England with his declaration that governments derived their powers from the consent of the governed.

With little thought of philosophy, Virginians engaged in two rebellions—one bloodless and one bloody—to defend that principle years before John Locke described it as the social contract theory of government.

By the middle of the eighteenth century, Virginia was led by an aristocracy that had assimilated English political philosophy from the time of Sandys to the era of Locke, and which used this knowledge to express the aspirations of the people.

It was not surprising, therefore, that Virginia should lead the American movement for independence, first by her Stamp Act Resolves and then by the resolutions for severance from Great Britain.

In this summer of 1776, one Virginian had given to America and the world a Declaration of Rights. Another had written the Declaration of Independence for the new American nation. Still another led the armies fighting to make those rights respected and that independence a reality.

Throughout America, men stood taller when they heard the words that a Virginian had written in Philadelphia:

"We hold these truths to be self-evident, that all men are created equal, that they are endowed by their Creator with certain unalienable rights, that among these are life, liberty and the pursuit of happiness. That to secure these rights, governments are instituted among men, deriving their just powers from the consent of the governed."

To the support of that declaration, the representatives of the thirteen colonies pledged their lives, their fortunes and their sacred honor.[107]

At that climactic moment in history—as once before, in 1607— the drama of Virginia was one with the story of America.

Chapter XIII

A PLACE CALLED YORKTOWN

(1776-1781)

Chapter XIII

~~~~~~

(1776-1781)

THE man hunched over the desk scrawled "P. Henry" at the bottom of another paper and laid it on a growing pile. Then, without bothering to dust the fresh ink with sand, he raised his head, thrust his spectacles up on his high forehead and looked out the window. His generous mouth sagged with weariness. The lean face was that of a harassed man.[1]

What did those deep-set eyes see? The view was limited. From the window of the Governor's office one could look across the little court to an almost identical small building, the guard house. The man stood up—he was tall and raw-boned—and in two strides was at the window. To the right, he could see the Georgian elegance of the entrance to the Governor's Palace, that former symbol of royal authority in Virginia, now his official residence as the head of a revolutionary government.

Head! The word was a mockery unless it was used as short for "figurehead." During the summer, as a member of the Virginia Convention of 1776, he had pleaded that the Governor be given veto power over legislation. Without such authority, he had pointed out, the executive "would be a mere phantom." He would "be ultimately a dependent, instead of a coordinate, branch of power."[2]

The advice was ignored by men who had learned to fear gubernatorial tyranny. Then Henry was elected Governor. Now the legislature was in session, and his prophecies of executive frustration were being fulfilled with himself as the victim.

To the left was another wall that blocked Henry's view. Beyond it was the Palace Green, where General Charles Lee had lately drilled raw Continental troops. Until recently, that eccentric military man had occupied the Palace as his headquarters while commanding Continental forces in Virginia. Money had been appropriated since for a refurnishing of the residence, and not unnecessarily either. Not only had there been the depredations of a revolution, but General Lee had insisted that his large pack of dogs share the habitation with him.[3]

441

At best, though, the Palace was not a fit dwelling place for Henry. Its chambers were spacious and so were its grounds. But everything was compartmentalized. There were walls and hedges everywhere. The formal maze of boxwoods was a good symbol of the Governorship. The Constitution had provided a maze of duties for the chief executive, and there was nothing that he could do but follow the formal paths provided. A choice of one path or another might delay, but could not change, the final result. The Governor would come out at the same place in the end. He could not alter the pattern in any way. He must simply learn the way and conform to the rules. Imagination would do him no good. Indeed, it made him miserable with the vast amount of routine paper work which he was required to perform.

Here he was "cribbed, cabined and confined," imprisoned in a little world of neat hedges. Back in Hanover County now, the blue October mists would lie like a thin drapery over the hills, sleeping in majestic indolence.

But Henry would not really wish to be in Hanover while the legislature met in Williamsburg. He would like to be less than half a mile away, at the eastern end of Duke of Gloucester Street. There the legislature was meeting in the capital. In the chamber of the House of Burgesses—now the House of Delegates—he had presented his resolutions against the Stamp Act eleven years ago and had captured the imagination of a continent.

His talents were legislative, not executive. He could move a vast assembly more easily than he could operate the machinery of administration. His faculty for improvisation was immense, but his capacity for detailed routine was exceeded by any competent clerk. Shunted into an executive position without executive powers, his massive intellect harnessed to the performance of minute tasks, and cut off from the legislature which was his source of strength, Henry helplessly watched the daily diminution of his influence.

In a comfortable brick home just off the Palace Green was another famous Virginian. This one was overjoyed to be where he was. Thomas Jefferson, returned to Virginia after representing its people in the Continental Congress of 1776, was living in the house of George Wythe, his old law teacher and mentor in many things. The learned Wythe was now a member of Virginia's delegation in Congress, and insisted that his pupil use the home as his own. Jefferson had had the satisfaction of writing the Declaration of Independence while in Philadelphia, but he had not enjoyed his stay in that city. He had been anxious about the health of his wife, who was now with him in Williamsburg. And he could hardly bear to be away from Virginia when a new instrument of government was being formed. He had worried, too, whether his chances of taking a prominent part in the affairs of the new Commonwealth would be jeopardized by his long absence. From Philadelphia, he had written to a friend, "It is a painful situation to be 300 miles from one's country, and thereby opened to secret [political] assassination without a possibility of self-defence."[4] Jefferson had resigned from Congress and declined appointment as a United States commissioner to France in order to return to Virginia.

If this thirty-three-year-old, red-headed giant paced the floor, it was not (as with Henry) in vexation, but in exuberance. Wythe had told Jefferson that the government established in Virginia required reformation, and he had said that Jefferson was the man to reform it.[5] There was no opportunity that the young man coveted more. Now he was in Williamsburg, the seat of government, and he discovered that his popularity and prestige had been increased by his activities in Philadelphia. He had a great work to do in Williamsburg. There was no place on earth that he would have preferred at this moment, not even his beloved mountain top in Albemarle County.

The difference between Henry's mood and Jefferson's was not solely a matter of position. True, Henry longed to be back in the legislature, as Jefferson was, and Jefferson would have been miserable if he had been responsible for the details of administration which plagued Henry. Nevertheless, Henry would not have plunged into the work of the legislature at this point with the youthful enthusiasm which animated Jefferson. Age did not make the difference either. Henry was only seven years older than the delegate from Albemarle, though the margin seemed greater. The fundamental difference between the two men was in their approach to revolution. Because of this difference, Henry was no longer a zealot while Jefferson now burned with greater zeal than he had ever known before.

Jefferson's imagination had been fired eleven years ago when, as a student at the College of William and Mary, he had stood in the doorway of the House of Burgesses and heard Henry denounce the Stamp Act with the thundering fervor and lightning words of an Old Testament prophet.

Jefferson's vision of revolution grew. It was fed by his studies in philosophy. The more he read of Utopias, the more he dreamed of building a civilization in harmony with philosophical concepts of good. Independence, he believed, merely opened the door to real revolution. Once freed from the Crown, the people of the colonies could build republics founded on the rights of man. They could reduce the strongholds of feudalism to rubble, and use only the best of the old materials to build a new structure of government.

Henry did not share the dream which he had inspired. A genius, but not nearly so learned as Jefferson, he did not long to realize the dreams of ancient philosophers. To his mind, the revolution would be over when independence was securely won. Little reform would be necessary after the western counties of Virginia had won a voice in the government commensurate with their population.

Henry had done as much as any man to bring the colonies to the verge of independence. He had been denied (wisely, many military men believed) the privilege of leading troops into battle for independence. Through success or failure, the revolution as he conceived it would soon be over. In any event, it no longer seemed to need him. The rest of life must be anticlimax. How could Henry be expected to summon the ardor of past days when his flaming words had set fire to a continent?[6]

After the decisive defeat of Royal Governor Dunmore at Gwynn's Island in the summer of 1776, Virginia ceased to wage offensive warfare in the Revolution. Virginia's sons were leaders of the Continental Army and one, George Washington, was its commander-in-chief. Many of Virginia's "common soldiers"—especially her riflemen—proved uncommonly effective in battle at a score of vital points. But Virginia's military operations as a colony or State were largely confined after Dunmore's flight to defense against sporadic British raids.[7]

Virginia's broad rivers—the James, York, Rappahannock and Potomac—and the many inlets indenting her coasts made the land peculiarly vulnerable to sudden and incisive attacks by British naval vessels operating in the Chesapeake Bay and along the Atlantic Seaboard. It would have been very hard, indeed, to convince a Tidewater planter of that day that these threats to his life and property did not constitute the most important phase of the revolution in Virginia.

Yet such was the case. A political revolution taking place with the quietness of accelerated evolution would have a far greater effect on the lives and fortunes of his descendants than anything that would be accomplished by a British man-of-war lying at anchor within range of his telescope.

Seventeen seventy-six was a crucial year of political revolution for all the colonies, since it produced (under Virginia's leadership) the Declaration of Independence of the United States, and saw the start of debate on the Articles of Confederation. It was no less critical a year of political revolution within the Commonwealth itself.

This revolution began in the Virginia Convention of 1776. There were many spectators—men and women who crowded the galleries and halls of the capitol in Williamsburg. Few if any, though, realized that they were witnessing not only the end of royal rule in Virginia, but also the beginning of the end for the Virginia they had known.

A great conservative leader, Edmund Pendleton—symbol of the old order, "aristocracy with the doors open"[8]—was elected chairman. With his leadership, and that of the astute Robert Carter Nicholas and the learned Richard Bland, Virginia's ancient oligarchy appeared to be firmly seated in the saddle. Patrick Henry, the agitator of earlier years, was elected governor. But his council was conservative, and he was no longer feared by the old guard for, like them, he was content to let revolution end with independence—to be a matter of foreign rather than domestic policy.[9]

Nevertheless, the very act of declaring independence necessitated the framing of a new government and invited experimentation by those who had glimpsed "a new Heaven and a new earth."

Henry had not caught the vision. He had no program to offer those who had. George Mason had the imagination and the intellect, but lacked the health and the disposition to be the leader of men who would build a new Jerusalem. Edmund Randolph and James Madison, able and well educated, lacked the experience and prestige. Richard Henry Lee had all of the requisite qualities except popularity. If Henry could no longer voice their aspirations, the mountain men were mute. These delegates from the hill country, together with the young liberals from Tidewater and the Piedmont, comprised a majority of the convention. But, lacking leadership, they could not dominate the proceedings.[10]

The constitution adopted for the new Commonwealth was much inferior to the Virginia Declaration of Rights which preceded it. The Declaration expressed the fondest hopes of the liberal majority and of far-seeing friends of freedom in every country. But the Constitution was a weak instrument, born of necessity and so flexible that it would accommodate the old oligarchy as easily as it would a new republic of inspired democrats. Whether the aspirations so nobly voiced would find expression within the society of the Commonwealth depended on whether the liberals would find leadership comparable to that which the oligarchy had enjoyed.

Before the end of the House session of 1776, it became evident that such leadership had been found. Jefferson was the man.

He goodnaturedly assumed the humdrum tasks of legislation that must have held no fascination for his imaginative mind. He drew bills to meet all sorts of minor requirements as uncomplainingly as if he had been drafting a declaration for the United States. His willingness to share so wholeheartedly in the humble tasks of the legislature increased his popularity. So did his deference to his elders.[11]

Unlike Richard Henry Lee, who was comparable to him in intellectual vigor and devotion to liberty, Jefferson could disagree strongly without inciting enmity. For example, Jefferson's relationship with Pendleton and other conservative leaders was as cordial as with Lee and members of the progressive faction.[12]

Moreover, Jefferson was a man of vision with a sense of urgency. He perceived that it would be easier to gain legislative assent to reforms while a war for liberty was in progress than later, when it would not "be necessary to resort every moment to the people for support."[13]

Jefferson did not have to search philosophical tomes for issues. The people were petitioning the House of Delegates for reforms. The House might act or fail to act on the proposals, but it could not shove the responsibility onto another legislative chamber or a coordinate branch of government. Despite what the Constitution said about the division of power, authority really resided in the House and Virginia voters knew it.[14]

In the first week of the October session, citizens of Prince Edward County appealed to the House to translate the noble sentiments of the Declaration of Rights into enforceable legislation. These dissenters, who were tired of paying taxes to support the Established Church, said that they hailed "the last article of the Bill of Rights as the rising sun of religious liberty, to relieve them from a long night of ecclesiastical bondage."[15] They called upon the legislators, who were the successors to the Convention of 1776, to "complete what is so nobly begun; . . . to raise religious as well as civil liberty to the zenith of glory, and make Virginia an asylum for free inquiry, knowledge and the virtuous of every denomination." The petitioners hoped "that, without delay, all Church establishments might be pulled down, and every tax upon conscience and private judgment abolished, and each individual left to rise or sink by his own merit, and the general laws of the land."

Anglicans held virtually all major offices in the Commonwealth, as they had in the Colony. There had been an occasional Presbyterian of great influence, but the Presbyterian Church was the established Kirk of Scotland and, as the colonists moved toward revolution, the Toryism of Scotch merchants brought odium on everything Scottish.[16] It would be an exaggeration to say that the Anglican, or Episcopal, Church dominated Tidewater. It would be more accurate to say that its members did. The vestries of colonial times had political as well as ecclesiastical authority. The political and social implications of vestry membership were as significant as the religious. Since the time of Commissary James Blair, who had died in 1743 at the age of eighty-eight, there had been no threat of theocracy.[17] Most Virginia leaders were men of sincere piety, whatever their faults, but they paid little heed to what was said by bishops in London. The church in Virginia was a Virginia institution, and they defended its forms and prerogatives with the tenacity of men fighting for the society which was their world.

But, while Virginia's leadership remained securely in the hands of members of her established church, dissenting sects multiplied within the colony. Scotch-Irish Presbyterians, German Lutherans and adherents of other denominations had moved into the Valley. Baptists had grown at a phenomenal rate. They had been inspired to new exertions by ruffians who had thrown hornets' nests and snakes in their midst at worship time. When Baptist ministers had been marched to jail for preaching without a license (a license which they could not obtain without pledging adherence to the Established Church), they had preached through the bars to fascinated congregations.[18] Baptists had made heavy inroads in Tidewater as well as in mountain sections. The bulk of their church in Virginia was composed of what were sometimes called "good, plain people." But the Baptists could also claim the support of some aristocrats who possessed wealth and influence. This was true especially in the Northern Neck where even Councillor Robert Carter, of Nomini Hall, grandson of "King" Carter and one of the richest and most cultivated of the "river barons," was listening with respect to Baptist teachings. Before long he would be a zealous Baptist.[19]

The Baptists and other dissenters maintained that an established church was inconsistent with the principles upon which the Commonwealth of Virginia was supposed to be founded. They had long been denied freedom of worship by honest conservatives who sincerely believed the influence of these religious radicals to be pernicious, and persecuted by unprincipled bullies who delighted in roughing up victims without incurring the serious displeasure of respectable men. Their patience was near exhaustion. Like Jefferson, they knew that now was the time to press for reform, and they would not be quieted by evasive answers.

Edmund Pendleton, speaker of the House, was alarmed at the growth of religious dissent.[20] This brilliant lawyer, who had borne the burden of administration in Virginia as chairman of the Committee of Safety during the first trying months of the revolution, was a stalwart fighter for independence but an equally determined defender of existing institutions. Even before formal presentation of the petition from Prince Edward County, he had appointed a Committee of Religion to take care of the anticipated move. To the chairmanship of this committee he had appointed Carter Braxton. He had also named to membership the most conservative man in the House, Robert Carter Nicholas. Pendleton had told Jefferson earlier that he counted upon these two to "assist in watching and breaking the spirit of party, that bane of all public councils."[21]

The committee was kept busy. From Albemarle, Amherst and Buckingham counties came the petitions of dissenters. Germans in Culpeper appealed for relief from supporting the Episcopal Church and asked that their parochial taxes might go to the support of their own church instead. The Presbytery of Hanover asked that county's delegates to "concur in removing every species of religious as well as civil bondage." It soon became apparent that the committee would hear from other dissenters in other parts of Virginia.

The Anglican clergy could not be expected to remain silent for long, and they counterattacked with a petition of their own. It was based on two principal arguments. The first was that it would be a violation of sacred trust to deprive of a livelihood ministers who had accepted charges in Virginia on the assurance that they would be supported from the public funds. The second argument was that ". . . the doctrines of Christianity have a greater tendency to produce virtue among men than any human laws or institutions, and that these can be best taught and preserved in their purity in an established church, which gives encouragement to men to study and acquire a competent knowledge of the scriptures. . . ." From their viewpoint, the clergymen clinched this argument when they declared, "If these great purposes can be answered by a religious establishment, the hardships which such a regulation might impose on individuals, or even bodies of men, ought not to be considered. . . ."[22]

Methodists, who liked to consider themselves reformers within the established church, rallied to the support of the Anglican clergy.[23]

The issue of the established church was debated daily in committee and in informal gatherings that included both conservatives and liberals. Formal debate was provoked by the presentation November 9 of a petition from dissenters in Augusta. The people of that area were tired of subordination to Tidewater and were talking seriously of secession.[24] These people could not be put off on a question so vital to them as their religion. The petition was referred to the Committee of the Whole. The question would now be debated openly by the delegates.

Jefferson was expected to take the lead in opposition to the established church, and he did. His task was a formidable one. Though an eloquent writer, he did not have a forceful or engaging delivery in public speech. Opposing him was Pendleton, one of Virginia's two ablest lawyers[25] and a master of polished argument. Standing with Pendleton was Nicholas, a man whose solidity seemed impregnable. Jefferson's task was further complicated by the fact that, though a majority of Virginians were dissenters, a majority of the legislators were members of the established church.

Debate revealed a variety of interpretations of statements on religion in the Declaration of Rights. George Mason had stated the principles of religious freedom in noble and lucid words in that document, but, like virtually all statements of principle, it did not include a detailed guide for application. The result was that defenders of the status quo could devise elaborate arguments to demonstrate that maintenance of the established church in its privileged position was not a violation of religious freedom.

Jefferson did not make a direct frontal assault on the institution of establishment. Instead he attacked several bastions separately and thus caused the fall of the fortress.[26] He secured the repeal of acts restraining preaching and worship by dissenters. Even the most subtle sophist was hard put to discover consistency between these acts and a declaration of religious freedom. But bitter controversy ensued when Jefferson pressed for a provision exempting dissenters from taxation for support of the established church. Nevertheless, he succeeded in pushing the measure through the House, and in suspending the salaries of all ministers of the establishment until the next session of the Assembly. The shock of sudden abolition had been avoided, but the establishment was on its way into limbo. The ministers' salaries could be suspended again at the next session and the next, and so on until the act of abolition would only put the seal of law on custom.[27]

In the 1776 session of the Assembly, Jefferson also launched an attack on the Virginia system of land tenure, which was part of the State's heritage from England. Land was the material basis and symbol of Virginia's aristocracy. A great landowner himself and an aristocrat, Jefferson nevertheless believed that the retention of large landed estates from generation to generation would be a means of perpetuating "un-natural distinctions" among the citizens of the Commonwealth. Virginia's aristocracy was remarkable for its ability and public spirit, but Jefferson feared that if it remained secure in the advantage of great property for successive generations it would eventually lose its sense of responsibility.[28]

He struck hard at the laws of entail and primogeniture. Under the laws of entail, a planter's lands could be inalienably settled upon his descendants. Under the law of primogeniture, the eldest son would inherit his father's entire landed estate if the parent died intestate.

The law of primogeniture seldom had to be invoked in Virginia, for the propertied men of that day were almost always careful to make wills. Nevertheless, Jefferson considered primogeniture a relic of feudalism and regarded its abolition as a matter of great symbolic significance.

But entails were his real target. He liked to think of his bill against entails, introduced October 14, as the "first blow" against the old order.

Not all of Virginia's large estates were entailed, but a planter, under Virginia law as under England's, could provide that all his lands would go to a particular son and would descend through him to the heirs "of his body begotten," or could even restrict the inheritance to the son's heirs by a particular marriage. By Virginia additions to English law, slaves could be entailed as well as land.[29] The planter could determine not only his own heirs, but also the heirs of those heirs. An entail could be set aside only by an Act of Assembly.

Pendleton, who had begun his career with a negligible inheritance, and who had no children to inherit his own estate,[30] was the chief defender of entails and primogeniture. He succeeded in postponing Jefferson's victory over primogeniture. He proposed a compromise measure to preserve the outstanding features of the entail system, and almost secured its passage, but again was defeated by Jefferson and the times.[31]

That acid-tongued arch-conservative, Landon Carter, spouted vitriol when he learned what Jefferson had accomplished. He said that abolishing entails was "overturning the very principles of justice on which [the contenders for liberty] built their very claim of freedom. This is what I call sowing the seeds of contention, which must spring up sooner or later, and all from the poisoned soil of popularity."[32]

But there was little excitement over the change. That fact was, in itself, a measure of the revolution that had taken place in men's minds before finding expression in law.[33]

Jefferson was one of the leaders who pushed through legislation to create out of Virginia's Western lands the huge county of Kentucky.[34] He had faith in the sun-browned men who made their homes in those green hills. He believed strongly in the destiny of the West. And he knew that its people, though largely strangers to Plato's *Republic* and Locke's empire of *Human Understanding*, would be more in sympathy with his ideas of democracy than most of the Tidewater planters who could speak familiarly with him of Attic glory and the empirical proofs of man's rights to freedom. He worked to establish representative government in the West and to give its citizens a voice in the affairs of the State.[35]

Jefferson's greatest opportunity for reform, however, came when the House passed a bill calling for a general revision of Virginia laws. He was named chairman of the committee to make recommendations. The group met for a preliminary conference in January 1777, at Fredericksburg.

Jefferson presided over a distinguished committee. There sat the great-headed George Wythe, whose brow seemed distended with its weight of knowledge. He had resigned from Congress to serve as a committeeman. At the same table was Pendleton, Wythe's only great rival at the bar. There, too, was George Mason, whose agile mind resided in a corpulent body. But an age that placed much faith in physiognomy would see the luster of genius in his large brown eyes. This man was the author of Virginia's constitution and of the Declaration of Rights. Completing the committee was Thomas Ludwell Lee, one of the most popular men in Virginia and a gentleman of liberal sentiments, but one who served the public despite an aversion for public life.[36]

Men with the intellect of a Pendleton or a Jefferson defy pigeon-holing. Theirs is a consistency above the labels of conservative or liberal. The committee had a striking demonstration of this fact when Pendleton, the conservative leader, proposed that the best way to proceed was "to abolish the whole existing system of laws and prepare a new and complete Institute."[37] Even more striking was the response of Jefferson, leader of Virginia's political revolution, who argued that the gentlemen should work to "preserve the general system, and only modify it to the present state of things."[38]

The younger man contended that "to compose a new Institute . . . would be an arduous undertaking, of vast research, of great consideration and judgment." He said, "No one of us probably would undertake such a work, which, to be systematical, must be the work of one hand."

He made a telling point when he said that, once a new Institute of laws had been reduced to a text, "every word of that text, from the imperfection of human language, and its incompetence to express distinctly every shade of idea, would become a subject of question and chicanery until settled by repeated adjudications." He predicted, "This would involve us for ages in litigation, and render property uncertain until, like the statutes of old, every word had been tried and settled by new decisions and by new volumes of reports and commentaries. . . ."

Lee agreed with Pendleton, but Wythe and Mason sided with Jefferson. Accordingly, it was decided that the common law was "not to be meddled with except where alterations are necessary."[39] It was generally agreed that change was necessary wherever the language of the statutes was "obsolete or redundant."

The committeemen decided to examine the Acts of the English Commonwealth and of the other American states with a view of adopting "any good ones."

When the work on proposed revisions was apportioned among the members, the criminal laws were assigned to Jefferson. He asked the guidance of the committee in framing these statutes, and found the opinions of the majority in harmony with his own.[40] Standards remarkably humane for the eighteenth century were agreed upon. The death penalty was to be invoked only in case of treason or murder. The branding iron was to be used no more. Suicide was "not to incur forfeiture, but [to be] considered as a disease." Castration would be`substituted for capital punishment in cases of rape.[41]

The final report of the committee was not submitted till two and one-half years later. The process of translating that report into effective legislation was a gradual one extending over more than a decade.[42]

When the committee's report was submitted to the General Assembly in 1779 in the form of one hundred twenty-six bills, many changes had befallen the committeemen themselves. Thomas Ludwell Lee was dead. Pendleton and Wythe were members of a judicial triumvirate created by legislation introduced by Jefferson. And Jefferson himself was Governor. Even the seat of government would soon be shifted, Williamsburg yielding to Richmond.

Under royal government in Virginia, the Governor and his Council had sat as the highest court of appeal. Dunmore's flight had put an end to Council and Court. County courts had continued to exist for the performance of such routine functions as the appointment of guardians and the qualification of executors and administrators. The Court of Admiralty still handled maritime cases. A court of Oyer and Terminer had tried prisoners confined to the public gaol in Williamsburg for offenses against the State. Remarkably enough, the people had attained such a level of political and social maturity that no wave of crime swept the Commonwealth during the many months while it was without a judicial system worthy of the name.[43]

Both liberal and conservative leaders, however, realized that such good fortune could not last forever. On October 30, 1777, Jefferson had been named chairman of three special committees assigned the respective tasks of preparing bills for establishing a General Court, a High Court of Chancery and a Court of Appeals.

As finally amended and passed, the bills retained the old county court system as it had existed before the Revolution and also the Court of Admiralty. A General Court and High Court of Chancery were created.

The General Court consisted of five judges and had jurisdiction over criminal and general common law cases.

The High Court of Chancery, the highest court in the new system until a supreme Court of Appeals should be created, consisted of three judges and exercised both original and appellate jurisdiction in equity cases.

Only three men were nominated in the House, and when Jefferson reported their names to the Senate January 13, 1778, they were unanimously elected the next day. The three were Pendleton, Wythe and Robert Carter Nicholas. All were gentlemen of superior mentality and high integrity. Pendleton was only fifty-six years old, but that made him past middle age by eighteenth century standards, and he was well on the way to becoming the grand old man of Virginia government. He had had considerable experience in both the legislative and judicial branches. It would have been hard to find in the American colonies two or three men so learned in the law as Wythe. As professor of law at the College of William and Mary, he soon would have the distinction of heading the first department of law in any American institution of higher learning. It was well known that, as an attorney, he would not take a case unless convinced that in so doing he would be on the side of moral right. Robert Nicholas, long the treasurer of Virginia, was a symbol of probity and a deeply religious man who united idealism with common sense. It is not strange that there were no further nominations after these three were named.[44]

During the time that the judicial system was being established, Jefferson was working hard for liberal reforms. With Mason, he led a movement to give small settlers (squatters though they might be) an advantage over speculative companies in the Western lands. The two idealists were defeated in 1778 by the conservatives, led by Pendleton and the bear-like and emphatic Benjamin Harrison. Many of the legislators were themselves land speculators. They were also influenced by the fact that rapid settlement of the West would decrease the value of their own Eastern lands. George Washington's statement that prospective soldiers would be diverted from the army by gifts of land in the West gave patriotic reinforcement to personal interest.[45] The defeat of Jefferson and Mason's plan was a foregone conclusion.

But their stout battling made possible a compromise measure framed by Mason in consultation with Jefferson. Providing for land purchases at nominal prices by those who had settled on the land before January 1, 1778, and creating buying opportunities for those who had settled since that date, the bills did provide a little more security for men of meager means who looked hopefully to the West. But the laws fell far short of their dreams, and the framers themselves were in no mood to celebrate when passage came in June 1779.[46]

Jefferson and his liberal associates in the legislature had plans for a group more unfortunate than the struggling settlers of the West. These liberals and some of the conservatives were convinced that the slaves must be freed. There were disagreements on the method and speed desirable in emancipation, but Virginia's leaders of thought were sure that evil consequences would flow from perpetuation of the institution.

Jefferson had wished to strike hard at slavery in the Declaration of Independence, but his indictment of the system was deleted to appease some Deep South delegates, some Yankees who were self-conscious about the slave trade, and other representatives who feared that debate on the subject would wreck the shaky structure of intercolonial unity.[47]

He still believed that slavery was destructive of the morals and industry of a society in which it existed. And he burned to do something about it.[48]

In proposing action to combat the menace of slavery, Jefferson was part of a Virginia tradition. As early as 1736, Colonel William Byrd, one of the two or three most powerful men in Virginia, criticized slavery on grounds of security, economics and morality. Having set forth arguments against it in a letter to Lord Egmont, who was a prominent promoter of English colonization in America, he concluded:

"It were therefore worth the consideration of a British Parliament, my Lord, to put an end to this unchristian traffick of making merchandise of our Fellow Creatures. At least, the further importation of them into our Colony should be prohibited. . . . All these matters duly considered, I wonder the legislature will indulge a few ravenous traders to the danger of the Publick Safety."[49]

There were many Virginians who defended slavery and the slave trade in Byrd's day. There doubtless were many on the eve of the Revolution. But defenders of the "unchristian traffic" were in the minority in the General Assembly of Virginia for many sessions. The colony's legislators repeatedly passed laws to restrain the importation of Negroes, and these laws were consistently vetoed by the Crown. On December 10, 1770, the King, weary of the whole business, instructed the Governor of Virginia, "upon pain of the highest displeasure, to assent to no law by which the importation of slaves should be in any respect prohibited or obstructed."[50]

In 1772, the House of Burgesses appealed to his Majesty to reconsider. Its petition declared:

"We implore your Majesty's paternal assistance in averting a calamity of a most alarming nature. The importation of slaves into the colonies from the coast of Africa hath long been considered as a trade of great inhumanity, and under its present encouragement we have too much reason to fear will endanger the very existence of your Majesty's American dominions. We are sensible that some of your Majesty's subjects may reap emoluments from this sort of traffic, but when we consider that it greatly retards the settlement of the colonies with more useful inhabitants and may in time have the most destructive influence, we presume to hope that the interests of a few will be disregarded when placed in competition with the security and happiness of such numbers of your Majesty's dutiful and loyal subjects. We, therefore, beseech your Majesty to remove all these restraints on your Majesty's Governor in this colony which inhibits their assenting to such laws as might check so pernicious a consequence."[51]

The committee which produced this petition included Pendleton, Richard Henry Lee and Benjamin Harrison.

In 1774, the Virginia Convention prohibited the importation of slaves in connection with its prohibitions on the importation of various commodities. But many Virginians were thinking of policies for the future as well as the exigencies of the moment. Resolutions adopted in Fairfax County said: "We take the opportunity of declaring our most earnest wishes to see *an entire stop forever* put to such a wicked, cruel and unnatural trade."[52]

When Jefferson advocated abolition of the slave trade, therefore, he was not generally considered radical. In 1778, the General Assembly enacted a law providing "that from and after the passing of this act no slaves shall hereafter be imported into this Commonwealth by sea or land, nor shall any slaves so imported be sold or bought by any person whatsoever." The law imposed a fine of one thousand pounds for every slave imported, and further declared that any slave brought into the State would automatically be freed upon arrival.[53]

Virginia's abolition of the slave trade preceded by thirty years similar action on the part of Britain. It must be admitted that fear and self-interest combined with humanitarianism to foster the Commonwealth's action and that the problem of slavery was not one of domestic urgency in Britain except as her traders were affected. But these considerations do not alter the fact that, as J. H. Ballagh asserted, "Virginia thus had the honor of being the first political community in the civilized modern world to prohibit the pernicious traffic."[54]

The next step, as Jefferson and his followers saw it, was the gradual and systematic abolition of slavery itself. Jefferson was fearful for reasons beyond purely practical consequences when he viewed in Virginia the subjection to the white race of a Negro race nearly as numerous. He wrote, "I tremble for my country when I reflect that God is just."[55]

But Jefferson could not press on with his legislative program. If he could have, the odds were against general agreement on any particular plan of emancipation. What Jefferson might have done as a legislative leader was to remain a subject for speculation. On June 1, 1779, by joint ballot, the two houses of the General Assembly elected him Governor of Virginia.

Jefferson was gratified that he should attain in his thirty-sixth year the chief office in the Commonwealth. But he foresaw that a high public post in such troubled times would entail "intense labor and great private loss."[56] Twenty-four days after his election he wrote, "The hour of private retirement, to which I am drawn by my nature with a propensity almost irresistible, will be the most welcome of my life."[57]

Jefferson's wish for retirement was partly due to his desire to be at his beloved Monticello and to devote himself to those scholarly pursuits which he always believed superior in importance to administrative activities. But there were other and stronger reasons why his job was onerous. Like Henry, he felt frustrated by the interruption in his legislative career. Though he lacked Henry's forensic gifts, Jefferson was an exceptionally effective committeeman. Thus, it was painful for him to mark time in an executive post while reforms which he had urged were pigeonholed. In at least one way, the experience was even more frustrating for Jefferson than for Henry, because Jefferson, unlike his predecessor, had a carefully formulated legislative program which he longed to put into action.

Though Jefferson had become the leader of the liberal faction in the legislature, he was not the head of a disciplined political organization that could push his measures through the Assembly. In general, he had the support of Henry's followers. The "forest-born Demosthenes"[58] had returned to his beloved hills after serving three terms as Governor and thus becoming ineligible to succeed himself under the Virginia constitution. Some of the young delegates from Tidewater also followed Jefferson, but more of the Tidewater legislators had voted for John Page and Thomas Nelson, Jr. when Jefferson was elected Governor. Jefferson had won on the second ballot, by 67 votes to Page's 61. The cleavage of sentiment was not so sharp as one might suppose. Jefferson and Page had been friends since boyhood, and were at great pains to reassure each other that the contest made no difference in their friendship. Acknowledging a letter of affectionate good wishes from Page, the victor wrote, ". . . the difference of the numbers which decided between us was too insignificant to give you a pain, or me a pleasure, had our dispositions toward each other been such as to admit those sensations."[59] While Jefferson was denied the advantage of an effective political organization,[60] he was also spared the obstruction of an organized opposition.

There were, however, even greater impediments to success. One was the nature of the office, the other the nature of the times.

The Governor was hedged in by innumerable constitutional restrictions even more binding upon a man of Jefferson's strict and scrupulous regard for the law than upon one of Henry's temperament. Jefferson saw himself as an administrator rather than a true executive.[61]

The times called for men of action more imperatively than for men of contemplation. Virginia's chief military officers and most of her soldiers were battling the British beyond the borders of the State. Ill-armored and poorly guarded, the Commonwealth was almost defenseless against attack, as was demonstrated in May 1779 when a seaborne British force raided Portsmouth and Suffolk. Yet it was the business of the Governor to provide a defense. As a student of Indian lore, Jefferson knew that some tribes had a war chief and a peace chief who alternated in authority according to the demands of the times. He must have felt like a peace chief called upon to perform the functions of his alternate.

To advise and assist him, Jefferson had a Council of State consisting of eight men who, like himself, owed their jobs to the General Assembly. In some ways, they hindered rather than helped him in the exercise of executive authority, for Jefferson believed that he did not have the right to go counter to the united opinion of the Council.[62]

Jefferson spent his first year in office in endless conferences and paper work. At the end of his term, he could point to no impressive achievements but had left an innocuous record of dignified and diligent performance of duty as he saw it. His integrity was widely respected and he had the confidence of Virginia's George Washington, whose relations with the war governors were important to his success as commander of the Continental Army. Jefferson was re-elected unanimously.

In the spring of 1780, the seat of government had been moved from Williamsburg to Richmond. As a legislator, Jefferson had advocated the move, partly because of a belief that the interior location would be safer from enemy attack and partly because of a desire to remove the capital from an area dominated by conservative Tidewater planters.

Problems that had vexed him in Williamsburg followed him to Richmond and grew more serious in his second term than they had been in his first. He must furnish money, supplies and soldiers for the war. As the need increased, the availability decreased.

A measure to procure money through the forfeiture and sale of property belonging to British subjects proved almost useless as the actual process became a matter of what Jefferson called "legal contestation . . . which may not be terminated in the present age."[63]

Jefferson realized that tax revenues could never catch up with the depreciation of currency, but he was as helpless to deal with the problem as colleagues who were sanguine in their ignorance. He could not halt the printing of a vast number of paper bills by presses that manufactured inflation.

British vessels patroling the Virginia coast prevented the shipment abroad of tobacco that would have brought desperately needed hard money, or equivalent credits, to the Commonwealth.

Nevertheless, amid all these vexations in the hot Virginia August of 1780, Jefferson did not lose his perspective. He wrote to the French minister, the Chevalier de la Luzerne, "Our own efforts to establish a force on the water have been very unsuccessful; and our trade has been almost annihilated by the most contemptible part of the enemy's force on that element." Even so, he did not ask that the friendly French fleet then in American waters make any move especially for Virginia's benefit. Instead, he said, "The interest of this State is intimately blended so perfectly . . . with that of the others of the confederacy that the most effectual aid it can at any time receive is where the general cause most needs it."[64]

Jefferson's national view in this time of emergency is particularly remarkable in one whose devotion to his State was such that he called it "my country." His high-mindedness in this respect commands the admiration of succeeding generations but probably irked many of his contemporaries.

Almost exactly a year before Jefferson wrote to the French minister, a very different attitude was displayed by the Council who, in his absence, detained a shipment of arms intended for disposition by the Continental Congress. By way of excuse, it should be recorded that Virginia's contributions to the Continental Army had reduced its own stands of arms to about three thousand.

Jefferson attempted to stimulate the manufacture of arms in Virginia, but his efforts were frustrated by legal objections and legislative obstacles.

Crop failures in 1779 had so far reduced the supply of foodstuffs that Virginia, far from being able to contribute to other States, was forced to import from them.

In the summer of 1780, Jefferson ruefully reflected that Virginia had not been able to comply "accurately in time, quantity and every other circumstance" with Congressional requisitions, but took comfort in the fact that her record did not suffer by comparison with those of the other States.

* * *

Early in the fall, Jefferson heard reports that the British planned to seize Portsmouth. But he was inclined to discredit the rumors. He was not a thoroughgoing optimist, however. He admitted that Virginia was virtually defenseless against a coastal attack in force. And, if he was not already convinced that Continental forces could not be spared to keep the war outside Virginia's borders, he soon would be made aware of that fact.

This unfortunate condition existed because of the hard facts of war and also because of considerations of grand strategy in which Virginians played a major part.

"The hard facts of war" is a comprehensive phrase, but the factors adverse to the colonial cause might be grouped under the one word "shortage." There was a shortage of munitions, clothing, medical supplies and food. There was also a severe shortage of naval power. There was even a shortage of dedicated patriots of the colonial cause, only about one-third of the population of the United States being earnest in the cause of freedom, while the remainder was divided between Loyalists and neutralists. And, among the troops who rallied to the revolutionary cause, there was a shortage of training and discipline. Short-term enlistments were the order of the day, and many men joined the army in the expectation of slipping back home in time for spring plowing.

Britain was strong in the things in which America was weak. She was rich in money and supplies. With her wealth, she could purchase Hessian mercenaries to augment her own well-equipped, thoroughly trained and superbly disciplined forces. Her lines of supply necessarily bridged the Atlantic, but they were guarded by the powerful navy which blockaded American ports and served as an invasion fleet.

One of Britain's military virtues was so overgrown that it assumed the proportions of a fault. Discipline became rigidity, as evidenced by the unwillingness of British officers to adapt European tactics to the necessities of American terrain and to the nature of their American foe. This British weakness was an old story to the commander in chief of the Continental Army, George Washington, who, as a young lieutenant colonel of Virginia forces, had accompanied Braddock on the road to the Monongahela and defeat.

One of the Continental Army's greatest assets was that it included many veterans of the French and Indian War who could teach the lessons of their experience to the mass of raw recruits.

The lack of training among most of the American troops was partly compensated by the colonists' almost universal familiarity with firearms. American children often had their own guns at an age when their British counterparts were still playing with toys. And in the hands of fighting men from Pennsylvania, Maryland and Virginia was a weapon unknown in Old England, and hitherto unknown even in New England—the rifle. Infinitely superior to the smooth-bore musket, it helped to make soldiers from these three States, as John Adams said, "the most accurate marksmen in the world."[65]

But none of these assets surpassed in importance the advantage of Washington's leadership.[66] That advantage had not been clearly apparent, even to his fellow Virginians, on June 15, 1775, when he was elected commander in chief of the Continental Army. His character and soldierly qualities were respected, but his appointment by the Congress was as much a tribute to the power and influence of his native State as to his own military prowess. Any American who might have been named would have been deficient in formal training as compared with British generals. Or, at least, any American with the possible exception of Major General Charles Lee. This eccentric newcomer to Virginia talked much about his experience on the battlefields of Europe, and there were many—in Congress and in the army itself—who shared his conviction that he was better suited to command than Washington.

But, in the hard months and years that followed, Washington revealed strengths of which he himself had been unaware. He had always been courageous, practical and persevering, and had nearly always been just. But his concept of honor, like that of many another proud planter, had been compounded almost equally of nobility and egotism. Now, for the first time, Washington was engaged in a cause for which his zeal burned so fiercely that it seemed to consume every element of personal vanity. All that was superfluous seemed to have been burned away, leaving him the clean, hard instrument of America's national aspirations.

Two weeks after the Battle of Bunker Hill, Washington arrived in Cambridge and took command of an army of 14,500. He must try to regain Boston from a growing army of unknown strength commanded by General Gage and three distinguished major generals, Howe, Clinton and Burgoyne. Washington was handicapped not only by the many shortages that plagued the Continental forces, but also by the fact that his duties and responsibilities were not clearly defined. Worse still, the area of his responsibility seemed to embrace all operations, while the area of his authority did not. In some situations where the opposing generals could command, he could only hope to persuade.

Washington's hardest battles were to keep up the morale of the troops, instill in them a modicum of discipline and obtain for them the barest minimum in supplies. To win unaided seemed impossible. The struggle was to keep going until help arrived from overseas— help that was far from certain. But Washington and his lieutenants won that battle. In February, with the aid of artillery brought from Fort Ticonderoga by General Henry Knox, Washington's army took Dorchester Heights, bringing Boston and most of its harbor under the Continental Army's guns. On March 7, the British began to evacuate the city. Ten days later the last of the troops, and about a thousand Loyalists, were aboard the ships of the Royal Navy. The fleet sailed March 26, and all New England heaved a sigh of relief.

Washington's contributions to the freeing of Boston had not been of the flamboyant sort that excites the Gallic imagination. But his success was a moral triumph with practical results—just the sort of thing to win the admiration of New Englanders. Massachusetts legislators were stirred to express their gratitude in terms not lightly used by Puritans. In a formal address, they declared:

". . . May future generations, in the peaceful enjoyment of that freedom, the exercise of which your sword shall have established, raise the richest and most lasting monuments to the name of Washington."

Here, indeed, was evidence of accomplishment by a man who, after fifteen years out of uniform, had been assigned one of the most difficult commands ever held by any human being. The tribute of the Massachusetts legislators speaks volumes of what Washington had learned about dealing with civil authority since the days when he had fired missives like missiles at Governor Dinwiddie, for many of the Massachusetts leaders had resented the appointment of a Virginian to command New England troops and had not bothered to conceal their feelings. The earning of the tribute also testified to the marvelous self-discipline of this man who was transforming mobs into regiments. His white-hot temper had been famous in some of his youthful haunts. Now many who met him for the first time were struck by his apparent impassivity and reflected upon the good fortune that a man exposed to such emotional stress was of a phlegmatic temperament.

Washington had little time for introspection. In the same month that the British evacuated Boston, General Henry Clinton and a British invasion force arrived off Cape Fear, North Carolina. Revising his plans because of a Loyalist defeat near Wilmington, he awaited the arrival of Cornwallis and additional troops in May. The two generals collaborated in an attack on Charleston, South Carolina, which was repulsed. General Charles Lee had commanded the successful defense, which discouraged British operations in that theater for more than two years, and his reputation soared.

Washington knew that this success, while important, had done little to relieve the general threat to the colonies. He also knew that his own army was not strong enough to take the offensive in any theater, or even to risk a general engagement with the enemy. Despite the goads and taunts of military-minded politicians and ambitious subordinates, he adhered, until May 1778, to a policy of skirmishing with the enemy at every opportunity while avoiding a general engagement.

Following the British evacuation of Boston, he correctly guessed that General Howe, who had succeeded Gage as commander of the British armies in America, would make New York City his base of operations. Washington quickly shifted his army from Boston. He could not prevent Howe's landing on Staten Island with 10,000 men.

He saw the odds were hopeless in July when the general's brother, Admiral Lord Richard Howe, arrived with a naval fleet and 150 transports. He helplessly watched the reinforcement of General Howe's command in July and August until it included about 32,000 men. Late in August, Howe landed about 20,000 men on Long Island, inflicted heavy casualties on a much smaller American force and captured two major generals, Israel Putnam and William Alexander. Under cover of darkness, and with great skill, Washington saved Putnam's troops by withdrawing them to Manhattan Island. Howe succeeded in occupying New York City, but Washington kept him uncomfortable.

Despite severe reverses, colonial morale was rising. Adoption of the Declaration of Independence, written by Virginia's Jefferson, had inspired a new consciousness of united resolve. More practical assurance came in the form of French promises of material aid, including munitions.

Then the picture abruptly changed. From November 18 to December 20, General Washington and General Nathanael Greene were forced to retreat across New Jersey before the superior forces of Lord Cornwallis. At Washington's command, General Charles Lee crossed the Hudson into New Jersey, where he was captured. By that time, Washington had crossed the Delaware into Pennsylvania. Congress had fled Philadelphia for Baltimore, abdicating its powers to Washington. American morale plummeted.

The year was dying, and the icy grip of winter was on the land. Howe had withdrawn the bulk of his army to winter quarters in New York, leaving garrisons at Trenton, Princeton, Bordentown, Perth Amboy and New Brunswick.

Washington celebrated Christmas in the traditional Southern way—with fireworks. On the night of December 25, he ferried 2,400 men across the Delaware River in long, flat boats, together with eighteen field cannon. The river was high, the wind was rising and the swift current bore chunks of ice that grated against the wooden craft like devouring jaws. Landing nine miles from Trenton, Washington split his forces, directing one division to move on the town by the lower road while he led the other by the upper. Through wind-driven snow, they marched over sleet-glazed roads until at eight o'clock in the morning they entered the town, surprised the sleeping Hessian garrison, and took the place with only five casualties.

After carrying 918 prisoners into Pennsylvania, Washington re-entered New Jersey and reoccupied Trenton.

On January 1, Howe sent General James Grant from New Brunswick to the Trenton area. Howe directed Cornwallis to leave New York for New Jersey and effect a junction at Princeton with Grant.

On January 2, Cornwallis' troops slogged through mud and unseasonably warm rain east of Trenton, and his advance made contact with American vedettes and forced them to retreat. Cornwallis deferred his attack until the next day, preferring to "bag the fox" at leisure.

His optimism seemed justified. The British greatly outnumbered Washington's army of 5,200 men, many of whom were held in service by the most tenuous of bonds following the recent expiration of their enlistment.

Once again, as in the move against Trenton, Washington demonstrated the imagination in which he had hitherto been thought deficient.

Leaving enough men in his camp to create by various devices the illusion that it was still occupied in force, Washington quietly led his army around Cornwallis' flank and was near Princeton by dawn. If Cornwallis had set out to bag a fox, Washington was proving himself one.

The first clash came when units led by Virginia's gallant Hugh Mercer, Washington's old comrade in arms, met a British column under Colonel Mawhood marching to join Cornwallis.

General Mercer's horse was shot from under him, but he sought to lead his men on foot. A blow from a rifle butt felled him, but he was back on his feet, trying to rally his men, when seven bayonet thrusts brought him down for the last time. A captain was killed before he could halt the rout of his men, and Colonel Daniel Neil, of New Jersey, was shot through the head while trying to rally them. Colonel Cadwallader, of Pennsylvania, boldly led his men within fifty yards of the British lines. But eventually his troops broke and ran to the woods for cover.

Suddenly a giant in blue appeared on a great white charger. It was Washington, always majestic on horseback. Waving his tricornered hat to Mercer's and Cadwallader's fleeing troops, and shouting cries of encouragement, he rode toward the enemy's guns. A volley rang out and Washington was hidden by the gunsmoke. Seasoned veterans hid their eyes. But, when they dared to look, the tall Virginian was still astride the great white horse. To some of the British, the sight was like an apparition.

Once again, Washington urged his men forward. They seemed too stunned and nerveless to obey. But there were other troops to follow the command. General Sullivan's forces had been close on Washington's heels, and units from Pennsylvania, Rhode Island and Virginia detached themselves from the division and dashed forward. Then troops from Mercer's and Cadwallader's commands rallied.

Led by the Virginians, the American units reformed and charged the British, who retreated. The Continentals poured a murderous fire at such close range that they could hear their victims' screams. Mawhood, though nearly surrounded, ordered another charge, then began an orderly retreat. But he was pursued by Washington with a troop of Philadelphia light horse, followed by infantry. This retreat, like the American one fifteen minutes before, became a rout.

On January 6, the Americans captured Hackensack and Elizabeth-Town. Washington had driven the enemy from most of New Jersey. He had accomplished this feat with a force half the size of the enemy's. He had executed swift marches with shoeless and illfed troops and, with his limited formal training in military science, he had bested not only the phlegmatic Howe, but also the vigorous and capable Cornwallis.

American morale soared. The sight of Hessian prisoners, marched into Pennsylvania and Virginia for safekeeping, was heartening. But, above all, the people had been hungry for a hero, and they had found one in Washington. The whole nation claimed Virginia's son. The story of his sudden appearance on a white charger, and his quick turning of defeat into victory, had elements of the supernatural. The tale of his personal solicitude for a wounded enemy soldier after the battle of Princeton appealed to a sense of chivalry not restricted to aristocrats. His courage made hearts beat faster in every State. His military skill, heretofore deemed less than adequate, was now hailed as genius. And the Middle Colonies joined in the chorus of praise as heartily as New England and the South. Of Washington, the *Pennsylvania Journal* said: "Had he lived in the days of idolatry, he had been worshipped as a god. One age cannot do justice to his merit, but the united voices of a grateful posterity shall pay a cheerful tribute of undissembled praise to the great asserter of their country's freedom."[67]

Washington was already "first in the hearts of his countrymen." When news of his campaign reached Europe, he became the first Virginian, and the first American, to be an international hero. As the British historian Trevelyan has written, "From Trenton onwards,

Washington was recognized as a far sighted and able general all Europe over—by the great military nobles in the Empress Catherine's court, by the French marshals and ministers, in the King's cabinet at Potsdam, at Madrid, at Vienna and in London."[68]

Washington knew that the rest of the way would not be an uninterrupted march of triumph. He may not have suspected that his greatest trials and bitterest disappointments lay ahead.

To a superficial observer, the prospect might seem promising. In March, Congress returned to Philadelphia, the city that it had fled less than three months before. Benjamin Franklin was in Paris as United States commissioner. Soon Virginia's Arthur Lee was appointed commissioner to Spain and his brother William was named diplomatic representative to Vienna and Berlin. The infant republic commanded the attention of powerful princes and their ministers. By March, Congress was receiving from foreigners so many applications for military commissions that it could afford to be very selective.

But Britain was planning to batter the States into submission by a series of quick blows. General John Burgoyne was the strategist for a three-pronged attack to cut off New England. One force would move down from Canada, another through the Mohawk Valley. The third army would be Howe's. Lord George Germain, Britain's Secretary of State for the Colonies, thought that Howe could execute his part of the scheme after taking Philadelphia.

Howe's campaign was not so quickly concluded. It began on July 23, and the city was not his till September 26. On October 3, Washington sought to recoup American losses by a Trenton on a grander scale. That night, he set in motion an elaborate pincer movement involving complex problems of timing. Before dawn, the American troops attacked the British army in the area of Germantown and won quick successes. But a dense fog rolled in and Americans mistakenly fired on Americans. The timing went wrong, and victory was turned into defeat. A long but orderly retreat followed.

Washington was disposed to regard the day's events as "rather unfortunate than injurious."[69] He did not know that the government of France would be so impressed with the Continental Army's near achievement of victory and with Washington and Nathanael Greene's skillful management of the retreat that they would think seriously of forming an alliance with the United States.[70]

On November 20, the American garrison at Fort Mercer, on the Delaware below Philadelphia, was compelled to evacuate by a vastly larger force led by Cornwallis. British ships could now sail up the river to Philadelphia without encountering serious opposition. Washington's army, which had withdrawn from Germantown, went into winter quarters at Valley Forge.

The military phrase "went into quarters" is here a euphemism. The word "went" makes the move sound deceptively easy. It required marching only from Whitemarsh to Valley Forge, thirteen miles away, but the effort took seven days—three in which the barefoot men were unable to march and four in which they plodded on through ice and snow until they could no longer tell whether their feet were freezing or burning, or even be sure that they were still appended to their aching legs. Washington said, "You might have tracked the army from Whitemarsh to Valley Forge by the blood of their feet." The word "quarters" is euphemistic too. There were no quarters for most of the men when they arrived. Thousands lacked even the comfort of a blanket.

Washington put the men to building log huts and initiated a contest to speed the work. But the logs were still standing timber and the men were weak, so that even Christmas Day found some of them still unhoused. Shirts were mere fringes of string, and in many cases breeches were little more than breechclouts. The itch came nearer than anything else to covering frostbitten skins.[71] Fire-cake—flour and water paste baked—was the staple article of diet—fire-cake for breakfast, fire-cake for dinner, fire-cake for supper, day after day. Occasionally the diet was varied by the introduction of spoiled salt herring. And all the while Washington and his officers knew that shoes and clothing, because of misdirection and want of transportation, were lying along roads and in many a wooded place.

Because of one man, the army did not mutiny. Washington remained patient and steadfast through the whole ordeal. And he was not supported by admiring and encouraging civil authorities. In fact, Congress, frightened by the turn of events, was disposed to blame Washington. It appointed his adjutant, Horatio Gates, president of the Board of War, evidencing greater confidence in him than in the commander in chief. Soon Washington had reason to believe that there was disloyalty among his own officers and a plot to depose him.

But nothing swayed him from the course of duty. And his example inspired worthy emulation. Nathanael Greene became an emergency quartermaster, the director of foraging operations in which Mad Anthony Wayne, Allen McLane and Virginia's Henry (Light

Horse Harry) Lee excelled. There were many desertions every day, but there was no mutiny, not even as winter deepened into January. In February, Baron von Steuben arrived from Germany with tales of his military exploits as a general under Frederick the Great. This stout, profane German had never attained a higher rank than captain, but he soon made in America as good a record as he had claimed for himself on arriving from Europe. Washington asked him to train the troops, and he trained them magnificently.

When the long winter was over, Washington's army was smaller, but stronger, than when it first went into quarters at Valley Forge. Credit for his achievement must go in part to Greene and Von Steuben, but even more to Washington. Through force of character united with good sense, the Virginian had achieved one of the greatest feats in military history.

Good news for the Continental cause had been made elsewhere. In the summer and fall of 1777, British General Burgoyne and Colonel St. Leger had waged a major campaign in the North. The American forces were commanded by General Philip Schuyler, who on August 4 was replaced by Gates. The British had enjoyed considerable success in New England until Burgoyne, pressed by a grave supply problem, detached about 700 of his men to capture American supplies at Bennington. The British were repulsed by American forces outnumbering them more than three to one. But the real reverse for Burgoyne came September 19 when, having crossed to the west side of the Hudson for a push on Albany, he was opposed by Colonel Daniel Morgan at Freeman's Farm. This large-framed, ruggedly handsome officer, who often wore a fringed hunting shirt and signaled his men with a turkey call, personally commanded the Virginia riflemen whose deadly aim had excited such terror among the British and admiration among the New Englanders. A roisterer and brawler until his marriage, he had become a substantial citizen under his wife's good influence and had been elected to the Virginia House of Burgesses. Though his energies had been rechanneled, his boisterous spirits had not been tamed, and they now found an outlet in fighting the British.[72] Morgan's forces, aided by Colonel Henry Dearborn, checked Burgoyne's advance and inflicted two British casualties for every one sustained by the Americans.

On October 7, General Gates, who incidentally was a Virginian who had emigrated from England only five years before after resigning from the British army, correctly saw that he had an opportunity to do great damage to a large reconnoitering force under

Burgoyne. Though an excellent organizer who rendered real service to the Continental cause, Gates was not a man of dashing action and desperate stratagems. It was fortunate, therefore, that he selected another Virginian, Colonel Morgan, to begin the action that became known as the Battle of Bemis Heights. Morgan skillfully maneuvered his men into attack position and then they "poured down like a torrent" on the flank and rear of the British right. Benedict Arnold, who was at this time without a command, spurred his horse forward into battle, leading the army in a fierce assault. That night the British withdrew. On October 17, Burgoyne's men laid down their arms.

International repercussions were quick. News of Burgoyne's surrender reached London early in December, and Lord North almost immediately began preparing a new offer of reconciliation. Afraid that America might accept the British offer, officers of the French government told the American commissioners in Paris that the King's Council had determined to recognize the independence of the United States. On January 8, France announced her willingness to enter into an alliance with America. In February, a treaty of amity and commerce, and a treaty of alliance (to become effective on the outbreak of war between France and Britain), were agreed upon by French and American negotiators.

Toward the end of 1777, the thirteen States had also moved a step nearer unity. When Richard Henry Lee, as spokesman for the Virginia delegation, had introduced in the Congress on June 7, 1776 a resolution for independence, he had coupled it with the proposal that "a plan of confederation be prepared and transmitted to the respective colonies for their consideration and approbation." A committee had been appointed and, under the able leadership of Pennsylvania's John Dickinson, had presented for action by Congress "Articles of Confederation and Perpetual Union." On November 15, 1777, after much argument, they were formally adopted, and two days later were dispatched to each State for ratification.

Thus, in the spring of 1778, the American States found themselves stronger in military readiness, in foreign support and in promise of unity than they had been a year before.

They were still weak economically and in naval strength.

But, in this spring of 1778, they found a naval hero. He was John Paul Jones.[73] A studious-looking little Scot, he had been known as John Paul when he fled Britain to escape the possible results of hostile testimony about his actions in a mutiny, one of two major

incidents that had plagued his short career as a captain. He had
made his home in Fredericksburg, Virginia, where his brother was
already settled, and had assumed the patronym of Jones. He was
confident that he had the ability to achieve distinction as a naval
officer, but this confidence apparently was not shared by the Congress, which did, however, commission him a lieutenant in the newly
organized Continental Navy in December 1775. In April 1778, now
Captain Jones, he sailed the *Ranger* into the Irish Sea, took two
prizes, and with supreme audacity landed at Whitehaven, England,
and spiked the guns of the fort. He set fire to a ship at anchor in
the harbor, landed that night on St. Mary's Island in Solway Firth,
sailed to the coast of Northern Ireland, captured the British sloop
Drake after an hour's battle, and early in May sailed with his prize
into the haven of Brest.

The next month, there were rumors that France would give more
than passive help to the Continental Navy. General Clinton, who
had succeeded to Howe's command of British forces based at Philadelphia, evacuated the city June 18 on hearing that a French fleet
was sailing toward America. He headed across New Jersey toward
New York City. Washington, glad to quit Valley Forge, broke camp
and pursued him. The American general gave command of a division
of three brigades to Charles Lee, who had been released from captivity by exchange, and ordered him to press home an attack on
Clinton's columns at the first opportunity. Lee, who was opposed to
Washington's plan, engaged the enemy near Monmouth, but failed
to follow up advantages gained and gave confused orders to two
subordinates, Wayne and the Marquis de Lafayette. When British
reinforcements arrived, Lee ordered a retreat.

When word of the retreat reached Washington, who had been
marching to Lee's support, he was so convinced of the impossibility
of such a thing that he had one informant arrested for spreading
false alarms. But, as his own eyes began to reveal the truth of the
report, Washington's temper blazed. When he came upon Lee, he
paused only long enough to demand an explanation and administer
a tongue lashing. Then, as before at Princeton, he suddenly burst
into view of the men. And, as before, he was mounted upon a great
white charger. As Lafayette reported, "His presence stopped the
retreat." All along the lines he rode, animated by indignation, shouting commands in a voice vibrating with wrath. The men stopped in
their tracks and broke into cheers. "I thought then, as now," Lafayette wrote, "that never had I beheld so superb a man."

Clinton attacked again and again, but the Continentals beat him back every time. That night the British withdrew and marched to Sandy Hook, where they boarded transports for New York.

The skillful British withdrawal was itself a triumph of sorts. But the fact remained that Clinton's army had suffered losses three to five times greater than those inflicted on the Americans.

The American army had for the first time held its own, and indeed it had more than held its own, in a full-scale engagement with the enemy. Washington had won his greatest personal success as a field commander. General Charles Lee, smarting under Washington's rebuke, demanded and got a court martial, but the result was evidently different from what he had anticipated. Found guilty of disobedience, misbehavior and disrespect to the commander in chief, he was suspended "from any command in the armies of the United States. . . ."

Lee's suspension came on July 4. Another Virginian, this one a native son, celebrated the second anniversary of the Declaration of Independence in an entirely different way. And, in so doing, he provided one of the high points of a Virginia expedition that became an epic of the Revolution. He himself became the greatest hero of the war for the West.

This man was George Rogers Clark.[74] Tall and strong, an impressive example of the American frontiersman, he had been born only twenty-six years before in Albemarle County and had been reared in Caroline County. Now he was Virginia's military commander in that part of her territory known as Kentucky. Though he despised academic routine, he had known greater cultural advantages than most of his fellows in deerskin and he was the equal of any of them in shrewdness and courage.

These qualities were important to survival and essential to leadership on Virginia's western frontier. The British post at Detroit was a center for the distribution of dangerous items—weapons, ammunition, liquor and propaganda—to dangerous customers—Indians of the Shawnee, Delaware, Miami and Ottawa tribes. The Ohio Valley was a vast battleground and the frontiers of Pennsylvania and Virginia were fields of slaughter. In the Kentucky part of Virginia, both Shawnees and Cherokees were perpetually on the warpath.

Twice the Continental Congress had sent expeditions into the Northwest Territory to strike at Detroit, but both attempts had been abandoned by force of necessity. Now Clark conceived a plan to conquer the Illinois country—the entire region east of the Mississippi, north of the Ohio, south of the Illinois, and west of the Wabash and the Miami. He reasoned that most of the white settlers, being of French origin, would not be inveterate enemies of the Americans and might even become allies. The key to his plans was the important settlement of Kaskaskia, which was the center of the region's French population. As early as the spring of 1777, he had sent spies into the town. His hopes confirmed by their reports, he had appealed to Governor Patrick Henry to authorize a Virginia expedition against the settlement.

Clark found eloquent advocates in Thomas Jefferson, George Mason, George Wythe and possibly Richard Henry Lee. They not only won Governor Henry's support, but with his aid persuaded the Virginia General Assembly to authorize the expedition—without most of the law-makers being permitted to share the secret of its destination. Clark was publicly instructed to raise seven companies of troops for the defense of Kentucky. He was privately ordered to effect that defense by attacking Kaskaskia.

On June 26, Clark and about one hundred seventy-five men left the falls of the Ohio in a flotilla of flatboats. At a point about ten miles below the mouth of the Tennessee River,[75] they landed, hid their boats, and began the overland march to Kaskaskia. One hundred twenty miles of varied landscape—rolling waves of prairie and dark labyrinths of forest—lay between them and their goal. Their stores of food upon their backs, they plodded on. They could take no comfort in the lessening of their burdens by the daily diminution of their supplies. At length, there was nothing to eat, but Clark still led them on. Late on the afternoon of July 4, they reached the Kaskaskia River, only three miles from the town. It seemed folly to press on for the attack when the men had not eaten for two days. But Clark thought that victory was in his grasp, and his enthusiasm was contagious.

About dusk, Clark and his men—moving shadows in the warm twilight—crept along the river bank until they stood like silent ghosts at a point across the water from Kaskaskia and about a mile above the town. A farmhouse was nearby, and there they learned that the Chevalier de Rocheblave, a French officer in the British service and the commander at Kaskaskia, had heard of the Virginia expedition and had called the militia to arms. Next they learned the good news that Rocheblave's spies had failed to confirm the presence of Clark's men in the area, and that the militia had been disbanded.

In high spirits, the Americans rounded up enough boats for a quick crossing of the river. The Virginian ordered one division of his troops to surround the town and took command of the other himself. So completely was the garrison surprised that Clark was able to lead his column through an open gate to the fort and march directly to Rocheblave's house. The astonished Frenchman promptly surrendered. Without the firing of a shot and within fifteen minutes after arriving on the scene, Clark was master of the fort in the name of the Commonwealth of Virginia.

The towns of Prairie du Rocher and Cahokia were also quick to submit.

Clark's magnanimity and gentlemanly treatment of the conquered, together with his assurances of religious freedom, quickly won over the French to such an extent that they proffered him their services. One of these volunteers, Father Pierre Gibault of Kaskaskia, became Clark's emissary in negotiations for the surrender of Vincennes. There were no British regulars in that town with its important stronghold, and Gibault and others from Kaskaskia spoke persuasively to the Frenchmen of Vincennes about Clark's ability and chivalry. Clark could be patient as well as swift. Early in August, conquered by diplomacy, Vincennes was his.

He had need of all the diplomacy he could summon. Though he commanded every French town in the Illinois region, his small force might very well be at the mercy of the great Indian tribes. In August and September, he held conferences at Cahokia with the Chippewas, Miamis, Foxes and other tribes whose very names were fearful even to brave men. Thousands of chiefs and warriors came to know the tall Virginian. They saw him gesture with a majesty which their great chiefs might envy. They heard eagerly the words of flattery which he spoke so eloquently, and they listened respectfully to the threats which he voiced solemnly, with dignity and restraint. They decided to make no trouble for this great white chief, at least for many months.

Meanwhile, Lieutenant Colonel Henry Hamilton, British agent at Detroit, was plotting a counteroffensive. On October 7, with one hundred seventy-five soldiers and sixty Indian warriors, he set out for Vincennes. By December 17, when he arrived at the town, his force had grown to five hundred or more. The officer left in charge by Clark could command the allegiance of the one American under him, but the French militia refused to fight. The post surrendered, and the French were once again "loyal" subjects of King George.

Panic seized the French at Kaskaskia and Cahokia. At this point,

Clark performed the amazing feat of whipping up their enthusiasm for a new offensive against Vincennes. On February 5, 1779, he sent an armed vessel up the Ohio and the Wabash to cut off a possible retreat by the British to the Mississippi. The next day he set out for Vincennes with one hundred twenty-seven men.

Hamilton must have felt secure from any attack such as Clark planned. A midwinter march across nearly two hundred miles of mud was a formidable task. The fact that nearly half of Clark's men were Frenchmen of uncertain allegiance made the attempt seem downright foolhardy.

But the Virginian was optimistic, and he kept up the spirits of his men. The weather was mild and there was singing around the campfires at night. After long days of slogging through the mud, the men still had energy enough to dance, and the Frenchmen probably enjoyed teaching some of the fine points of the art to American frontiersmen whose motions were as wild and uninhibited as the leaping flames.

On February 13, they reached the Little Wabash River, spent two days in ferrying across it, and encamped on high ground. They soon learned that, though less than twenty miles from their goal, they were in deadly peril. Flood waters had driven off the game and food supplies were dwindling. On the seventeenth, they reached the Embarrass River and found it too high to ford. With night lowering over its dark waters, a cold drizzle falling, and the chill cutting bone-deep, they sank down on the wet ground and tried to chase hunger with sleep.

In the morning, they heard the gun of the fort at Vincennes. It was only nine miles away, but it must have seemed no more accessible than the regions from which Heaven's thunder sounds. Not until the night of the twentieth were they able to ferry across the Wabash, to which they had wearily plodded after being frustrated by the Embarrass. Arrived on the other side, they were told that they could not possibly make their way across the flooded ground that lay between them and Vincennes.

The water was at times shoulder high, but Clark and his men managed to march three miles the next day. The next, some were too weak and hungry to move a step. Clark had them ride in the few canoes available, and his force moved on, almost treading water at times. On the morning of the twenty-third, his half-starved, half-frozen army lay on the ground like casualties after a battle. But the Virginian appealed to them to make one more determined push, then strode into the icy waters that soon were chest-deep, and called to the soldiers to follow. Forward they went. Such was Clark's inspiriting example—and such was the force of his order to Captain Bowman to shoot any man who refused to march. As before, the weakest were carried in canoes. But soon the canoes were filled, and other men were stumbling and staggering, clinging to trees and logs to keep their heads above water until hardier marchers could help them along.

At last, they emerged upon higher ground and found themselves only two miles from Vincennes.

Soon the men were thawing out around campfires and drinking the hot broth made from some buffalo meat "requisitioned" from a squaw. A captured Frenchman assured Clark that the expedition remained undetected. Of course, he also told him that two hundred Indians had joined Hamilton's British forces. But the Americans really had only one major thing to worry about—the fact that they had exhausted almost all their ammunition.

Clark decided without hesitation that the proper action in such circumstances was to push forward. Knowing that his army was much weaker than the well-fortified enemy, he counted on audacity and cunning. By the captured Frenchman, he sent word into town that he would take the fort that night, but had no desire to harm the townspeople. Those who wished to ally themselves with the United States should remain in their homes, and those who wished to stand with the British should repair to the fort. The excited citizens concluded that only the commander of a very strong army would dare so to forewarn his foes. At sunset, when the half-light made one buckskinned soldier look very much like another, Clark split his forces in two and marched the divisions to and fro in such a way that the townsmen were convinced he had an almost endless column of troops. The citizens did not join the British. Neither did the Indians. In fact, one chief was so impressed that he offered one hundred braves to Clark, and was even more impressed when the Virginian spurned the offer.

As Clark's men entered the town, they received gifts of ammunition from the citizens. Their drums beating, the Americans marched up the main street to the cheers of the inhabitants and then fired on the fort. Hamilton doubtless felt secure behind the eleven-foot walls with their twenty-three foot bastions. True, his force was reduced to fewer than a hundred, but he had twelve artillery pieces, plenty of ammunition and sufficient stores of food. He must have been surprised when the Americans threw up an intrenchment two hundred yards from the main gate. He was astounded when they suddenly sprang from cover only about thirty yards away and, with the cannon balls flying harmlessly over their heads, poured a deadly fire into the gunports. Soon after the break of day, the guns of Fort Sackville were silent. The only American casualty was one wounded man. About nine o'clock, Clark sent Hamilton a demand for surrender and received a proud refusal. Shooting resumed on both sides, but Clark's long rifles proved more effective than the British cannon. About eleven o'clock, Hamilton requested a truce for surrender negotiations.

Clark demanded unconditional surrender and Hamilton insisted on moderation of the terms. By bluffing tactics akin to those he had used before the battle, the Virginian triumphed in diplomacy. The following morning, the British surrendered and gave up their arms. Clark sent Hamilton to Virginia as a prisoner. Virginia now had complete control of the Illinois country, and the British were uneasy in Detroit.

In the South, things had not gone so well for the Americans. On December 29, 1778, Savannah had fallen to the British. It was now apparent that Clinton was shifting the center of British operations, and the South promised to be the major battleground in 1779. Full-scale war in the South would inevitably mean invasion of Virginia.

On January 29, Augusta, Georgia was taken by the British. Two defensive victories in South Carolina saved the Continentals from despair, but in March an American attempt to retake Augusta proved a costly failure. Washington sent General Benjamin Lincoln to Georgia with a detachment of Continental troops, but they were unable to regain Augusta or prevent further gains by the British. The only Southern successes of American arms in the spring were the isolated, but important, forays by Virginia and North Carolina troops against the Chickamauga Indians in Tennessee.

In May, General Clinton sent an expedition under the command of Admiral Sir George Collier from New York to Virginia.[76] On May 9, the fleet anchored in Hampton Roads, and the following day a landing force under General Matthews attacked the exposed rear of Fort Nelson, on the Elizabeth River. The garrison retreated and the British occupied Portsmouth without opposition. A raiding party dispatched from Portsmouth captured Suffolk, Virginia's chief depot of military supplies, and destroyed great quantities of naval stores and food. There was a great deal of sacking, burning and plundering. Governor Jefferson called out the militia, and two thousand recruits destined for the Continental Army were held back for Virginia's defense. But Collier abandoned Portsmouth and returned to New York, and Virginia's recruits were forwarded to South Carolina.

Momentarily, the center of interest shifted to the Middle States. On June 1, Clinton seized an uncompleted American fort at Stony Point. On that "defiant promontory," whose rocky face rose one hundred fifty feet above the Hudson, he erected two series of works and garrisoned the point with six hundred men under the command of Colonel Henry Johnson.

At first, Washington despaired of retaking Stony Point, saying, "All we can do is to lament what we cannot remedy."

Later he took hope and asked General Anthony Wayne to scout the defenses. Allen McLane, the "most active officer" in "Light Horse Harry" Lee's corps, was sent inside the fort as a spy and returned with valuable information. Then the approaches to the fort were carefully studied by Colonel Rufus Putnam, and by three Virginians—Lee, Major Thomas Posey and Washington himself.

On the basis of this reconnaissance, an attack was carefully planned. Specially assigned to Wayne's command for this expedition were four picked regiments, selected for courage and general military proficiency. Virginians, together with Pennsylvanians, had the honor of composing the First Regiment, which was commanded by Virginia's Lieutenant Colonel Christian Febiger. One of the two battalion commanders was Virginia's Major Thomas Posey, the other being the distinguished Frenchman Lieutenant Colonel François Louis de Fleury. One of the two captains of artillery for the expedition was Virginia's Captain James Pendleton, nephew of Edmund Pendleton. But the real, animating force of the expedition was the handsome, bold-featured man whose dark eyes burned with a passion that some called madness—Anthony Wayne. This Pennsylvanian, who insisted that his men be "fresh-shaved and well-powdered" on the day of battle, led them to victory over the British garrison at Stony Point on the night of July 15. It was one of the most dashing and daring triumphs, and also one of the best planned, of the Revolution. All America could be proud of Anthony Wayne, and Virginia could be proud of the vital role that her sons had played in the crowning accomplishment of his career.

A companion victory was won by Virginia's "Light Horse Harry" Lee in August. Across two miles of swampland, and at times through chest-deep water, he led an attack on the British garrison at Paulus Hook, a sandy point projecting into the Hudson opposite New York City. As notable as the victory itself was the way in which he led his troops safely back to the American lines after they had marched thirty miles "through mountains, swamps and deep morasses, without the least refreshment," and fought an historic battle, only to find that the boats intended for their escape were not available.

The twin victories of Stony Point and Paulus Hook disrupted the enemy's plans, but their chief value was the boost that they gave to American morale. The battle of Paulus Hook drove the British from their last major outpost in New Jersey and was the last active military operation in the North in 1779.[77]

Next came victory at sea. On September 23, John Paul Jones, commanding the *Bonhomme Richard*, sighted a fleet of thirty-nine merchant ships off the East coast of England. Convoying them were the British ships *Serapis* and *Countess of Scarborough*. Jones engaged the *Serapis* at close range and fought with skill and tenacity. But the contest seemed unequal and finally, when the *Bonhomme Richard* was aflame and sinking, the British captain demanded that the American surrender. It was then that Jones hurled back the reply "I have not yet begun to fight." The *Richard* sank, but Jones captured the *Serapis* in one of the greatest sea fights in world history. Virginia's adopted son, fighting against his native Britain, became one of the greatest naval heroes of all time.

But victories at Stony Point and Paulus Hook, and on the high seas, could not disguise the fact that America was losing the war in the South. In September and October, a French fleet under Admiral d'Estaing and American troops under General Lincoln sought to wrest Savannah from the British but failed and suffered heavy casualties. D'Estaing's fleet withdrew October 28, and the initiative passed to the British, who promised to make good use of it. Clinton evacuated Rhode Island to concentrate on the South, and the day after Christmas he sailed south from New York with about eight thousand men.

Clinton planned to invade South Carolina and move through North Carolina into Virginia. The conquest of Charleston was essential to the success of his scheme.

Arriving off the Carolina coast February 1, Clinton proceeded with a leisurely campaign against Charleston which brought the surrender of the city April 12. Suffering only 255 casualties, Clinton had captured, besides the vital seaport, a garrison of 5,400 men and four American ships. He had inflicted on the Americans their heaviest defeat of the war, and one which had damaging results far beyond the immediate military effects. North Carolinians remembered that their State, like Virginia, had seen the departure of all its Continentals in 1777 to reinforce Washington's army in the North. They could not understand why similar help could not be sent to the Carolinas when Charleston was threatened. Tories came forth from hiding, brandishing their swords. Regiments were formed to fight for the King, and a small civil war raged in the Carolinas. A Virginia regiment, fighting bravely against regulars and Tories under the command of Colonel Banastre Tarleton, was destroyed at Waxhaw Creek.

Early in June, Clinton, well-satisfied with the subjection of South Carolina, sailed for New York, leaving Cornwallis to direct operations in the South.

If the Carolinians could have known what Washington was enduring in May 1780, they would not have been critical of his failure to send reinforcements to the South. Encamped at Morristown, New Jersey, he had reason to fear that he might not be able to retain enough men to defend the place. He had just emerged from a winter that was a grim twin to Valley Forge. But spring had not brought the relief that had come to the Pennsylvania camp. Continental currency had plummeted, and only the most ardent patriots would sell supplies to the Continental Army. Rations were steadily reduced until at last they were one-eighth the normal allotment.

On May 25, Washington, much in the spirit of a man writing an obituary, penned a report to the committee of the Congress. ". . . The country exhausted; the people dispirited; the consequence and reputation of these States in Europe sunk; our enemies deriving new credit, new confidence, new resources"[78]—these were the words he wrote. As dusk settled on his miserable camp, a roll of drums came from the Connecticut Line. Then Washington learned that the fourth and eighth regiments were in armed mutiny. At such a time, and in such conditions, the whole army—regiment by regiment— might march away. The sufferings and privations endured at Valley Forge and Morristown, the fruits of daring at Trenton and Princeton, would count for nothing. The American cause would be lost.

The mutinous regiments were marching to the Connecticut Third and Sixth to solicit their support. But some of Washington's officers ran ahead and reached these two regiments first. Orders were given

for the men to parade immediately without arms. Thus the mutineers found no armed allies there.

But there was violence. One officer was stabbed with a bayonet,
and the mutineers were deaf to pleas that they lay down their arms.
The Pennsylvania Line was ordered to surround the Connecticut
men. No one knew whether the Pennsylvanians would obey orders
or join the mutiny. They obeyed, and a crisis that had international
implications passed.

Meanwhile, the British had very much their own way in South
Carolina and Georgia, hindered only by the skillful guerilla activity
of Andrew Pickens, Thomas Sumter and Francis Marion, "the
Swamp Fox."

On July 25, organized Continental opposition returned to the
South when Gates assumed command of a Southern Army, including
a nucleus of Continental troops, at Coxe's Mill, North Carolina. The
Virginian marched in easy stages toward Camden, South Carolina,
a British supply base. On August 16, the Americans met Cornwallis'
force just north of the town.[79] Raw troops from Virginia and North
Carolina broke in confusion before the enemy's fierce onslaughts.
Baron De Kalb, his head split by a saber stroke and his blood flowing
from nearly a dozen wounds, rallied his Maryland and Delaware
brigade again and again until at last he fell. Over and over, British
bayonets drove home. Over and over, the butts of British muskets
crashed down on American skulls. Tarleton's cavalry swept down
on the American remnants and the battle was over. Gates withdrew
to Hillsboro, North Carolina, one hundred sixty miles from Camden.

Two days after the Battle of Camden, Tarleton defeated another
American force—this one led by Sumter—at Fishing Creek, South
Carolina. With the way thus prepared for him, Cornwallis invaded
North Carolina September 8.

Conquest of Carolina would open the road to victory in Virginia.
Once Virginia was gained, all the colonies south of Pennsylvania
"would fall without much resistance and be retained without much
difficulty."

For the success of these moves, Cornwallis depended heavily on
Major Patrick Ferguson and his American volunteer regiment.
Though only thirty-six, Ferguson was already a veteran of twenty-
one years in the British army and many European engagements.
Not tall, and slight in build, he was nevertheless an impressive
athlete and his performances in hand-to-hand fighting were notable.
He was the inventor of a breech-loading rifle, and his ingenuity was

also evident in his tactical operations. With seven regiments of South Carolina Tories, he had dominated the hill country of that colony and had spared Cornwallis many headaches. Early in October he was at King's Mountain, on the border of the Carolinas, screening Cornwallis' left flank.

West of the mountains were the Wautauga settlements, which had been terrorized by Ferguson's Loyalists until the Scotch-Irish frontiersmen started slipping nooses around Tory necks. The leader of the settlers was William Campbell,[80] a young Virginia giant with fiery hair and a temper to match. Fierce in his pride of clan and race, and ferocious in defense of his land, this Campbell of the Virginia hills was a fit descendant of warriors whose battle axes had made the crags of Scotland ring.

Two other Virginia leaders of opposition to the marauding Tories were Colonel Isaac Shelby and Colonel John Sevier.[81] To them Ferguson sent word that, if they did not desist from opposition to his Majesty's supporters, "he would march his army over the mountains, hang their leaders and lay their country waste with fire and sword."

Shelby and Sevier knew that it was time for the patriots of the western counties to unite in their own defense. They sent a message to Campbell. Campbell, in turn, sent a message to the North Carolinians. On September 25, the three leaders, with their followers, assembled at Sycamore Shoals on the Wautauga. To the same spot, with 160 men, came Colonel Charles McDowell, of North Carolina. Sevier and Shelby each had about 240 "over-mountain men." Campbell commanded four hundred. Before moving against Ferguson, these covenanters invoked "the sword of the Lord and of Gideon."

In contrast was the spirit of Major Ferguson, who took his stand on King's Mountain, a sixty-foot high, level plateau, which lay like a giant club across the level landscape near King's Creek a mile and a half below the border of the two Carolinas. Ferguson said that he "defied God Almighty and all the rebels out of Hell to dislodge him."

The British officer drew confidence from the natural strength of his situation. The steep, rocky sides of the eminence and the thick woods lent protection. With him were about a hundred rangers and a thousand Tory militia. They were well trained and skilled in the use of the bayonet. Ferguson would be the only British soldier in the battle which was shaping up.[82] The fight would be between rebels and Loyalists, but with the one exception, entirely between Americans.

About noon on October 7, the rebel forces took up positions that almost surrounded the base of the mountain. The longest section of their lines was manned by Campbell's men. Opposite them were Shelby's forces. Sevier was next to Campbell. Joseph McDowell, Charles' Virginia-born brother, had succeeded to command of the main body of North Carolinians[83] and was next to Sevier. Next to McDowell were North Carolinians under the command of Joseph Winston, a native of Louisa County, Virginia, and a cousin of Patrick Henry.

The tense silence was broken by a war whoop that was the signal for Campbell and Shelby to attack. Up the mountain they clambered, Campbell yelling, "Here they are, boys! Shout like hell and fight like devils!" Ferguson's men brandished their bayonets, but these weapons could not prevail over well-aimed rifles firing from trees that almost encircled the exposed plateau.

The Tories were being slaughtered, but Ferguson was deaf to pleas that he surrender. Twice he cut down white flags raised by his men, and then he himself was felled by a bullet. In panic, his followers herded together and made futile efforts to surrender. Vainly Shelby and Campbell pleaded with the rebels to cease firing. At last Campbell brought most of them to their senses by riding to the front and shouting, "For God's sake, quit. It's murder to shoot any more!"

The moral quality of the victory was spoiled by the unnecessary slaughter and by the vengeance wreaked by a hastily convened military court, even though rebel rage was understandable in view of Tory atrocities committed in the hills. The Loyalists of the upcountry, in many cases, were quite different from their highly civilized counterparts of Tidewater.

Some of the victory's practical effectiveness was reduced by the escape of most of the captured Britishers in ensuing months.

Nevertheless, the rebel triumph was an event of monumental significance. The completeness of the British defeat was beyond dispute. A little over a thousand of Ferguson's men had been engaged in the battle. Of these, 157 had been killed, 163 had been left wounded on the field and 698 had been taken prisoner. The rebels lost only twenty-eight men, and only sixty-two of their number were wounded. They captured fifteen hundred muskets and rifles and valuable supplies and ammunition.

The rebel victory at King's Mountain was the turning point of the war in the South. Tory fears magnified the American forces. When the distorted reports reached Cornwallis, he concluded that he must abandon for the time his plans to subdue North Carolina and retreated from Charlotte to Winnsboro, South Carolina. On October 14, the day that the British general went into winter quarters, Nathanael Greene, one of the very ablest of the Continental officers, was named commander of the Southern department, succeeding Gates.

This same fall of 1780 brought a heavy blow to American morale in the North. Benedict Arnold, one of the bravest and most intelligent of American generals, deserted to the British. The physical force of the blow would soon be felt by Virginia.

* * *

In that autumn of 1780, the British proved what Jefferson had feared—that Virginia was virtually defenseless against an enemy attack in force. Because of the hard facts of war, the Continental Army could not intervene to mitigate the harshness of the lesson.

In October, General Leslie and three thousand British soldiers landed at Portsmouth to establish communications with Cornwallis. The militia assembled to oppose Leslie, but after a quiet occupation of Portsmouth and Suffolk for about a month he sailed for South Carolina.[84]

Virginia had suffered little but anxiety as a result of Leslie's landing, but the ease with which the expedition had occupied two towns encouraged the British to attempt an operation of much larger scope.

Benedict Arnold, now a brigadier general in his Majesty's service, entered the Virginia Capes December 30 with a force of sixteen hundred men and sailed up the James past Norfolk and Portsmouth. Meeting with only the feeblest resistance, he reached Richmond on January 5, 1781. There he destroyed the public buildings of the infant capital and, more important, its military stores.

A detachment of Arnold's forces, moving on Petersburg, had an entirely different experience. It was beaten back by militia under General William Smallwood.

Arnold himself found the return trip a little rougher. As he dropped down river, he was ambushed by George Rogers Clark, but even the wily hero of the Northwest was unable to inflict a defeat on the renegade's superior forces.

On January 20, Arnold went into winter quarters at Portsmouth. Reinforced by two thousand men, he began raiding the countryside with great thoroughness according to careful plan. A larger purpose lay behind Clinton's ordering Arnold to Virginia. Extensive raids could capture or destroy the stores of tobacco with which Virginia helped to support the shaky foreign credit of the Continental Congress and could prevent the sending of salt provisions to the Continental Army. But even more important was the actual possession of Virginia itself—the richest and most populous of the colonies and their acknowledged leader. Cornwallis, confident that possession of Virginia would bring control of all the American States, had proposed the abandonment of New York and the concentration in the Chesapeake area of all the royal forces.[85] Though not consenting to so risky a plan, Clinton had ordered Arnold to Virginia where he could seize parts of the State and prepare the way for Cornwallis. Not entirely trusting the man who had betrayed the Continental Army, Clinton placed with him the capable Colonels Dundas and Simcoe, "by whose advice he was to be guided in every important measure."[86]

The choice of Arnold to lead the expedition increased Virginia's chances of receiving outside aid. Washington, as commander of the Continental Army, conscientiously maintained a continental perspective. He did not spare forces for Virginia's defense even when his own beloved Mount Vernon and its neighbors were threatened. But Arnold, from the continental view, would be a most desirable prize. His capture, the Virginian wrote, would be "an event particularly agreeable to this country."[87]

To the aid of Virginia's four thousand militia, Washington sent Lafayette with three regiments of light infantry from New England and New Jersey. Lieutenant General de Rochambeau, commander of the French Army, and Admiral Detouches consented to send the French fleet and 1,200 soldiers to operate with Lafayette.

A British naval force intercepted the French ships under Detouches just off the Virginia capes and drove them back to Newport, Rhode Island. Thus Lafayette, marching to Virginia's aid, was left without the naval support which he so badly needed.

Other circumstances made the Frenchman's plight desperate. On March 26, Major General William Phillips arrived at Portsmouth with 2,600 men to add to Arnold's force. Phillips superseded Arnold in command.

In the Carolinas, the superb generalship of Nathanael Greene and the remarkable performances of two Virginians, Daniel Morgan and "Light Horse Harry" Lee, were giving events a turn that would soon have important effects in Virginia.

Realizing that he lacked the strength to justify an attack on Cornwallis' camp at Winnsboro, Greene violated the canons of British warfare by dividing his inferior force. But there was shrewdness in Greene's plan, and he allowed for the skill of two unusual subordinates to compensate for deficiency in numbers and equipment. Morgan led eight hundred men in a magnificent sweep to the west and Lee waged a brilliant guerilla campaign in the area between Cornwallis and Charleston.

When Morgan was ready to battle Banastre Tarleton's cavalry, which Cornwallis had sent in pursuit, he halted at a cattle grazing place called the Cowpens. The choice was not in many ways an advantageous one, but Morgan's disposition of his forces was unorthodox and ingenious. He made good his promise on the eve of battle that the "old wagoner" (himself) would crack his whip over Ban Tarleton. Aided by the cavalry of Colonel William Washington, a South Carolina cousin of the great commander in chief, Morgan won one of the most notable victories of the war. Suffering fewer than seventy-five casualties, the rebels killed 329 of the enemy and captured six hundred.

Cornwallis set out in pursuit of Morgan who, acting on Greene's orders, retreated northward to draw the Englishman farther from British supply lines and nearer to those of the Continental forces in Virginia. When Morgan's army got across the Dan River, Cornwallis turned back. Greene, with a greatly reinforced command, engaged Cornwallis at Guilford Courthouse, North Carolina, on March 15. Though the Americans lost the field, they inflicted losses that forced his lordship to abandon the campaign.

On April 25, Cornwallis, sure that the British could not regain domination of the Carolinas so long as Virginia remained a supply and training base for the Continental forces, set out from Wilmington to invade the Old Dominion.

By this time, the forces defending Virginia, deprived of the expected naval aid from France, had been frustrated in their plans to retake Portsmouth and were ill-prepared to resist a new invasion projected from that base.

In mid-April, the British moved up the James, occupying Williamsburg and proceeding up the Appomattox River. Muhlenburg, a Virginia Lutheran minister turned general,[88] opposed the British with the Virginia militia. After a brisk fight, the Redcoats entered Petersburg April 25. They burned warehouses there and in Warwick, and put the torch to the military supply depot at Chesterfield Courthouse.

The British next moved on Richmond. Baron von Steuben, who was commanding in Virginia with meager forces at his disposal, could only fight to delay the enemy's advance until Lafayette's arrival.

Events rushed forward at a melodramatic pace. Lafayette entered Richmond from the north just as the British reached the village of Manchester on the opposite bank of the James.[89] Though much stronger than the Americans, the British believed that it was unwise to attempt a crossing under fire. Lafayette, though able to prevent a crossing, was too weak to attack.

General Phillips died May 13 and Arnold succeeded to his command. Lafayette, knowing that Cornwallis was on the march to join Arnold, anxiously awaited the arrival of "Mad Anthony" Wayne, who was marching from Pennsylvania to reinforce the marquis.

General Greene had marched south and his troops could not help Virginia when Cornwallis joined forces with Arnold at Petersburg May 20. Lafayette, who had about three thousand ill-equipped men as opposed to about 7,200 well-equipped British troops, reported to Washington, "I am not strong enough even to get beaten."[90]

Cornwallis is said to have written, "The boy cannot escape me."[91]

Failing to provoke Lafayette into more than a skirmish, Cornwallis on June 4 sent the dreaded Tarleton with cavalry and mounted infantry to Charlottesville, which had become Virginia's temporary capital in Richmond's hour of peril. He hoped to capture Governor Jefferson and the Virginia legislators.

Learning of the plan, Captain Jack Jouett, a young officer of prodigious proportions, rode some forty miles from Cuckoo Tavern to Charlottesville to warn the Commonwealth's leaders.[92] Cutting through woodland trails, his scarlet coat (and perhaps even his flesh) torn by lashing branches, he galloped up to the steps of Monticello before sunrise and told Jefferson of Tarleton's approach. Next he warned the legislators. Because of Jouett's superb feat of horsemanship, British plans for a coup were thwarted.

The General Assembly reconvened in Staunton. Jefferson was absent because his term as Governor had expired. No successor had been elected amid confusion attending the flight from Charlottesville, and a misunderstanding public got the idea that their Governor had deserted them. On June 12, Thomas Nelson, Jr., was elected Governor, and on the same day the House of Delegates adopted a resolution "That at the next session of Assembly an inquiry be made into the conduct of the Executive of this State for the last twelve months." A desperate people needed a scapegoat. One measure of their desperation was the fact that Richard Henry Lee was in the forefront of a group proposing that Washington be sent or recalled to Virginia and entrusted with dictatorial powers.[93]

By the time the British had weighed the frustrations of Tarleton's campaign, Wayne's forces had joined Lafayette's and the Americans were now strong enough to prevent the conquest of most of Virginia. After several skirmishes, Cornwallis retired to Portsmouth. He had not succeeded in engaging the American forces in a large-scale battle and he held only the area at the mouth of the James.

Ordered by Clinton to fortify some point suitable to command a harbor for his Majesty's ships, Cornwallis seized Yorktown and Gloucester Point, which faced each other across the mouth of the York.[94]

In mid-August, Washington learned that Admiral De Grasse and his entire fleet, with three thousand French troops, had left the West Indies and should be available for operations in the Chesapeake Bay area until mid-October. The Virginian had already received the promise of Rochambeau's cooperation in a large scale attack on the British.

Duping Clinton into thinking that the Americans would attack New York, Washington led his and Rochambeau's troops southward across New Jersey toward Virginia. Washington was an avid huntsman and now he smelled victory.

Those who had supposed him phlegmatic now realized they had never known their chief. When he learned that De Grasse had arrived in Virginia waters, he ran down to the dock at Chester to tell the good news to Rochambeau. Waving his hat and handkerchief in his excitement and embracing the Frenchman, Washington displayed more Gallic enthusiasm than Rochambeau could muster. In his general orders, the Virginian declared of De Grasse's arrival, "As no circumstance could possibly have happened more opportunely in point of time, no prospect could ever have promised more important successes."[95]

On August 31, De Grasse had set up a naval blockade of the British garrison at Yorktown and landed his troops for the junction with Lafayette's force. The British fleet, under Admiral Thomas Graves, arrived September 5. De Grasse sailed out and a sharp action ensued. Three days of maneuvering followed. Then Count Barras arrived with the French squadron from Newport and on September 10 Graves withdrew his fleet to New York for repairs. The French now had undisputed command of the waters off Yorktown.

French ships sailed up Chesapeake Bay to take on the bulk of Washington's and Rochambeau's troops and transport them to Williamsburg. From that city, about nine thousand Americans in nondescript, faded and ragged uniforms and 7,800 Frenchmen resplendent in green, cream and silver marched to Yorktown, through sunlit Tidewater countryside, attended all the way by curious eyes and awe-struck exclamations.

On September 28, the allies began the siege of Yorktown. The dawn of the thirtieth revealed that Cornwallis had abandoned his outer line of fortifications under cover of darkness, drawing his garrisons into the town.

The Americans and French promptly occupied the abandoned redoubts. On October 9, heavy siege guns opened fire on the British. On October 14, redoubts on the left of the British line were seized in a daring assault. A British counterattack two days later failed to regain lost fortifications.

Knowing that promised help would not come in time but still seeking to save his army from surrender, Cornwallis decided to transport his troops to Gloucester in small boats that night. However, after the frail craft had made the first landing on the Gloucester side, a violent storm arose and the black, angry waters of the York swept the boats downstream.

That night meteors blazed across the sky like rockets,[96] and superstitious Virginians—like the first colonists in 1607—concluded that the celestial fireworks were portents.

The next day, Cornwallis opened negotiations for the surrender of his army. Articles of surrender were drawn up on the eighteenth.

At two o'clock on the nineteenth, the Allies were paraded in two lines under a bright blue October sky. The sun shone on the spotless white broadcloth of the French in one file and exposed the raggedness of the American ranks in the other. But there was a gleam in American eyes to match the glint on French silver. In the blue river, French, British and American vessels bobbed on the sparkling waves. Washington, clad in blue and buff and astride his white charger, was a great monument of a man. And then, wearing new scarlet coats with the stiff pride of haughty men in defeat, the British garrison marched out, its bands playing "The World Turned Upside Down."

To them, the world must have seemed topsy-turvy indeed when his Majesty's army surrendered to untrained colonials and backwoods rebels.

But, among the Americans, who saw the Stars and Stripes flying proudly in the crisp October air, there was assurance that the world was being righted. With blood and sacrifice, they had bought their citizenship in a new nation.

* * *

When news of Cornwallis' surrender reached Lord North in London on November 25, the Prime Minister cried out, "Oh God! It is all over!" That unfortunate statesman, who had been wrong so many times, was right at last.

Though a cessation of hostilities was not proclaimed until February 4, 1783, for all practical purposes the war between America and Britain had ended at Yorktown.[97]

Military revolution had been an expression of political revolution. Thirteen British colonies had become independent States and had formed the Confederation of the United States. This new nation had won an empire extending from the Atlantic to the Mississippi.

And, within the States themselves, there had been a revolution. In all, penal reforms and the disestablishment of the Anglican church had been achieved or were proceeding apace. Entail and primogeniture, the foundations of baronial estates, had been abolished. In Virginia, the ruling class had led the revolution, but in some States it had battled for the King and lost its power to a rising middle class.

In the Revolution, viewed as a military and political entity, Virginians had played a conspicuous role—even a dominant one.

Patrick Henry's Stamp Act Resolutions had, in the words of the British, "set fire to a continent." Virginia had taken the lead in the Continental Congress, and Peyton Randolph, speaker of the Virginia House, had been named its first president.

In 1776, Richard Henry Lee introduced the Virginia Resolutions for Independence, Thomas Jefferson gave the colonies their Declaration of Independence and George Mason gave them their Declaration of Rights.

Virginia's leadership was as notable in the field as in the forum. The commander in chief of the Continental Army was George Washington—the one "indispensable man" of the Revolution. Virginians fought from Canada to Georgia and from the Atlantic to the Mississippi. The Commonwealth itself had been the decisive battlefield of the war.

"Virginia excelled all her sister States in devoting 'land, property and manufacturing' to naval purposes,"[98] and John Paul Jones was the greatest naval hero of the Revolution.

In 1777, the martyred General Hugh Mercer was, next to Washington himself, the hero of the Battle of Princeton. Later the same year, General Daniel Morgan won the battle of Freeman's Farm.

In 1778, George Rogers Clark emerged as the greatest leader of the war in the West, winning control of the Ohio Country and subsequent tribute as "an architect of the United States."[99]

The next year was one of dashing triumph for Virginians on land and sea. "Light Horse Harry" Lee, winning the Battle of Paulus Hook, drove the British from their last outpost in New Jersey. John Paul Jones, commanding the *Bonhomme Richard*, captured the *Serapis*.

At the Battle of King's Mountain, in 1780, Colonel William Campbell and Colonel Isaac Shelby were the chief leaders. Among the foremost heroes, in addition to these two, were John Sevier, Joseph MacDowell and Joseph Winston. Sir Henry Clinton, commander in chief of his Majesty's forces in America, said that King's Mountain "proved the first link of a chain of evils that followed each other in unbroken succession until they at last ended in the total loss of America."

General Morgan, aided by the guerilla activity of "Light Horse Harry" Lee, won one of the war's most important victories at Cowpens.

All of these battles, and others in which Virginians played less conspicuous roles, led to the culmination at Yorktown. There, the confederation born of resolutions introduced by Richard Henry Lee, but born above all in the resolution expressed in patriotic acts of valor from New England to Georgia, stood up to be counted as an independent force in the world's affairs.

With dramatic appropriateness, the freedom of the American States became a reality in Virginia, where the first permanent English settlement in America was made and where the first colonial resolutions for independence originated.

The road from Jamestown to Williamsburg to Yorktown is short, less than twenty miles by the smooth highway.

But the road from Jamestown to Williamsburg to Yorktown *was* long, drenched in blood, paved with the bodies of martyrs and villains, checkered with the dark and light of human life and character. A nation traveled down that road and the journey took one hundred seventy-four years.

FOOTNOTES TO CHAPTERS

END NOTES TO CHAPTERS

FOOTNOTES TO CHAPTER I

1. It is interesting to note that the London Company advised each emigrant to provide himself with a monmouth cap (a flat, round cap), three shirts, one suit of canvas, one pair of garters, four pairs of shoes, three falling bands, one waistcoat, one suit of frieze, one suit of broadcloth, three pairs of silk stockings, and a dozen pairs of points. (Elisabeth McClellan: *History of American Costume*, p. 46.) Perhaps only pointed beards or, at most, lace collars distinguished "gentlemen" from artisans.

2. Captain John Smith afterwards wrote (John Smith, *The Generall Historie of Virginia*, etc., published by James MacLehose, Glasgow, vol. I, p. 91) that there were 100 "first Planters" of Jamestown. But a twentieth century researcher (C. W. Sams, *The Conquest of Virginia, the Second Attempt*, pp. 807-813) has compiled a list of 108 colonists, whose number was diminished by the death of one on the voyage to Virginia. A contemporary of Smith's, Samuel Purchas, reported that there were 105 colonists. (*Ibid.*)

3. Smith, vol. I, pp. 90-91.

4. There were on the voyage to Virginia about 40 sailors who returned to England with Newport. (C. Whittle Sams, *The Conquest of Virginia, the Second Attempt*, p. 813.)

5. Sketch of Smith based on Philip L. Barbour, *The Three Worlds of Captain John Smith*, entry in *Dictionary of American Biography*, portraits in early editions of his books, and his own autobiographical writings—*True Relations*, etc. Strangely enough, Smith has been credited with one accomplishment which he did not claim in his history. Henry Hudson's third voyage in search of a northern passage to the East, which carried him to the river that now bears his name, was prompted by "letters and maps which Captain Smith had sent him from Virginia, informing him of a sea leading into the Western Ocean." *The Geographical Magazine* (London), vol. XXVI, p. 197.

6. *Dictionary of National Biography*.

7. Matthew Page Andrews, *Virginia, the Old Dominion*, p. 15.

8. Queen Mary, of England, and Cardinal Pole had been god-parents to Wingfield's father.

9. D. A. B.

10. John Smith: *The Generall Historie of Virginia*, etc., vol. I, p. 60. Hereafter referred to as Smith.

11. Richard Hakluyt, foremost historian-geographer of his age, devoted so much of his monumental "Voyages" to praise of Virginia that Sir Philip Sydney called him "a good trumpet" for the new land, and a distinguished Scotch historian of a later generation, William Robertson, declared that to him "England is more indebted for its American possessions than to any man of that age." Michael Drayton, England's famous poet-patriot, ranked Hakluyt's paeans of praise with Homer's verses. Drayton himself, in his "Ode to the Virginian Voyage," labeled Virginia, "earth's only paradise." Edmund Spenser, in "The Faerie Queen," thought to be the subject of burlesque in Drayton's "Nymphidia," joined his supposed critic in praise of the new land. A reference to "fruitfullest Virginia" in Book II (second verse of the introductory portion) was perhaps inspired by Sir Walter Raleigh, father of the ill-fated expeditions of 1585 and 1587, to whom the entire work was dedi-

cated. Quicksilver's cynical comment on Virginia colonization in John Drayton's "Eastward Hoe!" doubtless was evoked by Raleigh's failures. Samuel Daniel, literary foe of Spenser, one of England's first metaphysical poets, one of her ablest sonneteers, and perhaps the forerunner of her realist school, was inspired to prophecy by the possibilities of the New World. He envisioned an English-speaking nation of influence "in the yet unformed Occident." Dr. Matthew Page Andrews, in an address delivered before the annual meeting of the Virginia Historical Society December 8, 1943 (published in *Virginia Magazine of History and Biography*, vol. LIII, p. 95), declared that all authors of the Elizabethan epoch, in so far as he knew them, wrote about Virginia.

12. Confusion regarding the names of the first two vessels has resulted from errors in transcription labeling them *Sarah Constant* and *Goodspeed*. Proof of correctness for the forms *Susan Constant* and *Godspeed* is given in Philip L. Barbour, ed., *The Jamestown Voyages Under the First Charter, 1606-1609*, vol. I, pp. 21-22, 55-59.

The "blazing Starre" was reported by George Percy in an account reprinted in Lyon G. Tyler's *Narratives of Old Virginia*, p. 5.

13. Charter of 1606.

14. Alexander Brown, *The First Republic in America*, p. 24.
Alexander Brown, *The Genesis of the United States*, vol. II, p. 1055.

15. First Charter of Virginia, April 10, 1606, Article I.

16. Charters of 1606 and 1609.
Matthew Page Andrews, *Virginia, the Old Dominion*, p. 17.

17. Smith, vol. I, p. 43. Early editions of Smith incorrectly listed "44" rather than 45 as extreme north boundary latitude. See Lyon G. Tyler's valuable compilation, *Narratives of Early Virginia*.

18. First Charter of Virginia, April 10, 1606, Article IV.

19. *Supra*. Captain John Smith described "that part which was planted by the English men" as lying "under the degrees 37. 38. and 39." (Smith, vol. I, p. 43.)

20. First Charter of Virginia, April 10, 1606, Article IV.

21. *Ibid.*, Article V.

22. Alexander Brown, *The First Republic in America*, p. 14.

23. Sometimes written "Sands." Information for the sketch of Sandys was derived primarily from the following sources: D.N.B.; Brown's *Genesis of the United States*; Stith's *History of the First Discovery and Settlement of Virginia*; Edward Channing, *A History of the United States*, (N.Y., Macmillan, 1933) vol. I, pp. 190-193; *Virginia Magazine of History*, vol. 29, pp. 237-242; *Records of the Virginia Company* (ed., Susan M. Kingsbury), vol. I, p. 212; vol. IV, p. 194; Wesley Frank Craven, *Dissolution of the Virginia Company*, pp. 27-28, 41-44, 46, 67, 136-139, 154-162.

• 24. Matthew Page Andrews, *Virginia, the Old Dominion*, p. 43. The same historian has referred to him as "the most far-sighted statesman of the seventeenth century" and the "founder-in-chief of representative government in America." (*Virginia Magazine of History and Biography*, vol. LII, p. 91

25. Though the informal organization of early universities makes it difficult to assign a definite date to the founding of Oxford, it seems to have received its impetus about 1170 from a group of English students who left the University of Paris because of the quarrel between Becket and Henry II. (Walter Phelps Hall, Robert G. Albion, *A History of England and the British Empire*, p. 136.)

26. The word "liberal" is so freely used and abused by extremists of Right and Left that any writer employing it is obligated to define its significance to him. As used in this book, the term is applied to one who seeks "the greatest

good for the greatest number" without sacrificing the rights of minorities. This definition holds true in the context of this work whether the minorities involved are aristocratic or proletarian.

27. Thomas J. Wertenbaker, *Virginia Under the Stuarts*, p. 8. (Hereafter cited as Wertenbaker, *Stuarts*.)

28. *Records of the Virginia Company*, vol. I, pp. 21-22.

29. Wertenbaker, *Stuarts*, pp. 3-4.

30. Though many historians long assumed that the "sickness" was malaria, the medical historian Wyndham B. Blanton in 1930 suggested that it was probably typhoid (Wyndham B. Blanton, M.D., *Medicine in Virginia in the Seventeenth Century*). Strong evidence of the probability of its being typhoid and of the Rev. Mr. Hunt's being the innocent carrier has since been presented in Gordon W. Jones, "The First Epidemic in English America," *Virginia Magazine of History and Biography*, LXXI (1963), pp. 3-10.

31. *Ibid.*, p. 4.

32. *Ibid.*, pp. 4-5.   33. *Ibid.*, p. 5.

34. *Ibid.*   35. *Ibid.*, p. 6.

36. *Ibid.*
Matthew P. Andrews, *Virginia, the Old Dominion*, p. 42.

37. Smith, vol. I, p. 123.   38. *Ibid.*, p. 149.

39. Transitions in government traced in *Records of the Virginia Company*, vol. I, pp. 11-25.

40. Charter of 1609. Flippin, *Royal Government in Virginia*, pp. 60-61.

41. Charter of 1609.   42. *Ibid.*

43. *Ibid.*

44. Matthew P. Andrews, *Virginia, the Old Dominion*, pp. 44-46.

45. Carefully collected evidence that Shakespeare based his description of the hurricane in *The Tempest* on Secretary William Strachey's account of the West Indian hurricane that wrecked the *Sea Venture* was published in 1917 by Charles Mills Gayley in a volume entitled *Shakespeare and the Founders of Liberty in America*. Some passages of the play so closely parallel Strachey's report that the narrative details are almost identical, though transferred from particular to universal significance by the transcendent creative genius of the poet.

46. Wertenbaker, *Stuarts*, p. 9.   47. *Ibid.*

48. Smith, vol. I, p. 193.   49. Tyler, *Narratives*, pp. 21-22.

50. Wertenbaker, *Stuarts*, p. 16. Gates had the honor of proclaiming ,'the first legal code ever put in practice in English-speaking America." (Oliver Perry Chitwood, *Justice in Colonial Virginia*, p. 13.

51. Some historians have advanced the theory that this settlement was on the Rappahannock or Potomac or even in North Carolina, and its location is uncertain. A convincing case for the James, however, is presented in Lewis and Loomie's *The Spanish Jesuit Mission in Virginia, 1570-72.*

52. The danger was very real. See Tyler, *Narratives*, pp. 217-224.

53. *William and Mary Quarterly* (2), vol. 19, pp. 513-514. The church here referred to is not to be confused with the brick church constructed *c.* 1639, whose ruined tower is the one prominent landmark that has survived the many vicissitudes that beset the early colonial capital.

54. *Ibid.*, p. 514.

FOOTNOTES TO CHAPTER II

1. Wertenbaker, *Virginia Under the Stuarts*, p. 18.
2. *Ibid.*, pp. 18-19.   3. *Ibid.*, pp. 19-20.
4. *William and Mary Quarterly* (2), vol. 18, p. 453.
5. *Ibid.*, p. 455.   6. *Ibid.*
7. *Ibid.*   8. *Ibid.*
9. *Ibid.*, p. 458.
   M. P. Andrews, *Virginia, the Old Dominion*, pp. 64-65.
10. "In Honour of Henry Prince of Wales"—Beverley, *History and Present State of Virginia*, p. 37.
11. *William and Mary Quarterly* (2), vol. 18, p. 466.
12. *Ibid.*, pp. 467-468.
    Wertenbaker's *Virginia Under the Stuarts*, pp. 21-22.
13. *William and Mary Quarterly* (2), vol. 18, pp. 466-467.
14. *Ibid.*, p. 467.
15. *Ibid.*, p. 466.
    Vagrancy was also severely punished in the mother country. One of the "Poor Laws" passed in Elizabeth's reign required that the vagrant, whether male or female, be "stripped naked from the middle upwards and shall be openly whipped until his or her body be bloodye."—Hall and Albion, *History of England and the British Empire*, p. 302.
16. *Ibid.*, p. 465.
17. Wertenbaker, *Virginia Under the Stuarts*, p. 23.
18. *Ibid.*
19. *Ibid.* Even under Dale, the harsh laws may not have been consistently enforced to the letter. (Oliver Perry Chitwood, *Justice in Colonial Virginia*, pp. 14-16.)
20. M. P. Andrews, *Virginia, the Old Dominion*, p. 68.
21. *Ibid.*, p. 65.
22. The account of the attack written by one of the French survivors, a Jesuit priest (Father Pierre Biard) has been translated from the original Latin and appears in Lyon G. Tyler, *Narratives of Early Virginia*.
    A translation from the French appears in Alexander Brown, *Genesis of the United States*, pp. 700-706.
23. *Library of Southern Literature*, vol. XIV, p. 639.
    Tyler, *Narratives of Early Virginia*, p. 240.
24. C. Whittle Sams, *The Conquest of Virginia, The Forest Primeval*. See map opposite p. 142, also pp. 269-270, 324.
    S. R. Hendren, *Government and Religion of the Virginia Indians*, pp. 5-6, 14.
25. Wertenbaker, *Virginia Under the Stuarts*, p. 26.
26. *William and Mary Quarterly* (2), vol. 18, pp. 464-465.
27. John Rolfe, *A True Relation of the State of Virginia Left by Sir Thomas Dale, Knight, in May Last 1616* (Yale University Press, 1951), p. 36.
28. *William and Mary Quarterly* (2), vol. 18, pp. 464-465.
29. *Ibid.*

FOOTNOTES TO CHAPTER III

1. Beverley, *The History and Present State of Virginia*, p. 39.
2. Virginia's first native historian. When enmity roused by his outspoken independence compelled him to retire from public life, he performed his greatest service to the colony by chronicling its history. His *History and Present State of Virginia*, first published in 1705, is prized today as an early American classic.
3. Beverley, pp. 44-45.
4. Wertenbaker, *Virginia Under the Stuarts*, p. 27.
5. *Ibid.*, p. 28.   6. Beverley, p. 45.
7. Hall and Albion, *A History of England and the British Empire*, p. 321.
8. *Ibid.*, p. 322.
9. Hall and Albion, *History of England and the British Empire*, p. 336.
10. Wertenbaker, *Virginia Under the Stuarts*, pp. 29-30.
11. M. P. Andrews, *Virginia, the Old Dominion*, p. 85.
12. Great Charter. The various transitions in the Company's role in Virginia government are sketched in *Records of the Virginia Company of London*, vol. I, pp. 11-25.
13. *Ibid.*
    Matthew Page Andrews, *The Soul of a Nation*, p. 250;
    Thomas J. Wertenbaker, *Virginia Under the Stuarts*, p. 36;
    Alexander Brown, *The First Republic in America*, p. 312.
14. Thomas J. Wertenbaker, *Virginia Under the Stuarts*, p. 38.
15. James Truslow Adams, *The March of Democracy*, vol. I, pp. 21-22; John Fiske, *Old Virginia and Her Neighbors*, vol. I, p. 186.
16. *Oxford English Dictionary.*
17. Alexander Brown, *The First Republic in America*, p. 312.
18. *Ibid.*   19. *Ibid.*, p. 315.
20. James Truslow Adams, *The March of Democracy*, vol. I, p. 22.
21. John Fiske, *Old Virginia and Her Neighbors*, p. 187.
22. Subsequent descriptions of the dress of the planters and their wives gathered in Jamestown for the convening of the first General Assembly are based on contemporary accounts and sketches included in Elizabeth McClellan's *History of American Costume*, vol. I, pp. 46-55, together with corroborating notes in *English Costume from the Fourteenth Through the Nineteenth Century*, by Iris Brooke and James Laver, pp. 186-192. That the women accompanied their husbands to Jamestown is a logical inference.
23. *Journals of the House of Burgesses of Virginia, 1619-1658/59*, p. 4.
    Proceedings of the General Assembly of Virginia, July 30-August 4, 1619, William J. Van Schreeven, ed. (facsimile), p. 14.
24. George Carrington Mason, *Colonial Churches of Tidewater Virginia*, pp. 6-7.
25. *Journals of the House of Burgesses of Virginia, 1619-1658/59*, p. 4.
    Proceedings of the General Assembly, pp. 14-15.
26. George MacLaren Brydon, *Virginia's Mother Church*, pp. 22-23.
27. Elizabeth McClellan, *History of American Costume*, pp. 49-53.
28. *Proceedings of the General Assembly*, p. 17.
29. *Ibid.*
30. *Ibid.*; also Alexander Brown, *The First Republic in America*, p. 316.
31. Governor's chair in the church was described as "green velvet" in 1610. G. M. Brydon, *Virginia's Mother Church*, p. 16.
    Other details are from McClellan's *American Costume*.

32. Matthew Page Andrews, *Virginia, the Old Dominion*, p. 112.
So far as we know there is no record of Lady Yeardley's attendance, but in such circumstances, what woman would stay away?

33. Alexander Brown, *The Genesis of the United States*, vol. II, p. 1065.

34. *Ibid.*, p. 970.

35. Matthew Page Andrews, *The Soul of a Nation*, p. 297.

36. *Journals of the House of Burgesses of Virginia, 1619-1658/59*, pp. 12, 16.

37. Thomas J. Wertenbaker, *Virginia Under the Stuarts*, p. 37.
Journals of the House of Burgesses of Virginia, 1619-1658/59, p. 4.

38. *Journals of the House of Burgesses of Virginia, 1619-1658/59*, pp. 4-5, 8-9.

39. *Ibid.*, p. 16.

40. Thomas J. Wertenbaker, *Virginia Under the Stuarts*, p. 39.

41. *Ibid.*   42. *Ibid.*, p. 40.

43. Samuel Eliot Morison and Henry Steele Commager, *The Growth of the American Republic*, vol. I, p. 41.

44. Robert Beverley, *The History and Present State of Virginia*, p. 238.

45. John Richard Green, *A Short History of the English People*, pp. 158, 232.
W. E. Lunt, *History of England*, pp. 152-153, 228-229.

46. John Richard Green, *A Short History of the English People*, pp. 60-61, 111.
W. E. Lunt, *History of England*, pp. 51, 53, 85-86, 100-102, 107, 113-114, 144, 195-198.

47. Information on which the account of Southampton's activities is based is derived from the following sources:
Matthew Page Andrews, *The Soul of a Nation*, pp. 40-41, 186, 236-237, 260;
John Richard Green, *A Short History of the English People*, pp. 433-434;
Dictionary of National Biography.
Evaluation of Sir Thomas Smith's role based on foregoing sources plus:
Richard L. Morton, *Colonial Virginia*, vol. I, pp. 3-4, 20-21, 56. Virginius Dabney, *Virginia the New Dominion*, pp. 16, 29.

48. Henry Steele Commager, *Documents of American History*, p. 13.

49. *Ibid.*   50. *Ibid.*

51. Information on which the account of Buckingham's activities is based is derived from the following sources:
John Richard Green, *A Short History of the English People*, pp. 487-488, 494;
W. E. Lunt, *History of England*, pp. 388, 396, 398-399;
Dictionary of National Biography.

52. Virginia Writers' Project, *The Negro in Virginia*, p. 1.

53. Matthew Page Andrews, *Virginia, the Old Dominion*, p. 88;
James C. Ballagh, *White Servitude in the Colony of Virginia*, pp. 22-49;
J. C. Ballagh, *A History of Slavery in Virginia*, pp. 28-33.

54. Virginia Writers' Project, *The Negro in Virginia*, p. 1.

55. Matthew Page Andrews, *The Soul of a Nation*, p. 224;
Matthew Page Andrews, *Virginia, the Old Dominion*, p. 89.

56. *Ibid.*

57. M. P. Andrews, *The Soul of a Nation*, p. 278.

58. *Ibid.*, p. 224.   59. *Ibid.*

60. Abbot Emerson Smith, *Colonists in Bondage*, pp. 139-140.

61. *Ibid.*

62. M. P. Andrews, *The Soul of a Nation*, p. 259.

63. *Ibid.*   64. *Ibid.*, pp. 259-260.

65. *Ibid.*   66. *Ibid.*, p. 261.

67. William Bradford, *Of Plymouth Plantation* (ed. by S. E. Morison, N. Y., Knopf, 1952), pp. 34, 39. 60, 75-76; *Virginia Magazine of History*, vol. 62, pp. 154-158.
68. Bradford, *Of Plymouth Plantation*, pp. 29, 31-32.
69. Matthew Page Andrews believed that the Stephen Hopkins aboard the *Mayflower* was the same who had been at Jamestown (*Virginia, the Old Dominion*, p. 59). Samuel Eliot Morison says "the two Stephen Hopkinses cannot positively be identified as the same person."—*Virginia Magazine of History*, vol. 62, p. 154.
70. Andrews, *Soul of a Nation*, p. 258.

FOOTNOTES TO CHAPTER IV

1. Alexander Brown, *First Republic in America*, p. 506.
2. Thomas J. Wertenbaker, *Virginia Under the Stuarts*, p. 46.
3. Edward Channing, *A History of the United States*, vol. I, pp. 206-207.
   This comment contrasts strangely with Captain Smith's statement: "In them nine ships that went with Sir Francis Wyat, not one passenger died." *Capt. Smith's Travels*, vol. I, p. 27.
4. Matthew Page Andrews, *Virginia, the Old Dominion*, p. 114.
5. *Ibid.*
6. Matthew Page Andrews, *The Soul of a Nation*, p. 297.
7. Thomas J. Wertenbaker, *Virginia Under the Stuarts*, p. 89.
8. *Ibid.*
9. Robert Beverley, *The History and Present State of Virginia*, p. 45.
10. Matthew Page Andrews, *Virginia, the Old Dominion*, p. 102.
11. Captain John Smith, *The Travels of Captaine John Smith*, vol. I, p. 281.
12. Alexander Brown, *The Genesis of the United States*, vol. II, p. 1031.
13. Captain John Smith, *The Travels of Captaine John Smith*, vol. I, p. 280.
14. Alexander Brown, *The First Republic in America*, pp. 468, 511; Alexander Brown, *The Genesis of the United States*, vol. II, p. 971; Captain John Smith, *The Travels of Captaine John Smith*, vol. I, p. 285.
15. Alexander Brown, *The First Republic in America*, pp. 466-467, 469; Captain John Smith, *The Travels of Captaine John Smith*, vol. I, p. 281; Robert Beverley, *The History and Present State of Virginia*, p. 51.
16. Captain John Smith, *The Travels of Captaine John Smith*, vol. I, pp. 282-283.
17. *Ibid.*, p. 283.   18. *Ibid.*, p. 282.
19. Thomas J. Wertenbaker, *Virginia Under the Stuarts*, p. 50.
   Captain Smith's estimate of 347 seems to have been inaccurate.
20. Philip Alexander Bruce, *Economic History of Virginia in the Seventeenth Century*, p. 71.
21. Alexander Brown, *The First Republic in America*, p. 508.
22. *Ibid.*, p. 475.   23. *Ibid.*, p. 576.
24. *Ibid.*, p. 475.   25. *Ibid.*, p. 576.
26. Matthew Page Andrews, *Virginia, the Old Dominion*, p. 106.
27. *Ibid.*
28. Alexander Brown, *The First Republic in America*, p. 475.
29. *Ibid.*, p. 510.   30. *Ibid.*, p. 514.

31. *Ibid.*, pp. 514-515.
32. Matthew Page Andrews, *Virginia, the Old Dominion*, p. 107.
33. *Journals of the House of Burgesses.*
34. Alexander Brown, *The First Republic in America*, p. 607.
35. *Ibid.*   36. *Ibid.*, pp. 607-608.
37. Thomas J. Wertenbaker, *Virginia Under the Stuarts*, p. 53.
38. Alexander Brown, *The First Republic in America*, p. 607.
39. *Ibid.*
　　The quotation is from a general letter of December 12, 1624.
40. *Ibid.*   41. *Ibid.*, pp. 437-439.
42. *Ibid.*   43. *Ibid.*, p. 393.
44. *Ibid.*, pp. 437-439.   45. *Ibid.*, pp. 435-437.
46. *Ibid.*, pp. 437-439, 542.   47. *Ibid.*, pp. 477-478.
48. *Ibid.*   49. *Ibid.*
50. *Ibid.*
51. Lyon G. Tyler, *Narratives of Early Virginia*, p. 411.
52. The full title was "The Unmasked face of our Colony in Virginia as it was in the Winter of the Yeare 1622."
53. Lyon G. Tyler, *Narratives of Early Virginia*, pp. 411-418.
　　Dr. Tyler records that charges against Captain Butler for allegedly extorting money from shipwrecked Spaniards while Governor of the Bermulas were dropped after he presented his broadside against Virginia to the king.
54. *Ibid.*
55. *Ibid.*, pp. 412-416.   56. *Ibid.*, p. 412.
57. *Ibid.*, pp. 412-413.   58. *Ibid.*
59. *Ibid.*, pp. 413-414.   60. *Ibid.*
61. *Ibid.*   62. *Ibid.*, p. 415.
63. *Ibid.*   64. *Ibid.*
65. *Ibid.*, p. 416.
　　The word "murders" refers to cannon.
66. *Ibid.*   67. *Ibid.*
68. *Ibid.*   69. *Ibid.*, p. 417.
70. *Ibid.*, pp. 417-418.
　　Spelling and punctuation in this passage, as well as in some subsequent ones, are modernized to avoid confusion.
71. *Ibid.*, p. 418.   72. *Ibid.*
73. Alexander Brown, *The First Republic in America*, p. 520.
74. *Ibid.*, pp. 540-541.   75. Brown, *First Republic*, p. 510.
76. Wertenbaker, *Virginia Under the Stuarts*, p. 57.
77. *Ibid.*, pp. 57-58.   78. *Ibid.*, p. 60.
79. Tyler, *Narratives*, p. 422. Subsequent quotations from this document are extracted from its text as printed in *Narratives*, pp. 422-426.
80. Wertenbaker, *Virginia Under the Stuarts*, p. 61.
81. Brown, *First Republic*, p. 510.
82. Wertenbaker, *Virginia Under the Stuarts*, p. 58.
83. *Ibid.*, p. 59.

FOOTNOTES TO CHAPTER V

1. Alexander Brown, *First Republic of America*, p. 634.
2. Thomas J. Wertenbaker, *Virginia Under the Stuarts*, p. 61.
3. *Ibid.*
4. Percy Scott Flippin, *The Royal Government in Virginia, 1624-1775*, pp. 151-152.
5. *Ibid.*, p. 31. On April 28, 1624, Sir Francis Wyatt had been "commended for his justice and equanimity towards all men" in a statement by Virginia planters to the Court of the Virginia Company (*Records of the Virginia Company of London*, ed. Susan M. Kingsbury, vol. II, pp. 536-537).
6. T. J. Wertenbaker, *Virginia Under the Stuarts*, p. 61.
7. Figure for general population furnished by the London Company and quoted in Tyler, *Narratives of Old Virginia*, p. 418. Number of Negroes recorded in muster of 1624-25, quoted in Philip Alexander Bruce, *Economic History of Virginia in the Seventeenth Century*, vol. II, p. 70.
8. *William and Mary Quarterly* (2), vol. XVIII, p. 493. There were, however, tenants on the "college lands" near Henrico City (*Ibid.*, p. 495).
9. Mary Newton Stanard, *The Story of Virginia's First Century* (Philadelphia, 1928), pp. 172-173.
10. Jennings Cropper Wise, *The Early History of the Eastern Shore of Virginia*, p. 35.
11. *Ibid.*
12. *William and Mary Quarterly* (2), vol. XX, p. 449.
13. *Ibid.*, p. 450.
14. G. MacLaren Brydon, *Virginia's Mother Church*, pp. 48, 419.
15. Philip Alexander Bruce, *Economic History of Virginia in the Seventeenth Century*, vol. I, pp. 91-92.
    Tyler, *Narratives of Early Virginia*, pp. 412-413.
16. Philip Alexander Bruce, *Economic History of Virginia in the Seventeenth Century*, vol. I, p. 86.
17. *Ibid.*, p. 143.   18. *Ibid.*, pp. 143-144.
19. *Ibid.*, p. 319.   20. *Ibid.*
21. *Ibid.*, pp. 319-320.
22. In 1619, Secretary John Pory wrote, "Our cowkeeper here of James City on Sundays goes accourtered all in fresh flaming silk; and a wife of one that in England had professed the black art, not of a scholar, but of a collier of Croydon, wears her rough beaver hat with a fair pearl hatband, and a silken suit thereto correspondent."—Tyler's *Narratives*, p. 285. A detailed discussion of the social origins of Virginia's great planters appears in P. A. Bruce, *Social Life of Virginia in the Seventeenth Century*, pp. 27-97.
23. Bruce, *Economic History of Virginia in the Seventeenth Century*, vol. I, p. 228.
24. *Ibid.*, p. 229.   25. *Ibid.*, p. 227.
26. Secretary John Pory's account—Tyler, *Narratives*, p. 285.
27. Burton Hendrick, *The Lees of Virginia*, pp. 14-16.
28. The role of the English manor in politics is discussed, with specific illustrations, in Sir Thomas Lawson-Tancred's *Records of a Yorkshire Manor*, pp. 198-200.
29. T. J. Wertenbaker, *The Planters of Colonial Virginia*, pp. 27-43.
30. *Ibid.*, pp. 60-62, 74-75, 82-83.
31. C. Whittle Sams, *The Conquest of Virginia, the Second Attempt*, pp. 807-813.

32. A. E. Smith, *Colonists in Bondage*, pp. 16-17.
33. A general discussion of indenture terms is in A. E. Smith, *Colonists in Bondage*, pp. 16-18.
34. A. E. Smith, *Colonists in Bondage*, p. 17.
35. *Ibid.*   36. *Ibid.*
37. *Ibid.*, pp. 238-241.   38. *Ibid.*
39. *Ibid.*, p. 226.   40. *Ibid.*, pp. 14-17.
41. *Ibid.*, p. 15.
42. *Journals of the House of Burgesses, 1619-1658/59*, pp. 1-16.
43. *Ibid.*
44. A. E. Smith, *Colonists in Bondage*, pp. 227, 275.
45. *Ibid.*, p. 253.
46. T. J. Wertenbaker, *Planters of Colonial Virginia*, pp. 75, 80.
    A. E. Smith, *Colonists in Bondage*, p. 297.
47. *The Negro in Virginia*, p. 10.
48. *Ibid.*   49. *Ibid.*
50. *Ibid.*, p. 11. He later became a slaveholder.
51. *Ibid.*, p. 13.
52. T. J. Wertenbaker, *Planters of Colonial Virginia*, p. 31.
53. *Ibid.*, p. 46.
54. Philip A. Bruce, *Economic History of Virginia*, vol. II, p. 495.
55. *Ibid.*, p. 496.   56. *Ibid.*
57. *Ibid.*   58. *Ibid.*
59. Philip A. Bruce, *Economic History of Virginia*, vol. I, p. 309.
60. *Ibid.*, p. 310.   61. *Ibid.*, p. 311.
62. *Ibid.*, pp. 313-315.
63. *Ibid.*, p. 317. Also called "worm fence."
64. *Ibid.*, p. 318.
65. T. J. Wertenbaker, *Planters of Colonial Virginia*, pp. 104-105.
66. *Ibid.*, p. 105.   67. *Ibid.*
68. Bruce, *Economic History of Virginia*, vol. II, pp. 149-150.
69. *Ibid.*   70. *Ibid.*, pp. 163-165.
71. *Ibid.*   72. *Ibid.*, p. 166.
73. *Ibid.*, pp. 166-167.   74. *Ibid.*, pp. 168-169.
75. Brass utensils and pewter tankards are frequently mentioned in inventories of the period. (Bruce, *Economic History of Virginia*, vol. II, pp. 164, 169.)
76. Tallow candles were frequently used in Virginia, but those molded from myrtle wax were more popular because they burned with a clear light and suffused the room with a pleasing fragrance. (Bruce, *Economic History of Virginia*, vol. II, p. 184.)
77. The traveler was Captain Devries, of the Netherlands, who recorded the incident in his *Voyages from Holland to America*. The Dutchman concluded that the Virginians were too shrewd as traders even for the merchants of his hard-bargaining nation. (Bruce, *Economic History of Virginia*, vol. I, p. 311.)
78. Hall and Albion, *A History of England and the British Empire*, p. 329; Hartwell, Blair and Chilton, *The Present State of Virginia and the College*, pp. XXXVII-XXXVIII. (The passage here alluded to occurs in the introduction written by H. D. Farish.)
79. William Waller Hening, *The Statutes at Large*, vol. I, p. 115; Hartwell, Blair and Chilton, *The Present State of Virginia and the College*, p. XLVI;
    T. J. Wertenbaker, *Planters of Colonial Virginia*, p. 15.

80. T. J. Wertenbaker, *Virginia Under the Stuarts*, p. 43.
81. *Ibid.;*
    P. A. Bruce, *Economic History of Virginia*, vol. II, pp. 448-449.
82. P. A. Bruce, *Economic History of Virginia*, vol. II, p. 440.
83. *Ibid.*
84. *Ibid.*, pp. 440-443. Some glass had been manufactured about a mile from Jamestown in 1608 (*Ibid.*, 440).
85. Wertenbaker, *Stuarts*, p. 44.   86. Hening's *Statutes*, vol. I, p. 116.
87. *Ibid.*   88. *Ibid.*
89. P. A. Bruce, *Economic History of Virginia*, vol. I, pp. 243-246.
90. Hening's *Statutes*, vol. I, p. 115.   91. *Ibid.*
92. *Ibid.*, p. 119.   93. *Ibid.*, p. 114.
94. *William and Mary Quarterly* (2), vol. 19, p. 27.
95. Robert Beverley, *The History and Present State of Virginia*, p. 67.
96. Hall and Albion, *A History of England and the British Empire*, p. 324.
97. Wertenbaker, *Stuarts*, pp. 61-62.
98. *Ibid.*, p. 62.   99. *Ibid.*
100. *Ibid.*   101. *Ibid.*
102. Alexander Brown, *First Republic in America*, p. 647.
103. *Ibid.*, p. 573.   104. *Ibid.*
105. T. J. Wertenbaker, *Virginia Under the Stuarts*, p. 64;
    Sir Francis' father had died in England.
106. *Ibid.*, p. 62.   107. *Ibid.*, p. 64.
108. Alexander Brown, *First Republic in America*, p. 648.
109. *Ibid.*   110. Wertenbaker, *Stuarts*, p. 63.
111. G. MacLaren Brydon, *Virginia's Mother Church*, p. 82.
112. *Ibid.*   113. *Ibid.*
114. *Ibid.*   115. *Ibid.*
116. *Ibid.*, pp. 81-82.   117. *Ibid.*, p. 83.
118. *Ibid.*
119. *Ibid.* Dr. Brydon notes: "This form of ecclesiastical or semi-ecclesiastical trial of gross offenders continued for a few years only, until courts with authority to try such cases were set up in the several counties. After the establishment of counties and the organization of county courts, presentments were made by the churchwardens to the courts and not to the minister."
120. *Ibid.*, pp. 83-84.   121. *Ibid.*, p. 85.
122. *Ibid.*   123. *Ibid.*
124. G. MacLaren Brydon, *Virginia's Mother Church*, vol. I, p. 85.
125. *Ibid.*   126. *Ibid.*, p. 86.
127. *Ibid.*   128. *Ibid.*, pp. 86-87.
129. *Ibid.*, pp. 87-88, 90-93.   130. *Ibid.*, p. 89.
131. *Ibid.*
132. T. J. Wertenbaker, *Virginia Under the Stuarts*, p. 64.
133. Hening's *Statutes*, vol. I, p. 117.
134. Fiske, *Old Virginia and Her Neighbors*, vol. I, pp. 251-252.
135. *Ibid.*, p. 253.   136. *Ibid.*, p. 252.
137. Dr. Pott was not appointed to the Council in September 1624 because of Warwick's request that the physician be omitted on grounds that "he was the poysoner of the salvages thear." (Alexander Brown, *The First Republic in America*, p. 639.
138. *Ibid.*
139. Fiske, *Old Virginia and Her Neighbors*, vol. I, p. 252.

140. M. P. Andrews, *Virginia, the Old Dominion*, p. 117.
141. T. J. Wertenbaker, *Virginia Under the Stuarts*, p. 65.
142. M. P. Andrews, *Virginia, the Old Dominion*, p. 118.
143. *Ibid.*
144. T. J. Wertenbaker, *Virginia Under the Stuarts*, pp. 65-66.
145. *Ibid.*   146. *Ibid.*
147. *Ibid.*
148. M. P. Andrews, *Virginia, the Old Dominion*, p. 119.
149. T. J. Wertenbaker, *Virginia Under the Stuarts*, p. 66.
150. *Ibid.*
151. *Alexander Brown, The First Republic in America*, p. 644.
152. M. P. Andrews, *Virginia, the Old Dominion*, p. 119.
153. T. J. Wertenbaker, *Virginia Under the Stuarts*, p. 67.
154. John Fiske, *Old Virginia and Her Neighbors*, vol. I, pp. 262-263.
155. *Ibid.*, p. 264.
156. *Documents of American History* (ed., Henry Steele Commager), p. 21.
157. M. P. Andrews, *Virginia, the Old Dominion*, p. 115.
158. Wertenbaker, *Virginia Under the Stuarts*, pp. 69, 71.
159. *Ibid.*, pp. 70-71.   160. *Ibid.*, p. 70.
161. *Ibid.*
162. John H. Latané, *The Early Relations between Maryland and Virginia*, pp. 11-15.
163. Andrews, *Virginia, the Old Dominion*, p. 122.
164. Wertenbaker, *Virginia Under the Stuarts*, p. 71; Latané, *The Early Relations between Maryland and Virginia*, pp. 18-19.
165. Wertenbaker, *Virginia Under the Stuarts*, p. 72.
166. *Ibid.*, p. 73.   167. *Ibid.*, p. 74.
168. *Ibid.*, p. 72.   169. Hening's *Statutes*, vol. I, p. 124.
170. Wertenbaker, *Virginia Under the Stuarts*, p. 73.
171. Words and gestures in this conference are reported in papers of the British Public Record Office, CO 1-8, quoted in Wertenbaker, *Stuarts*, pp. 73-74.
172. *Virginia Magazine of History*, vol. I, p. 416. A letter from Matthews (Mathews), dated May 25, 1635 and dealing with the Harvey controversy, is reprinted *ibid.*, pp. 416-424. It is on this letter, and on Harvey's declaration to the Lords Commissioners of Foreign Plantations (*Ibid.*, pp. 425-430), that our account of the struggle is chiefly based. Where the two accounts are at variance, we have made allowance for the prejudice of opponents.
173. Wertenbaker, *Stuarts*, p. 75. There is a possibility that, in accounts of the petition's circulation, Dr. John Pott has been confused with his brother, Francis. See *Virginia Magazine of History and Biography*, vol. I, p. 427.
174. Fiske, *Old Virginia and Her Neighbors*, vol. I, pp. 295-296.
175. Wertenbaker, *Virginia Under the Stuarts*, p. 75.
176. Fiske, *Old Virginia and Her Neighbors*, vol. I, p. 296; *Virginia Magazine of History and Biography*, vol. I, p. 418.
177. Session described by Matthews, *ibid.*, pp. 418-419. Minifie's name was also spelled Menifie and Menefy. He later acquired a large estate, and is credited with cultivating the first peach trees introduced into America, *ibid.*, pp. 86-87.
178. ". . . he demanded the reason that wee conceived of the countreye's Petition against him"—Matthews, *ibid.*, pp. 419-420.
179. "Mr. Menefee made answer, the chiefest cause was the detayning of the Letters to his Majestie and the Lords"—Matthews, *ibid.*, p. 420. The en-

suing description of this meeting is an attempt to reconcile according to logic the account by Matthews (*ibid.*, p. 420) and the one by Harvey (*ibid.*, pp. 426-427).

180. *Ibid.*, p. 470.   181. *Ibid.*, pp. 421-422.

182. Wertenbaker, *Stuarts*, p. 77.

FOOTNOTES TO CHAPTER VI

1. Wertenbaker, *Stuarts*, p. 78.   2. *Ibid.*

3. *Ibid.*, p. 79.   4. *Ibid.*

5. *Ibid.*   6. *Ibid.*, p. 80.

7. *Ibid.*   8. *Ibid.*

9. *Ibid.*, p. 81.   10. *Ibid.*

11. *Ibid.*, p. 82.   12. *Ibid.*

13. M. P. Andrews, *Virginia, the Old Dominion*, p. 126.

14. *Ibid.*   15. Wertenbaker, *Stuarts*, p. 85.

16. *Ibid.*   17. D. N. B.
                                                                  D. A. B.

18. Wertenbaker, *Stuarts*, p. 86.

19. T. J. Wertenbaker, *Torchbearer of the Revolution*, p. 14.

20. *Ibid.*, pp. 14-15.   21. Wertenbaker, *Stuarts*, p. 87.

22. Cheyney, *A Short History of England*, pp. 442-443.

23. *Journals of the House of Burgesses, 1619-1658/59*, p. 68.

24. *Ibid.*, p. 66.   25. Wertenbaker, *Stuarts*, p. 88.

26. *Ibid.*, p. 87.   27. *Ibid.*

28. G. MacLaren Brydon, *Virginia's Mother Church*, p. 120.

29. M. P. Andrews, *Virginia, the Old Dominion*, p. 128.

30. Beverley, *History and Present State of Virginia*, pp. 60-61.

31. *Ibid.*, pp. 61-62.   32. *Ibid.*, p. 62.

33. *Ibid.*   34. *Ibid.*

35. *Ibid.*   36. Wertenbaker, *Stuarts*, p. 94.

37. *Ibid.*, p. 96.

38. Governor Berkeley's speech is here quoted from *Journals of the House of Burgesses, 1619-1658/59*, pp. 75-76.

39. *Ibid.*, pp. 76-78.

40. *Ibid.*, p. 79.
    Wertenbaker, *Stuarts*, p. 99.

41. Beverley, *History and Present State*, p. 63.

42. *Journals of the House of Burgesses, 1619-1658/59*, p. 79.

43. *Ibid.*   44. *Ibid.*

45. *Ibid.*   46. *Ibid.*, p. 80.

47. *Ibid.*, pp. 79-80.   48. *Ibid.*, pp. 82-83.

49. *Ibid.*, p. 82.   50. Wertenbaker, *Stuarts*, p. 103.

51. *Journals of the House of Burgesses, 1619-1658/59*, p. 82.

52. *Ibid.*, p. 82.

53. Jennings Cropper Wise, *The Early History of the Eastern Shore of Virginia*, pp. 139-140;
    Whitelaw, *Virginia's Eastern Shore*, vol. I, pp. 28-31, 528-529. Members

of the committee were Stephen Charlton, Levin Denwood, John Nuthall, William Whittington, John Ellis, and Stephen Horsey.

54. *Ibid.*, p. 29.
54. Wise, *The Early History of the Eastern Shore of Virginia*, pp. 139-140.
55. *Journals of the House of Burgesses, 1619-1658/59*, p. 90.
56. Wise, *The Early History of the Eastern Shore of Virginia*, pp. 139-140.
57. *Journals of the House of Burgesses, 1619-1658/59*, p. 90.
58. *Ibid.*, p. 86.   59. *Ibid.*
60. *Ibid.*, p. 104.   61. *Ibid.*, p. 109.
62. *Ibid.*, p. 110.   63. *Ibid.*
64. *Ibid.*, pp. 110-111.   65. *Ibid.*, p. 111.
66. *Ibid.*   67. *Ibid.*
68. *Ibid.*   69. Wertenbaker, *Stuarts*, p. 108.
70. *Ibid.*, p. 109.   71. *Ibid.*, p. 110.
72. *Ibid.*, p. 111.   73. *Ibid.*
74. *Ibid.*   75. *Ibid.*, p. 113.
76. *Ibid.*
77. P. A. Bruce, *Economic History of Virginia in the Seventeenth Century*, vol. I, pp. 356-357.
78. Wertenbaker, *Stuarts*, p. 120.
79. P. A. Bruce, *Economic History of Virginia in the Seventeenth Century*, vol. I, p. 389.
80. *Ibid.*
81. *Ibid.*, pp. 390-391.   82. *Ibid.*, pp. 391-393.
83. Wertenbaker, *Stuarts*, p. 122.
    Wertenbaker, *Torchbearer*, pp. 20-21.
84. Wertenbaker, *Stuarts*, pp. 122-123.
85. Wertenbaker, *Torchbearer*, p. 18.   86. *Ibid.*, p. 19.
87. Angus McDonald Papers, Virginia State Library Archives.
88. P. A. Bruce, *Economic History of Virginia in the Seventeenth Century*, vol. I, pp. 397-400.
89. Wertenbaker, *Torchbearer*, p. 32.
90. *Ibid.*, p. 31.   91. *Ibid.*, pp. 23-24.
92. Wertenbaker, *Stuarts*, p. 127.   93. *Ibid.*, pp. 128-129.
94. Douglas S. Freeman, *George Washington*, vol. I, p. 447.
95. *Ibid.*, pp. 448-450.   96. *Ibid.*, pp. 454-455.
97. *Ibid.*, p. 455.   98. *Ibid.*, p. 456.
99. *Ibid.*, pp. 456-458.   100. *Ibid.*, p. 458.
101. *Ibid.*, p. 459.   102. *Ibid.*
103. *Ibid.*, p. 461.   104. *Ibid.*, pp. 461-462.
105. *Ibid.*, p. 462.   106. *Ibid.*
107. *Ibid.*, pp. 462-463.
108. Wertenbaker, *Torchbearer*, pp. 28-29.
109. Wertenbaker, *Stuarts*, p. 145.   110. Wertenbaker, *Torchbearer*, p. 33.
111. *Ibid.*
112. *Tracts and Other Papers, Relating Principally to the Origin, Settlement and Progress of the Colonies in North America* (collected and printed by Peter Force, Washington, D. C., 1836,), vol. I, p. 7. Hereinafter cited as Force's *Tracts*.
113. *Ibid.*, pp. 7-8.   114. Wertenbaker, *Torchbearer*, p. 75.
115. Force's *Tracts*, vol. I, p. 8.   116. *Ibid.*

117. *Ibid.*, pp. 8-9. Trying to make amends, Colonel Mason took home with him the Doeg chief's eight-year-old son. There the boy was nursed back to health.
118. Wertenbaker, *Torchbearer*, p. 78.   119. *Ibid.*
120. *Ibid.*
121.*Ibid.*, p. 79.
Freeman, *Washington*, vol. I, p. 23.
122. Wertenbaker, *Torchbearer*, p. 79.
Freeman, *Washington*, vol. I, pp. 23-25.
123. Freeman, *Washington*, vol. I, pp. 20-21.
124. *Ibid.*, pp. 2-3.
125. Wertenbaker, *Torchbearer*, pp. 79-80.
126. Freeman, *Washington*, vol. I, p. 24.
127. *Ibid.*
128. Wertenbaker, *Torchbearer*, p. 81; Force's *Tracts*, vol. I, p. 12.
129. Wertenbaker, *Torchbearer*, pp. 81-83.
130. *Ibid.*   131. *Ibid.*, pp. 83-84.
132. Wertenbaker, *Stuarts*, pp. 151-153. 133. Wertenbaker, *Torchbearer*, p. 85.
134. *Ibid.*   135. *Ibid.*
136. *Ibid.*, pp. 86-87.   137. *Ibid.*, pp. 87-88.
138. *Ibid.*, p. 88.   139. *Ibid.*
140. *Ibid.*, p. 59.   141. Force's *Tracts*, vol. I, p. 10.
142. Wertenbaker, *Torchbearer*, pp. 90-91.
143. Force's *Tracts*, vol. I, pp. 10-11.   144. Wertenbaker, *Torchbearer*, p. 91.
145. William Byrd, *Natural History of Virginia* (edited and translated from a German version by R. C. Beatty and W. J. Mulloy, Dietz Press, Richmond, Virginia, 1940), pp. VI-VII.
The Secret Diary of William Byrd of Westover, 1709-1712 (edited by L. B. Wright and M. Tinling, Dietz Press, Richmond, Virginia, 1941), p. IX.
L. B. Wright, *The First Gentlemen of Virginia*, pp. 312-322.

The William Byrd referred to in our text was the father of the William Byrd who founded Richmond and Petersburg and wrote the famous *History of the Dividing Line.*
146. Wertenbaker, *Torchbearer*, p. 92.
147. *Ibid.*, p. 93.   148. *Ibid.*
149. Beverley, *History and Present State of Virginia*, pp. 78, 81.
D. A. B.
150. Wertenbaker, *Torchbearer*, p. 125. 151. *Ibid.*, pp. 93-94.
152. *Ibid.*, p. 95.   153. *Ibid.*
154. The circumstances of this alliance were recorded by Councillor Philip Ludwell in a letter, June 28, 1676, to Secretary Williamson (*Virginia Magazine of History*, vol. I, pp. 180-181).
155. Wertenbaker, *Torchbearer*, p. 95.
156. *Virginia Magazine of History*, vol. I, p. 181.
157. Wertenbaker, *Torchbearer*, p. 95.
158. *Ibid.*, p. 97.   159. *Ibid.*
160. *Ibid.*   161. *Ibid.*, pp. 97-98.
162. *Ibid.*, p. 99.   163. *Ibid.*, p. 103.
164. *Ibid.*   165. *Ibid.*, pp. 103-104.
166. *Ibid.*, pp. 104-105.   167. *Ibid.*, pp. 105-106.
168. *Ibid.*, p. 106.   169. *Ibid.*, pp. 106-107.
170. *Ibid.*, p. 107.   171. *Ibid*
172. *Ibid.*   173. *Ibid.*, p. 108.

174. *Ibid.*, p. 109.   175. *Ibid.*
176. Wertenbaker, *Stuarts*, p. 163.   177. *Ibid.*
178. *Ibid.*, pp. 163-164.
179. *Ibid.*, p. 164.
    Peter Force, *Tracts*, Sect. VIII, pp. 13 and 18.
    Substantially the same words are quoted in a contemporary account by
    Thomas Mathews titled *Beginning, Progress and Conclusion of Bacon's
    Rebellion in Virginia in the Years 1675 and 1676.* This description was
    reprinted by G. P. Humphrey, Rochester, N. Y., in 1897. The portion
    dealing with the climax is reprinted in *The Heritage of America* (ed. by
    Henry Steele Commager and Allan Nevins, Little, Brown and Company;
    Boston, 1951), pp. 53-61.
180. *Heritage of America*, pp. 55-56.
181. *Virginia Magazine of History*, vol. I, pp. 182-183.
182. W. F. Craven, *The Southern Colonies in the Seventeenth Century*, vol. I,
    p. 385.
183. Wertenbaker, *Stuarts*, p. 165.   184. *Ibid.*, pp. 165-166.
185. Wertenbaker, *Torchbearer*, p. 119.
186. *Ibid.*
    Heritage of America, p. 56; Force's *Tracts*, vol. I, p. 16.
187. Wertenbaker, *Torchbearer*, p. 120.
188. Force's *Tracts*, vol. I, p. 17.
    Thomas Mathews, who quotes these words, was an eye witness.
189. Wertenbaker, *Stuarts*, p. 168; Force's *Tracts*, vol. I, p. 17.
190. *Ibid.* (both Wertenbaker and Force)
191. Wertenbaker, *Stuarts*, p. 169.
192. Wertenbaker, *Torchbearer*, p. 123. 193. Wertenbaker, *Stuarts*, p. 169.
194. Wertenbaker, *Torchbearer*, pp. 123-124.
195. Wertenbaker, *Stuarts*, p. 169.   196. *Ibid.*, p. 170.
197. Wertenbaker, *Torchbearer*, pp. 125-126.
198. *Ibid.*, p. 127.   199. *Ibid.*
200. *Ibid.*
    All but conclusive evidence indicates that Berkeley spoke from the saddle.
    He may have lost consciousness after mounting his horse following his
    appeal, but such a situation is not suggested by the report that, when his
    audience walked away from him, he "fainted away on horseback in
    the field."
201. *Ibid.*, p. 129.
202. *Virginia Magazine of History*, vol. I, p. 55.
203. Wertenbaker, *Torchbearer*, p. 130.
204. *Ibid.*, pp. 130-131.   205. *Ibid.*, p. 132.
206. Wertenbaker, *Stuarts*, p. 173.   207. *Ibid.*
208. Wertenbaker, *Torchbearer*, pp. 133-134.
209. *Ibid.*, pp. 141-142.   210. *Ibid.*, pp. 144-145.
211. *Ibid.*, p. 145.   212. *Ibid.*, pp. 146.
213. *Ibid.*, pp. 146-147.
214. Wertenbaker, *Stuarts*, pp. 174-175, 178.
215. *Ibid.*, pp. 178-179.
    Wertenbaker, *Torchbearer*, p. 150.
216. Wertenbaker, *Torchbearer*, pp. 150-156.
217. *Ibid.*, pp. 156, 158.
218. Wertenbaker, *Torchbearer*, p. 157. 219. Wertenbaker, *Stuarts*, pp. 178-179.

220. Wertenbaker, *Torchbearer*, p. 158. 221. *Ibid.*
222. Wertenbaker, *Torchbearer*, pp. 159-160.
223. Wertenbaker, *Stuarts*, pp. 179-180. 224. Wertenbaker, *Torchbearer*, p. 166.
225. *Ibid.*, p. 167.
    Wertenbaker, *Stuarts*, p. 182.
    Reconstruction of the burning of Jamestown is based also on examination of the site and archaeological findings there indicating the location of buildings.
226. Wertenbaker, *Torchbearer*, p. 167.
    Wertenbaker, *Stuarts*, p. 182.
227. Wertenbaker, *Stuarts*, p. 182.
228. Wertenbaker, *Torchbearer*, p. 169.
    Wertenbaker, *Stuarts*, pp. 182-183.
229. Wertenbaker, *Torchbearer*, pp. 170-171.
230. *Ibid.*, p. 171.
231. *Ibid.*
    Wertenbaker, *Stuarts*, pp. 183-184.
232. Wertenbaker, *Torchbearer*, pp. 171-172.
233. Wertenbaker, *Stuarts*, p. 184.
234. Wertenbaker, *Torchbearer*, p. 173.
235. *Ibid.*, pp. 173-174.
    Wertenbaker, *Stuarts*, p. 184.
236. Wertenbaker, *Torchbearer*, p. 177; Edward D. Neill, *Virginia Carolarum,* pp. 368-369.
237. Wertenbaker, *Torchbearer*, pp. 184-186.
238. *Ibid.*, pp. 187-189.   239. Wertenbaker, *Stuarts*, p. 191.
240. Wertenbaker, *Torchbearer*, pp. 189-190.
241. *Ibid.*, pp. 194-195.
242. *Ibid.*, p. 196.   243. *Ibid.*, pp. 196-197.
244. *Ibid.*, pp. 197-200.
    Wertenbaker, *Stuarts*, pp. 193-194.
245. Wertenbaker, *Stuarts*, p. 199.
    Wertenbaker, *Torchbearer*, p. 203.
246. Wertenbaker, *Torchbearer*, pp. 203-204.
247. *Ibid.*, pp. 204-205.   248. *Ibid.*, p. 206.
249. *Ibid.*   250. Wertenbaker, *Stuarts*, p. 211.
251. Craven, *The Southern Colonies in the Seventeenth Century*, vol. I, pp. 411-412.
252. *Ibid.*
    William Warren Sweet, *The Story of Religion in America*, pp. 81-82; H. E. Bolton and T. M. Marshall, *The Colonization of North America* (MacMillan, New York, 1936), p. 188.
253. Craven, *The Southern Colonies in the Seventeenth Century*, vol. I, p. 410.

FOOTNOTES TO CHAPTER VII

1. Wertenbaker, *Stuarts*, p. 212.   2. *Ibid.*
3. *Ibid.*, p. 221.
    Flippin, *Royal Government in Virginia*, pp. 108-110.
4. Louis B. Wright, *The First Gentlemen of Virginia*, p. 288.

5. *Journals of the House of Burgesses,* 1659/93, p. XXVIII.
6. Wertenbaker, *Stuarts,* p. 214.   7. *Ibid.*
8. *Ibid.,* pp. 214-215.   9. *Ibid.,* p. 215.
10. *Journals of the House of Burgesses,* 1659/93, p. XXIX.
11. Wertenbaker, *Stuarts,* p. 215.   12. *Ibid.*
13. *Ibid.,* p. 227.   14. *Ibid.,* p. 232.
15. *Ibid.,* p. 233.   16. *Ibid.,* pp. 233-234.
17. *Ibid.,* p. 234.   18. *Ibid.,* pp. 234-235.
19. Louis B. Wright, *The First Gentlemen of Virginia,* p. 289.
20. Wertenbaker, *Stuarts,* p. 238.
21. *Ibid.,* p. 239.   22. *Ibid.,* p. 241.
23. *Ibid.,* pp. 240-241.   24. *Ibid.,* p. 242.
25. *Ibid.*   26. *Ibid.,* pp. 242-243.
27. *Ibid.,* p. 243.   28. *Ibid.,* p. 244.
29. *Ibid.*   30. *Ibid.,* p. 245.
31. Some historians think it not absolutely certain that Monmouth was Charles' son (J. R. Green, *A Short History of the English People,* p. 630), but the duke was the son of Charles' mistress Lucy Walters and Charles acknowledged his paternity (Sir Charles Petrie, *The Stuart Pretenders,* p. 23).
32. Wertenbaker, *Stuarts,* pp. 243-244.
33. *Ibid.,* p. 244.   34. *Ibid.,* p. 246.
35. *Ibid.*   36. *Ibid.,* p. 249.
37. *Journals of the House of Burgesses,* 1659/93, p. LV.
38. Wertenbaker, *Stuarts,* p. 254.
39. *Ibid.,* p. 255.   40. *Ibid.,* pp. 255-256.
41. *Ibid.,* p. 255.   42. *Ibid.,* p. 256.
43. D.N.B. entry on William III.   44. *Ibid.*
45. Wertenbaker, *Stuarts,* p. 256.   46. *Ibid.*
47. *Ibid.,* pp. 257-258.   48. *Ibid.,* p. 258.
49. Beverley, *History and Present State of Virginia,* p. 118.
50. *Journals of the House of Burgesses,* 1659/93, pp. XLIV-XLV, 135, 137-138.
51. P. A. Bruce, *Economic History of Virginia in the Seventeenth Century,* vol. II, pp. 444-446.
52. *Ibid.,* pp. 553-554.   53. Wertenbaker, *Stuarts,* pp. 247-248.
54. M. P. Andrews, *Virginia, the Old Dominion,* pp. 170-171.
55. *Ibid.,* pp. 170-178.
    D.A.B.
56. M. P. Andrews, *Virginia, the Old Dominion,* p. 171;
    Beverley, *The History and Present State of Virginia,* pp. 97-98;
    Hartwell, Blair and Chilton, *The Present State of Virginia, and the College* (edited by H. D. Farish, Princeton University Press, 1940), pp. XXII-XXIII.
        This work, originally written in 1697 and published in 1727, is one of the most valuable sources of information during the period when Jamestown was yielding to Williamsburg as the political and social capital of the colony. Blair was Commissary James Blair, first president of the College of William and Mary.
    The descriptions of Blair here and elsewhere in *The Virginia Experiment* are sustained by the following: Morton, *Colonial Virginia,* pp. 350-351, 354, 376-387, 393-394, 467-469, 481.
    Parke Rouse, Jr. *James Blair of Virginia.*
57. Hartwell, Blair and Chilton, *The Present State,* p. XXIV.
58. *Ibid.*
59. *Ibid.,* p. XXVIII.   60. *Ibid.,* pp. XXIV-XXV.

61. These features are exhibited in the portrait by J. Hargreaves which is the property of the College of William and Mary.
62. M. P. Andrews, *Virginia, the Old Dominion*, p. 178.
63. *Ibid.*
64. M. P. Andrews, *Virginia, the Old Dominion*, p. 178.
65. *William and Mary Quarterly* (2), vol. XIX, p. 350.
66. *Ibid.*, pp. 347-350.   67. *Ibid.*, p. 351.
68. Hartwell, Blair and Chilton, *The Present State*, p. XXVII.
69. D.N.B. entry for George Hamilton, Earl of Orkney.
70. M. P. Andrews, *Virginia, the Old Dominion*, pp. 178-179.
71. Hening, *Statutes*, vol. III, pp. 197, 419-433.
72. M. P. Andrews, *Virginia, the Old Dominion*, pp. 177-178.
73. *Ibid.*
74. *Ibid.*, p. 173.
    William and Mary Quarterly (2), vol. 22, pp. 389-390.
75. M. P. Andrews, *Virginia, the Old Dominion*, p. 174.
76. *William and Mary Quarterly* (2), vol. 22, p. 390.
77. D.A.B.; M. P. Andrews, *Virginia, the Old Dominion*, pp. 177-178.
78. *Ibid.*, p. 176
79. *William and Mary Quarterly* (2), vol. XXII, pp. 389-390.
    Many histories have perpetuated the error that the Burwell daughter involved was Martha instead of Lucy, and that Henry Armistead rather than Edmund Berkeley was the groom.
80. *Ibid.*, p. 394.   81. *Ibid.*
82. M. P. Andrews, *Virginia, the Old Dominion*, p. 174.
83. *William and Mary Quarterly* (2), Vol. XXII, p. 395.
84. *William and Mary Quarterly* (3), vol. II, p. 62.
85. M. P. Andrews, *Virginia, the Old Dominion*, p. 174.
86. *A Handbook for the Exhibition Buildings of Colonial Williamsburg* (Willimsburg, 1936), p. 12.
87. *Ibid.*, pp. 68-69.
88. M. P. Andrews, *Virginia, the Old Dominion*, p. 179.
89. Beverley, *The History and Present State of Virginia*, p. 253.
90. *Ibid.*   91. *Ibid.*
92. *Ibid.*, p. 86.   93. *Ibid.*
94. *A Handbook for the Exhibition Buildings of Colonial Williamsburg*, p. 12.
95. This description is based on the meticulous reconstruction of the capitol by Colonial Williamsburg, Inc.
96. M. P. Andrews, *Virginia, the Old Dominion*, p. 172.
97. Based on Williamsburg Restoration.
98. Beverley, *The History and Present State of Virginia*, pp. 289-290.
99. Hartwell, Blair and Chilton, *The Present State*, p. LV.
100. *Ibid.*, p. 8.
101. Wertenbaker, *The Planters of Colonial Virginia*, pp. 101-133.
102. Hartwell, Blair and Chilton, *The Present State*, p. LXII.
103. S. E. Morison and H. Commager, *Growth of the American Republic*, vol. I, p. 87.
104. *Ibid.*, pp. 85-86.   105. *Ibid.*, pp. 88-89.
106. Louis B. Wright, *The First Gentlemen of Virginia*, p. 56.
107. *Ibid.*, pp. 56-57.   108. *Ibid.*, p. 69.

109. Durand, *A Huguenot Exile in Virginia*, p. 142.

110. Louis B. Wright, *The First Gentlemen of Virginia*, p. 193;
Philip Vickers Fithian, (Fithian's Diary, ed. by H. D. Farish), pp. XVIII-XXI.

111. Description of the Tidewater aristocrat's plantation home based primarily on: Wright, *First Gentlemen*; inventory of Robert (King) Carter's estate; inventory of Councillor William Churchill's estate.

112. Like all generalizations, this description of Virginia's land barons is inadequate. Allowance must be made for the extraordinary diversity among members of a class notable for their individuality. Our summary is based on study of the lives of certain representatives who are discussed elsewhere in this chapter and on a variety of other sources; *e.g.*:

> Charles S. Sydnor, *Gentlemen Freeholders*, pp. 1-10;
> David Mays, *Edmund Pendleton*, vol. I, pp. 3-12;
> Dumas Malone, *Jefferson the Virginian*, pp. 3-16;
> Hartwell, Blair and Chilton, *The Present State of Virginia and the College*, pp. XXII-XXXVI;
> *William Byrd's Natural History of Virginia*, pp. V-XXVI;
> Louis B. Wright, *The First Gentlemen of Virginia* in its entirety, but especially pp. 63-94;
> Douglas S. Freeman, *George Washington*, vol. I, pp. 1-47;
> *The Secret Diary of William Byrd of Westover*, 1709-1712, edited by L. B. Wright and M. Tinling;
> Burton J Hendrick, *The Lees of Virginia*, pp. 3-57;
> T. J. Wertenbaker, *The Planters of Colonial Virginia*, together with such original sources as the Robert Carter Letter Books in the archives of the Virginia Historical Society, the Richard Corbin Letter Book in the Virginia State Library, and the official records of Lancaster, Middlesex, Norfolk and Northampton Counties.

113. An excellent discussion of these factors appears in Charles S. Sydnor's *Gentlemen Freeholders*, pp. 1-10.

114. Col. William Byrd's activities in connection with his father-in-law's estate, together with a sketch of Col. Daniel Parke, are described in Douglas S. Freeman's *George Washington*, vol. II, pp. 279-290.

115. Wright, *First Gentlemen*, p. 192.   116. *Ibid.*, p. 54.

117. Durand, *A Huguenot Exile in Virginia*, p. 110.

118. *Ibid.*, p. 193.

119. Frequent quotations from classical sources appear in the papers of Col. William Byrd II. Col. Richard Lee II reportedly "spent almost his whole life in study and usually wrote his notes in Greek, Hebrew or Latin. . . ." Classical works constituted an important part of the library of a typical member of Virginia's ruling class. (See Wright's *First Gentlemen*, pp. 117-154.)

120. Wright's *First Gentlemen*, pp. 193-194;
The Secret Diary of William Byrd of Westover, 1709-1712, p. 98.

121. Material on Wormeley, unless otherwise indicated, is derived from Wright's *First Gentlemen*, pp. 187-211; Durand, *A Huguenot Exile in Virginia*, pp. 30-32, 110, 111, 154-155 and 158.

122. Hartwell, Blair and Chilton, *The Present State*, p. 71.

123. Wright, *First Gentlemen*, p. 193.

124. Date of death recorded by Col. William Byrd II (November 28, 1710 . . . Col. Churchill died this morning); *The Secret Diary of William Byrd of Westover*, 1709-1712, p. 264.

125. *William and Mary Quarterly* (2), vol. 4, pp. 284-285.

126. *Ibid.*, p. 285.

127. *William and Mary Quarterly* (1), vol. 7, p. 186.

128. *Virginia Magazine of History,* vol. I, p. 368.

129. He also became churchwarden (William Meade, *Old Churches, Ministers and Families of Virginia* (J. B. Lippincott, Philadelphia, 1857), p. 368.

130. Churchill's Middlesex estates are said to have extended across the width of the county (*Encyclopedia of Virginia Biography,* vol. I, p. 150).

131. *William and Mary Quarterly* (2), vol. 22, p. 157.

132. *Virginia Magazine of History and Biography,* vol. XVI, p. 82.

133. *Ibid.,* vol. VII, p. 21.

134. *Ibid.*

135. William Meade, *Old Churches, Ministers and Families of Virginia,* pp. 361, 368.

136. *Ibid.,* p. 361.

137. *William and Mary Quarterly* (1), vol. 7, p. 187.

138. For Churchill's public activities, see *Encyclopedia of Virginia Biography,* vol. I, p. 150; *Virginia Magazine of History,* vol. I, p. 368; *William and Mary Quarterly* (1), vol. 7, pp. 186-188.

139. *The Secret Diary of William Byrd of Westover,* 1709-1712; p. 98.

140. *Ibid.*   141. *Ibid.*

142. *Ibid.,* p. 101.   143. *Ibid.*

144. The variety of Col. Byrd's interests is attested by the secret diary of the years 1709-1712 and the journal entries and letters published in *Another Secret Diary of William Byrd,* 1739-1741, edited by Dr. Maude H. Woodfin. They are also discussed interestingly in Beatty and Malloy's introduction to *William Byrd's Natural History of Virginia,* pp. V-X.

145. *William Byrd's Natural History of Virginia,* pp. VI-VII.

146. *Ibid.,* p. VII.   147. *Ibid.,* pp. VII-VIII.

148. Wright, *First Gentlemen,* p. 324.   149. *Ibid.,* p. 322.

150. Witness the case of Martin's Brandon in Virginia's First Assembly: M. P. Andrews, *Virginia, the Old Dominion,* p. 86.

151. Wright, *First Gentlemen,* p. 325; *William Byrd's Natural History of Virginia,* p. VIII.

152. D.A.B.

153. *The Secret Diary of William Byrd of Westover,* 1709-1712, p. IX.

154. Wright, *First Gentlemen,* p. 317.

155. *Ibid.,* p. 326. Douglas S. Freeman, *George Washington,* vol. II, pp. 279-290.

156. *William Byrd's Natural History of Virginia,* p. VII.

157. *Ibid.,* p. XIX; Wright, *First Gentlemen,* pp. 333-336.

158. Some may see an exception to this record of probity in the fact that Byrd once offered £1,000 for appointment as lieutenant-governor of Virginia under the titular governor, the Earl of Orkney. It should be remembered, though, that it was long customary in England to buy even the command of armies, and baronetcies were once sold by a king.

159. Wright, *First Gentlemen,* pp. 336-339.

160. *The Secret Diary of William Byrd of Westover,* 1709-1712, pp. 234, 235, 241, 242.

161. Wright, *First Gentlemen,* pp. 343-344.

162. *Ibid.,* p. 330.

163. Robert Carter's estate at his death comprised "about 300,000 acres of land, about 1,000 Negroes and £10,000 in money" (Wright, *First Gentlemen,* p. 249).

Corotoman, sometimes spelled "Corrotoman," is pronounced Cûr'-o-tō-man. Variations through the years in the spelling and pronunciation of the word are discussed in *Virginia Magazine of History and Biography*, vol. LII, pp. 105-108.

164. Wright, *First Gentlemen*, p. 237.

165. *Ibid.*, p. 238. 166. *Ibid.*, p. 25.

167. The sketch of Col. John Carter is based on:
Wright, *First Gentlemen*, pp. 236-238; and the D.A.B. entry for Robert Carter.

168. Wright, *First Gentlemen*, p. 250.

169. *Ibid.*, p. 249. 170. D.A.B.

171. *Ibid.*
Wright, *First Gentlemen*, p. 250;
Louis Morton, *Robert Carter of Nomini Hall* (Princeton University Press, 1941), pp. 3-25;
Douglas S. Freeman, *George Washington*, vol. I, pp. 8-14, 488-500.

172. Louis Morton, *Robert Carter of Nomini Hall* (Princeton University Press, 1941), pp. 3-25.
Douglas S. Freeman, *George Washington*, vol. I, p. 10;
The Virginia Magazine of History and Biography, vol. LII, p. 108.

It is interesting to note that "King" Carter's descendants include U. S. Secretary of State Edmund Randolph, Governor John Page, Carter Braxton, President William Henry Harrison, President Benjamin Harrison and General Robert E. Lee. (*The Virginia Magazine of History and Biography*, vol. LII, pp. 108-109).

173. Wright, *First Gentlemen*, p. 250.

174. *Ibid.*, p. 251.
The quotation is from Carter's epitaph which may be read by visitors to Christ Church. The original is in Latin.

175. Wright, *First Gentlemen*, p. 251.

176. Manuscript inventory of the "Personal Estate of the Hon[ble.] Robert Carter late Count of Lancaster Esqr. Deceased," preserved among the Robert Carter Papers in the archives of the Virginia Historical Society.

177. Wright, *First Gentlemen*, p. 256.

178. *Ibid.*, pp. 213-214. 179. *Ibid.*, pp. 212-215.

180. Burton J. Hendrick, *The Lees of Virginia*, pp. 31-32.

181. *Ibid.*, p. 33. 182. *Ibid.*

183. Burton J. Hendrick, *The Lees of Virginia*, p. 42.

184. This library was analyzed at length in Wright, *First Gentlemen*, pp. 217-233.

185. Burton J. Hendrick, *The Lees of Virginia*, pp. 33-34.

186. *The Virginia Magazine of History and Biography*, vol. XVIII, p. 20 .

187. *Ibid.* 188. *Ibid.*
(through miscopying, Sir Edward Walter listed as Chief Justice of *North* Wales).

189. *Ibid.* 190. *Ibid.*

191. *Ibid.* 192. *Ibid.*

193. *Ibid.* 194. *Ibid.*, pp. 20-23.

195. *Ibid.*, p. 22. 196. Wright, *First Gentlemen*, p. 140.

197. The Littletons were also descended from Charlemagne in multiple lines, and from Henry II and William the Conqueror, as well as Ireland's King Brian Boru and Scotland's David I, and more than a third of the Barons of Runnymede.
The Virginia Magazine of History and Biography, vol. XVIII, pp. 20-23.
Ames, Susie M. *County Court Records of Accomack-Northampton, Virginia*, XXXIV-XXXVI.

Edward Coke, *The First Part of the Institute of the Laws of England; or, A Commentary upon Littleton,* pp. XXVII-XXXVII.
Sir Bernard Burke, *A Genealogical History of the Dormant, Abeyant, Forfeited, and Extinct Peerages of the British Empire,* pp. 341-343.
DNB entries for Sir Edmond Littleton, Baron Littleton of Mounslow, and Sir Thomas Littleton, K.B.
Arthur Adams and Frederick Lewis Weis, *The Magna Charta Sureties, 1215: The Barons Named in the Magna Charta, 1215, and Some of Their Descendants Who Settled in America, 1607-1650,* pp. 85, 123-124.

198. Wright, *First Gentlemen,* p. 47.   199. *Ibid.,* p. 77.

200. *Ibid.,* pp. 14-17.

201. The reader who doubts this fact need only turn to Samuel Pepys' *Diary.* Proof that matters had not changed very greatly by 1762 is to be found in *Boswell's London Journal* (edited by F. A. Pottle, McGraw-Hill, New York, 1950).

202. It must be admitted that Bacon was an aristocrat by birth, but his greatest public prominence was as the symbol of a yeoman's movement.

203. Marriage bonds of Lancaster and Northampton counties in the compilations of Stratton Nottingham; also the genealogies of the Churchills of Middlesex County, the Littletons of Nandua and the Scarboroughs of the Eastern Shore.

204. Douglas S. Freeman, *George Washington,* vol. I, p. 33.

205. The first volume of Dr. Freeman's *Washington* tells the story of the events that determined the family's rise.

206. Wright, *First Gentlemen,* p. 78.

207. M. P. Andrews, *Virginia, the Old Dominion,* pp. 88-89.

208. *The Negro in Virginia,* pp. 11-12.

209. *William Byrd's Natural History of Virginia,* p. 4.

210. *Ibid.,* p. 5.   211. *Ibid.*

212. Hartwell, Blair and Chilton, *Present State,* pp. 21-22.

213. Flippin, *Royal Government in Virginia,* pp. 95-96.

214. Charles S. Sydnor, *Gentlemen Freeholders,* p. 64.
The same historian points out that "only fifty-seven family names appear in a list of the ninety-one men appointed to the Council from 1680 to the Revolution," and adds, "nine family names account for almost a third of the Councillors during this century, and fourteen other names for almost another third."

215. Beverley, *The History and Present State of Virginia,* pp. 240-241.

216. Burton J. Hendrick, *The Lees of Virginia,* pp. 15-16, 70.

217. Hartwell, Blair and Chilton, *The Present State,* pp. 34-35.

218. Beverley, *The History and Present State of Virginia,* p. 245.

219. *Ibid.*   220. *Ibid.*

221. *Ibid.*   222. *Ibid.,* pp. 245-246.

223. *Ibid.,* p. 246.

224. Hartwell, Blair and Chilton, *The Present State,* p. 39.

225. *Ibid.,* p. 44.

226. *Ibid.,* pp. 46-47. The judicial powers of the Assembly are effectively described in Chitwood, *Justice in Colonial Virginia,* pp. 17, 19-32.

227. The physical description of Alexander Spotswood is based on a portrait by Charles Bridges.

228. Philip Alexander Bruce, *The Virginia Plutarch,* vol. I, p. 118; Leonidas Dodson, *Alexander Spotswood,* pp. 3-4; *The Official Letters of Alexander Spotswood,* pp. VII-XVI.

229. D.A.B.; Dodson, *Spotswood,* pp. 4-5.
Some insights into Spotswood's personality are provided by Walter Havighurst, *Alexander Spotswood: Portrait of a Governor.*

230. Bruce, *The Virginia Plutarch*, vol. I, p. 121.

231. D.A.B.

232. David I. Bushnell, Jr., *Germanna Ford: Cross-Roads of History* (Smithsonian Institution Series), p. 5, *et seq.*
    This grant included the present counties of Spotsylvania, Orange and Culpeper.

233. *Ibid.*; Kathleen Bruce, *Virginia Iron Manufacture in the Slave Era*, pp. 8-15; Dodson, *Spotswood*, pp. 228-230.

234. D.A.B.

235. The description of the men comprising the expedition is based largely on John Fontaine's journal as reproduced in *Memoirs of a Huguenot Family, Translated and compiled from the Original Autobiography of the Rev. James Fontaine* (ed., Ann Maury).

236. *William and Mary Quarterly* (2), vol. XXII, pp. 175-177, 180.

237. *Ibid.*, p. 177.

238. John Fontaine's journal entry for September 6, 1716: ". . . we drank the King's Health in Champagne, and fired a volley—the Princess's health in Burgundy, and fired a volley, and all the rest of the Royal Family in claret, and fired a volley. We drank the Governor's health and fired another volley. We had several sorts of liquors, viz., Virginia red wine and white wine, Irish usquebaugh, brandy, shrub, two sorts of rum, champagne, canary, cherry, punch, water, cider &c. . . ."

239. M. P. Andrews, *Virginia, the Old Dominion*, p. 186.

240. Spotswood presented to each gentleman participating in the expedition a miniature, diamond-studded, golden horseshoe inscribed *sic juvat transcendre montes*. See Hugh Jones, *The Present State of Virginia*, (Morton edition), p. 58.

241. M. P. Andrews, *Virginia, the Old Dominion*, p. 189.

242. *Ibid.*, pp. 196-197.   243. *Ibid.*

244. *Ibid.*, pp. 197-198.

245. Hartwell, Blair and Chilton, *The Present State*, p. XXV.

246. D.A.B.

247. M. P. Andrews, *Virginia, the Old Dominion*, p. 199.

248. *Ibid.*, p. 191.

249. P. A. Bruce, *History of Virginia*, vol. I, pp. 306-307.

250. M. P. Andrews, *Virginia, the Old Dominion*, p. 206.

251. *Ibid.*, pp. 190-191.   252. *Ibid.*, p. 190.

253. *Ibid.*

254. Spotswood was not alone in his concern over the Negro's role. The Virginia Assembly, in 1710-1711, imposed a virtually prohibitive tax on the importation of Negroes, but was overruled by London (M. P. Andrews, *Virginia, the Old Dominion*, p. 190).
    General references for Spotswood's character and accomplishments:
    Leonidas Dodson, *Alexander Spotswood*; *The Official Letters of Alexander Spotswood*, vol. I; D.A.B.; Hugh Jones, *The Present State of Virginia* (Morton edition), pp. 8, 45-46, 58-59, 70, 87, 124.

FOOTNOTES TO CHAPTER VIII

1. P. S. Flippin, *Royal Government in Virginia*, pp. 121-124.

2. Wright, *First Gentlemen*, pp. 235, 248-250.

3. Historians differ as to the date on which Gooch entered upon his duties as governor. September 11 is the date given in Alexander Wilbourne Weddell's *A Memorial Volume of Virginia Historical Portraiture* and in *A Hornbook of Virginia History*, published by the Division of History of the Virginia Department of Conservation and Development, under the editorship of J. R. V. Daniel. September 8 is given in P. S. Flippin, *The Royal Government in Virginia*, p. 124, and Morton, *Colonial Virginia*, pp. 497-498.

4. M. P. Andrews, *Virginia, the Old Dominion*, p. 202.
   D.A.B.

5. Freeman, *Washington*, vol. I, p. 87.

6. M. P. Andrews, *Virginia, the Old Dominion*, p. 204.

7. Freeman, *Washington*, vol. I, p. 88.

8. *Ibid.*, p. 87.   9. *Ibid.*, p. 88.

10. *Ibid.*, p. 87.

11. Gooch's comment on his seasickness is to be found in the Virginia Historical Society's collection of William Gooch's letters (typescript), vol. II. The quotation regarding his wounds is from a letter to his brother, October 13, 1741, in Gooch Letters, p. 90, archives of Colonial Williamsburg. An explicit description of his injury is contained in a letter written to his brother June 12, 1741 from Jamaica (Gooch Letters, p. 77, Colonial Williamsburg archives).

    Despite his fear that he was "quite disabled," Gooch rejoiced that no bones were broken and declared, "Never was so providential a shot known, nor so particular an instance of Divine favor." And, as he confessed to his brother, the governor was further cheered to discover that "the Virginians were mightily rejoiced at [his] return, day and night firing guns, bonfires and illuminations."

12. In Spotswood's administration. Morton, *Colonial Virginia*, pp. 428-435.

13. Freeman H. Hart, *The Valley of Virginia in the American Revolution*, 1763-1789, pp. 5-7.

14. *Ibid.*, pp. 5-7, 47, 169.

15. Louis K. Koontz, *Robert Dinwiddie*, p. 161.

16. Letter of December 28, 1727, Gooch Letters, Colonial Williamsburg archives.

17. Hartwell, Blair and Chilton, *The Present State*, p. XXV.

18. June 9, 1728, Gooch Letters, p. 13, Colonial Williamsburg archives.
    In a letter of October 15, 1740, Blair praised Gooch as "so good a governour." (William Gooch Letters (typescript), vol. II, No. 644, Virginia Historical Society archives.

19. Blair's interim service began June 14, 1740. See William Gooch Letters, vol. II, Nos. 644 and 645, Virginia Historical Society archives; also *Another Secret Diary of William Byrd of Westover*, p. 76.

20. Gooch Letters, p. 114, Colonial Williamsburg archives.

21. Letter of May 10, 1743, William Gooch Letters, vol. II, No. 726, Virginia Historical Society archives.

22. M. P. Andrews, *Virginia, the Old Dominion*, p. 208.

23. *Ibid.*

24. *Ibid.*
    David J. Mays, *Edmund Pendleton*, vol. I, p. 69;
    P. Abernethy, *Western Lands and the American Revolution*, pp. 5-8;
    Kenneth P. Bailey, *The Ohio Company of Virginia and the Westward Movement*, pp. 35-39.

25. Freeman, *Washington*, vol. I, p. 282;
    Virginia Cavalcade, vol. III, pp. 17-18;
    George Mercer Papers, (ed., Lois Mulkearn), pp. 7-40.

26. M. P. Andrews, *Virginia, the Old Dominion*, p. 207.

27. *A Hornbook of Virginia History*, p. 6.
28. *Virginia Cavalcade*, vol. III, p. 18;
Burton J. Hendrick, *The Lees of Virginia*, pp. 66-69.
29. *A Hornbook of Virginia History*, p. 101.
30. Koontz, *Dinwiddie*, pp. 39, 165, 167, 169-170.
31. Freeman, *Washington*, vol. I, p. 170.
32. Koontz, *Dinwiddie*, pp. 32-94.
33. The physical description of Dinwiddie is based on a photograph of a portrait in the National Portrait Gallery, London.
34. Koontz, *Dinwiddie*, p. 37.
Dinwiddie's contest for Council powers was described by Governor Gooch November 6, 1741 in a letter to the Rt. Hon. Lords Commissioners of Trade and Plantations (William Gooch Letters, vol. II, No. 670, Virginia Historical Society archives).
35. William Gooch Letters, vol. II, No. 558, Virginia Historical Society archives.
36. Freeman, *Washington*, vol. I, p. 173.
37. The English tradition of parliamentary representation for universities is explained in R. K. Gooch's *The Government of England*, pp. 156-157.
38. Freeman, *Washington*, vol. I, p. 173.
39. Freeman, *Washington*, vol. I, p. 185.
40. *Ibid.*   41. *Ibid.*
42. *Ibid.*, p. 158.   43. *Ibid.*, pp. 158-159.
44. W. H. T. Squires, *Through the Years in Norfolk*, p. 7.
45. *Ibid.*, pp. 16-17.
The mace was ordered in 1753, and this date is engraved on it, but the emblem was actually presented April 1, 1754.
46. Hening, *Statutes*, vol. VI, pp. 265-266.
Colonel Craford's name is sometimes spelled "Crawford."
47. Col. Byrd's notice about the laying off of Richmond appeared as an advertisement in the Williamsburg *Gazette* issue of Friday, April 29, to Friday, May 6, 1737, No. 40. An original copy is preserved in the archives of the Virginia Historical Society.
48. Freeman, *Washington*, vol. I, p. 160.
49. *Ibid.*, pp. 60-61.   50. *Ibid.*, p. 160.
51. *Ibid.*, pp. 232-233.
52. *The Secret Diary of William Byrd of Westover, 1709-1712*, p. XII
53. Freeman, *Washington*, vol. I, p. 161.
54. *Ibid.*   55. *Ibid.*
56. Freeman H. Hart, *The Valley of Virginia in the American Revolution*, p. 160.
57. Morison and Commager, *Growth of the American Republic*, vol. I, p. 119.
58. *Ibid.*, p. 120.
59. Herbert E. Bolton and T. M. Marshall, *The Colonization of North America* (N. Y., 1936), pp. 363-364;
Woodrow Wilson, *A History of the American People* (N. Y., 1902), vol. II, p. 71;
Morison and Commager, *Growth of the American Republic*, vol. I, p. 120.
60. W. H. T. Squires, *Through the Years in Norfolk*, p. 16.
61. Morison and Commager, *Growth of the American Republic*, vol. I, p. 120.
62. *Ibid.*, p. 121;
Edward Channing, *A History of the United States* (N. Y., 1936), p. 549;
The Treaty of Aachen is known also as the Treaty of Aix-la-Chapelle.
63. H. E. Bolton and T. M. Marshall, *The Colonization of North America* (N.Y., 1936), pp. 366-369.

64. Morison and Commager, *Growth of the American Republic*, vol. I, p. 122; Freeman, *Washington*, vol. I, p. 271.

65. *Ibid.*   66. *Ibid.*

67. *Ibid.;*
    Koontz, *Dinwiddie*, p. 158.

68. Logstown was eighteen miles west of the present site of Pittsburgh (Koontz, *Dinwiddie*, p. 135).

69. Freeman, *Washington*, vol. I, pp. 271-272.

70. *Ibid.*, p. 272.   71. *Ibid.*

72. *Ibid.*

73. Lawrence Washington was the half-brother of George Washington and the great-grandson of Col. John Washington, the famous Indian fighter.

74. Freeman, *Washington*, vol. I, pp. 264-266.

75. *Ibid.*, p. 266.   76. *Ibid.*

77. *Ibid.*, p. 268.   78. *Ibid.*, pp. 268-269.

79. *Ibid.*, p. 272.   80. *Ibid.*, p. 273.

81. *Ibid.*, p. 274.

82. *Ibid.*, p. 275. Early in 1754, Dinwiddie's correspondence with his fellow governors had grown apace (see Koontz, *Dinwiddie*, pp. 261-273).

83. Description of Washington's physical appearance based on Charles Willson Peale portrait at Washington and Lee University, Lexington, Virginia.

84. Freeman, *Washington*, vol. I, p. 276.

85. *Ibid.*

86. *The Diaries of George Washington* (edited by John C. Fitzpatrick, Houghton Mifflin, 1925), vol. I, p. 43.
    The "servitors" were "Barnaby Currin and John Mac-Quire, Indian traders, Henry Steward and William Jenkins."
    (*The Diaries of George Washington* are hereinafter referred to as *Washington Diaries.*)

87. Freeman, *Washington*, vol. I, p. 287.

88. *Ibid.*   89. *Washington Diaries*, vol. I, p. 44.

90. *Ibid.*, pp. 45-46;
    Freeman, *Washington*, vol. I, pp. 289-290.

91. Freeman, *Washington*, vol. I, p. 291;
    Washington Diaries, vol. I, pp. 45-47.
    Van Braam evidently mistook "Illinois" for "Isles Noires," because, after hearing the Dutchman's translation, Washington wrote "Black Islands."

92. Freeman, *Washington*, vol. I, pp. 292-294;
    Washington Diaries, vol. I, pp. 47-49.

93. Freeman, *Washington*, vol. I, pp. 300-301.

94. *Washington Diaries*, vol. I, p. 54.
    The hunter was described as "young" on p. 63 of the same volume.

95. *Ibid.*, pp. 54-55.

96. Freeman, *Washington*, vol. I, pp. 302-303.

97. *Washington Diaries*, vol. I, p. 55.

98. *Ibid.*
    Washington said that the French boasted they "knew their [English] motions were too slow and dilatory to prevent any undertaking" of King Louis' men.

99. *Ibid.*, pp. 55-56.
    The information which Washington secured was amazingly specific as to garrisons and the distance between forts.

100. *Ibid.*, p. 56.

101. *Ibid.*, p. 57.
Freeman, *Washington*, vol. I, pp. 305-306.

102. Gist's diary has been printed in *Massachusetts Historical Society Collections*, Series 3, vol. V. Gist's report on Joincare is quoted in *Washington Diaries*, vol. I, p. 57. Washington himself wrote that Gist had to use "great persuasion" to draw the Indians away from Joincare. (*Washington Diaries*, vol. I, p. 57.)

103. *Washington Diaries*, vol. I, p. 58;
Freeman, *Washington*, vol. I, pp. 307-308.

104. Freeman, *Washington*, vol. I, p. 308;
Washington Diaries, vol. I, p. 58.
Washington called Repentigny "Monsieur Riporti."

105. *Washington Diaries*, vol. I, pp. 58-59.

106. *Ibid.*, pp. 61-62;
Freeman, *Washington*, vol. I, p. 312.

107. *Ibid.*, p. 313;
Washington Diaries, vol. I, p. 61.

108. Freeman, *Washington*, vol. I, p. 309.

109. The quotation is from Washington's own account (Freeman, *Washington*, vol. I, p. 310).

110. *Washington Diaries*, vol. I, p. 59.

111. In Washington's phrase, "blocked out in readiness to make" (*Washington Diaries*, vol. I, p. 59).

112. Freeman, *Washington*, vol. I, p. 311.

113. *Washington Diaries*, vol. I, p. 63.

114. *Ibid.*, p. 64;
Freeman, *Washington*, vol. I, p. 318.

115. *Ibid.*, p. 325;
Washington Diaries, pp. 65-67.

116. Washington was later embarrassed to learn that his hastily prepared manuscript had been printed. (*Washington Diaries*, vol. I, p. 41.)

117. The dispute began when Governor Dinwiddie announced the imposition of an additional fee of one pistole (a Spanish coin) for the issuance of every land patent. The course of the quarrel is described at length in Koontz, *Dinwiddie*, pp. 201-235.

118. Koontz, *Dinwiddie*, pp. 237-256.   119. *Ibid.*, p. 240.

120. Freeman, *Washington*, vol. I, pp. 328-329.

121. *Ibid.*, p. 329.   122. *Ibid.*, p. 331
123. *Ibid.*   124. *Ibid.*
125. *Ibid.*, p. 332.   126. *Ibid.*

127. *Journal of the House of Burgesses*, 1752-1758, pp. 175-176.

128. Freeman, *Washington*, vol. I, pp. 332-333.

129. *Ibid.*   130. *Ibid.*, p. 333.

131. Koontz, *Dinwiddie*, p. 259.

132. Freeman, *Washington*, vol. I, pp. 333-334.

133. *Ibid.*, p. 336.   134. *Ibid.*
135. *Ibid.*, p. 337.   136. *Ibid.*
137. *Ibid.*   138. *Ibid.*

139. *Ibid.*, p. 342.

140. *Ibid.*, p. 338;
Koontz, *Dinwiddie*, pp. 261-262.

141. Freeman, *Washington*, vol. I, p. 338.

142. *Ibid.*;
Koontz, *Dinwiddie*, p. 275.

143. Freeman, *Washington*, vol. I, p. 338.

144. *Ibid.*, p. 339.   145. *Ibid.*, p. 340.

146. *Ibid.*, p. 341.   147. *Ibid.*, pp. 341-342.

148. *Ibid.*, p. 336.   149. *Ibid.*

150. *Ibid.*, p. 342.

151. *Ibid.*, pp. 343-344;
     Washington Diaries, vol. I, pp. 73-74.

     The *Washington Diaries* for the period of March 31—June 27, 1754 are an English translation of a French translation of Washington's memoranda. For this period, therefore, the entries are reliable in some particulars and unreliable in others. There is every reason to believe that there is little or no willful distortion by the French in translation of the earlier portion of the memoranda. An explanation of the sequence of translations appears in *Washington Diaries*, vol. I, p. 72. An explanation and valuable critique of this portion of the journals appears in Freeman, *Washington*, vol. I, appendix I-9.

152. Freeman, *Washington*, vol. I, pp. 348-349.

153. *Ibid.*, p. 349. The haste of the messenger is conjectured from his report that he bore letters from Captain Trent "demanding a reenforcement with all possible speed." (*Washington Diaries*, vol. I, p. 74.)

154. Freeman, *Washington*, vol. I, p. 343.

155. Trent wrote he "hourly expected a body of eight hundred French." (*Washington Diaries*, vol. I, p. 74.)

156. Freeman, *Washington*, vol. I, p. 350.

157. Washington had heard April 20 an unconfirmed report of the fort's capture (*Washington Diaries*, vol. I, p. 75).

158. Freeman, *Washington*, vol. I, p. 353.

159. *Ibid.*   160. *Ibid.*, pp. 352-353.

161. *Ibid.*, p. 353.   162. *Ibid.*, pp. 352-353.

163. *Washington Diaries*, vol. I, pp. 75-76.

164. Freeman, *Washington*, vol. I, p. 354.

165. *Ibid.*   166. *Ibid.*, pp. 354-355.

167. *Ibid.*, p. 355.   168. *Ibid.*, p. 356.

169. *Washington Diaries*, vol. I, p. 79.

170. *Ibid.*

     George Washington's Indian name was Conotocarious, or "Devourer of Villages." It was the same bestowed by the Indians upon his great-gandfather John.

171. Freeman, *Washington*, vol. I, pp. 356-358.

172. *Washington Diaries*, vol. I, p. 81.

     Washington reported that "many others" agreed with the two traders.

173. Freeman, *Washington*, vol. I, p. 358.

174. *Ibid.*, p. 359.

175. *The Official Records of Robert Dinwiddie*, vol. I, p. 141.

176. *Ibid.*, p. 447.

     The letter was dated January 2, 1755.

177. Hayes Baker-Crothers, *Virginia and the French and Indian War*, pp. 49-50.

178. Freeman, *Washington*, vol. I, p. 359.

179. *Ibid.*, pp. 358-361.   180. *Ibid.*, p. 361.

181. *Ibid.*, pp. 361-362.   182. *Ibid.*, p. 362.

183. *Ibid.*, p. 363.

184. *Washington Diaries*, vol. I, p. 83.

     The lieutenant was John West, Jr., Virginia Regiment.

185. Freeman, *Washington*, vol. I, p. 365.

186. *Ibid.*, p. 367.   187. *Washington Diaries*, vol. I, p. 85.

188. *Ibid.*
Freeman, *Washington*, vol. I, p. 368.

189. Freeman, *Washington*, vol. I, p. 368.

190. *Ibid.*, p. 369;
Washington Diaries, vol. I, pp. 84-85.

191. *Ibid.*

192. Freeman, *Washington*, vol. I, p. 369;
Washington Diaries, vol. I, p. 86.

193. Washington's journal (*Washington Diaries*, vol. I, p. 86) said 65, rather than
75, men, but the journal, distorted in translation from English into French
and back into English again, must yield in point of accuracy to a letter
cited by Dr. Freeman in *Washington*, vol. I, pp. 369-370.

Captain Hog's name was pronounced as it came to be spelled, "Hoge,"
rhyming with "brogue."

194. Freeman, *Washington*, vol. I, p. 170.

The journal states that the Indian runner arrived at eight o'clock.

195. *Washington Diaries*, vol. I, p. 87;
Freeman, *Washington*, vol. I, p. 371.

196. *Washington Diaries*, vol. I, p. 87.

Washington recorded that his party "set out in a heavy rain and in a
night as dark as pitch, along a path scarce broad enough for one man;
we were sometimes fifteen or twenty minutes out of the path before we
could come to it again, and we would often strike against each other in
the dark."

197. Freeman, *Washington*, vol. I, p. 371;
Washington Diaries, vol. I, p. 87.

198. Freeman, *Washington*, vol. I, pp. 371-372.

199. *Ibid.*, p. 372.

Stephen's troops had returned May 23 from reconnaissance. (Freeman,
Washington, vol. I, p. 366.)

200. *Ibid.*, pp. 372-373.

Stephen himself did not know which side fired first.

201. *Ibid.*   202. *Ibid.*, p. 373.

203. *Ibid.*   204. *Ibid.*, p. 374.

205. *Ibid.*, pp. 374-375.   206. *Ibid.*

207. *Ibid.*, pp. 375-376.   208. *Ibid.*, pp. 377-379.

209. *Ibid.*

210. Freeman, *Washington*, vol. I, p. 379.

211. *Ibid.*   212. *Ibid.*, pp. 379-380.

213. *Ibid.*, p. 380.   214. *Ibid.*, pp. 380-381.

215. *Ibid.*, p. 381.   216. *Ibid.*

217. *Ibid.*, pp. 382-383;
D.A.B. entry for Lewis.

218. Freeman, *Washington*, vol. I, pp. 381-383.

219. *Ibid.*, p. 384.   220. *Ibid.*

221. *Ibid.*, pp. 385-390.   222. *Ibid.*, p. 385.

223. *Ibid.*, pp. 385-386.   224. *Ibid.*, p. 390.

225. *Ibid.*, pp. 390-391.   226. *Ibid.*

227. *Ibid.*   228. *Ibid.*, pp. 391-401.

229. *Ibid.*   230. *Ibid.*, p. 400.

231. *Ibid.*, p. 401.   232. *Ibid.*

233. *Ibid.*
235. *Ibid.*, p. 403.
237. *Ibid.*, pp. 403-404.
238. *Ibid.*
 The quoted words are Washington's.
239. *Ibid.*, pp. 404-405.
241. *Ibid.*, pp. 406-407.
243. *Ibid.*, pp. 405-406.
245. *Ibid.*, p. 411.
247. *Ibid.*, p. 415.
249. *Ibid.*, p. 413.
251. *Ibid.*, p. 416.
253. *Ibid.*, p. 416.
255. *Ibid.*
257. *Ibid.*, pp. 423-424.
259. *Ibid.*
261. *Ibid.*
263. *Ibid.*, p. 441.
265. Freeman, *Washington,*vol. II, p. 5.
267. *Ibid.*, pp. 6-7.
269. *Ibid.*
271. *Ibid.*
273. *Ibid.*, p. 9.
275. *Ibid.*, p. 10.

234. *Ibid.*, pp. 402-403.
236. *Ibid.*
240. *Ibid.*, pp. 405-406.
242. *Ibid.*, p. 407.
244. *Ibid.*, pp. 408-409.
246. *Ibid.*, p. 410.
248. *Ibid.*, p. 407.
250. *Ibid.*, p. 415.
252. *Ibid.*, p. 432.
254. *Ibid.*, p. 422.
256. *Ibid.*
258. *Ibid.*, pp. 427, 431.
260. *Ibid.*, pp. 436-437.
262. *Ibid.*, p. 439.
264. *Ibid.*
266. *Ibid.*, pp. 5-6.
268. *Ibid.*, p. 7.
270. *Ibid.*, p. 8.
272. *Ibid.*, pp. 8-9.
274. *Ibid.*, pp. 9-10.

276. *Virginia Gazette*, Williamsburg, February 28, 1755.
 (Hunter, photostats in Virginia Historical Society archives.)
277. *Ibid.*
278. D.N.B.
279. Freeman, *Washington*, vol. II, pp. 15-16.
 James Thomas Flexner, *George Washington: The Forge of Experience*, pp. 114-131.
 For a very sympathetic estimate of Braddock's character and abilities, see Lawrence Henry Gipson, *The British Empire Before the American Revolution*, vol. VI, pp. 57-58, 78-79, 82-85.
280. Manuscript History of Virginia by Edmund Randolph, p. 102. (Virginia Historical Society archives.)
281. Freeman, *Washington*, vol. II, p. 17.
282. Mrs. Charlotte Browne's "Journal of a Voyage from London to Virginia," (Virginia Historical Society archives, photostated pages from Library of Congress photographs of the original journal, owned by S. A. Courtald of the Howe, Halstead Essex, England).
283. Freeman, *Washington*, vol. II, p. 11.
284. *Ibid.*, p. 21.
286. *Ibid.*
288. *Ibid.*
290. *Ibid.*, p. 23.
292. *Ibid.*, p. 25.
294. *Ibid.*, p. 26.
296. *Ibid.*, p. 35.
298. *Ibid.*, p. 45.
300. *Ibid.*, p. 47.
302. *Ibid.*, p. 95.

285. *Ibid.*
287. *Ibid.*
289. *Ibid.*, p. 16.
291. *Ibid.*, p. 24.
293. *Ibid.*
295. *Ibid.*, p. 34.
297. *Ibid.*, pp. 89-90.
299. *Ibid.*, pp. 46-47.
301. *Ibid.*, pp. 92-94.

303. M. P. Andrews, *Virginia, the Old Dominion*, p. 230.
304. Freeman, *Washington*, vol. II, p. 89.

305. *Ibid.*, p. 61.   306. *Ibid.*, p. 62.
307. *Ibid.*, pp. 62-63.   308. *Ibid.*, pp. 64-65.
309. *Ibid.*, pp. 66-67.
310. M. P. Andrews, *Virginia, the Old Dominion*, p. 222.
311. Freeman, *Washington*, vol. II, p. 68.
312. *Ibid.*, p. 72.
     The quoted words are approximately those that St. Clair spoke.
313. *Ibid.*, p. 76.   314. *Ibid.*
315. *Ibid.*, p. 78.   316. *Ibid.*, pp. 78-80.
317. *Ibid.*, p. 82.   318. *Ibid.*, pp. 82-83.
319. M. P. Andrews, *Virginia, the Old Dominion*, p. 223.
320. Freeman, *Washington*, vol. II, p. 86.
321. *Ibid.*
322. M. P. Andrews, *Virginia, the Old Dominion*, p. 224.
323. Freeman, *Washington*, vol. II, p. 381.
324. M. P. Andrews, *Virginia, the Old Dominion*, p. 226.
325. *Ibid.*   326. *Ibid.*
327. *Ibid.*   328. *Ibid.*, p. 227.
329. *Ibid.*, p. 228.   330. *Ibid.*, p. 230.
331. *Ibid.*   332. *Ibid.*
333. *Ibid.*   334. *Ibid.*, pp. 229-230.
335. Morison and Commager, *Growth of the American Republic*, vol. I, p. 123.
336. *Ibid.*   337. *Ibid.*
338. *Ibid.*, p. 124.
339. Cheyney, *A Short History of England*, p. 562.
340. Morison and Commager, *Growth of the American Republic*, vol. I, p. 123;
     George Macaulay Trevelyan, *A Shortened History of England* (Longmans,
     Green and Co., New York, 1942), pp. 374-376;
     John Richard Green, *A Short History of the English People* (American Book
     Co., New York, 1916), pp. 746-748;
     James Truslow Adams, *Building the British Empire*, p. 372;
     William B. Willcox (Knopf, New York, 1950), *Star of Empire*, pp. 137-138.
341. J. C. Long, *Mr. Pitt and America's* Birthright (Stokes, New York, 1940),
     pp. 236, 256-260;
     J. R. Green, *Short History of the English People*, p. 748;
     G. M. Trevelyan, *A Shortened History of England*, p. 378;
     J. T. Adams, *Building the British Empire*, p. 372.
342. J. C. Long, *Mr. Pitt*, pp. 226-265;
     G. M. Trevelyan, *A Shortened History of England*, pp. 376, 378-379;
     J. R. Green, *Short History of the English People*, pp. 749-753;
     William B. Willcox, *Star of Empire*, pp. 138-139;
     J. T. Adams, *Building the British Empire*, pp. 372-373.
343. Cheyney, *A Short History of England*, p. 563.
344. J. C. Long. *Mr. Pitt*, pp. 266-278;
     J. R. Green, *Short History of the English People*, pp. 754-755.
345. J. C. Long, *Mr. Pitt*, pp. 279-289;
     J. R. Green, *Short History of the English People*, pp. 755-756;
     G. M. Trevelyan, *A Shortened History of England*, p. 378.
346. Morison and Commager, *Growth of the American Republic*, vol. I, p. 125;
     J. C. Long, *Mr. Pitt*, pp. 274-277;
     G. M. Trevelyan, *A Shortened History of England*, p. 379;
     J. R. Green, *Short History of the English People*, pp. 755-757.
347. M. P. Andrews, *Virginia, the Old Dominion*, pp. 230-231.

348. *Ibid.*, p. 231.
349. J. R. Green, *Short History of the English People*, pp. 754-755.
350. J. R. Green, *Short History of the English People*, pp. 753-754;
    J. C. Long, *Mr. Pitt*, p. 313.
351. J. R. Green, *Short History of the English People*, p. 756.
352. *Ibid.*, pp. 756-757.
353. Morison and Commager, *Growth of the American Republic*, vol. I, p. 125.
354. *Ibid.*   355. *Ibid.*, p. 126.
356. G. M. Trevelyan, *A Shortened History of England*, p. 376.
    Trevelyan wrote of Pitt, "He alone of British statesmen carried the map
    of the empire in his head and in his heart."
357. J. R. Green, *Short History of the English People*, pp. 757-758, 764.
358. Koontz, *The Virginia Frontier, 1754-1763*, p. 53.
359. Marshall Davidson, *Life in America*, vol. I, p. 98.
360. M. P. Andrews, *Virginia, the Old Dominion*, p. 224.
361. J. R. Green, *Short History of the English People*, p. 757.

FOOTNOTES TO CHAPTER IX

1. M. P. Andrews, *Virginia, the Old Dominion*, p. 236.
2. Following Pontiac's offensive, Maj. Gen. Jeffrey Amherst proposed to Col.
   Henry Bonquet that germ warfare be used. The general's plan to distribute
   smallpox-laden blankets among the Indians was abandoned because of the
   danger of infection to the English.
       In all fairness to Pontiac, it should be noted that he remained personally
   loyal to the British after the Oswego Treaty of 1766.
3. The proclamation was signed by the king October 7, 1763 after being rushed
   through the cabinet and privy council. The document was prepared by the
   Earl of Hillsborough who the month before had succeeded William Petty,
   Lord Shelburne, as head of the Board of Trade.
4. Freeman, *Washington*, vol. I, p. 236;
   M. P. Andrews, *Virginia, the Old Dominion*, p. 234.
5. M. P. Andrews, *Virginia, the Old Dominion*, p. 235.
6. *Ibid.*, p. 243.   7. *Ibid.*, p. 233.
8. *Ibid.*, p. 235.
9. Freeman, *Washington*, vol. I, p. 236;
   T. P. Abernethy, *Western Lands and the American Revolution*, pp. 5-8.
10. Freeman, *Washington*, vol. I, p. 237;
    Mays, *Edmunds Pendleton*, vol. I, p. 69.
11. Mays, *Edmund Pendleton*, vol. I, pp. 69, 178.
12. *Ibid.*, p. 69.
13. *Ibid.*;
    Freeman, *Washington*, vol. I, p. 237.
14. Mays, *Edmund Pendleton*, vol. I, p. 69.
15. Colonial Williamsburg copy of unpublished Book 6, Folio 327 in North
    Papers, Bodleian Library.
16. Rev. Andrew Burnaby, *Travels through the Middle Settlements in North
    America in the Years 1759 and 1760* (second edition, T. Payne. London,
    1775), p. 34.
17. *Ibid.*

18. Mays, *Edmund Pendleton*, vol. I, pp. 142-143.

19. *Ibid.*, p. 143.

The quote is from Mays himself.

20. *Ibid.*   21. *Ibid.*

22. *Ibid.*, pp. 143-144.   23. Burnaby, *Travels*, p. 34.

24. *Ibid.*, p. 33.

A native Virginia leader, Edmund Pendleton, censured his fellow Virginians for "extravagance." (Mays, *Edmund Pendleton*, vol. II, p. 204.)

25. Burnaby, *Travels*, p. 19.   26. *Ibid.*, p. 31.

27. Mays, *Edmund Pendleton*, vol. I, pp. 144-146.

28. *Ibid.*, p. 146.   29. *Ibid.*, p. 147.

30. *Ibid.*, p. 148.

31. *Ibid.*, pp. 148-149.

The tax was to cease if sufficient money reached the Virginia treasury before the end of 1769 out of money previously granted by Parliament.

32. *Ibid.*, pp. 149, 150, 328 (note 35).

33. A convincing picture of "the precarious situation of credit" in Virginia is given in the letters of Col. Richard Corbin, especially those to the Messrs. Hanbury, Robert Cary, Esq. & Co., and James Buchanan & Co. These letters are available in manuscript "Letter Book, 1761-1768, of Col. Richard Corbin, Receiver General of Virginia," in the Virginia Historical Society archives. This manuscript letter book was copied in 1901 from the original in the possession of James Parke Corbin of Fredericksburg, Virginia.

34. Mays, *Edmund Pendleton*, vol. I, p. 150.

35. *Journals of the House of Burgesses*, 1761-1765, p. 173.

36. *Ibid.*   37. *Ibid.*

38. Mays, *Edmund Pendleton*, vol. I, p. 151.

39. *Ibid.*   40. *Ibid.*

41. *Ibid.*, pp. 151-152.   42. *Ibid.*, p. 152.

43. *Ibid.*, pp. 152-153.

44. *Encyclopedia of American History* (ed. Richard B. Morris), p. 72.

45. John C. Miller, *Origins of the American Revolution* (Little, Brown and Co., Boston, 1943), pp. 100-106;

Claude H. Van Tyne, *The Causes of the War of Independence* (Houghton-Mifflin, Boston, 1922), pp. 244-245.

46. John C. Miller, *Origins of the American Revolution*, pp. 84-86.

47. Mays, *Edmund Pendleton*, vol. I, p. 156.

48. *Ibid.*, p. 157.   49. *Ibid.*

50. *Ibid.*, p. 157.

51. Freeman, *Washington*, vol. III, p. 114.

52. *Ibid.*, p. 113.   53. *Ibid.*

54. *Ibid.*, p. 114.   55. *Ibid.*, pp. 118-119.

56. *Ibid.*, p. 123.   57. *Ibid.*

58. *Ibid.*

Jefferson thought that the memorial was written by Richard Bland or Edmund Pendleton. William Wirt Henry thought it was written by Richard Henry Lee (See Mays, *Edmund Pendleton*, vol. I, p. 158).

59. Freeman, *Washington*, vol. III, p. 123.

60. *Ibid.*, pp. 123-124.

61. Mays, *Edmund Pendleton*, vol. I, p. 158.

62. J. R. Green, *Short History of the English People*, p. 769.

63. *Ibid.*, pp. 768-769;
    Mays, *Edmund Pendleton*, vol. I, p. 159.
64. Mays, *Edmund Pendleton*, vol. I, p. 160.
65. *Virginia Cavalcade*, vol. III, p. 18.
66. Freeman, *Washington*, vol. III, pp. 130-131.
67. *Ibid.*   68. *Ibid.*, p. 130.
69. Manuscript "History of Virginia," by Edmund Randolph, pp. 104-105 (Virginia Historical Society archives). Of course, some of the Piedmont leaders were of aristocratic descent (see Carl Bridenbaugh, *Seat of Empire*, pp. 51-52), but the frontier influence fostered democracy.
70. Henry was apparently sworn in either May 18 or May 20. See Freeman, *Washington*, vol. III, p. 128, note 16.
71. D. A. B.
72. Freeman, *Washington*, vol. III, pp. 104-106.
73. *Ibid.*, p. 106.
74. The quotations are from Edmund Randolph's manuscript "History of Virginia."
75. *Ibid.*
76. C. S. Sydnor, *Gentlemen Freeholders*, p. 78.
77. Freeman, *Washington*, vol. III, pp. 129-130.
78. *Ibid.*, pp. 130-131.
79. The description of Henry's voice and manner is based on those furnished by his contemporaries, such as Thomas Jefferson, and quoted in such works as William Wirt Henry's *Patrick Henry* and William Wirt's *The Life of Patrick Henry*.
    Standard biography is Robert Douthat Meade, *Patrick Henry,* 2 vols.
80. The wording here is essentially that used by Henry, but may not be exactly the same in all phrases. For a concise explanation of the possible differences, see Freeman, *Washington*, vol. III, p. 131, note 29; also Appendix III-3, pp. 592-595.
81. Freeman, *Washington*, vol. III, pp. 131-132.
    We may judge the reactions of Henry's audience from the statements made in the debate following his speech.
82. *Ibid.*, pp. 133, 592. This statement is Henry's own, though he was doubtless influenced by colleagues, especially John Fleming.
83. *Ibid.*, p. 134.
    Many historians have listed Edmund Pendleton as among the speakers against Henry's resolutions, but apparently he should not be included. See Mays, *Edmund Pendleton*, vol. I, p. 163.
84. Freeman, *Washington*, vol. III, p. 134.
85. *Ibid.*
86. The effect of Henry's oratory is not exaggerated. Some men used to become sick with excitement when they heard him, and one asked to be buried on the spot where he had first heard him speak.
87. The version here used is that given by Edmund Randolph in his manuscript "History of Virginia," preserved in the archives of the Virginia Historical Society. An intelligent scholar well versed in the colony's history, Edmund Randolph lived in the home of his uncle, Peyton Randolph, who was one of the chief actors in the legislative drama enacted May 29, 1765 in the House of Burgesses. Chief authority for the more dramatic version that has Henry demanding, "If this be treason, make the most of it," is William Wirt Henry, whose *Patrick Henry, Life, Correspondence and Speeches,* valuable work though it is, relies heavily on uncertain family traditions and is marred by notable errors. Randolph's account of Henry's backing down a bit when

charged with treason is corroborated by the journal of an unknown Frenchman quoted in Volume XXVI of the *American Historical Review*, in Claude H. Van Tyne's *The Causes of the War of Independence*, pp. 155-156, and very briefly in Mays' *Edmund Pendleton*, Vol. I, p. 329. Van Tyne, in *Causes*, etc. says that the unidentified Frenchman was a "French agent seeking to sound the colonial loyalty and find how deep it was." The historian reports, pp. 155-156, that the journal was discovered by M. Abel Doysie in the *Archives* of the Hydrographic Service of the Ministry of the Marine in Paris, in the course of an investigation for the Carnegie Institute of Washington.
The Frenchman's account is reprinted in full in Edmond S. Morgan, *Prologue to Revolution*, pp. 46-47. Morgan cites the account as "the only direct road that we can follow back to those critical days when Virginia pointed the way to freedom" in Edmund S. Morgan and Helen M. Morgan, *The Stamp Act Crisis*, p. 90, arguing the case succinctly, pp. 89-91. Meade, though admitting the genuineness of the Frenchman's journal, still argues for the more dramatic traditional account, Meade, *Patrick Henry*, vol. I, pp. 175-181. Dabney, largely out of respect for Meade's scholarship, accepts the traditional version (Dabney, *Virginia the New Dominion*, p. 114).

88. Freeman, *Washington*, vol. III, p. 136.

89. D. A. B.

90. The description of Randolph's physical appearance is based on the portrait in the possession of the Virginia Historical Society. The quotation was recalled by Jefferson in correspondence with Wirt, who used it in his *Life of Henry*.

91. Freeman, *Washington*, vol. III, p. 136.

92. *Journal of the House of Burgesses*, 1761-65, p. 359.

93. C. S. Sydnor, *Gentlemen Freeholders*, pp. 102-103.

94. Freeman, *Washington*, vol. III, p. 137.

95. *Ibid.*   96. *Ibid.*, p. 139.

97. *Ibid.*

98. Mays, *Edmund Pendleton*, vol. I, pp. 163-164.

99. Freeman, *Washington*, vol. III, p. 140.

100. Mays, *Edmund Pendleton*, vol. I, pp. 164, 330, note 41.

101. Letter of September 20, 1765 to Francis Dandridge, quoted in Freeman, *Washington*, vol. III, pp. 143-144.

102. *Ibid.*, pp. 111-112, 114-115, 125, 140.

103. Arthur M. Schlesinger, *The Colonial Merchants and the American Revolution*, p. 62.

104. Letter to Messrs. Hanbury, Richard Corbin Letter Book, Virginia Historical Society archives.

105. Letter of August 8, 1763, Richard Corbin Letter Book. The same sentiment was expressed in similar words in a Corbin letter of the same date to James Buchanan & Co.

106. Colonial Williamsburg, Inc. microfilm of *Virginia Gazette*, October 25, 1765, printed by J. Royle & Co.

107. Freeman, *Washington*, vol. III, p. 142.

108. *Ibid.*, p. 146.

109. *Virginia Magazine of History*, vol. LX, p. 407.
Alfred Procter James, *George Mercer of the Ohio Company*, pp. 35-36.

110. *Ibid.*, pp. 405, 409-410.

111. *Ibid.*, p. 410.
The testimonial was dated June 16, 1763.

112. *Ibid.*, p. 412.

The quotation is from Mercer's Memorial of April 11, 1766 to the Marquis of Rockingham.

113. *Ibid.*   114. *Ibid.*

115. Freeman, *Washington*, vol. III, p. 143.

116. C. S. Sydnor, *Gentlemen Freeholders*, p. 82.

117. *Ibid.*, p. 80.

118. *Ibid.*;
Freeman, *Washington*, vol. I, p. 175.

119. C. S. Sydnor, *Gentlemen Freeholders*, pp. 81-82.

120. *Ibid.*, p. 83.   121. *Ibid.*

122. *Ibid.*, p. 82.

123. Freeman, *Washington*, vol. III, p. 143.

124. *Ibid.*   125. *Ibid.*, p. 147.

126. The quotation is from Fauquier's report to the Lords of Trade, November 3, 1765, printed in *Journal of the House of Burgesses, 1761-65*, p. LXIX.

127. *Ibid.*

128. Fauquier wrote, "They met Col. Mercer on the way, just at the capitol." (*Journal of the House of Burgesses, 1761-65*, p. LXIX.)

129. In his memorial of April 11, 1766, Mercer wrote that he was "surrounded by more than 2,000 People." (*Virginia Magazine of History*, vol. LX, p. 412.)

130. There is no guarantee that the question was phrased exactly as it is here, but the wording must have been substantially the same. Fauquier wrote: "There they stop'd and demanded of him an answer whether he would resign or *act* in this office as Distributor of the Stamps." (*Journal of the House of Burgesses, 1761-65*, p. LXIX.)

131. Mercer's exact words apparently were not preserved. But Fauquier's report of them seems to be an indirect quotation. Hence, Mercer's actual statement must have been substantially as here given.

132. *Journal of the House of Burgesses, 1761-65*, p. LXIX.
The remainder of the description of Mercer's experience with the mob, except where otherwise indicated, is based on Fauquier's report to the Lords of Trade.

133. The quotations are from Mercer's memorial of April 11, 1766. (*Virginia Magazine of History*, vol. LX, p. 412.)

134. Mercer's speech is quoted from the *Pennsylvania Gazette* of November 21, 1765 in Freeman, *Washington*, vol. III, p. 149.

135. The courtroom scene is described in Fauquier's report, *Journal of the House of Burgesses, 1761-65*, p. LXX.

136. *Ibid.*, p. LXXII.

137. *Virginia Magazine of History*, vol. LX, p. 413. The quotation is from Fauquier.

138. *Journal of the House of Burgesses, 1761-65*, p. LXX.

139. Mays, *Edmund Pendleton*, vol. I, pp. 167-168.

140. Fauquier to Conway, November 24, 1765. Quoted in Mays, *Edmund Pendleton*, vol. I, p. 167.

141. *Ibid.*, p. 168.

142. Letter of December 11, 1765 to Col. James Madison, a justice of Orange County and father of President Madison. Mays, *Edmund Pendleton*, vol. I, pp. 168-169.

143. *Ibid.*, p. 169.

144. Letter of February 15, 1766 to Col. James Madison. *Ibid.*, p. 170.

145. *Ibid.*   146. *Ibid.*

147. Whitelaw, vol. I, pp. 40-41.

148. Mays, *Edmund Pendleton*, vol. I, p. 168.
149. Descriptions of the events at Leedstown and Hobbs Hole are based on Freeman, *Washington*, vol. III, pp. 153-156, and Mays, *Edmund Pendleton*, vol. I, pp. 171-172.
150. The letter itself was dated November 9, 1765. It was printed in Royle's *Virginia Gazette*, No. 772, March 7, 1766; microfilm in Colonial Williamsburg archives.
151. Purdie and Dixon's *Virginia Gazette*, No. 773, March 14, 1766; photostat in Colonial Williamsburg archives.
152. Royle's *Virginia Gazette*, No. 668, November 4, 1763, p. 2, under dateline "New York, October 13"; microfilm in Colonial Williamsburg archives.
153. Alexander Walker to William Allason, January 11, 1766. Quoted in Mays, *Edmund Pendleton*, vol. I, p. 173.
154. *Ibid.*
    The letter had been written in February 1766.
155. Freeman, *Washington*, vol. III, p. 163.
156. Mays, *Edmund Pendleton*, vol. I, p. 173.
157. Freeman, *Washington*, vol. III, p. 164.
158. Description from Rind's *Gazette*, May 16, 1766, quoted in Freeman, *Washington*, vol. III, p. 164.
159. Purdie and Dixon's *Virginia Gazette*, June 20, 1766, quoted in Mays, *Edmund Pendleton*, vol. I, p. 173.
160. Freeman, *Washington*, vol. III, p. 164.
161. Mays, *Edmund Pendleton*, vol. I, pp. 177-178.
162. Fauquier's letter of May 12, 1761; Mays, *Edmund Pendleton*, vol. I, p. 178.
163. Edmund Randolph's manuscript "History of Virginia," quoted in Mays, *Edmund Pendleton*, vol. I, pp. 64-65.
164. Mays, *Edmund Pendleton*, vol. I, p. 178.
165. *Ibid.*, pp. 174-175.
166. Freeman, *Washington*, vol. I, pp. 181-182.
167. Fauquier's letter of September 7, 1763; quoted in Mays, *Edmund Pendleton*, vol. I, p. 174.
168. Mays, *Edmund Pendleton*, vol. I, pp. 174-175.
169. *Ibid.*, p. 175.   170. *Ibid.*, p. 174.
171. *Ibid.*, p. 331, note 4.   172. *Ibid.*, p. 175.
173. *Ibid.*, pp. 166-167.   174. *Ibid.*, p. 181.
175. *Ibid.*, pp. 181-185, 358-375.   176. *Ibid.*, pp. 185-186.
177. The Robinson estate's indebtedness to Virginia was not paid in full until 1781.
178. Mays, *Edmund Pendleton*, vol. I, p. 188.
179. *Ibid.*
180. Freeman, *Washington*, vol. III, pp. 166-167, 169-172.
181. Miller, *Origins of the American Revolution*, p. 242;
    Van Tyne, *The Causes of the War of Independence*, pp. 244-245.
182. *Encyclopedia of American History* (ed. Richard B. Morris), p. 76.
183. Miller, *Origins of the American Revolution*, p. 242.
184. Freeman, *Washington*, vol. III, p. 197.
185. *Journal of the House of Burgesses, 1766-69*, pp. 145-146.
186. *Ibid.*, p. 158. It was a 12-man committee.
187. *Ibid.*, pp. 168, 170-171.   188. *Ibid.*, p. 171.
189. *Ibid.*, pp. 173-174.
190. Mays, *Edmund Pendleton*, vol. I, p. 249.
191. *Ibid.*

192. The description of the governor is based on D. A. B.; *Virginia Magazine of History*, vol. 63, pp. 379-409; and the statue of him which stands on the campus of the College of William and Mary.

193. Mays, *Edmund Pendleton*, vol. I, p. 251.

194. *Ibid.*   195. *Ibid.*

196. *Ibid.*, p. 250.

197. D. A. B.; Mays, *Edmund Pendleton*, vol. I, p. 252.

198. *Ibid.*

199. *Journal of the House of Burgesses, 1766-69*, p. 188.

200. *Ibid.*, p. 189.

201. Freeman, *Washington*, vol. III, p. 217.

202. Forty-six years later, August 5, 1815, Jefferson wrote William Wirt: "Being a young man as well as a young member, it made on me an impression proportioned to the sensibilities of that time of life." Quoted in Freeman, *Washington*, vol. III, pp. 217-218.

203. *Journal of the House of Burgesses, 1766-69*, p. 214.

204. *Ibid.*, p. 214.   205. *Ibid.*

206. *Ibid.*, p. 215.   207. *Ibid.*, p. 216

208. *Ibid.*   209. *Ibid.*, p. 218.

210. The description of the Apollo Room is based on its appearance as a meticulously restored part of Colonial Williamsburg. Detailed descriptions and illustrations of the room are available in a *Handbook for the Exhibition of Colonial Williamsburg, Inc.* (1936), pp. 45-46; and Fiske Kimball and Susan Higginson Nash, *The Restoration of Colonial Williamsburg in Virginia*, pp. 454-456.

211. Robert A. Rutland, ed., *The Papers of George Mason*, vol. I, pp. 93-113.

212. *Ibid.*

213. *Journal of the House of Burgesses, 1766-69*, pp. XL-XLII.

214. Freeman, *Washington*, vol. III, p. 224.

215. *Journal of the House of Burgesses, 1766-69*, pp. XLII-XLIII.

216. Freeman, *Washington*, vol. III, p. 225.

217. *Ibid.*, pp. 228-230.

218. Mays, *Edmund Pendleton*, vol. I, p. 260.

219. John Fiske, *The American Revolution*, vol. I, pp. 64-65;
Encyclopedia of American History (ed., Richard B. Morris), p. 78.
The Virginia Association itself had been influenced by a Philadelphia model.

220. *Journal of the House of Burgesses, 1766-69*, pp. 226-227.

221. *Ibid.*, p. 227.

222. Freeman, *Washington*, vol. III, pp. 241-242.

223. *Ibid.*, p. 250.   224. *Ibid.*

225. Carter's diary, May 29, 1770; quoted in Mays, *Edmund Pendleton*, vol. I, p. 258.

226. Mays, *Edmund Pendleton*, vol. I, p. 259.

227. Freeman, *Washington*, vol. III, p. 251.

228. J. C. Miller, *Origins of the American Revolution*, pp. 293-298;
C. H. Van Tyne, *The Causes of the War of Independence*, pp. 283-289;
George Eliot Howard, *Preliminaries of the Revolution* (N. Y., 1907), pp. 203-205.

229. Mays, *Edmund Pendleton*, vol. I, p. 260.

230. *Virginia Cavalcade*, vol. I, p. 20.
The description of the flood is based on facts reported in pp. 20-22 of the same work.

231. Freeman, *Washington*, vol. III, p. 273.

232. *Journal of the House of Burgesses, 1770-72*, pp. 119, 122-123, 127-129, 131, 134-136, 137-138.

233. Freeman, *Washington*, vol. III, p. 276.

234. *Ibid.*, p. 277.   235. *Ibid.*, p. 282.

236. The physical description of Dunmore is based on the portrait by Sir Joshua Reynolds, a copy of which, by Charles X. Harris, is owned by the Virginia Historical Society.

237. *Virginia Cavalcade*, vol. II, p. 42.

238. Freeman, *Washington*, vol. III, pp. 289-290.

239. *Ibid.*, p. 289.

240. *Virginia Magazine of History*, vol. LXII, pp. 17-18.
The general story of this counterfeiting and the measures taken against it is given in pp. 15-26 of the same publication.

241. The Burgesses made it a felony "to prepare, engrave, stamp or print" counterfeits of the notes of other British colonies, and set up a committee of correspondence to request similar action from other colonies. Maryland and Georgia complied.

242. *Journal of the House of Burgesses, 1773-76*, p. 22.

243. *Ibid.*, p. 33.

244. Freeman, *Washington*, vol. III, p. 313.

245. Jefferson's relationship with Carr is discussed by Dumas Malone, *Jefferson the Virginian*, pp. 160-161.

246. Jefferson's description of Carr's manner of speaking is quoted in Freeman, *Washington*, vol. III, p. 316.

247. *Journal of the House of Burgesses, 1773-76*, p. 28.

248. *Ibid.*

249. Malone, *Jefferson the Virginian*, p. 170.

250. *Ibid.*, pp. 170-171.   251. *Ibid.*

252. *Ibid.*, p. 170.

253. Freeman, *Washington*, vol. III, p. 316.

254. *Ibid.*   255. *Ibid.*

256. The ensuing explanation of the Boston Tea Party, though contrary to the popular account, is supported by such excellent sources as Freeman, *Washington*, vol. III, pp. 339-341; Edward Channing, *A History of the United States*, vol. III (N. Y., 1912), pp. 129-134, especially pp. 131-132, n. 5; C. H. Van Tyne, *The Causes of the War of Independence*, pp. 375-388.

257. Freeman, *Washington*, vol. III, p. 341.

258. John Fiske, *The American Revolution* (Boston, 1901), vol. I, pp. 83-84; C. H. Van Tyne, *The Causes of the War of Independence*, pp. 388-390; Edward Channing, *A History of the United States*, vol. III, p. 131.

259. John Fiske, *The American Revolution*, vol. I, p. 91.

260. Mays, *Edmund Pendleton*, vol. I, p. 272.

261. *Ibid.*   262. *Ibid.*

263. The description of the meeting of May 23 is based on Freeman, *Washington*, vol. III, p. 351; Malone, *Jefferson the Virginian*, pp. 171-172; Mays, *Edmund Pendleton*, vol. I, pp. 269-270.

264. *Journals of the House of Burgesses, 1773-76*, p. 124.

265. *Ibid.*, p. 132.   266. *Ibid.*

267. Freeman, *Washington*, vol. III, pp. 353-354.

268. *Journals of the House of Burgesses, 1773-76*, p. XIV.

269. Freeman, *Washington*, vol. III, p. 354.

270. *Journals of the House of Burgesses, 1773-76*, p. 138.

271. *Ibid.*, pp. 143-148.   272. *Ibid.*, p. 148.

273. Freeman, *Washington*, vol. III, pp. 355-356.
274. *Ibid.*, pp. 357-358.   275. *Ibid.*, p. 361.
276. *Encyclopedia of American History* (ed. Richard B. Morris), p. 82.
277. Arthur M. Schlesinger, *The Colonial Merchants and the American Revolution*, p. 311.
278. Letter of March 18, 1774, *American Archives* (4th series), vol. I, Peter Force and M. St. Clair Clarke, Washington, 1837, pp. 228-229.
279. The resolutions are quoted and discussed in Malone, *Jefferson the Virginian*, pp. 181-190.
280. *Ibid.*, pp. 181, 183.
281. Freeman, *Washington*, vol. III, pp. 368-369.
282. *Ibid.*, p. 369.   283. *Ibid.*
284. *Ibid.*, p. 370.
     Malone, *Jefferson the Virginian*, p. 181.
285. Mays, *Edmund Pendleton*, vol. I, p. 278.
286. *Ibid.*
287. *Journals of the House of Burgesses, 1773-76*, p. 152.

FOOTNOTES TO CHAPTER X

1. Adams' excitement and curiosity are amply exhibited in his diary and letters, *e.g.*, Edmund Cody Burnett, ed., *Letters of Members of the Continental Congress* (8 vols., Washington, 1921-36), vol. I, pp. 2-3. Hereinafter cited as Burnett, *Letters.*
2. Adams wrote, "Randolph is a large, well looking man. . . ."
   Burnett, *Letters*, vol. I, p. 2.
   Silas Deane, of Connecticut, described Randolph as "of an affable, open and majestic deportment, large in size, though not out of proportion," and added, "he commands respect and esteem by his very aspect." Edmund Cody Burnett, *The Continental Congress* (New York, 1941), p. 29.
   Our description of Randolph is based on these comments and on the portrait by Charles Willson Peale which hangs in Independence Hall, Philadelphia.
3. Mays, *Pendleton*, vol. I, p. 279.
   Burnett, *Letters*, vol. I, p. 28.
4. Adams' diary, September 2, 1774—Burnett, *Letters*, vol. I, p. 2.
5. Grigsby, *Virginia Convention of 1776*, p. 57.
6. Burton J. Hendrick, *The Lees of Virginia*, pp. 80, 86-87, 100-102.
7. John Adams described Lee as a "tall spare man" (Burnett, *Letters*, vol. I, p. 2). Lee's features were portrayed by Charles Willson Peale.
8. Burnett, *Letters*, vol. I, p. 2.
9. John Adams' diary, entry of Wednesday, August 31, 1774.
   The quotation may be conveniently found in H. S. Commager and Allen Nevins' *The Heritage of America*, p. 139.
10. Mays, *Pendleton*, vol. I, p. 281.
    Philadelphia was then the largest city on the continent.
11. This facial description is based on the miniature painted by Lawrence Sully in 1795. Henry's figure was described as tall and lean by a great many contemporaries.
12. Henry's manner and voice are minutely described in Edmund Randolph's manuscript, "History of Virginia," Virginia Historical Society archives.

13. Freeman, *Washington*, vol. III, p. 377.
14. Description based on portrait in possession of Virginia Historical Society and on Mays, *Pendleton*, vol. I, p. 229.
15. Letter of September 9, 1774 to Thomas Rodney—Burnett, *Letters*, vol. I, p. 27.
16. Letter of September 10, 1774—Burnett, *Letters*, pp. 28-29.
17. Letter of September 1-3, 1774 to Mrs. Deane—Burnett, *Letters*, p. 4.
18. *Journals of the Continental Congress* (ed., W. C. Ford), vol. I, p. 14.
19. Letter of Silas Deane to Mrs. Deane, September 1-3, 1774:
    "The city have offered us the Carpenters Hall, so called, to meet in, and Mr. Galloway offers the State House, insists on our meeting there, which he says he has a right to offer as Speaker of that House. The last is evidently the best place, but as *he* offers, the other party oppose." Burnett, *Letters*, vol. I, pp. 5-6.
20. John Adams' diary entry of September 5, 1774—Burnett, *Letters*, vol. I, pp. 6-7; also, *Journals of the Continental Congress*, vol. I, p. 13.
21. *Journals of the Continental Congress*, vol. I, p. 24. It is difficult to determine whether the ensuing debate took place on September 5 alone or on the succeeding day as well. See *Journals*, vol. I, p. 25.
22. John Adams' diary entry of September 5—Burnett, *Letters*, vol. I, p. 7.
23. Quotation from contemporary description quoted in Freeman, *Washington*, vol. III, p. 374.
24. See David John Mays' comment on Henry's apparent nationalism, *Pendleton*, vol. I, p. 284: "This part of his speech was so much rhetoric, for he was always a Virginian, and when he said 'my country,' he always meant Virginia."
25. John Adams' diary entry of September 5—Burnett, *Letters*, vol. I, p. 7.
26. *Ibid.*   27. Burnett, *Letters*, vol. I, p. 14.
28. John Adams' diary entry of September 5—Burnett, *Letters*, vol. I, p. 7.
    Both of Sullivan's parents were natives of Ireland—D.A.B.
29. Burnett, *Letters*, vol. I, p. 13.
30. Lynch apparently used, at least approximately, the words here quoted. Mays, *Pendleton*, vol. I, p. 284.
    Journals of the Continental Congress, vol. I, p. 25.
31. Mays, *Pendleton*, vol. I, p. 284.   32. *Ibid.*, pp. 284-285.
33. *Journals of the Continental Congress*, vol. I, p. 25.
    The words here quoted are from John Adams' diary, entry of September 5 (Burnett, *Letters*, vol. I, p. 8), and must be substantially those which he spoke in augment.
34. Mays, *Pendleton*, vol. I, p. 285.
35. The description of Jay is based on portraits and on his D.A.B. entry.
36. Mays, *Pendleton*, vol. I, p. 285.
37. Report of Connecticut delegates, October 10, 1774, in *Journals of the Continental Congress*, vol. I, p. 25.
38. Burnett, *Letters*, vol. I, p. 29.   39. *Ibid.*, p. 11.
40. *Ibid.*, p. 27.
41. *Journals of the Continental Congress*, vol. I, p. 26.
42. Silas Deane wrote, "The bells toll muffled, and the people run as in a case of extremity, they know not where or why."
    John Adams wrote, "War! War! War! was the cry. . . ."
43. The Psalter for the seventh of September included the Thirty-fifth Psalm.
44. John Adams wrote of Duché, "He filled every bosom present."
45. Mays, *Pendleton*, vol. I, p. 350, n. 25.
46. Both quotations are from *Journals of the Continental Congress*, vol. I, p. 28.

47. Burnett, *Letters*, vol. I, p. 22.
48. *Journals of the Continental Congress*, vol. I, p. 28.
49. Burnett, *Letters*, vol. I, p. 22.
50. *Journals of the Continental Congress*, vol. I, p. 28.
51. *Ibid.*   52. *Ibid.*, p. 41.
53. *Ibid.*, pp. 31 and 38.
    Burnett, *The Continental Congress*, pp. 42-43.
54. Burnett, *The Continental Congress*, pp. 33-34.
55. *Ibid.*, p. 34.   56. *Ibid.*, p. 42.
57. *Ibid.*, p. 43.   58. *Ibid.*
59. *Journals of the Continental Congress*, vol. I, p. 41.
60. *Ibid.*   61. *Ibid.*, p. 45.
62. *Ibid.*, p. 42.   63. Mays, *Pendleton*, vol. I, p. 288.
64. A good presentation of the Galloway plan is to be found in Burnett, *The Continental Congress*, pp. 47-50.
65. Burnett, *The Continental Congress*, pp. 48-49.
66. *Ibid.*, pp. 33, 49-50.
67. Mays, *Pendleton*, vol. I, pp. 290-291.
68. Burnett, *The Continental Congress*, p. 49.
    The description of Rutledge's manner of speaking is based on the description by John Adams. (See Burnett, *The Continental Congress*, p. 104.)
69. Mays, *Pendleton*, vol. I, p. 290.   70. *Ibid.*
71. Burnett, *The Continental Congress*, pp. 50-51.
72. *Ibid.*, p. 51.
    On October 21, Congress decided to send addresses to the North American colonies of Quebec, St. Johns, Georgia and East and West Florida.
73. *Ibid.*
    The assumption that Lee was chairman is based on the fact that he was the first man named to the committee.
74. *Ibid.*   75. *Ibid.*
76. *Ibid.*, p. 53.
    Freeman, *Washington*, vol. III, p. 388.
    The declaration is reprinted in Commager's *Documents of American History*.
    Jay's address was read by Livingston.
    Journals of the Continental Congress, vol. I, p. 28.
77. A comparison of the two texts should be convincing to any reader. Brief discussions of, or references to, the similarity appear in: Burnett, *The Continental Congress*, pp. 54-57; *Encyclopedia of American History*, p. 84; Mays, *Pendleton*, vol. I, pp. 295-296.
78. Freeman, *Washington*, vol. III, pp. 388-389.
79. Burnett, *The Continental Congress*, p. 55.
80. Freeman, *Washington*, vol. III, p. 390.
    Mays, *Pendleton*, vol. I, p. 296.
    Randolph, Bland and Harrison may actually have left Philadelphia October 24. See *Virginia Gazette* (Purdie and Dixon, November 3, 1774) photostats in library of the College of William and Mary.
81. Freeman, *Washington*, vol. III, p. 391.

FOOTNOTES TO CHAPTER XI

1. This scene is reconstructed from November issues of the *Virginia Gazette*, information on life in colonial Williamsburg compiled by Colonial Williamsburg, Inc., and inferences that may logically be drawn from observations of human behavior. It is, of course, impossible to say exactly how a particular shopkeeper or artisan acted on November 3, 1774.

2. *Virginia Gazette* (Purdie and Dixon), November 3, 1774; photostats in library of the College of William and Mary.

3. Commager, *Documents of American History*, p. 86.

4. *Ibid.*
   Burnett wrote in *The Continental Congress*, p. 56: "The conclusion is inescapable that some of these associated frowns were motivated by ethical rather than economical purposes."

5. M. P. Andrews, *Virginia, the Old Dominion*, pp. 182-183.

6. For example, see Lancaster, Westmoreland and Middlesex County wills.

7. For an exposition of the influence of the local "great man" in Virginia politics, see Charles S. Sydnor, *Gentlemen Freeholders*, pp. 78-93.

8. *Virginia Gazette* (Purdie and Dixon), November 17, 1774; William and Mary photostats.

9. *Virginia Gazette* (Purdie and Dixon), November 24, 1774; William and Mary photostats.

10. The meeting took place November 10.
    Mays, *Pendleton*, vol. I, pp. 297-298.

11. Nicholas was elected chairman for James City County November 25, 1774—*Virginia Gazette* (Purdie and Dixon), December 1, 1774; William and Mary photostats.
    Other committees were headed by Archibald Cary, Joseph Jones, Peyton Randolph, Richard Bland, Landon Carter, and Benjamin Harrison—H. J. Eckenrode, *The Revolution in Virginia*, p. 43.

12. Mays, *Pendleton*, vol. I, pp. 301-302.

13. *Ibid.*, pp. 302-303.

14. Jerdone Letters (apparently written by Thomas Jett, of Leedstown, Virginia, representative of John Morton Jerdone and Company and of Perkins, Buchanan and Brown, Merchants, in London, 1769-1776), archives of the College of William and Mary.

15. Arthur M. Schlesinger, *The Colonial Merchants and the American Revolution, 1773-1776*, p. 519.
    Dartmouth was Secretary of State.

16. Mays, *Pendleton*, vol. I, p. 303. 17. *Ibid.*, pp. 305-306.

18. Supplement to *Virginia Gazette* (Purdie and Dixon), December 8, 1774; William and Mary photostats.

19. Mays, *Pendleton*, vol. I, p. 304.

20. Freeman H. Hart, *The Valley of Virginia in the American Revolution*, pp. 69-70.

21. *Ibid.*, pp. 75-76.

22. Indian scalps were proudly exhibited by white men passing through Winchester in 1765.
    Ibid., p. 77.

23. *Ibid.*, pp. 77-78. 24. *Ibid.*, p. 79.

25. *Ibid.*

26. In 1765, Lewis reported the killing of friendly Indians to Governor Fauquier.
    Ibid., p. 78.

27. Matthew Page Andrews, *Virginia, the Old Dominion*, p. 238.

28. *Ibid.*, p. 239.
29. *Ibid.*, pp. 238-239.
    F. H. Hart, *The Valley of Virginia in the American Revolution*, p. 81.
    Freeman, *Washington*, vol. III, p. 394.
30. Freeman, *Washington*, vol. III, p. 394.
31. Lynn Montross, *The Reluctant Rebels*, p. 60.
32. Mays, *Pendleton*, vol. I, p. 305.
33. In many colonies, a large proportion of the population was Tory. Many New England aristocrats inclined toward Toryism, and the revolutionary movement in that region was led largely by representatives of the middle class. Of course, many Northern Tories were mechanics, as Montross and other historians have proved.
34. Mays, *Pendleton*, vol. I, pp. 303-304.
35. *Ibid.*, p. 305.
36. *Virginia Gazette*, February 3, 1775.
37. Force, *Archives*, Series 4, vol. II, p. 167.
38. *Ibid.*, p. 167.   39. *Virginia Gazette*, March 17, 1775.
40. *Virginia Gazette* (Purdie), February 3, 1775; William and Mary photostats.
41. Force, *Archives*, Series 4, vol. II, p. 167.
42. *Ibid.*
43. A description of Band as he appeared one year later is given in Hugh Blair Grigsby, *The Virginia Convention of 1776*, pp. 57-58.
44. Description of Nicholas based on Grigsby, *The Virginia Convention of 1776*, p. 65.
45. Description of Harrison based on that by John Adams (Burnett, *Letters*, vol. I, p. 2) and other delegates to the Continental Congress of 1774.
46. Description of Pendleton based on Mays, *Pendleton*, vol. I, pp. 229, 241, 283, 355; vol. II, pp. 126-127.
47. The quotations that follow are from Henry's speech as it is given in William Wirt's *Sketches of the Life and Character of Patrick Henry*. Doubtless only a few phrases are exactly the same as those used by Henry, but the substance and style are probably faithful to the original. Wirt relied on the recollections of John Tyler and St. George Tucker, witnesses of unusually high caliber, as well as accounts by others. The most famous quotations, "We must fight" and the last sentence of Henry's speech, are reasonably well verified. For a discussion of the authenticity of Wirt's account, see Freeman, *Washington*, vol. III, p. 404.
48. Force, *Archives*, Series 4, vol. II, p. 168.
49. Dumas Malone, *Jefferson the Virginian*, pp. 194-195.
    The description of Jefferson's appearance and manner is based on the same volume, especially p. 48.
50. Mays, *Pendleton*, vol. II, p. 7.
    One account says Nicholas called for 10,000 men, another that he called for 20,000. See Mays, *Pendleton*, vol. II, pp. 353-354, n. 18.
51. Force, *Archives*, Series 4, vol. II, pp. 167-168.
52. *Ibid.*, p. 168.   53. *Ibid.*
54. *Ibid.*, pp. 168-170.   55. *Ibid.*, p. 170.
56. Freeman, *Washington*, vol. III, p. 407.
57. Mays, *Pendleton*, vol. II, p. 354, n. 34.
58. Freeman, *Washington*, vol. III, pp. 410-411.
59. Force, *Archives*, Series 4, vol. II, pp. 371-372.
60. Mays, *Pendleton*, vol. II, p. 14.

61. Freeman, *Washington*, vol. III, p. 414.
62. The debate and decision regarding the messages from Pendleton, Lee and Washington were by a council of 102 representing the troops. It included some members of the Virginia Convention as well as officers and other representatives of the different companies.
    Freeman, *Washington*, vol. III, p. 414.
63. There are several contradictory accounts of the Fredericksburg affair, but a careful study of the evidence has been made by Freeman, who presents his findings in *Washington*, vol. III, pp. 414-415.
64. Supplement to April 29, 1775 issue of *Virginia Gazette* (Dixon and Hunter).
65. It is quite possible that the first shot came from the colonial ranks. Both British and American accounts of the incident appear in Commager, *Documents of American History*. A fair-minded description of the battle is given in Christopher Ward, *The War of the Revolution*, vol. I, pp. 32-39.
66. Mays, *Pendleton*, vol. II, p. 16.
67. Freeman, *Washington*, vol. III, pp. 422-423.
68. *Ibid.*, p. 423.
    Mays, *Pendleton*, vol. II, p. 16.
69. Mays, *Pendleton*, vol. II, p. 16.
70. The description of the following scene is based on pertinent passages in Christopher Ward, *The War of the Revolution*, vol. I, especially pp. 106-107; Mays, *Pendleton*, vol. II; Burnett, *The Continental Congress*; Lynn Montross, *The Reluctant Rebels* and Elisabeth McClellan, *History of American Costume*.
71. Freeman, *Washington*, vol. III, pp. 422-423.
72. Mays, *Pendleton*, vol. II, p. 19.
73. Freeman, *Washington*, vol. III, p. 420.
74. *Journals of the Continental Congress*, vol. II, pp. 11-22.
75. Freeman, *Washington*, vol. III, p. 421.
76. *Ibid.*
77. Ward, *The War of the Revolution*, vol. I, p. 63.
78. There are several variations of Allen's demand, all of similar tone and import. See *ibid.*, p. 68.
79. *Journals of the Continental Congress*, vol. II, p. 56.
80. Ward, *The War of the Revolution*, vol. I, p. 68.
81. Freeman, *Washington*, vol. III, p. 425.
82. D.A.B.
83. *Journals of the Continental Congress*, vol. II, p. 67.
84. The uniform worn by Washington at this time is often described as buff and blue, but evidence suggests that it was the red and blue uniform which he wears in the famous portrait by Charles Willson Peale. See Freeman, *Washington*, vol. III, p. 426.
85. *Ibid.*
86. *Ibid.*, p. 429.
87. *Ibid.*, p. 427.
88. *Ibid.*, pp. 433-434.
89. Charles Lee was the choice of Elbridge Gerry and Joseph Warren, powerful Massachusetts leaders. Washington was their second choice.
90. The ensuing incident, including the actual conversation, was recorded by John Adams in his diary. It appears in *The Works of John Adams*, vol. II, p. 417, *et seq.*, but may be more conveniently found in Commager and Nevins, *The Heritage of America*, pp. 144-145.
91. The date of the day's events, here given as June 14, may actually have been June 10. The record on this point is not clear. For explanation, see Freeman, *Washington*, vol. III, p. 434, n. 73.
92. In our account of this speech, we have simply transposed the words of John Adams' diary from past to present tense. See *The Works of John Adams*, also *The Heritage of America*, pp. 145-146.

93. In a letter of August 6, 1822, John Adams referred to "the Frankfort advice" as an important factor in the Continental Congress. *The Heritage of America*, p. 150.
94. Freeman, *Washington*, vol. III, p. 436.
95. The delegate was Eliphalet Dyer. See *ibid.*
96. Mays, *Pendleton*, vol. II, p. 24.
97. That fellow delegates joined Washington for dinner is not certain, but highly probable. See Freeman, *Washington*, vol. III, p. 436.
98. Freeman, *Washington*, vol. III, pp. 437-438.
99. *Ibid.*, p. 438.   100. *Ibid.*, pp. 439-440.
101. *Encyclopedia of History*, p. 84.
102. Dumas Malone, *Jefferson the Virginian*, pp. 198-199.
103. *Ibid.*, p. 199.   104. *Ibid.*, p. 200.
105. *Ibid.*, p. 199.
106. Ironically enough, Livingston's letter criticizing Jefferson's Declaration was written July 4. Quoted in Malone, *Jefferson the Virginian*, p. 205.
107. *Ibid.*, pp. 205-206.
108. Congress formally adjourned August 2, but for all practical purposes, the session had ended August 1 when Jefferson left town. Other Virginians had left earlier.
109. Malone, *Jefferson the Virginian*, pp. 203-204.
110. *Ibid.*

FOOTNOTES TO CHAPTER XII

1. The physical description of George Mason is based on Guillaume's copy of Boudet's copy of the portrait by Hesselius.
     The psychosomatic nature of some of Mason's afflictions may be inferred from his own writings, as quoted in Kate Mason Rowland, *The Life of George Mason* (vols. I and II), though the biographer does not state this conclusion.
2. Letter of October 14, 1775; Rowland, *The Life of George Mason*, vol. I, pp. 210-211.
3. D.A.B.
4. Mays, *Pendleton*, vol. II, p. 34. Rowland, *Mason*, vol. I, p. 211.
5. Mays, *Pendleton*, vol. II, p. 35.   6. *Ibid.*, pp. 35-36.
7. Our estimate of Pendleton is based largely on Mays, *Pendleton*, especially vol. I, pp. 57, 66, 122-123, 196, 261, 357, and vol. II, pp. 126, 347.
8. Richard Hildreth said, "The signature of the Association may be considered as the commencement of the American Union." The quotation appears in Commager, *Documents of American History*, pp. 84-85.
9. Mason's learning is amply attested by contemporary evidence. See Rowland, *Mason*, vol. I, pp. 52-53, and vol. II, pp. 368-378. H. J. Eckenrode compared the learning of Mason and Bland in *The Revolution in Virginia*, p. 125.
10. Hening's *Statutes*, vol. IX, pp. 49-53.
11. Mays, *Pendleton*, vol. II, p. 38.   12. *Ibid.*, p. 42.
13. *Ibid.*   14. *Ibid.*, p. 43.
15. *Ibid.*   16. D.A.B.
17. Mays, *Pendleton*, vol. II, p. 48.   18. *Ibid.*, pp. 46-47, 49.
19. Moreau de St. Méry, *The American Journey*, pp. 68-69.
20. M. W. Butt, *Norfolk Naval Shipyard, a Brief History*, pamphlet published by Shipyard's P.I.O., April 1951.

21. Mays, *Pendleton*, vol. II, p. 50.
22. H. J. Eckenrode, *The Revolution in Virginia*, p. 64.

Dunmore published on shipboard his own edition of the *Virginia Gazette*, complaining with little exaggeration, "All the presses upon the continent (very few excepted) are as much engaged in the service of the popular leaders as ever hireling wretch has been accused of being at the devotion of the most venal minister." This sentence is part of an interesting statement by his lordship which appeared in the *Virginia Gazette* (Norfolk), February 3, 1776. The only known copy of this or any other issue of Dunmore's paper is preserved in the archives of the Virginia Historical Society.

23. Mays, *Pendleton*, vol. II, pp. 52-53.
Eckenrode, *The Revolution in Virginia*, pp. 59-60.

Capt. Squire's name has also been spelled "Squier."

24. Eckenrode, *The Revolution in Virginia*, pp. 67-69.
25. Mays, *Pendleton*, vol. II, p. 57.   26. *Ibid.*, pp. 57-58.
27. According to a report of John Mitchel and Company, Portsmouth, to James Wilson and Son, Kilmarnock.
Ibid., p. 57.
28. *Ibid.*, p. 58.
29. *Ibid.*, p. 56.

For an account of Toryism in the Norfolk-Portsmouth area, see Eckenrode, *The Revolution in Virginia*, pp. 91-93, 140.

30. Mays, *Pendleton*, vol. II, pp. 53-54.
31. *Ibid.*, p. 55.   32. *Ibid.*, p. 61.
33. Page, Bland, Digges, Cabell, Braxton and Tabb.
Ibid., p. 55.
34. *Ibid.*, p. 63.   35. *Ibid.*, p. 55.
36. The story of the engagement at Great Bridge is based on the following sources: Mays, *Pendleton*, vol. II, pp. 55-84; Eckenrode, *The Revolution in Virginia*, pp. 80-83; Christopher Ward, *The War of the Revolution*, vol. II, pp. 847-848, Benjamin Quarles, *The Negro in the American Revolution*, p. 13.
37. Up to that time, of course.   38. Mays, *Pendleton*, vol. II, p. 70.
39. Ward, *The War of the Revolution*, vol. II, p. 849.
Actually, according to records of the Committee of Safety, more dwellings in Norfolk were burned by the patriots than by Dunmore.
40. Malone, *Jefferson the Virginian*, pp. 212-213.
41. Ward, *The War of the Revolution*, vol. I, pp. 106-107.
42. Both Burton J. Hendrick and Edmund Jennings Lee call Arthur Lee "the first diplomatic representative of the American nation." For evaluations of his great influence on Congress, see Hendrick, *The Lees of Virginia*, p. 214, and E. J. Lee in the *Northern Neck Historical Magazine*, vol. II, pp. 161-166.
43. *Virginia Cavalcade*, vol. II, p. 46.   44. Mays, *Pendleton*, vol. II, p. 76.
45. *Ibid.*, p. 77.   46. *Ibid.*, p. 84.
47. *Ibid.*   48. *Ibid.*, p. 85.
49. The negotiations are described in *ibid.*, pp. 87-90.
50. *Ibid.*, p. 89.   51. *Ibid.*, p. 91.
52. *Ibid.*   53. *Ibid.*, pp. 91-92.
54. Lewis incorrectly believed that Dunmore had intentionally led Virginia's Indian fighters into a trap in the war against Cornstalk. The fact that Lewis' brother had been slain in the Battle of Point Pleasant intensified his animosity. *Virginia Cavalcade*, vol. II, p. 44.
55. Mays, *Pendleton*, vol. II, p. 101.
56. Eckenrode, *The Revolution in Virginia*, pp. 91-93.
Mays, *Pendleton*, vol. II, pp. 101-102.

57. Mays, *Pendleton*, vol. II, p. 102.
58. Hugh Blair Grigsby, *The Virginia Convention of 1776*, p. 9.
59. Van Tyne, *The War of Independence*, p. 344.
60. Randolph had died of apoplexy the October before while in Philadelphia for the Continental Congress.
61. Grigsby, *The Virginia Convention of 1776*, pp. 66-67.
62. *Ibid.*, p. 79.
63. The physical description of James Madison is based on Grigsby, *The Virginia Convention of 1776*, p. 79; Irving Brant, *James Madison, Father of the Constitution*, p. 14; and on the miniature of Madison as a young man by Charles Willson Peale.
64. Grigsby, *The Virginia Convention of 1776*, pp. 54, 65.
65. *Ibid.*, p. 57.   66. *Ibid.*, pp. 35-36.
67. The figures of the vote are not known.
68. Mays, *Pendleton*, vol. II, pp. 107-111.
69. *Ibid.*, p. 107.   70. Mays, *Pendleton*, vol. II, p. 109.
71. Regardless of Massachusetts wishes in the matter, it was not expedient for that colony to advocate independence since, as an invaded province, it might seem to be attempting selfishly to draw others into the struggle in which it was already engaged.
72. For a discussion of the primacy of Virginia's actions, see Grigsby, *The Virginia Convention of 1776*, pp. 16-33.
73. A detailed description of the celebration was printed in the May 17, 1776 issue of Purdie's *Virginia Gazette*.
74. *Virginia Cavalcade*, vol. II, p. 46.
75. Then a part of Gloucester County, but now a part of Mathews.
  The description of Dunmore's activities at Gwynn's and of the battle that followed is based on Eckenrode, *The Revolution in Virginia*, pp. 93-94, and *Virginia Cavalcade*, vol. II, pp. 46-47.
76. Mays, *Pendleton*, vol. II, pp. 120-122.
  Mason had been detained by a "smart fit of the gout." (*Virginia Cavalcade*, vol. I, p. 7.)
77. Eckenrode, *The Revolution in Virginia*, p. 164.
  Rowland, *Mason*, vol. I, pp. 244-251, 433-442.
78. Rowland, *Mason*, vol. I, pp. 52-54.
79. The qualifying phrase "when they enter into a state of society" was inserted by Edmund Pendleton to quiet the objections of those who feared that Mason's bold declaration was inconsistant with anything less than immediate emancipation of the slaves. See Mays, *Pendleton*, vol. I, pp. 121-122.
80. Randolph's "Manuscript History of Virginia," Virginia Historical Society archives.
81. *Virginia Cavalcade*, vol. I, p. 14.
82. *Ibid.*   83. Mays, *Pendleton*, vol. II, p. 123.
84. The quotation is from Eckenrode, *The Revolution in Virginia*, p. 162.
85. Malone, *Jefferson the Virginian*, p. 235.
86. Letter to Thomas Nelson, Jr., May 16, 1776, quoted in Malone, *Jefferson the Virginian*, p. 235.
87. *Ibid.*, pp. 235-236.
  The knowledge that Randolph made the presentation is enough to insure that it was polished.
88. *Ibid.*, p. 236.
  The constitution proposed by Jefferson is reprinted in Thomas Jefferson, *Notes on the State of Virginia* (University of North Carolina Press, Chapel Hill, 1955), pp. 209-222. Jefferson's criticisms of the constitution adopted appear in the same volume, pp. 118-129.

89. Malone, *Jefferson the Virginian*, p. 245.

90. He was reelected anyway. See *ibid.*, p. 240.

91. *Ibid.*, p. 242.

92. The description of Richard Henry Lee's manner is based on Hendrick, *The Lees of Virginia*, pp. 100-101.

93. The North Carolina Convention on April 12 had authorized its delegates to vote for a Declaration of Independence if one should be proposed in Congress. Some persons have confused this move and construe it to be the equivalent of the Virginia Convention's action in instructing its delegates to offer a resolution for independence.

94. Malone, *Jefferson the Virginian*, p. 219.

95. John Adams said that Richard Henry Lee was not placed on the committee for preparing a Declaration of Independence because he was already on one for preparing articles of confederation, and "it was not thought convenient that the same person should be upon both." (Commager and Nevins, *The Heritage of America*, p. 150.) Malone suggests (*Jefferson the Virginian*, pp. 219-220) that Jefferson may have envied Lee the opportunity to return to Virginia instead of serving on this committee. Historians have persisted in saying that Jefferson was placed on the committee instead of Lee to play up the young man's prestige at the expense of his elder's. As a possible refutation of this view, it is interesting to note that Lee, after Jefferson's manuscript was edited by Congress, wrote to the author: "I wish sincerely, as well for the honor of Congress, as for that of the states, that the manuscript had not been mangled as it is. However, the thing in its nature is so good that no cookery can spoil the dish for the palates of free men." The letter was signed, "Your affectionate friend, Richard Henry Lee." (*Northern Neck Historical Magazine*, vol. II, p. 158.)

96. Malone, *Jefferson the Virginian*, pp. 219-220.

97. John Adams wrote: "You inquire why so young a man as Mr. Jefferson was placed at the head of a committee for preparing a Declaration of Independence. I answer: It was the Frankfort advice to place Virginia at the head of everything." (Commager and Nevins, *The Heritage of America*, p. 150.) Despite this evidence from one of Jefferson's contemporaries, Carl T. Becker concludes that Jefferson was chosen chiefly "because he was known to possess a 'masterly pen.'" (Becker, *The Declaration of Independence*, p. 194.)

98. The ensuing conversation was reported by Adams himself years later (1805 and 1822). The intervening years may have confused his memory of some circumstances, as Jefferson later claimed, but there is no reason to doubt the essential validity of the conversation as reported. Adams' account is quoted in Becker, *The Declaration of Independence*, p. 135.

99. The author's insertions and deletions are visible on Jefferson's manuscript, and have been analyzed by Becker to illustrate the Virginian's writing procedure. See Becker, *The Declaration of Independence*, pp. 140-184.

100. Malone, *Jefferson the Virginian*, p. 220.

101. Becker, *The Declaration of Independence*, p. 198.

102. *Ibid.*, pp. 212-213.

103. It is possible that some committee member other than Adams agreed with Jefferson about including the passage on slavery, but if so, the record is silent on this point. Some who voted for excision of the reference to slavery doubtless disapproved the institution. Like Lincoln in the following century, they placed national union before the issue of slavery.

104. In 1818, Jefferson gratefully recalled this experience. Becker, *The Declaration of Independence*, p. 208.

105. *Ibid.*, pp. 209-213.

106. *Ibid.*, p. 79.

The philosophical origins of the Declaration of Independence are discussed in Becker, *The Declaration of Independence*, pp. 24-134, and Van Tyne's *The War of Independence*, pp. 351-355.

107. Most of the signatures were affixed August 2, but Matthew Thornton, of New Hampshire, signed in November.

FOOTNOTES TO CHAPTER XIII

1. This description of Patrick Henry is based primarily on the 1795 miniature by Lawrence Sully, which was perhaps the only portrait of him painted from life. The gestures here attributed to Henry are those described as typical of him by such biographers as William Wirt and William Wirt Henry.
2. Mays, *Pendleton*, vol. II, p. 123.
3. These dogs excited as much comment in the other colonies as in Virginia. A caricaturist included them in his picture of Lee, and Benjamin Rush wrote, "A troop of dogs which he permitted to follow him everywhere seemed to engross his whole heart."
4. Malone, *Jefferson the Virginian*, p. 240.
5. *Ibid.*, p. 239.
6. Eckenrode, *The Revolution in Virginia*, pp. 167-168.
7. Ward, *War of the Revolution*, vol. II, p. 867.
8. Ralph Waldo Emerson's phrase describing the British class system was particularly applicable to the Virginia society which had produced Edmund Pendleton. The descendant of long forgotten gentry, he served so well as an apprentice in one of the Old Dominion's great families that he himself came to be one of the chief leaders of the aristocracy. See Mays, *Pendleton*, vol. I, pp. 3-5, 12-24, 355-357.
9. Eckenrode, *The Revolution in Virginia*, pp. 167-169.
10. *Ibid.*
11. Malone, *Jefferson the Virginian*, p. 248.
12. *Ibid.*, pp. 248-249; also *Northern Neck of Virginia Historical Magazine*, vol. II, p. 158.
13. Thomas Jefferson, *Notes on the State of Virginia*, p. 161.
14. Eckenrode, *The Revolution in Virginia*, p. 165.
15. Mays, *Pendleton*, vol. II, p. 133.
16. Correspondence of the period is full of caustic references to Scots.
17. This ecclesiastic's role in colonial policy is well told in Hartwell, Blair and Chilton, *Present State of Virginia and the College*, pp. XXII-XXVIII.
18. J. M. Cramp, *Baptist History*, pp. 532-533, 536-537.
    David Benedict, *A General History of the Baptist Denomination in America* (Boston, 1813), pp. 64-77.
19. Carter joined the Baptist Church in 1778. He contributed to churches of that denomination even outside his native Northern Neck, and at his own expense educated young men for the Baptist ministry. Louis Morton, *Robert Carter of Nomini Hall*, pp. 236-237.
20. Mays, *Pendleton*, vol. II, p. 265. 21. *Ibid.*, p. 372, n. 23.
22. *Journal of the House of Delegates of Virginia, 1776* (Shepherd), p. 47.
23. Mays, *Pendleton*, vol. II, p. 135. 24. *Ibid.*
25. The other was George Wythe. Patrick Henry was the greatest orator in Virginia and a great pleader before juries, but he was not so good an all-round lawyer as Wythe and Pendleton.
26. Eckenrode, *The Revolution in Virginia*, p. 171.
27. *Ibid.*
28. Malone, *Jefferson the Virginian*, pp. 251-252.
29. *Ibid.*, p. 253.

30. He did, however, adopt his nephew Edmund and felt that the boy had "a filial claim" upon him. Mays, *Pendleton*, vol. II, p. 325.
31. *Ibid.*, vol. II, p. 138.
32. Malone, *Jefferson the Virginian*, p. 255.
33. John Adams, it will be recalled, observed that the American Revolution began in men's minds before it did on the battlefield.
34. Malone, *Jefferson the Virginian*, p. 257.
35. *Ibid.*
36. George Wythe told John Adams that Thomas Ludwell Lee was the most popular man in Virginia. *Northern Neck of Virginia Historical Magazine*, vol. II, p. 153.
37. The quoted words were used by Jefferson to describe Pendleton's stand. Mays, *Pendleton*, vol. II, p. 139.
38. *Ibid.*, pp. 139-140.
39. Mason's phrase. His memorandum "Plan settled by the Committee of Revisors, in Fredericksburg, January 1777," preserved in the archives of the Virginia State Library is reprinted in part in Mays, *Pendleton*, vol. II, pp. 373-376, n. 55.
40. Mays, *Pendleton*, vol. II, p. 40.
41. Criminal law section of Mason's memorandum.
42. Malone, *Jefferson the Virginian*, pp. 261, 263.
43. Mays, *Pendleton*, vol. II, p. 151.
44. *Journal of the House of Delegates*, pp. 114-115.
45. Malone, *Jefferson the Virginian*, pp. 258-259.
46. *Ibid.*, p. 259.
47. Becker, *The Declaration of Independence*, pp. 212-213.
48. Jefferson, *Notes on the State of Virginia*, pp. 162-163.
49. Letter of July 12, 1736. Beverley B. Munford, *Virginia's Attitude Toward Slavery and Secession*, pp. 16-17.
50. *Ibid.*, p. 17.   51. *Ibid.*, p. 18.
52. *Ibid.*, p. 21.   53. *Ibid.*, p. 25.
54. *Ibid.*
55. Jefferson, *Notes on the State of Virginia*, p. 163.
56. Malone, *Jefferson the Virginian*, p. 301.
57. *Ibid.* Letter to Major General William Phillips.
58. George Gordon, Lord Byron's phrase.
59. Malone, *Jefferson the Virginian*, pp. 302-303.
60. *Ibid.*, p. 303.   61. *Ibid.*, pp. 304-307.
62. Jefferson's theory of the proper relation between governor and council is diametrically opposed to Abraham Lincoln's concept of the relationship between President and cabinet. Lincoln is said to have ruled, "The ayes have it," after polling his cabinet on a proposition to which they all voted "No." The ensuing account of Jefferson's gubernatorial administrations is based largely on:
   Malone, *Jefferson the Virginian*, pp. 301-369;
   Eckenrode, *The Revolution in Virginia*, pp. 262-264.
63. Malone, *Jefferson the Virginian*, pp. 314-315.
64. Letter to Chevalier de la Luzerne. *Ibid.*, p. 317.
65. Ward, *The War of the Revolution*, vol. I, p. 31.
66. The account of Washington's trials and achievements as Commander of the Continental Army is drawn largely from:
   Ward, *The War of the Revolution*, vol. I, pp. 24-31, 99-134, 202-431; vol. II, pp. 543-554, 557-564, 570-586, 879-895;

Freeman, *Washington*, vol. III, pp. XII-XXXVIII, 440-586, vols. IV and V; Van Tyne, *The War for Independence*.

Henry P. Johnston, *Yorktown Campaign and the Surrender of Cornwallis, 1781*.

Our estimate of Washington, essentially the same as Freeman's, is generally supported by Flexner's *George Washington: The Forge of Experience* and *George Washington: In the American Revolution*.

67. Freeman, *Washington*, vol. IV, pp. 358-359.
68. Quoted in Ward, *The War of the Revolution*, vol. I, p. 316.
69. Freeman, *Washington*, vol. IV, p. 517.
70. Ward, *The War of the Revolution*, vol. I, p. 371.
71. Washington wrote Governor Patrick Henry: "I look with the greatest concern upon the sufferings of our soldiers for the remainder of this year; and as for the next, I view them as naked except some measures can be fallen upon to collect from the inhabitants of the different states part of their stock of clothing, which I fear is but scanty." Freeman, *Washington*, vol. IV, pp. 569-570.
72. Morgan became a brigadier-general. The description of him is based largely on those in the D.A.B. and Ward, *The War of the Revolution*.
73. Description based on D.A.B. entry.
74. Description of Clark based largely on D.A.B. entry; Ward, *The War of the Revolution*, vol. II, pp. 852-853; and James A. James, *The Life of George Rogers Clark*.

    The story of his campaign is based largely on Ward, *The War of the Revolution*, vol. II, pp. 850-865; James, *The Life of George Rogers Clark*, pp. 109-146.
75. Site of the present city of Louisville, Kentucky.
76. The account of Collier's raid on Virginia is based largely on Eckenrode, *The Revolution in Virginia*, pp. 262-264; Ward, *The War of the Revolution*, vol. II, p. 267.
77. Though Paulus Hook ended formal military operations between British and American forces in the North in 1779, Sullivan's expedition against the Indians along the frontiers of New York and Pennsylvania was as important as such operations.
78. Freeman, *Washington*, vol. V, p. 163.
79. Advanced forces had met the night before but had withdrawn following a brief clash.
80. Description of Campbell based on D.A.B. entry.
81. Sevier later became the first governor of Tennessee, and Shelby was elected to Congress from North Carolina.
82. Ward, *The War of the Revolution*, vol. II, p. 741.
83. D.A.B. entries on both Charles and Joseph McDowell. Other noteworthy American officers in the battle were Col. Benjamin Cleveland of North Carolina, Lacey, Williams and Hambright.
84. Eckenrode, *The Revolution in Virginia*, p. 264.
85. *Clinton-Cornwallis Controversy* (ed. Benjamin Franklin Stevens, London, 1888), vol. I, pp. 10-13, including n. 25.
86. Ward, *The War of the Revolution*, vol. II, p. 868.
87. *Ibid.*, p. 870.
88. In January 1776 he had preached his farewell sermon at Woodstock and then had shed his robes in the pulpit to reveal an officer's uniform.
89. Eckenrode, *The Revolution in Virginia*, p. 268.
90. Henry P. Johnston, *Yorktown Campaign and the Surrender of Cornwallis, 1781*, p. 37.
91. *Ibid.*, p. 38.

92. An excellent, brief account of Jouett's ride is given in Malone, *Jefferson the Virginian*, pp. 355-357; also John Daly Burk, *History of Virginia*, vol. IV, pp. 499-500.

In terms of physical endurance and lasting benefit to the nation, the Virginian's ride was a greater feat than the one which Paul Revere was able to complete. To admit this fact is not to detract in any way from Paul Revere's courage as a patriot, skill as a silversmith, or acumen as a pioneer industrialist. But Jouett has not been accorded the credit that is his due. His equestrian accomplishments were far more impressive than Revere's but, unlike the New Englander, he did not have a famous and popular descendant firmly mounted on Pegasus.

93. Malone, *Jefferson the Virginian*, pp. 357-359.

Jefferson was vindicated by the investigation.

94. Freeman, *Washington*, vol. V, pp. 341-342, 345.

95. *Ibid.*, p. 322.   96. *Ibid.*, p. 379.

97. One of Washington's great fears was that people would decide that the war was over after victory at Yorktown without waiting for events to prove the assumption true. Skirmishing continued after that battle. On February 12, 1783—eight days after the cessation of hostilities was proclaimed, but before the news reached America—Colonel John Mapp, County Lieutenant for Northampton, reported to Commodore Barron the capture of "near sixty prisoners of war." He wrote: "A captain of a barge and four privates of the number were captured on Hog Island by my militia; the remainder are the officers and crew of the British privateer called the *Digby*, mounting eighteen guns, and lately run on shore near Cape Charles." (*Calendar of Virginia State Papers*, vol. III, p. 435.)

98. M. P. Andrews, *Virginia, the Old Dominion*, p. 300.

99. Ward, *The War of the Revolution*, vol. II, p. 865.

BIBLIOGRAPHY

BIBLIOGRAPHY

I. Manuscripts, Photostats, Typescripts and Old Newspapers

Angus McDonald Papers, Virginia State Library, Richmond, Virginia.

Colonial Williamsburg copy of unpublished Book 6, Folio 327 in North Papers, Bodleian Library, Oxford, England.

Gooch Letters, Colonial Williamsburg, Inc., archives, Williamsburg.

Jerdone Letters, Library of the College of William and Mary.

"Letter Book, 1761-1768, of Col. Richard Corbin, Receiver General of Virginia," Virginia Historical Society archives, Richmond.

Manuscript history of Virginia by Edmund Randolph, Virginia Historical Society.

Mrs. Charlotte Browne's "Journal of a Voyage from London to Virginia," (photostated pages from Library of Congress photographs of the original journal, owned by S. A. Courtald of the Howe, Halstead, Essex, England), Virginia Historical Society archives.

Official records (some original records at county seats and some in photostat or typescript at Virginia State Library) of Accomack, Lancaster, Middlesex, Norfolk, Northampton, Northumberland and Westmoreland Counties.

Richard Corbin Letter Book, Virginia State Library.

Robert Carter Letter Books, archives of the Virginia Historical Society.

Virginia Gazette (Williamsburg, original), 1737, Virginia Historical Society archives.

Virginia Gazette (Williamsburg, Hunter, photostats), 1755, Virginia Historical Society archives.

Virginia Gazette (Williamsburg, J. Royle, micrifilm), 1765, Colonial Williamsburg, Inc.

Virginia Gazette (Williamsburg, J. Royle, microfilm), 1766, Colonial Williamsburg, Inc.

Virginia Gazette (Williamsburg, Purdie and Dixon, photostats), 1766, Colonial Williamsburg, Inc.

Virginia Gazette (Williamsburg, Purdie and Dixon, photostats), 1774, Colonial Williamsburg, Inc. and Library of the College of William and Mary.

Virginia Gazette, individual issues, especially for 1775-1776, Virginia Historical Society archives and Colonial Williamsburg, Inc.

Virginia Gazette (Norfolk), Feb. 3, 1776, only known copy, Virginia Historical Society archives.

William Gooch's Letters (typescript), Vol. II, Virginia Historical Society.

II. Official and Semi-Official Collections

Ames, Susie M., ed. *County Court Records of Accomack-Northampton, Virginia, 1632-1640. American Legal Records,* vol. VII, Washington, D.C., The American Historical Association, 1954.

Calendar of Virginia State Papers, Richmond, 1875.

Documents of American History (ed. by Henry Steele Commager), New York, 1949.

Executive Journals of the Council of Colonial Virginia.

George Mercer Papers Relating to the Ohio Company of Virginia (ed. Lois Mulkearn), Pittsburgh, 1954.

Journals of the Continental Congress (ed. by W. C. Ford), Vols. I and II.

Journals of the Council of the State of Virginia, Vols. I-III, Richmond, 1931.

Journals of the House of Burgesses of Virginia (1619-1776), Richmond, 1905-1915.

Journals of the House of Delegates of Virginia, 1776, Richmond, 1828.

Official Letters of the Governors of the State of Virginia, Vols. I-III, Richmond, 1926-1929 (General Editor H. R. McIlwaine); Vol. I, *The Letters of Patrick Henry*; Vol. II, *The Letters of Thomas Jefferson*; Vol. III, *The Letters of Thomas Nelson and Benjamin Harrison.*

The Official Records of Robert Dinwiddie, Vol. I.

Proceedings of the General Assembly of Virginia, July 30-August 4, 1619 (facsimile edited by William J. Van Schreeven and George H. Reese). Jamestown, Va.: Jamestown Foundation, 1969.

The Records of the Virginia Company of London, the Court Book, from the Manuscript in The Library of Congress (ed. Susan Myra Kingsbury, Vols. I-IV, Washington, 1906, etc.)

The Statutes at Large, Being a Collection of All the Laws of Virginia (ed. by W. W. Hening), N. Y., Philadelphia, Richmond.

Tracts and Other Papers, Relating Principally to the Origin, Settlement and Progress of the Colonies in North America, (collected and printed by Peter Force, Washington, D. C. 1836-1837), American archives 4th series, Vols. I and II.

III. CONTEMPORARY WRITINGS (Original Printings and Reprints)

Beverley, Robert, *History and Present State of Virginia*, Chapel Hill, 1947. (Reprint of 1705 London edition.)

Bland, Richard, *An Inquiry into the Rights of the British Colonies,* Williamsburg, Alexander Purdie & Co., 1776 (Reprint, Richmond, Virginia, The Appeals Press, 1922.)

Boswell's London Journal (ed. F. A. Pottle), N. Y., 1950.

Bradford, William, *Of Plymouth Plantation* (ed. by S. E. Morison), New York, 1952.

Brown, Alexander, *The Genesis of the United States*, Boston, 1891.

Burnaby, Rev. Andrew, *Travels through the Middle Settlements in North America in the Years 1759 and 1760* (second edition, London, 1775).

Burnett, Edmund Cody, (ed.) *Letters of Members of the Continental Congress* (Washington, 1921).

Byrd, William, *Another Secret Diary of William Byrd of Westover, 1739-1741* (ed. by Dr. Maude H. Woodfin), Richmond, 1942.

Byrd, William, *Natural History of Virginia* (ed. and translated from the German version by R. C. Beatty and W. J. Mulloy, Richmond, 1940)

Byrd, William, *The Secret Diary of William Byrd of Westover, 1709-1712* (ed. by L. B. Wright and M. Tinling), Richmond, 1941.

Carter, Landon, *The Diary of Colonel Landon Carter of Sabine Hall, 1752-1778*, 2 vols. (ed., Jack P. Greene), Charlottesville, Va., 1965.

Durand de Dauphiné, *A Huguenot Exile in Virginia, or Voyages of a Frenchman Exiled for His Religion with a Description of Virginia and Maryland* (from the Hague edition of 1687 with an introduction and notes by Gilbert Chinard), N. Y., 1934.

An Exact Reprint of Six Rare Pamphlets on the Clinton-Cornwallis Controversy with Very Numerous Important Unpublished Manuscript Notes by Sir Henry Clinton, K. B., Vols. I and II (ed. by Benjamin Franklin Stevens), London, 1888.

Fithian, Philip Vickers, *Journal and Letters of Philip Vickers Fithian, 1773-1774* (ed. by H. D. Farish), Williamsburg, 1943.

Fontaine, Rev. James, et al., *Memoirs of a Huguenot Family* (ed. Ann Maury), N. Y., 1872.

Hartwell, Blair and Chilton, *The Present State of Virginia and the College* (ed. by H. D. Farish), Princeton, 1940.

Jefferson, Thomas, *Notes on the State of Virginia*, Chapel Hill, 1955.

John Norton & Sons, Merchants of London and Virginia, Being the Papers from Their Counting House for the Years 1750-1795 (ed. Frances Norton Mason), Richmond, 1937.

Jones, Hugh, *The Present State of Virginia*, London, 1724; also (ed. Richard L. Morton), Chapel Hill, 1956.

Mathews, Thomas, *Beginning, Progress and Conclusion of Bacon's Rebellion in Virginia in the Years 1675 and 1676*, Rochester, 1897.

Oswald, Richard, *Memorandum on the Folly of Invading Virginia, The strategic Importance of Portsmouth, and The Need for Civilian Control of the Military* (ed. W. Stitt Robinson, Jr., Charlottesville, Virginia, 1953.

Pepys, Samuel, *Diary*.

Rolfe, John, *A True Relation of the State of Virginia Left by Sir Thomas Dale, Knight, in May Last, 1616* (Yale, 1951).

St. Méry, Moreau de, *The American Journey*, Garden City, N. Y., 1947.

Sams, C. W., *The Conquest of Virginia, the Forest Primeval*, New York, 1916.

Sams, C. W., *The Conquest of Virginia, the Second Attempt*, Norfolk, 1929.

Smith, John, *The Generall Historie of Virginia*, etc., Glasgow.

Spotswood, Alexander, *The Official Letters of Alexander Spotswood*, Vol. I (ed. R. A. Brock), Richmond, 1882.

Stith, William, *The History of the First Discovery and Settlement of Virginia*, Williamsburg, 1747.

Tyler, Lyon G., *Narratives of Early Virginia, 1606-1625*, New York, 1907 and 1952.

Washington, George, *The Diaries of George Washington* (ed. John C. Fitzpatrick), Boston and New York, 1925.

IV. SECONDARY SOURCES

Abernathy, P., *Western Lands and the American Revolution*. New York, 1937.

Adams, Arthur and Frederick Lewis Weis, *The Magna Charta Sureties, 1215: The Barons Named in the Magna Charta, 1215, and Some of Their Descendants Who Settled in America 1607-1650*. Boston, Massachusetts, 1955.

Adams, James Truslow, *Building the British Empire.* New York and London, 1938.

—————————. *The March of Democracy.* Vol. I,New York, 1933.

Allen, Gardner W., *A Naval History of the American Revolution.* 2 vols. New York, 1962.

Ambler, Charles Henry, *Sectionalism in Virginia from 1776 to 1861.* Chicago, 1910.

Andrews, Matthew Page, *The Soul of a Nation.* New York, 1943.

—————————. *Virginia, the Old Dominion.* Garden City, 1937.

Bailey, Kenneth P., *The Ohio Company of Virginia and the Westward Movement.* Glendale, Calif., 1939.

Baker-Crothers, Hayes, *Virginia and the French and Indian War.* Chicago, 1928.

Ballagh, James Curtis, *A History of Slavery in Viriginia.* Baltimore, 1902.

—————————. *White Servitude in the Colony of Virginia.* Baltimore, 1895.

Barbour, Philip L., ed., *The Jamestown Voyages Under the First Charter, 1606-1609.* Vol. I, Cambridge, 1969.

—————————. *The Three Worlds of Captain John Smith.* Boston, 1964.

Becker, Carl, *The Declaration of Independence.* New York, 1940.

Benedict, David, *A General History of the Baptist Denominations in America.* Boston, 1813.

Blanton, Wyndham B., M. D., *Medicine in Virginia in the Eighteenth Century.* Richmond, 1931.

—————————. *Medicine in Virginia in the Seventeenth Century.* Richmond, 1930.

Bolton, H. E. and T. N. Marshall, *The Colonization of North America.* New York, 1936.

Brant, Irving, *James Madison, Father of the Constitution.* Indianapolis and New York, 1950.

Bridenbaugh, Carl, *Seat of Empire.* Williamsburg, 1958.

Brock, R. A., *Virginia and Virginians.* Vol. I, Richmond and Toledo, 1888.

Brooke, Iris and James Laver, *English Costume from the Fourteenth through the Nineteenth Century.* New York, 1937.

Brown, Alexander, *The First Republic in America.* Boston and New York, 1898.

Brown, Robert Eldon and B. Katherine Brown, *Virginia, 1705-1786: Democracy or Aristocracy?* East Lansing, Michigan, 1964.

Bruce, Kathleen, *Virginia Iron Manufacture in the Slave Era.* New York and London, 1931.

Bruce, Philip Alexander, *Economic History of Virginia in the Seventeenth Century.* Vols. I and II, New York, 1895-1896.

—————————. *History of Virginia.* Vol. I, Chicago and New York, 1924.

—————————. *Social Life of Virginia in the Seventeenth Century.* Lynchburg, 1927.

—————————. *The Virginia Plutarch.* Vol. I, Chapel Hill, 1929.

Brydon, George MacLaren, *Virginia's Mother Church and the Political Conditions Under Which It Grew . . . 1607-1727.* Richmond, 1947.

Burk, John Daly, *The History of Virginia.* 4 vols. Petersburg, Va., 1804-1816.

Burke, Sir Bernard, *A Genealogical History of the Dormant, Abeyant, Forfeited, and Extinct Peerages of the British Empire.* London, 1883.

Burnett, Edmund Cody, *The Continental Congress.* New York, 1941.

Butt, Marshall W., *Portsmouth Under Four Flags, 1752-1970.* Portsmouth, Va., 1971.

Campbell, Charles, *History of the Colony and Ancient Dominion of Virginia.* Philadelphia, 1860.

Carrier, Lyman, *Agriculture in Virginia, 1607-1699.* Williamsburg, 1957.

Channing, Edward, *A History of the United States.* Vol. I, New York, 1936.

——————. *A History of the United States.* Vol. III, New York, 1912.

Cheyney, Edward, *A Short History of England.* Boston, 1937.

Chitwood, Oliver Perry, *Justice in Colonial Virginia.* Baltimore, 1905.

——————. *Richard Henry Lee, Statesman of the Revolution.* Morgantown, West Virginia, 1967.

Clendening, A. Elizabeth, *The Dunaways of Virginia.* Ogunquit, Maine, 1959.

Coke, Edward, *The First Part of the Institute of the Laws of England; or, a Commentary upon Littleton.* Philadelphia, 1853.

Cramp, J. M., *Baptist History.* Philadelphia (n.d.)

Craven, Wesley Frank, *Dissolution of the Virginia Company, the Failure of a Colonial Experiment.* New York, 1932.

——————. *The Southern Colonies in the Seventeenth Century.* Vol. I, Louisiana State University, 1949.

Dabney, Virginius, *Virginia the New Dominion.* Garden City, New York, 1971.

Daniel, J. R. V. (ed.), *A Hornbook of Virginia History.* Richmond, 1949.

Davidson, Marshall, *Life in America.* Vol. I, Boston, 1951.

Davis, Burke, *A Williamsburg Galaxy.* Williamsburg, 1968.

Davis, Richard Beale, ed. *William Fitzhugh and His Chesapeake World, 1676-1701.* Chapel Hill, 1963.

Dodson, Leonidas, *Alexander Spotswood.* Philadelphia, 1932.

Dowdey, Clifford, *The Golden Age: A Climate for Greatness, Virginia 1732-1775.* Boston, 1970.

——————. *The Great Plantation.* New York, 1957.

——————. *The Virginia Dynasties.* Boston, 1969.

Eckenrode, H. J., *The Revolution in Virginia.* Boston and New York, 1916.

Eichelberger, N. Pierce, *The Mapp Family of the Eastern Shore of Virginia.* Quinby, Virginia, 1972.

Fiske, John, *Old Virginia and Her Neighbors.* Vol. I. Boston and New York, 1899.

——————. *The American Revolution.* Vol. I. Boston and New York, 1901.

Fitzhugh, Georgianna, *The Life of Dr. John Tankard.* Hampton, Virginia, 1907 (reprint, 1965).

Flexner, James Thomas, *George Washington: The Forge of Experience (1732-1775).* Boston, 1965.

——————. *George Washington: In the American Revolution (1775-1783).* Boston, 1967.

Flippin, Percy S., *Royal Government in Virginia, 1624-1775.* New York, 1919.

Forman, Henry Chandlee, *Virginia Architecture in the Seventeenth Century.* Williamsburg, 1957.

Frantz, John B., *Bacon's Rebellion: Prologue to the Revolution?* Lexington, Massachusetts, 1969.

Freeman, Douglas Southall, *George Washington.* Vols. I-V. New York, 1948-1952.

Gipson, Lawrence Henry, *The British Empire before the American Revolution.* Vols. I-XIII. New York, 1936-1967.

——————. *The Coming of the Revolution, 1763-1775.* New York: Harper & Brothers, 1954.

Gooch, R. K., *The Government of England.* New York, 1937.

Green, John Richard, *A Short History of the English People.* N. Y., 1916.

Greene, Jack P., *The American Colonies in the Eighteenth Century, 1689-1763.* New York, 1969.

——————. *The Quest for Power: The Lower Houses of Assembly in the Southern Royal Colonies, 1689-1776.* Chapel Hill, 1963.

Griffith, Lucille, *The Virginia House of Burgesses, 1750-1774* (Revised edition). University, Alabama, 1970.

Grigsby, Hugh Blair, *The History of the Virginia Federal Convention of 1788,* vols. I and II. Richmond, 1890-1891.

——————. *The Virginia Convention of 1776.* Richmond, 1855.

Hall, Walter Phelps and Robert G. Albion, *A History of England and the British Empire.* Boston, 1937.

A Handbook for the Exhibition Buildings of Colonial Williamsburg. Williamsburg, 1936.

Hart, Freeman H., *The Valley of Virginia in the American Revolution, 1763-1789.* Chapel Hill, 1942.

Havighurst, Walter, *Alexander Spotswood: Portrait of a Governor.* New York, 1967.

Hendren, Samuel Rivers, *Government and Religion of the Virginia Indians.* Baltimore, 1895.

Hendrick, Burton J., *The Lees of Virginia: Biography of a Family.* Boston, 1935.

Henry, William Wirt, *Patrick Henry, Life, Correspondence and Speeches.* New York, 1891 (3 vols.).

Howard, George Eliot, *Preliminaries of the Revolution.* New York, 1907.

Howe, Henry, *Historical Collections of Virginia.* Charleston, S. C., 1852.

James, Alfred Procter, *George Mercer of the Ohio Company.* Pittsburgh, 1963.

James, James Alton, *The Life of George Rogers Clark.* Chicago, 1928.

Jester, Annie Lash, *Domestic Life in Virginia in the Seventeenth Century.* Williamsburg, 1957.

Johnston, Henry P., *The Yorktown Campaign and the Surrender of Cornwallis, 1781.* New York, 1881.

Kilham, Austin D. and Fannie M. Clark, *Badger and Tankard Families of the Eastern Shore of Virginia.* Charlottesville, Virginia, 1973.

Kimball, Fiske and Susan Higginson Nash, *The Restoration of Colonial Williamsburg in Virginia.* New York, 1935.

Koontz, Louis K., *Robert Dinwiddie: His Career in American Colonial Government and Westward Expansion.* Glendale, Calif., 1941.

——————. *The Virginia Frontier, 1754-1763.* Baltimore, 1925.

Latané, John H., *The Early Relations Between Maryland and Virginia.* Baltimore, 1895.

Lawson-Tancred, Sir Thomas, Bart., *Records of a Yorkshire Manor.* London, 1937.

Long, J. C., *Mr. Pitt and America's Birthright.* New York, 1940.

Lonn, Ella, *The Colonial Agents of the Southern Colonies.* Chapel Hill, 1945.

Lunt, W. E., *History of England.* New York and London, 1947.

Malone, Dumas, *Jefferson the Virginian.* Boston, 1948.

Mays, David, *Edmund Pendleton,* Vols. I and II. Cambridge, 1952.

Mason, George Carrington, *Colonial Churches of Tidewater Virginia.* Richmond, 1945.

McClellan, Elisabeth, *History of American Costume.* New York, 1937.

Meade, Robert D., *Patrick Henry: Patriot in the Making*. Philadelphia, 1957.

——————————. *Patrick Henry: Practical Revolutionary*. Philadelphia, 1969.

Meade, William, *Old Churches, Ministers and Families of Virginia*. Philadelphia, 1857.

Middleton, Arthur Pierce, *Tobacco Coast*. Mariners' Museum, 1953.

Miller, John C., *Origins of the American Revolution*. Boston, 1943.

Montross, Lynn, *The Reluctant Rebels*. New York, 1950.

Morgan, Edmund S., *Prologue to Revolution*. Chapel Hill, 1959.

Morgan, Edmund S. and Helen M. Morgan, *The Stamp Act Crisis*. Chapel Hill: The University of North Carolina Press, 1953.

Morison, Samuel Eliot and Henry Steele Commager, *The Growth of the American Republic*, vol. I. New York, 1942.

Morton, Louis, *Robert Carter of Nomini Hall*. Princeton, 1941.

Morton, Richard L., *Colonial Virginia*, vols. I and II. Chapel Hill, 1960.

Munford, Beverley B., *Virginia's Attitude Toward Slavery and Secession*. Richmond, 1909.

Neill, Edward D., *Virginia Carolarum: The Colony Under the Rule of Charles the First and Second . . . 1625-1685*. Albany, 1886.

Petrie, Sir Charles, *The Stuart Pretenders*. Boston and New York, 1933.

Quarles, Benjamin, *The Negro in the American Revolution*. Chapel Hill, 1961.

Rouse, Parke, Jr., *Virginia: The English Heritage in America*. New York, 1966.

——————————. *James Blair of Virginia*. Chapel Hill, 1971.

Rowland, Kate Mason, *The Life of George Mason*, vols. I and II. New York, 1892.

Rutland, Robert A., ed., *The Papers of George Mason*, vols. I and II. Chapel Hill, 1970.

Sams, C. Whittle, *The Conquest of Virginia, the Forest Primeval*. New York, 1916.

Scheer, George F. and Hugh F. Rankin, *Rebels and Redcoats*. Cleveland and New York, 1957.

Schlesinger, Arthur M., *The Colonial Merchants and the American Revolution, 1763-1776*. New York, 1957.

Smith, Abbot Emerson, *Colonists in Bondage*. Chapel Hill, 1947.

Squires, W. H. T., *Through the Years in Norfolk*. Portsmouth, 1937.

Stanard, Mary Newton, *The Story of Virginia's First Century*. Philadelphia, 1928.

Sweet, William Warren, *The Story of Religion in America*. New York, 1950.

Sydnor, Charles S., *Gentlemen Freeholders*. Chapel Hill, 1952.

Trevelyan, George Macaulay, *A Shortened History of England*. New York, 1942.

——————————————. *History of England*. 1926.

Tyler, Lyon G., *History of Virginia*, vol. II. Chicago and New York, 1924.

Van Tyne, Claude H., *The Causes of the War of Independence*. Boston, 1922.

Virginia Writers' Project, *The Negro in Virginia*. New York, 1940.

Ward, Christopher, *The War of the Revolution*, vols. I and II. New York, 1952.

Washburn, Wilcomb E., *The Governor and the Rebel: A History of Bacon's Rebellion in Virginia*. Chapel Hill, 1957.

Weddell, Alexander Wilbourne, *A Memorial Volume of Virginia Historical Portraiture.* Richmond, 1930.

Wertenbaker, Thomas J., *Patrician and Plebeian in Virginia.* Charlottesville, 1910.

——————————. *Torchbearer of the Revolution: the Story of Bacon's Rebellion and Its Leader.* Princeton, 1940.

——————————. *Virginia Under the Stuarts, 1607-1688.* Princeton, 1914.

Whitelaw, Ralph T., *Virginia's Eastern Shore,* vols. I and II. Richmond, 1951.

Wilcox, William B., *Star of Empire.* New York, 1950.

Wilson, Woodrow, *A History of the American People,* vol. II. New York, 1902.

Wirt, William, *Sketches of the Life and Character of Patrick Henry.* Philadelphia, 1836.

Wise, Jennings Cropper, *Ye Kingdome of Accawmacke or the Eastern Shore of Virginia in the Seventeenth Century.* Richmond, 1911.

Wright, Louis B., *The First Gentlemen of Virginia: Intellectual Qualities of the Early Colonial Ruling Class.* San Marino, Calif., 1940.

Wrong, George M., *The British Nation.* New York, 1903.

V. GENERAL REFERENCES

Dictionary of American Biography.

Dictionary of National Biography.

Encyclopedia Americana.

Encyclopaedia Britannica

Encyclopedia of Virginia Biography.

Library of Southern Literature.

Oxford English Dictionary.

Swem, Earl Gregg, *Titles of the Manuscripts and Published Maps Relating to Virginia,* Richmond, 1914.

Swem, Earl Gregg, *Virginia Historical Index* (2 vols.), Roanoke, Virginia, 1934-1936.

VI. MAGAZINES AND PERIODICALS

The Geographical Magazine, London, Vol. XXVI, 1953.

Lower Norfolk County Virginia Antiquary, Vols. I-IV, 1895-1906.

Northern Neck of Virginia Historical Magazine, Montross, 1951-.

Tyler's Quarterly Historical and Genealogical Magazine, Vols. I-X, Richmond, 1919-1929.

Virginia Cavalcade (published quarterly by the Virginia State Library), 1951-.

Virginia Magazine of History and Biography, Richmond, 1893-.

William and Mary College Quarterly Historical Magazine (1st, 2nd and 3rd series), Williamsburg, 1892-.

INDEX

INDEX

561

G

W